The Reception of Vatican II

The Reception
of Vatican II

EDITED BY
MATTHEW L. LAMB AND
MATTHEW LEVERING

OXFORD
UNIVERSITY PRESS

OXFORD
UNIVERSITY PRESS

Oxford University Press is a department of the University of Oxford. It furthers
the University's objective of excellence in research, scholarship, and education
by publishing worldwide. Oxford is a registered trade mark of Oxford University
Press in the UK and certain other countries.

Published in the United States of America by Oxford University Press
198 Madison Avenue, New York, NY 10016, United States of America.

Library of Congress Cataloging-in-Publication Data
Names: Lamb, Matthew L., editor. | Levering, Matthew, 1971– author, editor.
Title: The reception of Vatican II / edited by Matthew L. Lamb and Matthew Levering.
Other titles: Vatican 2
Description: New York, NY : Oxford University Press, 2017. | Includes index.
Identifiers: LCCN 2016021256 | ISBN 9780190625801 (pbk. : alk. paper) |
ISBN 9780190625795 (cloth : alk. paper)
Subjects: LCSH: Vatican Council (2nd : 1962-1965 : Basilica di San Pietro
in Vaticano) | Catholic Church—Doctrines.
Classification: LCC BX830 1962 .R383 2017 | DDC 262/.52—dc23
LC record available at https://lccn.loc.gov/2016021256

9 8 7 6 5 4 3 2 1

Paperback printed by Webcom, Inc., Canada
Hardback printed by Bridgeport National Bindery, Inc., United States of America

Contents

PART THREE: THE DECLARATIONS

Acknowledgments

Our gratitude goes first to the contributors to this volume. We were blessed to find such superb contributors. David Augustine, now a doctoral student at Catholic University of America, carefully standardized the footnotes and checked for typos prior to our final submission of the manuscript. He also prepared the index. Many thanks to him for his meticulous work. Matthew Kuhner, a doctoral student at Ave Maria University, graciously assisted us in the copy-editing. Without the support of Theo Calderara, there could have been no book, and it is always a delight to work with him and his assistant Glenn Ramirez. The editorial staff of Oxford University Press merits our warm thanks for bringing this book to publication. Matthew Levering's wife, Joy, deserves thanks for her warmth of spirit and hard work in fostering projects such as this one. Finally, we dedicate this book to all the men and women who are presently enrolled in doctoral programs of Catholic theology. It will be their task to assist the Church in the ongoing interpretation of the Second Vatican Council, and we pray that this book points them anew to the good news of salvation from sin and death and participation in the very life of the triune God in Christ Jesus and his Spirit.

Abbreviations

Contributors

Robert Barron is Auxiliary Bishop of Los Angeles and the founder of Word on Fire Catholic Ministries. He is the author of numerous books, including *Vibrant Paradoxes: The Both/And of Catholicism*, *The Priority of Christ*, and *The Strangest Way*.

Sara Butler, MSBT, taught for many years at Mundelein Seminary of the Archdiocese of Chicago. A distinguished ecumenist, she has served as president of the Academy of Catholic Theology and as a member of the International Theological Commission, among numerous other positions. She is the author of *The Catholic Priesthood and Women: A Guide to the Teaching of the Church*.

Gavin D'Costa is a Professor of Catholic Theology at the University of Bristol. An advisor for the Pontifical Council for Interreligious Dialogue, he is the author or editor of numerous books, including *Vatican II: Catholic Doctrines on Jews and Muslims* and *Christianity and World Religions: Disputed Questions in the Theology of Religions*.

Adam A. J. DeVille is an Associate Professor of Theology and Departmental Chair at the University of Saint Francis. He is the author of *Orthodoxy and the Roman Papacy: Ut Unim Sint and the Prospects of East-West Unity*. He serves as editor of *Logos: A Journal of Eastern Christian Studies*.

Jeremy Driscoll, OSB, is the abbot of Mount Angel Abbey in Oregon. He previously taught for many years at the Pontifical Atheneum of St. Anselm in Rome. He is the author of numerous books, including *What Happens at Mass, Revised Edition, Theology at the Eucharistic Table*, and *Steps to Spiritual Perfection: Studies on Spiritual Progress in Evagrius Ponticus*.

Nicholas J. Healy, Jr., is Associate Professor of Philosophy and Culture at the Pontifical John Paul II Institute for Marriage and the Family at the Catholic University of America. He is the author of *The Eschatology of Hans Urs von Balthasar: Being as Communion*. With David L. Schindler, he co-authored *Freedom, Truth, and Human Dignity: The Second Vatican Council's Declaration on Religious Freedom*. Since 2002 he has served as an editor of *Communio: International Catholic Review*.

Paige E. Hochschild is Assistant Professor of Theology at Mount St. Mary's University. She previously taught philosophy at Mount St. Mary's Seminary for five years, and she teaches and writes in both systematics and patristics. She is the author of *Memory in Augustine's Theological Anthropology*.

Matthew L. Lamb is the Cardinal Maida Professor of Theology at Ave Maria University. He is the author or editor of numerous books, including most recently *Catholicism and America, Theology Needs Philosophy*, and *Eternity, Time, and the Life of Wisdom*. In addition to his earned doctorate from Muenster, he holds an honorary doctorate from the Franciscan University of Steubenville.

Matthew Levering holds the James N. and Mary D. Perry Jr. Chair of Theology at Mundelein Seminary. He is the author or editor of over thirty books, including most recently *Proofs of God: Classical Arguments from Tertullian to Barth* and *Engaging the Doctrine of the Holy Spirit*.

Guy Mansini, OSB, is a monk of Saint Meinrad Archabbey and Professor of Systematic Theology at Saint Meinrad School of Theology. He is the author of *The Word Has Dwelt among Us: Explorations in Theology* and *Promising and the Good*. With James G. Hart, he edited *Ethics and Theological Disclosures: The Thought of Robert Sokolowski*.

Ralph Martin is President of Renewal Ministries and is the Director of Graduate Theology Programs in the New Evangelization at Sacred Heart Major Seminary. He is the author of numerous books, including *Will Many be Saved? What Vatican II Actually Teaches and its Implications for the New Evangelization* and *The Fulfillment of All Desire*.

David Vincent Meconi, SJ, is Associate Professor of Historical Theology and Director of the Edmund Campion Centre for Catholic Studies at Saint Louis University. He is the author or editor of numerous books, including *The One Christ: St. Augustine's Theology of Deification, The Cambridge Companion to Augustine, On Earth as It Is in Heaven: Cultivating a Contemporary Theology of Creation*, and *Called to Be Children of God: The Catholic Theology of Deification*.

Matthew J. Ramage is Associate Professor of Theology at Benedictine College. He is the author of *Reading the Gospels with Bart Ehrman and Benedict XVI: The Debate behind the Debate* and *Dark Passages of the Bible: Engaging Scripture with Benedict XVI and Thomas Aquinas*.

Michele M. Schumacher is a private docent in the theology faculty of the University of Fribourg. In addition to numerous journal articles, she is the author of *A Trinitarian Anthropology: Adrienne von Speyr and Hans Urs von Balthasar in Dialogue with Thomas Aquinas* and the editor of *Women in Christ: Toward a New Feminism*.

Thomas Joseph White, OP, is Associate Professor of Systematic Theology at the Dominican House of Studies in Washington, DC. He is the author of numerous books, including *The Incarnate Lord: A Thomistic Study in Christology*, *Wisdom in the Face of Modernity: A Study in Thomistic Natural Theology*, and *Exodus*.

William M. Wright IV is Associate Professor of Theology at Duquesne University. With Francis Martin, he recently co-authored *The Gospel of John*. He is the author of *Rhetoric and Theology: Figural Reading of John 9*, as well as numerous journal articles.

Daniella Zsupan-Jerome is Assistant Professor of Theology at Notre Dame Seminary. A consultant for the USCCB's Committee on Communication, she is the author of *Connected Toward Communion: The Church and Social Communication in the Digital Age*.

The Reception of Vatican II

Introduction

Matthew L. Lamb and Matthew Levering

In a recent commemoration of the Second Vatican Council, John O'Malley appreciatively observes that "Vatican II continues to be a reality very much alive in the church today."[1] The present volume bears witness to this ongoing life of Vatican II by reflecting upon the reception—past, present, and future—of the sixteen documents (four Constitutions, nine Decrees, and three Declarations) that the Council produced. In preparing this sequel to our *Vatican II: Renewal within Tradition*,[2] we have assembled contributors from a variety of contemporary schools of thought and perspectives. They are united by a shared commitment to Vatican II as a "renewal within Tradition" rather than as a rupture with previously defined doctrine. Far from representing a monolithic view of what the Council was and how to carry it forward, however, our contributors exhibit quite an array of interests and at times divergent viewpoints with respect to the constructive task of how best to receive the Council today.[3]

In our previous volume, we gathered eminent Catholic scholars to write about each of the sixteen documents of the Council from the perspective of "renewal within Tradition." We were guided by Pope Benedict XVI's distinction between a "hermeneutic of discontinuity" and a "hermeneutic of reform."[4] The former hermeneutic envisions Church history and the Second Vatican Council in terms of doctrinal ruptures and re-inventions, so that what the Church today formally defines as included in divine revelation may tomorrow be cast out as erroneous. By contrast, the latter hermeneutic involves the task (in St. Pope John XXIII's words) of transmitting the "substance of the ancient doctrine of the deposit of faith" in a manner that is "pure and integral, without any attenuation or distortion" but also "in a way that corresponds to the needs of our time."[5]

In the present volume, our contributors are committed to the latter hermeneutic. Rather than calling upon the same authors for this new volume—which would have been impossible, not least because some have been called to the Lord—we have generally chosen members of the next generation of Catholic scholars, that is to say, students of those who were young scholars in Rome during the Council. Thus the contributors to the present volume largely belong to the third generation after the Council—the students of the students of the great *periti* who helped to prepare the conciliar documents.

In offering some background to our volume's perspective and goals, this Introduction will proceed in four steps. First, we will discuss the relationship of Tradition and reform in interpreting the Council. In this regard, we will point especially to the writings of Joseph Ratzinger and Yves Congar both before and during the Council. Second, we will examine areas of concern with regard to post-conciliar theological understandings of the Church's Tradition. Here we note that for a significant body of Catholic theologians, the Church no longer is able to proclaim and interpret the Gospel authoritatively for believers, and indeed the Gospel itself is stripped of its authoritative doctrinal and moral (cognitive) content, since Jesus appears simply as an exemplar of liberative praxis. Third, we reflect upon how best to interpret what happened at Vatican II and how the reception of the Council should proceed today. We engage here with the 1985 Extraordinary Synod, whose focus was Vatican II, and with some contemporary interpreters who move in directions different from our own. Finally, as a fourth step, we reflect upon our interest in Magisterial and theological "reception" of Vatican II, and we interact briefly with theologians who contributed to similar reception-focused books especially during the mid-1980s.

I. Vatican II, Tradition, and Reform

The well-known historian of Vatican II, Giuseppe Alberigo, entitled one of the final sections of his five-volume compendium on the history of the Council "Vatican II and Tradition." In this section, Alberigo notes that in accord with the stated wishes of Pope John XXIII and Pope Paul VI, the Council understood itself in a traditional manner. Thus, as Alberigo observes, "In dealing with the various subjects it faced," the Council aimed not to produce doctrinal change, let alone a rupture with definitive Church teaching, but rather "devoted itself to developing formulations that were ever more faithful to revelation and more suited to the understanding of educated contemporaries."[6] This does not mean, of course, that these new formulations involved no change.

In 1963, looking back upon the just-completed first session of the Council, Joseph Ratzinger (the future Pope Benedict XVI), who served at the Council as an influential *peritus* and a representative of the *nouvelle théologie*,[7] described what he perceived to be the stakes in the controversy at the outset of the Council over the original schema for what became the Dogmatic Constitution on Divine Revelation. Ratzinger remarks, "What was the central issue? Among the theological questions open to serious discussion were the relationship of scripture to tradition and the way in which faith is related to history. Also under discussion was a proper understanding of inspiration and of the historicity of events narrated in scripture."[8] In addition to these historical issues, which had been suppressed by the papal response to the Modernist crisis of the early twentieth century, Ratzinger states that beyond any particular "quarrel about theological differences," there was a deeper issue: "The real question behind the discussion could be put this way: Was the intellectual position of 'anti-Modernism'—the old policy of exclusiveness, condemnation and defense leading to an almost neurotic denial of all that was new—to be continued?"[9]

Ratzinger's generation and many members of the generation prior to his (Henri de Lubac, Karl Rahner, Otto Semmelroth, Yves Congar, Hans Urs von Balthasar, Jean Daniélou, Louis Bouyer, Bernard Lonergan, John Courtney Murray, Gérard Philips, et al.)[10] were tired of what Ratzinger calls "cramped thinking, once so necessary as a line of defense" and "the old pattern of 'anti-ism.'"[11] They were eager to begin "abandoning the defensive and really undertaking a Christian 'offensive.'"[12] This Christian "offensive" or new positive proclamation of the Gospel did not mean, for Ratzinger or his friends, giving in to the Modernist historicizing and relativizing of the Church's dogmatic mediation of divine revelation. On the contrary, Ratzinger affirms in 1963 that the Church must take "all the necessary precautions to protect the faith" even as the Church also comes to "turn over a new leaf and move on into a new and positive encounter with its own origins, with its brothers and with the world of today."[13] Against any possible misunderstanding, Ratzinger insists that "'pastoral' should not mean nebulous, without substance, merely 'edifying'" and that "'ecumenical' must not mean concealing truth so as not to displease others."[14]

In this move from defense to offense during the first half of the twentieth century, not only the above-named theologians but also a number of other important Catholic philosophers and intellectuals were engaged in promoting a dialogue with modernity. For example, Jacques Maritain, Étienne Gilson, Maurice Blondel, Gabriel Marcel, George Lemaître, Erich Przywara, Romano Guardini, Jean Ladrière, and Josef Pieper—just to name a few—worked to disentangle the great schoolmen of the Middle Ages from the often rather superficial treatments found in the manuals used to teach philosophy and theology in Catholic schools and seminaries.[15] These manuals promoted the "anti-isms" through their lists of "adversaries," whose positions were reduced to a few sentences and then condemned.[16] In contrast to such manuals, the writings of the scholars mentioned above displayed how modern questions in the natural and human sciences, including history, politics, and the arts, could be enlightened by reference to the resources of the patristic, scholastic, renaissance, and later periods.

What Ratzinger and his friends wished to affirm by means of their contributions to the documents of the Second Vatican Council was that "to be a Catholic is not to become entangled in separatism, but to be open to the fullness of Christianity."[17] Like their philosopher colleagues, these theologians had shifted from the manualist style dominant in many schools and seminaries to a dialogic mode of expression that sought appreciatively to engage the questions of modern times. As Ratzinger wrote in 1966, this dialogic mode should not be interpreted "as a sudden switchover, a sudden shift from 'conservatism' to 'progressivism' in the Church."[18] Since Catholic theology cannot be rightly interpreted in terms of modern materialist and mechanistic understandings of "progress," true theological progress according to Ratzinger occurs precisely by means of a return to (or a retrieval of) the past, the privileged sources that bear divine revelation to us today and that faithfully communicate, therefore, the living and reigning Jesus Christ. Ratzinger explains that "the measure of the renewal is Christ, as scripture witnesses him. And if the renewal seeks to think through and to speak the Gospel of Christ in a way understandable to contemporary man—i.e., in a contemporary fashion (*aggiornamento* means bringing up to date), the objective is precisely that Christ may become understood."[19]

Already in 1950, in his then-controversial but now quite tame *True and False Reform in the Church*, Yves Congar had noted among the pressing needs of the day "the synthesis of Christianity and liberalism (inescapable and already begun), an updated conception of the role of humanity in the universe and in evolution, and (on a more practical level) the search for a meaningful religious life."[20] Congar made clear that what he was talking about was not a dogmatic error in the Church's mediation of divine revelation, let alone a denial that divine revelation has identifiable, binding, and permanent cognitive content. He observes, "Some things in the church are unchangeable because they are of divine institution and they represent the very foundations upon which the church is built. Among these, for example, are dogma, the sacraments, and the essential structure of the church."[21] In addition to these unchangeable realities, Congar adds further elements that should not be changed: "Other realities ... are so deeply linked to the essence of the church that they cannot be fundamentally changed; they demand our docility and our respect. (Here, for example, are found formulas of doctrine, even those that are not dogmatic formulas properly so called.)"[22]

The defensiveness or "old pattern of 'anti-ism'" that Ratzinger bemoaned shows up in Congar's journal entry of November 30, 1962, where he describes a meeting with Cardinal Ottaviani at the Holy Office. According to Congar, "The Cardinal said: as you are being watched and are under suspicion to such an extent, you ought to be so much more careful and align yourself with the authentic Magisterium."[23] In response, Congar pointed out that he was doing nothing that was not requested of him by bishops participating in the Council. In his journal entry, however, he adds a more combative observation, indicative, no doubt, of the self-understanding of many of the great theologians of the *nouvelle théologie* whose impact on the Council's documents can be found everywhere: "My work displeases them because they realise very well that its whole aim is to bring back into circulation certain ideas, certain things that they have been endeavouring to shut out for four hundred years, and above all for the past hundred years."[24]

Is this Congar's confession that in his view the Church had not faithfully mediated divine revelation during the four hundred years prior to Vatican II? On the contrary, Congar states that his effort to "bring back into circulation certain ideas" is "my vocation and my service in the name of the Gospel and of the Tradition."[25] It is not "the Gospel and . . . the Tradition," but rather certain aspects of the Tradition's formulation and of the Church's pastoral stance over the past few centuries that Congar seeks to change. Thus, in *La tradition et la vie de l'Église*, published during the Council as a summary of his two masterful volumes on Tradition and traditions, Congar remarks that for the Fathers of the Church (and in his own view as well), "tradition presents first the content of the Scriptures, which contain in one way or another all that is necessary to live as God wishes us to (the details of which will be given later), and it interprets the meaning of the Scriptures."[26]

In *La tradition et la vie de l'Église*, Congar joyfully proclaims that the Catholic Church has now been "cured of the siege mentality she has known at times" and that the Church "has regained the initiative with increasing determination"—an initiative that is not progress beyond an archaic past but rather a deeper penetration into divine revelation.[27] With the Church's teaching authority in view, Congar insists that "the material book called 'The Holy Bible', which can be bought as such at any bookseller's, is only the true Bread of Life for God's People when it is interpreted correctly, according to the meaning implanted in it by God, and . . . this is possible only in the Church, in and by her tradition."[28] When Congar wrote these words, he was a bold reformer but certainly not an advocate of rupture in defined doctrine: he affirms that the Holy Spirit "is enough to ensure a certain continuity running through tradition and the Scriptures; we have seen that the Fathers, Schoolmen and Council of Trent have in fact proved the value of tradition in God's economy for revealing himself and his plan by the action of the Holy Spirit."[29]

In his section on "Vatican II and Tradition," Alberigo sheds light on the way in which the Council, inspired not least by Congar (whose prominence among the *periti* is well known), sought to renew and reform the Church so as to make the Gospel more present to the modern world, without producing doctrinal relativism or a rupture in defined doctrine. Alberigo states, "A comparison of the texts of the preparatory schemas with the documents finally accepted helps us measure the substantial continuity with Christian tradition as understood in Catholicism, but also the discontinuity with the Catholicism of the medieval Christian centuries and the post-Tridentine period."[30] This "discontinuity" is not a denial of the fidelity of the post-Tridentine Church's mediation of the Gospel. As Alberigo explains, "No substantial novelties emerged, but an effort was made (even if not always satisfactory) to restate the ancient faith in language intelligible to contemporary humanity and freed of the more or less parasitical encrustations that had hardened in place over the centuries."[31] Alberigo here echoes, without needing to cite, Ratzinger's and Congar's views of the achievement of the Council. With respect to the proper understanding of *aggiornamento* (in the context of *Sacrosanctum Concilium*, but in a manner applicable to the whole Council), Alberigo adds that "[t]he notion people sometimes have that Vatican II set out in a radically new direction springs from hasty and superficial reading that mistakes the return to ancient liturgical practices for subversive innovation."[32]

Making his point even clearer, Alberigo emphasizes the centrality of Tradition for *Dei Verbum* and indeed the centrality of *Dei Verbum* for the unfolding of the whole Council.[33] He appreciates that far from repudiating the Catholic Tradition, "the Council composed a constitution [*Dei Verbum*] that was devoted to tradition in the deepest meaning of the word: tradition is the transmission of Christian revelation itself. It is significant that *Dei Verbum* was one of its major and most telling documents, and the only one the composition of which lasted through the entire duration of the assembly, from 1962 to 1965."[34] Admittedly, Alberigo turns in his next paragraph to an assessment of the Council that suggests that the Council's main focus is the human condition rather than Jesus Christ. He speaks of the task of "refocusing Christian thought on the constitutive elements of the human condition as seen in the light of gospel revelation"— certainly a crucial task of theology, but not the "focus" of "Christian thought" in the view of the conciliar Constitutions or the great majority of the theological contributors to Vatican II.[35]

II. The Post-Conciliar Situation and Tradition

As is well known, events moved quickly after the Council, more quickly than any of the theologians or bishops who participated in the Council could have anticipated. Congar's response to the post-conciliar situation was one of surprise and even a certain amount of defensiveness. He observes in a hasty afterword to the 1968 edition of *True and False Reform in the Church*, "The council was not responsible for either the current problems or the new attitudes. It is unjust and even stupid to attribute to the council the difficulties that we are having today, or even the disquiet and pain about matters of faith."[36]

What "difficulties" did Congar have in mind? Although he notes specific issues—and indeed remarks that "[e]verything is being called into question at the same time"—he makes clear that his fundamental concern is a new attitude of protest, "a revolutionary climate" (including the Paris student uprising of May–June 1968) in which "things that yesterday appeared certain and solid suddenly seemed outdated or at least uninteresting."[37] For theology and for Western culture, he warns, "The danger of *horizontalism* is not a fantasy!"[38] By "horizontalism" he means anthropocentrism, the focus on "the contemporary world and ... humanity's role in the world," a focus that conflicts with the Second Vatican Council's insistence upon the primacy of Jesus Christ and the mysteries of divine life that the Gospel contains.[39]

Rather than turning his back on the protesters, however, Congar sought to extend a dialogic hand to them, in order to work with them to develop solutions to their concerns. In this dialogue, Congar insists upon certain givens of faith: protest, insofar as it wishes to remain in the Church, "can never call into question the hierarchical structure of the church's pastoral life, given to us by the Lord's own institution" and "can never deny or question in a hasty, superficial, or irresponsible way the articles of doctrine, for which one rather ought to be willing to give one's life."[40] In fact, Congar was already worried about some kind of schism in the Church resulting from doctrinal dissent. As he says, "The possibility that the church will be split in two is not mere fantasy: either because, within the framework of an externally preserved institutional unity, the church might really become a community of the Right and of the Left ... or because the division might go even further and end in formal schism."[41] Congar calls for "peace making," for moderation in all things, for weighing all sides of difficult questions, and for "the full participation of everyone in those affairs and activities that concern everyone"—something that will require the clergy to be deeply "conscious of the lives, the ideas, the concerns, and the desires of the faithful" and that will require the Church "to create or multiply structures for participation."[42]

Fifty years after Vatican II, the aspects that Congar says cannot be given up—"the hierarchical structure of the church's pastoral life, given to us by the Lord's own institution" and "the articles of doctrine, for which one rather ought to be willing to give one's life"—are no longer easily insisted upon in the Catholic academic circles that Congar knew so well. Describing the postconciliar vision of Edward Schillebeeckx, with which a significant proportion of professional Catholic theologians agree today, a recent author proposes that "theological dissent and critical communities not only need each other, but they are a necessary part of a living church."[43] On this view, "since the Spirit's authority calls the church to imitate the 'vulnerable rule of God' made flesh in Jesus, there is no room for 'master-slave' relationships within the church"; and it follows that "a democratic form is a better, even if imperfect, model for creating a church in which the Spirit's impulse can be expressed by all Christians."[44] The hierarchical structure is here not "given to us by the Lord's own institution" (as Congar says it is). From this perspective, then, "theologians in their role as critical mediators can dissent from the received language and praxis of the present by arguing that current church doctrine and praxis do not actually take into full account the subversive memory of Jesus. Alternatively, theologians can also criticize any absolutization of language or praxis in the church in the name of the eschatological proviso."[45]

Given this new view of the Church as simply an "anticipatory sign of the redeemed and just human community," there inevitably are numerous defined doctrines and hierarchical forms that no longer truthfully mediate the Gospel of Jesus Christ (newly conceived not as cognitive content but as egalitarian praxis), and Catholic theologians are now encouraged and expected "to express and defend formulations of [Christian] experience that go beyond (or against) the received expressions for possible experience in the church contained in doctrine and magisterial teaching."[46] In fact, for a significant number of academic Catholic theologians today, rupture with what Congar presented as the unchangeable givens is the fundamental purpose of theology, namely instantiating an egalitarian ecclesiastical form joined to an understanding of the Gospel as Jesus's exemplary liberative praxis. In many culture-shaping Catholic colleges and universities, undergraduates have been learning to conceive their faith along these lines since the late 1960s.

Terrence Tilley, who presently holds the Avery Cardinal Dulles Chair at Fordham University, sums up the new perspective on Catholic Tradition: "Crucial for identity through change is *not* remembering *what* the past said or did.... Our fidelity is constituted not by a 'what' but by 'how.' Our faithful memories are not preserved in practices frozen in the past but in living performances that warm our hearts and enlighten our minds."[47] For Tilley, we must ever keep in mind that the Catholic Church's "practices and the doctrines that are the grammar of its practices will change in response to internal and external changes."[48] One recalls here Avery Dulles's own observation, in his foreword to the English edition of Congar's *La tradition et la vie de l'Église*, that "the Modernists devised an evolutionary theory of doctrine in which tradition functioned as a principle of transformation," so that "Christ became a mere point of departure for a revelatory process that went far beyond him and the apostles."[49] Tilley seems to think that a Catholic Christianity conceived in this way is not only true but also salutary.

Tilley's viewpoint is reflected in some recent historiography of the Council's origins. In an essay arguing that Henri de Lubac's unconscious nostalgia for a mythic French past led ultimately to "the council fathers ... unwittingly set[ting] in motion an engine of nostalgia" through their promotion of patristic renewal, the patristics scholar Robin Darling Young issues a caution against our previous volume, *Vatican II: Renewal within Tradition*.[50] Referring both to Pope Benedict XVI's December 2005 address to the Curia and to Avery Dulles's chapter in our volume, Young argues that "the historian can observe that more than one of *ressourcement*'s own architects came to regret the effects of the very council their work helped to stimulate, as in the development of recent Catholic theology and culture, patristic 'inspiration' was left far behind," with the result that "some of *ressourcement*'s defenders were forced to take rearguard action and emphasize the 'hermeneutic of continuity.' "[51] It seems to us, however, that the documents of the Second Vatican Council themselves emphasize that the Church has faithfully, without rupture in defined doctrine, mediated divine revelation so that each generation has been able to encounter the Gospel of Jesus Christ, in Scripture as interpreted in the Church's Tradition. Young's portrait indicates the situation in some portions of the Catholic academy, where an insistence upon the fidelity and truth of the Church's dogmatic transmission of the Gospel over the centuries is often presented as a nostalgic and conservative political stance rooted in something other than a radical and life-changing faith in Jesus Christ and the action of the Holy Spirit.

More nuanced, but still troubling, is Joseph Komonchak's critique of Benedict XVI's December 2005 address to the Curia. Komonchak states, "The Church, he [Benedict] claims, is a single historical subject, and its journey is one of continuous progress toward deeper understanding of the faith; it is not marked by fractures or breaks, or by leaps either."[52] Komonchak challenges this claim on two grounds. First, he casts doubt on the view that the Church can be understood to be "a single historical subject" moving through time, since, after all, there are multiple "actual communities of believers who have constituted the Church in the past and constitute it today."[53] The question then is where the single Church could possibly exist, given that what we see on the ground are multiple particular churches. Surely, however, the answer is that due to the action of the Holy Spirit, the multiple churches found across time and space are the one "body of Christ": "For just as the body is one and has many members, and all the members of the body, though many, are one body, so it is with Christ. For by one Spirit we were all baptized into one body—Jews or Greeks, slaves or free—and all were made to drink of one Spirit" (1 Cor 12:12–13, 27). This spiritual unity in a hierarchically organized, sacramental Body of Christ is elaborated upon frequently in the documents of Vatican II, and indeed one wonders how the Church could even have an authoritative Council (let alone, over the centuries, many authoritative Councils) if such spiritual and institutional unity did not in fact exist across the generations, just as Benedict XVI—in accord with *Lumen Gentium* and other documents of the Council—says it does.

Secondly, Komonchak challenges Benedict XVI's claim on the grounds that Benedict disallows any "fractures or breaks" or "leaps." In fact, however, what Benedict disallows is the notion that the Church has definitively taught error and thereby corrupted the divine revelation that the Church, guided by the Holy Spirit, hands on and proclaims for the salvation of the world in each generation. In Newman's sense of development of doctrine (as opposed to doctrinal corruption), there surely will be "breaks" and "leaps," because certain truths will be neglected for a time and certain truths will be newly ascertained; but there will not be definitive erroneous teaching about faith and morals.[54] Komonchak holds that Benedict XVI is guilty of presenting an "abstract description of a Church that never leaps forward and never has to break with its past,"[55] but this is due to Komonchak's faulty reading of Benedict, whose vision of the Church is not "abstract" but Pauline, and who rules out not breaks and leaps per se but solemn false teaching that corrupts the apostolic deposit of divine revelation.

III. What Happened at Vatican II and Its Reception Today

We can easily agree, then, in answering John O'Malley's question "Did Anything Happen at Vatican II?" with a resounding yes, and we note that not only did something happen, but great things happened.[56] In this volume, we hope to show that many significant advances were put forward in the documents of Vatican II, and that many of these advances still need to be better received today, just as would be expected of an important Church Council after the passage of only fifty years. In our view, however, the reception of Vatican II must not be separated from receiving its full teaching on divine revelation and the Church, since the cost of such a mis-reception would be to turn the

Catholic Church into a human construct that cannot mediate the salvation won by Jesus Christ.

It is not possible to appeal to the authority of the Second Vatican Council while proclaiming freedom from the authority of the doctrinal and moral teaching of the Church as contained in the Church's Magisterial Tradition. One finds a recent example of this problem in Massimo Faggioli's invocation of Pope Francis's authority (and the Council's) to rule out "the use of the triad abortion-contraception-homosexuality as a test for entering, staying in, or leaving the Church."[57] Surely, however, *Gaudium et Spes* condemns abortion as illicit killing of an innocent human being, as do later (and earlier) Magisterial texts, and as Pope Francis has also done. Why, then, suppose that proper belonging to the Church can be decisively separated from what one believes about the licitness of abortion? Such a separation would surely count as an "ideologization of the Catholic tradition" (in Faggioli's words).[58] For Faggioli, the fundamental post-conciliar problem with the Church has been St. John Paul II and Benedict XVI themselves. He states, "The bishops of Vatican II have been 'outvoiced,' especially in the last thirty years, by a theologically activist papacy."[59] It is as though a squabble over papal power were the real issue, when in fact Catholic communities since the Council (as Congar already in 1968 saw would be the case) have been divided by the question of whether the Church really has a divinely revealed and salvific faith handed down from the apostles, a doctrinal and moral teaching that unites the people of God in worship. Fortunately, as the present volume will emphasize, the Council has been wonderfully received in all sorts of ways, and it has been received as authoritative teaching on the part of the Church as the Body of Christ.

In the ongoing reception of the Council, as John O'Malley observes, the study of each separate document should "pave the way for the further, absolutely essential step of considering the documents as constituting a single corpus and thus of showing how each document is in some measure an expression of larger orientations and part of an integral and coherent whole."[60] O'Malley recognizes that the documents "implicitly but deliberately cross-reference and play off one another—in the vocabulary they employ, in the great themes to which they recur, in the core values they inculcate, and in certain basic issues that cut across them."[61] One sees this implicit cross-reference and coherence even by simply reading the opening paragraphs of the Constitutions. The common themes in these opening passages are many, but it is not surprising that the Extraordinary Synod of Bishops of 1985 focuses on the shared theme of communion in Christ. As the Synod's "Message to the People of God" affirms, a central thread that ties the four Constitutions together is believers' being "in communion with Christ present in the Church (*Lumen gentium*), in listening to the Word of God (*Dei Verbum*), in the holy liturgy (*Sacrosanctum concilium*), in the service of mankind, especially the poor (*Gaudium et spes*)."[62] In this light, the Synod describes the Church's aim as a "civilization of love" whose primary agent is the Holy Spirit, who unites the Church and enables it to give thanks "to God the Father, through his Son."[63]

The topics that the 1985 Synod's "Final Report" lists as particularly significant in the documents of Vatican II include the distinction beteen the secular
and the sacred; the mystery of God through Jesus in the Holy Spirit; the mystery of the Church; the universal vocation to holiness; Scripture, Tradition,
Magisterium; evangelization; the relationship between the Magisterium and
theologians; renewal of the liturgy; the meaning of communion; unity and
pluriformity in the Church; the Oriental Churches; collegiality; the episcopal
conferences; participation and co-responsibility in the Church; ecumenical
communion; the theology of the Cross; *aggiornamento*; inculturation; dialogue
with non-Christian religions and non-believers; and the preferential option
for the poor and human promotion. With regard to all these areas, the Synod
aptly finds that "[t]he ecclesiology of communion is the central and fundamental idea of the Council's documents," specified as "communion with God
through Jesus Christ, in the Holy Spirit" through "the Word of God and . . .
the sacraments."[64]

O'Malley's consideration of the documents as a whole emphasizes not particular shared themes but a shared *style*. He notes that the documents "are
striking in that they express themselves in a style different from the legislative, judicial, and often punitive style employed by previous councils"; and he
attributes this style to the *nouvelle théologie*'s shift from a neo-scholastic mode
of discourse to a discourse modeled on that of Scripture and the Fathers.[65]
Certainly, the documents have an inviting and dialogic style that differs from
the terser and more combative style found in other councils. For O'Malley,
Vatican II's style "conveyed a values shift that was also a system shift or a paradigm shift."[66] As Ratzinger put it in the passage we quoted above, the bishops
and the theologians who wrote the documents were tired of "anti-ism," and
the shift to a positive tone was quite deliberate. But we hesitate nonetheless to
invoke the phrases "system shift" or "paradigm shift," because these phrases
might seem to imply that a new paradigm has replaced the old Christian
paradigm—which surely was likewise centered upon the Gospel, upon communion in Christ rooted in obedient response to the word of God as mediated
by the Church under the guidance of the Spirit. Furthermore, caustic denun-
ciations remain part of the Church's repertoire when needed, as can be seen,
for example, in Pope Francis's homiletic words of correction.

O'Malley consistently emphasizes that "to press continuity to the exclusion of any discontinuity is in effect to say that nothing happened. As applied
to Vatican II, it reduces the council to a non-event."[67] We agree that there is at
points some demonstrable discontinuity between Vatican II's teachings and
those of other time periods, but not discontinuity in the sense of a rupture
in definitive doctrine, which is the kind of discontinuity that many scholars
have insisted happened.[68] In the sense of Congar's *True and False Reform in the
Church*, which is the sense adopted by Benedict XVI, there is no doubt that the
Second Vatican Council should be interpreted, as O'Malley says, through "the
lens of reform," and we fully agree that the Council "was animated by a *spirit of
reform*."[69] But "reform" here does not mean fundamental revision of definitive

doctrine so as to introduce a rupture in the Church's faithful handing on of the truth of divine revelation, as the phrase "spirit of reform" has sometimes come to mean.

Insofar as the Council's true "spirit of reform" involves a greater effort to dialogue with outsiders, as Ormond Rush argues,[70] it seems quite clear that this is indeed the case. The essays in our volume demonstrate the positive and fruitful ecumenical and interreligious advances promoted by the Council's documents, even while, at the same time, this did not mean for the Council a Christological or doctrinal relativism or a watering down of the contents of faith and holiness for Catholic believers. On the contrary, if anything, the Council emphasized more than ever the universal call to holiness and the demands of the life of faith and charity.

IV. An Evaluation of Reception and an Exercise in Reception

The present volume focuses on the reception of Vatican II in Magisterial teaching and in theological work, and in this way it constitutes both an evaluation of the reception of Vatican II and an exercise in theological reception. Although we deliberately have not imposed uniformity upon the perspectives or formats of the essays, theological works available in English are given preference both because of the vast array of literature (which would have overwhelmed the limited space available to the essays in the volume) and because of our authors' situatedness in the American and Western European contexts. In the future, we hope to undertake work devoted to the reception of the Council around the world.[71] The focus of the present volume is on the ways in which the documents of Vatican II, as interpreted by the Magisterium and also by theologians, have contributed to the handing on of the Gospel. As Karl Barth puts it in his *Ad Limina Apostolorum*, both "Rome and the non-Roman churches . . . live to the extent that they are living communities of the living Jesus Christ."[72] The Catholic Church must be "living"; this means reform and change, which Barth recognized and appreciated in the documents of Vatican II. The Catholic Church must also be proclaiming the true Gospel "of the living Jesus Christ," and thus proclaiming the truth of history precisely within history. This can only be done if "history" is not a historicist solvent that dissolves all truth claims. A judgment about the Holy Spirit's work is needed for hearing the Gospel as interpreted at Vatican II as the word of God for all generations.

We can conclude this introduction, then, by hearkening back to some earlier efforts in the reception of the Second Vatican Council, and reflecting once more upon the central issue at stake. In an essay in *Vatican II: The Unfinished Agenda*, a book published in 1987 to evaluate the reception of the Council, Leo O'Donovan urges that Vatican II be received via the work of the eminent Jesuit *peritus* Karl Rahner, who in O'Donovan's view "sought a radically temporal and historical conception of God and the people of God."[73] For O'Donovan, the results that Rahner achieved remain firmly rooted in "[t]he paschal mystery of Christ": "To a rising tide of relativism he [Rahner] offered the Gospel of a traditional faith newly conceived."[74] Fifty years after the Council, the question has become whether "a radically temporal and historical conception of God and the people of God" can avoid becoming not only radically historical but historicist. In the same volume, Lucien Richard astutely observes, " 'Mission to the world' sums up adequately the purpose of Vatican II," but "[d]efining the words 'mission' and 'world' was not an easy task for the Council—the past twenty years have seen the Church and theologians grappling with the same basic questions."[75] Put simply (not from Richard's perspective but from our own), if there is a divinely given mission, does it involve the proclamation of the apostolic message of salvation to all generations, and is the Church authoritatively the bearer of that apostolic message, so that the Church is distinct even in the midst of a shared history from the "world" and its history?

René Latourelle highlights the relationship of faith and history in his contribution to his three-volume Jesuit collection, *Vatican II: Assessment and Perspectives: Twenty-Five Years After (1962–1987)*. Latourelle states, "Theology cannot escape the need to reflect on the relationship between faith and history, and on the unity of the glorified Christ and Jesus of Nazareth. The Christian faith presumes a link of continuity between the phenomenon of Jesus and the interpretation of this phenomenon by the early Church."[76] The credibility of the early Church's (scriptural) interpretation of Jesus and of the creedal and conciliar interpretations offered in the course of the Church's history (including at Vatican II) stands or falls upon the possibility of true historical communication and development of the cognitive content of the Gospel. As Dulles argues in his contribution to *The Reception of Vatican II*, a balanced interpretation of the Council's documents should conclude—as does the 1985 Synod—that "notwithstanding some real shifts and developments, Vatican II is fundamentally self-consistent, stands in substantial continuity with earlier church teaching, and remains valid in its essentials for our own day."[77]

Dulles's insistence on the relationship of Vatican II to earlier Church teaching is not a present-day exhibition of restorationist tendencies or "anti-ism." On the contrary, it belongs inherently to the joyful reception of Vatican II's documents as truth about divine revelation. Of course, neither the Council nor any Church Synod should be simplistically described by "a picture of a bland Synod in which peace reigned."[78] No one imagines the bishops at Vatican II sitting around serenely agreeing with each other on everything, and so our insistence upon the ongoing reception of the apostolic deposit of faith is not a ploy to disseminate an imaginary Vatican II that reprises the wondrous peace of the Church as described in Acts 2. Something happened at Vatican II, and it significantly, positively, and tumultuously changed the Church. Given that Vatican II "was a beautiful work of the Holy Spirit," as Pope Francis said in a homily on 17 April 2013,[79] the Church does not dare suppose either that it has yet done all that the Holy Spirit wished to be done through the Council's Constitutions, Decrees, and Declarations, or that all that the Church has done has been done rightly. The task of the ongoing reception of the Council after fifty years, indeed, is not least to sift and evaluate what has been done thus far, so as to see better the true paths of development.[80] As the 1985 Synod put it, "Unanimously and joyfully we ... verify that the Council is a legitimate and valid expression and interpretation of the deposit of faith as it is found in Sacred Scripture and in the living tradition of the Church. Therefore we are determined to progress further along the path indicated to us by the Council."[81] The two points go together: it is precisely because the Council leads us deeper into the "deposit of faith as it is found in Sacred Scripture and in the living tradition of the Church" that we must boldly proceed along the true path of reform and renewal that the Council documents set forth.[82]

NOTES

1. John O'Malley, SJ, "Introduction: Trajectories and Hermeneutics," in *After Vatican II: Trajectories and Hermeneutics*, ed. James L. Heft, SM with John O'Malley, SJ (Grand Rapids, MI: Eerdmans, 2012), x–xxii, at xxii. O'Malley notes, "Although studies in this volume could well be considered under the rubric of 'reception,' I suggest that 'trajectory' might better catch the reality. The dictionary defines *trajectory* as the path of a moving body. We can take it here as almost a synonym for development, that is, for shifts or changes that have taken place that probably would not have done so except for the council but that cannot easily be traced to a specific provision of the council. Whereas 'reception' generally indicates a direct application (or nonapplication) of explicit norms or directives, such as the revised liturgical forms, 'trajectory' suggests something less obviously based on the council's norms and directives. It is related to reception, and perhaps can be considered a species of it. Introduction of it as a category of interpretation expands what we usually mean by reception" (xii). The risk of the term "trajectory" is that it may indicate any direction of a projectile and need not indicate a "development" (in the sense of a true unfolding of the revealed mystery). Therefore, in the present volume, we retain the term "reception," although we include not only the magisterial reception but the theological (and, when appropriate, the pastoral) reception of the documents of Vatican II.

2. See *Vatican II: Renewal within Tradition*, ed. Matthew L. Lamb and Matthew Levering (Oxford: Oxford University Press, 2008).

3. For discussion of the concept of "reception," see Yves Congar, OP, "La reception comme réalité ecclésiologique," *Revue des sciences philosophiques et théologiques* 56 (1972): 369–403. See also Gilles Routhier, *La réception d'un concile* (Paris: Cerf, 1993); *Réceptions de Vatican II. Le Concile au risqué de l'histoire et des espaces humains*, ed. Gilles Routhier (Leuven: Peeters, 2004).

4. Pope Benedict XVI, "A Proper Hermeneutic for the Second Vatican Council," in *Vatican II: Renewal within Tradition*, ed. Matthew L. Lamb and Matthew Levering (Oxford: Oxford University Press, 2008), ix–xv, at xi; excerpted from Pope Benedict XVI's December 22, 2005 address to the Roman Curia, "Ad Roman Curiam ob omnia natalicia," *Acta Apostolicae Sedis* XCVIII (January 6, 2006): 40–53.

5. Pope Benedict XVI, "A Proper Hermeneutic for the Second Vatican Council," xi, quoting Pope John XXIII's speech inaugurating the Second Vatican Council on October 11, 1962. This view differs, we think, from the proposal for renewal offered by Paul Lakeland when, consciously going well beyond the teaching of *Lumen Gentium*, he advises, "The recovery of a healthy presence in the developed world may be a matter of standing down from the sense of religious superiority and placing ourselves

firmly and equitably in the ranks of the many Christian churches, all of us at one and the same time bearers of revealed truth and yet incomplete and sinful institutions, needing one another for our completeness" (Lakeland, *A Council That Will Never End: Lumen Gentium and the Church Today* [Collegeville, MN: Liturgical Press, 2013], 149). Insofar as Lakeland is calling for an end to triumphalist arrogance and for an appreciation for the insights and contributions of non-Catholic Christians, we fully agree; but the problem is that given the doctrinal differences among Christians, if all "the many Christian churches" are in the same way "bearers of revealed truth," then which church is correct about which doctrine? Lakeland seems to be suggesting that all are correct and incorrect in various ways, with the result that prior to the eschaton we cannot know what is doctrinally correct, that is to say what belongs truly to divine revelation. In thus rejecting the teaching of *Lumen Gentium* on this matter, he puts into question the truth of the teachings of Vatican II. He allows for Christian "humility" but at the high cost of being unable to identify, in the ecumenical and interreligious (and non-theist) context of the modern world, the content of divine revelation. The problem has been well put by Thomas G. Weinandy, OFM Cap.: "While the Council Fathers probably did not fully realize it at the time, this call for a renewed presentation, theologically and pastorally, of the unchanging Gospel contained an inbuilt tension as well as a complementary relationship. What changes were needed for creating a truly renewed articulation and presentation of the Gospel, and, simultaneously, what could not be altered so as to insure that it is actually the Gospel that is being renewed? The struggles within the post-Vatican II Church have been over maintaining the proper balance and interrelationship between these two concerns" (Weinandy, "Vatican II Today: Forty Years Later: Struggles and Initiatives," in *After Forty Years: Vatican Council II's Diverse Legacy*, ed. Kenneth D. Whitehead [South Bend, IN: St. Augustine's Press, 2007], 1–11, at 2–3).

6. Giuseppe Alberigo, "Vatican II and Tradition," in *History of Vatican II*, vol. 5, *The Council and the Transition: The Fourth Period and the End of the Council, September 1965–December 1965*, ed. Giuseppe Alberigo, trans. Matthew J. O'Connell, English version ed. Joseph A. Komonchak (Leuven: Peeters, 2006), 592–95, at 593. See also Alan Schreck's popular introduction to the Council, which responds to the Council's critics: *Vatican II: The Crisis and the Promise* (Cincinnati, OH: Servant Books, 2005).

7. For background to the role of the *periti* and to Ratzinger's own role, see, for example, Karl Heinz Neufeld, SJ, "In the Service of the Council: Bishops and Theologians at the Second Vatican Council (for Cardinal Henri de Lubac on His Ninetieth Birthday)," trans. Ronald Sway, in *Vatican II: Assessment and Perspectives: Twenty-Five Years After (1962–1987)*, vol. 1, ed. René Latourelle, SJ (New York: Paulist Press, 1988), 74–105; Jared Wicks, SJ, "Six Texts by Prof. Joseph Ratzinger as *Peritus* before and during Vatican Council II," *Gregorianum* 89 (2008): 233–311. See also Gérard Philips, *Carnets conciliaires de Mgr. Gérard Philips, Secrétaire adjoint de la Commission doctrinale*, ed. Karim Schelkens (Leuven: Peeters, 2006).

8. Joseph Ratzinger, *Theological Highlights of Vatican II*, trans. the Missionary Society of St. Paul the Apostle (New York: Paulist Press, 1966), 43. In his preface to the English edition of *Theological Highlights of Vatican II*, Ratzinger explains that "[t]his book was originally published in four separate booklets which appeared after each of the four sessions of Vatican Council II. In each I tried to give an account of what had happened during that particular session and a preview of what still remained to be done. The four parts of the present book correspond to the four original booklets. Thus this book clearly has its own specific character. It is not an attempt to appraise past events from the detached viewpoint of the historian. Rather, it is the account of

a personal journey through the landscape of each session, with an open view toward future developments. Therefore, the various parts invite the reader to reacquaint himself with the Council, moving through it again from its beginnings. He is invited to reexperience the step-by-step movement from present to future rather than merely contemplate the end result from afar" (preface to the English edition, vii–ix, at vii). For a historical study of the development and content of the Schema that suggests that it was somewhat closer to the emphases of the *nouvelle théologie* than Ratzinger realized at the time, see Karim Schelkens, *Catholic Theology of Revelation on the Eve of Vatican II: A Redaction History of the Schema* De fontibus revelationis *(1960–1962)* (Leiden: Brill, 2010); but see Jared Wicks, SJ's critical review of this book in *Zeitschrift für Kirchengeschichte* 123 (2012): 408–9.

9. Ratzinger, *Theological Highlights of Vatican II*, 44.

10. See Gerald O'Collins, SJ's chapter on "*Ressourcement* and Vatican II" in his *The Second Vatican Council: Message and Meaning* (Collegeville, MN: Liturgical Press, 2014). O'Collins sums up: "Called by Pope John XXIII of blessed memory, Vatican II was the most significant religious event in the twentieth century. One generation has now passed, and a second is well established since the Council ended in 1965. Its teaching is still being received and tested in the lives of believers. In major ways that teaching was shaped by theologians of the *ressourcement* movement: Chenu, Congar, Daniélou, de Lubac, Philips, Rahner, Ratzinger, Smulders, and others. They left the whole Christian Church a life-giving legacy in what they retrieved from the Scriptures and the great tradition for the documents of Vatican II" (24).

11. Ratzinger, *Theological Highlights of Vatican II*, 42–43.

12. Ibid. 43.

13. Ibid. 44.

14. Ibid. 45.

15. See Maritain's writings on the degrees of knowledge from the sciences to metaphysical wisdom, on art, and on the need for modern democracies to cultivate the intellectual and moral virtues; Gilson's reflections upon the history of scholasticism and his involvement in parliamentary democracy; Lemaître's contributions to cosmology and the distinctions and relations between science and religion; Przywara's developments of the analogy of being in light of modern philosophical questions; Ladrière's important mathematical contributions and his work on the relations of scientific knowledge and religious knowledge; the many varied and pivotal contributions of Pieper to the renewal of contemporary cultures; and so forth. In listing these figures, we do not intend to propose an exhaustive list or to privilege any particular "school of thought."

16. The manuals of theology were often referred to as "*Schultheologie*," which was then rendered in English as "scholastic theology" or "school-theology." Unlike the question-structures of the medieval *Summae*, the manuals used a thesis-structure. The succinct presentations of the manuals were well suited for covering the many subjects of theology from apologetics through Scripture to doctrines, schools of systematics, moral, and pastoral fields. But their concise style in dismissing opposed or different positions tended to promote the "anti-ist" mentality among students and teachers.

17. Ratzinger, *Theological Highlights of Vatican II*, 46.

18. Ratzinger, preface to the English edition, *Theological Highlights of Vatican II*, viii.

19. Ibid. ix.

20. Yves Congar, OP, *True and False Reform in the Church*, trans. Paul Philibert (Collegeville, MN: Liturgical Press, 2011), 298.

21. Ibid. 150.

22. Ibid. 150–51.

23. Yves Congar, OP, *My Journal of the Council*, trans. Mary John Ronayne, OP and Mary Cecily Boulding, OP, ed. Denis Minns, OP (Collegeville, MN: Liturgical Press, 2012), 222.

24. Ibid.

25. Ibid. See also Henri de Lubac, SJ, *Carnets du Concile*, 2 vols. (Paris: Cerf, 2007).

26. Yves Congar, OP, *The Meaning of Tradition*, trans. A. N. Woodrow (San Francisco: Ignatius Press, 2004), 90.

27. Ibid. 96.

28. Ibid.

29. Ibid. 99.

30. Alberigo, "Vatican II and Tradition," 593.

31. Ibid.

32. Ibid. See also Joseph Ratzinger, *Milestones: Memoirs 1927–1977*, trans. Erasmo Leiva-Merikakis (San Francisco: Ignatius Press, 1998), 123–24.

33. Similarly, in "The Ongoing Agenda: A Council Unlike Any Other," in *The Second Vatican Council: Celebrating Its Achievements and the Future*, ed. Gavin D'Costa and Emma Jane Harris (London: Bloomsbury, 2013), 19–34, Godfried Cardinal Danneels states, "The Constitution on Divine Revelation is perhaps the most important doctrinal document of the Council.... *Verbum Dei*, which consumed so much time and discussion, is unfortunately barely read today. This Constitution is however a pillar for conciliar work and, from a doctrinal point of view, is the crown of Vatican II" (26).

34. Alberigo, "Vatican II and Tradition," 594.

35. Ibid.

36. Congar, *True and False Reform in the Church*, 341.

37. Ibid.

38. Ibid.

39. Ibid.

40. Ibid. 344.

41. Ibid. 343–44n5.

42. Ibid. 345–46.

43. Daniel Speed Thompson, *The Language of Dissent: Edward Schillebeeckx on the Crisis of Authority in the Catholic Church* (Notre Dame, IN: University of Notre Dame Press, 2003), 157.

44. Ibid. 160.

45. Ibid. 153–54.

46. Ibid. 154.

47. Terrence W. Tilley, *Inventing Catholic Tradition* (Maryknoll, NY: Orbis Books, 2000), 185.

48. Ibid.

49. Avery Cardinal Dulles, SJ, forward to *The Meaning of Tradition*, by Yves Congar, vii–x, at ix.

50. Robin Darling Young, "A Soldier of the Great War: Henri de Lubac and the Patristic Sources for a Premodern Theology," in Heft and O'Malley, *After Vatican II: Trajectories and Hermeneutics*, 134–63, at 137.

51. Ibid. 161.

52. Joseph A. Komonchak, "Interpreting the Council and Its Consequences: Concluding Reflections," in Heft and O'Malley, *After Vatican II: Trajectories and Hermeneutics*, 164–72, at 167.

53. Ibid.

54. See Ian Ker, *Newman on Vatican II* (Oxford: Oxford University Press, 2014), esp. chap. 2 on "The Hermeneutic of Change in Continuity." Ker here defends *Dignitatis Humanae* as a true development of doctrine in Newman's sense.

55. Komonchak, "Interpreting the Council and Its Consequences," 168.

56. This is the title of one of the essays contained in John W. O'Malley, SJ, *Vatican II: Did Anything Happen?*, ed. David G. Schultenover (New York: Continuum, 2007).

57. Massimo Faggioli, *A Council for the Global Church: Receiving Vatican II in History* (Minneapolis, MN: Fortress Press, 2015), 322.

58. Ibid.

59. Ibid. 94.

60. John W. O'Malley, SJ, "'The Hermeneutic of Reform': A Historical Analysis," in *50 Years On: Probing the Riches of Vatican II*, ed. David G. Schultenover, SJ (Collegeville, MN: Liturgical Press, 2015), 3–34, at 29. For important corrections of O'Malley's *What Happened at Vatican II* (Cambridge, MA: Harvard University Press, 2008), see John M. McDermott, SJ, "Did That Really Happen at Vatican II? Reflections on John O'Malley's Recent Book," *Nova et Vetera* 8 (2010): 425–66.

61. O'Malley, "'The Hermeneutic of Reform,'" 29.

62. *The Extraordinary Synod—1985: Message to the People of God* (Boston, MA: Daughters of St. Paul, n.d.), 32.

63. Ibid. 35–36.

64. Ibid. 53.

65. O'Malley, "'The Hermeneutic of Reform,'" 29–30.

66. Ibid. 30.

67. Ibid. 31.

68. In our view, however, it is also important to appreciate the developments in Magisterial teaching in the three decades leading up to the Council. The degree of discontinuity between Vatican II's documents and pre-conciliar Magisterial teaching has at times been greatly exaggerated: pre-conciliar Magisterial teaching anticipated aspects of a number of the significant developments of Vatican II, without thereby rendering Vatican II "a non-event." See, for example, the essays in *La théologie catholique entre intransigeance et renouveau. La reception des mouvements préconciliaires à Vatican II*, ed. Gilles Routhier, Philippe J. Roy, and Karim Schelkens (Leuven: Maurits Sabbebibliotheek, 2011).

69. O'Malley, "'The Hermeneutic of Reform,'" 34.

70. Ormond Rush, "Toward a Comprehensive Interpretation of the Council and Its Documents," in Schultenover, *50 Years On*, 35–60; Rush, *Still Interpreting Vatican II: Some Hermeneutical Principles* (New York: Paulist Press, 2004).

71. For steps in this direction, see the essays by Agbonkhianmeghe E. Orobator, SJ, Peter C. Phan, and O. Ernesto Valiente in Schultenover, *50 Years On*, and the bibliographical resources identified in these essays; as well as the nine brief essays in section 12 (entitled "The Effect of the Council on World Catholicism") of *Modern Catholicism: Vatican II and After*, ed. Adrian Hastings (New York: Oxford University Press, 1991). Yet we note with concern that the conclusion of Orobator's essay, for example, lumps together "[f]orms of this resurgent clericalism and conservatism . . . in matters of sexual morality, control of liturgical development, gender discrimination, and the exercise of ecclesial authority" (291). Here one fears that the sexual morality in

question is none other than the Church's sexual morality as set forth in *Gaudium et Spes* and later Magisterial documents, since it is unclear what other kind of teaching on sexual morality—as distinct from gender discrimination—would be here deemed out of line. More precision is needed, since the assumption (against "resurgent clericalism and conservatism") that Vatican II is always on the side of elite liberal views is erroneous.

72. Karl Barth, *Ad Limina Apostolorum: An Appraisal of Vatican II*, trans. Keith R. Crim (Edinburgh: The Saint Andrew Press, 1969), 72–73.

73. Leo J. O'Donovan, SJ, "For Church and World: A Messenger of Faith and Hope," in *Vatican II: The Unfinished Agenda: A Look to the Future*, ed. Lucien Richard, OMI with Daniel Harrington, SJ, and John W. O'Malley, SJ (Mahwah, NJ: Paulist Press, 1987), 3–8, at 4. O'Donovan has in view not least Rahner's "Towards a Fundamental Theological Interpretation of Vatican II," trans. Leo O'Donovan, SJ, in Richard, Harrington, and O'Malley, *Vatican II: The Unfinished Agenda: A Look to the Future*, 9–21. Rahner praises *Gaudium et Spes* while singling out *Lumen Gentium* and *Dei Verbum* for criticism, along lines that are rather astounding given the crucial subject matter of these two Dogmatic Constitutions: "As far as the doctrinal decrees of the Council are concerned, those namely on the Church and divine revelation, it may be that they speak largely from a specifically European horizon of understanding and that they consider problems that are vital only for a European theology" (13). With faint praise, Rahner adds, "And still we can say that these decrees strive for statements that are not entirely conditioned by the linguistic style of a Neo-Scholastic theology and can be made more easily understandable in the entire world" (13). The real contribution of the Council, Rahner argues, is to interreligious dialogue (with the corresponding impact on ecclesiology, Christology, and the doctrine of revelation): "doctrinally the Council did two things which are of fundamental significance for a world-wide missionary effort. In the Declaration on the Relation of the Church to Non-Christian Religions, a truly positive evaluation of the great world religions is initiated for the first time in the doctrinal history of the Church. Furthermore, even from an infralapsarian perspective (as the Scholastics say), the documents on the Church, on the missions, and on the Church in the modern world proclaim a universal and effective salvific will of God which is limited only by the evil decision of human conscience and nothing else. This implies the possibility of a properly salvific revelation-faith even beyond the Christian revelatory world" (13–14). On this view, the "message of salvation" taught by the Council, not least vis-à-vis the "world," seems perhaps redundant.

74. O'Donovan, "For Church and World," 4.

75. Lucien Richard, OMI, "Vatican II and the Mission of the Church: A Contemporary Agenda," in Richard, Harrington, and O'Malley, *Vatican II: The Unfinished Agenda: A Look to the Future*, 57–70, at 68.

76. René Latourelle, SJ, "Absence and Presence of Fundamental Theology at Vatican II," in *Vatican II: Assessment and Perspectives: Twenty-Five Years After (1962–1987)*, ed. René Latourelle, SJ, vol. 3, trans. Leslie Weane (New York: Paulist Press, 1989), 378–415, at 390.

77. Avery Dulles, SJ, "The Reception of Vatican II at the Extraordinary Synod of 1985," appendix to *The Reception of Vatican II*, ed. Giuseppe Alberigo, Jean-Pierre Jossua, and Joseph A. Komonchak, trans. Matthew J. O'Connell (Washington, DC: Catholic University of America Press, 1987), 349–63, at 350. Dulles raises concerns, however, regarding the implementation of the Extraordinary Synod: see ibid. 363. See also Dulles's important observations in his contribution, entitled "Catholic Ecclesiology Since Vatican II," to the otherwise generally critical volume *Synod*

1985: An Evaluation, ed. Giuseppe Alberigo and James Provost, English language ed. Marcus Lefébure (*Concilium* 188 [6/1986]), 3–13, at 11–12: "Some commentators proposed that *a proper hermeneutics* would find the key to the Council's meaning in its innovations. Wherever the Council simply repeated what had been previously taught, this was attributed to inertia, to perfunctory rhetoric, or to the necessity of placating the conservative minority. Conservative interpreters, by contrast, tended to use the Council's reaffirmations of the positions of Trent, Vatican I, and Pius XII as the hermeneutical key for understanding all other passages. In the second decade after the Council these *one-sided interpretations have been vigorously challenged.* Theologians such as Walter Kasper and Hermann-Josef Pottmeyer have protested against selective interpretations that seek to perpetuate the very battles which the Council, through its consensus, overcame in principle. The spirit of Vatican II cannot be urged against the letter, nor can it be plausibly maintained that the majority of the bishops wished to break with the earlier Catholic tradition. The Council's documents must therefore be understood *not selectively but integrally,* not in opposition to, but in continuity with, the Catholicism of earlier centuries. Where the Council was content simply to juxtapose traditional and innovative formulations, the interpreters are challenged to seek a *coherent synthesis that does justice to both.*" Dulles goes on to credit the Synod with providing "eminently sane *hermeneutical principles,*" including the need to understand Vatican II "in continuity with the great tradition of the Church" (12).

78. Hebblethwaite, *Synod Extraordinary,* 125.

79. See http://www.catholicculture.org/news/headlines/index.cfm?storyid=17610.

80. In an interview with Gavin D'Costa, for example, Godfried Cardinal Danneels amply praises the Council and its implementation, but also grants that "[t]here have been exaggerations, certainly, since the Council. The progress afterwards has from time to time not been good" ("Cardinal Godfried Danneels Interviewed by Gavin D'Costa," in D'Costa and Harris, *The Second Vatican Council: Celebrating Its Achievements and the Future,* 165–71, at 167).

81. *The Extraordinary Synod—1985,* 38.

82. For an example of this balance, see Paul D. Murray's argument that "far from the Council's remarkable articulation of a distinctively Catholic theology and practice of ecumenism being in tension with its understanding—commensurate with previous Catholic tradition—of the catholicity of the Church, the former is properly rooted in and flows from a recovered sense of the full implications of the latter" (Murray, "Vatican II: On Celebrating Vatican II as Catholic and Ecumenical," in D'Costa and Harris, *The Second Vatican Council: Celebrating Its Achievements and the Future,* 85–103, at 85). Murray is quite right that "a concern for the integrity ('continuity') of the Catholic tradition of Vatican II requires also due appreciation for its appropriate freshness and renewal ('reform')" (102).

PART ONE

The Constitutions

1

Sacrosanctum Concilium

Jeremy Driscoll, OSB

Introduction

After a number of years in which the Church prepared for the great Jubilee celebration of the year 2000 and when the Jubilee celebration itself was completed, Pope John Paul II said, "Now that the Jubilee has ended, I feel more than ever in duty bound to point to the Council as *the great grace bestowed on the Church in the twentieth century*: there we find a sure compass by which to take our bearings in the century now beginning."[1] Some twelve years later, on October 12, 2012, the fiftieth anniversary of the opening of the Council was celebrated in a joyous Mass in St. Peter's Square that was a significant part of the Synod on the New Evangelization, which had just begun several days before. I was privileged to take part in this Mass. At a certain point I was suddenly invaded by an overwhelming sense of gratitude and wonder for the gift of the Council. I felt its greatness. I saw its amazing achievements. I thought, "Yes, surely the work of the Holy Spirit in our times!" I know, of course—we all do—that there have been serious, even terrible, disputes about the meaning and application of the Council. Difficulties of this sort have followed virtually all the councils of the Church. Even so, in the teachings of all of the councils, there is the possibility of rising above the skirmishes and clashes that follow a Council and seeing it from a different perspective. Faith reminds us that in the give and take of a community's coming to decisions, we can trust that the Holy Spirit is at work in the Church.

The first of the documents of Vatican Council II to be promulgated was the document on the sacred liturgy, *Sacrosanctum concilium* (henceforth *SC*), the subject of this essay. Now more than fifty years have passed since its promulgation on December 4, 1963; and here in particular what I just called serious and even terrible disputes about the Council's teachings have occurred around the changes in the liturgy that the document called for. In part, at least, these are disputes about the liturgy itself and the ways it has been celebrated or should be celebrated since the reform of the liturgical books called for by this document. But I think to some extent the problem in the disputes has been losing sight of some of the principle theological ideas expressed in *SC*. I am hoping that a review here of some of those principal ideas will remind us that in this document there is articulated for our own times some of the richest wisdom of the Church around her experience of the encounter with God through the sacred liturgy.

1. Preparation and Reception

To consider the theology of liturgy in this document, it is important to realize that it was not something produced in hasty preparation for that Council that caught everyone by surprise when John XXIII announced it. Rather, its thought is the fruit of a liturgical movement that preceded it by at least sixty or seventy years, articulating theological positions of a trustworthy pedigree: Pius X in *Tra le Sollecitudini* in 1903, the Benedictine Lambert Beauduin in the movement he ignited by his brief but stirring summons at the Congress of Malines in 1909, the work of outstanding theologians in pre- and post-war years (of whom we can let the name Romano Guardini remind us of the rest),[2] the intense interest of Pius XII in the liturgical movement expressed authoritatively in *Mediator Dei* and in his reforms of the Paschal Vigil and Holy Week liturgies, the international congress of scholars held at Assisi in 1956 that received strong approbation from Pius XII in an audience at Rome that concluded it. Nor is it a document that suffers because the Council's vision had not yet grown mature.[3] It is the point of arrival of decades of serious thought and experience to which the bishops gathered solemnly together in Council gave virtually unanimous approval.

If seventy years or more led up to *SC*, there are now more than fifty years of the history of its reception. By reception I mean something more than who likes it and who does not. Although that is important—important enough, apparently, for people to fight about—reception is an ecclesial question deeper than who wins a fight. Reception means tracing in the Church the effects of the document, watching how her leaders have referred to it, and taking account of how her people have responded to it.

The document's immediate reception is seen in the renewed liturgical books. On the basis of the theological positions that will be reexamined here shortly, the Council called for this renewal, and it has been accomplished. It is a huge achievement. It has borne abundant fruit in the lives of the faithful and will continue to do so for decades and even centuries to come.

By the time twenty years had passed from the close of the Council, the beginnings of a historical perspective could show itself. Pope John Paul II named the question of the reception of the Council as the topic for the Synod of 1985. The Final Report of that synod declared, "The liturgical renewal is the most visible fruit of the whole conciliar effort." It was the Synod of 1985 that also gave rise to the idea of producing a new *Catechism of the Catholic Church*, which was eventually promulgated in 1992. I think the *Catechism* is a splendid gift to the Church, not least because it is massively saturated with the documents of Vatican II, which a glance at the index will demonstrate. Consulting the index for references to *SC* is to discover a program for how this document's treasures can be delivered in catechetical settings. All this is part of the story of reception.[4]

Three years after the Synod of 1985, which marked the twentieth anniversary of the close of the Council, Pope John Paul wrote *Vicesimus Quintus Annus* on the twenty-fifth anniversary of the promulgation of *SC*. In that letter he put all his apostolic authority behind further advancing its agenda. In one paragraph he lists what he sees as the fruits of the liturgical reform for which we must be grateful, namely, "For the fact that the table of the word of God is now abundantly furnished for all; for the immense effort undertaken throughout the world to provide the Christian people with translations of the Bible, the Missal and other liturgical books; for the increased participation of the faithful by prayer and song, gesture and silence, in the Eucharist and the other sacraments; for the ministries exercised by lay people and the responsibilities that they have assumed in virtue of the common priesthood into which they have been initiated through Baptism and Confirmation; for the radiant vitality of so many Christian communities, a vitality drawn from the wellspring of the Liturgy."[5] What the Pope said after twenty-five years about the fruits of this liturgical reform could be redoubled now more than fifty years after. These fruits are part of the story of reception.

The Mass to celebrate the fiftieth anniversary of the opening of the Council, which I mentioned at the beginning of this essay, took place as part of the Synod on the New Evangelization. In his homily at that Mass and again at the closing Mass of the Synod, Pope Benedict XVI urged again in the strongest terms a new and deeper appropriation of the grace-filled event of Vatican Council II, with the *CCC* (Catechism of the Catholic Church) as a key for its interpretation. He spoke of the need for the same again on February 14, 2013 in his informal discussion about Vatican II with the priests of the diocese of Rome, just three days after announcing his resignation. In all three of these talks, he stressed a renewed attention to the *texts* of the Council, as opposed to versions of what the *event* of the Council may have meant.[6] But *event* and *text* are both important. There is a way of approaching *texts* that in fact protects the *event* itself. This is the rich *con-text* in which I want to consider some of the most important parts of the *text* of *SC*. What graces are there still to be mined there?

2. Taking Up the Text Again

We do well to begin our examination of the text itself with the very first paragraph of the document. There it is clearly stated that the reform of the liturgy is tied up with the purpose of the entire Council. It is important for us to measure the significance of this claim. The Council's liturgy and the Council's teaching are inextricably intertwined. (Both opponents and defenders of the Council seem to operate from a profound intuition that such is the case.) This intimate connection between the reform of the liturgy and the whole Council is solidly indicated at the outset in the document's title, which has no specific reference to liturgy, but is simply *Sacrosanctum Concilium*, "This Sacred Council." The word *sancrosanctum* is already an expression of faith by the Council Fathers. Theirs is not just a meeting of a group of corporate leaders. Something holy is underway. The gathering is God's doing. And what do they discern to be the purpose for which God has gathered them? The purpose is stated in four interrelated dimensions as being (1) to impart vigor to the Christian life of the faithful, (2) to adapt to our own times those structures subject to change, (3) to promote unity among Christians, and (4) to strengthen whatever serves to call all people into the embrace of the Church. On the basis of this they state, "The Council therefore sees particularly cogent reasons for undertaking the reform and promotion of the liturgy."[7]

So, the "reform and promotion of the liturgy" have these broader goals of the Council in view. And the rest of the Council's documents were developed in the light of this first document that the Council's bishops approved. From this perspective, I want to examine now three major theological ideas of the document that speak of the liturgy in a general way and are relevant to many different types of sacramental and liturgical celebration. I do not pretend to be exhaustive with this choice. These ideas are all found in the Introduction and important first chapter, but they likewise run through the entire document.[8] Taking account of them will not only indicate the direction a closer reading of the document should take, but will also allow us to encounter some of the key concepts that can help us to continue to pray and celebrate the renewed liturgy with profit and to avoid inappropriate celebrations that mistakenly name the Council as their warrant. These are among the theological reasons for undertaking the reform. The three ideas I have chosen are (1) liturgy founded in the Paschal Mystery, (2) the work of our redemption communicated through the liturgy, and (3) full, active, and conscious participation in the liturgy. After examining these key general ideas, I will look at how they appear in what the document says on the Holy Eucharist, on the Liturgy of the Hours, and on the Liturgical Year. I will conclude with reflections on the renewal of the whole Church envisioned by the renewal of the liturgy.

Before examining particular texts where these ideas are found, something should be said about the kind of language employed in this document and, in fact, in all the documents of the Council. This style of language is already part of the Council's message, indeed, a considerable part of the message. It is well described by Pope John Paul in *TMA* (Tertio Millennio Adveniente): "The Council's enormously rich body of teaching and *the striking new tone* in the way it presented this content constitute as it were a proclamation of new times. The Council Fathers spoke in the language of the Gospel, the language of the Sermon on the Mount and the Beatitudes."[9] When we remember that the Pope had been a bishop-participant in the Council, we can think he is perhaps recalling that many of the bishops at the Council were surprised when they first saw drafts of documents in this new style. They were expecting a more juridical style—language that excluded errors and defined truths in our troubled times, just as previous councils had done.[10] But the Pope notes that what he calls "the striking new tone" of the documents is a proclamation of new times. Here, I think, the problem of "event" and "text" actually meet each other and perhaps can be reconciled. Careful attention to the striking new tone of the texts leads us to the event of the Council that wanted to declare new times in the life of the Church and in the life of the Church for the world.

This new tone, among other things, is the language of Scripture, a tapestry of citations and allusions woven together in such a way that what the Council teaches will appear ultimately as Scripture applied to the point in question. In this way Scripture becomes the ultimate authority for what the Council authoritatively teaches.[11]

2.1 Liturgy Founded in the Paschal Mystery

Let us turn now to some of that rich teaching in chapter 1 of *SC*. The first key idea that I want to consider is liturgy founded in the Paschal Mystery. Chapter 1 begins at Paragraph 5. Paragraphs 5 and 6 are formed by a well-crafted combination of scriptural texts that are a description of God's redemptive work as culminating in the Paschal Mystery. It begins as follows: "God who 'wills that all men and women be saved and come to the knowledge of the truth' [1 Tim. 2:4], 'who in many and various ways spoke in times past to the fathers by the prophets' [Heb. 1:1], when the fullness of time had come sent His Son [allusion to Gal 4:4], the Word made flesh [John 1:14], anointed by the Holy Spirit, to preach the gospel to the poor, to heal the contrite of heart [allusions to Isaiah 61:1 and Luke 4:18], to be a 'bodily and spiritual medicine' [Ignatius of Antioch], the Mediator between God and human beings [1 Tim 2:5]."[12]

As the text continues its movement, it arrives at a first climax by using for the first of many times an expression that will be of major importance for the theology developed here and for the renewed liturgy. It is the expression "Paschal Mystery." Its careful placement within the whole development is striking: "The wonderful works of God among the people of the Old Testament were but a prelude to the work of Christ the Lord in redeeming mankind and giving perfect glory to God. He achieved His task principally by the paschal mystery of His blessed passion, resurrection from the dead, and the glorious ascension, whereby 'dying, he destroyed our death and, rising, he restored our life.' For it was from the side of Christ as He slept the sleep of death upon the cross that there came forth 'the wondrous sacrament of the whole Church.'"[13] Paschal Mystery, then, is the central work of Christ; it is usefully delineated here as his passion, resurrection, and ascension. But not only that—this work is immediately associated with us. His dying destroyed *our* death; his rising restored *our* life. Then an explicit and crucial piece of ecclesiology is inserted into the text, which is based in a vivid Gospel image and well developed by the Fathers; namely, "the wondrous sacrament of the whole Church" emerges from the crucified Lord's pierced side. The Church is born as part of the Paschal Mystery. This is a first step in a development that wants to arrive at the claim that the Church's liturgy likewise springs forth from that same Paschal Mystery. She is called a "wondrous sacrament."

Paragraph 6 develops this by focusing on the risen Lord's relationship to his apostles. I like to say—in part to catch people's attention, but I mean it— that the words "as" and "so" are the most important words of Jesus's teaching. "*As* the Father has loved me, *so* have I loved you." "*As* you and I are one, Father, *so* may they be one in us." "*As* the Father sent me into the world, *so* do I send you" (John 15:9; 17:21; 20:21). And so forth. There are many of these. When we take them seriously, we see that a tremendous transfer is being revealed and accomplished: nothing less than the divine relationship between Father and Son completely transferred to us. This "as and so" construction, so crucial to Jesus's own revelation, is used to open Paragraph 6. "Just *as* Christ was sent by the Father, *so* also He sent the apostles, filled with the Holy Spirit."

Something wonderful is being claimed here. Just *as* Christ was sent, *so* also the apostles are sent. This is the tremendous transfer. And the transfer will find its climax in the Church's liturgy. Christ sent the apostles to proclaim his death and resurrection to every creature so that, the document continues, "they might accomplish the work of salvation which they had proclaimed, by means of sacrifice and sacraments, around which the entire liturgical life revolves" (*SC* 6). This too is an enormous transfer. The work of salvation accomplished in the death and resurrection of Christ is still being accomplished through "sacrifice and sacraments." Baptism is named and described as our being "plunged into the paschal mystery of Christ" (*SC* 6). Then the Eucharist is named as a proclamation of the death of the Lord until he comes. The development reaches a beautiful conclusion with Pentecost, which is called the day "when the Church appeared before the world." And what does this Church look like? Its liturgical form is described. Those who heard Peter's preaching were baptized, and—the document still proceeds just to talk Scripture—"they continued steadfastly in the teaching of the apostles and in the communion of the breaking of bread and in prayers . . . praising God and being in favor with all the people" (Acts 2:41–47).

In the final move of this paragraph, the Council document strikingly declares the Church's direct continuity with these apostolic beginnings. It says, "From that time onwards the Church has never failed to come together to celebrate the paschal mystery." And those celebrations are a description of our liturgy: ". . . reading those things 'which were in all the scriptures concerning him' (Luke 24:27), celebrating the eucharist in which 'the victory and triumph of his death are again made present,' and at the same time giving thanks 'to God for his unspeakable gift' (2 Cor. 9:15) in Christ Jesus, 'in praise of his glory' (Eph. 1:12), through the power of the Holy Spirit." In 1963 this was an "enormously rich... teaching" in "a striking new tone."[14] We have absorbed a good deal of it in fifty years, but precisely because the teaching is so saturated in Scripture, we dare not claim that we have exhausted its meaning and can go on now to further thoughts. This way of conceiving things is of perennial importance for the Church.[15]

The concept of Paschal Mystery has had enormous influence on the shaping of the new liturgical books and celebrations. Later in this document, the Council Fathers will call for a revision of the liturgical year with a clear center in the Paschal Mystery as exposed during Lent and Paschaltide. A renewed sense of Sunday is likewise called for, because "the Church celebrates the paschal mystery every eighth day."[16] The rite of burial should be revised to show more clearly the paschal character of Christian death.[17] The revision of sacraments and sacramentals is to be done so that the faithful "are given access to the stream of divine grace which flows from the paschal mystery of the passion, death, the resurrection of Christ, the font from which all sacraments and sacramentals draw their power."[18] The restoration of the Rites of Christian Initiation for Adults flows from this principle and is specifically called for by SC.[19] And there can be no question that one of the great theological achievements of the Missal of Paul VI is the way in which the Paschal Mystery emerges with clarity as the center of the liturgical year and, indeed, as the center of every celebration of the Eucharist. Measuring this achievement is done by studying individual texts and gaging their cumulative effect,[20] but a simple statistic can indicate what I am pointing to. In the Missal of Paul VI, the word "paschal," in its various forms, occurs in 120 texts, many of which are repeated numerous times. In the preconciliar missal of 1962 it occurs in 17 texts.[21]

2.2 The Work of Our Redemption Communicated Through the Liturgy

Let us turn now to the second key idea that I propose for our consideration: the Council's teaching that the work of our redemption is communicated through the liturgy. Paragraph 7 begins, "To accomplish so great a work [opus], Christ is always present in His Church, especially in her liturgical celebrations." The "so great a work" to be accomplished is a reference to the previous paragraph, which states that "the Church has never failed to come together to celebrate the paschal mystery." Now it becomes clear that this work is not something accomplished simply by human beings deciding to put some liturgy together. It is actually Christ's deed that he works through his Church, and he does it especially in the liturgy. Next, the document gives examples of different ways in which Christ is present in the liturgy: in the person of his minister, in the eucharistic species, in the reading of the Word, in the praying and singing of the whole assembly. All this is Christ associating the Church with himself in what is called, for a second time, "this great work." After this, that work is described in two of its dimensions: it is the "great work [opus] wherein [1] God is perfectly glorified and [2] men and women are sanctified."

It could be said that the document is at pains here to indicate that something is actually occurring and accomplished when the liturgy is celebrated.

namely, the glorification of God and the sanctification of human beings. For this reason, the document declares, "Rightly, then, the liturgy is considered an exercise of the priestly office of Jesus Christ." The word "exercise" (*exercitatio*) is like the twofold use of the word "work" (*opus*)—it indicates Christ's activity during the liturgy. Christ the priest (1) glorifies the Father, and Christ the priest (2) sanctifies human beings. The reason for the liturgy's signs and symbols is explained in this context. "In the liturgy the sanctification of human beings is signified by signs perceptible to the senses, and is effected in a way which corresponds with each of these signs." "Effected" (*efficitur*) is yet another word associated with the idea that something very concrete is actually occurring during the celebration of the liturgy.

That Christ is at work in the liturgy, communicating to us the work of our redemption, is certainly being stressed in this paragraph. But just as important is the stress that Christ associates the Church with himself in all that he is doing. The subject acting is not simply Christ or the ordained priest representing him. Rather, "Christ indeed always associates the Church with Himself in this great work ... in the liturgy the whole public worship is performed by the Mystical Body of Jesus Christ, that is, by the Head and His members." This formulation further clarifies the strong start of the introduction to the whole document, in line with what we already saw to be the reasons "this sacred council" sought to reform and promote the liturgy. Liturgy is "the outstanding means by which the faithful may express in their lives, and manifest to others, the mystery of Christ and the real nature of the true Church." The real nature of the true Church is that she is associated with Christ in his glorifying the Father and his work of accomplishing human redemption. It is enormous. There is nothing bigger. Paragraph 7 concludes by saying so: "From this it follows that every liturgical celebration, because it is an action of Christ the priest and of His Body which is the Church, is a sacred action surpassing all others; no other action of the Church can equal its efficacy by the same title and to the same degree."

The strong sense that Christ is at work in the liturgy actually communicating the work of our redemption, together with the notion that the subject acting in the liturgy is the whole Christ, head and members, is very definitely one of the major pieces of thinking from the liturgical movement in the first half of the century preceding the Council.[22] The authoritative statement of such thinking in this first chapter of *SC* makes it one of the principles for guiding the reform of the liturgical books. That is surely what we see in the shape of the rites and in the language of the prayers of the reformed liturgy. The whole Church is active in the liturgy with Christ at its head.[23]

2.3 Active Participation

The third key idea I propose for consideration occurs not only in the document's first chapter but is a theme that runs through the entire document as a leitmotif, namely, active participation on the part of all in the liturgy. That it is a leitmotif is why it has been so widely discussed and also probably why disagreements about its interpretation seem so crucial to the disputants. In any case, active participation of all in the liturgy is without question one of the main themes and concerns of *SC*, and understanding it rightly is crucial to what the Council intended.

Obviously, I cannot be exhaustive here, but I will reflect on a few pivotal points that I find important in this ample discussion. A way in is offered, perhaps, by the great Belgian Benedictine pioneer of the liturgical movement, Bernard Capelle, with his simple definition for active participation: "a presence sustained by an intention."[24] There is something elegant about this. It holds in tension the exterior and interior dimensions of what "active participation" might mean and represents each of these dimensions with words that require a good deal from the one who would enact them. "Presence" is more than just physically being in a place and doing something there. It suggests a personal engagement, an energy emanating from the participant, an atmosphere, deep engagement. "Intention" is what sustains this atmosphere and energy, and it implies understanding and the pointing of one's understanding toward a goal.

A definition like this can help us sort through what is in fact a fairly broad range of levels of meaning around the document's use of the notion of active participation. Sometimes it is applied to external forms and at other times to the mystery celebrated. So, the risk of confusion is potentially considerable; but if it can be avoided, then a treasure is found.

It seems best to begin with a paragraph that is certainly crucial to understanding it correctly: paragraph 14, which opens the second subtitled section of chapter 1 of the document, entitled, "The Promotion of Liturgical Instruction and Active Participation." There we read, "Mother Church earnestly desires that all the faithful should be led to that full, conscious, and active participation in liturgical celebrations which is demanded by the very nature of the liturgy." First of all, the three adjectives—full, conscious, and active—give shape to what participation means.[25]

I find it useful to comment on these adjectives with paragraph 11, which precedes this. That it precedes it is a reminder that "participation" may well be at issue even when that particular word, in its noun form, is not used; for participating is also a verb. Paragraph 11 claims that the liturgy cannot produce its full effects unless "the faithful come to it with proper dispositions, that their minds should be attuned to their voices."[26] It reminds pastors that "something more is required [in the liturgy] than the mere observation of the laws governing valid and licit celebration; it is their [pastors'] duty also to ensure that the faithful take part fully aware of what they are doing, actively engaged in the rite, and enriched by its effects." The Latin is strong and concise here: "ut fideles scienter, actuose et fructuose eandem participent." The Council here articulates an enormous program, with significant responsibility for its implementation assigned to "pastors of souls." Indeed, pastors would do well regularly to measure themselves by how well they are accomplishing what is asked of them here.

Returning to paragraph 14, it is helpful to notice the passive form of the verb in the opening sentence: "that all the faithful should be led [*ducatur*] to that ... participation." Perhaps something in the modern spirit rankles at this; nevertheless, we must try to get past it, for the passive verb form helps us to see what the bishops of the Council envisioned. It is the nature of the liturgy itself, they say, that demands this active participation; but they are speaking to a situation where, in many cases, this is understood poorly or not at all. It is a question of formation, of "being led." Many of the faithful—and perhaps, unfortunately, some of their pastors—do not know that "such participation ... is their right and duty by reason of their baptism." Only when that is understood can participation be full, conscious, and active. This is at the heart of what the Council intended by the liturgical reform. In this paragraph it is stated in the clearest possible terms: "In the restoration and promotion of the sacred liturgy, this full and active participation by all the people is the aim to be considered before all else; for it is the primary and indispensable source from which the faithful are to derive the true Christian spirit." I am explaining why the bishops at the Council were speaking this way in 1963. Now, more than fifty years later, we can use their language to measure our own current pastoral scene. Is it yet the case that "active participation by all [in the liturgy] ... is the primary and indispensable source" by which the faithful are actually nourished in their Christian lives? Much progress has been made. Much remains to be accomplished.

More systematic attention to the texts of the Missal of Paul VI might help us solve the debates around what full, active, and conscious participation means in Vatican II's program. The word *particeps*, together with related forms like *participatio* and *participare*, is a root found 111 times in the reformed Missal as opposed to 17 times in the previous Missal. A whole semantic field of suchlike words is much more abundant in the Missal of Paul VI: *commercium, societas, consortium*, and *communio*.[27] Careful attention to these words would reveal that they all serve to express again and again the fact that, through *participation* in the liturgy, we are made *participators* of the divine life. Participating in the divine life is the true, ultimate active participation. Or to say the same in the theological categories examined here: participation in the liturgy is nothing less than participation in the Paschal Mystery of Jesus. Through participation in the liturgy, the work of our redemption is communicated to us. Full, conscious, and active participation in the liturgy by all the faithful in the one Eucharist offered by the one high priest "is the outstanding means whereby the faithful may express in their lives, and manifest to others, the mystery of Christ and the real nature of the true Church."[28]

3. The Key Ideas Brought to Bear on Particular Liturgies

I want now to consider several different sections of *SC* where the three key ideas we have considered—Paschal Mystery, the work of our redemption, and active participation—are brought to bear on particular and different liturgical celebrations in which the document calls for reform. In speaking of the Paschal Mystery, I have already listed a number of areas in which the Council called for it to be more clearly set in relief in particular liturgies.[29] Likewise, what is said of the work of our redemption being accomplished through the liturgy and of the crucial importance of active participation is now applied to particular liturgies. Let us look more systematically now at some of these. We can examine three: the Eucharist, the Liturgy of the Hours, and the Liturgical Year.

3.1 "The Most Sacred Mystery of the Eucharist"

The title of this section of the essay is the same as the solemn title that opens chapter 2 of *SC*. Having established general principles in the first chapter, from which I have taken the material considered so far, the document now turns to what is the central and most important dimension of the Church's liturgical life, namely, the most sacred mystery of the Eucharist. This is treated in paragraphs 47–58. Naturally, the document does not attempt in any way to be exhaustive in presenting the treasures of the centuries of the Church's rich theological reflection and experience, nor does it deal with any problematic or heretical positions regarding the Eucharist, as, for example, Trent had to do. Instead, a few crucial ideas are articulated—in beautiful language, it should be noted—in order to explain why the Council sees fit to decree that the rite of the Mass be revised.

It is no accident that paragraph 47 uses "sacrifice" as its first word and concept for the Eucharist. What is said here about the eucharistic sacrifice will later be cited near the beginning of the *General Instruction of the Roman Missal* (GIRM), itself a product of the reform called for by *SC*. As such, the citation from *SC* sets the tone for the whole Missal, presenting it not only as the product of this ecumenical council, but in continuity with the eucharistic teaching of Trent and, indeed, of the universal Church through the centuries. It says, "The sacrificial nature of the Mass, solemnly asserted by the Council of Trent in accordance with the Church's universal tradition, was reaffirmed by the Second Vatican Council, which offered these significant words about the Mass: 'At the Last Supper our Savior instituted the Eucharistic Sacrifice of his Body and Blood, by which he would perpetuate the Sacrifice of the Cross throughout the centuries until he should come again, thus entrusting to the Church, his beloved Bride, the memorial of his death and resurrection.'"[30] In fact, in the *General Instruction*, where dense eucharistic theology is expressed in the pithy style characteristic of *praenotandae*, there are scores of citations from *SC*. This is significant. *SC* would have been a dead letter and of no interest fifty years later were it not for the renewed liturgical books that resulted from this document. *SC* speaks in broad, general terms. The renewed liturgical books give concrete and detailed expression to these broad strokes.

So, the eucharistic sacrifice perpetuates the sacrifice of the Cross through the centuries. To speak of the Eucharist, *SC* begins with this thought in its opening paragraph on the Eucharist, and so does the *Roman Missal*. But *SC* in fact wanted to use more than this one word and concept to speak of the mystery.

The whole of the opening paragraph, not cited in its entirety in the *General Instruction*, actually heaps up a list of different names for the Eucharist, and in doing so, the document expresses the Church's awe, the Church's joy, in so great a reality. In the citation from the *General Instruction*, we see the words "sacrifice" and "memorial of his death and resurrection." *SC* 47 goes on to call it "a sacrament of love, a sign of unity, a bond of charity, a paschal banquet in which Christ is eaten, the mind is filled with grace, and a pledge of future glory is given to us." These are six different names for the Eucharist, and the last of this list—paschal banquet—speaks of three different dimensions of the banquet: Christ consumed, grace in the mind, and future glory.[31] The next paragraph will employ yet another name for the Eucharist: the mystery of faith. Clearly something enormous is being considered, and it is addressed in effusive language.

The next paragraph, 48, is perhaps one of the most important and influential paragraphs of the entire document; indeed, it exercised considerable influence on the shaping of new rites for the Mass. It begins with the phrase, "The Church, therefore, earnestly desires that Christ's faithful, when present at this mystery of faith, should not be there as strangers or silent spectators." We should first observe the logic expressed in the word "therefore" (in Latin, *itaque*). The desire of the Church flows from the overwhelming reality of the Eucharist, expressed in the litany of six different names used for this mystery. It is a pastoral desire that addresses a problem present in the Church at the time of the document's writing, and which is still potentially present for us today. The problem was (and still can be) that it is possible for the faithful to be present at Mass in such a way that it is foreign to them and they are not personally involved. In what follows, the Church's earnest desire is expressed in positive terms: "on the contrary, through a good understanding of the rites and prayers they [the faithful] should take part [*participent*] in the sacred action conscious of what they are doing, with devotion and full collaboration." In effect, these carefully crafted words outline a program.

The verb form—*participent*—is used, but it is qualified both before and after.[32] First, it speaks of participating "through a good understanding of the rites and prayers [*per ritus et preces id bene intelligentes*]." This is a high, and perhaps distant, goal; but what an excellent desire it describes. One need only look at the over-sized beautifully bound book we call the *Roman Missal* and begin to leaf through its hundreds and hundreds of pages of prayers (*preces*)— what would it mean for the vigor that "this sacred Council" desires to impart to the life of the Church if Christ's faithful really came to understand more fully, more deeply, all that these prayers say and accomplish—the presidential prayers, the prefaces, the eucharistic prayers, the antiphons? And one need only call to mind some of the rich rites that this Missal's rubrics describe, or again, call to mind a eucharistic liturgy beautifully celebrated and enacted— what would it mean if Christ's faithful really came to understand more fully, more deeply, the unfathomable divine realities incarnated in these ritual actions and use of symbols? I call it a program, a desire, a high and distant goal. But what a vision for the Church is described and hoped for here! This is what is meant by active participation.

The verb "participate" is further qualified by three adverbs, *conscie, pie et actuose*—translated, "conscious of what they are doing, with devotion and full collaboration." It is qualifiers like these that help us to understand that the question of active participation as conceived by this document is far more than just more standing up and moving around and doing something or saying something. Capelle's phrase mentioned earlier, "a presence sustained by an intention" (n. 24), is particularly well illustrated here. "Intention" connects especially with *conscie*, "sustained" connects with *pie*, and "presence" connects with *actuose*, and indeed with *conscie* and *pie* as well.

Furthermore, what the faithful are participating in is called a "sacred action," an expression that further underlines the point. What is this sacred action? Surely, this question is the heart of the matter concerning the Eucharist itself and the reality of active participation in it. For the participation of which we are speaking is not grounded so much in the community's initiative, as in God's. Both passive and active verbs express the action that all are called to participate in: being instructed (*instituantur*) by God's word, being nourished (*reficiantur*) by the Lord's body, giving thanks (*gratias agant*), and—most striking of all—"by offering [*offerentes*] the Immaculate Victim, not only through the hands of the priest, but also with him, they should learn also to offer themselves." The deepest center of the eucharistic mystery is presented here as the object of active participation. The priest is not alone in offering the sacrifice, but it is underlined (*non tantum ... sed etiam*) that the faithful are to do it with him, through his hands, and, in so doing, are to offer themselves. This is not newly invented theology but a putting forward of some of the best fruits of the *ressourcement*.[33]

This is the most theologically dense of the document's paragraphs on the Eucharist. From it, from the "earnest desire" that all this should come about in the Church, the document sets forth what the Council decrees for the reform of the eucharistic liturgy. The language of paragraph 49 is solemn and is careful to use once again a connector word (*quapropter*) to show how the logic of what is to be decreed flows from this desire: "For this reason [*quapropter*] the sacred Council [*Sacrosanctum Concilium*]... has made the following decrees in order that the sacrifice of the Mass ... may become pastorally efficacious to the fullest degree." The document's very title is used again inside this sentence with the same import that I drew attention to above; namely, that what is decreed here is intricately connected with the purposes of the entire Council, a Council that dares to use the adjective "sacred" to describe itself because it believes itself guided by the Holy Spirit. And the goal of the reform is that the celebration of the Mass be "pastorally efficacious to the fullest degree."

The nine paragraphs that follow touch briefly on some particular parts that need attention, but all flows from the basic principle of paragraph 50 that "the rite of the Mass is to be revised" so that its nature and parts "may be more clearly manifested, and that devout and active participation by the faithful may be more easily achieved." All that is decreed here is realized in the Missal of Paul VI. In several of these paragraphs, apparently simple sentences contain points of considerable theological import. Paragraph 56 says, "The two parts which, in a certain sense, go to make up the Mass, namely, the liturgy of the word and the eucharistic liturgy, are so closely connected with each other that they form but one single act of worship." Perhaps that sounds obvious to us; but if it does, it is a measure of the success of the pastoral initiatives of this Council. At the time of SC's writing, it was not uncommon for some among the Catholic faithful to fulfill their Sunday Mass obligation by showing up on time only for the Liturgy of the Eucharist proper, in the process missing the preceding Liturgy of the Word in whole or in part. This is why the sentence in Paragraph 56, cited above, is followed by an exhortation to pastors to "insistently teach them [the faithful] to take their part in the entire Mass, especially on Sundays and feasts of obligation."

The General Instruction, as it introduces the structure of the whole Mass, cites this paragraph from SC and then adds, "For in the Mass the table both of God's word and of Christ's Body is prepared, from which the faithful may be instructed and refreshed."[34] The new Lectionary, called for by SC 51, is most certainly one of the great treasures of the reform. It has made possible a celebration of the Eucharist in which the celebration of the Liturgy of the Word truly forms an intrinsic part of "one single act of worship." SC 52 emphasized that the homily "is to be highly esteemed as part of the liturgy itself," and, in the decades since its promulgation, it has become increasingly clear and is increasingly urged that the homilist should make it clear "that the divine word read and proclaimed by the Church in the Liturgy has as its one purpose the sacrifice of the New Covenant and the banquet of grace, that is, the Eucharist."[35]

Paragraph 55 contains another deceptively simple sentence that is full of theological consequences. It says, "That more perfect form of participation in the Mass whereby the faithful, after the priest's communion, receive the Lord's body from the same sacrifice, is strongly commended." This point is stressed even more strongly by the General Instruction (85) with a theological explanation added: "so that even by means of the signs Communion will stand out more clearly as a participation in the sacrifice actually being celebrated." "Through a good understanding of the rites and prayers [per ritus et preces id bene intelligentes]," the importance of this point becomes clear. The bread and wine that are brought by the faithful into the hands of the priest so that they may be transformed into the body and blood of Christ (and all the language and action that accompany these) have as their clear aim that the faithful should have communion "in the sacrifice actually being celebrated." When this is done with good understanding and with the faithful receiving communion "conscious of what they are doing, with devotion, and with full collaboration," then indeed the desires of the reform are being achieved. To serve the faithful communion from the tabernacle instead is to destroy the trajectory of "the rites and prayers," and is a practice that betrays an alarming lack of understanding of the whole eucharistic mystery.[36]

3.2 The Divine Office

"For he [Christ Jesus] continues His priestly work through the agency of His Church, which is ceaselessly engaged in praising the Lord and interceding for the salvation of the whole world. She does this, not only by celebrating the eucharist, but also in other ways, especially by praying the divine office."[37] In discussing paragraph 7 above on how the work of our redemption is accomplished through the liturgy, it was noted how much is contained in the statement, "Rightly, then, the liturgy is considered an exercise of the priestly office of Jesus Christ." This concept is used throughout the document and, in a significant way, to discuss the Divine Office in the comparatively ample discussion of chapter 4, paragraphs 83 to 101. Here, crucial reforms are called for "in order that the divine office may be better and more perfectly prayed."[38] Those reforms have subsequently been enacted to the enormous benefit not only of clerics and religious who were and are bound by their state in life to such prayer, but also to the benefit of many of the faithful, whom the reformed rites encourage to practice this treasury of prayer. The particulars of what the Council decreed be reformed are found in paragraphs 88 to 101, but these are preceded by—and flow from—several theologically rich paragraphs that describe the deep reality of what is occurring in this prayer. It is these paragraphs that I want briefly to examine here. This is the same pattern of proceeding that was noted in the paragraphs on the Eucharist: first, theology, and then the reforms that would better embody that theology.

The chapter begins solemnly, elegantly striking a noble tone that confidently declares the rich mystery of this prayer. This prayer—indeed, all Christian prayer—is far more than some sort of "we better think of something to say to God." No, here is the deep reality underway in the Divine Office: "Christ Jesus, high priest of the new and eternal covenant, taking human nature, introduced into this earthly exile that hymn which is sung throughout all ages in the halls of heaven. He joins the entire community of mankind to Himself, associating it with His own singing of this canticle of divine praise."[39]

In this beginning, the priesthood of Christ is introduced immediately, and it is characterized as the priesthood of a "new and eternal covenant." This new covenant means a new way of prayer, prayer at a new level, a way and level of prayer that touches what is "eternal." All this is implied just with the titles: "Christ Jesus, high priest of the new and eternal covenant." He is the subject of this sentence. The verbs describe with vivid imagery his exercise of this priesthood. The Church's faith in Christ's divine nature taken as a given, he is here described as "taking human nature" and introducing "into this earthly exile that hymn which is sung throughout all ages in the halls of heaven." This is a very effective description of the mystery of Incarnation, formulated precisely for the purposes of understanding the kind of prayer that happens in the Divine Office. The eternal Son's taking a human nature effectively introduces on earth the eternal relationship of the divine Son with his Father. A hymn of praise that is sung eternally in the halls of heaven now sounds within the context of our earthly exile. It is not just Christ alone who sounds that eternal hymn, though by nature it has eternally been his to do so. But in the new way of prayer that his Incarnation accomplishes, "He joins the entire community of mankind to Himself, associating it with His own singing of this canticle of divine praise." This speaks of Christ's "own singing." He *is* praise of his Father. But now he has associated all mankind with "His own singing." This is the enormous exercise of his priesthood under discussion here.

The idea is developed in the citation with which I opened this section: "For he continues His priestly work through the agency of His Church." This is a specific application to the Divine Office of what was noted in general terms in paragraph 7: "Christ indeed always associates the Church with Himself in this great work ... in the liturgy the whole public worship is performed by the Mystical Body of Jesus Christ, that is, by the Head and His members."

The sentence that I referred to as the solemn beginning of this chapter is later cited in the *General Instruction on the Liturgy of the Hours*, which very effectively builds upon and elaborates this image provided by *SC*.[40] This whole *General Instruction* develops a profound theology of prayer for the Divine Office. As such, it too is part of the reception of the Council and its fruits. But the seeds of this development are planted in the opening paragraphs of chapter 4 of *SC* on the Divine Office. In addition to the effective imagery with which the mystery of Incarnation is described in paragraph 83, we find in paragraph 84 the statement that "the divine office is devised so that the whole course of the day and night is made holy by the praises of God." This is the reason why later paragraphs will urge that "the traditional sequence of the hours is to be restored so that once again they may be genuinely related to the time of the day when they are prayed."[41] But the center of the mystery, both day and night, is that "when this wonderful song of praise is rightly performed ... then it is truly the voice of the bride addressed to her bridegroom; it is the very prayer which Christ Himself, together with His body, addresses to the Father." This is the shape of prayer in the new and eternal covenant made possible by the priesthood of Christ Jesus and the Church's share in the same. Two levels or directions of this prayer are described. The Church as bride speaks to her bridegroom, and the Church speaks together with Christ the very prayer that he addresses to the Father. It is this key idea also that is so marvelously developed in the *General Instruction*.

These ideas are thoroughly rooted in the tradition and practice of the Church. Yet in 1963 a good many of those bound by obligation to this way of prayer had not been instructed effectively in these rich theological ideas that could help them to pray the Divine Office with profit. This state of affairs would certainly be among the "particularly cogent reasons for undertaking the reform and promotion of the liturgy," which *SC* mentions in its opening paragraph. The new shape of the Divine Office, reflecting the decrees of the conciliar reform, has greatly enriched the prayer life of those bound by obligation to this way of prayer; and it has become the practice of large numbers of the lay faithful to celebrate the same. We would do well to hope for and work toward a deepening of the spirituality of prayer seeded here in *SC* and splendidly developed in the *General Instruction of the Liturgy of the Hours*. This is the Council's vision: "Hence all who render this service are not only fulfilling a duty of the Church, but also are sharing in the greatest honor of Christ's spouse, for by offering these praises to God they are standing before God's throne in the name of the Church their Mother."[42]

3.3 The Liturgical Year

SC's chapter on the Divine Office is followed by a chapter on the liturgical year—chapter 5, paragraphs 102–11—shaped once again according to the pattern of declaring key theological ideas and then decreeing reforms in their light. The three theological ideas examined in the first part of this essay are all very much present here. (1) The clear paschal center of Sunday and Easter is emphasized. (2) The work of our redemption accomplished through the liturgy takes place concretely in the mystery of Christ, as unfolded in the course of the year's Sundays and feasts. (3) Active participation and understanding are urged. As with the Eucharist and the Divine Office, what is decreed here in brief form has been realized in the reform of the liturgical calendar, a work carried out in close coordination with the reform of the Missal and the Liturgy of the Hours. *Universal Norms on the Liturgical Year and Calendar* is the document that reflects this reformed calendar, and it achieves the same theological depths that the *praenotandae* of the Missal and the Divine Office do in their respective general instructions. The seeds of all these developments were planted in *SC*.

The chapter begins with the emphasis strongly placed on the Paschal Mystery. "Holy Mother Church is conscious that she must celebrate the saving work of her divine Spouse by devoutly recalling it on certain days throughout the course of the year. Every week, on the day which she has called the Lord's day, she keeps the memory of the Lord's resurrection, which she also celebrates once in the year, together with His blessed passion, in the most solemn festival of Easter."[43] This, of course, is simply the tradition as always practiced. But the Council is anxious that the clarity of this structure shine through in the minds of the faithful and the practice of the Church in our times. Every week has Sunday as its center and "keeps the memory of the Lord's resurrection." What the Church celebrates on Sunday, she also celebrates annually at Easter, called here "the most solemn feast."

With Sunday and Easter put into clear relief in this way, a single sentence follows that magnificently displays the whole sweep of the year: "Within the cycle of a year, moreover, she unfolds the whole mystery of Christ, from the incarnation and birth until the ascension, the day of Pentecost, and the expectation of blessed hope and of the coming of the Lord."[44] It is Christ himself who is celebrated, and we recognize in this formulation the beginning of his coming among us ("incarnation and birth") and its culmination ("the ascension, the day of Pentecost"). But there is a second culmination, as it were, one still to be realized and which is to be looked for within the course of the year, namely "the expectation of blessed hope and the coming of the Lord."

The next sentence of this rich opening paragraph of chapter 5 can be considered an explanation of how the work of our redemption is accomplished through the liturgy, in this case, through the liturgical year. "Recalling thus the mysteries of redemption, the Church opens to the faithful the riches of her Lord's powers and merits, so that these are in some way made present for all time, and the faithful are enabled to lay hold upon them and become filled with saving grace." The work of our redemption, accomplished by Christ in one time and place, is made available in every time and place through liturgically "recalling the mysteries of redemption." The faithful can thus lay hold of these riches and become filled with grace. Active participation in these—this is the Council's vision!

After this strong opening paragraph, paragraph 103 mentions the special place of the Mother of God in the annual cycle, and paragraph 104 mentions the role of the saints. Paragraph 105 touches upon the seasons and concludes in a way similar to what we have seen before: "Accordingly [*quapropter*] the sacred Council [*Sacrosanctum Concilium*] has seen fit to decree as follows."

Sunday is the first consideration of what is decreed, and in the Latin the first sentence of paragraph 106 opens with the words *Mysterium paschale*, not possible as a beginning in an English construction. In any case, it is clear that Sunday's meaning *is* the celebration of the Paschal Mystery: "By a tradition handed down from the apostles which took its origin from the very day of Christ's resurrection, the Church celebrates the paschal mystery every eighth day; with good reason this, then, bears the name of the Lord's day or Sunday."[45] What follows urges the active participation of the faithful in this celebration of Sunday and echoes the language developed earlier in the document that was examined above concerning the Eucharist. "On this day Christ's faithful are bound to come together into one place so that; by hearing the word of God and taking part in the eucharist [*verbum Dei audientes et Eucharistiam participantes*], they may call to mind the passion, the resurrection and the glorification of the Lord Jesus, and may thank God who 'has begotten them again, through the resurrection of Jesus Christ from the dead, unto a living hope' (1 Pet. 1:3)." The two parts of the eucharistic liturgy are specified here, liturgy of the word and liturgy of the Eucharist, and the central content of these as well; namely, "the passion, the resurrection and the glorification of the Lord Jesus." On Sunday and by means of these celebrations we give thanks for our share in the same. "Hence [*itaque*] the Lord's day is the original feast . . . the foundation and kernel of the whole liturgical year."

Limitations of space do not permit our examination of the other dimensions of the liturgical year for which reform is decreed here. Suffice it to say that the strong paschal center of the whole is what is clearly achieved. Sunday and Easter show up as the clear center of the liturgical year, just as they do as the clear center of the celebration of Eucharist and the Divine Office. As mentioned above, all this is clearly reflected in the *praenotandae* of these liturgies and the document that reforms the calendar. Pope John Paul II very much took to heart what is said in *SC* 106 and developed it in his beautiful apostolic exhortation *Dies Domini*. The *CCC* is no less clear in this regard.[46] All this forms part of the history of the reception of *SC* and its enormous influence.

4. A Renewed Liturgy and Renewal in the Church

It can hardly be disputed that a renewed vision of the Church was a major question at the Second Vatican Council. It is at issue in virtually all of the documents. *SC*, in the vision of liturgy it promotes, makes a crucial contribution to this ecclesial project of the Council.[47] Indeed, this intention is expressed from its very first words: "This sacred Council has several aims in view." And among those listed we find the desire to impart increasing vigor to the life of the faithful, "to foster what can promote union among all who believe in Christ," and, finally, "to strengthen whatever can help to call the whole of mankind into the household of the Church." These are the aims for which the reform of the liturgy is undertaken.[48]

We have already read that liturgy is "the outstanding means by which the faithful may express in their lives, and manifest to others, the mystery of Christ and the real nature of the true Church."[49] The real nature of the true Church—meant to be manifested ever more clearly in a renewed liturgy—is that the Church is associated with Christ in his glorifying the Father and in his work of accomplishing human redemption.

Numerous other texts could be cited in which there is a direct correlation between the renewal of the liturgy and a renewed vision of Church, not only in this document but in other documents of the Council. I want to examine one that is both very concrete and full of theological consequences. Precisely because of its concreteness and theology, it can also serve as a fitting conclusion to this essay.

I have in mind paragraphs 41 and 42, which bear the laconic, understated title of "Promotion of Liturgical Life in Diocese and Parish." Much more than that is accomplished in these powerful paragraphs. But they should be read in conjunction with a principle enunciated in paragraph 26: "Liturgical services are not private functions, but are celebrations of the Church, which is the 'sacrament of unity,' namely, the holy people united and ordered under their bishops. Therefore liturgical services pertain to the whole body of the Church; they manifest it and have effects upon it; but they concern the individual members of the Church in different ways, according to their differing rank, office, and actual participation."[50] The vision of Church expressed here is intimately joined to a way of celebrating the liturgy that manifests the Church as "the holy people united and ordered under their bishops." Consequently, liturgical services are not a concern of only bishops and priests; they "pertain to the whole body of the Church."

This principle of involving the whole body of the Church, expressed in what may be understood as virtually juridical tones, stands behind what is concretely urged in paragraphs 41 and 42. These paragraphs urge a recovery of the sense of local church gathered in unity under the bishop and expressed in the bishop's Eucharist.

Let us observe the theological steps involved as the document outlines them. It begins with an important theological principle, stating, "The bishop is to be considered as the high priest of his flock, from whom the life in Christ of his faithful is in some way derived and dependent." The use of the term "high priest" reminds us that in the Church there is only one priest, Jesus Christ. The bishop is sacrament and image in a local Church of this one priesthood, and unity with the bishop is the concrete means and verification of the unity of the faithful in that local church with Christ. Thus, rightly does the document state that the life in Christ of the faithful is "in some way derived and dependent" upon the relationship with the bishop. But this is not a unity primarily achieved by moods, feelings, acquiescence, or right attitudes in the relationship between a bishop and his faithful, even though, of course, these play a part. Rather, it is a unity fundamentally *given* to the Church by God in the divine action of the liturgy. It is for us to recognize that this unity is achieved there and not to betray it. Thus, the document continues, "Therefore all should hold in great esteem the liturgical life of the diocese centered around the bishop, especially in his cathedral church; they must be convinced that the pre-eminent manifestation of the Church consists in the full active participation of all God's holy people in these liturgical celebrations, especially in the same eucharist, in a single prayer, at one altar, at which there presides the bishop surrounded by his college of priests and by his ministers."[51]

There is an important footnote at the end of this paragraph, referring the reader to three passages from the letters of St. Ignatius of Antioch. The authority of this Father of the Church, who wrote early in the second century, is invoked for the vision promoted here. Thus, this is not a new idea invented by liturgists but a very, very old one. There is one bishop, one same Eucharist, one single prayer, one altar—but, of course, in the Church there are many; and what achieves the unity of the many in the one Christ, what would be, in the document's words, "the pre-eminent manifestation of the Church," is "the full active participation of all God's holy people in these liturgical celebrations."[52]

It is hard to imagine that in 1963 an average Catholic, including an average Catholic theologian, would spontaneously think that the pre-eminent manifestation of the Church is to be found in the full active participation of all the faithful in the one Eucharist of the bishop. Every word here is important: *full, active, participation, all*. What a vision of Church! What renewal! Some may quip that we are still far from it, but I answer that we are closer than we were and that the vision is clearly stated here for our continued reception of the Council.

Paragraph 42 addresses the practical reality of the fact that in any given local church it is usually not possible for the majority of the faithful to be present at the bishop's Eucharist in the cathedral. But this practical reality is addressed in theological terms. We read, "But because it is impossible for the bishop always and everywhere to preside over the whole flock in his Church, he cannot do other than establish lesser groupings of the faithful. Among these the parishes, set up locally under a pastor who takes the place of the bishop, are the most important: for in some manner they represent the visible Church constituted throughout the world." This too, in very practical terms, expresses a renewed vision of the Church directly realized in the relationship between the bishop and priests who preside over "lesser groupings of the faithful." Priests act in the bishop's place (*vices episcopi*), that is, as sacraments or images that effect a "lesser grouping's" communion with the one bishop, who represents the one priest, Jesus Christ. This chain of relationships "represents the visible Church constituted throughout the world."

This detail of what I am here calling a renewed vision of Church requires fostering, as the document clearly urges. "And therefore the liturgical life of the parish and its relationship to the bishop must be fostered theoretically and practically among the faithful and clergy." Here the word "theoretically" means understanding the profound significance of these ancient structures. "Practically" means that gatherings of the faithful will be the actual context in which this communion of the one Church will be effected and experienced. This will show itself—"practically"—in what the document calls "a sense of community within the parish, above all in the common celebration of the Sunday Mass."[53]

From the perspective of many decades after the promulgation of *SC*, the expression "common celebration of the Sunday Mass" reveals itself as a sleeper phrase. Yes, all the sacramental celebrations have been renewed as directed by the Conciliar document, as well as all the other liturgical rites of the Church. But in the week by week it is probably in the "common celebration of the Sunday Mass" where the liturgical renewal has most fully occurred and continues to occur in a sustained manner. This was already observed in the final report of the 1985 Synod: "The liturgical renewal is the most visible fruit of the whole conciliar effort."

Conclusion

I want to finish this essay quietly, peacefully, with an image, a vision. It is the image of a reality underway and a vision still to be achieved. The image is of the common celebration of Sunday Mass, of tens of thousands of Sunday Masses celebrated throughout the world. Seeing this beautiful image in our mind's eye, we can quietly let ring again some of the phrases that summarize the Spirit-guided vision of "this sacred Council," of *SC*. Sunday Mass: the original feast, the kernel of the whole liturgical year. Tens of thousands of Sunday Masses: the visible Church constituted throughout the world. Sunday Mass: the Church never failing to come together to celebrate the Paschal Mystery. Sunday Mass: where God is perfectly glorified and men and women are sanctified. Sunday Mass: where the faithful, through a good understanding of rites and prayers, take part in the sacred action, conscious of what they are doing and with full collaboration. Sunday Mass: celebrated by clergy and laity alike who are formed day by day and hour by hour through the Divine Office, joined to Christ's own singing of his canticle of praise. Sunday Mass: where the faithful are instructed by God's word and nourished at the table of the Lord's body. Sunday Mass: a sacrament of love, a sign of unity, a bond of charity, a paschal banquet.

This was the Council's hope and achievement. It still asks for our adherence, for purification, for deepening. But it is a magnificent vision and the gift of a Spirit-guided sacred Council.

NOTES

1. *Novo Millennio Ineunte (NMI)* 57. See also *Tertio Millennio Adveniente (TMA)* 18: "We can affirm that *the Second Vatican Council was a providential event, whereby the Church began the more immediate preparation* for the Jubilee of the Second Millennium"; and *TMA* 36: "This great gift of the Spirit to the Church at the end of the second millennium." (All translations are taken from www.vatican.va.)

2. Other important names would include: O. Casel, I. Herwegen, B. Neunheuser, B. Botte, B. Capelle, A. Nocent, C. Vagaggini, S. Marsili, A. G. Martimort, L. Bouyer, V. Michel, G. Diekmann, and many more.

3. On this, see John O'Malley, *What Happened at Vatican II* (Cambridge, MA: Harvard University Press, 2008), 129–41 on why *SC* was the first of the documents to pass the approval of the Council Fathers. *SC* 43 affirms, "Zeal for the promotion and restoration of the liturgy is rightly held to be a sign of the providential dispositions of God in our time, as a movement of the Holy Spirit in His Church." (All translations of *SC* are taken from the Vatican's website) Pope Benedict XVI spoke of this as recently as September 26, 2012 in the Wednesday General Audience, where he said that the draft for *SC* was the "least controversial" of the various drafts and could consequently "serve as an exercise in learning conciliar methodology." See http://www.vatican.va/holy_father/benedict_xvi/audiences/2012/documents/hf_ben-xvi_aud_20120926_en.html.

4. Naturally some parts of the *CCC* (Catechism of the Catholic Church) seem more satisfactory to the academically trained theologian than others. For the purposes of catechetical questions around liturgy, I signal out nn. 1066–1209 as especially well done.

5. *Vicesimus Quintus Annus (VQA)* 12.

6. In this he shows himself leaning more toward Tübingen-styles of interpretation rather than toward the Bologna school. For an ample discussion of the difference in these two schools of interpretation, see C. Theobald, *La réception du concile Vatican II. I. Accéder à la source* (Paris: Cerf, 2009), 515–43.

7. Cf. *SC* 1.

8. Paul De Clerck ("La réforme liturgique: ce qui reste à faire," *Questions Liturgiques* 91 [2010]: 64–75) suggests that chap. 1 of *SC* and the "General Instructions" of the liturgical books should be read again as a good program for entering into the spirit of the liturgy.

9. *TMA* 20.

10. See J. O'Malley, *What Happened at Vatican II*, 11–12, 306–7. J. A. Jungmann, in a commentary on *SC* published immediately after the close of the Council, said, "Many Fathers were astonished at this manner of speech about the Church, which differs from the view especially as developed by Bellarmine during the struggle of post-Tridentine theology with the Reformation" (cited by M. Faggioli, *True Reform, Liturgy and Ecclesiology in* Sacrosanctum Concilium [Collegeville, MN: Liturgical Press, 2012], 66).

11. The Fathers of the Church used Scripture in this same way, and it is their style of doing so that is used now to express what Pope John Paul called "the Council's enormously rich body of teaching." See also the references in the previous note.

12. Oddly, the official footnote of the text does not indicate the allusions to Gal 4:4 and John 1:14, which I have taken the liberty to insert into the text that I cite. In any case, it is clear that the style here is the language of scripture, a tapestry of citations and allusions.

13. *SC* 5. The phrase "dying, he destroyed our death" is from the Easter Preface of the Roman Missal in use at the time of the Council.

14. *TMA* 20.

15. Nearly fifty years later, on September 26, 2012 Pope Benedict XVI was stressing this very point again in the Wednesday General Audience, where he said, "Thus the Paschal Mystery of the death and resurrection of Christ is the center of the liturgical theology of the Council." See http://www.vatican.va/holy_father/benedict_xvi/audiences/2012/documents/hf_ben-xvi_aud_20120926_en.html.

16. *SC* 102–11.

17. *SC* 81.

18. *SC* 61.

19. *SC* 64–71.

20. A excellent example of this is found in P. Regan, *Advent to Pentecost: Comparing the Seasons in the Ordinary and Extraordinary Forms of the Roman Rite* (Collegeville, MN: Liturgical Press, 2012).

21. Even if *Mediator Dei* (*MD*) did much to prepare the way for *SC*, one of the ways of measuring the difference and the progress between the two documents is to note that "Paschal Mystery" is never mentioned in *MD*. Some critics of the reformed liturgy are unhappy precisely with this point of the strong introduction of the Paschal Mystery into the Missal. Joseph Ratzinger forcefully demonstrated that such criticism is theologically unsound. See his "Theology of the Liturgy," in *Looking Again at the Question of the Liturgy with Cardinal Ratzinger*, ed. Alcuin Reid (Farnborough: St. Michael's Abbey Press, 2003), 18–31. In the English-speaking world, the impact of what the Missal of Paul VI intended was weakened by the habitual translation of *paschale* as "Easter." But "Easter" means only resurrection, whereas, "paschal" means death, resurrection, ascension, and the wondrous sacrament of the Church all at once. In the new translation, the word "paschal" is heard again and again in conformity to what the reformed liturgy intends.

22. This is beautifully detailed in the classic article by Yves Congar, written in the first generation of commentaries on *SC* and now recently available in English as "The *Ecclesia* or Christian Community as a Whole Celebrates the Liturgy," in *At the Heart of Christian Worship, Liturgical Essays of Yves Congar*, trans. and ed. Paul Philibert (Collegeville, MN: Liturgical Press, 2010), 15–68.

23. The key ideas of paragraph 7, among other things, gave rise already twenty-five years ago to the list from Pope John Paul that I already cited of things to be grateful for as fruits of this document. See *VQA* 12, as cited above at n. 5.

24. For this and for several other of the observations I make here, I am indebted to P. Prétot, "Retrouver la 'participation active,' une tâche pour aujourd'hui," *La Maison-Dieu* 241 (2005/1): 151–77.

25. In other paragraphs, still other adjectives or adverbs are used, e.g., full, conscious, devout, intelligent. By far the most frequent is "active." See *SC* 11, 14, 19, 27, 30, 41, 48, 50, 79, 113, 114, 121, 124.

26. The language here is constructed on *The Rule of St. Benedict*, chap. 19.

27. *Consortium* occurs in thirty-four texts, and *consors* in three; *societas* in fifteen texts, *sociare* in thirty-three texts; *socius* in twenty; *communio* in twenty-five; *commercium* in sixteen.

28. *SC* 2.

29. See above with references to the liturgical year, Christian death, the Sacraments of Initiation, etc.

30. *GIRM* 2.

31. Footnote 37 of the document shows that this last image comes from the Magnificat antiphon of Second Vespers of the Solemnity of Corpus Christi.

32. Actually, in the Latin all the qualification come before the verb, but English translations generally have arranged them both before and after.

33. This is amply illustrated in model works of *ressourcement*, such as, for example, the essay by Congar cited above in n. 22 or the ample collection of ancient texts that forms the argument for J.-M.-R. Tillard's *Flesh of the Church, Flesh of Christ: At the Source of the Ecclesiology of Communion*, trans. Madeleine Beaumont (Collegeville, MN: Liturgical Press, 2001).

34. *GIRM* 28, with footnote references to *SC* 56, 48, 51, as well as *Dei Verbum* 21 and *Presbyterorum Ordinis* 4.

35. *Ordo Lectionum* (*OL*) 10. See also *OL* 24. *OL* 10 also cites *SC* 51, 56. *SC* is cited some forty times in *OL*.

36. I am confounded by the fact that in many parts of the Church what was urged here by *SC* and what remains in force through the *General Instruction* is simply not practiced. But what is urged is not some new idea fashioned by overly enthusiastic liturgists. It was strongly urged by Benedict XIV as long ago as 1742 and by Pius XII in *Mediator Dei* 118. For a theological analysis of the whole problem, see Robert Taft, "'Communion' from the Tabernacle—A Liturgico-Theological Oxymoron," *Worship* 88, no. 1 (2014): 2–22.

37. *SC* 83.

38. *SC* 87.

39. *SC* 83.

40. See *GILH* (General Instruction on the Liturgy of the Hours) 3–11.

41. *SC* 88. See also the whole of *SC* 88–89.

42. *SC* 85. Although the new shape of the Divine Office in the reformed liturgical books is a significant improvement over the pre-conciliar *Breviary* generally prayed only by priests and the religious bound to it by obligation, the reformed *Liturgy of the Hours* probably stands in need of further review so that it can become a form of prayer for even more of the lay faithful and a richer experience for those bound to it by their state in life.

43. *SC* 102.

44. *SC* 102.

45. *SC* 106.

46. *Dies Domini* cites *SC* some twelve times. For *CCC*, see nn. 1163–78; 2174–88.

47. Let the remarks of Paul VI suffice as an authoritative confirmation of this ecclesial center of the Council. See his address during the last general meeting of the Council on December 7, 1965 at http://www.vatican.va/holy_father/paul_vi/speeches/1965/documents/hf_p-vi_spe_19651207_epilogo-concilio_en.html. G. Dossetti, commenting immediately after the close of the Council on the influ-ence of SC on the renewed vision of the Church, offers the following statistics: sev-enteen citations of SC in other conciliar documents that followed it: three in LG; one in OE, CD, and GS; four in PO, two in OT, AA, AG. See G. Dossetti, Per una "chiesa eucaristica." Rilettura della portata dottrinale della Costituzione liturgica del Vaticano II. Lezioni del 1965, ed. Giuseppe Alberigo and Giuseppe Ruggieri (Bologna: Il Mulino, 2002), 34n11. For a useful discussion of this question, see M. Faggioli, True Reform, Liturgy and Ecclesiology in Sacrosanctum Concilium (Collegeville, MN: Liturgical Press, 2012).

48. In the document's own words, "The Council therefore [because of these aims] sees particularly cogent reasons for undertaking the reform and promotion of the lit-urgy" (SC 1).

49. SC 7.

50. SC 26.

51. SC 41.

52. Cited favorably by VQA n. 9 in a section called "Self-manifestation of the Church." This vision is also taken up in CD 15. The Church is not primarily an idea; it is a concrete assembly. See also LG 26. This vision is further appropriated in the Ceremonial of Bishops, nn. 1–17.

53. SC 42.

2

Lumen Gentium

Guy Mansini, OSB

The reception of the Dogmatic Constitution on the Church, *Lumen Gentium (LG)*, over the past fifty years has been practical, catechetical, magisterial, and theological. Its catechetical reception is manifested preeminently in the *Catechism of the Catholic Church* (1992) but also in all the books and series of books for catechesis inspired by the *Catechism*. Just by itself, *Lumen Gentium* has provided an orderly, scripturally and patristically rich, and rhetorically satisfying way to provide catechesis on the Church, and has influenced such reforms as *The Rite of Christian Initiation for Adults* (1972). Its practical reception appears in the new *Code of Canon Law* (1983) and has taken place in a host of ways, from formal and officially sponsored ecumenical dialogues to the vigorous exercise of the teaching and ruling competence of national bishops' conferences, from the erection and functioning of parish pastoral councils to local ecumenical contact and hospitality and common action. Catechetical reception is ordered first to the good functioning of the Church in transmitting revelation, second, to the exercise of faith by the Christian faithful, and ultimately to sharing the glory of God. Practical reception, the good governance of the People of God at whatever level of their organization, is ordered to the exercise of charity so that we may all share in the resurrection of Christ on the last day, but the exercise of charity includes the exercise of justice and prudence, both in governing and being governed, and in the Church's relations with state and society.

There is also magisterial and theological reception, to which these pages are devoted. "Magisterial reception" is the reception of *Lumen Gentium* in subsequent acts of magisterial teaching, and here it refers to such teaching as directed to the universal Church, whether that teaching be papal, synodical, or such as has been undertaken by the dicasteries of the Holy See, especially the

Congregation for the Doctrine of the Faith. Magisterial reception is logically prior to theological reception, insofar as magisterial teaching, together with tradition and Scripture, are the fonts of theology, and so will be treated first.

A. Magisterial Reception of *Lumen Gentium*

Reception of some teaching is a matter both of the simple reiteration or reca-pitulation of such teaching in a time and circumstance subsequent to the original teaching and also of deepening, explaining, or reinforcing such teach-ing. Since *Lumen Gentium* is a *dogmatic* constitution, its reception has been profound and profuse.[1] The following remarks, however, concentrate only on what might be called "fundamental ecclesiology," insofar as they regard the nature and properties of the Church. Questions about ecclesial structure and operation taken up by other documents of Vatican II are left to the discussion of those documents: episcopacy, priesthood, the actualization of the holiness of the Church in religious life, the mission of the Church, the mission of the laity. Three issues of the magisterial reception of *Lumen Gentium* bearing on fundamental ecclesiology are highlighted here: the interpretation of what it means to say the Church of Christ subsists in the Catholic Church; the rela-tion between the universal Church and particular churches; and the Church as the universal instrument of salvation.

1. *Lumen Gentium Article 8: The Church of Christ Subsists in the Catholic Church*

Article 8 of *Lumen Gentium* determines two relations: first, the relation between the Catholic Church and "the unique church of Christ," the Church "set up [erected—*erexit*] by Christ" and committed to Peter and the other apos-tles; and second, the relation between "the unique church of Christ," subsist-ing in the Catholic Church, and variously organized non-Catholic Christians. The council further states in this article:

> This church [of Christ], set up and organized [*constituta et ordinata*] in this world as a society, subsists in the catholic church, governed by the successor of Peter and the bishops in communion with him, although outside its structure many elements of sanctification and of truth are to be found which, as proper gifts to the church of Christ, impel towards catholic unity.[2]

As to the second relation, the fact that there are elements of sanctifica-tion and truth outside the Church that subsists in the Catholic Church makes ecumenical dialogue possible; there is something to talk about since there is ecclesial reality common to Catholics and non-Catholics. *Unitatis Redintegratio* (*UR*), the Decree on Ecumenism, insists on the desirability of such dialogue "for restoring the unity of all Christians" (*UR*, no. 1) in fulfillment of the will of Christ. *Lumen Gentium* certainly implies that desirability, however, for the "although" in the above citation from article 8 indicates a state of affairs contrary to the founding will of Christ, and Catholics cannot be indifferent to their own good or the good of non-Catholics who possess the elements that "impel towards catholic unity." The Catholic reception of *Lumen Gentium* at this point is therefore to be read in the long account of post-conciliar ecumenical dialogues.

The reception of the first relation, however, the relation between the Church established by Christ and the Catholic Church has not been uncontentious. What was the import of changing the draft statement that the Church established by Christ "is" the Catholic Church to saying that it "subsists in" the Catholic Church, the move from *est* to *adest* and finally to *subsistit in*?[3] Is Pius XII's *Mystici Corporis* (1943) being corrected?[4]

As to that second question, it might be said that magisterial reception of *Lumen Gentium* began even before the council ended and even before the promulgation of *Lumen Gentium* itself (November 21, 1964) if we look to Paul VI's *Ecclesiam Suam* (*ES*) of August 6, 1964. *Mystici Corporis* is recommended to us as a "highly authoritative text," and Pope Paul quotes its opening words, characterized as a "splendid utterance," where Pius XII identifies the Church established by Christ and the Catholic Church: "the Mystical Body of Christ . . . is the Church."[5] Pope Paul urges the "rediscovery" of the doctrine of the Church as the Mystical Body of Christ on the grounds that then we will discover Christ within the Church, directing it, and manifested by it (*ES*, no. 35). Paul VI, obliquely but unmistakably, is receiving *Lumen Gentium* in continuity with *Mystici Corporis*.

Neither Paul VI's indication of the continuing relevance of *Mystici Corporis*, nor the warning of the Congregation for the Doctrine of the Faith in 1966 against a "pernicious irenicism" in ecumenical dialogue, prevented an interpretation of *Lumen Gentium* at odds with its intent.[6] The Congregation's *Mysterium Ecclesiae*, a Declaration in Defense of the Catholic Doctrine on the Church (1973), insists that the Church of Christ has not passed away into various ecclesial splinters, none of which is integrally the Church established by Christ.[7] To the contrary, Catholics belong to the Church that Christ founded, which exists today, and the unity of the Church does not consist in lumping together churches and ecclesial communities into one collection.

Such early recapitulations of article 8 of *Lumen Gentium* did not prevent its continued misreading by many theologians, according to which the identity of the Church founded by Christ and the Catholic Church is not complete. A more pointed and terminologically significant intervention came in 1985 with the Notification on the work of Leonardo Boff, who did not want to distinguish the relation of the Church of Christ to the Catholic Church from its relation to other churches and ecclesial communions. The Congregation paraphrased article 8 as follows:

> The Council had chosen the word *subsistit*—subsists—exactly in
> order to make clear that one sole "subsistence" of the true Church

exists, whereas outside her visible structure only *elementa Ecclesiae*—elements of Church—exist; these—being elements of the same Church—tend and conduct toward the Catholic Church.[8]

In saying that the council means that only the Catholic Church is the unique "subsistence" of the Church of Christ, the Congregation implies two things. First, it is unique because the subsistence of the Church established by Christ in many communities or churches not in communion with one another and differing in doctrine or sacramental agency or the claim to define doctrine would offend against that visible unity and integral fullness of saving powers, which the council understands Christ intended for the Church at her foundation and which he maintains to this day until the end of the age. Second, the introduction of the noun "subsistence" intends a philosophically richer understanding of the council's teaching. It is tantamount to conceiving the Church in its unity as comparable to an individual—a hypostasis or person. This reading of the council has been strenuously resisted. "Subsists in" is taken to mean no more than "continues to exist in," and no appeal to some scholasticized use of "subsistence" need or can be made.

That is the view of Francis Sullivan, SJ, who has doggedly argued that the transition from *est* to *subsistit in* must mean a correction of *Mystici Corporis*, that "subsists in" can mean no more than "continues to exist in," that the Congregation's paraphrase in its notification on Boff is wrong, since it implies that "church" cannot be truly predicated of any non-Catholic body; and that the "big box" view of the Church, according to which the Church founded by Christ embraces the Catholic Church and other ecclesial communities, is entirely legitimate.[9] If the big box view is correct, however, it is hard to see what point there is to ecumenical dialogue; the unity of the Church seems to be achieved by theological legerdemain.

Joseph Komonchak, another influential ecclesiologist, recognizes that, with the "subsists" formula, the council is saying something that is proper to the Catholic Church, namely, that only there can be found all the means of salvation that Christ left his Church.[10] But he also says the following:

> The doctrinal commission explained that it had replaced the verb "is" (used in earlier drafts) with the term "subsists in," not because of a deep philosophical concept of "subsistence," but simply because the latter was a more appropriate phrase, given the council's affirmations ... of the existence of ecclesial elements in other Christian communities.[11]

This can make us think the commission excluded a philosophical understanding of subsisting. However, the commission said absolutely nothing about "subsistence" or a philosophical understanding of *subsistere* one way or another, but only that "subsists in" fits better with the recognition of ecclesial elements outside the visible structure of the Catholic Church.

There are two arguments, however, that lead us to a philosophical concept of subsistence. First, that it is the connotation that Joseph Ratzinger, a *peritus* at the time of the council, says that everyone understood upon hearing that the Church of Christ subsists in the Catholic Church:

> The Council Fathers, who were trained in neoscholastic philosophy and theology, were quite well aware that *subsistere* is a narrower concept than that of *esse*: ... *subsistere* is the form of existence of a being resting in itself, as in particular occurs in the case of an "active agent."[12]

Second, it is demanded by the logic of affirming that "the fullness of the means of salvation" is found alone in the Catholic Church (*UR*, no. 3). For part of this fullness is the ability so to act as to define the doctrine of faith for all Christians, and so to act as to bind all Christians to a common governance. This unique and complete capacity to act is located only in the Catholic Church; it makes of her an agent in a unique sense as compared with all other churches and ecclesial communities. This unique agency, moreover, connotes existence as of a hypostasis or individual—subsistence in the philosophical sense.

Ten years later, Saint John Paul II rehearsed the language and teaching of *Lumen Gentium* in his encyclical *Ut Unum Sint* (*UUS*) of 1995.[13] The Church of Christ subsists only in the Catholic Church, and so only there with all the means of salvation and the visible unity Christ desired for his Church. Precisely because of the many elements of truth and sanctification outside the visible confines of the Catholic Church, however, there is no "ecclesial vacuum" beyond these confines, as the Holy Father says energetically (*UUS*, no. 13). There is also this (*UUS*, no. 11):

> To the extent that these elements are found in other Christian Communities, the one Church of Christ is effectively present in them. For this reason the Second Vatican Council speaks of a certain, though imperfect communion. The Dogmatic Constitution *Lumen Gentium* stresses that the Catholic Church "recognizes that in many ways she is linked" (no. 15) with these Communities by a true union in the Holy Spirit.

The Church of Christ is not said to subsist in separated Churches and ecclesial communities, but is rather said to be effectively present in them, and this is a matter of degree ("to the extent"). The language of "subsisting in" continues to be reserved for the Catholic Church. That the one Church of Christ is said to be "effectively present in" the separated Churches and ecclesial communities brings forward the language of the relator of *Unitatis Redintegratio* at the time of the council, according to which the Church of Christ is present and operative in "ecclesial" communities in virtue of the elements of truth and sanctification they possess.[14]

The same explanation by the Congregation as to how to read article 8 first articulated in the Notification on Boff is repeated in its Declaration on the Unicity and Salvific Universality of Christ and the Church, *Dominus Iesus* (*DI*) of 2000.[15] *Dominus Iesus* notes that it is the single Church of Christ subsisting in the Catholic Church that is "operative" for salvation—exercising agency—in those churches and communities not in full communion with her (*DI*, no. 17). The explanation is repeated again in 2007, in the Congregation's Responses to Some Questions Regarding Certain Aspects of the Doctrine of the Church, the second question, which refers us to *Mysterium Ecclesiae, Dominus Iesus*, and the Notification on Boff.[16]

Responses to Some Questions also addresses another terminological issue, that of "identity." The Congregation here denies that *Lumen Gentium* changed the Church's doctrine on herself (first question), and maintains that to say the Church subsists in the Catholic Church "indicates the full identity of the Church of Christ with the Catholic Church" (Responses, third question). This claim is well supported by citations from the *Expensio Modorum* for the first chapter of *Unitatis Redintegratio*, which does nothing itself but state the meaning of *Lumen Gentium*'s dictum. "Full identity," moreover, does not deny that there are many elements of truth and sanctification outside the visible confines of the Catholic Church. That might be indicated by saying "total identity."[17] But "full identity" means that the Church of Christ is fully, integrally the Catholic Church, and the Catholic Church is fully, integrally the Church of Christ. Or we could say that the Mystical Body of Christ is the Catholic Church and the Catholic Church is the Mystical Body, and come full circle to Paul VI's *Ecclesiam Suam*, itself recalling *Mystici Corporis*.[18] "Subsists" is therefore said unqualifiedly: the Church of Christ subsists in the Catholic Church, and only there, because only there are all the means of salvation, including the full recognition of the office of the papacy as defined at both Vatican councils: "the word 'subsists' can only be attributed to the Catholic Church alone precisely because it refers to the mark of unity that we profess in the symbols of the faith (I believe . . . in the 'one' Church); and this 'one' Church subsists in the Catholic Church" (Responses, second question).

This quite constant line of interpretation on the part of popes and the Congregation for the Doctrine of the Faith provides an indispensable orientation to all thinking about the nature of the Church where due measure is taken of the fact that Christians are divided by differences of doctrine and sacrament. That is its dogmatic function. But it also poses a problem for understanding. Beyond the repetition of the phrases of the council, beyond their paraphrase, beyond the bare introduction of "subsistence" and "identity" into the argument, there is also a call for systematic insight.

2. Universal Church and Particular Churches

Writing in 1961, Yves Congar opined that the conception of the Church as a communion between God and men, a communion structured and organized as a society, a *politeia*, might have a bright future before it in ecclesiology.[19] Writing also in 1961, Karl Rahner sought to clarify the relation between the episcopate and the pope, and did so by raising the question of the relation of the individual, local church to the universal Church: "The Church as a whole, where she becomes 'event' in the full sense of the term, is necessarily the local Church," and this full actualization of the whole Church occurs in the necessarily local celebration of the Eucharist, "the most intensive event of the Church."[20] Both these themes, the Church as communion, and the local church as the realization of the Church, making present in every location, every diocese, what the Church is as a whole, come together in *Lumen Gentium*. The fact of the Church as a communion of particular churches is stated in article 13 (where a "particular church" is a grouping of dioceses).[21]

> So also, within the ecclesiastical communion, there are lawfully particular churches which enjoy their own proper traditions, while the primacy of the see of Peter remains intact, which presides over the universal communion of charity and safeguards legitimate differences while taking care that what is particular not only does no harm to unity but rather is conducive to it.[22]

Then there is article 23 of *Lumen Gentium*:

> This variety of local churches [churches enjoying "their own discipline, their own liturgical usage and their own theological and spiritual patrimony"], in harmony among themselves, demonstrates with greater clarity the catholicity of the undivided church.[23]

Thus was instigated the great tide of "communion ecclesiology" of the post-conciliar era, the fundamental rightness of which the Extraordinary Synod of 1985 recognized when it said that "the ecclesiology of communion is the central and fundamental idea of the Council's documents."[24] The council teaches that the local celebration of the Eucharist makes present the very reality which the Church is principally ordered to effect, and which, in her own nature as a communion with God, she is.

> In any community of the altar, under the sacred ministry of the bishop, there is made manifest the symbol of that charity and "unity of the mystical body without which there can be no salvation."[25]

Article 23 of *Lumen Gentium*, however, poses a problem for a coherent ecclesiology of communion. On the one hand, particular churches are "formed in the likeness of the universal church." This bespeaks the priority of the universal Church, insofar as a likeness is dependent on what it is a likeness of. On the other hand, "in and from these particular churches there exists the one unique catholic church."[26] And this suggests rather the priority of the particular churches, out of which there comes to be the universal Church.

These dicta of the council provoked an extensive and fruitful theological examination, a many-sided discussion that itself invited further magisterial teaching on the relation of the universal Church to the particular churches. Nor was it possible for theologians to resist thinking about the local church in the age of "globalism" and "multi-culturalism" subsequent to the council.[27]

It is hard to find someone who entertains the idea that the great Church is a federation of independently existing particular churches, or, on the other hand, anyone who thinks that the particular churches are dependent administrative units of a prior whole. These two ways make the Church a this-worldly social or political reality. The most insightful people who took up the invitation to think through the apparent paradox with which article 23 presents us end up saying that there is no priority to be asserted, but that the universal Church and particular churches are simultaneous realities.

J.-M. R. Tillard's *Church of Churches* suggests by its title and its development the priority of the local and Eucharistically established "concrete" church to the great communion of such churches, which is the one universal Church.[28] This is how Avery Dulles reads him.[29] Joseph Komonchak takes him to be making the less controversial point that whatever theological richness we ascribe to the universal Church is available to us only in a particular church.[30]

In fact, Tillard's position is hard to state vis-à-vis the question of the relation of the local church to the one Church of Christ. Pentecost is the first full manifestation of the Church, where—at Jerusalem, a place—the community possesses in fullness that final gift of the messianic age, the Spirit of God who makes Jesus the Christ. It is then perfectly the *"Ekklesia tou Theou."*[31] The spread of this Church must be carefully appreciated: each subsequent community will also be rightly called the *Ekklesia tou Theou*, and "the Church will multiply itself without being divided."[32] In each local community, the full reality of the Church is revealed, and all together are the one Church of God.[33] As soon as there is more than one local church, the one Church is the communion of churches. Evidently, however, the first Church is destined and ordained to this repetition of her full reality in other places, and we might say that the communion of churches is already inscribed in her finality, her destiny. Does this view overly privilege the local church? It seems that, originally, by force of the circumstance that human beings are always "circumstanced"—standing in a place—it is simultaneously particular and "universal."[34] This view is continued in his contribution to the 1991 Salamanca conference on "The Local Church and Catholicity."[35] "Catholic" means first of all that the Church bears "the entirety of the plan of God for his People," which is not the same as the "geographical universality" of the Pentecost assembly; the Church is catholic in that it possesses "the entirety of divine gifts," and it is this "rather than their extension that is essential."[36] In its very nature as possessing this all, the local church "cannot exist as a local church except in communion with the other churches of God scattered throughout the world," and the Catholic Church just is "the *koinonia* of local churches mutually recognizing themselves as churches of God."[37] The relation of the local churches with Rome, moreover, is simply in the service of the mutual recognition of local churches.[38]

Komonchak also argues for simultaneity powerfully and persuasively:

> To try to solve problems by asserting a priority on either side is surely
> a mistake. It is mistaken historically because the Church which first
> emerged at Pentecost was at once local and catholic, gathered in
> Jerusalem but already speaking the one message in all languages, and
> because the Churches generated from that mother-church are the same
> Church, becoming catholic now concretely, in various other places.
> "Ontologically," the mistake lies in imagining that the constitutive
> principles of the Church can ever realize the universal Church except
> in a local Church or a local Church except as the universal Church.[39]

Historically, the first Church was "at once" local and universal—they are
simultaneous. Ontologically, there are no principles of the universal Church
"except" in a local church, and there is no local church "except" as universal—
they are simultaneous. Evidently, this simultaneity is a function of the fact that
all the elements that constitute the Church are present in the local church,
"the call of God, the Word of Christ, the grace of the Spirit, the Eucharist,
the apostolic ministry."[40] It is easy to understand the presence of the whole
in each because of the mutual indwelling of charity. But this presence is also
properly ecclesial and therefore visible, both in the Eucharist, which is not
what it should be unless it is an open Eucharist, hospitable to all the faithful
of whatever local church, and in the fact that the bishop who presides over the
local church is not a bishop except in view of his membership in a college that
has responsibility for the whole.[41]

The universal Church, after all, is nothing but the communion of all local
churches, and "is not a distinct subject of existence, attributes, or activities."[42]
Given this premise, Komonchak finds remarkable corroboration of his view in
John Paul II's Speech to the Curia of December 21, 1984, where the interiority
of the universal Church in each particular church means the mutual interiority of *all* the particular churches in one another. Commenting on *Lumen
Gentium* (no. 13), the Holy Father says,

> It would be difficult to express oneself with greater clarity and depth:
> the universal Church is present as a communion of (particular)
> churches and, indirectly, as a communion of nations, languages,
> cultures. Each of these brings its own proper "gifts" to all the oth-
> ers, just as they bring along each generation and human epoch, each
> scientific and social achievement, the goals of civilization gradually
> achieved.[43]

Such a recognition promises a "sane pluralism," one that does not detract from
the unity of the one Church but makes it catholic.

> In fact among the individual particular churches there is an onto-
> logical relationship of mutual inclusion: every particular Church, as a
> realization of the one Church of Christ, is in some way present in all

the particular Churches "in which and out which the one and unique catholic Church has its existence" (*Lumen Gentium*, no. 23). This ontological relation must be translated on the dynamic level of concrete life, if the Christian community does not wish to be in contradiction with itself: the basic ecclesial choices of believers in one community must be able to be harmonized with those of the faithful in the other communities, in order to allow that communion of minds and hearts for which Christ prayed at the Last Supper.[44]

And the Holy Father continues that it is especially the office of Peter to maintain the harmony just mentioned.

The Congregation for the Doctrine of the Faith took up the relation between particular churches and the universal Church in its Letter on Some Aspects of the Church Understood as Communion, *Communionis Notio* (*CN*) published in 1992.[45] The Letter responds to suggestions that local churches may set their own standards for accession to communion, and that, in effect, they may pursue the genius of their "locale" independently of concern for the whole. The Letter begins by noting that the communion is both communion with God and communion with men (*CN*, no. 3; cf. *LG*, no. 1), something both visible and invisible (*CN*, no. 4; cf. *LG*, no. 8). As to the relation of one particular church to another, and to the universal Church, this relation is grounded both in the Eucharist, which "renders all self-sufficiency on the part of the particular Churches impossible" (*CN*, no. 11), and in the unity of the episcopate, where each bishop in a local church reminds that church of the responsibility of the college of bishops for the whole and therefore for each part (*CN*, nos. 12–13), and where the college is not independent of its primate, the pope (*CN*, nos. 12–13). The mutual interiority of the universal and particular churches is stated: the council asserted that particular churches are in the universal Church and vice versa (see *Christus Dominus*, nos. 6 and 11); therefore they enjoy a relation of "mutual interiority," according to John Paul II (*CN*, no. 9).[46] Further, since the universal Church just is "a Communion of churches" (*CN*, no. 8), the interiority of the universal in the particular church seems to entail the presence of all particular churches in each. As to the formula of *Lumen Gentium* (no. 23) that "the Church [is] in and formed out of the Churches," it is balanced with another formula from John Paul II: "The Churches [are] in and formed out of the Church."[47] After noting the mutual interiority of particular church and the universal Church, the congregation concludes with John Paul II, unsurprisingly, that the universal Church is not a federation, and then, quite surprisingly for many, that the universal Church, "in its essential mystery . . . is a reality *ontologically and temporally* prior to every *individual* particular Church" (*CN*, no. 9).

This last claim famously became a bone of contention between Cardinal Ratzinger and Cardinal Walter Kasper, who defended the simultaneity of the universal and local churches.[48] Does the statement make of the Church itself some pre-existent, celestial hypostasis, independent of any and all particular churches? Does it contradict the concreteness of mutual interiority which Komonchak, and indeed John Paul II, were concerned to bring to the fore?

Worst, if the church of Rome, the pope's church, succeeds to the church of Jerusalem, is the Letter anything more than a re-assertion of pre-conciliar centralization and Roman authority? [49]

The Letter explains the ontological priority of the universal Church by noting that, for the Fathers, "the Church that is one and unique, precedes creation" (CN, no. 9, with reference to Shepherd of Hermas and Clement of Rome). The temporal priority of the universal Church is demonstrated by the Pentecostal assembly in which all the nations, who have yet to enjoy any local assembly of Christians, are represented.

Ratzinger replied to these criticisms of the Congregation's Letter in his own voice. [50] He is unmoved by the contention of Komonchak, Kasper, and Tillard that the first church of Jerusalem is both local and universal, since the entire reality of the Church is concentrated there, with the Twelve, with the fullness of the Spirit of Pentecost, a place that, for a while, is the unique location of the Eucharist. The temporal priority of the universal Church is not just in itself an historical thesis, but a theological one that includes a bearing on history:

> What comes first in Saint Luke's account is not any original community at Jerusalem; what comes first is that, in the Twelve, the old Israel, which is one, becomes the new and that through the wonderful gift of tongues this new Israel of God is then shown, before there is any question of constituting a local community in Jerusalem, to be a unity encompassing every time and place. [51]

As to ontological priority, he holds the following:

> This ontological precedence of the Church as a whole, of the one Church and the one body, of the one bride, over the empirical and concrete realizations in the various individual parts of the Church seems to me so obvious that I find it difficult to understand the objections raised against it. [52]

We have a clue as to what is "so obvious" to Ratzinger where he mentions the "one bride." No particular church *in her particularity* can claim to be the "one bride" or the "one body" of Christ. Only of the universal Church can we say "bride of Christ," "body of Christ." Here, the universal Church is a distinct subject of attributions different from the particular church. [53]

Both theses, that the universal Church is "prior" to the particular churches, and that the universal Church and the particular churches are "simultaneous" realities, have something to recommend them. There is a call here for speculative insight.

3. The Church as Universal Instrument of Salvation

Lumen Gentium begins with the assertion that the Church is the sacrament of salvation, the "sign and instrument of intimate union with God." Since there is but one such sign and instrument, the council can add that that it is the sign and instrument of "the unity of the whole human race," and so has a universal mission (*LG*, no. 1). This is repeated in article 9, where the Church is "for one and all the visible sacrament of this saving unity," and in article 48, where the Church is "the universal sacrament of salvation." These are strategic assertions, where the council treats of the mystery of the Church (no. 1 in chapter 1), the Church in history as the pilgrim People of God (no. 9 in chapter 2), and the eschatological consummation of the Church (no. 48 in chapter 7).

Lumen Gentium (no. 16) teaches further that those who search for God, even in ignorance of Christ and his Church, can be saved. Therefore a question arises—or rather three questions. First, there is the issue of instrumentality. How does the Church save those who are ignorant of the Church? The instrumentality of the Church for salvation, and the universality of this instrumentality, such that no one who is saved is saved apart from the Church, has been repeated in magisterial acts subsequent to the council. Still, if someone possesses grace and charity, but not through the preaching of the Gospel and not through baptism, how is the Church the instrument of his salvation?

Second, there is the question of the exclusivity of the Church's instrumentality for salvation. The universality of the Church's instrumentality for salvation, and therefore, for the salvation of all, seems to settle this issue already. If the Church is the universal instrument, it would seem to be the exclusive instrument, and there would therefore be no other instrumentality unto salvation except the Church's. So in article 8 of *Lumen Gentium*, Christ, the "unique" mediator, establishes a "unique" Church. And in article 9, as we have noted, the Church is "for one and all the visible sacrament of this saving unity." *Ad Gentes* (nos. 5 and 7) seems to repeat this teaching. How can there be another instrumentality unto salvation except that of Christ and his Church?

Third, there is the question of visibility. According to *Lumen Gentium* (no. 8), the one Church is visible and invisible. If someone belongs to the Church by possessing the interior goods of grace and charity, unseen things, and is ignorant of the Gospel and of the Church, how does he yet belong to a *visible* Church?

One way to conceive of the Church as effecting the salvation of non-Christians is to suppose that Christian prayers and intercessions mediate the grace of Christ to those who are being saved, and if this is so, it is so especially for the mass, which is offered for men of good will and "all who were pleasing to you at their passing from this life" (Eucharistic Prayer III). So Charles Journet, before the council, taught that non-Christians can be saved by the priestly offering of Christians.[54] In the same vein, Francis Sullivan noted the teaching of Pius XII in *Mystici Corporis*, according to which Christ is helped in the work of redemption by the prayers and penances of the members of his Body.[55]

Another way to answer these questions is to conceive of non-Christian religions as somehow participating in Christianity. If Gospel elements of truth and sanctification can work unto salvation outside the visible confines of the Catholic Church, cannot there be some participation of these elements in non-Christian religions (ordered, to be sure, to completion in what they are participations of), which, in their social availability and visibility, could be instruments for the salvation of the adherents of these religions? This is the way that Jacques Dupuis has explored. For instance, divine inspiration can be understood to operate beyond the confines of Judeo-Christian history and tradition, producing a true word of God and genuinely holy scriptures,[56] although in a secret and "non-official" way.[57] As such, the concepts of inspiration and the word of God and scripture can be analogized, and the holy writings of other religions can be understood also to be inspired—if not in the same sense as the Old and New Testaments, then at least in some way—providing a word complementary to the Bible,[58] and as a real participation in the mediation of the word of God.[59] Similarly, just as there is extra-biblical revelation, so there are extra-Christian sacraments that mediate the presence and saving action of God.[60]

Dupuis's proposal is that the Church is exclusively the perfect instrument of salvation, and that while non-Christian religions may be imperfect, they are nonetheless real instruments of salvation, according as they participate in the elements of truth and sanctification revealed to and established for Christians in the Church. Insofar as they really are instruments unto salvation, they are willed just as such by God. They are "ways" and "means" of salvation.[61]

The third issue of the visibility of the Church is not addressed by speaking of the prayers of Christians. But in Dupuis's way, the extra-ecclesial and non-Christian statements of revealed truth, and the extra-ecclesial and non-Christian sacramental mediations of grace would share in the visibility of the Church, strange as this may sound, so that wherever there is salvation, there is the Church in her one reality, composed of visible and invisible elements.

The post-conciliar magisterial reception of Lumen Gentium and Ad Gentes addressed some of the questions raised by Dupuis and others. In addition to the notification on Dupuis's Toward a Christian Theology of Religious Pluralism, the chief texts are John Paul II's Redemptoris Missio (RM) of 1990 and Dominus Iesus, published in 2000 by the Congregation for the Doctrine of the Faith.[62]

Redemptoris Missio celebrated the twenty-fifth anniversary of Ad Gentes, and it re-asserted the council's call for a renewal of missionary activity. The grace of Christ can save those ignorant of the Gospel, just as Lumen Gentium asserted (no. 16), but such grace maintains a "mysterious relationship to the Church" (RM, no. 10), which remains the universal sacrament of salvation (RM, no. 9). What is the relation of those so touched by grace to the Church? It does not make them "formally a part of the Church" (RM, no. 10), and the encyclical leaves things at that. If we absolutely have to have a name for their relationship to the Church, we could say that, since their relation to the communion of grace and charity is more than potential, but since they have not been baptized and have no express desire to be baptized (see RM, no. 55), they are "virtually" members of the Church.

As to the value of non-Christian religions, the encyclical acknowledges their "spiritual riches" at no. 55:

He does not fail to make himself present in many ways, not only to individuals but also to entire peoples through their spiritual riches, of which their religions are the main and essential expression, even when they contain "gaps, insufficiencies and errors" [quoting Paul VI, to the Council, September 29, 1963].

This certainly seems to say that God makes himself present for salvation through non-Christian religions, as Dupuis wants to say: if he makes himself present through the "spiritual riches" that the religions "express," then surely he makes himself present through the religions. This is not, however, to recognize a regime of the Spirit separable from that of the Incarnate Word (*RM*, no. 29). "Seeds of the Word" there may be in these religions, as Paul VI taught,[63] but they do not make non-Christian religions ordinary, "normal" ways of salvation, and at this point in the reception of *Lumen Gentium*, it is to be wondered whether they can be considered ways *at all*.[64]

The Notification of 2001 on Dupuis's book by the Congregation for the Doctrine of the Faith defends the exclusive and universal mediation of Christ, the completeness of revelation in Christ, the co-extensivity of the missions of Son and Spirit, and the ordination of all mankind to the Church. The Notification declares further at no. 8 that there is "no foundation in Catholic theology" for considering non-Christian religions as "ways of salvation," despite whatever elements of truth and goodness they contain, and despite the Spirit's ability to use these elements for the salvation of their adherents.

The Notification was but an application of the much longer Declaration on the Unicity and Salvific Universality of Jesus Christ and the Church, *Dominus Iesus*, which at much greater length reviewed the above issues.

Dominus Iesus is difficult to construe coherently and in its entirety without keeping two distinctions in mind. First, there is a distinction between what is *good* in non-Christian religions, and which must therefore come from God, and things that proceed from God precisely as *Christian* things (*DI*, no. 22). Second, there is a distinction between the order of *revelation* on the one hand, the order communicating truth, and the order of effective, saving *grace*, the order that accomplishes salvation in grace (cf. nos. 8 and 22). As to the order of revelation, God makes himself present in truth "not only to individuals, but also to entire peoples through their spiritual riches," and non-Christian religions express these very riches, albeit not without "gaps, insufficiencies and errors" (*DI*, no. 8, quoting *Redemptoris Missio*, no. 55). Thus, I conclude, God is not being considered here as the *author* of these riches, as he is of the riches of the Old and New Testament, although these riches are truly received "from the mystery of Christ" (*DI*, no. 8). Christ, who in his divinity is the express Truth of God and of all things in God, must be the origin of every truth; but he does not *speak* every truth that we come to know, even though every truth comes from him, and so not every truth is dignified with the title "word of God." Nonetheless, just because these truths are true, he can use them to make himself present to the minds of the adherents of non-Christian religions.[65] As to the order of grace, "the various religious traditions contain and offer religious elements which come from God" (*DI*, no. 21), things that the "the Spirit brings about in human hearts and in the history of peoples, in cultures and religions" (*DI*, no. 21), things that prepare for the Gospel and prompt the heart "to be open to the action of God" (*DI*, no. 21). But these things have no *ex opere operato* efficacy—that is, they are not non-Christian equivalents of sacraments, and the text explicitly evokes the council of Trent at just this point.

Thus, Christ uses things of which he is not the author but which come from him in the order of revelation. In the order of grace, once again, good things come from God, as all good things must, but not as Christian things do, with the warrant of their provenance, and they are not used for the conferral of grace but for rightly disposing men to it.

If Dupuis's proposal is rejected, then the solution it contains for the visibility of the Church wherever someone is saved also goes by the boards. But this is a serious matter too. If it is possible that the community of the saved need have no visible relations to the Church whatsoever, then we are squarely back in the sixteenth century, where the community of the saved and the community of those who visibly belong to the Church could be two quite separable communities. And then we cannot really uphold the teaching of article 8 of *Lumen Gentium*, according to which the one Church is both visible and invisible.

B. Theological Reception of *Lumen Gentium*

It is time to turn to the theological reception of *Lumen Gentium*. This reception, too, is ordered to the same end as its catechetical and practical reception, and is supposed to do that by helping these receptions. It is to do so, however, by first passing through, as we usually count them, two acts of contemplation. First, there is the challenge to behold *Lumen Gentium* in its Scriptural, patristic, and theological antecedents, and to appreciate how they are re-read, and with what new emphases, insights, and applications. This work is, I think, well in hand—a lot of it is pre-conciliar—such that, if we want to know the background in Scripture and tradition to whatever central idea or image *Lumen Gentium* uses, we have only to take and read about the Body of Christ, or the People of God, or the distinctions between laity and clergy and clergy and religious, or the complicated relations between the task of governing and episcopal jurisdiction, or acting in the person of Christ, and so on.

There is also a second act of theological contemplation, the sapiential act of beholding the intrinsic intelligibility of a revealed mystery from its analogy to naturally known things, its connection to other revealed mysteries, and its relation to our final end.[66] The text of *Lumen Gentium* invites such a contemplative act. The Church is indeed a "mystery," and this is meant in a properly theological sense, where, explaining the title of chapter one, the Theological Commission explained that a mystery is "a divine, transcendent, and saving reality which is revealed and manifested in a visible way."[67] Just as the other mysteries, the mystery of the Church gives rise to systematic thought.

Yet, if we look for mature speculative accounts that successfully unfold the mystery of the Church in the unity of her divine and human elements (*LG*, no. 8) and that can deal insightfully with such questions as the instrumentality and visibility of the Church, her subsistence in and identity with the Catholic Church while doing speculative justice to non-Catholic churches and communions, and the relation of the local to the universal Church, it is easy to exhaust our search. Writing just over ten years ago, Avery Dulles said,

> It would be gratifying to be able to report that the theology of the Church has been developing in healthy ways. But I do not find much progress in the last forty years. The renaissance that should have followed Vatican II has not yet occurred except here and there in isolated cases. Whatever development has occurred may be found most clearly in official teaching.[68]

This is a sobering assessment. Post-conciliar systematic theology was, in general, starved, strangled, and suffering. It was starved of the dogmatic truths it is ordered to understand. Once "dogma" was taken out of play because of the recrudescence of modernism and theological liberalism after the council, then systematic theology, untethered to revelation, became infinite and uninteresting. It was strangled by the post-conciliar aversion to an explicitly avowed metaphysics. It suffered chills of resentment of Church authority alternating with fevers of enlisting in the various wills to power in the postmodern, openly Nietzschean age of the fifty years following the council.

So perhaps it is not really surprising that there has been little systematic ecclesiology worthy of the name, where the nature of the Church is articulated, insofar as any mystery can be so given to reason illumined by faith, and in such a way as therein to behold those principles whereby we see the properties of the Church unfold, the *convenientiae* of her structures, and the solutions of such various problems as the three touched on in the first part of this essay.

That being said, I divide this part into three sections that treat, first, useful if not particularly systematic recapitulations of *Lumen Gentium*, second, older but genuinely systematic theological contemplations of the Church, and third and notwithstanding Dulles's assessment, a new light to engage our attention.

1. *Useful Things that Make No Speculative Contribution*

The scope of Johann Auer's *The Church: The Universal Sacrament of Salvation* is broad, and the discussion of each topic always informative.[69] This is a work of immense erudition and contains masterful historical summaries, concise and precise. But it is systematically unambitious: the Church is a communion; and the Church is a sacrament. But how these aspects of the Church are related to one another in detail is not even stated, much less developed. There is no real speculative attempt here.

Similarly well informed and erudite is Miguel M. Garijo-Guembe's *Communion of the Saints*.[70] The biblical ecclesiological images and ideas are thoughtfully presented. This study is regularly attuned to Orthodox and Protestant views of whatever is being discussed. Bibliographical resources for each section are very handy.

Also useful is *The Gift of the Church*, edited by Peter Phan.[71] Distinguished contributors include Joseph Komonchak, Avery Dulles, Susan K. Wood, Francis A. Sullivan, Hermann Pottmeyer, and Sara Butler. The volume is styled a textbook, and could serve as one for the "many voices, many perspectives" manner of theological education in the United States. Evidently, as the product of many hands, there is no systematic unity expressed or attempted, but the collection is thoroughly informed by a consciousness of *Lumen Gentium*.

Avery Dulles became instantly famous in 1974 for his *Models of the Church*, where he attempted a new style of theological reflection inspired by the philosopher of science, Thomas Kuhn.[72] *Models* is a sort of meta-theological study that lines up many efforts at understanding the Church and then exercises judgment according to standard theological criteria (Scripture, tradition, pastoral effectiveness, contemporaneity, theological fruitfulness). Subsequently, but without the apparatus of any appeal to paradigms and paradigm changes, Dulles continued to assess, weigh, and render judgment on a host of ecclesiological proposals, studies, trends, and projects.[73] In this way, for over forty years, he carefully followed the reception of *Lumen Gentium*, rendering his assessment of post-conciliar ecclesiology reported above particularly weighty. While he gave special attention to the theory and practice of magisterial teaching authority,[74] his judgment was always informed historically and dogmatically, whatever he addressed, conscious of all the alternatives. His most comprehensive and satisfying study in a like vein was his *The Catholicity of the Church*.[75]

2. *Older Things That Do Make a Speculative Contribution, Briefly Noted*

Louis Bouyer's *The Church of God* contains a thoughtful, not uncritical analysis of *Lumen Gentium*, and proposes to supply some of its lacuna: a meatier treatment of the Holy Spirit and the Church, as well as a lengthier appreciation of the local church.[76] He takes up all the themes of the Constitution, as near as I can see, and receives them in his comprehensive awareness of Christian theology, culture, and history. Someone might object that Bouyer gives us no more than an erudite discussion of these themes, and no systematic treatment. But this is to forget that *The Church* is the second part of a trilogy whose overarching theme is the presence of the Triune God to the creation: first, in a human person, the Mother of the Word; second, in redeemed humanity, the Church, whose personality is Marian; third, in the cosmos, called to eschatological nuptials with the Word.[77] Bouyer's study is also noteworthy for the attention it gives, both historically and dogmatically, to the Orthodox, and to the question of their reception of the ecumenical councils at which they were not present.

Should Heribert Mühlen's *Una Mystica Persona* really count as a reception of *Lumen Gentium*?[78] The basic ecclesiological vision was worked out in the 1964 edition, and the 1967 edition simply adds material on *Lumen Gentium*. Is there a real act of reception here? Yes, there is, even though the council's teaching is received into a developed ecclesiology. The aim of this ecclesiology, it will be recalled, was to provide a dogmatic formula for the Church as fundamental and illuminating as those for the Trinity ("three Persons in one nature") and Christology ("two natures in one Person"). The proposal, "one Person in many persons," or "one Spirit in Christ and in us," is a satisfying systematic move, one that turns to ecclesiological use St. Augustine's conception of the Holy Spirit in the *De Trinitate*, and one that finds an expression for the mission of the Spirit of equivalent conciseness, articulateness, and fundamentality as Chalcedon's formula for the mission of the Son. Moreover, Mühlen's addition to the 1967 edition is substantial, at four chapters and more than two hundred pages; if it is an afterthought, it is a long and well-developed afterthought. Grist for his mill is article 8 of *Lumen Gentium*, the analogy between Incarnation and Church, the missions of Word and Spirit. He turns his theology of the Holy Spirit also to a consideration of the council's ecumenical thrust; the one Spirit in many Christians making the Church is the one Spirit in many churches, too. This remains a thoughtful and thought-provoking systematic achievement.

Jean-Hervé Nicolas's *Synthèse dogmatique* is a classically conceived theology that aspires to the scientific and so certain knowledge of God and the works of God by the light of revelation.[79] The treatise on the Church occupies the place most Thomists suppose it would have had in the *Summa* had Thomas needed to write one, after Christology and before the sacraments, and Nicolas devotes 100 pages of the 1260 of the entire work to the Church.[80] Nicolas reads *Lumen Gentium* as surely offering an invitation to consider the Church as a sacrament—an invitation that he accepts, making it the architectonic concept under which he considers the Church. But this is more than a barely asserted statement of its preeminence, since he devotes a good deal of space to showing how "sacrament" completes the images of People, Body, Bride, Temple, and absorbs the ideas of the Church as institution and society.

His central systematic contribution is to develop an idea suggested after the council by Journet, and developed by Jean-Guy Pagé, that the analogy of the Church to a sacramental reality needs to do more than speak of two things, a visible thing manifesting an invisible thing, since this does not provide a way to avoid the total separation of sign and signified, of visible society and communion of charity. Between the ecclesial *signum tantum*, the visible society of the Church, and the *res tantum*, shared Trinitarian life, there is also a *res et sacramentum*, namely, the objective holiness of sacramental character in each of the members of the Church, and the objective bonds of the preaching and profession (not mere confession) of faith, and the exercise and recognition of apostolic authority. The ecclesial *res et sacramentum* makes available the presence of grace as always offered in the Church. This idea will find further elaboration in one of Nicolas's Dominican *confrères* and is revisited at more length below.

Nicolas is attentive to the language of Church membership, according to which we do better speaking of belonging invisibly or visibly to the one visible/invisible Church, than of belonging to its soul or body. His discussion of the holiness of the Church, indebted to Charles Journet but not uncritical of him, is very worthwhile, and especially so when we remember the many apologies and reckonings with the past undertaken by St. John Paul II.

3. Benoît-Dominique de La Soujeole, OP

The best comprehensive systematic ecclesiology of recent years is to be found in the work of Benoît-Dominique de La Soujeole, OP, which should be considered at greater length. His work includes a monograph on "fundamental ecclesiology," *Le sacrement de la communion* (1998), an *Introduction au Mystère de l'Église* (2006)—a "textbook," but what a textbook!—and many articles.[81] He brings forward into his work the legacy of Charles Journet and Yves Congar within a framework ordered by a comprehensive insight generated by *Lumen Gentium*. The *Introduction* comprises an essay in positive theology followed by a consideration of the real definition and properties of the Church.

A. CHURCH: SACRAMENT OF COMMUNION De La Soujeole thinks that article 8 of *Lumen Gentium* brings to a close the long-lasting, post-Tridentine difficulty over the unity of the Church.[82] Article 8 does not distinguish the Church from the Mystical Body of Christ; rather, the hierarchically structured society and the Mystical Body, the visible assembly and the spiritual community of faith and charity, the earthly Church and the Church endowed with divine gifts are not two things, not two communities, but only one reality, one congregation of those who on this earth are being saved, just as the Lord Jesus himself, though human and divine, is one person, one Word of God incarnate.[83] In this way, as was noted with Nicolas, we can no longer speak of belonging to the soul of the Church but not to the body, nor vice versa, as did Robert Bellarmine, using a distinction never received into the Magisterium, as de La Soujeole points out, a distinction finally seen as unsuited for the description of ecclesial reality.[84]

How distressing it was, therefore, that the Final Report of the Extraordinary Synod in 1985 was bound to report "a partial reading of the Council, a unilateral presentation of the Church as a purely institutional structure devoid of her Mystery" (I.4). This separation "between the institution [of the Church] and charity," de La Soujeole writes, "is one of the most important causes of the current ecclesial malaise."[85] It is indeed astonishing that the "century of the Church" (Otto Dibelius) should have ended in the popular perception that "spirituality" and "religion," charity and the Church, need have, and for some people cannot have, anything to do with one another. Post-conciliar indifference to the unique subsistence of the Church in the Catholic Church, the readiness to downplay the universal instrumentality of the Church for salvation, and the readiness to impute sin to the Church herself, the "institutional Church," are all manifestations of the separation the Synod and de La Soujeole name.

The Church is a mystery, according to the council, and *mysterion* is also rendered by *sacramentum*. So the council teaches that the Church is "in Christ as a sacrament or instrumental sign of intimate union with God and of the unity of all humanity" (*LG*, no. 1). The phrase "in Christ [the Anointed]" relates the Church to the missions of both Son and Spirit: the sacrament of the altar unites the faithful in Christ (no. 3); the Church is the Body of Christ (no. 7); yet we are "in" Christ only through the gift of the Holy Spirit (no. 4), who can be said to "vivify" the Church as does a soul a body (no. 7) because he "gives life, unity and movement to the whole body" (no. 7). This unity is the unity of the members of the Church. This Spirit is moreover related to "the social struc-ture of the Church" in the way the divine Word is related to the humanity of Christ (no. 8). But union with God and the unity of humanity (no. 1), effected by the Spirit (no. 7), can be designated as *communion*, too. Thus, it is just one step beyond the text of *Lumen Gentium* to say that the visible and societal ele-ments of the Church can be understood as the sacramental and effective sign of communion in grace and charity with God and men, which is salvation taken in its communal scope, whence the Church is "the universal sacrament of salvation" (no. 48).

This invitation to systematic thought was already afoot before the coun-cil, in the plethora of studies devoted to the Church as sacrament, and in Congar's prediction of the theological serviceability of the concept of com-munion.[86] For Rahner in 1961, the Church has "an intrinsically sacramental structure,"[87] where the "juridically organized society" is the sign of "the people of God."[88] Rahner insists that sign and signified are here inseparable. Pieces also appeared almost immediately after the council on the sacramentality of the Church.[89]

The invitation of the conciliar text can be thought to be met too easily, how-ever, if we but briskly slap together the Church as sacrament and the Church as communion. The Church as the sacrament of communion can be respon-sibly asserted only if we take into account the council's insistence that the Church is one thing. However the sacramentality of the Church is understood, it cannot imply that the "visible assembly" and the "spiritual communion" are two things—that is, two assemblies, two communities, two societies—else we return to the deadend of the sixteenth century. But it is hard not to do this: wit-ness Walter Kasper (who is appealing to Karl Rahner):

> It is part of the unity between the sign and the thing signified, that the church in its actual, specific form, unlike the synagogue, cannot fundamentally fall away from God's truth and love. . . . Yet in spite of this inherent connection, the visible church is not simply identi-cal with the thing to which it testifies. In extreme cases the outward sign and the inward salvific reality can also be sundered. The outward sign, though retaining its reality, may become empty and unfruitful; and conversely, the saving reality can be conveyed even without the external ecclesial sign.[90]

This seems to mean that, despite the "inherent connection" of sign and signified, some visible ecclesial assembly can be untouched by grace, and the communion of those enlivened by grace can be divorced from any external assembly. This seems to mean, as well, that we are squarely immobilized in the sixteenth century, where the Protestants openly, and Bellarmine despite himself, entertained the separation of ecclesial assembly and the assembly of grace. The one reality of the Church is not maintained. Kasper notes that this view is one with the possibility of Rahner's "anonymous Christian."[91] Ecclesially, it is one with the question of the visibility of the Church: the assembly of anonymous Christians is an invisible Church.

De La Soujeole is well aware of the difficulty of thinking out the sacramentality of the Church.

> There are ... different ways of deploying the sacramentality of the Church. The dominant line before Vatican II maintained that by *sacramentum*, we must understand the exterior sensible reality, and by the *res sacramenti*, we must understand the interior reality of grace. And it is then maintained that the society is the sacrament (sign and instrument) of communion (the reality). The sacramentality of the Church is then susceptible of being used within the line of a social analogy founded on the intuitions of modern social philosophy; it is not considered in a more directly theological way. This conception maintains the limitation of ecclesial visibility to the signs-means of grace, and holds that communion is a purely interior reality.[92]

Theological borrowings from modern sociology, de La Soujeole thinks, have been wholly without warrant in Scripture or tradition or magisterial statement (including *Lumen Gentium*) and mostly disastrous. Society and communion, the *Gesellschaft* and *Gemeinschaft* of Ferdinand Tönnies, become the visible and structured society of the Church and the interior communion of faith and charity. It will be claimed there is a "dialectical tension" between these two poles of ecclesial reality, and while the necessity of the visible and structured society may be reluctantly admitted, generally things turn out badly for the institution and the hierarchy, and there is a tacit permission to cultivate the communion of charity according to one's own lights and capacities. In fact, the unity of the Church is not maintained.[93]

There is furthermore the question of the holiness of the Church. If the sacramental sign of the Church is purely the socially related congregation of some place (diocese), and if all the members of the congregation are liable to be sinners, what assurance is there that this society really does make available the sanctification of Christ in the Spirit?[94]

To meet this problem, de La Soujeole receives *Lumen Gentium* in three strategic ways. First, he realizes an ecclesiology of communion grounded in concise but thorough studies of *ekklesia* and *koinonia* in the New Testament and tradition: "The ecclesiological notion of *koinonia-communio* expresses the divine community insofar as it is shared by man according to a Christological economy, an economy that conforms man to Christ."[95] Second, although the sacramentality of the Church specifies its generic reality, it is the analogy with the Eucharist that provides the key to unlock the sixteenth-century puzzle over how the social and the theologal communities of the Church are related. This requires some exposition.

De La Soujeole thinks to work out the sacramentality of the Church in a more successful way, and one that addresses the question of the sinfulness of the members of the Church, by adapting the Eucharistic distinction of the *sacramentum tantum* (the appearances of bread and wine and the words of consecration), the *res et sacramentum* (the true Body and Blood of the Lord), and the *res tantum* (charity). These moments must find communal instantiations, doubtless, if the Church is to be the sacrament of *communion*.

The ecclesial identification of the ecclesial *res tantum* is easy to specify: it is "the community of those who live now the life of God that has been communicated to them."[96] The ecclesial *sacramentum tantum* will be "the common life of Christians," a social whole distinct from other such realities, the whole community composed of both clerical and lay members.[97] Materially, it is available to the inspection of all; as a sign of salvation, it is available only to faith. Still, de La Soujeole says, the reality of sin can disturb the "perfect correspondence" between the community that enjoys the ecclesial *res* and the society that is its sign.[98] It is here that the identification of the ecclesial *res et sacramentum* serves to assure the grace-filled reality of the Church. "What is it, truly signified by the social sign and borrowing its visibility from it," de La Soujeole asks, "that is really established in the Church in order that she be *unfailingly* the reality and the means of living the communitarian theologal life?"[99] It is something that can be perceived only by faith, and it is necessarily communitarian in nature, although rooted in each member of the community.

> At the level of individuals, it will be of the *charismatic* order, a common *gratia gratis data* and not reserved to some, according to the unforeseeable freedom of the Spirit. It will thus be a matter, in our opinion, of the characters imprinted by the sacraments of baptism, confirmation, and orders. At the level of the community, this ecclesial *res et sacramentum* denotes the presence of sanctifying grace as giving itself: the community is the instrument that the Spirit of Christ uses in order to pour out what is in the incarnate Word, he who, according to his humanity, is the Head.[100]

Evidently, the ministers of word and sacrament play a principal role in constituting this the community of the Church as a community guaranteeing the availability of grace, but it is the entire community that constitutes this role, since there is no word except it be heard, and there is no sacrament except it be received.

This way of viewing the Church solves no problems unless it is firmly kept in mind that the three communities constituting the *res*, the sign, and the intermediate reality of sign and reality, are the one Church, the one reality of the Church. "The *signum tantum* bears the *res et sacramentum* that engenders the *res tantum*."[101]

I mentioned a third strategic reception of the council, and this has to do with the visibility of the Church, something mostly overlooked by studies subsequent to the council. The economy of communion is Christological, in that Christ effects communion with God through the sacraments of the Church. It is also Christo-conforming, in that those who are saved look like Christ and do the works of Christ. In both these ways, the Church is visible, and not only in the first way of preached word and celebrated sacrament. Now, this too was observed by the council.[102] Moreover, it links us up with a much older way of thinking about the visibility of the Christian economy, that of St. Thomas, for whom the invisible communion of grace and charity is preceded by the visible economy of the means of grace, and is followed by the visible works of Christian love.[103]

What is also recovered is the older way of speaking about membership in the Church. Those invisibly in grace belong spiritually or mentally to the Church; those visibly touched by baptism belong visibly to the Church, *and so do those who do the works of charity*. There cannot be two separable ecclesial communities; rather, "the principle of ecclesiality is within the person," as de La Soujeole says, and there is a great difference between saying one belongs to the *body* of the Church or *bodily* to the Church.[104] The Church is always both visible and invisible, for she is one thing, although a member's belonging may include belonging to the community of grace, or the visible social group, or both.

We revisit the three issues we privileged in the first part of this essay.

B. THE CHURCH SUBSISTS IN THE CATHOLIC CHURCH   De La Soujeole interprets article 8 of *Lumen Gentium* pretty much as Joseph Ratzinger does: to say the Church subsists in the Catholic Church asserts an identity, but a non-exclusive one, in that ecclesial reality is to be recognized outside the visible confines of the Catholic Church.[105] In explaining the relation of non-Catholic churches and communions to the Catholic Church, he deploys a trope of scholastic theology, useful for capturing the relationship:

> The Roman Catholic Church is in act the unique Church of Christ;
> the separated communities are that Church in potency, not purely
> and simply, but progressively actualized according as they follow the
> dynamism of the ecclesial elements that they have kept.[106]

Subsequently, he develops this in a more technically satisfying way by characterizing the separated churches and communities as potential parts of the

Church. In each of them the essence of the Church is verified, but they do not possess all the powers with which Christ endowed the Church.[107]

C. PARTICULAR CHURCH AND UNIVERSAL CHURCH De La Soujeole has a nuanced answer to the question of the relative priorities of the universal and particular Churches, based on his distinction between the Church as a sociologically available assembly and the Church as the communion of service in word and sacrament. As to the *signum tantum*, therefore, the sociologically describable society of Christians, the Church as a whole is, as it were, federally composed of its parts, the particular churches.[108] But this is not the most important perspective to take for de La Soujeole. The communion of service in preaching and sanctifying, what de La Soujeole calls the "diaconal communion" of the Church and which evokes the faith and bestows the charity of the Holy Spirit—this communion begins in Jerusalem.[109]

> Thus, what is first, as an ontological condition of possibility presupposed to every local church, is the group of the Twelve of which Peter is the head. This group is the source and rule of diaconal communion.[110]

"Universal Church" is thus seen to designate two things, according as one considers it before or after the local church. Antecedent to the local church, the universal Church is the originating apostolicity of the Church, the source and norm of every church. Posterior to the local church, the universal Church is apostolicity "as effectively received and lived."[111]

Thus, local churches are from the universal Church insofar as it is the source of their foundation and rule of life; but "local churches united by their identity of source and of regulation are the universal Church considered as the effect that happens by them and from them."[112]

D. UNIVERSAL SACRAMENT OF SALVATION De La Soujeole adopts the language proposed by Jacques Maritain to speak of the relation of non-Christians to the Church: they are not purely potential members, but, according as they are touched by grace, "virtual" members, and this is not discordant with *Lumen Gentium* (no. 16), which refuses a contradictory choice between wholly in and wholly out.[113] How are they touched by grace? Very definitely through the Church herself, as de La Soujeole reads *Lumen Gentium*, though the council does not specify the exact nature of this mediation.[114] This mediation of grace renders a non-Christian a member *merito vel mentaliter tantum*, in the language of St. Thomas.[115] Further, it enables us to speak of non-Christian religions themselves as sharing in the one way that is Christ and the Church, according as their doctrines, rites, and rule of life participate in the mystery of the Church.[116] These elements do not work *ex opere operato*, but dispose someone for grace, and are in that way instruments of the Holy Spirit.[117]

De la Soujeole proposes here a genuine development of the teaching of *Lumen Gentium*, though in continuity with it. The council found a way to speak of the ecclesiality of individuals, both non-Catholic and non-Christian who are being saved (nos. 15 and 16); it also found a way to speak of the ecclesiality of non-Catholic Christian groups (no. 8). He proposes a way to speak of the ecclesiality of non-Christian religions, where their visible rites and manners of life substitute for the visible elements of Christianity.[118] This is not an insignificant proposal: it allows us to recognize the providential role of non-Christian religions without denying that Christianity is the unique and only way ordained by God, just as recognizing the elements of truth and sanctification in non-Catholic Christian societies enables us to speak of the unique subsistence of the Church of Christ in the Catholic Church.

There are further studies promised by de La Soujeole, completing the *Introduction*, on the action of the Church and its end, studies eagerly to be awaited.

4. Joseph Ratzinger

For several reasons, it is difficult to categorize the achievement of Joseph Ratzinger, so I leave him in solitary splendor. To be sure, he was admirably prepared to become a great theologian of the Church, on the Church. His doctoral dissertation delimited St. Augustine's use of "people of God" and "house of God." The Old Testament "people of God," to be sure, is transformed into the new people of the New Testament by becoming the Body of Christ. The first chapter of *Lumen Gentium* takes up the mystery of the Church, and especially as the Body of Christ. Ratzinger's *Habilitationshrift* studied the theology of history in St. Bonaventure, the center of whose progress is Christ. The second chapter of *Lumen Gentium* considers the display of the Church throughout history. Who better prepared than Ratzinger, therefore, to take the theological measure of these foundational chapters? Second, Ratzinger was a *peritus* at the council for Cardinal Frings, fully lived the event of the council, and knew the players, the pressures, the dangers, and the graces. This meant, among many other things, that he was present at the meeting of the Doctrinal Commission where the shift was proposed from saying the Church of Christ is the Catholic Church to saying it subsists in the Catholic Church. By providence, therefore, Ratzinger was uniquely prepared to write an ecclesiology of matchless theological insight and peerless contemporary authority.

Providence evidently had other plans for him, and his contribution to the life and understanding of the Church is surely greater than any theological treatise could contribute. Still, we miss the treatise. Even so, it is supplied for us piecemeal in a vast collection of its various *membra*, scattered *disiecta* throughout Ratzinger's theological literary career, made by Maximilian Heim.[119] Heim organizes Ratzinger according to the plan of the conciliar text. And this is not so extrinsic to Ratzinger's own mind if we consider his professional preparation, as I have tried to indicate. Heim is generous with exposition. So, for instance, we have not just names and references, but explications of such things as Ratzinger's detailed understanding of the New Testament concept of the *soma tou Christou*. There is ample exposition of the Eucharistically based theology of communion, too.

It is hard to communicate the quality of Ratzinger's mind in a short notice like this. But I think it fair to say that he tries to let the biblical and patristic material themselves suggest the conceptual framework in which to express them today. This is not always successful, to my way of thinking, as he sometimes presses some category beyond its inherent virtualities (as he does with relationality in theological anthropology and the theology of the Trinity). On the other hand, this gives his theology a freshness not otherwise easily found in the post-conciliar theological world. In ecclesiology, I think his divination that the essence of the Church is comprehensively stated as the mystery of forgiveness and reconciliation is one such fresh and fruitful thought, especially as he develops it in an understanding of apostolic office.[120]

NOTES

1. For the dogmatic force of the Constitution, see Umberto Betti, OFM, "Qualification théologique de la constitution," in *L'Église de Vatican II. Études autour de la Constitution conciliare sur l'Église*, ed. G. Baraúna, OFM, and Y. Congar, OP (Paris: Cerf, 1966), 2:215: "Toute la doctrine contenue dans la Constitution n'est pas un condensé de simples opinions théologiques, mais, en certains points, elle dit le dernier mot sur tout ce qui avait été jusqu'à present controversé, elle en représente la solution avec autorité, exprimée en des formules doctrinales certaines, dont il n'est pas permis de douter."

2. In addition to *Lumen Gentium*, I will also cite the council's Decree on Ecumenism, *Unitatis Redintegratio (UR)*, its Decree on Bishops, *Christus Dominus (CD)*, and its Decree on Missionary Activity, *Ad Gentes (AG)*. I will cite by article number and will quote the translation of the documents of Vatican II to be found in *Decrees of the Ecumenical Councils*, ed. Norman Tanner, SJ, vol. 2 (Washington, DC: Georgetown University Press, 1990).

3. For the history of the text, see Alexandra von Teuffenbach, *Die Bedeutung des subistit in (LG 8): Zum Selbstverständnis der katholischen Kirche* (Munich: Herbert Utz Verlag, 2002), esp. 375–88. Teuffenbach holds to the meaning of *subsistere* to be found in a good Latin dictionary—"continues to exist in"—and resists any scholasticized sense according to which it means a hypostasis or agent (90–98), resisting too its German translation as *verwirklicht in* (108–10, 393). Since *subsistit in* was introduced at the suggestion of Sebastian Tromp, SJ, who drafted *Mystici Corporis*, it is difficult, to say the least, to find in it any repudiation or "correction" of the teaching of Pius XII.

4. Pius XII, *Mystici Corporis* (http://w2.vatican.va/content/pius-xii/en/encyclicals/documents/hf_p-xii_enc_29061943_mystici-corporis-christi.html), no. 13: the true Church of Jesus Christ "is the One, Holy, Catholic, Apostolic and Roman Church."

5. Paul VI, *Ecclesiam Suam* (http://w2.vatican.va/content/paul-vi/en/encyclicals/documents/hf_p-vi_enc_06081964_ecclesiam.html), no. 30. For the converse identification, see no. 13 of *Mystici Corporis*.

6. Congregation for the Doctrine of the Faith, Letter to the Presidents of Episcopal Conferences of July 24, 1966 (http://www.vatican.va/roman_curia/congregations/cfaith/documents/rc_con_cfaith_doc_19660724_epistula_en.html); the phrase recalls

Pius XII's encyclical, *Humani Generis* (http://w2.vatican.va/content/pius-xii/en/encyclicals/documents/hf_p-xii_enc_12081950_humani-generis.html), no. 12.

7. Congregation for the Doctrine of the Faith, *Mysterium Ecclesiae* (http://www.vatican.va/roman_curia/congregations/cfaith/documents/rc_con_cfaith_doc_19730705_mysterium-ecclesiae_en.html).

8. Congregation for the Doctrine of the Faith, Notification on the book *Church: Charism and Power* by Father Leonardo Boff, OFM (http://www.vatican.va/roman_curia/congregations/cfaith/documents/rc_con_cfaith_doc_19850311_notif-boff_en.html).

9. Francis A. Sullivan, SJ, *The Church We Believe In: One, Holy, Catholic and Apostolic* (New York: Paulist, 1988), correctly reads *Lumen Gentium* with *Unitatis Redintegratio* as to the uniqueness of the Catholic Church and as alone possessing all the means of salvation given by Christ with the unity desired by Christ (25–28), and yet suggests in the same book the "big box" view (63–65). Sullivan thinks the Notification on Boff misreads *Lumen Gentium*, no. 8 (29–31), and holds that the council corrects *Mystici Corporis* (107–8). See also Sullivan, "The One Church in Current Ecclesiology," *Ecumenical Trends* 38.1 (2009): 1, 5–6, 14, where strict identity as in *Mystici Corporis* is denied (4); "subsists in" means no more than "continues to exist in" (5); the "big box" view is asserted (6); and the Notification on Boff misreads the council (5). For a carefully argued and documented reply to this line of interpretation, see Christopher Malloy, "*Subsistit In*: Nonexclusive Identity or Full Identity?," *The Thomist* 72 (2008): 1–44.

10. Joseph Komonchak, "The Significance of Vatican Council II for Ecclesiology," in *The Gift of the Church: A Textbook on Ecclesiology in Honor of Patrick Granfield, OSB*, ed. Peter C. Phan (Collegeville, MN: The Liturgical Press, 2000), 79, rightly reads *LG*, no. 8, with *UR*, no. 3.

11. Ibid. 79.

12. Joseph Ratzinger, "The Ecclesiology of the Constitution *Lumen Gentium*," in *Pilgrim Fellowship of Faith: The Church as Communion*, trans. Henry Taylor (San Francisco: Ignatius, 2005), 148n18. See also the discussion in Maximillian Heinrich Heim, *Joseph Ratzinger: Life in the Church and Living Theology: Fundamentals of Ecclesiology with Reference to Lumen Gentium*, trans. Michael J. Miller (San Francisco: Ignatius, 2007), 74–76, 310–30.

13. John Paul II, *Ut Unum Sint* (http://w2.vatican.va/content/john-paul-ii/en/encyclicals/documents/hf_jp-ii_enc_25051995_ut-unum-sint.html).

14. See Karl Becker, *Origins* 35, no. 31 (January 2006): 520.

15. Congregation for the Doctrine of the Faith, *Dominus Iesus* (http://www.vatican.va/roman_curia/congregations/cfaith/documents/rc_con_cfaith_doc_20000806_dominus-iesus_en.html), no. 16, note 56.

16. Congregation for the Doctrine of the Faith, Responses to Some Questions Regarding Certain Aspects of the Doctrine on the Church (http://www.vatican.va/roman_curia/congregations/cfaith/documents/rc_con_cfaith_doc_20070629_responsa-quaestiones_en.html).

17. Joseph Ratzinger, *Principles of Catholic Theology: Building Stones for a Fundamental Theology*, trans. Sister Mary Frances McCarthy, SND (San Francisco: Ignatius, 1987), 230–31: the council's formula indicates a "full concreteness of the Church" in the Catholic Church, "but this does not mean that every other Church can be only a non-Church." No, there are ecclesial elements outside the visible confines of the Catholic Church. Thus, Ratzinger says, the identity of the Catholic Church and ecclesial reality is not "mathematical."

18. Responses to Some Questions also obliquely takes up the argument that, since the council dignifies the eastern churches not in communion with Rome with the name "churches," it must be the mind of the council to say that the Church of Christ subsists in these churches, too, just as it does in the Catholic Church. See, for instance, Francis Sullivan, "Further Thoughts on the Meaning of *Subsistit In*," *Theological Studies* 71 (2010): 136. The Congregation says about eastern churches not in full communion with Rome, "However, since communion with the Catholic Church, the visible head of which is the Bishop of Rome and the Successor of Peter, is not some external complement to a particular Church but rather one of its internal constitutive principles, these venerable Christian communities lack something in their condition as particular churches" (Responses, question four).

19. Yves Congar, OP, "Peut-on definir l'Église?," in *Sainte Église: Études et approaches ecclésiologiques* (Paris: Cerf, 1963), 39. He is reporting Frédéric Pilgram's proposal in his *Physiologie de l'Église* of 1864.

20. Karl Rahner, SJ, *The Episcopate and the Primacy*, in *Inquiries*, trans. Kenneth Barker et al. (New York: Herder and Herder, 1964), 315, 317.

21. For the terminology "local" and "particular," see Henri de Lubac, SJ, *Particular Churches in the Universal Church*, ch. 1, published with *The Motherhood of the Church*, trans. Sr. Sergia Englund, Cis.D. (San Francisco: Ignatius, 1982 [French, 1971]).

22. "Inde etiam in ecclesiastica communione legitime adsunt Ecclesiae particulares, propriis traditionibus fruentes, integro manente primatu Petri Cathedrae, quae universo caritatis coetui praesidet, legitimas varietates tuetur et simul invigilat ut particularia, nedum unitati noceant, ei potius inserviant."

23. "Quae ecclesiarum localium in unum conspirans varietas indivisae ecclesiae catholicitatem luculentius demonstrat."

24. Final Report of the Extraordinary Synod of 1985 (http://www.nytimes.com/1985/12/08/world/text-of-final-report-adopted-by-synod-of-bishops-in-rome.html), Section C, "The Church as Communion."

25. *Lumen Gentium*, no. 26; the quotation is from St. Thomas, *Summa theologiae* III, Q. 73, a. 3.

26. This is partially repeated at *Lumen Gentium*, no. 26: the one Church of Christ "is truly present in all the lawful local congregations of the faithful which . . . are themselves called churches in the New Testament."

27. Some of this thinking about particularities and the Church was sophisticated and some of it was silly; cf. International Theological Commission, "Select Themes of Ecclesiology" (1984), in *International Theological Commission: Text and Documents, 1969–1985* (San Francisco: Ignatius, 1989), 278–82, on "The People of God and Inculturation"; and Ellen Leonard, "Experience as a Source for Theology," *CTSA Proceedings* 43 (1988): 44–61.

28. J.-M. R. Tillard, OP, *Church of Churches: The Ecclesiology of Communion*, trans. R. C. De Peaux, O. Praem (Collegeville, MN: The Liturgical Press, 1992 [French, 1987]), 28–29, 216.

29. Dulles, "Trends in Ecclesiology," in *Called to Communion and Holiness: Vatican II on The Church*, ed. Steven Boguslawski, OP, and Robert Fastiggi (Scranton, PA: University of Scranton Press, 2009), 5–6, citing Tillard, *Church of Churches*, 29–33.

30. Joseph Komonchak, "The Local Church and the Church Catholic: The Contemporary Theological Problematic," *The Jurist* 52 (1992): 416–47, at 432 and note 39. See Tillard, *Church of Churches*, 12–28.

31. Tillard, *Church of Churches*, 13–14.

32. Ibid. 13.

33. Ibid. 14.

34. Tillard later avoids the term "universal" as logically misleading; see J.-M. R. Tillard, OP, *L'Église locale: Ecclésiologie de communion et catholicité* (Paris: Cerf, 1995), 28–29.

35. The papers were published in *The Jurist* 52 (1992), edited by Hervé Legrand et al.

36. J.-M. R. Tillard, OP, "The Local Church and Catholicity," *The Jurist* 52 (1992): 449.

37. Ibid. 453.

38. Ibid. Tillard attacked the problem again in *L'Église locale*, along much the same lines, e.g., "la catholicité se trouve, non seulement de par son origine mais aussi de par son essence, dans la grâce d'une Église locale, l'Église apostolique de Jérusalem" (41); "L'Église de Rome a pour tâche de garantir le maintien des traits de Pentecôte en toutes les Églises locale, afin qu'elles puissant 'se reconnaître' et se 'recevoir,' mutuellement" (92).

39. Komonchak, "The Local Church and the Church Catholic," 431–32.

40. Ibid. 420.

41. See Henri de Lubac, SJ, *Particular Churches in the Universal Church*, writing in 1971: "It is not merely the unity of the people gathered around him which is realized in the Eucharist celebrated by the bishop. . . . What is realized at one and the same time, indivisibly, is the unity of this people with all others who, in other places around their bishop, participate in the same mystery" (206); and for apostolic office: "A Christian becomes bishop only through his admission to this undivided body of the episcopacy," and "it is the whole Church, in her undivided episcopacy, which makes him a bishop" (204–5).

42. Komonchak, "The Local Church and the Church Catholic," 433.

43. John Paul II, Speech to the Curia of December 21, 1984 (http://w2.vatican.va/content/john-paul-ii/it/speeches/1984/december/documents/hf_jp-ii_spe_19841221_cardinali-curia-romana.html), no. 3: "Sarebbe difficile esprimersi con maggiore chiarezza e profondità: la Chiesa universale è presentata come una comunione di Chiese (particolari) e, indirettamente, come una comunione di nazioni, di lingue, di culture. Ciascuna di esse porta i propri 'doni' all'insieme, così come li portano le singole generazioni ed epoche umane, le singole conquiste scientifiche e sociali, i traguardi di civiltà via via raggiunti." My translation appears in the text.

44. Ibid., no 5: "V'è infatti tra le singole Chiese particolari un rapporto ontologico di vicendevole inclusione: ogni Chiesa particolare, in quanto realizzazione dell'unica Chiesa di Cristo, è in qualche modo presente in tutte le Chiese particolari 'nelle quali e dalle quali ha la sua esistenza la Chiesa cattolica una ed unica' (*Lumen Gentium*, no. 23). Questo rapporto ontologico deve tradursi sul piano dinamico della vita concreta, se la comunità cristiana non vuole entrare in contraddizione con se stessa: le scelte ecclesiali di fondo dei fedeli di una comunità devono potersi armonizzare con quelle dei fedeli delle altre comunità, così da dare luogo a quella comunione di menti e di cuori, per la quale Cristo pregò nell'ultima Cena." Komonchak's translation, in "The Local Church and Church Catholic," 441, appears in the text.

45. Congregation for the Doctrine of the Faith, Letter on some Aspects of the Church Understood as Communion, *Communionis Notio* (http://www.vatican.va/roman_curia/congregations/cfaith/documents/rc_con_cfaith_doc_28051992_communionis-notio_en.html).

46. John Paul II, Speech to the Curia, December 20, 1990 (http://w2.vatican.va/content/john-paul-ii/it/speeches/1990/december/documents/hf-jp-ii_spe_19901220_curia.html), no. 9.

47. Citing his own Speech to the Curia, December 20, 1990.

48. Kasper was already on record as one warning against the centrifugal effects of an over-concentration on the local church, and the tendency to exalt socio-cultural differences over what makes the Church one; see his "The Church as Communion: Reflections on the Guiding Ecclesiological Idea of the Second Vatican Council," in *Theology and Church*, trans. Margaret Kohl (New York: Crossroad, 1989), 148–65. The essay first appeared in German in 1986.

49. This would be contradicted by the Note of the Congregation on the use of the term "sister churches" (a phrase that appears in *Ut Unum sint*) published in 2000 (http://www.vatican.va/roman_curia/congregations/cfaith/documents/rc_con_cfaith_doc_20000630_chiese-sorelle_en.html). The Note observes that while the particular church of Rome may be a church sister to the orthodox churches, the universal Church is Mother relative to all particular churches.

50. See the discussion in Heim, *Joseph Ratzinger*, 373–82.

51. Joseph Ratzinger, "The Ecclesiology of the Constitution *Lumen Gentium*," 137–38.

52. Ibid. 134–35.

53. The priority of the universal Church finds corroboration in the identity of the bishop, in which his concern for the universal takes precedence over his care of his particular church. Dulles ("Trends in Ecclesiology," 11) says on the basis of *Lumen Gentium*, nos. 21 (all bishops are members of the college) and 24 (some bishops receive charge of a diocese), that "the episcopal office is most fundamentally a relationship to the universal, not the particular, Church." In *Christus Dominus*, the council treats a bishop's responsibility for the whole (no. 6) before taking up the role of the diocesan bishop (nos. 11ff.).

54. Charles Journet, *The Church of the Word Incarnate*, trans. A. Downes (New York: Sheed and Ward, 1955), 1:59–60, 123.

55. Francis Sullivan, SJ, *The Church We Believe In* (New York: Paulist Press, 1988), 126; see *Mystici Corporis*, no. 44.

56. Jacques Dupuis, SJ, *Toward a Christian Theology of Religious Pluralism* (Maryknoll, NY: Orbis Books, 1997), 244–48.

57. Ibid. 250.

58. Ibid. 251–252.

59. Jacques Dupuis, SJ, *Christianity and the Religions: From Confrontation to Dialogue* (Maryknoll, NY: Orbis Books, 2002), 132–37.

60. Jacques Dupuis, *Christian Theology of Religious Pluralism*, 317–19; *Christianity and the Religions*, 188–89.

61. Jacques Dupuis, *Christian Theology of Religious Pluralism*, 319; *Christianity and the Religions*, 188.

62. Congregation for the Doctrine of the Faith, Notification on the book *Toward a Christian Theology of Religious Pluralism* by Fr. Jacques Dupuis, S.J., January 24, 2001 (http://www.vatican.va/roman_curia/congregations/cfaith/documents/rc_con_cfaith_doc_20010124_dupuis_en.html); John Paul II, *Redemptoris Missio* (http://w2.vatican.va/content/john-paul-ii/en/encyclicals/documents/hf_jp-ii_enc_07121990_redemptoris-missio.html).

63. Paul VI, Apostolic Exhortation, *Evangelium Nuntiandi* (http://w2.vatican.va/content/paul-vi/en/apost_exhortations/documents/hf_p-vi_exh_19751208_evangelii-nuntiandi.html), no. 80.

64. For the proposal that non-Christian religions are ordinary ways of salvation for their adherents, see Heinz Robert Schlette, *Towards a Theology of Religions*, trans. W. J. O'Hara (New York: Herder and Herder, 1966 [German, 1963]), 102–3.

65. Recall the distinction of Newman that, while there may be many revelations in the world, it is only the Christian revelation that comes to us as revelation, and, in this context, we should add that it comes to us as the revelation *of the Triune God*. For Christians, therefore, the Old and New Testaments, the revelation of Christ, must stand as the only standard of revelation there is, just as, for Muslims, the Qur'an is the only standard according to which what is really revealed in the New Testament can be discerned.

66. See Vatican I, *Dei Filius*, chap. 4 in *Decrees of the Ecumenical Councils*, ed. Norman Tanner, SJ, vol. 2 (Washington, DC: Georgetown University Press, 1990).

67. See *Concilii Vaticani II Synopsis: Constitutio Dogmatica De Ecclesia Lumen Gentium*, ed. Francissco Gil Hellín (Vatican City: Libreria Editrice Vaticano, 1995), 2, the note to the emended version of the second draft, "De voce mysterii," from the Relatio: "Vox 'mysterium' non simpliciter indicat aliquid incognoscibile aut abstrusum, sed ... designat realitatem divinam transcendentem et salvificam, quae aliquo modo visibili revelatur et manifestatur."

68. Dulles, "Trends in Ecclesiology," 16. See also his earlier article, "A Half Century of Ecclesiology," *Theological Studies* 50 (1989): 419–32.

69. Johann Auer, *The Church: The Universal Sacrament of Salvation*, trans. Michael Waldstein (Washington, DC: The Catholic University of America Press, 1993 [German, 1988]).

70. Miguel M. Garijo-Guembe, *Communion of the Saints: Foundation, Nature, and Structure of the Church*, trans. Patrick Madigan (Collegeville, MN: The Liturgical Press, 1994 [German, 1988]).

71. Peter Phan, ed., *The Gift of the Church: A Textbook on Ecclesiology in Honor of Patrick Granfield, OSB* (Collegeville, MN: The Liturgical Press, 2000).

72. Avery Dulles, SJ, *Models of the Church: A Critical Assessment of the Church in All Its Aspects* (Garden City, NY: Doubleday, 1974). A second edition followed in 1989 with a new "model," and an expanded edition in 2002.

73. See Avery Dulles, SJ, *The Resilient Church: The Necessity and Limits of Adaptation* (Garden City, NY: Doubleday, 1977); *A Church to Believe In: Discipleship and the Dynamics of Freedom* (New York: Crossroad, 1982); *The Reshaping of Catholicism: Current Challenges in the Theology of the Church* (San Francisco: Harper & Row, 1988).

74. There are relevant essays in all the just-cited titles; see also Avery Dulles, *Magisterium: Teacher and Guardian of the Faith* (Naples, FL: Sapientia Press, 2007).

75. Avery Dulles, *The Catholicity of the Church* (Oxford: The Clarendon Press, 1985).

76. Louis Bouyer, *The Church of God: Body of Christ and Temple of the Holy Spirit*, trans. Charles Underhill Quinn (Chicago: Franciscan Herald Press, 1982 [French, 1970]).

77. For the first and third parts, see Louis Bouyer, *The Seat of Wisdom: An Essay on the Place of the Virgin Mary in Theology*, trans. A. V. Littledale (New York: Pantheon, 1962 [French, 1957]), and *Cosmos: The World and the Glory of God*, trans. Pierre de Fontenelle (New York: Fordham University Press, 1988 [French, 1982]).

78. Heribert Mühlen, *Una Mystica Persona: Die Kirche als das Mysterium der Identität des Heiligen Geistes in Christus und den Christen: Eine Person in Vielen Personen*, 2nd ed. (Munich: Verlag Ferdinand Schöningh, 1967).

79. Jean-Hervé Nicolas, OP, *Synthèse dogmatique: De la Trinité à la Trinité* (Paris: Beauchesne, 1985).

80. I do not include in this hundred pages the last chapter in the section devoted to the Church, since it is more of a treatise on *De sacramentis in genere* than anything else.

81. In English, see Benoît-Dominique de La Soujeole, OP, "The Mystery of the Church," *Nova et Vetera* 8 (2010): 827–37, which is a good summary of his ecclesiological view; and "The Economy of Salvation: Entitative Sacramentality and Operative Sacramentality," *The Thomist* 75 (2011): 537–53.

82. Benoît-Dominique de La Soujeole, OP, *Le sacrement de la communion: Essai d'ecclésiologie fondamentale* (Paris: Cerf, 1998), 8–9, 80–82.

83. *Lumen Gentium*, no. 8: "Christ, the one mediator, set up his holy Church here on earth as a visible structure, a community of faith, hope and love.... This society, however, equipped with hierarchical structures, and the mystical body of Christ, a visible assembly and a spiritual community, an earthly church and a Church enriched with heavenly gifts, must not be considered as two things [*duae res*], but as forming one complex reality [*unam realitatem complexam*] comprising a human and a divine element."

84. Benoît-Dominique de La Soujeole, OP, *Introduction au Mystère de l'Église*, *Bibliothèque de la Revue Thomiste* (Toulouse: Éditions Parole et Silence, 2006), 364–5, 382–3. The translations of de La Soujeole in the text are my own. However, I will also refer in the notes to the recent translation by Michael J. Miller, *Introduction to the Mystery of the Church* (Washington, DC: The Catholic University of America Press, 2014). *Mystère* refers to the French edition, *Mystery* to Miller's translation. For the above citation, see *Mystery*, 362–3, 380–1.

85. *Mystère*, 42–43; *Mystery*, 38–39.

86. See Congar's notice of communion, *Sainte Église*, 39. One of the most significant pre-conciliar recognitions of the Church as communion was Ludwig Hertling's *Communio: Church and Papacy in Early Christianity*, trans. Jared Wicks, SJ (Chicago: Loyola University Press, 1972 [German, 1943]). For Church as sacrament, see the pre-conciliar studies of Otto Semmelroth, Eduard Schillebeeckx, *et al.*

87. Karl Rahner, *The Church and the Sacraments*, in *Inquiries* (New York: Herder and Herder, 1964), 200.

88. Ibid. 194, 200–201.

89. See, e.g., Piet Smulders, SJ, "L'Église sacrement du salut," in *L'Église de Vatican II*, ed. G. Baraúna, OFM and Y. M. J. Congar, OP, vol. 2, which explores the sacrament as *mysterion*; the Church as "primordial sacrament," which especially follows from considering the Church as the Body of Christ (330); the Church as "permanent and visible presence of the glorified Lord" (330); as instrument (331–32); and as the anticipation of salvation, of the kingdom (332), and where the society or communion of the Church is the effective sign of salvation in Christ (333).

90. Walter Kasper, "The Church as a Universal Sacrament of Salvation," in *Theology and Church* (New York: Crossroad, 1989), 121–22. The article first appeared in German in 1984. See the note to Rahner's *Das Grundwesen der Kirche* after "sundered."

91. Kasper, "The Church as a Universal Sacrament of Salvation," 122.

92. De La Soujeole, *Le sacrement de la communion*, 59.

93. Ibid. 195–210; de La Soujeole, *Mystère*, 379–82, 415–26, with attention to Hegel; *Mystery*, 376–9, 411–22.

94. De La Soujeole, *Mystère*, 442–43; *Mystery*, 439–40.

95. *Mystère*, 465; *Mystery*, 464.

96. *Mystère*, 445; *Mystery*, 442.

97. *Mystère*, 446; *Mystery*, 443–4.

98. *Mystère*, 448; *Mystery*, 445.

99. *Mystère*, 448; *Mystery*, 445–6.

100. *Mystère*, 449; *Mystery*, 446–7.

101. *Mystère*, 45; *Mystery*, 449.

102. De La Soujeole, *Le sacrement de la communion*, 154–61. See for instance *Sacrosanctum concilium*, no. 2, and *Lumen Gentium*, no. 39.

103. De La Soujeole, *Le sacrement de la communion*, 164–69. De La Soujeole relies here on the previous work of Congar.

104. De La Soujeole, *Mystère*, 367; *Mystery*, 365.

105. De La Soujeole, *Le sacrement de la communion*, 83–88.

106. Ibid. 88; de La Soujeole is inspired here by Journet.

107. De La Soujeole, "The Mystery of the Church," 836.

108. De La Soujeole, *Mystère*, 586; *Mystery*, 582–3.

109. *Mystère*, 587; *Mystery*, 584.

110. *Mystère*, 587; *Mystery*, 584.

111. *Mystère*, 588; *Mystery*, 585.

112. *Mystère*, 589; *Mystery*, 585.

113. *Mystère*, 252; *Mystery*, 250.

114. See Benoît-Dominique de La Soujeole, OP, "Être ordonné à l'unique Église du Christ," *Revue Thomiste* 102 (2002): 5–41, at 19.

115. Ibid. 36.

116. Ibid. 38.

117. Ibid. 33, 38, with *Mystère*, 254; *Mystery*, 252.

118. Ibid. 39.

119. See note 12 above.

120. For which see especially Joseph Ratzinger, *Called to Communion: Understanding the Church Today*, trans. Adrian Walker (San Francisco: Ignatius, 1996 [German 1991]).

3

Dei Verbum

William M. Wright IV

The *Dogmatic Constitution on Divine Revelation*, more commonly known by its Latin title *Dei Verbum* (henceforth *DV*), is a theologically rich and wide-ranging document of the Second Vatican Council.[1] Over the course of its six chapters and twenty-six sections, *DV* sets forth normative Catholic doctrine on a number of topics, all pertaining to divine revelation. It opens with a presentation of God's self-revelation to human beings in the course of salvation history (nos. 1–6) and proceeds to the transmission of that revelation (i.e., the Word of God) through the divinely instituted and guaranteed means of Scripture and Tradition and its interpretation by the Church's magisterium (nos. 7–10). The text then moves to the doctrine and interpretation of Sacred Scripture (nos. 11–13), the two biblical testaments (nos. 14–16; nos. 17–20), and then the role of Scripture in the Church's faith and life (nos. 21–26).

The breadth and depth of the contents of *DV* as well as the immense volume of secondary literature on this text require that any essay-sized account of its reception history be selective.[2] The present essay will focus on the reception of *DV* in post-conciliar Catholic biblical interpretation insofar as this text figures into major magisterial and curial documents as well as significant scholarly works on the interpretation of Scripture.

This essay will unfold in three major sections. First, in order to provide a point of departure for the reception of *DV*, I will provide a brief sketch of its major teachings on the interpretation of Scripture and identify some tensions within the conciliar text that, it seems, help account for some unevenness in its reception. In the second section, I will map out some major landmarks (magisterial, curial, and scholarly) in the reception of *DV*'s teachings on the interpretation of Scripture. In the third section, I will conclude with some prospective remarks concerning future directions for continued Catholic reception and implementation of this conciliar text.

I. *Dei Verbum* on Biblical Interpretation

A. *Context and Content*

Discussion of the interpretation of Scripture does not appear in *DV* until no. 12. The placement of this topic in the middle of the text is significant because it shows that *DV* embeds the practice of biblical interpretation within the larger theological context, articulated in nos. 1–11. The compositional structure of *DV* thus points to the interpretation of Scripture as a theological practice, which needs to be conducted in light of the preceding teachings on divine revelation (nos. 1–6) and its transmission (nos. 7–10) as well as the doctrine of Scripture (no. 11).

When *DV* finally arrives at the interpretation of Scripture in no. 12, it sets forth an interpretive program, comprised of two sets of interpretive principles, both of which are informed by theological tenets. The first set of principles may be classified as historical and literary. These historical and literary principles are themselves founded upon a theological premise: "God speaks in Sacred Scripture through men in human fashion" (no. 12).[3] Since God speaks through the human authors of Scripture and those human authors employed various literary genres and modes of discourse characteristic of their historical and cultural situations, attention to the historical and literary situation of the human authors is an essential ingredient in determining what God sought to communicate through the people who composed the biblical books. In this regard, the text speaks of the importance of the correct identification of different literary genres in Scripture and modes of discourse by which the biblical authors communicated their intended meaning and "what God wanted to manifest by means of their words" (no. 12).

DV also prescribes a second set of interpretive principles, which merit "no less serious attention" than the historical and literary ones. These principles may be classified as theological and ecclesial, for they "all arise from. the beliefs and practices of the Church as a historically continuous community of interpretation,"[4] which the Holy Spirit, who inspired the Scriptures, indwells and guides to a deeper understanding of divine revelation. The text places these principles under the heading of interpreting Scripture "in the same Spirit in Whom it was written" (no. 12).[5] This phrase, which according to de la Potterie comes from St. Jerome and very likely goes back to Origen, refers to certain theological principles, which are characteristic of patristic exegesis.[6]

The text specifies three such theological-ecclesial principles of interpretation. The first principle is "the content and unity of the whole of Scripture" (no. 12), that is, the sense that emerges when the biblical books are taken in light of the larger canonical setting. The second principle is "the living tradition of the whole Church" (no. 12). Although *DV*, no. 12 does not elaborate on it, statements from elsewhere in *DV* suggest several aspects of this interpretive principle. For instance, in its discussion of Tradition, *DV*, no. 8 speaks of "growth in the understanding of the realities and the words which have been handed down." This growth in understanding, which progresses through the Spirit's work, comes by way of such means as "the contemplation and study made by believers, ... through a penetrating understanding of the spiritual realities which they experience, and through [apostolic] preaching." Similarly, for the Spirit-guided Church "to move ahead toward a deeper understanding of the Sacred Scriptures," *DV*, no. 23 "encourages the study of the holy Fathers of both East and West and of sacred liturgies." The third theological-ecclesial principle given in *DV*, no. 12 is "the harmony which exists between elements of the faith [*analogiae fidei*]." As Gerald O'Collins explains, the analogy of faith "has been traditionally used to recall the unity in the whole of revelation."[7] Applied to exegesis, this principle holds that "biblical passages and specific Christian beliefs should be interpreted in the complete context of definitive revelation and integral faith."[8]

In articulating these two sets of interpretive principles, *DV* continues the interpretive program, which has been developing from Pope Leo XIII in *Providentissimus Deus* (1893) and Pope Pius XII in *Divino Afflante Spiritu* (1943). While there are differences between them, both *Providentissiumus Deus* and *Divino Afflante Spiritu* encourage Catholic biblical scholars to study the Bible with attention to its historical context, while also accounting for the Church's tradition, "the analogy of faith," and the biblical interpretation of the Church Fathers.[9]

B. *Two Key Tensions in Dei Verbum*

As a document that underwent multiple redactions and involved multiple authors in its composition, it should not be surprising that *DV* contains some subtle tensions between its sections on certain topics. Regarding the interpretation of Scripture, there are two internal tensions, which, while certainly not irreconcilable, can nevertheless move interpreters of *DV* in somewhat different directions, depending on how these tensions are negotiated. These tensions, I suggest, help account for some of the unevenness in the reception of *DV* in Catholic biblical interpretation.

The first tension concerns what exactly is the primary object of biblical interpretation; that is, what exactly does the exegete pursue in interpreting Scripture. On the one hand, *DV*, no. 12 speaks of the need to "investigate what meaning the sacred writers really intended, and what God wanted to manifest by means of their words."[10] Accordingly, the biblical texts and language should be studied in their ancient contexts of composition in order to grasp "what meaning [*sensum*] the sacred writer intended to express and actually expressed" (no. 12). Here, *DV* focuses on the biblical text as a mode of communication by which the biblical writers convey an intended meaning (which one might fairly construe as an idea or message). The object sought by the biblical interpreter, on this account, is the human authors' intended meaning (i.e., their ideas or message), which the interpreter attains through the analysis of the biblical texts in their historical contexts of composition.

But a slightly different account of the object of biblical interpretation appears in *DV*, no. 2. This paragraph speaks of God's revelation given in the realities and words in salvation history, which are "intrinsically connected to each other [*intrinsece inter se connexis*]" (no. 2; translation mine). The text elaborates on this intrinsic relationship: "The deeds [*opera*] wrought by God in the history of salvation manifest and confirm the teaching and realities [*res*] signified by the words, while the words proclaim the deeds [*opera*] and clarify the mystery contained in them" (no. 2). This statement places the interpretive attention on the realities (broadly understood) in salvation history, which both conceal and reveal the divine mystery. The words of the biblical texts present those realities and interpret them in a manner accurate and appropriate to their revelatory significance.[11] On this account, the task of the interpreter is to penetrate the mystery-bearing realities of salvation history by means of their verbal presentation and interpretation in the biblical text.

Thus, *DV*, nos. 2 and 12, while similar in many respects, can nevertheless be read as pulling its readers in somewhat different directions. The account given in no. 12 focuses on the biblical text as communicative means of the human authors' intended meanings, ideas, or message. The account given in no. 2 focuses on the mystery-bearing realities of salvation history, which the biblical texts present and accurately interpret. The first account operates on a theory of text and communication. The second operates on a sacramental theology of history.[12] While these two are not irreconcilable, they do offer somewhat different visions of what constitutes the object of biblical interpretation: the authors' ideas and intended meanings or the realities of salvation history, what the text says or what the text is about.[13]

Closely related to this first tension is a second one concerning those two sets of interpretive principles: the historical-literary and the theological-ecclesial.[14] While *DV* prescribes these two sets of principles for Catholic biblical interpretation, it does not offer much direction as to how they are to be integrated or what a successful integration would look like in practice. Writing in 1982, Joseph Ratzinger observed that the "peaceful juxtaposition" of both sets of principles in the conciliar text "conceals the antagonism of two basic attitudes that are diametrically opposed to one another in both origin and purpose."[15] The theological and ecclesial principles, with their emphasis on the canonical whole and the harmony of Scripture with the Church's Tradition and faith, articulate "the fundamental concept of patristic exegesis . . . [which] was unity—the unity that is Christ himself."[16] By contrast, the goal of modern historical-critical analysis "is not first of all to unite but to distinguish: not to seek for a pneuma that faith knows is actively present in the whole Bible, but to ask about the many individuals who, each in his own way, have worked on this many-faceted composition."[17] Nevertheless, the Council affirms that, despite fundamental differences in their contexts of origin, presuppositions, reading practices, and goals, both modern biblical criticism and premodern interpretation have positive and abiding value for Catholic biblical exegesis today.

This tension between interpretive principles interfaces with the first tension over the primary object of biblical interpretation. For those who focus primarily on the account of *DV*, no. 12 with its concern for the author's intended meaning communicated through the biblical text, the historical and literary principles predominate. These techniques are geared toward the analysis of biblical texts in their context of origin in order to grasp the message or idea, which the human authors—as people of particular historical and cultural settings—sought to communicate through them. Those who focus on the account in *DV*, no. 2 with its sacramental theology of history are better positioned as regards the theological-ecclesial principles of interpretation. These principles—unity of the canon, the Church's tradition, and analogy of faith—are all elements in the traditional doctrine of the spiritual sense, which, as Francis Martin has so insightfully put it, "is based, not on a theory of text, but on a theology of history."[18] These principles are ordered toward discerning the depths of divine mystery that the realities, presented by the text, conceal and reveal. These mystery-bearing realities have depths, which historical and literary analysis by themselves are unable to access but which the theological-ecclesial principles can access. By these theological and ecclesial principles and the corresponding reading practices, those same mystery-bearing realities of salvation history are contemplated, lived, and experienced in the ecclesial life of faith.[19]

With this sketch of *DV*'s teaching on biblical interpretation in place, I will turn to examine some major instances of its reception. In the course of doing so, I will consider how these internal tensions about the proper object of biblical interpretation and the two sets of interpretive principles help account for some of the unevenness and ongoing tensions in the reception of this text.

II. *Dei Verbum* in Post-Conciliar Catholic Biblical Interpretation

A. Pope Paul VI

Two statements by Pope Paul VI on biblical matters appeal to *DV* as giving direction to post-conciliar Catholic biblical interpretation. While these statements are not highly significant in themselves, they give evidence for how *DV* was being received and employed by the pope in the decade after its promulgation.

On June 27, 1971, Paul VI issued the Apostolic Letter *Sedula Cura*, which reconstituted the Pontifical Biblical Commission under the auspices of the Congregation for the Doctrine of the Faith. In the introductory paragraphs that lead into the new rules and regulations for the Biblical Commission, the pope references a few allusions to *DV*. He begins by speaking of the Church's need for "an ever more profound understanding of the Sacred Scriptures," so that the Church may do the work of "nourishing her children with the Divine Word."[20] He then cites the Council's directive that "the Word of God be made more widely and plentifully accessible to the faithful, for the purpose of more earnestly fostering the Christian life."[21] With these references to *DV*, no. 23,

Paul VI continues the text's interest in promoting the place of the Bible in Catholic faith and life. The reference to the Scriptures as providing nourishment also picks up the relationship between the Scripture and the Eucharist in *DV*, no. 21 ("the two tables" passage) and the text's presentation of Scripture in quasi-sacramental terms.[22]

Paul VI later makes a general appeal to the two sets of interpretive principles prescribed by *DV*, no. 12 and the need for both sets to inform Catholic exegesis. He speaks of the need for Catholic scholars "to pursue their studies in accordance with recent scientific method," presumably referring to the historical-literary principles. But since "God has entrusted the Sacred Scriptures not to the private judgment of scholars but to his Church," Paul VI writes, there is the attendant need that Scripture "must always be interpreted according to the norms of the Christian tradition and hermeneutics under the guardianship [of the magisterium]."[23] Paul VI here continues the interpretive program of *DV* according to which Catholic biblical interpretation should integrate the historical-literary principles and the theological-ecclesial ones.

The influence of *DV* likewise continues in Pope Paul VI's 1974 Address to the Pontifical Biblical Commission.[24] An overarching motif of this address is the "essential connection between the Bible and the Church," which has been the case from the Bible's very origins to the present day.[25] Paul VI calls on exegetes to interpret the Bible within and for the Church, and he speaks of the need to "actualize" the biblical text for the present life of the Church—a concept that will appear in the Biblical Commission's 1993 document, *The Interpretation of the Bible in the Church*. The pope speaks approvingly of certain conclusions of the historical-critical method, those analytical "approaches that we have encouraged with the necessary methodological corrections."[26] At the same time, the pope warns against certain pitfalls for exegetes, such as the move "to regard any method as absolute, pretending that it alone gives access to divine revelation."[27] As a safeguard, Paul VI appeals to what he calls "the golden rule of theological hermeneutics," and this is the set of traditional-ecclesial principles given in *DV*, no. 12: "The content and unity of the whole of Scriptures, taking into account the entire living Tradition of the Church and the analogy of faith."[28] The pope also cites the Christological center of Scripture and the exegete's own personal faith and relationship with God as essential elements to the interpretive task. The latter point about the exegete's personal faith, piety, and relationship with God proves significant for Paul VI, for without it, the interpretive task remains quite incomplete: "Without a real, existential openness to the mystery of the God of love, our exegesis, no matter how scholarly it may be, will certainly remain shrouded in darkness."[29]

B. *Dei Verbum* and the Conventional Narrative of Twentieth Century Catholic Biblical Interpretation

Not long after the promulgation of *DV* in 1965, there appeared two major one-volume commentaries on the entire Bible and related issues produced by two groups of Anglophone Catholic scholars. In 1968, there appeared *The Jerome*

Biblical Commentary (United States), which was edited by Raymond E. Brown, SS, Joseph A. Fitzmyer, SJ, and Roland E. Murphy, O. Carm.[30] In 1969, there appeared *A New Catholic Commentary on Holy Scripture* (Great Britain), a new updated edition of a pre-conciliar commentary, which was edited by Reginald Fuller, Leonard Johnson, and Conleth Kearns, OP.[31] While these two commentaries differ in tone and theological outlook, they are both instances of the flourishing of Catholic biblical scholarship in the early post-conciliar period.

In the early 1970s, there began to be formulated what has come to be a conventional, three-part narrative of official Catholic stances toward modern biblical criticism in the twentieth century. This account, which (to the best of my knowledge) was first formulated by Raymond Brown, tells the story of the slow, embattled acceptance of the historical-critical method into Catholic biblical interpretation.[32] Across the three major stages in this account, there occurred a sea change in official Catholic stances toward modern biblical criticism. After the measured encouragement of Pope Leo XIII in *Providentissimus Deus* (1893) for Catholic scholars to employ certain critical methods, the first major phase in twentieth-century Catholic attitudes toward modern biblical criticism (1900–1940) was one of defensiveness and suspicion. This was due in large part to the condemnations of Modernism and the employment of modern biblical criticism on the part of certain Modernists (e.g., Alfred Loisy) to articulate and support heretical positions. From 1905–1915, the recently founded Pontifical Biblical Commission issued fourteen *responsa*, "often phrased with perception and nuance," which pertained to exegetical questions and to which Catholic scholars were obliged to assent.[33] Brown writes, "Though the decrees of the PBC, when interpreted with juridic insight, allowed a certain room for scholarly investigation, the atmosphere was not conducive to this."[34] The most famous example of the inhibiting of Catholic biblical studies during this time was the suspicion that fell upon Marie-Joseph Lagrange, OP.

The second major phase (1941–1965) featured a marked shift in official Catholic attitudes away from suspicion and toward an appreciative encouragement of Catholic scholars to employ critical methods to exegete Scripture. The watershed moment was the promulgation of Pope Pius XII's 1943 encyclical, *Divino Afflante Spiritu*, which Raymond Brown has called "a Magna Carta for biblical progress."[35] In this encyclical, Pius XII exhorts Catholic biblical scholars to study the biblical texts in their historical contexts of origin with recourse to archaeology, ancient history, and ancient modes of discourse.[36] Following on this encyclical with its magisterial encouragement of Catholic historical biblical exegesis, this second phase saw a flourishing of critical scholarship from Catholic exegetes. The 1948 Letter of the Biblical Commission's Secretary to Cardinal Suhard of Paris interpreted two of those early *responsa* of the Biblical Commission in a nuanced way so as to permit "Catholic scholars to study these problems, without prepossession, in the light both of sound criticism and of the findings of other sciences connected with the subject-matter."[37] This time period, however, was not without controversy, as evidenced in the conflicts between the certain biblical professors based in Rome and the Vatican's Holy Office in the late 1950s and early 1960s.[38]

The third major phase (1966–1990) comprises approximately the last third of the twentieth century. With its instruction for Catholic exegetes to study the biblical texts in their historical and literary contexts of origin, *DV* continued an appreciation and endorsement of modern biblical criticism by Catholic scholars, initiated by Pius XII. Accordingly, the historical-critical method secured its place in Catholic biblical interpretation. But as Brown puts it, this period "has involved the painful assimilation of those implications [of modern biblical criticism] for Catholic doctrine, theology, and practice."[39]

This conventional narrative highlights several things for our present purposes. First, while it has a noticeably triumphalist ring, this account illustrates that the status of historical biblical criticism has been the predominant issue in formal discussions of Catholic biblical interpretation throughout the twentieth century. Second, within this account, it is Pius XII's *Divino Afflante Spiritu*, not *DV*, that plays the most prominent role. In contrast to magisterial defensiveness at the start of the twentieth century, this encyclical gave magisterial authorization for Catholic scholars to employ modern biblical criticism in a rigorous and confident manner and opened the way for its formal acceptance in Catholic circles. Third, given these first two points—the ongoing centrality of modern biblical criticism as an issue and the watershed that was *Divino Afflante Spiritu*—it is not surprising that *DV* is treated here in light of *Divino Afflante Spiritu* and lauded as continuing and securing the trajectory set by Pius XII. Hence, Raymond Brown concludes, "The modern Catholic biblical movement inaugurated by Pius XII and confirmed by Vatican II is now too much a part of the church to be rejected."[40] Not surprisingly, those sections of *DV* that have garnered most attention in scholarly circles are those that fit most neatly with this trajectory to incorporate historical biblical criticism into Catholic exegetical practice.

Accordingly, the historical-literary principles of interpretation, along with the attendant identification of the object of biblical interpretation as the human authors' intended meaning or ideas communicated through the biblical texts, have dominated post-conciliar Catholic scholarly exegesis. The application of these historical-literary principles by Catholic scholars has produced an immense corpus of critical scholarship that has greatly increased our understanding of the biblical texts within their contexts of origin. Any attempt to provide even a representative sampling of major scholarly works by Catholic exegetes, which does justice to the contributions in English-, French-, German-, Italian-, and Spanish-speaking Catholic scholarship (among others), would itself be an immense effort. Nevertheless, to illustrate the caliber of scholarship produced by Catholic scholars in the post-conciliar period, one may point not only to the aforementioned *Jerome Biblical Commentary* (1968), its 1990 update *The New Jerome Biblical Commentary*, and *The New Catholic Commentary on Holy Scripture* (1969), but also to works of the individual scholars who contributed to those one-volume commentaries.

At the same time, it would be inaccurate to say that the course of Catholic biblical exegesis in the times after *DV* was not without controversy. As one

Catholic scholar has put it, "Once the inhibitions—and, we might add, the censures—of the preconciliar Church in matters of exegesis vanished (or were reduced to the point of imperceptibility), Catholic biblical scholarship became engaged in wide-scale experimentation, laying hands on all the results of modern critical scholarship, including some of the forbidden fruits of modernism."[41] Within post-conciliar Catholic scholarship, there also emerged a smaller line of learned inquiry, which took a non-reactionary, critical stance toward modern biblical criticism and sought to separate the methodological wheat from the chaff. Influenced by the *Ressourcement* movement, many scholars in this trajectory sought to retain the genuine goods of modern historical-critical analysis and integrate them with certain theological and spiritual principles at work in classic Christian hermeneutics found in patristic and medieval exegesis. Put differently, this line of scholarship devotes sustained attention to those theological-ecclesial principles of interpretation set forth in *DV*, no. 12 and how they might be synthesized with the historical-literary ones.

C. Reading "in the Same Spirit" and the Philosophical Critique of Modern Exegesis

Despite appeals to the aforementioned "golden rule of theological hermeneutics" spoken of by Paul VI and again by Pope St. John Paul II, the theological-ecclesial principles of interpretation given in *DV*, no. 12 have received nowhere near the attention that the historical-literary principles have in post-conciliar Catholic exegesis.[42] That said, the attention these principles have received has been very substantive intellectually and spiritually. While others could be cited, I will survey briefly four representative figures, who have contributed to this lesser known line of reception.

Denis Farkasfalvy, O. Cist. approaches the issue of Christian biblical hermeneutics with special attention to canon formation and the doctrine of biblical inspiration, considered both historically and theologically.[43] In his historical works, Farkasfalvy discerns the basic structures of Christian biblical hermeneutics being set in the processes of Christian canon formation, which are subsequently developed in patristic exegesis. With its affirmation of the unity of the divine economy centered in Christ and its own formation within the Church's tradition and *regula fidei*, the Christian biblical canon "becomes the theological framework for interpretation."[44] He continues, "Since [the canon] was produced by the Rule of Faith, it subordinates exegesis to faith. Because it was the product of Church tradition, it constrains the use of Scripture to the service of the Church."[45] Farkasfalvy has also made significant contributions to the doctrine of biblical inspiration and its implications for interpretation when taken together with modern biblical criticism.[46] In doing so, he interacts extensively with *DV*, calling attention to where the conciliar text advances the discussion, where it stalls, and what tasks require further work.

A longtime professor at the Pontifical Biblical Institute, Ignace de la Potterie, SJ, is well known in New Testament studies for his scholarship on the Fourth Gospel, especially his massive study, *La Vérité dans Saint Jean.*[47] De la Potterie's scholarship on John provides an example of what a synthesis of classic Christian and modern biblical interpretation can be. He does the conventional historical-critical analysis of the Gospel texts and interacts with other modern critical scholars. He also reads with special concern for the theological teachings and realities set forth by the text, which he explores with extensive reference to patristic and medieval exegetes. In some programmatic essays, de la Potterie set forth a basic case for how and why modern Catholic exegetes should retrieve certain theological sensibilities of patristic exegesis.[48]

With regard to *DV* in particular, de la Potterie published the nonpareil study of the theological-ecclesial principles, which the conciliar text places under the principle of interpretation "in the same Spirit in Whom it was written" (no. 12).[49] De la Potterie observes that these principles have been largely "ignored" in post-conciliar Catholic scholarship and have "received almost no echo in the years since the Council."[50] His lengthy study of the historical background and theological substance of this principle in the conciliar text seeks to remedy the widespread neglect of these teachings of *DV.*

The American biblical scholar Francis Martin is another significant figure in this line of scholarship.[51] Martin's scholarly writings feature a high-level integration of historical-critical exegesis, theological and philosophical analysis, literary theory, and a keen interest in the Christian spiritual life. Very important for Martin are the philosophical and theological principles that inform both ancient and modern biblical interpretation.[52] Martin recognizes the genuine goods in both ancient and modern biblical exegesis: the increase of our knowledge about the Bible afforded by modern historical criticism as well as the theologically and spiritually powerful way of reading the Bible practiced by the Church Fathers and continuing in monasticism. The real divide between these two modes of interpretation stems from key intellectual shifts, many of which are typified in Immanuel Kant, that have adversely affected how biblical history and language are understood theologically.[53] For Martin, the work of integrating these two modes of exegesis must first be set on a more robust philosophical account of history and language, which is also more consistent with revealed truth.

The refooting of modern biblical exegesis on a better philosophical and theological basis also informs Martin's effort to retrieve the genuine goods in the tradition of spiritual exegesis.[54] The integration of what is truly good in both premodern and modern Christian exegesis will help Christians read the Bible as mediating an encounter with realities of salvation history and their power to transform lives and communities. This is precisely what *DV* commends to Catholic scholars. Martin writes that in "§12 of *Dei Verbum* ... we find there, in an unmistakable manner, the challenge issued to theologians of the Bible to avail themselves of all the resources provided by modern critical historiography while at the same time retaining the faith approaches that have nourished the Church for two millennia."[55]

The most well-known figure in this line of receiving *DV* is Cardinal Joseph Ratzinger (later Pope Benedict XVI). In 1988, Ratzinger delivered his famous lecture, "Biblical Interpretation in Conflict: On the Foundations and the Itinerary of Exegesis Today," a text which might prove in time to be the most significant work in Catholic biblical hermeneutics in the second half of the twentieth century.[56] Ratzinger observes that historical-biblical criticism has been a deeply ambiguous phenomenon for modern Christianity. On the one hand, it has produced immense learning about the biblical books in light of their historical and social contexts of origin. But on the other hand, it has created very serious problems: "forbidding the uninitiated [i.e. the non-exegete] access to the Bible"; the rupture between theological studies and exegesis; the corrosiveness to the faith of Christians.[57]

Ratzinger goes on to make the case for integration of historical exegesis and Christian doctrine in a manner that speaks to contemporary believers. He argues that *DV*, when read in its entirety, can provide the substance and direction for "a synthesis between historical method and theological 'hermeneutics,' but the coherence between them does not simply lie ready to hand."[58] According to Ratzinger, this lack of ready-made coherence between the historical-literary and the theological-ecclesial principles accounts for why the teachings on biblical interpretation in *DV* have been received in such a selective and partial manner: "This explains why the post-conciliar reception of the document has practically set aside the theological portion of the document as a concession to the past and has understood the text exclusively as an unrestricted official approval of the historical-critical method."[59]

For Ratzinger, the real work of integrating biblical exegesis and theology will not be done at the level of history or exegetical method. Rather, he recognizes that the root of the problem is philosophical: "The debate about modern exegesis is not at its core a debate among historians, but among philosophers."[60] Ratzinger thus calls for "a criticism of the criticism" whereby the philosophical architecture that undergirds modern biblical criticism should be critically examined.[61] Among the philosophical presuppositions underlying conventional historical-critical analysis that Ratzinger cites are the importing into exegesis of models and habits of thinking proper to the natural sciences and, even more profoundly, the enduring influence of Kantian epistemology.[62] A philosophically renovated (and chastened) mode of biblical criticism would allow for a more fruitful synthesis of the indisputable goods produced by modern biblical studies with Christian doctrine and practice.

E. The Catechism of the Catholic Church (1992)

The *Catechism of the Catholic Church* (henceforth, *CCC*) is another significant instance in the reception history of *DV*.[63] This text, the composition of which followed upon requests from the 1985 Synod of Bishops, first appeared in 1992 with a second edition based on the Latin typical edition appearing in 1997.[64] In his Apostolic Constitution *Fidei Depositum*, promulgating its publication, Pope St. John Paul II authoritatively defines the *CCC* as "a statement of the Church's faith and of catholic doctrine" and "a sure norm for teaching the faith and thus a valid and legitimate instrument for ecclesial communion."[65]

DV figures most prominently in part 1, section 1, chapter 2 of the *CCC*, entitled "God Comes to Meet Man" (no. 50), which contains teaching on divine revelation, its transmission, and Sacred Scripture. The *CCC*'s presentation of these topics in nos. 51–141 follows the sequence and content of *DV* so closely that one could think of it as a kind of commentarial elaboration on the conciliar text. The chapter's first article—"The Revelation of God" (nos. 51–73)—follows *DV* chapter 2 (esp. nos. 2–4).[66] The article opens by quoting *DV*, no. 2 with the statement of God revealing Himself and His will for the sake of human salvation (*CCC*, no. 51). Following *DV*, nos. 3–4, the *CCC* states that this revelation is a process of divine pedagogy (no. 53), which is given over to the course of salvation history (nos. 54–56) and culminates in Christ (no. 66).

DV figures even more prominently in the chapter's second article—"The Transmission of Divine Revelation" (nos. 74–100). Once again, the structure and content of *DV* informs the *CCC*'s exposition. The *CCC* treats the apostolic mandate to preach the received Word of God as well as apostolic succession (nos. 74–77; cf. *DV*, no. 7). Continuing to follow *DV*, the *CCC* speaks of sacred Tradition as a special mode of revelation's transmission (nos. 78–79; cf. *DV*, no. 8) and its relationship with Sacred Scripture (nos. 80–82; cf. *DV*, no. 9). Scripture and Tradition together bear the "'Sacred deposit' of the faith" (no. 84), which the Church's magisterium has both the responsibility and authority to interpret normatively (nos. 85–93; cf. *DV*, no. 10). Working through the entire Church, the Holy Spirit guides the faithful into a deeper understanding of divine revelation, transmitted by Scripture and Tradition and interpreted by the Magisterium (nos. 94–95).

It is in the chapter's third article—"Sacred Scripture" (nos. 101–41)—that the *CCC*'s use of *DV* is most concentrated—nearly half of the references to *DV* in the *CCC* appear here.[67] Especially significant for present purposes are the ways in which the *CCC* emphasizes certain sections of *DV* and expands on its teaching on the interpretation of Scripture.

The article on Sacred Scripture has five subsections. As suggested by its title, "Christ—The Unique Word of Sacred Scripture," the first subsection (nos. 101–4) provides an account of Scripture that is Christocentric and also generically sacramental. Quoting *DV*, no. 13, *CCC*, no. 101 speaks of the "condescension" of God to communicate Himself to human beings through human language. What the many words in Scripture give is the one Word of God, Christ himself (no. 102). Drawing on *DV*, nos. 21 and 24, the *CCC* presents Scripture as a means by which the faithful can truly encounter God and be fed by Him (nos. 103–4). The second subsection, "Inspiration and Truth of Sacred Scripture" (nos. 105–8), consists largely of quotations of *DV*, no. 11 pertinent to these two topics. The last paragraph in this subsection (no. 108) plays an important role in the *CCC*'s exposition of teaching on Sacred Scripture. It looks backwards to nos. 101–4, with their two motifs of Christocentrism and Scripture as a place of present encounter with the Word of God. It also speaks of the essential role of Christ and the Holy Spirit in bringing the reader to understand Scripture: "If the Scriptures are not to remain a dead letter, Christ, the eternal Word of the living God, must, through the Holy Spirit, 'open [our] minds to understand the

Scripture'" (no. 108, citing Luke 24:45). In this way, no. 108 leads into the third subsection where the *CCC* takes up the interpretive program of *DV*, no. 12 and also offers its most substantial expansion of the conciliar text.

The *CCC* here speaks to the importance of both the historical-literary and theological-ecclesial principles prescribed by *DV*, no. 12. However, as set up by the subsection's title, "The Holy Spirit, Interpreter of Scripture," the *CCC* places great emphasis on the theological-ecclesial principles and the need to interpret Scripture "in the same Spirit in Whom it was written" (*DV*, no. 12). Referencing *DV*, no. 12, the *CCC* affirms the need to grasp what the human authors of the Bible sought to communicate and what God sought to communicate through them (no. 109). Accordingly, the historical-literary principles of interpretation, as techniques for discerning the human authors' "communicative intention," are very important for a proper interpretation of Scripture (no. 110).[68] After these two paragraphs on historical-literary principles, the *CCC* turns to the theological-ecclesial principles and devotes the next eight paragraphs to them.

The *CCC* introduces the theological-ecclesial principles by stating, "Since Sacred Scripture is inspired, there is another and no less important principle of correct interpretation without which Scripture would remain a dead letter. 'Sacred Scripture must be read and interpreted in the light of the same Spirit by whom it was written'" (no. 111; quoting *DV*, no. 12.3).

Two things stand out here regarding biblical interpretation. First, the theological-ecclesial principles follow upon and are correlated with the doctrine of biblical inspiration—the same Spirit who inspired the Scripture also works in the faithful to bring them to a deeper understanding. Second, these principles are essential for hearing Scripture as the living Word of God, speaking to readers in the present moment.

The *CCC* goes on to devote a paragraph to each of the three theological-ecclesial principles: the unity of the canon (no. 112), reading within the Church's Tradition (no. 113), and the analogy of faith (no. 114). Then, the *CCC* goes beyond *DV* by incorporating into its exposition the traditional doctrine of the fourfold sense of Scripture (nos. 115–18). The inclusion of the doctrine of the fourfold sense is a significant development, for while much of its substance was present in *DV*, the conciliar text itself did not explicitly mention the fourfold sense. The presence of the fourfold sense, along with the amount of attention given to them, exemplify a concerted interest in the *CCC* to direct Catholic hermeneutical attention to the theological-ecclesial principles of interpretation (perhaps because of their neglect in the post-conciliar period).

In the remaining two subsections, the *CCC* continues to follow the structure and content of *DV*. It affirms the permanent value of the Old Testament on its own terms as well as in light of its typological relation to Christ (nos. 128–30; cf. *DV*, nos. 14–16). It also holds up the New Testament (nos. 124–27; cf. *DV*, nos. 17–20) as that place where the Word of God is given preeminently, and in particular the Gospels, which the *CCC* calls "the heart of all the Scriptures" (no. 125). The *CCC*'s presentation on Scripture closes with a treatment of its place in the life of the Church (nos. 131–33; cf. *DV*, nos. 21–26).

As a formal statement of Catholic doctrine, the *CCC* is a significant instance in the reception history of *DV*. The *CCC* closely follows the structure and content of the conciliar text, while also expanding upon certain elements of its teaching. The *CCC* places a decided emphasis on the theological-ecclesial principles of interpretation. Consistent with this interest (and the aforementioned tensions in *DV*), the *CCC* likewise references those sections of *DV* where the sacramentality of Scripture and the divine economy appear. On several occasions, the *CCC* references the sacramental economy comprised of those intrinsically connected words and realities in salvation history (nos. 53, 1103; cf. *DV*, no. 2). The words of Scripture serve to "proclaim [God's] works and bring to light the mystery they contain" (no. 2587; citing *DV*, no. 2). The *CCC* also repeatedly references the Scripture-Eucharist comparison and the "two tables" stated in *DV*, no. 21 (*CCC*, nos. 103, 141, 1346). It speaks of Scripture as a place where the faithful can encounter God in the present and be fed and strengthened by him (nos. 104, 131). As will be discussed below (II.G), such attention to the theological-ecclesial principles, as well as the sacramentality of the divine economy and Scripture, will be further developed by Pope Benedict XVI in *Verbum Domini*.

E. The Pontifical Biblical Commission, The Interpretation of the Bible in the Church (1993)

In 1993, the Pontifical Biblical Commission issued the document *The Interpretation of the Bible in the Church* (henceforth, 1993 PBC).[69] While not a document of the Magisterium, this text of the Pontifical Biblical Commission sets forth an interpretive program of both critical exegesis and theological application, which goes beyond *DV* by intensifying the place of historical-critical exegesis with respect to other modes of interpretation and Catholic life.[70]

The 1993 PBC text has four major sections of unequal length.[71] The first (and lengthiest) section, "Methods and Approaches for Interpretation," reviews about a dozen different interpretive methods and approaches (which the document defines as being categorically different) and evaluates the strengths and weaknesses of each.[72] Within this survey, the historical-critical method, which the PBC defines as the combination of text, source, form, and redaction criticism(s), has the unparalleled pride of place.[73] The body of the 1993 PBC text opens with these statements: "The historical-critical method is the *indispensable* method for the scientific study of the meaning of ancient texts," and given that the Scripture was composed by historically conditioned human beings, the Scripture's "proper understanding not only admits the use of this method but actually *requires* it."[74]

The second section of the 1993 PBC text, "Hermeneutical Questions," takes up two sets of concerns: first, the contributions and challenges posed by general hermeneutics, notably the philosophical work of Hans-Georg Gadamer and Paul Ricoeur; second, the multiple meanings in Scripture, such as in classic accounts of the senses of Scripture. The third section of the document, "Characteristics of Catholic Interpretation," deals with a range of topics such as the dynamics of inner-biblical exegesis, the interpretation of the Bible within the Church's tradition, and the present work of biblical exegesis on its own and in relation to other theological fields. By my count, there are twenty-eight references to *DV* in the 1993 PBC text, and twenty of those twenty-eight references appear in section 3. This section draws from all but one chapter of *DV*, and the greatest number of references comes from chapter 6, "Sacred Scripture in the Life of the Church." The concentrated use of *DV* in section 3 of the 1993 PBC text speaks to a concern to integrate modern biblical criticism (especially the historical-critical method) into a Catholic vision of Scripture and Church life. The fourth section, "Interpretation of the Bible in the Life of the Church," addresses the role that the Bible should presently play in the Church's liturgy, spirituality, work of inculturation, pastoral ministry, and ecumenical endeavors. Especially important in this section is the notion of "actualization," which refers to the bringing of the literal sense to bear in a present set of lived circumstances.[75]

The 1993 PBC document can be read as a sustained methodological effort to integrate historical-biblical criticism with Catholic theology and tradition (the 1993 PBC text, however, never references the theological-ecclesial principles in *DV*, no. 12). But it tries to achieve this integration on grounds dictated by a particular construal of the historical-critical method. The 1993 PBC text unambiguously privileges the historical-critical method as the sine qua non of Catholic exegesis. The text speaks of the historical-critical method as "indispensable," and the "proper understanding [of Scripture] ... actually requires it."[76] The privileging of the historical-critical method is accompanied by the notion that the object of interpretation is the human authors' ideas communicated through the text. The 1993 PBC text uses a number of phrases to articulate the object of interpretation on this model: for instance, "meaning expressed by the biblical authors"; "the intention of the authors"; "a message communicated by the author to his contemporaries."[77] The task of the historical-critical method is to ascertain this meaning or message, which is in turn identified with the literal sense of Scripture: "that which has been expressed directly by the inspired human authors."[78] The 1993 PBC text holds that the literal sense is basically singular—the authors generally communicate a single idea or message in a text.[79] But the line of author's thinking expressed in the literal sense also contains the potential for new, organically related meanings in later contexts via the notion of *"dynamic aspect."*[80]

This notion of "dynamic aspect" is how the 1993 PBC text links the literal sense and more-than-literal meanings. For instance, the document defines the spiritual sense as the meaning *of texts*: it is "the meaning expressed by the biblical texts when read, under the influence of the Holy Spirit, in the context of the paschal mystery of Christ and of the new life which flows from it."[81] Since the literal sense is the historically-conditioned expression of the authors' ideas, the spiritual sense is the extension or development of the original authors' thinking within the context of Jesus's death and resurrection. The 1993 PBC text provides the following example: the thinking at work in the covenantal promise that David's throne would endure forever (2 Sam. 7:16) is developed and extended beyond its original setting to literal fulfillment in Christ.[82] The Church's post-biblical interpretation of Scripture in its faith and Tradition is effectively the Christian equivalent of the "re-readings," characteristic of inner-biblical exegesis, whereby earlier biblical texts are re-read in later contexts.

Within this model, the author's original intention or message acts as a reservoir of meaning. The authors' original meaning contains the potential for new meaning, and this potency is actualized when reread in later contexts. This is how the 1993 PBC text works in the Church's interpretation of the Bible in its tradition. Thus, instead of speaking of the moral or anagogical senses, the 1993 PBC text introduces the concept of "actualization" to discuss how Christians can read and apply the Bible to their lives.[83] Any legitimate actualization of Scripture extends the ideas communicated by the human authors, which are determined by historical-critical analysis.[84] In this way, the 1993 PBC text basically espouses a version of Krister Stendahl's distinction between "what *did* [the Bible] mean" and "what *does* [the Bible] mean."[85]

The 1993 PBC text is a very ambitious document, and there is much of value in it. The document contains also some problematic issues and internal tensions, which complicate the resulting synthetic picture. These will be explored in a bit more depth here because they put into relief some of the internal tensions in *DV* itself.

Many of these complications arise from the way in which the 1993 PBC defines the historical-critical method and makes it the arbiter of textual meaning. The document speaks of the historical-critical method as "a group of scientific procedures," employing "scientific criteria," and is thus methodologically neutral—"It is a method which, when used in an objective manner, implies of itself no a priori."[86] Clearly, the document conceives of the historical-critical method as akin to the methods proper to the natural sciences.

But this particular construal of the historical-critical method is deficient in several respects. First, as Ayres and Fowl write, it is "simply incorrect to speak as if there were a single thing called 'the historical-critical method' whose practices all cohere and whose practitioners all share a vision of a common project."[87] A walk through the biblical studies section of any academic library can lead one to the conclusion that the practice of historical-critical exegesis over its history from the 1830s to the present has not produced much in the way of "scientific" conclusions or that historical-critical exegetes conceive of or go about their task in the same way. Similarly, as we have seen, one of the points of Ratzinger's philosophical critique of modern biblical criticism was its misappropriation of methods and models from the natural sciences. To conceive of biblical exegesis, a discipline at home in the humanities, along the lines of the natural sciences, is a distorting category mistake. As Dale Allison, one of the most well-respected historical-critical New Testament scholars, has written, "We are under the illusion that exegesis progresses like the hard sciences."[88] In particular, he takes issue with the idea that biblical exegesis is a cumulatively growing body of knowledge, where new results build upon, subsume, and displace the old.[89] Furthermore, Olivier-Thomas Venard has pointed out a variety of conceptual weaknesses that beset the "historical-psychological" notion of the literal sense, such as that employed in the 1993 PBC text.[90] He writes, "The historical-psychological definition of the literal sense has a very naïve confidence in a Romantic conception of *the author*: for example, who is the author of a Gospel? The final redactor? The composer of the first accounts? Does the presumed author of the hypothetical Q source hold the key to the literal sense of the passages in question?"[91] Venard argues that this account of the literal sense "also exaggerates the scientific capacities to explore the intentions of a man of the distant past and *a fortiori* his message. . . . Is it possible to reconstruct a psychological state? To infer the *states of consciousness* which one produces from a *text*?"[92]

The way in which the 1993 PBC defines the historical-critical method and its object creates hermeneutical problems with regard to modes of more-than-literal interpretation. This point has been made by Ayres and Fowl.[93] For example, they call attention to this passage about the notion of *sensus plenior*: "The Holy Spirit, the principal author of the Bible, can guide human authors in the choice of expressions in such a way that the latter will express a truth the fullest depths of which the authors themselves do not perceive."[94] Ayres and Fowl argue that this claim cannot be coherently squared with other claims in the document about authors, texts, and meaning: "Having already tied textual meaning to the intention of the human author, *Interpretation* now asserts that a text's fullest truth might have nothing to do with that text's meaning."[95] Similarly, the 1993 PBC document also expresses a very high regard for the liturgy, which it calls "the most perfect actualization of the biblical texts."[96] The document likewise speaks positively of the spiritual reading of Scripture known as *lectio divina*.[97] Indeed, the liturgical use of Scripture and *lectio* are two instances in which the premodern interpretation of Scripture survives and thrives today. And yet, how can such interpretation or "actualization" be reckoned as legitimate when neither are based on historical-critical analysis?

The same tensions that appear in *DV* regarding the object of biblical interpretation appear in the 1993 PBC text. As mentioned previously, there is a subtle tension in *DV* as to what constitutes the proper object of biblical interpretation: the intrinsically connected words and realities in salvation history (no. 2) or the human authors' ideas or message communicated by the text (no. 12). The 1993 PBC text clearly prefers the account given in *DV*, no. 12 and posits the human authors' ideas or message communicated by the text as the object of biblical interpretation. However, as in *DV*, other passages in the 1993 PBC text do not locate revelation in the authors' ideas or texts, but in the realities that Scripture presents or to which it bears witness. For example, in its discussion of hermeneutical theory, the 1993 PBC text specifies the object of biblical interpretation as "the person of Jesus Christ and the saving events accomplished in human history."[98] The same passage speaks of the "the meaning that is given in the events and ... in the person of Jesus Christ."[99] Similarly, when talking about the relationship of the Testaments, the 1993 PBC text recalls, but does not reference, the sacramental theology of history in *DV*, no. 2: "Scripture reveals the meaning of events and that events reveal the meaning of Scripture."[100] Passages such as these identify the primary *locus* of revelation, and thus the object of interpretation, as God's revelatory and saving action in the course of human events. The biblical texts themselves are not revelation per se, but they bear uniquely inspired, authoritative witness to those revelatory events.

Although the document never cites *DV*, no. 2, these statements are congruent with the latter's sacramental theology of history with its intrinsically connected words and deeds in salvation history. The 1993 PBC text's lack of attention to the sacramental theology of history given in *DV*, no. 2, which is so characteristic of premodern biblical interpretation, coheres with its general sheepishness (if not outright embarrassment) over the biblical exegesis of the Church Fathers.[101] While the 1993 text does see some value in patristic exegesis and is very concerned about the role of the Bible in the Church's tradition, faith, and practice, the strong interest to secure the interpretive primacy of its construal of the historical-critical method and its discernment of the human authors' intended meaning shapes its reception of *DV* so as to favor one set of elements in the conciliar text and play down (or ignore) others.

F. Contributions to Ecumenical and Interfaith Relations

The interpretive program of *DV*, especially the historical-literary principles, has also made positive contributions in ecumenism and inter-faith relations. First, one may point to *The Joint Declaration on the Doctrine of Justification* (henceforth, *JDDJ*) signed by the Lutheran World Federation and the Catholic Church in 1999.[102] This ecumenical milestone states that between the two signatories there is "a consensus on basic truths concerning the doctrine of justification," with the result that "the corresponding doctrinal condemnations of the sixteenth century do not apply to today's partner."[103] The *JDDJ* cites the important contribution made by the "insights of recent biblical studies" in negotiating the historic differences of interpretation between Lutherans and Catholics and thus assisting in the formation of the ecumenical agreement.[104] The first major section of the *JDDJ* comprises a brief survey of pertinent biblical evidence, which incorporates and reflects the shared reading of Scripture, especially Paul, in light of modern exegetical interests.

Another significant contribution is the document *The Jewish People and Their Sacred Scriptures in the Christian Bible*, issued by the Pontifical Biblical Commission in 2001 (henceforth, 2001 PBC).[105] This lengthy document has three major sections, which take up the essential place of Israel's Scriptures in the Christian biblical canon (nos. 2–18), major themes established in the Hebrew Bible and which are received and interpreted in the New Testament (nos. 19–64), and lastly, the presentation of Jews in the New Testament and its historical context (nos. 66–83). Affirming "the supremacy of the historical-critical method," this text covers much exegetical ground and seeks to negotiate a number of complex topics.[106] It acknowledges the legitimacy and value of a Jewish reading of the Hebrew Bible and encourages Christian and Jewish scholars to learn much from each other.[107] At the same time, it also maintains the legitimacy of the Christian reading of the Old Testament, which arises from faith in Christ. This Christological reading of the Old Testament

> is a retrospective perception, whose point of departure is not located in the texts as such, but in the events of the New Testament, proclaimed by the Apostolic Preaching. One should not say, therefore, that the Jewish [reader] does not see that which was announced in the texts, but that the Christian [reader], in the light of Christ and in the Spirit, discovers in the texts a surplus of meaning, which was hidden there.[108]

While one may be justifiably critical of various aspects of this curial text, one must also recognize that it is a significant contribution in post-conciliar Jewish-Catholic relations and Catholic biblical interpretation.[109] Indeed, as Reinhard Hütter says of the 2001 PBC text (which we might also say of the *JDDJ*), this document "would have been unthinkable had not . . . the historical-critical method become a vital interpretive tradition among Roman Catholic biblical scholars."[110]

G. Pope Benedict XVI, Verbum Domini (2010)

In September 2010, Pope Benedict XVI promulgated his Apostolic Exhortation *Verbum Domini*.[111] This text followed upon the October 2008 meeting of the Synod of Bishops, devoted to "The Word of God in the Life and Mission of the Church" (§1).[112] *Verbum Domini* is a text of great significance for post-conciliar Catholic biblical interpretation. Unlike the documents issued by the Pontifical Biblical Commission, *Verbum Domini* is a text of magisterial status, and it is the first major magisterial text on the interpretation of Scripture since the promulgation of *DV* in 1965. Moreover (to the best of my knowledge), it is the lengthiest, most substantial magisterial text on the interpretation of the Bible and its place in the Church's life to have ever been issued in the entire history of the Church.

Benedict specifies that his goal in this text is "to point out certain fundamental approaches to a rediscovery of God's word in the life of the Church as a wellspring of constant renewal" (§1). The text is divided into three major parts, which are composed of chapter-like subsections. The first major part, *Verbum Dei* (nos. 6–49), sets forth the theological setting within which Scripture and its interpretation have their proper place. The first chapter subsection, "The God Who Speaks" (nos. 6–21), sets forth an account of divine revelation framed in terms of dialogue. Benedict writes, "The novelty of biblical revelation consists in the fact that God becomes known through the dialogue which he desires to have with us" (no. 6). The revelation of God through the eternal Word proceeds from the inner-trinitarian "dialogue of love between the divine persons" (no. 6), and it is into the divine communion that the triune God invites human beings to share. The Father speaks his Word both in creation, which "indelibly bears the mark of the *creative Reason which orders and directs it*" (no. 8), and especially in the course of salvation history, culminating in the Word's incarnation in Jesus (nos. 7, 11–13). The revealed Word of God, the understanding of which is enabled by the Holy Spirit who indwells the believing Church (nos. 15–16), is delivered to the Church and is preserved and transmitted through Scripture and Tradition (nos. 17–19).

The second chapter subsection, "Our Response to the God Who Speaks" (nos. 22–28), builds upon the dialogical motif and treats the human response(s) to divine revelation. Benedict writes, "The word of God draws each of us into a conversation with the Lord" (no. 24), and through this dialogue, "we come to understand ourselves and we discover an answer to our heart's deepest questions" (no. 23). Human beings are free to refuse God's Word or, with the help of grace, to receive the Word in faith (nos. 25–26). According to Benedict, such obediential faith "arises from an encounter with Christ," who is himself "present today in history, in his body which is the Church" (no. 25). And "for this reason," Benedict concludes, "our act of faith is at once both personal and ecclesial" (no. 25). This theological horizon, given in chapter subsections 1–2, provide the setting for Benedict's programmatic discussion, "The Interpretation of Sacred Scripture in the Church" (nos. 29–49), which is most pertinent for our purposes and to which I will return below.

The second major part, *Verbum in Ecclesia* (nos. 50–89), treats the place of Scripture in the Church's life. Among the topics discussed here are the relationship between the Bible and the Church's liturgy and sacraments, its pastoral ministry, and private prayer. Following the template of the transmission of revelation given in part 1 (i.e., from God to the Church and through the Church to the world), the third major part, *Verbum Mundo* (nos. 90–120), expands its scope to treat the Bible and the Church's place in its mission to the world and addresses the Church's work for peace, justice, practical care for the poor, inculturation, and interreligious dialogue.

DV plays a very prominent role in *Verbum Domini*. Benedict references *DV* twenty-six times throughout *Verbum Domini*, and he appeals to all chapters of the conciliar text (except chapter 5). The greatest concentration of references to *DV* is in part 1, subsection 1, "The God Who Speaks" (nos. 6–21), where Benedict appeals to all but one chapter of *DV*. Structurally, the first major part of *Verbum Domini* follows the basic scheme of divine revelation and its transmission given in *DV* chapters 1–2: salvation-directed revelation of the triune God in creation and in salvation history, culminating in the Incarnation; the obedience of faith as the proper human response to revelation; the transmission of God's Word through Tradition and Scripture. Just as *DV* places its discussion of the interpretation of Scripture within a larger theological setting, so too does Benedict by placing the sub-section "The Interpretation of Sacred

Scripture in the Church" after his teaching on divine revelation and the ecclesial setting of its transmission and human response.

In this chapter subsection, Benedict openly and extensively makes reference to the interpretive program given in *DV*, no. 12. A basic premise of Benedict's teaching is that *"the primary setting for scriptural interpretation is the life of the Church"* (no. 29).[113] According to Benedict, this is an object-appropriate interpretation. The books of the Bible were composed within the context of a faith community: they were "written by the People of God and for the People of God" (no. 30). Within this historically-continuous community of God's people and their faith, the biblical books are recognized as Sacred Scripture, not simply as a collection of religious writings from the ancient world (no. 29). The same Holy Spirit, who inspired the Scriptures, also indwells the Church as a whole and enables the Church to arrive at an understanding of the inspired books. Accordingly, a genuine understanding of the Scriptures requires the interpreter's participation in the ecclesial communion, its faith, and its practices (no. 30).

Benedict thus teaches that the interpretation of the Bible as Scripture is a theological and ecclesial practice. It properly takes place within the historically-continuous community of God's people in keeping with its normative doctrines and practices. This same theological and ecclesial matrix provides the proper context for receiving and applying the interpretive program given in *DV*, no. 12, both the historical-literary principles and the theological-ecclesial ones.

Benedict recognizes the good that modern historical-critical exegesis has produced for the Church.[114] Like the 1993 PBC text, Benedict affirms that historical methods of analysis follow upon the reality of the Incarnation. Essential to Christian faith are certain realities that occurred within the course of human events. He writes the following: "The historical fact is a constitutive dimension of the Christian faith. The history of salvation is not mythology, but a true history, and it should thus be studied with the methods of serious historical research" (no. 32). These claims, along with Benedict's appeal to the encyclical teachings of Leo XIII and Pius XII, which gave (varying) degrees of approval to modern historical analysis, lead into Benedict's discussion of the interpretive program in *DV*, no. 12.

Consistent with previous papal teachings, *DV*, Benedict notes, "emphasizes the study of literary genres and historical context as basic elements for understanding the meaning intended by the sacred author" (no. 34). And yet, Benedict also reminds his audience that these historical-literary principles comprise only part of *DV*'s interpretive program, and he goes on to list the three theological-ecclesial principles. While acknowledging the benefits produced by historical and literary analysis, Benedict also observes that the reception of *DV*, no. 12 has been very one-sided in favor the historical-literary principles to the neglect of the theological-ecclesial ones. He writes in *Verbum Domini*, no. 34:

> While today's academic exegesis, including that of Catholic scholars,
> is highly competent in the field of historical-critical methodology

and its latest developments, it must be said that comparable attention needs to be paid to the theological dimension of the biblical texts, so that they can be more deeply understood in accordance with the three elements indicated by the Dogmatic Constitution *Dei Verbum*.

Much work remains to be done regarding the integration of the two sets of interpretive principles. Benedict states that this is a vitally important task: "Only where both methodological levels, the historical-critical and the theological, are respected, can one speak of a theological exegesis, an exegesis worthy of this book [i.e., the Bible]" (no. 34).

In the following sections (esp. nos. 35–41), Benedict gives some direction for the work of integrating these two sets of interpretive principles. Much of his teaching recalls and develops content from his 1988 Erasmus Lecture, "Biblical Interpretation in Conflict," which was discussed above (II.C). While much can be said about Benedict's teaching in these sections, two significant aspects stand out. First, the work of integrating these principles must proceed from a strong (and accurate) sense of *"the harmony between faith and reason"* (no. 36).[115] Benedict acknowledges that all modes of reading and interpreting Scripture involve philosophical presuppositions of various kinds.[116] According to Benedict, much modern biblical exegesis operates with a truncated account of human reason, which reduces biblical exegesis to historical and philology (i.e., a restriction to things empirical). More specifically, Benedict speaks of a "secularized hermeneutic" (no. 35), which denies (or, one might say, deems unknowable) any activity by God in the world. As he did in the Erasmus Lecture, Benedict teaches that the integration of interpretive principles requires a critical engagement with the philosophical make-up of modern critical exegesis. In particular, the proper interpretation of Scripture requires a more capacious, healthy account of human reason, which "is marked by openness [esp. to the transcendent] and does not reject *a priori* anything beyond its own terms of reference" (no. 36).[117]

Second, Benedict teaches that the work of integration should involve a more rigorous and sustained engagement with the biblical exegesis of the Church Fathers (no. 37). In an approving citation of the 1993 PBC text, Benedict applauds patristic exegesis for entering into the biblical texts "to find the reality of faith there expressed, ... [and then] to link this reality to the experience of faith in our present world" (no. 37).[118] Among the other aspects of patristic exegesis that Benedict commends are its essential identification with patristic theology (i.e., patristic theology *is* the exegesis of Scripture) and the doing of this exegesis within the ecclesial communion of the Church and its faith (no. 37). Benedict also writes of the need for "transcending the letter" (no. 38), that is, to go beyond the literal to the Christological (or spiritual) senses. This interpretive move involves reading individual texts within the larger whole that is the divine economy of salvation in Christ (nos. 38–41), and it also involves the action of the Holy Spirit within the exegete (no. 38).

Consistent with Benedict's focus on the theological-ecclesial principles as essential to Catholic biblical interpretation is his appeal to the texts of *DV* that speak of the sacramentality of Scripture and the divine economy. Benedict addresses both in *Verbum Domini*, nos. 52–56, which treat the relationship between the Bible and liturgy. Referencing the *DV*, nos. 21 and 26, Benedict speaks to the close relationship between the Eucharist and Scripture, a relationship which is grounded in Scripture itself (no. 54; citing Luke 24; John 6). Similar to claims made in the *CCC* (cf. nos. 103–4, 112), Benedict speaks of Scripture as a locus of present encounter with God.[119] He writes, "The proclamation of God's word at the celebration entails an acknowledgement that Christ himself is present, that he speaks to us, and that he wishes to be heard" (no. 56). According to Benedict, the liturgical proclamation of inspired Scripture is a kind of divine presence, analogous to Christ's Eucharistic presence: "Christ, truly present under the species of bread and wine, is analogously present in the word proclaimed in the liturgy" (no. 56). Underpinning these claims is what Benedict, using the words of Pope St. John Paul II, calls "the *'sacramental* character of revelation'" (no. 56).[120] Benedict connects the sacramentality of Scripture to *DV*, no. 2 with its sacramental account of the divine economy: "A deeper understanding of the sacramentality of God's word can thus lead us to a more unified understanding of the mystery of revelation, which takes place through 'deeds and words intimately connected'" (no. 56).

III. The Future of *Dei Verbum*

The preceding survey reveals that the reception of *DV* in discussions of Catholic biblical interpretation has been both positive and partial. It has been quite positive in that it has contributed to a flourishing of Catholic exegesis and an enhancing of the Bible's place in Catholic faith and practice. But it has also been partial in that certain elements in *DV* (e.g., the historical-literary principles and the object of interpretation as the human authors' message communicated through the texts) have received far more attention and have been assigned greater hermeneutical priority than others. This has led to a marginalization or neglect of other key teachings in the conciliar text (e.g., the theological-ecclesial principles and the object of interpretation as the intrinsically related words and realities, given in the sacramental economy of salvation). This unevenness in the reception of *DV* owes something, I suggest, to subtle tensions within the conciliar text itself.

Given its substance and magisterial status, Benedict XVI's *Verbum Domini* has set the agenda for the future reception of *DV*. It acknowledges both the genuine goods produced by Catholic biblical scholarship and the deficiencies in the reception of the conciliar text. By so identifying these deficiencies and offering some direction toward remedying them, Benedict has set the stage for a fuller and more holistic reception of *DV* in the future. By way of conclusion, I would like to offer some brief remarks as to where the continued reception of *DV* might go.

To begin with, one can certainly agree with the conclusion of Raymond Brown: "The modern Catholic biblical movement inaugurated by Pius XII and confirmed by Vatican II is now too much a part of the church to be rejected."[121] Modern biblical criticism has greatly increased the understanding of the biblical texts in their contexts of origin, and it would be both impossible and foolish to do away with such analysis. Accordingly, the study of biblical texts in light of their contexts of origin should continue to thrive as an integral part of Catholic biblical interpretation. But also to be encouraged in this regard are further refinements both of individual methods and of the larger task and place of historical-literary analysis in Catholic interpretation (so as to avoid some of the complications arising in the 1993 PBC text from its particular construal of the historical-critical method and its role in the interpretive process).[122]

At the same time, as Joseph Ratzinger/Benedict XVI provocatively states, "If scholarly exegesis is not to exhaust itself in constantly new hypotheses, becoming theologically irrelevant, it must take a methodological step forward and see itself once again as a theological discipline, without abandoning its historical character."[123] For Catholic biblical interpretation, as *DV* presents it, to thrive as a theological and ecclesial practice, it needs to be embedded consciously within a theological context. Consider, for instance, that in *DV* and *Verbum Domini*, discussions about proper method and interpretive practices do not appear until those respective documents first articulate a theological context within which the interpretation of Scripture occurs. Much of the rationale for situating biblical interpretation within a strong theological context is given by Benedict in *Verbum Domini*: the books of the Bible were produced in and for the People of God; it is through the Church's faith that these books are recognized as Scripture; the same Spirit who inspired the Scripture also indwells Christ's ecclesial body, guiding it to a deeper understanding of what God has revealed. Among the topics meriting further study in this regard are the nature and place of Scripture as a theological reality in relation to divine revelation, the place and function of Scripture in the divine economy that includes the Church, the inspiration of both biblical texts and authors, the relationship between inspiration and interpretation, and the sacramentality of Scripture.

Benedict also spoke of the need to integrate the historical-literary principles with the theological-ecclesial principles of interpretation. If, as argued above, the tension between these two sets of principles also relates to a tension between their objects of interpretation, then the integration of interpretive principles must also involve an integration of the objects of biblical interpretation: the human authors' message communicated through the text (*DV*, no. 12) with the intrinsically related words and realities in the sacramental economy of salvation history (*DV*, no. 2). Put differently, the work of integration is not to be worked out solely at the level of methodologies. Rather, the work of integrating the interpretive principles and the objects of interpretation requires work at the deeper level of philosophical principles, for involved here are the interrelationships between human language (both written and spoken), human cognition and intentionality, and the extra-mental world. Important work on aspects of this topic has already been done by Robert

Sokolowski, Francis Martin, and in a postmodern key by Olivier-Thomas Venard.[124]

Throughout its first fifty years of reception, *DV* has provided both substance and direction for Catholic biblical interpretation. And yet, many aspects of this text still remain to be received and implemented robustly. Looking to the future of *DV*, we might work for a fuller reception of this conciliar text and a stronger realization of its stated goals: "by hearing the message of salvation the whole world may believe, by believing it may hope, and by hoping it may love" (*DV*, no. 2).[125]

NOTES

1. Historians of Vatican II have documented the complex and often tumultuous composition history of this particular text. A helpful summary of this text's composition history is provided in Ronald D. Witherup, SS, *Scripture:* Dei Verbum (New York: Paulist Press, 2006), 15–31. As Witherup notes (134n14, 143), the most thorough account appears across the volumes of Giuseppe Alberigo and Joseph A. Komonchak, eds., *History of Vatican II*, 5 vols. (Maryknoll and Leuven: Orbis and Peeters, 1995–2006). Also very illuminating is Jared Wicks, SJ, "Vatican II on Revelation—From Behind the Scenes," *Theological Studies* 71 (2010): 637–50.

2. For instance, in *Retrieving Fundamental Theology*, Gerald O'Collins and Joseph Cassar provide a bibliography of secondary works on *DV*, which comprises nearly 450 items only up to 1991. See Gerald O'Collins, *Retrieving Fundamental Theology: Three Styles of Contemporary Theology* (New York and Mahwah: Paulist Press, 1993), 178–217.

3. Unless otherwise noted, all citations of *DV* (English and Latin) will be taken from the texts available at the website of the Holy See: (English) http://www.vatican.va/archive/hist_councils/ii_vatican_council/documents/vat-ii_const_19651118_dei-verbum_en.html; (Latin) http://www.vatican.va/archive/hist_councils/ii_vatican_council/documents/vat-ii_const_19651118_dei-verbum_lt.html. Accessed April 6, 2015. Citations of *DV* will be given parenthetically in the body of the text.

4. William M. Wright IV, "Pre-Gospel Traditions and Post-Critical Interpretation in Benedict XVI's *Jesus of Nazareth: Volume 2*," *Nova et Vetera* (English Edition) (2012): 1018. See also Francis Martin, "Joseph Ratzinger, Benedict XVI, on Biblical Interpretation: Two Leading Principles," *Nova et Vetera* (English Edition) 5 (2007): 285–99.

5. English translation is my own from the Latin text of *DV* §12: "cum Sacra Scriptura eodem Spiritu quo scripta est etiam legenda et interpretanda sit." Essential for understanding this phrase is Ignace de la Potterie, SJ, "Interpretation of Holy Scripture in the Spirit in Which It Was Written (*Dei Verbum* 12c)," in *Vatican II: Assessment and Perspectives—Twenty-Five Years After (1962–1987)*, ed. René Latourelle (Mahwah, NJ: Paulist Press, 1988), 220–66. See also O'Collins, *Retrieving Fundamental Theology*, 139–42.

6. See de la Potterie, "In the Spirit in Which It Was Written," 223–33. De la Potterie (258nn7–8) adduces Jerome's *Commentary on Galatians* 5: 19–21 as evidence of this claim, as well as Jerome's claim in the Prologue of this work to be drawing on a (now lost) commentary of Origen's on Galatians.

7. O'Collins, *Retrieving Fundamental Theology*, 141.

8. Ibid.

9. See Pope Leo XIII, *Providentissimus Deus*, §§14–15, 17–20; Pope Pius XII, *Divino Afflante Spiritu*, §§23–30, 33–41. For the text of *Providentissimus Deus*, see http://w2.vatican.va/content/leo-xiii/en/encyclicals/documents/hf_l-xiii_enc_18111893_providentissimus-deus.html. For the text of *Divino Afflante Spiritu*, see http://w2.vatican.va/content/pius-xii/en/encyclicals/documents/hf_p-xii_enc_30091943_divino-afflante-spiritu.html.

10. The Latin text reads, "Attente investigare debet, quid hagiographi reapse significare intenderint et eorum verbis manifestare Deo placuerit." Note that the Latin text uses the disclosive language of "signify" (*significare*) and "manifest" (*manifestare*), not "meaning."

11. See William M. Wright IV, "Inspired Scripture as a Sacramental Vehicle of Divine Presence in the Gospel of John and *Dei Verbum*," *Nova et Vetera* (English Edition) 13 (2015): 175–78.

12. Wicks ("Vatican II on Revelation," 649) points out that the concern for "revelation in words and deeds intimately interrelated" is a contribution to *DV* stemming from Jean Daniélou, a well-known figure in the Catholic *Ressourcement*. The sacramental theology of history is very much at home within the broader interests of this theological movement and Daniélou in particular; see Hans Boersma, *Nouvelle Théologie and Sacramental Ontology: A Return to Mystery* (New York: Oxford University Press, 2009), 168–80.

13. I am indebted here to Francis Martin, "Revelation and Its Transmission," in *Vatican II: Renewal within Tradition*, ed. Matthew L. Lamb and Matthew Levering (New York: Oxford University Press, 2008), 68.

14. The remainder of this paragraph is taken from Wright, "Pre-Gospel Traditions and Post-Critical Interpretation," 1018–19.

15. Joseph Cardinal Ratzinger, *Principles of Catholic Theology: Building Stones for a Fundamental Theology*, trans. Sister Mary Frances McCarthy, SND (San Francisco: Ignatius Press, 1987), 135 (both quotations from this page).

16. Ibid. 136.

17. Ibid. 136.

18. Francis Martin, "Election, Covenant, and Law," *Nova et Vetera* (English Edition) 4 (2006): 867.

19. See Maurice Blondel, *The Letter on Apologetics & History and Dogma*, trans. Alexander Dru and Illtyd Trethowan (Grand Rapids: Eerdmans, 1994), 221–87. For secondary discussion, see Marcellino D'Ambrosio, "Critique of Scientific Exegesis," *Communio* 19 (1992): 365–88; William M. Wright IV, "The Literal Sense of Scripture according to Henri de Lubac: Insights from Patristic Exegesis of the Transfiguration," *Modern Theology* 28 (2012): 267–71.

20. Pope Paul IV, "Apostolic Letter Issued *motu proprio* on New Laws Regulating the Pontifical Biblical Commission, *Sedula Cura*," in *The Scripture Documents: An Anthology of Official Catholic Teachings*, ed. and trans. Dean P. Béchard (Collegeville, MN: The Liturgical Press, 2002), 147. References to page numbers in Béchard's anthology will be given parenthetically.

21. Ibid.

22. See Wright, "Inspired Scripture as a Sacramental Vehicle of Divine Presence in the Gospel of John and *Dei Verbum*," 172–78.

23. Pope Paul VI, *Sedula Cura* (Béchard 147–48). AR: *Sedula Cura* is very short and does not have any internal system of references (e.g. paragraph numbers).

24. Pope Paul VI, "Address to Members of the Pontifical Biblical Commission on the Ecclesial Role of Biblical Studies," in Béchard, *Scripture Documents*, 151–56.

25. Pope Paul VI, "Ecclesial Role of Biblical Studies," §5 (Béchard 153).

26. Ibid. §3 (Béchard 152).

27. Ibid. §6 (Béchard 154).

28. Ibid. §7 (Béchard 154).

29. Ibid. §10 (Béchard 156).

30. Raymond E. Brown, SS, Joseph A. Fitzmyer, SJ, and Roland E. Murphy, O. Carm., eds., *The Jerome Biblical Commentary* (Englewood Cliffs, NJ: Prentice-Hall, Inc., 1968).

31. Reginald C. Fuller, Leonard Johnson, and Conleth Kearns, OP, eds., *A New Catholic Commentary on Holy Scripture* (London: Thomas Nelson and Sons, Ltd., 1969).

32. See Raymond E. Brown, SS, *The Virginal Conception and Bodily Resurrection of Jesus* (New York: Paulist Press, 1973), 2–15; *Biblical Reflections on Crises Facing the Church* (New York: Paulist Press, 1975), 6–12; *The Critical Meaning of the Bible* (New York and Mahwah: Paulist Press, 1981), ix. In the next three paragraphs, I summarize the developed version of this account given in Raymond E. Brown, SS, and Thomas Aquinas Collins, OP, "Church Pronouncements," in *The New Jerome Biblical Commentary*, ed. Raymond E. Brown, SS, Joseph A. Fitzmyer, SJ, and Roland E. Murphy, O. Carm. (Englewood Cliffs, NJ: Prentice Hall, 1990), 72:3–9 (pp. 1167–68).

33. Brown and Collins, "Church Pronouncements," *NJBC* 72:5 (p. 1167). For the text of these *responsa*, see Béchard, 187–208. In an appendix to his anthology (pp. 318–29), Béchard offers a helpful sketch of these *responsa*, the debated measure of their authoritativeness, and their eventual nuancing of their status. On their obligatory status, see Heinrich Denzinger, *Compendium of Creeds, Definitions, and Declarations on Matters of Faith and Morals*, 43rd ed., ed. Peter Hünermann, Robert Fastiggi, and Anne Englund Nash (San Francisco: Ignatius Press, 2010), 3503.

34. Brown and Collins, "Church Pronouncements," *NJBC* 72:5 (p. 1167).

35. Ibid. *NJBC* 72:6 (p. 1167).

36. See Pope Pius XII, *Divino Afflante Spiritu* §§23–24, 31–41.

37. Pontifical Biblical Commission, Letter to Cardinal Suhard, January 16, 1948 (Béchard 222). A comparable, nuanced understanding of these *responsa* would later be given by Cardinal Joseph Ratzinger, while serving as the head of the Congregation for the Doctrine of the Faith. Commenting on the 1990 text *Donum Veritatis* ("Instruction Concerning the Ecclesial Vocation of the Theologian"), Ratzinger writes the following: this 1990 document holds "that there are magisterial decisions which cannot be the final word of a given matter as such but, despite the permanent value of their principles, are chiefly also a signal for pastoral prudence, a sort of provisional policy. Their kernel remains valid, but the particulars determined by circumstances can stand in need of correction. In this connection, one will probably call to mind ... the anti-Modernist decisions of the beginning of this century, especially the decisions of the then Biblical Commission" (cited from Joseph Cardinal Ratzinger, *The Nature and Mission of Theology*, trans. Adrian Walker [San Francisco: Ignatius Press, 1995], 106).

38. See also Joseph A. Fitzmyer, SJ, *The Interpretation of Scripture: In Defense of the Historical-Critical Method* (Mahwah, NJ: Paulist Press, 2008), 17–36.

39. Brown, *Critical Meaning of the Bible*, ix.

40. Brown and Collins, "Church Pronouncements," *NJBC* 72:9 (p. 1168).

41. Denis Farkasfalvy, "The Case for Spiritual Exegesis," *Communio* 10 (1983): 335.

42. See Pope John Paul II, General Audience, May 1, 1985. Spanish text available at http://w2.vatican.va/content/john-paul-ii/es/audiences/1985/documents/hf_jp-ii_aud_19850501.html. My thanks to Michael Niebauer for his translation assistance with this text.

43. Some of his writings on this topic are Denis Farkasfalvy, O. Cist., *Inspiration and Interpretation: A Theological Introduction to Sacred Scripture* (Washington, DC: The Catholic University of America Press, 2010); "In Search of a 'Post-Critical' Method of Biblical Interpretation for Catholic Theology," *Communio* 13 (1986): 288–307; "The Case for Spiritual Exegesis," 332–50; "A Heritage in Search of Heirs: The Future of Ancient Christian Exegesis," *Communio* 25 (1998): 505–19; "How to Renew the Theology of Biblical Inspiration," *Nova et Vetera* (English Edition) 4 (2006): 231–54; "Biblical Foundations for a Theology of Inspiration," *Nova et Vetera* (English Edition) 4 (2006): 719–46; William R. Farmer and Denis M. Farkasfalvy, O. Cist., *The Formation of the New Testament Canon: An Ecumenical Approach* (New York: Paulist Press, 1983), 97–178.

44. Farkasfalvy, "Case for Spiritual Exegesis," 340.

45. Ibid.

46. See Farkasfalvy, *Inspiration and Interpretation*.

47. Ignace de la Potterie, SJ, *La Vérité dans Saint Jean*, 2 vols., Analecta Biblica 73–74 (Rome: Biblical Institute Press, 1977).

48. For instance, Ignace de la Potterie, "Reading Holy Scripture 'in the Spirit': Is the Patristic Way of Reading the Bible Still Possible Today?," *Communio* 13 (1986): 308–25; "La vérité de l'écriture et l'herméneutique biblique," *Revue théologique de Louvain* 18 (1987): 171–86; "The Spiritual Sense of Scripture," *Communio* 23 (1996): 738–56; "Biblical Exegesis: A Science of Faith," in *Opening Up the Scriptures: Joseph Ratzinger and the Foundations of Biblical Interpretation*, ed. José Granados, Carlos Granados, and Luis Sánchez-Navarro, essay trans. Michelle Borras (Grand Rapids: Eerdmans, 2008), 30–64.

49. Translation mine. See de la Potterie, "In the Spirit in Which It Was Written," 220–66.

50. Ibid. 221, 255 respectively.

51. See Francis Martin, *Sacred Scripture: The Disclosure of the Word* (Naples, FL: Sapientia Press of Ave Maria University, 2006); "Election, Covenant, and Law," 857–90.

52. See Francis Martin, *The Feminist Question: Feminist Theology in the Light of Christian Tradition* (Grand Rapids: Eerdmans, 1994), 168–94; "Revelation as Disclosure: Creation," in *Wisdom and Holiness, Science and Scholarship: Essays in Honor of Matthew L. Lamb*, ed. Michael Dauphinais and Matthew Levering (Naples: Sapientia Press, 2007), 205–47; "Reflections on Professor Bockmuehl's 'Bible versus Theology,'" *Nova et Vetera* (English Edition) 9 (2011): 49–74; "Joseph Ratzinger, Benedict XVI, on Biblical Interpretation," 301–11.

53. For a brief sketch of Martin's views on these issues, see Francis Martin, introduction to *Acts*, Ancient Christian Commentary on Scripture, New Testament vol. 5 (Downers Grove, IL: InterVarsity Press, 2006), xxii–xxvi.

54. See Francis Martin, "Spiritual Sense," in Kevin J. Vanhoozer, ed., *Dictionary for Theological Interpretation of the Bible* (Grand Rapids: Baker Academic, 2005), 769–72; "The Spiritual Sense (*Sensus Spiritualis*) of Sacred Scripture: Its Essential Insight," in *Sacred Scripture*, 249–75; "Spiritual Understanding of Scripture," in *Verbum Domini and the Complementarity of Exegesis and Theology*, ed. Scott Carl (Grand Rapids: Eerdmans, 2015), 12–25.

55. Martin, "The Contribution and Challenge of *Dei Verbum*," in *Sacred Scripture*, 228.

56. Joseph Cardinal Ratzinger, "Biblical Interpretation in Conflict: On the Foundations and the Itinerary of Exegesis Today," in *Opening Up the Scriptures*, essay trans. Adrian Walker, 1–29.

57. Ibid. 1–3; quotation from p. 2.

58. Ibid. 7.

59. Ibid. 7

60. Ibid. 19.

61. Ibid. 8.

62. Ibid. 17–19. In addition to these two, many of Ratzinger's other critiques have since become standard in biblical studies (e.g., the impossibility of unbiased analysis and interpretation, the importance of the reader's subjectivity and location in the interpretive process).

63. *Catechism of the Catholic Church*, 2nd ed. (Vatican City: Libreria Editrice Vaticana, 1997).

64. In his Apostolic Letter *Laetamur Magnopere*, John Paul II indicates that the 1997 Latin typical edition is the "definitive text" of the *CCC*; John Paul II, *Laetamur Magnopere*, in *CCC* xiii. Accordingly, this English translation based on the 1997 Latin typical text will be used in this essay, and references to the *CCC* will be given parenthetically in the body of this essay.

65. Pope John Paul II, *Fidei Depositum* §3, cited from *CCC*, no. 5.

66. Discussion of the obedience of faith in *DV* §5 appears in *CCC*, no. 143, 153, and the teachings in *DV* §6 on natural revelation and the illumination of human reasoning by revelation appear in *CCC*, no. 36, 38.

67. A helpful (and sympathetic) analysis is in Ignace de la Potterie, "The *Catechism of the Catholic Church*: The Section on Sacred Scripture," *Communio* 21 (1994): 450–60.

68. On communicative intention, see Stephen E. Fowl, "The Role of Authorial Intention in the Theological Interpretation of Scripture," in *Between Two Horizons: Spanning New Testament Studies and Systematic Theology*, ed. Joel B. Green and Max Turner (Grand Rapids: Eerdmans, 2000), 71–87. Fowl (74n6) here draws on Mark Brett, "Motives and Intentions in Genesis 1," *Journal of Theological Studies* 42 (1991): 1–16.

69. All references and quotations of this text are from the Pontifical Biblical Commission, *The Interpretation of the Bible in the Church*, trans. John Kilgallen and Brendan Byrne (Boston: St. Paul Books and Media, 1993; Vatican City: Libreria Editrice Vaticana, 1993). References to *The Interpretation of the Bible in the Church* will be given according to the document's internal outline structure with page numbers to the St. Paul Books and Media edition given parenthetically. For substantive analysis of this text, see Peter S. Williamson, *Catholic Principles for Interpreting Scripture: A Study of the Pontifical Biblical Commission's* The Interpretation of the Bible in the Church, Subsidia Biblica 22 (Rome: Editrice Pontifico Instituto Biblico, 2002). Expository commentary is given in Joseph A. Fitzmyer, SJ, *The Biblical Commission's Document "The Interpretation of the Bible in the Church": Text and Commentary*, Subsidia Biblica 18 (Rome: Editrice Pontifico Instituto Biblico, 1995).

70. See Lewis Ayres and Stephen E. Fowl, "(Mis)Reading the Face of God: *The Interpretation of the Bible in the Church*," *Theological Studies* 60 (1999): 513–28.

71. Based on the English translation: part 1 = 38 percent; part 2 = 11 percent; part 3 = 27 percent; part 4 = 17 percent.

72. *Interpretation of the Bible in the Church* (Introduction, B, n.1) makes a categorical distinction between "method" and "approach": "By an exegetical 'method' we understand a group of scientific procedures employed in order to explain texts. We

speak of an 'approach' when it is a question of an enquiry proceeding from a particular point of view" (34).

73. Biblical Commission, *Interpretation*, I.A.1 (pp. 35–38).

74. Ibid. I.A.1 (p. 35) (emphasis added).

75. Ibid. IV.A (pp. 117–21). This notion of "actualization" owes much to François Dreyfus, OP; for instance, his "L'actualisation à l'Intérieur de la Bible," *Revue Biblique* 83 (1976): 161–202; "L'actualisation de L'Écriture I.—Du texte á la vie," *Revue Biblique* 86 (1979): 5–58; "L'actualisation de L'Écriture II.—L'action de L'Espirit," *Revue Biblique* 86 (1979): 161–93; "L'actualisation de L'Écriture III—La place de la tradition," *Revue Biblique* 86 (1979): 321–84. For secondary discussion and bibliography, see Ugo Vanni, SJ, "Exegesis and Actualization in the Light of *Dei Verbum*," in Latourelle, *Vatican II: Assessment and Perspectives*, 1:344–63; Aidan Nichols, "François Dreyfus on Scripture Read in Tradition," in *Scribe of the Kingdom: Essays on Theology and Culture*, 2 vols. (London: Sheed & Ward, 1994), 1:32–77.

76. Biblical Commission, *Interpretation*, I.A, 35.

77. Quotations from Biblical Commission, *Interpretation*, I.A.4 (p. 42); I.A.1 (p. 38); I.A.3 (p. 40) respectively.

78. Ibid. II.B.2 (p. 82). For an account of the many different ways in which the "literal sense" of Scripture has been defined throughout Christian history, see Brevard S. Childs, "The Sensus Literalis of Scripture: An Ancient and Modern Problem," in *Beiträge zur Alttestamentlichen Theologie: Festschrift für Walther Zimmerli zum 70. Geburtstag*, ed. Herbert Donner, Robert Hanhard, and Rudolf Smend (Göttingen: Vandenhoeck & Ruprecht, 1977), 80–93.

79. Biblical Commission, *Interpretation*, II.B.1 (p. 82).

80. Ibid. II.B.1 (p. 83) (emphasis PBC). The document does admit some multiplicity to the literal sense because authors can intend multiple meanings through a single statement, or divine providence can lead human words to mean other things; see II.B.1 (pp. 82–83).

81. Ibid. II.B.2 (p. 84).

82. Ibid. II.B.2 (pp. 84–85).

83. Ibid. IV.A.1–3 (pp. 117–21).

84. Ibid. IV.A.2 (p. 119).

85. See Krister Stendahl, "Biblical Theology, Contemporary," in *The Interpreter's Dictionary of the Bible: An Illustrated Encyclopedia*, ed. George Arthur Buttrick et al., 4 vols. (New York and Nashville: Abingdon Press, 1962), 1:418–32, quote from 419; cf. Brown, *Critical Meaning of the Bible*, 23–44.

86. Quotations from Biblical Commission, *Interpretation*, Introduction.B (p. 34n1); I.A.2 (p. 38); and I.A.4 (p. 40) respectively.

87. Ayres and Fowl, "(Mis)reading the Face of God," 516n10. To be fair, while the 1993 PBC text does reify the historical-critical method, it also acknowledges the method's being made up of text, source, form, and redaction criticism; see *Interpretation*, I.A.1–3 (pp. 35–40).

88. Dale C. Allison, Jr., "Forgetting the Past," *Downside Review* 120 (2002): 255.

89. Ibid.

90. Olivier-Thomas Venard, OP, "Problématique du sense littéral" in *Le sens littéral des Écritures*, ed. Olivier-Thomas Venard, OP (Paris: Éditions du Cerf, 2009), 312.

91. Ibid. 312 (emphasis Venard's, translation mine).

92. Ibid. 312 (emphasis Venard's, translation mine).

93. Ayres and Fowl, "(Mis)reading the Face of God," 521.

94. Biblical Commission, *Interpretation*, II.B.3 (p. 87). On *sensus plenior*, see Raymond E. Brown, SS, and Sandra M. Schneiders, IHM, "Hermeneutics," *NJBC* 71:49–51 (p. 1157).

95. Ayres and Fowl, "(Mis)reading the Face of God," 520.

96. Biblical Commission, *Interpretation*, IV.C.1 (p. 124).

97. Ibid. IV.C.2 (pp. 126–27). I am indebted to Lewis Ayres for calling my attention to the role of *lectio divina* as regards this issue.

98. Ibid. II.A.2 (p. 80).

99. Ibid. II.A.2 (p. 80).

100. Ibid. III.A.2 (pp. 91–92).

101. On the last point, the document (III.B.2) states, "The allegorical interpretation of Scripture so characteristic of patristic exegesis runs the risk of being something of an embarrassment to people today" (p. 101).

102. Lutheran World Federation and the Catholic Church, *Joint Declaration on the Doctrine of Justification*. October 31, 1999. English translations taken from http://www.vatican.va/roman_curia/pontifical_councils/chrstuni/documents/rc_pc_chrstuni_doc_31101999_cath-luth-joint-declaration_en.html. Accessed March 3, 2015. I owe this reference to Jared Wicks.

103. *Joint Declaration on the Doctrine of Justification*, 13.

104. Ibid. 13.

105. As Charles Miller has amply documented, the English translation of the French original of this text contains numerous flaws. Accordingly, all quotations of this text will be my own translation from the French original, available at http://www.vatican.va/roman_curia/congregations/cfaith/pcb_documents/rc_con_cfaith_doc_20020212_popolo-ebraico_fr.html. Accessed March 5, 2015. For discussion of the problems in the English translation, see Charles H. Miller, "Translation Errors in the Pontifical Biblical Commission's 'The Jewish People and Their Sacred Scriptures in the Christian Bible,'" *Biblical Theology Bulletin* 35 (2005): 34–39.

106. Biblical Commission, "Jewish People and Their Sacred Scriptures," §20.

107. Ibid. §22.

108. Ibid. §21.

109. For evaluations of this document, which are appreciative in some respects and critical in others, see Denis Farkasfalvy, O. Cist., "The Pontifical Biblical Commission's Document on Jews and Christians and Their Scriptures: Attempt at an Evaluation," *Communio* 29 (2002): 715–37; Roch Kereszty, O. Cist., "The Jewish-Christian Dialogue and the Pontifical Biblical Commission's Document on 'The Jewish People and Their Sacred Scriptures in the Christian Bible,'" *Communio* 29 (2002): 738–45; Amy-Jill Levine, "Roland Murphy, the Pontifical Biblical Commission, Jews, and the Bible," *Biblical Theology Bulletin* 33 (2003): 104–13; Roland E. Murphy, "The Biblical Commission, the Jews, and Scriptures," *Biblical Theology Bulletin* 32 (2001): 145–49.

110. Reinhard Hütter, "'In.' Some Incipient Reflections on *The Jewish People and Their Sacred Scriptures in the Christian Bible*," *Pro Ecclesia* 13, no. 1 (2004): 21.

111. Benedict XVI, *The Word of the Lord—Verbum Domini* (Vatican City and Boston: Libreria Editrice Vaticana and Pauline Books and Media, 2010); references will be given parenthetically.

112. Italics removed from the printing of the Synod's title.

113. Italics Benedict's.

114. He writes, "We need to acknowledge the benefits that historical-critical exegesis and other recently-developed methods of textual analysis have brought to the life of the Church" (§32).

115. Italics Benedict's.

116. Contra Biblical Commission, *Interpretation*, I.A.4.

117. On the importance of reason's openness to the transcendent in Benedict's thought, see William M. Wright IV, "Echoes of Biblical Apocalyptic in the Encyclical Teaching of Benedict XVI," *Gregorianum* 95 (2014): 535–57.

118. Citing Biblical Commission, *Interpretation*, II.A.2.

119. The remainder of this paragraph is an adapted version of material, previously published in Wright, "Inspired Scripture," 178–79.

120. Benedict here cites John Paul II, *Fides et Ratio* §13.

121. Brown and Collins, "Church Pronouncements," *NJBC* 72:9 (p. 1168).

122. Very helpful here is the distinction between "historical method" and "historical model" made by Luke Timothy Johnson in *The Writings of the New Testament: An Interpretation*, 3rd ed. (Minneapolis: Fortress Press, 2010), 6–9; cf. Luke Timothy Johnson, *The Real Jesus: The Misguided Quest for the Historical Jesus and the Truth of the Traditional Gospels* (New York: HarperCollins, 1996), 81–104.

123. Joseph Ratzinger (Pope Benedict XVI), *Jesus of Nazareth*, vol. 2, *Holy Week: From the Entrance into Jerusalem to the Resurrection*, trans. Philip J. Whitmore (Vatican City and San Francisco: Libreria Editrice Vaticana and Ignatius Press, 2011), xiv.

124. See the works of Francis Martin cited in n55–58; Robert Sokolowski, *Eucharistic Presence: A Study in the Theology of Disclosure* (Washington, DC: The Catholic University of America Press, 1994), 138–58; "God's Word and Human Speech," *Nova et Vetera* (English Edition) 11 (2013): 187–210; Olivier-Thomas Venard, OP, "'La Bible en ses Traditions': The New Project of the *École biblique et archéologique française de Jérusalem* Presented as a 'Fourth-Generation' Enterprise," *Nova et Vetera* (English Edition) 4 (2006): 142–59; "Literary Mediation of Knowledge and Biblical Studies," *Nova et Vetera* (English Edition) 4 (2006): 761–86; *Pagina sacra: Le passage de l'Écriture sainte à l'écriture théologique* (Paris: Ad Solem, 2009).

125. I would like to thank Lewis Ayres, Nathan Eubank, Michael Niebauer, and Jared Wicks, SJ, for their various forms of assistance with this essay.

4

Gaudium et Spes

Thomas Joseph White, OP

What is the central subject of the *Pastoral Constitution on the Church in the Modern World* (*Gaudium et Spes*)? What is its chief significance for the Catholic Church at the beginning of the twenty-first century? Certainly these are demanding questions. The first confronts us with the issue of thematic unity in *Gaudium et Spes*. "Schema XIII," as it was called in the Conciliar years, was subject to a complex process of redaction, with diverse and multi-layered conflictual influences.[1] Identifying the profound center of the finished document is challenging. Nor can we ignore the issue of its extremely diversified reception in the years following the Council. Consider, for example, the interpretive stance of the theologian-editors of the journal *Concilium*, as contrasted with those of the journal *Communio*.[2] Most importantly, one must note the detailed interpretation that this document received in the pontificate of Pope John Paul II. Not only did he help author the *Pastoral Constitution*, but he also referred to it authoritatively many times in his magisterial teaching, a development of teaching that cannot be reduced in Catholic theology to the mere level of one theological opinion among others.[3] And yet not even a pope-saint gives the unique and final interpretation to a Council, since such a document lives on within the larger life of the Church. We are confronted, then, with a serious set of hermeneutical questions. Can we derive a unified teaching of the Council out of this complexity?

The second question raises similarly challenging issues. The *Pastoral Constitution* was composed in order to present Christianity to non-Christians in the modern world, setting forth a biblical and theological understanding of the human being (anthropology), seen in light of Christ (Christology). How truly "contemporary" is this document today, however, in light of important historical changes that have occurred since its publication? One can think here of the fall of communism, the political triumph of capitalist liberalism, the growth of Christianity in the global South, the wide-scale secularization of Europe and North America, the philosophical influence of post-modernity on ontology and ethics, the sexual revolution (stemming from the widespread use of contraception, the prevalence of abortion, co-habitation, divorce, and the increasing cultural acceptance of homosexuality), the discovery of the human genome and the bioethical practices it has given rise to, the rise of militant Islam, the widespread crisis in Catholic religious orders, the cultural transformation enacted by modern social media, especially through the use of the computer and internet. None of these events were foreseen by the Council, and all of them are more central to the culture of the twenty-first century than many of the "signs of the times" alluded to in *Gaudium et Spes.* Consequently, we may ask fairly and honestly fifty years after its publication if, despite all intentions to the contrary, the document has any unambiguous relevance to the Church in the modern world?

No single interpreter can claim to offer a comprehensive answer to these questions. Furthermore, in a domain like this one, the hermeneutical task is inevitably deeply conditioned by one's fundamental convictions regarding the nature of Catholic dogma, sacred Tradition, post-conciliar Church teaching, and the practice of Catholic theology. Not everything can be justified in the space of an essay. Therefore in the argument below certain things are presupposed: the doctrinal significance of the Second Vatican Council as a definite act of the Church inspired by the Holy Spirit, the human tensions inherent in *Gaudium et Spes* (i.e., a complex redactional history still reflected in the text), the irreversible contribution of the teaching pontificate of Pope John Paul II for a right interpretation of the document, and the perennial relevance of the scholastic ontology and theological analysis of St. Thomas Aquinas as the *Doctor Communis* of Catholic theology. *Gaudium et Spes* is arguably a very "Thomistic" document, but in what sense?[4] I will return to this issue below.

In what follows I will analyze the document in two parts, each with a view to its significance for Catholic theology in a twenty-first century setting. The first part is concerned with what I take to be the two central thematic principles: first, a Christological illumination of the human condition and of the natural law, second, a Christian anthropology of the human being made in the image of God. Here I will argue that the Council needs to be read in profound continuity with the "transformationist" accounts of grace that the Church articulated in the Council of Trent and in the condemnations of Jansenism in the seventeenth century. The "anthropological optimism" of the Pastoral Constitution can thus be read in a "hermeneutic of continuity" with the traditional theology of grace of the early modern Catholic Church, as well as her Thomistic heritage.

The second part of the essay notes key ethical teachings in *Gaudium et Spes* that inevitably will be of importance to the life of the Catholic Church in the coming century. In particular: the issue of the soteriological universality of Jesus, the contested question of what a human person is particularly in relation to the modern sciences, the nature of human marriage, the inviolable dignity of the human person in the face of new biotechnologies, and last, the promotion of a comprehensive, non-reductive political understanding of the common good.

In both of these sections I will underscore at multiple junctures why the ontology and anthropology of Aquinas are important for a balanced interpretation of *Gaudium et Spes* in its ongoing significance.

I. Central Thematic Principles

By all accounts, the goal of *Gaudium et Spes* in its final redacted form is to present to a modern audience an authentic Christian vision of the human person understood in light of the mystery of Christ, with an emphasis on common human experience as it points toward our need and capacity for redemption.[5] The document is fundamentally about theological anthropology, then, but Jesus, who is the perfect man, forms the capstone of the presentation, since all human beings—in their rational nature and deepest aspirations—can only be understood fully in the light of Christ.[6] Here we will reverse the genetic order of presentation, beginning with the Christological universalism of the Council and its understanding of human nature and grace. We can then consider the human person made "to the image of God" (*GS*, no. 12), subject to death and sin, but capable of great good, especially in the concrete order of redeemed history.

A. Christocentrism, Grace and Nature

At the center of *Gaudium et Spes* is its teaching regarding the person of Jesus Christ, as he who illumines from within the mystery of the human condition. The "Introductory Statement" of the document announces this theme unambiguously: "Under the light of Christ, the image of the unseen God, the firstborn of every creature, the council wishes to speak to all men in order to shed light on the mystery of man."[7] Of greatest significance in this respect is section 22 in the document, central to the subsequent magisterial teaching of Pope John Paul II.

Section 22 presents the essential Christological vision of *Gaudium et Spes*, and the location of the section is significant. It comes after paragraphs 12–21, which set out a fundamental theological anthropology, treating subjects such as the human being made in the image of God, the reality of sin, the essential nature of man as body and spiritual soul, the dignity of the human intellect, conscience and moral freedom, the mystery of death and various forms of atheism. These sections are comprised from a mixture of experiential observations regarding the human condition, scholastic philosophical perspectives, and biblical-theological teachings. They present the human being as possessing a nature oriented toward spiritual transcendence, but as simultaneously wounded by acute forms of moral and physical misery. The presentation of Christology is, therefore, apologetic as well as analytic: Christ helps us decrypt the enigmatic quality of human existence. The presupposition is that the human condition cannot be fully explained by natural reason alone, and we must have recourse to the revelation given in Jesus Christ.

There are two dimensions to this claim, one formal or essential and the other final or teleological. Christ reveals man to himself *essentially* because he is the perfect man. Without the mystery of Jesus, it is difficult to see perfectly well "what" the human being is. Second, Christ illumines the mystery of the human condition *teleologically* because the deepest desire of the human heart objectively tends toward beatitude or ultimate happiness in God alone, and only in the grace of Christ does this desire find its existentially adequate rest:

> The truth is that only in the mystery of the incarnate Word does the mystery of man take on light. For Adam, the first man, was a figure of Him Who was to come, namely Christ the Lord. Christ, the final Adam, by the revelation of the mystery of the Father and His love, fully reveals man to man himself and makes his supreme calling clear. It is not surprising, then, that in Him all the aforementioned truths find their root and attain their crown. He Who is "the image of the invisible God" (Col. 1:15), is Himself the perfect man. . . . He restores the divine likeness which had been disfigured from the first sin onward. Since human nature as He assumed it was not annulled, by that very fact it has been raised up to a divine dignity in our respect too. For by His incarnation the Son of God has united Himself in some fashion with every man. He worked with human hands, He thought with a human mind, acted by human choice and loved with a human heart. Born of the Virgin Mary, He has truly been made one of us, like us in all things except sin. (*GS*, no. 22)

We should note several theological claims that are made in this important passage. First, Christ who is both God and man reveals the human being's nature to himself *in its originally intended integrity*, not affected by sin, but whole and entire, subject to God and at the service of the authentic love of other human beings. What human nature is essentially is accessible to us most perfectly or "formally" in the historical mystery of Christ.

Second, however, the nature in question does not exist concretely without grace, nor was it ever meant to. Here the Council alludes implicitly to an important medieval debate. In the thirteenth century, Catholic theologians differed on the question of whether angels and men were first created "in a state of grace" or whether they were first created "in a state of pure nature" (i.e., absent the gift of grace) and offered grace only subsequently.[8] St. Bonaventure, for example, held the latter position.[9] Aquinas, however, argued for the former position.[10] The Council seems clearly to follow an opinion closer to that of St. Thomas.[11] The paragraph just cited clearly implies that in Jesus we see what human nature was meant to be "from the beginning" in a historical state of grace. Human beings existing without grace, then, exist in a wounded or incomplete state, not *naturally or formally incomplete*, but affected in their *mode of being* and as regards their *true end*, which is found in God alone. Christ has *essentially* the same human nature as Adam, who is wounded by the consequences of sin, but Christ possesses this nature in a restored, sinless *state* or *mode*.[12] Just as grace does not destroy human nature but heals and elevates it, so the human life Jesus possesses is more *naturally* perfect because it is free from sin, and the most perfectly *graced* human life.[13]

Third, then, this anthropological truth points us toward the significance of the language of "the mystery of man." "Mystery" is a technical term pertaining to Catholic theology, denoting a reality that transcends the knowledge available to unaided human reason. It indicates something that is intelligible only due to the gift of supernatural faith, which grants insight into the special effects of God's work of grace and sanctification in Christ.[14] Considered philosophically, the nature of the human being is not a "mystery" in the strong sense (but perhaps an "enigma"). What is denoted here, then, is not human nature per se, but human nature receiving the divine gift of filial adoption in grace, and the supernatural beatitude toward which that grace tends. The human being is made for the supernatural vision of God, a mystery that can only be discovered by the grace of faith. The grace of Christ thus reveals something present in a hidden way within the fundamental experience of man: that we were meant to live in a higher friendship of life with God. The destiny, or teleological end of the human person, is made manifest to us in the Incarnation and the Paschal Mystery.[15]

Last, we can note the explicit universality of the teaching under consideration. "[B]y His incarnation the Son of God has united Himself in some fashion with every man" (*Gaudium et Spes*, no. 22). Here we touch upon the question of the *extension* of the grace of Christ. The next section of the document could not be more explicit:

> The Christian man, conformed to the likeness of that Son Who is the firstborn of many brothers, received "the first-fruits of the Spirit" (Rom. 8:23) by which he becomes capable of discharging the new law of love. . . . Pressing upon the Christian to be sure, are the need and the duty to battle against evil through manifold tribulations and even to suffer death. But, linked with the paschal mystery and patterned on the dying Christ, he will hasten forward to resurrection in the strength which comes from hope. All this holds true not only for Christians, but for all men of good will in whose hearts grace works in an unseen way. For, since Christ died for all men, and since the ultimate vocation of man is in fact one, and divine, we ought to believe that the Holy Spirit in a manner known to God offers to every man the possibility of being associated with this paschal mystery. (*Gaudium et Spes*, no. 22)

Here we come to the heart of the matter. The grace of Christ is at work in the world in hidden ways, even outside the visible life of the Catholic Church and the sacraments. We should note various features of the universal vision of Christological grace promoted in the Council. First, it is grounded in the principled developments of early modern Catholic theology of the sixteenth and seventeenth centuries. The key doctrinal touchstone is one that was articulated during the seventeenth century in the time of the Jansenist controversies. Jansenius in his *Augustinus* was condemned by the Catholic Church for teaching a doctrine of "restricted atonement," the idea that Christ did not die for all human beings, but only for the elect, those who are predestined and who persevere in the grace of God.[16] At the Council of Trent, the Catholic Church had already clarified (against contrary affirmations of Calvin and Luther) that the grace of God can be offered to human beings who refuse or resist it, thus reiterating a biblical notion and traditional teaching of medieval Catholic theology.[17] In the Jansenist controversy, then, the idea was taken a step further in an organic fashion. Christ has died for all human beings, and consequently all human beings are offered the possibility of salvation by the hidden workings of the grace of God, down through history. If some human beings are not saved, this is not because they were not offered the grace that could lead them to salvation, but because they refused or resisted this grace culpably.[18]

What the Council does with this traditional teaching is to interpret it in a social, dynamic, and historical way. The grace of Christ is at work in the whole historical sweep of human life and society. Just as our human nature is not meant to exist outside of the sphere of a relationship with God in the order of grace, so concrete history is a place where fallen human nature is perpetually affected in concrete ways by the hidden presence and work of grace.[19] Consequently, the broad anthropological vision that *Gaudium et Spes* promotes is not purely "philosophical" but profoundly theological in kind. Even secular modern human beings are not only made for God (whether they acknowledge it or not) but are moved interiorly by the occasional promptings of grace. This is true for us not only as individuals but also in our communitarian nature, and so it occurs in and through the fabric of human culture. The hidden work of grace can be promoted in and through the spiritual forces of culture (be they religious, political, or artistic), but it can also be resisted and thwarted by those same forces as well.

Consequently, the teaching of *Gaudium et Spes* does not mean to suggest that all human beings are in a state of grace independently of their moral condition or the presence and absence of Christian faith, nor should it be taken to suggest that the visible Catholic Church is merely one manifestation of grace or one visible way toward union with God among others.[20] Least of all should it be interpreted to affirm that every instance of human culture is the latest manifestation of the zeitgeist of the Holy Spirit in history.[21]

On the contrary, the thinking in this text is profoundly ecclesiocentric. Its necessary parallel text in Vatican II—without which it cannot be rightly interpreted—is found in *Lumen Gentium*, no. 14–16. There we find the ancient dictum "No salvation outside the Church" reaffirmed, but also rearticulated positively. All those who are saved are saved by the grace of Christ, and in direct relationship, and by eventual incorporation into, the visible Catholic Church (whether in this life of the next).[22] The teaching of *Lumen Gentium* then goes on to draw a set of concentric circles around the visible Catholic Church as so many exterior "ripples" where the grace of Christ *might be present* throughout the historical and social sphere of human culture. First in the Eastern Orthodox Churches, then the Protestant ecclesial communities, then in non-Christian monotheists (Jews, then Muslims), in other religious traditions (Hinduism, Buddhist wisdom traditions), and in various spheres of secular humanism where human beings genuinely seek to find the truth and to accomplish the moral good, in response to the hidden action of the grace of God.[23] The presupposition is that the fullness of the means of salvation are found in the visible communion of the Catholic Church, but that elements of Catholic sacramental life and teaching can be found in different degrees in communities, cultures, and individuals outside the visible Church.[24] Grace can be operative in those domains of human society in ways that are more seemingly evident or more hidden. It must be noted that the teaching in *Lumen Gentium* does not ignore the real possibility of eternal damnation that threatens each human being, and it clearly intimates that this danger exists more concretely the more the person is estranged from the ordinary means of salvation that are to be found in the visible Catholic Church, her teaching, and her sacraments.[25]

If we pair these two texts together, then we see that the vision is at once deeply Christocentric and ecclesiocentric. Christ has died for all human beings. The grace of God has always been active in the world, both prior to and subsequent to the time of the coming of Christ, who came to call all human beings into the visible communion of the Catholic Church, the body of Christ. Grace does continue to work in the lives of all human beings, even outside the sphere of the visible Church, and can do so more profoundly there where deeper elements of Christian and religious truth are to be found. However, where the grace of the Holy Spirit is present, it is also "tendential," calling all human beings inwardly toward ontological conformity to the Paschal Mystery of Jesus, and toward the visible communion of the Catholic Church.[26] All grace is not only mediated by the sacred humanity of Jesus, who died for all, but is also ordered in its effects toward the sacramental life of the visible Church, the mystical body of Christ.

Two important principles follow from this theological perspective, both of which impact directly the anthropology of *Gaudium et Spes*. The first we might call a modern apologetic point. The Council wishes to underscore that the widespread modern aspiration to some form of universal secular humanism has many positive features, but that no fully authentic humanism can exist other than one that is Christian.[27] The reason for this is that the grace that alone heals our wounded human nature effectively is found only in Christ and within the ambit of the sacramental economy that derives from him.

Here we can see the overtly "restorationist" aim of *Gaudium et Spes*: the Council aspires to a harmony of Church and state that respects the distinction between the two, but that also envisages Catholic Christianity as the deepest formative element within the moral conscience of any authentically moral civilization.[28] This harmony is not cast in the traditional terms of establishment Christianity and pre-revolutionary, monarchical government. Rather, it is envisaged within the context of modern secular governments in which some form of separation of Church and state is a de facto given, but in which theological faith and the motivations of charity are permitted to *inform from within* the activity of Christians in the civil sphere.[29] We should note the conceptual harmony between this idea and the one we find in *Dignitatis Humanae* regarding both the rights of the Church to preach the Gospel within the civil sphere, and regarding the rights of the religious conscience of each human person within the context of a secularized, pluralistic society.[30] The presupposition is not that all religious traditions are equal, or that they are equally irrelevant to human flourishing. On the contrary, the theological presupposition of *Gaudium et Spes* is that in the concrete fallen state we live in, the graces transmitted from within a Catholic ethos are the condition sine qua non for the ethical transformation of humanity according to our own best capacities and desires. While secular European humanism may aspire to certain goals that are noble and authentic, the purification, plenary identification, and effective realization of those same aspirations are only possible with Christ.

Second, it also follows from the principles of grace and nature mentioned above that the presentation of "natural law" given in *Gaudium et Spes* is complex. On the one hand, the Council does appeal unambiguously to a wide variety of principles drawn from the natural law, as well as to the overarching notion of universal natural law, which is mentioned several times.[31] On the other hand, the principles we have noted above would suggest that the natural moral law—inscribed in the human being both by natural inclination and reflexive conscience—can be rendered obscure to the human intelligence in the fallen state.[32] Catholic theologians classically have held a wide variety of permitted opinions on this subject. Aquinas himself is willing to envisage a fairly radical erosion of the true perception of the moral law in human hearts dimmed by sin, at least in many times and places.[33] However, the radical *capacity* or potency for moral awareness does remain endemic to natural human reason, and grace can act within the moral conscience to restore and heal the full scope of moral practical reasoning, from the clear perception of first principles ("do good and avoid evil"), to middle-term principles ("never take innocent human life"), to the extension to particular cases ("never kill innocent human life in the womb at any stage, and no matter what circumstances obtain").[34]

What this means is that there is no profound discord or methodological inconsistency in the teaching of *Gaudium et Spes*. The document enunciates moral teachings regarding just war, the human family, the inviolable dignity of human life, sound principles of economic practice, the right to education, and so forth, which are considered universal and naturally accessible to human reason in ways formally distinct from revelation.[35] The document also underscores the significance of the grace of Christ for a right understanding of the moral principles of human civilization, such that only in the light of Christ is man able to perceive fully the dignity of his moral vocation to contribute ethically to the common good.[36] The presupposition here is neither that non-Christians are wholly immoral (an exaggerated theory of radical depravity) or that Christianity alone by divine revelation provides the premises of the moral law (an exaggerated form of revelatory positivism and practical fideism). Rather, the presupposition is that man has in his nature as such essential inclinations toward life in society and the moral law, which remain intact in the fallen state, but that these inclinations are *wounded* and rendered in great part *ineffective* due to the effects of personal and social sin.[37] Consequently, they can only be fully awakened and effectively realized under the influences of the grace of Christ. This rendering of the human condition is not particularly novel. It seems to constitute a creative representation in a modern setting of the classical teaching of Aquinas, although similar ideas can be found in both late medieval and early modern Catholic scholastic literature.[38]

B. Anthropology: Sin, Grace, and Transformation in Modern Catholicism

I have argued above that the theological anthropology of *Gaudium et Spes* must be interpreted in the light of its Christology, and the universalist doctrine of operative grace that it espouses. However, this also means that this anthropology must be understood in light of thematic notions of original sin, and the necessary role of grace in the healing and elevation of human personal and spiritual acts and operations.

It is at this juncture that we do well to note the deep points of continuity between the teaching of *Gaudium et Spes* and the measured doctrines of human fallenness and of the transformative power of grace that were formulated doctrinally by the Catholic Church in the sixteenth century at the Council of Trent. We have already noted the line of interpretation that leads from the condemnations of Jansenism to the espousal of the universality of the doctrine of grace (and its resistibility). Those same seventeenth-century debates were echoes of the earlier disputes between Rome and the Reformers. Most notably, the questions arose as to whether the fallen human being was capable of aspiring effectively to any moral good whatsoever (a question that radical Augustinians tended to answer negatively) and whether the human being was justified by faith alone (the Lutheran doctrine of "*sola fidei*") or whether justification also entailed the transformation of the human will by the infused virtues of theological hope and charity.[39] The Council of Trent unequivocally stated the matter thus: in the economy of salvation, the human being is not so radically depraved as to be incapable of some basic natural desires and choices in view of some authentic natural moral goods.[40] Likewise, the human being is placed "in a state of grace" or rendered justified not by faith alone, but only by faith, hope, and love, transforming the human intellect *and will* from within.[41] We might note the *moderate* optimism regarding *both* fallen human nature *and* the Christian life under grace that these two distinct teachings represent. To this we can add a third idea related to the grace-universalism noted above: the Council of Trent insisted that human beings can (at times at least) refuse or resist graces offered to them by God (against the Lutheran and Calvinist insistence on irresistible grace and the selective offer of grace only to the predestined).[42]

If we resituate these various ideas within the context of *Gaudium et Spes*, we can interpret correctly the anthropological principles of that document. Clearly the Council Fathers wished to acknowledge many positive inclinations toward the good that are present in the modern secular age.[43] It is not always clear which of these inclinations spring concretely from the impulses of grace operating in the theater of human history, and which spring from the fundamentally good orientations that remain within (non-radically depraved) human nature. However, it is clear that much that the Council underscores (the good of political peace, the nature of human marriage, the right to education) pertains to goods that human beings can aspire to *imperfectly* even in a fallen state. Correspondingly, then, the document also emphasizes wounds of sin that haunt the human heart and undermine the human aspirations toward authentic love, political progress, and so forth. The reality of original sin is admitted and integrated into the overall perspective of the document.[44] Finally, there is the "answer" of grace that is able to heal the wounds of sin, and transform the human condition internally by the virtues of hope and charity. And thus the specific difference of *Christian* humanism: charity is at the heart of the social ethic that the Church proposes to the world, both individually and collectively.[45]

It is in light of this modern Catholic theology of the effects of original sin as wounds (rather than radical depravity) and of grace as transformative (rather than merely declarative or forensic) that we can make a great deal of sense of the anthropology of *Gaudium et Spes*. The human being is able in part to understand the meaning of his life, but remains a question or enigma to himself (*Gaudium et Spes*, no. 10). As rational animals, we are made in the Image of God, invited by grace into communion with God and other persons (no. 12). And yet:

> Examining his heart, man finds that he has inclinations toward evil too, and is engulfed by manifold ills which cannot come from his good Creator.... As a result, all of human life, whether individual or collective, shows itself to be a dramatic struggle between good and evil, between light and darkness. Indeed, man finds that by himself he is incapable of battling the assaults of evil successfully, so that everyone feels as though he is bound by chains. (no. 13)

The human being can be identified by reason as a composite being, one entity consisting of both a spiritual soul and an animal body, the soul being the form of the body (no. 14). As such, the human being is made to seek the truth in reality, and is capable of profound moral interiority (no. 15–16). He or she is endowed with the dignity of freedom in his or her decision-making (no. 17), and yet he is also subject to death, which makes the spiritual character of his existence enigmatic (no. 18). The human being is ordered toward life in society (no. 31), and yet the permanent temptations to individualistic selfishness and collective tribalism always risk undermining the right understanding and effective realization of the common good (no. 41–43). All of these characterizations, then, are reminiscent of Pascal's Augustinian apologetics.[46] The human being is subject to profound tensions, between spiritual desires and temporal needs, between embodied existence-unto-death and the desire for eternal life, between the dignity of individual freedom of conscience and collective participation in the common good, between the collective ethical strivings of humanity throughout history, and the profound, perpetual human complicity with sin and evil. The answer to this tension is the mystery of Christ, whose life and whose grace alone can resolve the paradox of human existence, especially in and through the ecclesial form of life in charity:

> Christ, to be sure, gave His Church no proper mission in the political, economic or social order. The purpose which He set before her is a religious one. But out of this religious mission itself come a function, a light and an energy which can serve to structure and consolidate the human community according to the divine law. . . . The Church recognizes that worthy elements are found in today's social movements, especially an evolution toward unity, a process of wholesome socialization and of association in civic and economic realms. The promotion of unity belongs to the innermost nature of the Church, for she is, "thanks to her relationship with Christ, a sacramental sign and an instrument of intimate union with God, and of the unity of the whole human race" (*Lumen Gentium*, no. 1). Thus she shows the world that an authentic union, social and external, results from a union of minds and hearts, namely from that faith and charity by which her own unity is unbreakably rooted in the Holy Spirit. For the force which the Church can inject into the modern society of man consists in that faith and charity put into vital practice, not in any external dominion exercised by merely human means. (*Gaudium et Spes*, no. 42)

Here, then, we arrive at the heart of what is sometimes perceived to be the optimism in the document *Gaudium et Spes*. In fact, we may speak rightly of "a tale of two optimisms" that are distinct in the text. The fundamental "optimism" is grounded in a traditional Catholic vision of the transformative dimensions of grace. Grace when it is fully at work in the world does internally heal, renew, and elevate all human actions from within, especially by the infused habit of charity, in such a way as to transform not only individuals, but the social character of human existence and the fundamental orientation of human life in society.[47] This kind of "optimism" has roots in the Church fathers (Greek and Latin), the Thomist doctrine of grace, and the teachings of the Council of Trent. It is applied by the Second Vatican Council to modern secular society in a more social and historical way, but in a manner that is arguably consonant with what has come before.

The second "optimism" would regard the viability of promoting this vision of grace-nature integration and of "Catholic humanism" in the context of mid-twentieth-century, post-World War II, modern secular Europe. Clearly the Council fathers did aspire optimistically to promote an alternative vision of modern social life that would contrast both with emergent atheist communism and with the idea of a return to the establishment Catholicism of the pre-revolutionary monarchical age. This second form of optimism may have been warranted within the context of the Christian democratic socialism emergent in Germany, France, and Italy in the 1950s and '60s. Whether it was in fact warranted or not, one could argue that the grounds for such optimism of a profound Church-state harmony in Europe and the Americas have largely evaporated in the fifty years following the Council, due to the intensive secularization that has taken place in those regions.

Even if such political judgments were unwarranted, however, the "first order optimism" of the ideal of the transformation of the human community by the power of grace remains normative for Catholic theological anthropology. This is why one might argue that there is in some real sense a *profound and strict continuity of principles* between the theological vision of *Gaudium et Spes* and the moral vision of Pope John Paul II, who made such extensive appeal to the Pastoral Constitution. For example, in *Redemptor Hominis* he appealed to the document in order to underscore—against the Soviet communist regime—the requirement that every government respect the human dignity of its subjects and permit a legitimate participation of all citizens in the public life of the nation.[48] This freedom is grounded, he insisted, on the freedom of the human being to respond to the call of grace that is given to each human person by virtue of the incarnation of God in history.[49]

Likewise, in *Veritatis Splendor*, the same pope made an appeal to the anthropology of the human conscience from *Gaudium et Spes* so as to oppose theoretical relativism and to affirm that grace works in the intellect and heart of each human being, calling them to respond in implicit or explicit ways to the natural inclinations of the moral law, and to the natural promptings of the moral conscience.[50] In *Evangelium Vitae*, he appealed to the Constitution's notion of each person's inherent human dignity from conception until natural death, which can be recognized by natural reason, and which is the basis for the declaration in *Gaudium et Spes* that "abortion and infanticide are unspeakable crimes" (no. 51).[51] In each of these cases, the post-conciliar teaching of Pope John Paul II appeals in reality *to the anthropological optimism of the Council and of traditional Catholic theology*, which affirms that the human being and human culture more generally truly can be transformed by grace and by the power of charity, including through the rational recognition and effective, freely chosen realization of the norms of the natural law. It is because of the recognition of this principle of optimism (the transformative power of grace) that this pope could call the largely altered moral terrain of Western Europe and the Americas a "culture of death" in light of the widespread practice of technological abortion.[52] Such a terminology does not represent a break from the teaching of *Gaudium et Spes*, but a very accurate and faithful rendering of its essential teaching in a distinct, profoundly altered context and circumstances. Similar things could be said of the defense of Christian marriage as a sacramental, indissoluble bond, consisting in the union of one man and one women and open to life through the procreation and education of children.[53] This teaching, also avidly elaborated throughout the course of the pontificate of John Paul II, has its most proximate modern doctrinal grounding in the explicit teaching of *Gaudium et Spes*, and the traditional and Tridentine vision that it contains of the power of charity to transform the natural good of marriage sacramentally.[54]

This is not to say that all the notes of "second order optimism" regarding the compatibility of Catholicism with the modern secular ethos need simply to be dismissed within the context of post-conciliar developments in human culture. There are many places where the aspirations of the council and those of modern secular liberalism may still overlap at least in modest ways. However, on the reading I am offering, it is simply not realistic to say that the aspirations of the prevalent zeitgeist of modern secular liberalism somehow transmit historically the inner essence of the aspirations of *Gaudium et Spes*, nor that the Pastoral Constitution aspired fundamentally toward this kind of naïve, Pelagian historicism.[55] To make either affirmation (stemming either from uncritical progressivism or excessively despairing traditionalism) is to read the Council outside of the context of previous Catholic tradition and thought, thus consigning it (in one way or another) to inevitable theological irrelevance. Since this instinct is most certainly not in concordance with authentic Catholic theology and spirituality, it is to be dismissed, and the reading I am offering should be granted a cogency and vitality that is not present in either of these alternative, intellectually unviable options.

II. Central Ethical Topics

If what we have argued up to this juncture is true, then a fundamental question still remains as to what significance the deep Christological and anthropological principles of *Gaudium et Spes* could have in the era of the Church that is currently emerging. What importance does the reception of the document have to the Catholic Church in the twenty-first-century modern world? Here we should turn to the principles of natural law that the document emphasizes (in the light of Christology and a Catholic humanism of grace). Where do these principles clearly continue to speak to the contemporary tensions in Catholicism's internal identity and theology and to the missionary challenges and possibilities of the Church in her modern cultural setting? Here I will not attempt to draw up a comprehensive list, but will only identify briefly five "poles" or areas of tension that were mentioned in the introduction to this essay: (1) the issue of the soteriological universality of Jesus, (2) the contested question of what a human person is particularly in relation to the modern sciences, (3) the nature of human marriage, (4) the inviolable dignity of the human person in the face of new biotechnologies, and (5) the promotion of a comprehensive, non-reductive political understanding of the common good. I will say a brief word concerning each of these topics, indicating ways that the teaching of *Gaudium et Spes* should continue to inspire and guide Catholic thinking in each of these domains.

A. *The Soteriological Universality of Jesus*

The edifice of *Gaudium et Spes* stands or falls on the presupposition of its Christology and the universality of the vision of grace and humanity that it affords. And yet we can immediately note a central difficulty that this raises in a contemporary context. The core aspiration of post-Enlightenment, modern liberalism is to create a form of government and a conception of individual and state rights that is free from any immediate dependence upon religious confessional commitments. (This is the case generally, whether or not a particular post-Enlightenment government or culture tends to be more welcoming or hostile to the Catholic tradition.) Furthermore, in many contemporary secular governments, there is an increasing tendency to preclude any normative, public appeal to moral commitments derived *even indirectly* from the Christian tradition. This problem is compounded by the fear of inter-religious strife, particularly due to conflicts that arise between Muslim cultures and Western liberal states, and due to the perceived necessity of a secularization model for international relations that can keep at bay the negative effects of religious violence, while making space for the very real religious pluralism that characterizes the inhabitants of modern democracies and their existentially sustaining financial markets, which require civic concord for their stability.

In this context, how is the Christocentricism of *Gaudium et Spes* meant to function meaningfully? Here we might answer briefly by noting two important principles. First, Catholic Christocentrism cannot be dissolved profitably by modern theologians into a general religious anthropology. Here I mean that the Catholic tradition rightly eschews all attempts to reduce the Incarnation and the uniqueness of Jesus Christ into a mere symbol of a more general process of grace acting in all human beings, of which Christ is only the deepest or most intensive instantiation. This latter strategy was attempted by nineteenth-century modern Protestantism (for example, in Friedrich Schleiermacher) and it can be found (at least according to certain readings) in the transcendental anthropology of Karl Rahner.[56] Such theologies might hold that Jesus is only the most intensive realization of the ethical religious life, under grace, so that there is merely a difference of degree between his grace and that of all other persons, not a difference of kind (i.e., the grace of hypostatic union).[57] It is a short step from this theology to one that sees in the Christian tradition only one vehicle for the salvation of human beings, alongside and in some ways equal to the mediations provided by other religious traditions, their founders, and their sacred texts.[58] If Christ is only a particular instantiation of holiness alongside others, and if the Church is only one collective witness to the work of grace in history among others, then the vision of *Gaudium et Spes* breaks down fundamentally.

Against this threat, then, we can see the profound continuity between the vision of the Council and the pivotal doctrinal document, *Dominus Iesus*, in 2000, which emphasized the centrality and uniqueness of Christ as the God-man and of the soteriological uniqueness of his life, death, and resurrection.[59] This document also emphasized, of course, that the Catholic Church was founded by Christ and is the unique authentic locus in which the objective plenitude of the visible means of salvation is fully realized and maintained.[60] Far from being in discord with the teaching of the Pastoral Constitution, *this doctrinal teaching is its very presupposition and center, without which the document loses all unity and teaching authority.*

Second, then, we might speak of two forms of imbalance that a right interpretation of *Gaudium et Spes* must avoid in a contemporary context. The first would result from opposing the mystery of grace with the principles of human nature, and of opposing Christology with general anthropology, particularly within the context of the relationship between the Church and modern secular culture. Such an imbalance would obtain if one were *either* to claim that in a post-religious age the teachings of the natural law are *wholly inaccessible* to human reason, save from within the domain of faith alone, and by virtue of the work of grace, *or* if one were to hold that the natural law can be "read off" of the climate of contemporary secularism, as if the cultural "progress" of post-religious society should basically dictate evolving moral norms to the Catholic tradition which should in turn assimilate them passively. The first stance implies an unwarranted fideism (a kind of pure grace-extrinsicism) while the latter typically entails a progressivist capitulation to various errors of secular, anti-Christian culture (a kind of Pelagian intrinsicism). The vision of *Gaudium et Spes* rightly underscores that a non-religious liberalism is necessarily incomplete, wounded, and profoundly blind as to the true destiny of man, but that the grace of Christ also addresses the heart of modern man by speaking directly to his own desires for happiness, moral responsibility, forgiveness, and human meaning.[61] There are no simple solutions, then, to the tension between the Church and the modern secular state. Modern evangelization must make manifest to human beings that their authentic salvation and enduring happiness are only made possible by life in Christ.

Analogously, the Church has to enunciate a form of humanism within a modern context that makes room for Christian confessional identity within pluralistic cultures and in the face of secular governments. She must do so while also challenging both Christians and non-Christian religionists to forms of peaceful co-existence that respect the civic rights of non-religious persons and that allow for genuine presentation of and discussion between religious alternatives in accord with the differentiated consciences of diverse citizens.[62] In short, the Church has to mediate between the extreme of a secular anti-religious mentality that would constrict religious freedom unduly, and various forms of anti-liberal religious absolutism that would seek to deny de jure any possibility of civic co-existence between diverse religious and non-religious sub-cultures.

In all these domains, no political utopianism is possible, but the principles elaborated by the Pastoral Constitution can be upheld in ways that are meaningful and powerful, in a context very different from that in which the document was originally drafted.

B. What is a Human Person?

At the center of *Gaudium et Spes* is a conception of the human person made in the Image of God, and characterized by human spiritual faculties of intellect and will. Consequently, as a unified soul-body composite, the human person enjoys a substantive dignity that is unique to man as a spiritual animal.[63] This conception of the person is primarily metaphysical, but of course it has important ethical consequences.

The challenge that this Christian vision of the human person faces in a contemporary context stems from the important expansion of modern scientific knowledge about the cosmos and the human body that has been produced over the past 150 years. Most specifically, modern big-bang cosmology, evolutionary theory, genetic discovery, and cognitive neuro-science all heavily condition the fundamental understanding of the human being that is communicated typically within the context of the modern Western university system. Does the traditional Christian vision of the human person that *Gaudium et Spes* elaborates stand in fundamental tension with the progress and insights of the modern sciences and the history of the cosmos and of evolving life forms that the sciences seek to identify in increasing degrees of explanation and detail?[64]

The answer to this question should be negative, but only if it is based upon a conditional set of premises. There is no inherent conflict between traditional Christian anthropology and the modern scientific ethos, so long as one establishes a series of responsible philosophical mediations along the way in the conversation between the two disciplines. Here the retrieval of themes that are central to Thomism is essential to the future health of Catholic theology in a scientific age. Aquinas's followers typically insist upon the distinct methodologies of theology, philosophy, and natural sciences, as objectively differentiated but also profoundly inter-related forms of scientific learning.[65] If the modern sciences obtain to a certain "level" of reality in accord with their premises and methods, they do not replace the distinctive vantage point of philosophy, particularly the analyses of the philosophy of nature and metaphysics.[66] These disciplines analyze reality at a deeper level or a more intensive degree of depth than the modern sciences, and in turn demonstrate the possibility of discourse about immaterial realties, such as the soul and God the creator. In this way, they also "make room" for the rational possibility of revealed knowledge of God and the human person, and the "science" of theology that stems from the analysis of divine revelation.[67]

The recovery in modernity of a profound, non-reductive vision of the human person requires a return to this more inclusive, sapiential vision of human learning that integrates the full sweep of modern scientific learning into a deeper philosophical and metaphysical analysis of reality, and that distinguishes this in turn from the knowledge of God and creation that is obtained only by revelation, but which also insists that Christian theology assimilate in a non-reductive way the plenary acquisitions of modern science and sound perennial philosophy. In the absence of this kind of broader vision of human learning, what results is a terrible disjuncture between a modern scientistic culture that has a wholly inadequate, reductive vision of the human person, and a religious personalism that is fideistic and rationally arbitrary, and which communicates the idea that religious notions of human dignity are rationally arbitrary and anti-scientific. Within this context, the intellectual heritage of the Catholic scholastic tradition is precious for its capacity to see the deeper harmony that exists among the sciences and to mediate between the false extremes that risk undermining the spiritual unity of modern intellectual life.

C. *The Nature of Human Marriage*

Gaudium et Spes's substantive teaching on the natural and sacramental dimensions of marriage (no. 47–52) followed after Pius XI's famous encyclical *Casti Connubii* (1930), building upon many of the premises of that document. Both documents attempt to find a "middle way" that affirms, on the one hand, the traditional teaching that the generation and education of children is the true, final end of marriage, and which, on the other hand, affirms the inherent meaningfulness and value of the friendship of the spouses and their shared conjugal life together. *Casti Connubii* did this by speaking of diverse "ends" of marriage in which some were subordinate to or ordered toward others, such that the unitive dimension of the marriage might be ordered ultimately toward its procreative dimension.[68] *Gaudium et Spes* famously dropped the language of multiple ends, and resorted instead to the mature teaching on Aquinas on marriage, in which the conjugal friendship of the two spouses is seen as the "formal cause" or essence of the marriage, while children and their education are seen as the "final cause," or teleological end of the friendship.[69] On this rendering, the friendship of the spouses and their conjugal life cannot be maintained essentially, or integrally, unless their conjugal life is ordered toward the transmission of life.[70] Metaphysically speaking, the formal cause is "for" or "in view of" the final cause, and so ethically and psychologically, the essence of a marriage changes if procreation is not intended in the union. But at the same time, if the couple wishes to have children but are involuntarily infertile, the essence of marriage is still present formally, even if this friendship cannot attain the ultimate perfection that it aspires to. Aquinas's definition, which the Pastoral Constitution seems to adopt, has the advantage of identifying a kind of relative integrity to the friendship of the spouses while also maintaining plausibly that the goal of conceiving and raising children is at the heart of the friendship and of the marital nature of the conjugal act.

Gaudium et Spes was not meant to provoke controversy on the topic of marriage, even if the Council fathers were well aware of attempts by nineteenth-century European states and of various twentieth-century communist regimes to redefine marriage civilly in ways that trampled upon the Church's teaching and sacramental authority.[71] However, it is unquestionably the case that the teaching of the Council on this point is in the twenty-first century context irreducibly traditional in nature, and inherently controversial. This is due, not least, to the widespread prevalence in modern culture of divorce as well as same-sex marriage, to say nothing of contraception. Each of these practices presumes a definition of marriage that radically contrasts with that of the Catholic tradition and of the natural law as traditionally conceived.

It is at this juncture that the tension between the natural law teaching in the Pastoral Constitution and its Christocentric doctrine of grace becomes most acutely felt and most interesting. For on the one hand, there is a clear basis in sound philosophy and in traditional Catholic theology for the affirmation that human marriage (traditionally conceived, between one man and one woman for life, open to the bearing and raising of children) is an institution that is fundamentally natural to human beings, and that is the foundation of any civic polity, presupposed by the state as its genuine basis.[72] On the other hand, in a culture in which the traditional forms of marriage are genuinely threatened and eroded existentially, can genuine human marriage be even rightly understood, let alone lived out effectively, without the revelation and grace of Jesus Christ, and the explicit knowledge of the mystery of the Church and the sacraments?[73] Contemporary Catholic theology will continue to develop thinking precisely on this topic as the nexus of debates on nature and grace, faith and the natural law, Church and state, sacrament and civic society. We may conclude, however, with two central ideas.

First, Aquinas's definition is of the utmost importance for any right understanding of the Council in a modern context. If procreation *is not* the unique ultimate end of marriage, then the traditional definition of marriage and the Church's longstanding moral reflection on the subject become unintelligible. But *because it is the case* that procreation is the final end of marriage, *therefore* the essence of the conjugal friendship between the spouses as *married* spouses must be heterosexual, open to life, exclusive, and permanent. The internal logic of the Church's teaching as a rational perception into the essence of marriage and its dignity can only be maintained if this teleological conception of marriage is rightly maintained.

Second, Aquinas's doctrine of the wounds of nature is most pertinent to the consideration of this teaching within the context of a skeptical, secular age. St. Thomas rightly underscores that the wounds of original sin do not obliterate the inclinations toward basic human goods, such as the good of procreation and life in the family.[74] However, these inclinations can be weakened in their moral center, and the intellectual perception of them as goods (both theoretically and practically) can be deeply compromised by the indulgence of intemperate passions and the dissemination of erroneous teaching.[75] If this is true, then the remedies to a false or superficial under-standing of the nature of marriage are not the remedies of grace and faith alone, nor of rational instruction and philosophical reason, but of both simultaneously. Just as the Council prolongs the Church's anti-Jansenist insistence on the universal, hidden presence of operative grace, so it is pos-sible to believe with *Gaudium et Spes* that hidden graces from Christ can accompany the teaching of the natural law, helping the human mind to see its inherent natural truth.[76] Likewise, an integral presentation of the Gospel is accepted not only in faith, but invites human reason to cooperate fully with the mystery of the faith by means of a philosophically grounded under-standing of the moral teachings of the Catholic Church. Faith and reason work as an ellipse with two foci, in which the intellect moves fluidly from one to another, and not in a form of dialectic that would oppose revelation with natural law reasoning, placing the entire weight of the enterprise only upon one side of the polarity.

D. *Technology and the Dignity of Human Life*

The Council fathers were virtually unanimous in their desire to respond theo-logically to anthropological questions arising from developments in modern technology. Already in no. 5–6, *Gaudium et Spes* discusses population growth, industrialization, urbanization, modern social media, and the new income inequalities that arise from historic changes in human society. Eventually the document also addresses the topics of total war and atomic weaponry, the potentially harmful effects of widespread use of artificial birth control, philo-sophical positivism and the skeptical mentality it creates, and the dangers of a cultural preference for technological innovation over the transmission of a patrimony of wisdom.[77] In all of this, the Council contains its own original theological echoes of Martin Heidegger, who warned that the rise of techno-logical progress in modernity could also lead to an eclipse of philosophical contact with the deeper meaning of existence.[78]

One can only think that this aspect of *Gaudium et Spes* is of equal or greater relevance to modern culture fifty years after the conclusion of the Council. No doubt the development of technology has done an immense amount to assist in the widespread fostering of human health, agricultural productivity, educa-tion, and wealth creation, as well as media information and a sense of com-mon human solidarity across time and place. However, we must also note the ecological crises that have arisen in the face of modern industrialization, the problems of serious economic imbalances that can be created in an interde-pendent, worldwide economy, brutal forms of modern technological warfare and terrorism, the morally damaging effects of modern reproductive technolo-gies, genetic testing and the widespread prevalence of abortion, mass internet use (often in substitution for contact with classical sources of culture), and pornography addictions that risk undermining healthy relationships between the sexes. Technology is not an indiscriminate good in the modern age.

Here the aspirations of the Council are greatly helped by recourse to the eudaimonist ethics of the Thomist tradition.[79] The latter emphasizes several anthropological truths that underscore effectively the ideas that the Council seeks to convey. First, there is a substantial dignity to the human being simply by virtue of the fact that he or she exists, independently of one's state of consciousness or degree of mental development. This ontological truth of fundamental human dignity accords each person a right to life that is irreducible and that modern technological developments cannot rightfully suppress or ignore.[80] Second, Thomistic ethics conveys the notion of responsible freedom, of that "freedom of excellence" that is teleologically directed toward spiritual love and moral truth. From this analysis (which insists that the human being is made to love others spiritually in a prudent, just, temperate way), one can derive canons of virtue and vice that permit the right evaluation of the uses of technology for human flourishing or to the detriment of human moral life.[81] Third, then, the moral psychology of Aquinas allows us to see how authentic human beatitude requires the integration of sensible goods and enjoyments into a deeper spiritual and rational pattern of life, so that the use of technological benefits is temperate and humane, and so that the emotional life of the human person is at the service of authentic human love.[82] It is only in light of a deeper anthropological vision of the moral life that the Council's vision of the human person can be meaningfully articulated and advanced in an age saturated with the effects of modern technological developments and our newfound cultural dependencies upon them.

E. The Politics of the Common Good: Non-Reductive Views

Finally, we might mention the politics of the common good. One striking feature of theoretical liberalism is the absence of any commitment to a normative theory of what the human person is. While freedom is highly valued, no metaphysical foundations can be clearly referred to upon which to base this primal respect for human autonomy. This suspension of speculative commitment is meant to allow a broad array of participants to adopt liberal theories of practical reason, but it has the disadvantage of retreating in advance from any settled philosophical account of why human freedom matters. This paradox is the sign of a deeper malaise: there is the more fundamental loss in the modern capitalist, liberal society of any clear way in which to evaluate the diverse goods that comprise the life of any political society and to discuss the hierarchical arrangement among them. Civic laws still seek to provide protections for what are traditionally perceived to be important moral goods. Here I mean to allude to goods that *Gaudium et Spes* underscores: the good of the family, the good of life in a larger political culture, the good of participation in government procedures, the good of education and access to meaningful work, the good of public works. However, there is little understanding theoretically of how these goods are to be arranged in relation to one another, or why they are considered significant in principle. The inevitable temptation is to treat

basic common goods (such as family life, education, or religion) as mere utilitarian goods that facilitate individual autonomy, emotional satisfaction, or participation in the economic market (or worse: which inhibit them). The deeper
goods of life can then be seen as readily discarded when they are no longer of
utilitarian interest in the service of individual freedom and market-dominated
choice-making.

Within this context, those who promote traditional Catholic social philosophy have at least two important contributions to make. First, they must
seek to articulate non-reductive theories of the political common good that
demonstrate the complexity of goods that comprise human society, and hierarchical status (of at least some) of these goods. Why, for example, is marital
commitment a fundamental good for the political life of society? Not first and
foremost because of the economic benefits it provides to the spouses and to
society (though these are genuinely real), but because of the happiness and
sense of personal wellbeing that it provides for children within marriage, and
because of the happiness and moral nobility that it confers upon the spouses.
These qualities of the common life affect the deeper health of a society more
than any economic factors, which remain secondary. Similarly, an academic
education is successful when it facilitates an integrated, profound understanding of reality and of human existence understood in the light of God and the
fundamental vocation of the human being to seek the truth. Practical indexes
of educational goals are extremely important but only in a secondary sense, in
light of the deeper vocation to human wisdom.

Second, Catholic social teaching can and must inculcate in modern society (and among Catholic political personnel first and foremost) a stronger
sense of the distinction between fundamental principles of practical reason
(including moral principles regarding intrinsic evils) versus prudential decisions that are conjectural and that require expert opinion as well as complex,
fallible estimations. For example, it is one thing to argue that each person who
works should not be exploited and should receive a living wage that allows him
and his family to live effectively. It is another thing to ask whether a given min-
imum wage in this or that country at this or that time may help best to bring
more people into the workforce or to permit a significant rise in the quality of
life, or effect the exact opposite of either of these two outcomes. The former
principle is one that is based on universal justice, while the latter discernment
is prudential and conjectural.[83] In a society in which few are able to determine
the difference between these two kinds of reflections, there is the permanent
temptation either to believe that all concerns are merely prudential in kind
(and so practical reason is rooted in a kind of moral relativism regarding first
starting points), or that all prudential decisions must have the same certitude
as first moral principles, in which case moral judgments frequently are made
by appeal to the evolving policy stances of a given political party as if they
were a matter of principle. These two erroneous forms of thinking feed each
other in ways that are politically noxious. It is a profound quality of traditional
Catholic political and social thought that it avoids such forms of intellectual

caricature, and is able, due to this fact, to facilitate rational thinking about the authentic common good in a consistent and profound way.

III. Conclusion: The City of God, the City of Man, and the Return to a Theology of History

The reflections I have offered above are of course topical and cursory in nature, by necessity. However, if the basic arguments of this essay are true, then the teaching of *Gaudium et Spes* remains deeply relevant to the Catholic Church in the modern world of the twenty-first century. However, this relevance does have to be identified with some concern for the discontinuity of historical circumstances between the age in which the document was composed and the age that has emerged henceforth, not least due to the challenges of contemporary secularization. At the heart of *Gaudium et Spes* lies its Christocentric vision of human existence and its profound Catholic realism regarding the potentially transformative power of grace and charity in the life of each person and culture in human history.

These doctrinal truths of the Catholic faith can be understood to have been rearticulated in *Gaudium et Spes* in a somewhat naïve fashion, based on the illusory wish that a vibrant Catholicism might blossom in the midst of the modern, secular world, just as it was in fact taking leave of the Catholic faith in a very profound fashion. However, it is more realistic to say the following: that in *Gaudium et Spes* the Catholic Church was effectively taking leave of the defensive stance adopted in previous centuries in the face of the breakdown of a unified Christendom and of the established Church. However, in doing so the Church was also adopting an evangelical stance in a new historical context, and was making a *first constructive attempt* to articulate the principles of evangelical engagement at the dawn of a new era. Understood in this light, the positive and optimistic tone of the document is the sign of a healthy realism regarding the new sociological condition of the Church in the modern (secular) world and is indicative of a desire to communicate genuine hope to intellectually and existentially disoriented human beings within a modern cultural context. That the Council failed to adequately predict the complete conditions and final consequences of the historical age that was unfolding is inevitable. However, progressivists who cling to the Council in intellectually rigid, theologically reductive ways, and traditional Catholics who utterly dismiss the document both make essentially the same error. They each believe it was meant to provide a final, comprehensive analysis of the Church's mission within a modern historical context, and then, based on this shared premise, either deny aspects of its impermanence or utterly dismiss it. The key, however, is to identify the deeper Christological and anthropological content of *Gaudium et Spes*, its perennial principles of natural law and Catholic social philosophy, and its inner spiritual aspiration: that the Church should seek to evangelize constructively in the modern world as it in fact exists in our own epoch. If these principles are rightly identified and preserved, the heart of the document remains of ongoing significance for the Church, particularly in an era of new evangelization.[84]

What I have also suggested, however, is that the affirmation of the essential principles of *Gaudium et Spes* in our own era might require a commitment not only to the "joy and hope" of the Gospel, but also to the second phrase of the document, *"luctus et angor,"* that is to say, grief and anxiety.[85] It seems clear in our own era that the Church does not escape the challenge of living within the city of man, walking through a valley of tears, in pilgrimage toward the city of God. Augustine's theology of history has as much pertinence today as it did during the collapse of the Roman empire under the weight of northern European invaders.[86] The central point that he sought to convey to Western Christianity was that the Church militant in her earthly sojourn has no abiding home in this world, and that the Eucharistic sacrifice of the Church's liturgy, and the sacrificial life of the Christian, remain the normative signs of communion with God in this world.[87] These measures decide the success or failure of Christian life in the *seculum*, and not those of political influence, worldly honor, or temporal power. Certain problematic interpretations of *Gaudium et Spes* tempt members of the Catholic Church—not to forsake directly the mission to the nations, *ad gentes*, but to evaluate the success of the Church's mission in terms that are alien to the normative foundations of sanctification that God wills for the Church in this world. These foundations are sacramental, and their fruit is charity. The Church *can transform the world from within* due to the power of charity at work in history, but *even when the world is not transformed effectively by the charity of Christ*, the Church can still live her vocation in a plenary way, by worshiping God, loving her neighbors in Christ, and by bearing witness to Christ unto death. Understanding this distinction is of vital importance for Catholic Christians in the twenty-first century. Sanctification can have political effects in the world, but it must never be identified with the latter effects as such. Arguably, it is only by regaining a sense of the life of the Church militant as a communion of authentic charity in the midst of a non-religious world that the Church can *safeguard* the vision of *Gaudium et Spes* and live it effectively, in great numbers or in small, even in the midst of the pagan city of man, and always in view of the eternal city of God, a city that knows no end.

NOTES

1. The best account of the history of the composition of the document is given by Charles Moeller, *Commentary on the Documents of Vatican II*, ed. H. Vorgrimler, trans. W. J. O'Hara, vol. 5, *Pastoral Constitution on the Church in the Modern World*, (New York: Herder and Herder, 1969), 1–76.

2. Compare, for example, the theology of Marie-Dominique Chenu, "Une constitution pastorale de l'Église," in *Peuple de Dieu dans le monde* (Paris: Cerf, 1966), 11–34, with that of Joseph Ratzinger, "The Dignity of the Human Person," in *Commentary on the Documents of Vatican II*, 115–63.

3. For some thematic examples, see John Paul II, *Redemptor Hominis*, no. 8–9, 13–14; *Redemptoris Missio*, no. 6, 9–10, 18, 28; *Veritatis Splendor*, no. 2–3, 28–29, 48–50, 61–64; *Evangelium Vitae*, no. 2–3, 21, 2; *Fides et Ratio*, no. 12, 60. (All references to ecclesiastical documents in this essay are taken from http://vatican.va/ unless otherwise noted.)

4. This was the view of Yves Congar in his essay, "La Théologie au Concile. Le 'théologiser' du Concile," in *Situation et taches présentes de la théologie* (Paris: Cerf, 1967), 41–56. See Joseph A. Komonchak, "Thomism and the Second Vatican Council," in *Continuity and Plurality in Catholic Theology: Essays in Honor of Gerald A. McCool, S.J.*, ed. A. J. Cemera (Fairfield, CT: Sacred Heart University Press, 1998), 53–73.

5. The theme is announced in *Gaudium et Spes*, no. 2: "[T]his Second Vatican Council, having probed more profoundly into the mystery of the Church, now addresses itself without hesitation, not only to the sons of the Church and to all who invoke the name of Christ, but to the whole of humanity. For the council yearns to explain to everyone how it conceives of the presence and activity of the Church in the world of today." For discussion of the apologetical form of the document, see, on this point, Joseph A. Komonchak, "Augustine, Aquinas or the Gospel *sine glossa*: Divisions over *Gaudium et spes*," in *Unfinished Journey: The Church 40 Years after Vatican II. Essays for John Wilkins*, ed. Austen Ivereigh (New York: Continuum, 2003), 102–18.

6. See the analysis of Ratzinger, "The Dignity of the Human Person," in *Commentary on the Documents of Vatican II*, 159–63, at 159: "The attempt to pursue discussion with non-believers on the basis of the idea of 'humanitas,' ... culminates in the endeavor to interpret being human Christologically and so attain the 'resolutio in theologiam' which, it is true, also means 'resolutio in hominem' (provided the sense of 'homo' is understood deeply enough).... On the basis of Christ this dares to present theology as anthropology and only becomes radically theological by including man in discourse about God by way of Christ."

7. *Gaudium et Spes*, no. 10.

8. See the study of this subject by Jean-Pierre Torrell, "Nature and Grace in Thomas Aquinas," in *Surnaturel: A Controversy at the Heart of Twentieth-Century Thomistic Thought*, ed. S. T. Bonino, trans. R. Williams, trans. revised by Matthew Levering (Naples, FL: Sapientia Press, 2009), 155–90.

9. See, for example, Bonaventure, *In II Sent.* dist. 29, q. 2, a. 2, resp., and the analysis of Christopher Cullen, "Bonaventure on Nature Before Grace: A Historical Moment Reconsidered," *American Catholic Philosophical Quarterly* 85 (2011): 161–76.

10. See most notably in his mature work, *Summa theologiae* [ST] I, q. 62, a. 3; q. 95, a.1.

11. Consider especially *Lumen Gentium*, no. 2, and the subsequent interpretation of the *Catechism of the Catholic Church*, no. 374–75, and *Gaudium et Spes*, no. 22, which speaks of the "restoration" of the Adamic likeness to God that takes place in Christ. Commenting on no. 22, John Paul II takes a similar interpretation to the one I am offering here in *Redemptor Hominis*, no. 13: "Accordingly, what is in question here is man in all his truth, in his full magnitude. We are not dealing with the 'abstract' man, but the real, 'concrete,' 'historical' man. We are dealing with 'each' man, for each one is included in the mystery of the Redemption and with each one Christ has united himself for ever through this mystery.... Man as 'willed' by God, as 'chosen' by him from eternity and called, destined for grace and glory—this is 'each' man, 'the most concrete' man, 'the most real'; this is man in all the fullness of the mystery in which he has become a sharer in Jesus Christ."

12. Aquinas, *ST* I-II, q. 85, aa. 1–2.

13. Aquinas, *ST* I-II, q. 109, aa. 2–4, 8–9; III, qq. 7–8; 14–15.

14. Consider the use of the term "mystery" in Vatican I, *Dei Filius*: "The perpetual agreement of the Catholic Church … maintains … that there is a twofold order of knowledge, distinct not only as regards its source, but also as regards its object. With regard to the source, we know at the one level by natural reason, at the other level by divine faith. With regard to the object, besides those things to which natural reason can attain, there are proposed for our belief mysteries hidden in God which, unless they are divinely revealed, are incapable of being known." See the analysis of the concept of mystery in Catholic theology by Matthias Joseph Scheeben, *The Mysteries of Christianity*, trans. Cyril Vollert (New York: Herder and Herder, 1946), 3–21.

15. On this topic, see Thomas Joseph White, "The 'Pure Nature' of Christology: Human Nature and *Gaudium et Spes* 22," *Nova et Vetera* (English edition) 8 (2010): 283–322; Benoît-Dominique de La Soujeole, *Le sacrament de la communion. Essai d'ecclésiologie fondamentale* (Fribourg: Éditions Universitaires Fribourg Suisse, 1998), 223–25.

16. Pope Innocent X, in his 1658 document *Cum Occasione*, demarcated as "impious … dishonoring to divine piety, and heretical" the proposition of the *Augustinus*: "It is semi-Pelagian to say that Christ died or shed His blood for all men without exception." Denz. 1096. [*The Sources of Catholic Dogma*, trans. by R. J. Deferrari from the Thirteenth Edition of Henry Denzinger's *Enchiridion Symbolorum* (Fitzwilliam, NH: Loreto Publications, 1955).] This was the fifth of the five condemned propositions of the *Augustinus*. Aquinas, like many other traditional Catholic doctors, clearly taught that Christ died for all human beings. See, for example, *ST* III, q. 48, a. 2, and q. 46, a. 6, ad 4. As a seventeenth-century representative of the Thomist school, Jean-Baptiste Gonet offers a thorough defense of Aquinas's teaching against the charge of restrictive atonement (as found in Jansenism) by appealing to a range of such texts. See his *Clypeus Theologiae Thomisticae*, vol. 1 (Paris: Vivès, 1875), "Depulso Jansenismi," art. X, sect. CXL–CXLIV, 583–84.

17. Council of Trent, Decree on Justification, canon 17, Denz. 827: "If anyone shall say that the grace of justification is attained by those only who are predestined unto life, but that all others, who are called, are called indeed, but do not receive grace, as if they are by divine power predestined to evil: let him be anathema." Note three different affirmations that seem to be implied: God offers grace even to those who are not predestined. Even among those justified by grace, some may culpably fall from grace. God is not the cause of moral evil and predestines no one to eternal damnation. On the distinction between the divine will of the good alone and the divine permission of sin, see the Decree on Justification of the Council of Trent, can. 6, Denz. 816. Both Luther (in *The Bondage of the Will*, WA 18, 614–20, 630–39) and Calvin (*Institutes*, III, c. 23, no. 8 and c. 24) expressly refused the distinction between God's will and his permissions. [*Martin Luthers Werke: kritische Gesammtausgabe. Weimarer Ausgabe*, 121 vols. (Weimar: H. Böhlaus Nachfolger, 1883–2009); John Calvin, *Institutes of the Christian Religion*, 2 Vol., trans. by F. Battles (Philadelphia: Westminster Press, 1960).]

18. See in this respect the second condemnation of the *Augustinus*, Denz. 1093. Qualification must be added with respect to the question of the salvation of children who died without baptism, prior to the age of reason. On this issue (regarding limbo), traditional theologians advanced a variety of theories. See Serge-Thomas Bonino, "La théorie des limbes et le mystère du surnaturel chez saint Thomas d'Aquin," *Revue thomiste* 101 (2001): 131–66.

19. By "operative" I mean graces that do not presuppose "cooperative" grace, and, therefore, from the Augustinian and Thomist point of view, graces that need

neither presuppose nor immediately effectuate justification on the part of recipient. For Aquinas, operative graces may or may not be accepted, but as they are effective in a person's life, they do progressively incline a person toward justification and sanctification. See *ST* I-II, q. 111, aa. 2–3.

20. See the problematic argument in this respect of Jacques Dupuis, *Toward a Christian Theology of Religious Pluralism* (Maryknoll, NY: Orbis, 1997), 330–57. A helpful and more sober discussion of the problem is offered by Charles Journet in his *The Meaning of Grace* (New York: P. J. Kenedy, 1960); and *L'Église du Verbe Incarné*, vol. 4, *Essai de théologie de l'histoire du salut* (St-Just-La-Pendue: St. Augustin, 2004). See the study of Alexandra Diriart, *Ses frontières sont la charité: l' Église Corps du Christ et Lumen Gentium* (Paris: Lethielleux et Desclée De Brouwer, 2011).

21. Chenu does seem to suggest this kind of fusion in "Une constitution pastorale de l'Église."

22. See in particular, *Lumen Gentium*, no. 14: "Basing itself upon Sacred Scripture and Tradition, [this Sacred Council] teaches that the Church, now sojourning on earth as an exile, is necessary for salvation.... Whosoever, therefore, knowing that the Catholic Church was made necessary by Christ, would refuse to enter or to remain in it, could not be saved." For a helpful historical treatment of the *extra Ecclesiam nulla salus* tradition, see Bernard Sesboüé, *Hors de l'Église pas de salut; Histoire d'une formule et problèmes d'interprétation* (Paris: Desclée de Brouwer, 2004).

23. *Lumen Gentium*, no. 15–16.

24. This idea is organically connected in turn with the teaching of *Unitatis Redintegratio*, no. 3 on visible elements of Christian life that are present in Christian communities not in communion with the Catholic Church, and with the affirmation of *Nostra Aetate*, no. 2 that other religious traditions "often reflect a ray of that Truth which enlightens all men."

25. See in particular *Lumen Gentium*, no. 16, and the study of Ralph Martin, *Will Many Be Saved?: What Vatican II Actually Teaches and Its Implications for the New Evangelization* (Grand Rapids, MI: Eerdmans, 2012), as well as Thomas Joseph White, "Von Balthasar and Journet on the Universal Possibility of Salvation and the Twofold Will of God," *Nova et Vetera* (English edition) 4 (2006): 633–66.

26. In contrast to the Bellarminian emphasis on ecclesial unity as occurring by means of visible structures (creed, sacraments, jurisdiction), Thomistic ecclesiology insisted that participation in the Church's theological virtues is constitutive of the Church's essence. The idea stems from Aquinas himself and is reproduced in commentators such as Cajetan, John of St. Thomas, and more recently, Journet, Congar, and Tillard. See the historical reflections on this doctrine by Yves Congar, "L'idée de l'Église chez saint Thomas d'Aquin," in *Esquisses du Mystère de l'Église* (Paris: Cerf, 1941): 59–91; and "Ecclesia ab Abel," in *Abhandlungen über Theologie und Kirche. Festschrift für Karl Adam*, ed. Marcel Reding (Düsseldorf: Patmos-Verlag, 1952), 79–108. Aquinas develops the idea by explaining how (for both Christians and non-Christians) a more profound, explicit belief about Christ can be contained implicitly in a less profound, less explicit assent to divine truth. See, for example, *ST* II-II, q. 2, aa. 5–8. In II-II, q. 2, a. 7, ad 3, he claims that the grace of "implicit faith" can be operative in and through the natural religious dimensions of human culture: "If, however, some were saved without receiving any revelation, they were not saved without faith in a Mediator, for, though they did not believe in him explicitly, they did, nevertheless, have implicit faith through believing in Divine providence, since they believed that God would deliver mankind in whatever way was pleasing to Him, and according to the revelation of the Spirit to those who knew the truth, as stated in Job 35:11: 'He who

teaches us more than the beasts of the earth'" (trans. by English Dominican Province, *Summa Theologica* [New York: Benziger, 1947]). Obviously Aquinas was aware that the Scriptures regard Job as a pagan. For a helpful contemporary restatement of the theology of "implicit faith," see Francois Daguet, "L'unique Église du Christ en act et en puissance," *Nova et Vetera* (French edition) 79 (2004): 45–70.

27. *Gaudium et Spes*, no. 11: "The People of God believes that it is led by the Lord's Spirit, Who fills the earth. Motivated by this faith, it labors to decipher authentic signs of God's presence and purpose in the happenings, needs and desires in which this People has a part along with other men of our age. For faith throws a new light on everything, manifests God's design for man's total vocation, and thus directs the mind to solutions which are fully human." See the pertinent remarks of Ratzinger, "The Dignity of the Human Person," in *Commentary on the Documents of Vatican II*, 118: "What is to be demonstrated, therefore, is that precisely by Christian faith in God, true humanism, i.e. man's full development as man, is attained, and that consequently the idea of humanism which present-day atheism opposes to faith can serve as the hinge of the discussion and a means of dialogue.... The whole Pastoral Constitution might therefore be described in this light as a discussion between Christian and unbeliever on the question who and what man really is."

28. See the argument of R. R. Reno in "Rahner the Restorationist: Karl Rahner's Time Has Passed," *First Things*, May 2013, http://www.firstthings.com/article/2013/05/rahner-the-restorationist.

29. It is frequently conjectured that this aspect of *Gaudium et Spes* is inspired in part by Jacques Maritain's *Man and the State* (Chicago: University of Chicago Press, 1951).

30. *Dignitatis Humanae*, no. 2.

31. The overt references are in *Gaudium et Spes*, no. 74, 79, and 89, though it would not be difficult to show that references to rationally accessible universal moral principles abound throughout the document. I have sought to offer an argument to this effect in "The 'Pure Nature' of Christology: Human Nature and *Gaudium et Spes* 22."

32. This is a point already made by Pius XII in *Humani Generis* in 1950. No. 2–3: "It is not surprising that such discord and error should always have existed outside the fold of Christ. For though, absolutely speaking, human reason by its own natural force and light can arrive at a true and certain knowledge of the one personal God, Who by His providence watches over and governs the world, and also of the natural law, which the Creator has written in our hearts, still there are not a few obstacles to prevent reason from making efficient and fruitful use of its natural ability. The truths that have to do with God and the relations between God and men, completely surpass the sensible order and demand self-surrender and self-abnegation in order to be put into practice and to influence practical life. Now the human intellect, in gaining the knowledge of such truths is hampered both by the activity of the senses and the imagination, and by evil passions arising from original sin. Hence men easily persuade themselves in such matters that what they do not wish to believe is false or at least doubtful. It is for this reason that divine revelation must be considered morally necessary so that those religious and moral truths which are not of their nature beyond the reach of reason in the present condition of the human race, may be known by all men readily with a firm certainty and with freedom from all error."

33. *ST* I-II, q. 94, aa. 4 and 6.

34. *ST* I-II, q. 85, aa. 1–2.

35. See, for example, *Gaudium et Spes*, no. 47, 50, 64–72, 73–75, 79–82, 86–87.

36. See, for example, *Gaudium et Spes*, no. 10, 22, 41.

37. *Gaudium et Spes*, no. 37: "For a monumental struggle against the powers of darkness pervades the whole history of man. The battle was joined from the very origins of the world and will continue until the last day, as the Lord has attested. Caught in this conflict, man is obliged to wrestle constantly if he is to cling to what is good, nor can he achieve his own integrity without great efforts and the help of God's grace." No. 78: "The human will is unsteady and wounded by sin."

38. Compare *ST* I-II, q. 85, and the Council of Trent, Decree on Original Sin, Denz. 787–91.

39. Consider, for example, Luther's 1525 work, *The Bondage of the Will*, and Calvin's *Institutes of the Christian Religion*, III, c. 11, but also the views of the Louvain theologian Michael de Bay (Baius) condemned by Pius V in his 1567 bull "Ex omnibus afflictionibus" (Denz. 1001–80).

40. See, for example, the Council of Trent, Decree on Justification, chap. 2 and can. 25, Denz. 804, 835.

41. Council of Trent, Decree on Justification, chap. 7 and can. 11, Denz. 799–800, 821.

42. Council of Trent, Decree on Justification, can. 4, 6, 17, Denz. 814, 816, 827.

43. *Gaudium et Spes*, no. 11: "This council, first of all, wishes to assess in this light those values which are most highly prized today and to relate them to their divine source. Insofar as they stem from endowments conferred by God on man, these values are exceedingly good. Yet they are often wrenched from their rightful function by the taint in man's heart, and hence stand in need of purification."

44. *Gaudium et Spes*, no. 13: "Although he was made by God in a state of holiness, from the very onset of his history man abused his liberty, at the urging of the Evil One." Komonchak explores the debates in the drafting process regarding the inclusion of a sober estimation of the power of sin in human history in "Augustine, Aquinas or the Gospel *sine glossa*: Divisions over *Gaudium et spes*."

45. *Gaudium et Spes*, no. 38: "To those, therefore, who believe in divine love, He gives assurance that the way of love lies open to men and that the effort to establish a universal brotherhood is not a hopeless one."

46. *Gaudium et Spes*, no. 13: "The call to grandeur and the depths of misery, both of which are a part of human experience, find their ultimate and simultaneous explanation in the light of this revelation." See the reflections on Pascal's theology and its modern heritage by Charles Journet, *Verité de Pascal: essai sur la valeur apologétique des "Pensées"* (St. Maurice: Éditions de l'oeuvre St. Augustin, 1951).

47. See Aquinas, *ST* I-II, q. 110; II-II, q. 23.

48. See, for example, *Redemptor Hominis*, no. 8 and 16–18.

49. *Redemptor Hominis*, no. 12.

50. *Veritatis Splendor*, no. 2–3.

51. *Evangelium Vitae*, no. 58.

52. *Evangelium Vitae*, no. 12, 19, 21.

53. See, for example, the 1981 document *Familiaris Consortio*, and the June 3, 2003 document of the Congregation of the Doctrine of the Faith, *Considerations Regarding Proposals to Give Legal Recognition to Unions between Homosexual Persons*, which, as is noted in the text, was approved by Pope John Paul II.

54. See, for example, the explicit appeal in *Familiaris Consortio*, no. 29 to *Gaudium et Spes*, no. 50, which in turn echoes the anthropological vision of the Council of Trent, session 24, on the Sacrament of Matrimony (Denz. 969–82).

55. On this topic, see the important essay of Richard Schenk, "*Officium signa temporum perscrutandi*. New Encounters of Gospel and Culture in the Context of

the New Evangelisation," in *Scrutinizing the Signs of the Times in Light of the Gospel* (*Bibliotheca Ephemeridum Theologicarum Lovaniensium*, CCVIII), ed. Johan Verstraeten (Leuven: Leuven University Press and Peeters, 2007), 167–203.

56. See the influential and helpful argument of Hans Urs von Balthasar in *Cordula or The Moment of Christian Witness* (San Francisco: Ignatius Press, 1994).

57. On this subject, see Thomas Joseph White, *The Incarnate Lord: A Thomistic Study in Christology* (Washington, DC: The Catholic University of America Press, 2015), prolegomenon and chap. 1.

58. See in this respect the arguments in John Hick, *God Has Many Names* (Philadelphia: The Westminster Press, 1980); Jacques Dupuis, *Toward a Christian Theology of Religious Pluralism*.

59. *Dominus Iesus*, no. 15: "One can and must say that Jesus Christ has a significance and a value for the human race and its history, which are unique and singular, proper to him alone, exclusive, universal, and absolute. Jesus is, in fact, the Word of God made man for the salvation of all. In expressing this consciousness of faith, the Second Vatican Council teaches: 'The Word of God, through whom all things were made, was made flesh, so that as perfect man he could save all men and sum up all things in himself. The Lord is the goal of human history, the focal point of the desires of history and civilization, the centre of mankind, the joy of all hearts, and the fulfilment of all aspirations. It is he whom the Father raised from the dead, exalted and placed at his right hand, constituting him judge of the living and the dead' (*Gaudium et Spes*, no. 45)."

60. *Dominus Iesus*, no. 16–17.

61. See the complementary views that are present in the 1994 *Catechism of the Catholic Church*, no. 1877–1948.

62. See in this respect the address of Pope Benedict XVI to the British parliament, Westminster Hall, Friday, September 17, 2010, and his University of Regensburg Address, Tuesday, September 12, 2006.

63. *Gaudium et Spes*, no. 12, 14, 16, 17. See the complementary reflections of Aquinas in *ST* I, qq. 75–83, 95, as well as the study of Yves Floucat, "Enjeux et actualité d'une approche thomiste de la personne," *Revue Thomiste* 100 (2000): 384–422.

64. See, for example, in this respect, Daniel C. Dennett, *Darwin's Dangerous Idea: Evolution and the Meanings of Life* (New York: Simon & Schuster, 1995).

65. See Aquinas, *Commentary on Boethius' De Trinitate*, qq. 5–6 [*The Division and Methods of the Sciences: Questions V and VI of his Commentary on the De Trinitate of Boethius*; trans. by A. Maurer (Toronto: PIMS, 1986)], and the analysis of Benedict Ashley, *The Way toward Wisdom: An Interdisciplinary and Intercultural Introduction to Metaphysics* (Notre Dame: Notre Dame University Press, 2009).

66. See, in this respect, the recent arguments of David S. Oderberg, *Real Essentialism* (London: Routledge, 2003).

67. See the restatement of this classical vision by Ralph McInerny, *Praeambula Fidei: Thomism and the God of the Philosophers* (Washington, DC: The Catholic University of America Press, 2006).

68. *Casti Connubii*, no. 59.

69. *Gaudium et Spes*, no. 50: "Marriage and conjugal love are by their nature ordained toward the begetting and educating of children.... Marriage to be sure is not instituted solely for procreation; rather, its very nature as an unbreakable compact between persons, and the welfare of the children, both demand that the mutual love of the spouses be embodied in a rightly ordered manner, that it grow and ripen. Therefore, marriage persists as a whole manner and communion of life, and maintains its value

and indissolubility, even when despite the often intense desire of the couple, offspring are lacking." On the formal and final causes of marriage, see Aquinas, *ST* III, q. 29, a. 2: "Marriage or wedlock is said to be true by reason of its attaining its perfection. Now perfection of anything is twofold; first, and second. The first perfection of a thing consists in its very form, from which it receives its species; while the second perfection of a thing consists in its operation, by which in some way a thing attains its end. Now the form of matrimony consists in a certain inseparable union of souls, by which husband and wife are pledged by a bond of mutual affection that cannot be sundered. And the end of matrimony is the begetting and upbringing of children: the first of which is attained by conjugal intercourse; the second by the other duties of husband and wife, by which they help one another in rearing their offspring." On the theological implications of this teaching for modern Catholic theology, see M. Leblanc, "Amour et procréation dans la théologie de saint Thomas," *Revue Thomiste* 92 (1992): 433–59.

70. See the pertinent argument of John Paul II in *Familiaris Consortio*, no. 32.

71. As argued by Leo XIII in *Arcanum* in 1880 and in *Immortale Dei* in 1885.

72. A point underscored forcefully by Leo XIII in *Immortale Dei*, no. 17 and 27.

73. See in this respect Benedict XVI, "Address to the Roman Rota," Jan. 26, 2013: "Contemporary culture, marked by accentuated subjectivism and ethical and religious relativism, places the person and the family before pressing challenges.... It escapes no one that the basic decision of each person to enter into a lifetime bond, influences the basic view of each one according to whether or not he or she is anchored to a merely human level or is open to the light of faith in the Lord. It is only in opening oneself to God's truth, in fact, that it is possible to understand and achieve in the concrete reality of both conjugal and family life the truth of men and women as his children, regenerated by Baptism."

74. *ST* I-II, q. 85, a. 2.

75. *ST* I-II, q. 85, a. 1.

76. Pius XI warned already in *Casti Connubii*, no. 62 against a modern iteration of Jansenism that would argue (falsely) that the natural goods of marriage are existentially inaccessible to modern man, who is in fact helped by the aid of grace.

77. *Gaudium et Spes*, no. 15, 33, 51, 56, 57, 62, 80.

78. Consider in this respect the influential essay of Martin Heidegger, "Die Frage nach der Technik," first published in *Vorträge und Aufsätze* (Pfullingen: G. Neske, 1954).

79. I am thinking in particular of the work of Servais Pinckaers, *The Sources of Christian Ethics*, trans. M. T. Noble (Washington, DC: The Catholic University of America Press, 1995); and Alasdair MacIntyre, *After Virtue: A Study in Moral Theory* (Notre Dame: Notre Dame University Press, 2007).

80. See David Albert Jones, *The Soul of the Embryo: An Enquiry into the Status of the Human Embryo in the Christian Tradition* (London: Bloomsbury, 2004).

81. See Michael Sherwin, *By Knowledge & By Love: Charity and Knowledge in the Moral Theology of St. Thomas Aquinas* (Washington, DC: The Catholic University of America Press, 2011); and Nicanor Austriaco, *Biomedicine and Beatitude: An Introduction to Catholic Bioethics* (Washington, DC: The Catholic University of America Press, 2011).

82. See Nicholas E. Lombardo, *The Logic of Desire: Aquinas on Emotion* (Washington, DC: The Catholic University of America Press, 2010).

83. See the *Catechism of the Catholic Church*, no. 2426–36.

84. The idea of a "New Evangelization" of Europe and America is thematic in John Paul II's 1990 Encyclical *Redemptoris Missio*.

85. As noted by Schenk, "*Officium signa temporum perscrutandi*. New Encounters of Gospel and Culture in the Context of the New Evangelisation."

86. See Augustine, *City of God*, XIX, 12–15, 17, 25–28; XXII, 29–30. [St. Augustine, *City of God*, trans. H. Bettenson (London: Penguin, 1972).]

87. Augustine, *City of God*, X, 6.

PART TWO

The Decrees

5

Christus Dominus

Matthew Levering

According to John Linnan's assessment, published twenty years after the close of the Council, *Christus Dominus*—the decree on the Pastoral Office of the Bishops in the Church—"suffers from the rapidity with which it was assembled and from the lack of clarity which resulted from combining the two preceding schemas. It breaks no new ground from a theological perspective."[1] Linnan finds that its main contributions are canonical in nature, and he focuses on the balance of power in the Church. Indeed, for Linnan, "The concept of permanent office holders needs to be re-examined as one means of limiting clericalism and making ministry in an ecclesial office a service and not a position in the hierarchy," and Linnan considers the whole distinction between laity and clergy (including bishops) to be rather suspect.[2] For Linnan, therefore, *Christus Dominus* makes its main contribution in raising questions about power relations and especially in supporting more autonomous power for the local church.

More recently, Brian Ferme has presented *Christus Dominus* as "an especially canonically oriented decree," and he finds in the 1983 *Code of Canon Law* evidence of a thorough and fruitful implementation of *Christus Dominus*. Ferme states, "The postconciliar process of the legal application of *Christus Dominus* reflects an important element in the hermeneutics of reform understood as the necessary and ongoing translation into legal language of the doctrines proposed by the council and in a particular fashion by *Christus Dominus*."[3] Ferme argues that *Christus Dominus* builds upon the theological insights of *Lumen Gentium* to renew the work of bishops and the canonical standing of the bishops.

Given Linnan's and Ferme's emphasis on *Christus Dominus* as a canonically oriented decree—despite their otherwise divergent perspectives—I will attend briefly to how the 1983 *Code of Canon*

Law receives *Christus Dominus*. I will focus, however, upon how *Christus Dominus* has been received magisterially and theologically. Specifically, I concentrate upon Pope John Paul II's Apostolic Exhortation *Pastores Gregis* and upon the approaches taken by three theologians, Richard Gaillardetz, Massimo Faggioli, and George Tavard. These writings strike me as representative of the main lines of the theological reception of the decree, although of course many more magisterial and theological texts could be referenced, including Pope Francis's recent encyclical *Laudato Si'*, which takes pains to cite appreciatively the documents produced by a variety of bishops' conferences. In my constructive section, I suggest that the ongoing reception of *Christus Dominus* should focus on the diocesan bishop's concrete *tasks* rather than on measuring how the power of the bishop (and the local church) compares with that of the pope/Curia. This focus on episcopal tasks will help the Church identify further areas in which the episcopal power still needs enhancing, and I think it will also show that the relative power of the bishops and the pope/Curia is no longer, thanks not least to Vatican II, the central issue facing episcopal ministry.[4] I will begin with a short summary of the document, for the benefit of readers for whom *Christus Dominus* may be unfamiliar.

I. A Survey of *Christus Dominus*

In its Preface, *Christus Dominus* takes its bearings from Christ Jesus's own mission from the Father, namely to save us from sin and to sanctify us. Christ sends the apostles by giving them a participation in his mission from the Father. Among the apostles, Christ gave to Peter the responsibility of "feeding His sheep and lambs" (cf. John 21:15–17), and this entails—both for Peter and Peter's successors the bishops of Rome—"supreme, full, immediate, and universal authority over the care of souls by divine institution" (§2). The mission received from Christ by Peter (and his successors) includes "a primacy of ordinary power" not merely over the whole Church in general, but "over all the churches" in a concrete way (§2). Christ gave Peter (and Peter's successors) a unique mission to care for both "the common good of the universal Church and for the good of the individual churches" (§2).[5]

Christus Dominus goes on to affirm both that all the apostles received a mission from Christ, and that all the bishops are successors of the apostles. All the bishops, and not solely the bishop of Rome, are sent by Christ for the purpose of continuing Christ's mission to the world. Just as the apostles were anointed at Pentecost for their mission, so also the bishops are "appointed by the Holy Spirit [*positi a Spiritu sancto*]" and are given power by the Holy Spirit to teach, govern, and sanctify the Church (§2). Like the apostles vis-à-vis Peter, therefore, the bishops receive their authority directly from Christ and the Holy Spirit rather than from the bishop of Rome.

What then should be the relationship between the bishop of Rome (the pope) and the other bishops? The answer involves both equality and subordination. The bishops act "together with the supreme pontiff," and yet the bishops are "under his authority" (§2). They act together with the pope insofar as they exercise episcopal office and insofar as they care not only for their local church but "for all the churches," as members of the college of bishops (§3). They are subordinate to the pope insofar as he holds primacy over each and every local church.

The Preface concludes by stating that it will seek to set forth the office of bishop in light of "the conditions of human association which have brought about a new order of things in our time" (§3). Before examining the body of the document, it is worth noting two further points: the Preface agrees with *Lumen Gentium* §21 that the bishops receive their office through "episcopal consecration," and bishops rightly exercise their office not only separately, but also by "jointly providing for certain common needs of various churches" (§3).

Chapter 1 examines the role of the bishops in the universal Church. Bishops belong to an episcopal body or college whose head is the pope. This college, as long as it operates together with and under its head, has full power over the universal Church. Although all bishops have a right to participate in an ecumenical Council, the pope can convene a "Synod of Bishops" that involves selected bishops from around the world, so as to assist the pope in his care for the universal Church.[6] *Christus Dominus* emphasizes that bishops should be concerned for all the churches rather than solely for the local church entrusted to their care.

Chapter 1 then turns specifically to the relationship of bishops to the pope and to the Roman Curia. So long as it is recognized that the pope has supreme authority in all cases, it should also be recognized that the bishop in his diocese is no mere figurehead, but rather has "all the ordinary, proper, and immediate authority" that is required for the bishop to exercise his office of teaching, governing, and sanctifying (§8). The pope rightly makes use of the Curia in the administration of the Church, but *Christus Dominus* urges that the Curia be streamlined, better integrated, more representative of the universal Church in terms of the nationalities of its officials, inclusive of more bishops, and more attentive to outstanding laypeople.

Chapter 2 addresses the work of bishops in their particular churches/dioceses. Through the power of the Holy Spirit, a diocese or particular church is gathered together by the bishop through the Gospel and the Eucharist. In each particular church, "the one, holy, catholic, and apostolic Church of Christ is truly present and operative" (§11). In this particular church, the bishop is the ordinary pastor with the authority to teach, govern, and sanctify, under the authority of the pope. The bishop should nourish the faithful and reach out to those who do not accept the Gospel and/or are not in communion with the Church. Focusing first on the bishops' teaching office, *Christus Dominus* urges the bishops, in proclaiming the Gospel, to teach primarily about "the whole mystery of Christ" as well as about the contours of a life in Christ that leads to eternal beatitude. Bishops should also not neglect to teach about the human goods that, while not specific to the Gospel, conduce to building up the body of Christ, such as the human person's freedom and bodily life, the family, art, and technology, economics, and peace and just war. Bishops should teach in an accessible and dialogic manner without diluting doctrine; should privilege the poor; should make use of the full variety of modes of communication; and should ensure good catechesis, not least by renewing the way in which adult catechumens are instructed.

Secondly, *Christus Dominus* discusses the bishops' sanctifying office. Bishops "are the principal dispensers of the mysteries of God, as well as being the governors, promoters, and guardians of the entire liturgical life in the church committed to them" (§15). Their goal should be the sanctification of the clergy, religious, and laity of the churches in their diocese, and they should seek to encourage vocations to priesthood and religious life. In a spirit of loving care, they should truly come to know the people whom they serve as bishop. This is especially the case with regard to the priests in their diocese, whom bishops should treat "as sons and friends" (§16) and whose spiritual and intellectual welfare the bishops should provide for, not least by means of educational institutes and spiritual retreats. *Christus Dominus* adds that "with active mercy bishops should pursue priests who are involved in any danger or who have failed in certain respects" (§16). In addition, bishops should pay special attention to societal needs and should be sure to welcome strangers and foreigners into the diocese; should ensure that the lay faithful are able to collaborate actively in the affairs of the Church; should have a spirit of generous ecumenism; should reach out in love to those who are not Christian; should encourage apostolic works and organizations; should benefit from sociological research regarding contemporary needs; and should take care to provide pastoral care to those whose way of life separates them in some manner from regular parish life.

In this section, *Christus Dominus* also touches upon the relationship of bishops to the state. They should encourage social progress and prosperity, obedience to just laws, and respect for legitimately constituted authorities. They should insist upon their rightful absolute independence from civil authority in the carrying out of their apostolic office for the salvation of souls. In the nomination and appointment of bishops, the state must not interfere. In the future, no rights or privileges "of election, nomination, presentation, or designation for the office of bishop" may be given to civil authorities (§20). *Christus Dominus* encourages bishops to be willing to resign due to age or illness. In large dioceses, auxiliary bishops will be needed. Guidelines for coadjutor bishops, who have right of succession, are also provided here, as are guidelines for the diocesan curia and committees that support the bishop's ministry. With respect to the latter, *Christus Dominus* notes, "It is greatly desired that in each diocese a pastoral commission will be established over which the diocesan bishop himself will preside and in which specially chosen clergy, religious and lay people will participate" (§27).

Christus Dominus next treats the relationship of the bishop to the priests of his diocese, both diocesan priests and priests of religious orders. All diocesan priests "form one presbytery and one family whose father is the bishop" (§28). *Christus Dominus* praises the work of priests who are assigned to schools and other apostolates, but it notes that pastors are especially the collaborators of the bishop. Pastors have the office (*munus*) of teaching, sanctifying, and governing the people of their parishes, in such a way that the faithful "will truly realize that they are members both of the diocese and of the universal Church" (§30), and also with a missionary and evangelistic spirit. With respect to parish priests, *Christus Dominus* recommends living in community. Parish priests should proclaim the word of God so as to nourish the people's life in Christ; should impart and oversee catechetical instruction; should ensure that "the celebration of the Eucharistic Sacrifice is the center and culmination of the whole life of the Christian community"; should hear the confessions of the people; and should visit people in their homes, and especially visit the poor, the sick, and the lower classes (§30). With respect to the filling of vacancies for parishes, the bishop must have full control, with the exception of parishes staffed by religious orders. The bishop also possesses full control over decisions regarding establishing parishes or suppressing parishes. *Christus Dominus* also seeks to provide for pastors' "stability of office" and remarks that "the distinction between removable and irremovable pastors is to be abrogated and the procedure for transferring and removing pastors is to be re-examined and simplified" (§31).

What is the relationship between the bishop and the members of a religious order? *Christus Dominus* sets forth six fundamental principles in this regard. First, whenever the bishop calls upon consecrated religious (who are not dedicated to the contemplative life) to perform works of the apostolate, such as pastoral ministry, "they are obliged to discharge their duties as active and obedient helpers of the bishops" (§35). When making such requests, of course, bishops should attend to the particular character of the religious order. Second, when religious assist the bishop in this way, they should nonetheless "remain faithful to the observance of their rule and spirit of submissiveness due to their own superiors" (§35). Third, although some religious orders are exempt from the jurisdiction of bishops and instead report to the pope, this exemption "does not exclude Religious in individual dioceses from the jurisdiction of bishops in accordance with the norm of law, insofar as the performance of their pastoral office and the right ordering of the care of souls requires" (§35). Fourth, all religious are subject to the authority of the bishop (and to any binding decisions made by episcopal conferences) with regard to public divine worship, the care of souls, public preaching, catechesis, decorum, and public works of the apostolate. *Christus Dominus* notes, "Catholic schools conducted by Religious are also subject to the authority of the local Ordinaries for purposes of general policy-making and vigilance, but the right of Religious to direct them remains intact" (§35). Fifth, religious orders should coordinate with the diocesan clergy, and this coordination should be encouraged by the pope, bishops, and episcopal conferences. Sixth, bishops should meet regularly with the superiors of the religious orders in their diocese.

The third and final chapter of *Christus Dominus* has to do with the cooperation of bishops, notably in synods, councils, and episcopal conferences, all of which *Christus Dominus* hopes will "flourish with fresh vigor" (§36). *Christus*

Dominus observes that episcopal conferences have been established in many nations, and it urges that every nation or region have an episcopal conference. In a formal way, *Christus Dominus* defines what an episcopal conference is, who its members are, and who has a deliberative vote. When an episcopal conference makes a decision that has been approved by two-thirds of the voting bishops at the conference and that has been approved by the Apostolic See, this decision only has juridically binding force (upon the bishops of the conference) when it receives a special mandate from the Apostolic See. Episcopal conferences should be sure to communicate with each other regularly. The Eastern Catholic Churches, in their synods, should be sure to keep in view the other rites, rather than solely focus on the needs of their own rite.

Christus Dominus concludes by mandating a revision of the Code of Canon Law so as to update it in light of the decree, by mandating "general directories ... treating of the care of souls" (§44), by mandating particular directories regarding pastoral care in particular nations or regions, and by mandating a directory containing basic catechetical principles.

II. 1983 Code of Canon Law: The Impact of *Christus Dominus*

In the new *Code of Canon Law* promulgated by Pope John Paul II in 1983, there is a chapter devoted to episcopal conferences. *Christus Dominus* states, "Wherever special circumstances require and with the approbation of the Apostolic See, bishops of many nations can establish a single conference" (§38). Canon 449 of the *Code of Canon Law* draws from this section of *Christus Dominus* and addresses an aspect about which *Christus Dominus* had not been completely clear, namely the extent of the authority of the pope over episcopal conferences. Thus Canon 449 states, "It is only for the supreme authority of the Church to erect, suppress, or alter conferences of bishops, after having heard the bishops concerned."[7] This fits, of course, not only with *Christus Dominus*'s insistence upon the necessity that the Apostolic See approve the constitutions and juridically binding decisions of each episcopal conference, but also with the first chapters of *Christus Dominus*, which emphasize the pope's authority.

With respect to episcopal conferences, too, Canon 451 of the *Code of Canon Law* follows *Christus Dominus* in teaching that the statutes of an episcopal conference must "provide for a permanent council of bishops, a general secretariat of the conference, and also other offices and commissions."[8] Canon 452 offers additional instructions: "Each conference of bishops is to elect a president for itself, is to determine who is to perform the function of pro-president when the president is legitimately impeded, and is to designate a general secretary."[9] In Canon 453, *Christus Dominus*'s recommendation that the episcopal conference meet "at fixed times" (§37) is specified to require at least an annual meeting.[10]

Regarding *Christus Dominus*'s discussion of the bestowal of a "special mandate" by the Apostolic See (§38), Canon 455 states that such a mandate is required in order for a decision of an episcopal conference to bind authoritatively each diocesan bishop in the conference. But Canon 456 adds, with a greater specification than one finds in *Christus Dominus*, that "when a plenary meeting of a conference of bishops has ended, the president is to send a report of the acts of the conference and its decrees to the Apostolic See so that the acts are brought to its notice and it can review the decrees if there are any."[11] This ensures that the Apostolic See always reviews the acts and especially the decrees of each plenary meeting of an episcopal conference.

A similar case has to do with Catholic schools. Recall that paragraph 35 of *Christus Dominus* remarks, "Catholic schools conducted by Religious are also subject to the authority of the local Ordinaries for purposes of general policy-making and vigilance, but the right of Religious to direct them remains intact." Paragraph 39 of Pope Paul VI's *Sanctae Ecclesiae* also addresses this point, as does paragraph 66 of the Congregation for Bishops's *Directorium de Pastorali Ministerio Episcoporum* (February 22, 1973).[12] In the *Code of Canon Law*, we find a canonical precept specifying the relationship of the bishop to any school operated by a religious order in his diocese. Canon 806 observes, "The diocesan bishop has the right to watch over and visit the Catholic schools in his territory, even those which members of religious institutes have founded or direct."[13] What this watching over (*invigilandi*) entails, in terms of concrete governing power, is then made clear, or at least somewhat clear: "He [the diocesan bishop] also issues prescripts which pertain to the general regulation of Catholic schools; these prescripts are valid also for schools which these religious direct, without prejudice, however, to their autonomy regarding the internal direction of their schools."[14] When the *Code of Canon Law* turns from Catholic schools to Catholic universities, the *Code of Canon Law* adds a responsibility of episcopal conferences and diocesan bishops that is not explicitly found in *Christus Dominus*. Canon 810 states, "The conferences of bishops and diocesan bishops concerned have the duty and right of being watchful so that the principles of Catholic doctrine are observed faithfully in these same universities."[15]

With regard to the duties of a bishop, the *Code of Canon Law* draws extensively upon *Christus Dominus*, as we would expect. For example, Canon 383 encourages pastoral solicitude toward those who have fallen away from the Catholic faith, as well as toward those who are unable (presumably because of age or infirmity, or perhaps because they are living in a state of sin) "to make sufficient use of ordinary pastoral care because of the condition of their life."[16] Canon 383 reprises what paragraph 16 of *Christus Dominus* teaches with regard to non-Catholic Christians and non-Christians. Canon 394 emphasizes that the bishop should encourage and harmonize the various works of the apostolate ongoing in his diocese, just as we found in paragraph 17 of *Christus Dominus*. Drawing upon paragraph 21 of *Christus Dominus* and paragraph 11 of *Ecclesiae Sanctae*, Canons 401 and 402 propose norms for the resignation of bishops due to age or ill health; indeed Canon 401, going beyond *Christus Dominus*, states that "[a] diocesan bishop who has completed the seventy-fifth year of age is requested to present his resignation from office to the Supreme Pontiff, who will make provision after he has examined all the circumstances."[17]

III. Apostolic Exhortation *Pastores Gregis* (October 16, 2003): Further
Magisterial Reception

In 2001, the Synod of Bishops reflected on the topic of "The Bishop, Servant
of the Gospel of Jesus Christ for the Hope of the World." Two years later, Pope
John Paul II issued his post-synodal Apostolic Exhortation *Pastores Gregis*,
whose purpose was to explore the ministry of bishops, in accord with the
Second Vatican Council's focus on "the ecclesiology of communion and mission," and with special reference to the virtue of hope (§2). In the background
was, among other things, John Paul II's praise in his encyclical *Redemptor
Hominis* of the postconciliar "process of consolidation of national episcopal
conferences throughout the Church and of other collegial structures of an
international or continental character," which "should pulsate in full awareness of their own identity and, at the same time, of their own originality
within the universal unity of the Church" (§5). In *Pastores Gregis*, John Paul
II observes specifically that "the work of the Synod made constant reference
to the teaching of the Second Vatican Council on the episcopate and the ministry of Bishops, especially as set forth in the third chapter of the Dogmatic
Constitution on the Church *Lumen Gentium* and in the decree on the Pastoral
Office of Bishops *Christus Dominus*" (§2). By my count, *Pastores Gregis* cites
Lumen Gentium forty-six times and *Christus Dominus* thirteen times.

The first citation of *Christus Dominus* appears in *Pastores Gregis*'s discussion of "the spirit of collegiality" (§8) and of the care that bishops have for
neighboring dioceses and indeed for the whole Church. Recall that *Christus
Dominus* teaches that bishops share "in the solicitude for all the churches"
and "are united in a college or body" (§3), and it adds that "bishops should
realize that they are bound together and should manifest a concern for all
the churches" (§6). *Pastores Gregis* therefore is well justified in referring to
Christus Dominus with regard to what *Pastores Gregis* calls "the Bishops' concern for the other particular Churches and for the universal Church" (§8), even
though the word "collegiality" is avoided in *Christus Dominus*.[18] As *Pastores
Gregis* states, "The spirit of collegiality is realized and expressed in different
degrees and in various modalities, including institutional forms such as, for
example, the Synod of Bishops, Particular Councils, Episcopal Conferences,
the Roman Curia, *ad Limina* visits, missionary cooperation, etc." (§8). These
institutional forms of collegiality, we will recall, were strongly encouraged by
Christus Dominus.

Pastores Gregis next refers to *Christus Dominus* with regard to bishops who
are not in charge of a particular diocese, but who instead do other tasks in
the Church. Not least through their cooperation with diocesan bishops, these
bishops too represent Christ in his governing authority. In chapter 3, *Pastores
Gregis* quotes *Christus Dominus*'s insistence that bishops, strengthened by the
Holy Spirit, have the task of calling people to faith and nourishing people's
faith. Recall that evangelization, which is a central theme in *Pastores Gregis*, is
also an important theme in paragraphs 11–14 of *Christus Dominus*.

At the outset of chapter 5, *Pastores Gregis* quotes both *Lumen Gentium* and *Christus Dominus* to emphasize that the bishop's governance must be one of service and self-sacrifice. With a biblical emphasis that is generally missing from *Christus Dominus* itself, *Pastores Gregis* quotes the Gospels' references to Jesus as the good shepherd who came to serve rather than to be served, as well as John 13:1–15, which recounts Jesus's washing of his disciples' feet, and Philippians 2:7, on Jesus's taking the form of a servant. *Pastores Gregis* also cites *Christus Dominus*'s observation that a diocese is gathered together by the bishop "through the Gospel and the Eucharist in the Holy Spirit" (*Christus Dominus* §11)—although *Pastores Gregis* orients this passage around the ecclesiology of communion by stating that the bishop "is to help his people to grow as a reality of communion in the Holy Spirit" (§43). In the same context, *Pastores Gregis* remarks that the bishops, like the apostles, are "sent in Christ's name" (§43), and here *Pastores Gregis* cites paragraph 8 of *Christus Dominus*, which states that the bishops are "successors of the Apostles" who, in their dioceses, have "all the ordinary, proper, and immediate authority which is required for the exercise of their pastoral office."

When it comes to how to treat a priest who has failed in some way or who is thinking of leaving the priesthood, *Pastores Gregis* exhorts, "The Bishop will also follow with prayer and genuine compassion priests who for whatever reason are questioning their vocation and their fidelity to the Lord's call and have in some way failed in the performance of their duties" (§47). This passage echoes the remark that we noted in *Christus Dominus* §16.

In its sixth chapter, paragraph 56, *Pastores Gregis* quotes a significant text from paragraph 8 of *Christus Dominus*, in which bishops are described as "successors of the Apostles" and given "all the ordinary, proper, and immediate authority which is required for the exercise of their pastoral office," without thereby infringing on the power of the pope to exercise direct authority in any situation. *Pastores Gregis* notes that, during the Synod, a question was raised regarding whether this text would support "a greater decentralization" in accord with the principle of subsidiarity, so that the Roman Curia would have a lesser role and the bishops a greater one (§56). *Pastores Gregis* answers by differentiating between the principle of subsidiarity, which applies to civil society, and the principle of communion (see §56). Civil society, however tight its bonds, does not enjoy communion in the same way or to the same degree that the Church does. Therefore, as *Pastores Gregis* goes on to say, the bishop's power is never extrinsic to or autonomous from the pope's, because the pope is the head of the college of bishops and each bishop's power is exercised in intrinsic union with the head. This differs from subsidiarity in civil society, where distinct entities are not necessarily intrinsically joined to each other. Thus *Pastores Gregis* observes that "the functions of teaching (*munus docendi*) and governing (*munus regendi*)—and hence the corresponding power of magisterium and of governance—are by their nature to be exercised in the particular Church by each Diocesan Bishop in hierarchical communion with the Head of the College and the College itself" (§56). *Pastores Gregis* denies that this weakens the power of the bishop in his diocese, since the bishop's power is precisely that of one who is in communion with the other bishops and with the pope. *Pastores Gregis* concludes this section by underscoring that communion involves mutual reciprocity, which means that neither the bishops nor the pope can exercise power as though the relationship of bishops and pope were an extrinsic reality.

In its discussion of the regular visit of each bishop *ad Limina Apostolorum* (to the church of Rome), *Pastores Gregis* further examines the constitutive elements of the communion of the Church. One such element is the church of Rome, which "safeguards legitimate differences and yet is vigilant to ensure that particularity not only does not harm unity but serves it" (§57). There is a strong sense in this paragraph of the fragility of unity, a sense that is not found in *Christus Dominus*. After treating the *ad Limina* visits as an expression of collegiality, *Pastores Gregis* discusses the Synod of Bishops, which was instituted by Pope Paul VI's motu proprio *Apostolica Sollicitudo* (September 15, 1965) and which received attention in paragraph 5 of *Christus Dominus*. Regarding the Synod of Bishops, *Pastores Gregis* explains that "during the Second Vatican Council the need was felt for the Bishops to be able to assist the Roman Pontiff more effectively in the exercise of his office" (§58). *Pastores Gregis* goes on to praise the contributions that these Synods have made, while defending "the fact that the Synod ordinarily has only a consultative role" as not undermining the Synod's standing as a "participation in the governance of the universal Church" (§58).

Paragraph 62 of *Pastores Gregis* quotes a passage from paragraph 36 of *Christus Dominus*, where the Council Fathers state their desire "that the venerable institution of synods and councils flourish with fresh vigor. In such a way faith will be deepened and discipline preserved more fittingly and efficaciously in the various churches, as the needs of the times require." *Pastores Gregis* argues that regional Councils are an effective way both of enhancing the communion of bishops from a particular region, and of involving priests, deacons, religious, and laity of the region in a consultative manner.

How to sum up the reception of *Christus Dominus* in *Pastores Gregis*? On the one hand, there is a strong appreciation for the bishop's pastoral role— including the pastoral role of bishops who are not in charge of a diocese, such as auxiliary bishops. The bishop is sent in Christ's name as a successor of the apostles; the bishop calls people to faith and nourishes faith; the bishop leads by self-sacrificial service to the people of his diocese; the bishop gathers together the people through the Gospel and the Eucharist in the Holy Spirit; the bishop has mercy and compassion for wayward or troubled priests; the bishop cares for the financial and priestly needs not only of his diocese, but also of neighboring dioceses and of the whole Church. *Pastores Gregis* touches all of these themes with reference to *Christus Dominus*. On the other hand, the issue of episcopal power is also central in *Pastores Gregis*'s reception of *Christus Dominus*. *Pastores Gregis* attempts to place the issue of power within a more properly theological frame, namely that of the principle of communion, which is able to account better for the unique reality that the Church is.

IV. Theological Reception of *Christus Dominus*: Gaillardetz, Faggioli, Tavard

In histories of the composition of *Christus Dominus*, the emphasis tends to be on matters having to do with the power relations between the bishops and the pope/Curia. Thus, in Giuseppe Alberigo's discussion of the results of the conciliar debates of September 1963 through September 1964, he notes that "there were repeated proposals for the creation of a collegial body, comparable to the permanent synod of the Eastern Churches, which would regularly assist the pope in decisions of greater moment for the universal Church."[19] As Alberigo observes regarding the early stages of the Council, "Vatican II was feeling the effects of impulses toward an active involvement of the bishops in the leadership of the Church, something the aged Pope John had fostered in the letter *Mirabilis ille*, which he had addressed to the entire episcopate on Epiphany 1963."[20] Similarly, in the historical section of his essay on *Christus Dominus*, Klaus Mörsdorf remarks, "From the beginning the subject of the bishops, and especially their relation to the Pope, was one of the main themes to be discussed by the Council."[21] Mörsdorf devotes a helpful excursus to the topic of the Synod of Bishops, in which he notes that when Pope Paul VI announced at the opening of the fourth session of the Council (September 14, 1965) his plans to establish a Synod of Bishops, "all the Fathers broke into spontaneous applause."[22]

The historical section of Richard Gaillardetz's *The Church in the Making: Lumen Gentium, Christus Dominus, Orientalium Ecclesiarum* follows the same path. Gaillardetz states, "It is only in the second millennium that the papacy began to displace the college of bishops as the principal ministry in service of the unity of the church."[23] Even so, Gaillardetz finds that there were always efforts to stop the slide. He points out, "The gradual weakening of episcopal authority from the eleventh to the sixteenth centuries did not go unnoted. The Council of Trent addressed this situation, with council fathers engaging in a lively debate regarding the authority and ministry of the bishop."[24] The Spanish bishops led this reform effort at the Council of Trent, but they failed on a key issue that therefore had to wait for resolution by Vatican II, namely the question of whether episcopal jurisdiction comes from the pope or from Christ. Gaillardetz also notes the reform movement at the First Vatican Council. He concludes that "as the church moved toward Vatican II, Catholic ecclesiology seemed to suffer, if not from any fundamental defect, then certainly from a pronounced imbalance in its treatment of the relationship between papal authority and episcopal authority. This imbalance was uppermost on the minds of those who undertook preparations for Vatican II."[25]

This power-struggle came to the fore, Gaillardetz suggests, during the debates regarding the schema that served as a first draft of what eventually became *Christus Dominus*. He observes that during these debates, "Many bishops expressed their desire for a strong assertion of the rights of individual bishops, particularly over against the authority of the Roman curia."[26] He also points to the intervention of Melkite Patriarch Maximos IV Saigh, who suggested "the creation of a synodal body to assist the pope in governance of the universal church," a suggestion that, as Gaillardetz says, "echoed a number of similar proposals that had been floated by various bishops who were looking for ways to enhance the participation of the bishops in decisions involving the universal church."[27] Indeed, Gaillardetz notes that during these deliberations, "a letter requesting the creation of a synod was sent to the pope with the signatures of some five hundred bishops."[28]

Gaillardetz is somewhat disappointed with *Christus Dominus*'s presentation of episcopal conferences. Despite strong support from Jerome Hâmer and Joseph Ratzinger, "the council would content itself with only a few muted references to episcopal conferences."[29] *Christus Dominus*'s discussion of collegial cooperation among bishops also appears to Gaillardetz to be rather muted, due to the interventions of more than one prominent bishop. In his assessment of the implementation of *Christus Dominus*, Gaillardetz observes that while "the bishops at the council were eager to see a substantive reform of the Roman curia"—a desire that finds expression in paragraphs 9 and 10 of *Christus Dominus*—the reform of the Curia that Pope John Paul II set in motion in his apostolic constitution *Pastor Bonus* (1988) deviated from *Christus Dominus*'s conception of the Curia as performing its duties in the pope's "name and with his authority for the good of the churches and in the service of the sacred pastors [the bishops]" (§9). Instead, *Pastor Bonus* followed the 1983 *Code of Canon Law* (Canon 360) by teaching, in Gaillardetz's words, "that the curia serves the pontiff directly and the local churches indirectly" and by "making no mention of the pastors (bishops)."[30] Gaillardetz makes clear that he regards *Pastor Bonus* to have been a failure both with respect to streamlining the Curia, and with respect to bringing a halt to the "consistent pattern of curial interventionism in the affairs of regional and local churches beyond that demanded by the legitimate concerns for the unity of the church."[31]

Gaillardetz also notes that the status of episcopal conferences, since the promulgation of *Christus Dominus*, seems to have declined in certain ways. Drawing upon arguments made by Henri de Lubac, both Hâmer and Ratzinger changed their minds about episcopal conferences after the Council. As Gaillardetz says, both came to fear "that the enhanced role of episcopal conferences could bring about a return to the kind of church nationalism that had appeared in times past under the guise of Gallicanism and Febronianism," and they also feared that the ministry of the bishop might become bureaucratized and hidden "behind episcopal committees."[32] In 1998 Pope John Paul II addressed the status of episcopal conferences in his apostolic letter *Apostolos Suos*. This apostolic letter, on the positive side, stated clearly that the episcopal conferences (in Gaillardetz's words) "were partial expressions of collegiality."[33] But *Apostolos Suos* put limits on the conditions under which the episcopal conferences could issue binding doctrinal statements. Gaillardetz observes that some, notably Francis Sullivan, have complained that the need for a *recognitio* or formal approval from Rome in order for a teaching of an episcopal conference to be binding doctrinally (a need that is waived if the document has

received unanimous approval) undermines the claim of the episcopal conferences to possess real authority.

Regarding the implementation of the Synod of Bishops, Gaillardetz is
again not particularly sanguine. He argues that Pope Paul VI's motu proprio
itself violated the spirit of collegiality; the Synod of Bishops should have been
decided upon by the bishops themselves at Vatican II. Since Vatican II, there
have been three kinds of synods: ordinary (meeting every three to four years),
extraordinary (convened to address special topics), and special or regional synods. Gaillardetz notes that those who, like Ratzinger, "would grant collegiality only to an exercise of the whole college generally would not attribute any
collegial authority to the world synod," and those who take this position have
favored limiting these synods to a consultative role.[34] As Gaillardetz points out,
"This view is reflected in the treatment of the synod of bishops in the Code
of Canon Law. In canons 342–48, there is no reference to the relationship
between the synod of bishops and the whole college of bishops nor is there any
consideration of the extent to which synods might be expressions of collegiality. Rather, the synod is related to the primacy of the bishop of Rome (c. 344)."[35]
Drawing upon the work of James Coriden, Gaillardetz recounts various concerns about the implementation of synods, and almost all of these concerns
have to do in some way with the overbearing role of the pope.[36]

Gaillardetz also comments briefly on the principle of subsidiarity, recalling that the 1967 Synod of Bishops "recommended that the principle of subsidiarity guide the process of revising the code of canon law" and that the preface
to the 1983 *Code of Canon Law* confirms "the applicability of the principle
of subsidiarity to the life of the church even though the principle is largely
avoided in the code itself."[37] In favor of applying subsidiarity more fully to the
Church are such theologians as Oswald von Nell-Breuning, Walter Kasper,
and Joseph Komonchak. As an example, Gaillardetz points to the German
bishops' desire to allow their pastoral counseling centers to provide certifi-
cates indicating that a woman had received abortion counseling, a certificate
that was needed in Germany for a legal abortion. He suggests that Rome's
rejection of the German bishops' request was a violation of subsidiarity. He
indicates that it was Cardinal Jérôme Hamer who defeated efforts to apply subsidiarity more fully to the Church, especially at the 1985 Extraordinary Synod
that established the principle of communion as the hermeneutical lens for
understanding the Second Vatican Council.[38]

Massimo Faggioli, in his historical and theological reflections on *Christus
Dominus*, similarly emphasizes the power relations of the bishop and pope
(and Curia). Writing in 2004, he argues that *Christus Dominus*'s descriptions
of the bishops' rightful authority have been undermined in recent years. The
reformist or radical impetus of both *Christus Dominus* and *Lumen Gentium* has
been obscured, in his view. With respect to *Christus Dominus*, a key problem
was Pope Paul VI's untimely intervention in *Apostolica Sollicitudo* to create the
Synod of Bishops himself, an intervention that caused the Council Fathers
to modify and weaken *Christus Dominus*. Looking back on the documents
of Vatican II in general and *Christus Dominus* in particular, the question of

interpretation for Faggioli is as follows: "Is the conciliar text a limit, that is, was *Christus Dominus* to be viewed as constituting the final stage of Vatican II's reform of the episcopacy? Or, on the contrary, was *Christus Dominus* to be viewed as only the 'incipit,' the beginning of the special reforms of the episcopacy envisioned by Vatican II?"[39] Faggioli contends that the latter must be the answer. He argues that by contrast to the consultative and ad hoc synodal form that emerged from *Christus Dominus* as shaped by *Apostolica Sollicitudo*, in fact "a *core, collegial, stable, and permanent* episcopal board involved in universal church government . . . was envisioned by a large part of the council fathers."[40]

Along these lines, Faggioli states that "with respect to the pope's powers, more than once the bishops called for the creation of an *executive, collegial episcopal government body*."[41] Obviously, as he says, "there is a real difference between a *core, collegial-synodal, stable, and permanent* church governmental body with the pope and above the Roman Curia, and an assembly made up of hundreds of bishops called every few years in order to debate some pastoral problem."[42] Influenced by *Apostolica Sollicitudo, Christus Dominus* instituted the latter, but at the Council there was a good bit of movement toward the former. Faggioli argues, therefore, that what emerged in the text of *Christus Dominus* is not what the majority of the Council Fathers truly had in mind when they called for a Synod of Bishops. As he puts it, "It is also clear that the mind of the conciliar fathers was to diminish the monarchical principle in ordinary universal church government, and not to provide for the consultation of the global episcopate about some particular pastoral problems."[43] According to Faggioli, a close reading of *Christus Dominus* shows the intended direction of its teaching. For example, "Paragraph 8 on the bishops' powers and the relation between them and the pope's power attempted to invert the historical trend of faculties being conceded by Rome to the bishops."[44] Even the members of "the 'conservative' minority" at the Council were generally in favor of "a new balance of powers between the papacy and the episcopacy, between the Roman Curia and the episcopacy."[45]

Faggioli calls for "radical, profound reforms of the structure and role of the Roman Curia in the Catholic Church."[46] Episcopal power, not papal power, must be at the center. Faggioli also argues that *Christus Dominus* envisioned a balance between episcopal conferences and regional synods/councils, but in fact episcopal conferences have crowded out such synods. A further key problem is that in a globalized Church with the influence of the global media, the charismatic leadership of the pope threatens to sweep away the practical authority of bishops and episcopal conferences.

In a nutshell, for Faggioli one cannot simply consult the final text of *Christus Dominus*, but one must also know its "history" and "mind," which show it to be on a more radical trajectory than might otherwise appear.[47] Fundamentally, *Christus Dominus* can only be understood "as a document pointing to the future," and we must be aware of "the betrayal of conciliar fathers' expectations" and of the ongoing persistence of a Curial "structure lasting from the Tridentine period."[48] Not only the conciliar majority but also most of the minority expected real changes in power relations, but these have not sufficiently appeared, and as a result *Christus Dominus* has been inadequately received. Faggioli concludes that "maintaining fidelity to Vatican II's mentality of *aggiornamento* and to the ecumenical destiny of Christians makes the possibility of collegial-synodal reforms in the Catholic Church of the twenty first century more than a hypothesis; rather they are a continuing imperative."[49]

In an essay that he wrote just before his death, "The Task of a Bishop in His Diocese: *Christus Dominus* 11–21," George Tavard agrees that Paul VI's motu proprio establishing the Synod of Bishops overrode the Council's desire for a permanent, collegial episcopal synod and ensured that the resulting synod "would be strictly controlled by the pope and the Roman Curia."[50] Tavard, however, focuses upon other matters in *Christus Dominus*, especially ones that he considers to be of ecumenical significance. He notes, for example, that *Christus Dominus* teaches that the bishop gathers his people together around the Gospel and the Eucharist in the Holy Spirit. This conception of the Church, Tavard thinks, could be accepted by the signers of the Augsburg Confession. Tavard also points to the way in which *Christus Dominus* (like *Lumen Gentium*) employs the threefold office of priest, prophet, and king, which was a favorite image of Calvin's. Examining what *Christus Dominus* has to say about the bishop's prophetic office or preaching, he remarks that "one may wonder how many bishops are qualified to engage in such a range of teaching."[51] He also considers that *Christus Dominus*'s presentation of faith and doctrine should have shown more clearly how they relate, with attention to the stability and development of doctrine.

Commenting on the bishop's sanctifying mission, Tavard points out that more attention should be paid here to the role of priests and deacons, and he observes that more attention should be given to the importance of prayer and spiritual direction. He argues that the bishop's sanctifying or perfective role in his diocese tells against the idea of auxiliary bishops. He notes that the model of servant-rule employed in *Christus Dominus* is still indebted to the model of the "ideal patriarchal family" and needs adjustment—or radical change, given problems with "the patriarchal structure of the Catholic priesthood and episcopate"—in light of feminist concerns.[52] He deeply appreciates *Christus Dominus*'s understanding of the bishop's role in encouraging lay apostolates, and he also comments positively upon its teaching about the pastoral care of migrants and immigrants. He concludes by warning that the bishop's three roles—in his diocese, at the national episcopal conference, and vis-à-vis the universal Church—"entails a permanent temptation to focus on immediate local problems and to rely on others for the other two levels: on the bishop of Rome and the Roman curia for the universal Church, and on the designated officials of the national episcopal conference."[53]

V. Future Reception of *Christus Dominus*: Retrieving the Neglected Paragraphs

To my mind, Tavard's essay, inasmuch as it focuses on the pastoral paragraphs of *Christus Dominus*, follows the most appropriate path of ongoing reception of

Christus Dominus—a path that we also found in *Pastores Gregis*. This attention to the pastoral paragraphs of *Christus Dominus* is important not least because the Church can easily wear itself out with internal power struggles. Consider the historical oddity of Nicholas Lash's claim, in the very midst of the crisis over episcopal authority due to archbishops' moving of priest-pedophiles from one parish to another, that "there are, at present, few more urgent tasks facing the Church than that of realizing the as-yet unrealized program of Vatican II by throwing into reverse the centralization of power which accrued during the twentieth century, and restoring episcopal authority to the episcopate."[54]

Faggioli's pursuit of radical decentralization seems to me to offer very limited returns. What happens when bishops are independent in the sense that he requires? Such independence can hardly be given to bishops alone, and so the very power that the bishop has thereby gained will in fact be lost, since priests will assert independence from their bishop, and laypeople from priests, bishops, and pope alike.[55] Indeed, this rejection of the doctrinal and moral demands of ecclesial authority—whose purpose is to interpret and communicate the demands of the Gospel to the whole Church—is the situation that the Church is often facing in actual parish life.[56] Catholic laypeople widely discount the bishop's supposed authority on everything from sexual matters to the real presence of Christ in the Eucharist and the very existence of a personal God.[57] The balance taught by *Christus Dominus* involves not only insisting that "to bishops, as successors of the Apostles, in the dioceses entrusted to them, there belongs per se all the ordinary, proper, and immediate authority which is required for the exercise of their pastoral office" (§8), but also insisting equally that "this never in any way infringes upon the power which the Roman pontiff has, by virtue of his office, of reserving cases to himself or to some other authority" (§8).[58]

As *Christus Dominus* emphasizes, the authority of bishops is for the purpose of enabling the bishops to perform their Spirit-appointed task of teaching, sanctifying, and governing with more zeal and credibility. Power relations are merely a means to the goal of the episcopal ministry fully serving the purpose that Jesus Christ wills for it. *Christus Dominus* states that Christ sent the Apostles (and thus also the bishops) by "conferring on them the Holy Spirit, so that they also might glorify the Father upon earth and save men, 'to the building up of the body of Christ' (Eph. 4:12), which is the Church" (§1). The fruitfulness of changes in power relations will be manifest, then, only in the spread of the good news of salvation and in the building up of the Church in faith and charity.

Insofar as bishops have recognized more clearly the authority that they have received from the Lord Jesus, and insofar as this newfound understanding has led them to collaborate more effectively with each other and with the pope in matters pertaining to their particular churches, their ecclesiastical regions, and the universal Church, the fruitfulness of this development will be apparent in a Church that embodies more fully the ministry of the forgiveness of sins and of the sanctification of believers in Christ. Curial reform and influential roles for episcopal conferences and for the Synod of Bishops are evident in the Church's life under Pope Francis. This situation indicates the ongoing reception of the sections of *Christus Dominus* that deal with power relations between the bishops and pope. If the reception of *Christus Dominus* is going to bear its most important fruit, these reforms with respect to the power relations between the bishops and the pope/Curia cannot be given the disproportionate place that they possess in the theological literature about *Christus Dominus*.[59]

In fact, only a handful of *Christus Dominus*'s paragraphs relate directly to these power relations. Sanctification and holiness are the real center of *Christus Dominus*, and calibrating the right balance of internal Church power, while it has a place in such matters, cannot have the central place. The central purpose of *Christus Dominus*, as we would expect from a decree on the bishops' pastoral office, has to do with the day-to-day work of evangelization.

Since this is so, ongoing reception of *Christus Dominus*, especially among theologians, can learn a great deal from *Pastores Gregis*. *Pastores Gregis* attends to what *Christus Dominus* says about power relations—though with an enhanced appreciation, in light of the post-conciliar experience, of the fragility of Church unity. But *Pastores Gregis* devotes the majority of its attention to the paragraphs of *Christus Dominus* that explore the mundane responsibilities of bishops. For example, after stating that "bishops should realize that they are bound together and should manifest a concern for all churches" (§6), *Christus Dominus* draws implications that have to do not with power but with an evangelistic concern about spreading the Gospel to places where it has not yet been fully proclaimed and about places in the world that lack priests. In this same section, too, *Christus Dominus* urges bishops to "make every effort to have the faithful actively support and promote works of the apostolate" (§6). *Christus Dominus* notes that the bishop's evangelistic concern cannot be limited to his own diocese. In undertaking his office, it is not power that should be first on the bishop's mind. Rather, the primary thing is the bishop's own holiness "as witness of Christ before all men" (§11). This witness requires that the bishop bring the message of Christ's mercy to all, and especially to those who are not yet evangelized or who have fallen away. As teachers, bishops "should announce the Gospel of Christ to men, calling them to faith in the power of the Spirit or confirming them in a living faith. They should expound the whole mystery of Christ to them" (§12).

Christus Dominus's list of things that a bishop should teach makes clear that bishops in the contemporary world inevitably teach about controversial matters. A bishop who today teaches the "great value" of the bodily life of humans, the stability of the family, and the procreation and education of children will have to address such issues as abortion, marriage as between a man and a woman, the impact of contraception and pornography, and the secularizing tendency in much of Catholic higher education. *Christus Dominus* urges the bishop to attend especially to the poor, whose right to receive care, love, and the full preaching of the Gospel must be recognized. With regard to the office of sanctifying, bishops should "constantly exert themselves to have the faithful know and live the paschal mystery more deeply through the Eucharist and thus become a firmly-knit body in the unity of the charity of Christ" (§15). Caring for and overseeing the diocese's priests and parishes is a huge part of the bishop's ministry, and so theological and practical attention to the later paragraphs of Christus Dominus will also continue to be important.

It may seem that my suggestions for the ongoing reception of Christus Dominus are simply a new attempt to continue the frustration that, according to John O'Malley, the Council majority consistently felt "in its efforts to make its will felt through the establishment of real structural changes."[60] O'Malley recognizes that "aggiornamento, development, and ressourcement plunge us into the dynamics of the council. Updating as such was not a problem to either party. It became a problem only in terms of its limits (how far could it legitimately go?) and its pastoral appropriateness (would it accomplish what it promised?)."[61] In the fifty years since the Council, the reception of Christus Dominus by theologians has focused mainly on how far, in terms of power relations between bishops and the pope (and Curia), the development undertaken by Christus Dominus has gone and should go. I suggest that ongoing theological reception of Christus Dominus will now be best served, not by ignoring the issues of power relations, but by concentrating on what Christus Dominus has to say about the daily pastoral tasks of the episcopal ministry, especially vis-à-vis the poor and those who are enduring spiritual poverty due to secularization. When, as is inevitable, the issues regarding power relations arise, they must be addressed with the balance that marks Christus Dominus itself, which affirms both the bishops' authority and the primacy and authority of the pope.

Ultimately, if episcopal authority is to be taken seriously, it can only be taken seriously from within a renewed appreciation of the pastoral value and necessity of such authority. The authority of bishops shows itself in the proclamation of the Gospel in word and deed (above all in the Eucharistic liturgy) and in the call to live out the Gospel's twin pillars of mercy and holiness in bringing about the sanctification of the whole world through the power of the Holy Spirit.

NOTES

1. John Linnan, CSV, "Dogmatic Constitution on the Church Lumen Gentium, 21 November, 1964 and Decree on the Pastoral Office of Bishops in the Church Christus Dominus, 28 October, 1965," in Vatican II and Its Documents: An American Reappraisal, ed. Timothy E. O'Connell (Wilmington, DE: Michael Glazier, 1986), 39–61, at 45.

2. Ibid. 60. Linnan states, "The laity (the People of God) should be given priority in the next Council's reflection on the nature of the Church. The distinction between work in the world and pastoral ministry should be re-thought and the practice of defining a particular group of persons by the work they do be reconsidered" (60). Linnan's essay, written during the twentieth anniversary of the Council's work, looks toward a future Council in which Vatican II will "be completed and perhaps replaced" (61). See also Paul Lakeland, The Liberation of the Laity (New York: Continuum, 2003).

3. Brian Ferme, "The Decree on the Bishops' Pastoral Office in the Church, *Christus Dominus*," in *Vatican II: Renewal within Tradition*, ed. Matthew L. Lamb and Matthew Levering (Oxford: Oxford University Press, 2008), 187–204, at 188. With respect to Pope Benedict XVI's December 22, 2005 address to the Roman Curia, a portion of which appears as "A Proper Hermeneutic for the Second Vatican Council," in *Vatican II: Renewal within Tradition*, ix–xv, Joseph A. Komonchak has argued that "Pope Benedict's view has been oversimplified into a contrast between a hermeneutic of discontinuity and one of continuity and interpreted as a rejection of any approach that would speak of the council as a difference-making event in any sense other than spiritual" (Komonchak, "Interpreting the Council and Its Consequences: Concluding Reflections," in *After Vatican II: Trajectories and Hermeneutics*, ed. James L. Heft, SM, with John O'Malley, SJ [Grand Rapids, MI: Eerdmans, 2012], 164–72, at 166). Certainly the Council made a huge difference in ways "other than spiritual," including the development of doctrine in various respects. The real issue, as Komonchak well knows, is whether one can speak of discontinuity in the sense of rupture with a defined doctrine of the Church. For the claim that the Church has repudiated previously defined doctrine, see Francis Oakley, "History and the Return of the Repressed in Catholic Modernity: The Dilemma Posed by Constance," in *The Crisis of Authority in Catholic Modernity*, ed. Michael J. Lacey and Francis Oakley (Oxford: Oxford University Press, 2011), 29–58; see also in the same volume Komonchak's "Benedict XVI and the Interpretation of Vatican II," 93–110. For further discussion see Ian Ker, *Newman on Vatican II* (Oxford: Oxford University Press, 2014).

4. For the view that the affirmation that the one, holy, catholic, and apostolic Church is present and realized in every local church is the main contribution of *Christus Dominus*, and indeed perhaps the most significant new development offered by the Second Vatican Council, see Karl Rahner, "The New Image of the Church," in *Theological Investigations*, vol. 10, *Writings of 1965–67, Part 2*, trans. David Bourke (London: Darton, Longman & Todd, 1973), 3–29. I agree with Richard R. Gaillardetz and Catherine E. Clifford that "an ultramontane view had crept into large sectors of Catholic theology that claimed bishops were little more than priests who were given a special task by the pope for the administration of the diocese. The powers or 'faculties' needed to carry out this task were said to be 'delegated' to them by the pope, who was viewed as the source and center of all power and authority in the church" (Gaillardetz and Clifford, *Keys to the Council: Unlocking the Teaching of Vatican II* [Collegeville, MN: Liturgical Press, 2012], 115).

5. In his evaluation and critique of the 1983 *Code of Canon Law*'s reception of Vatican II, Eugenio Corecco criticizes, mistakenly in my view (and certainly mistakenly if *Christus Dominus* is any indication), the fact that "the Code unvaryingly gives priority to the pope over the college" (Corecco, "Aspects of the Reception of Vatican II in the Code of Canon Law," in *The Reception of Vatican II*, ed. Giuseppe Alberigo, Jean-Pierre Jossua, and Joseph A. Komonchak, trans. Matthew J. O'Connell [Washington, DC: Catholic University of America Press, 1987], 249–96, at 277–78). Corecco argues, "The Council . . . at least in passages in which the ecclesiological problem is not looked at primarily from a collegial institutional standpoint but remains imbedded in broader theological reflection, repeatedly does not hesitate to give the college of the apostles priority over Peter and the college of bishops over the pope. The consistent way in which the Code has instead put the pope before the college (can. 330ff., 746, 749, 782) gives the impression that, at least for itself, it preferred to ignore the doctrine of the one subject of supreme power in the Church" (278).

6. A little more than a month before the promulgation of *Christus Dominus*, Pope Paul VI announced the formation of this Synod of Bishops in his motu proprio *Apostolica Sollicitudo*, promulgated on September 15, 1965 (see www.vatican.va).

7. *Code of Canon Law*, Latin-English edition, trans. by the Canon Law Society of America (Washington, DC: Canon Law Society of America, 1998 [Latin edition copyright 1983]), 147.

8. Ibid. 148.

9. Ibid.

10. Ibid.

11. Ibid. 149.

12. See www.vatican.va for these two documents and all other Vatican documents not cited otherwise.

13. Ibid. 263.

14. Ibid.

15. Ibid. 264.

16. Ibid.

17. Ibid. 131.

18. See Klaus Mörsdorf's commentary on paragraph 38 of *Christus Dominus*: "An episcopal conference is, as it were, a council in which the bishops of a given nation or territory jointly exercise their pastoral office [*munus suum pastorale coniunctim exercent*] to promote the greater good which the Church offers mankind." Mörsdorf states, "It cannot be doubted that the bishops are to exercise their pastoral office in the episcopal conference *coniunctim*, but this word does not express the characteristics of this exercise of authority. The reason why the Council has here avoided the only appropriate term *collegialiter exercent* seems to be that the majority of the Fathers did not approve of the principle of collegiality for the particular Churches. Nevertheless, the principle of collegiality has been accepted as a formal structural principle [in §4, according to Mörsdorf]" (Mörsdorf, "Decree on the Bishops' Pastoral Office in the Church," in *Commentary on the Documents of Vatican II*, ed. Herbert Vorgrimler, trans. Hilda Graef [New York: Herder and Herder, 1968], 2:165–300, at 286).

19. Giuseppe Alberigo, "Conclusion: The New Shape of the Council," in *History of Vatican II*, ed. Giuseppe Alberigo, English version ed. Joseph A. Komonchak, vol. 3, *The Mature Council. Second Period and Intersession: September 1963–September 1964* (Maryknoll, NY: Orbis Books, 2000), 491–513, at 499.

20. Ibid. 495.

21. Mörsdorf, "Decree on the Bishops' Pastoral Office in the Church," 165.

22. Ibid. 214. Mörsdorf also points to Paul VI's motu proprio *Pastorale Munus* (November 30, 1963), which, as Mörsdorf says, "granted the diocesan bishops a large number of new powers and to all bishops several privileges.... Though the motu proprio did not yet clear up the basic principles, the granting of forty faculties was nevertheless of great practical importance, because many matters which till then had to be submitted to the Holy See could now be settled by the bishops" (183–84). Regarding *Christus Dominus*, Mörsdorf observes that it "affects the legal order of the Church much more than any other document of the Council, especially as regards the Latin Church; hence it is understandable that it will become fully effective only with the reform of canon law" (197).

23. Richard R. Gaillardetz, *The Church in the Making: Lumen Gentium, Christus Dominus, Orientalium Ecclesiarum* (New York: Paulist Press, 2006), 28.

24. Ibid.

25. Ibid. 30.

26. Ibid. 33.

27. Ibid.

28. Ibid.

29. Ibid. 36.

30. Ibid. 134.

31. Ibid. 135.

32. Ibid. 129.

33. Ibid. 130.

34. Ibid. 131; see Joseph Ratzinger, "The Structure and Task of the Synod of Bishops," in *Church, Ecumenism and Politics: New Essays in Ecclesiology* (New York: Crossroad, 1988), 46–62.

35. Gaillardetz, *The Church in the Making*, 131.

36. Ibid. 131–32; see James Coriden, "The Synod of Bishops: Episcopal Collegiality Still Seeks Adequate Expression," *The Jurist* 64 (2004): 116–36.

37. Gaillardetz, *The Church in the Making*, 132. See Bonaventure Kloppenburg, OFM, *The Ecclesiology of Vatican II*, trans. Matthew J. O'Connell (Chicago: Franciscan Herald Press, 1974), 189–94.

38. On the 1985 Extraordinary Synod, see Avery Dulles, SJ, "The Reception of Vatican II at the Extraordinary Synod of 1985," in Alberigo, Jossua, and Komonchak, *The Reception of Vatican II*, 349–63. At this stage of his career, Dulles appears to have been rather dismayed by Cardinal Hamer's remarks. As Dulles points out, despite the Synod's "Final Report" having contained a recommendation for a study of whether the principle of subsidiarity can be applied to the Church, Pope John Paul II did not mention this recommendation in his closing address and argued instead, in a speech to the Curia on June 29, 1986, that more time would be needed to determine "the precise state of the question and the point at issue" (362). Dulles asks, "Will there be free and open processes based on a recognition of the desirability of input from below? More specifically, will subsidiarity be utilized or excluded in the conduct of the study of subsidiarity?" (363). For a highly negative response to the study of episcopal conferences undertaken after the 1985 Extraordinary Synod, complaining that the *instrumentum laboris* "assigns priority or primacy to the whole college of bishops, presiding in the universal church, over the individual diocesan bishop, presiding in his particular church," see Joseph A. Komonchak, "The Roman Working Paper on Episcopal Conferences," in *Episcopal Conferences: Historical, Canonical, and Theological Studies*, ed. Thomas J. Reese, SJ (Washington, DC: Georgetown University Press, 1989), 177–204. For an evaluation of the teaching and role of episcopal conferences, see Dulles's excellent "Doctrinal Authority of Episcopal Conferences," in Reese, *Episcopal Conferences*, 207–31. See also James P. Green, *Conferences of Bishops and the Exercise of the "Munus Docendi" of the Church* (Rome: P. Graziani, 1987).

39. Massimo Faggioli, "Institutions of Episcopal Collegiality-Synodality after Vatican II: The Decree *Christus Dominus* and the Agenda for Collegiality-Synodality in the 21st Century," *The Jurist* 64 (2004): 224–46, at 229.

40. Ibid.

41. Ibid. 230.

42. Ibid. 231.

43. Ibid.

44. Ibid. 233.

45. Ibid. 235.

46. Ibid. 236.

47. Ibid. 245.

48. Ibid. 245–46.

49. Ibid. 246. See also Daniele Menozzi, "Opposition to the Council (1966–84)," in Alberigo, Jossua, and Komonchak, *The Reception of Vatican II*, 325–48. Menozzi comments upon "more subtle forms of anti-conciliarism," and as an example gives the post-conciliar concerns of the great *Ressourcement* theologians and their followers (327). See also Giuseppe Alberigo, "Cristianesimo e storia nel Vaticano II," *Cristianesimo nella storia* 5 (1984): 577–92. Menozzi grants that "progressives, too, not only held and acted on anticonciliar positions but had been consolidating them at the levels of both of ideological development and of organization" ("Opposition to the Council [1966–84]," 341), but here he focuses on Socialist groups that deemed the Council to be a neocapitalist ploy.

50. George Tavard, "The Task of a Bishop in His Diocese: *Christus Dominus* 11–21," *The Jurist* 68 (2008): 361–81, at 372.

51. Ibid. 374.

52. Ibid. 379–80.

53. Ibid. 381.

54. Nicholas Lash, *Theology for Pilgrims* (Notre Dame: University of Notre Dame Press, 2008), 234, cited in Faggioli, "Between Documents and Spirit," 16.

55. See the representative remark of Christian Duquoc, in his evaluation of *Presbyterorum Ordinis* written twenty years after the Council: "Priests continue to occupy an ambiguous position: they resent the exclusion felt by the laity as a result of decisions by higher authorities over which they have no control. At the same time, however, they themselves exercise an unrestricted hierarchical power over the laity, analogous to that which higher authorities exercise over them. The conciliar document in no way corrects this situation; instead it aggravates it by proclaiming principles that do not produce any corresponding theology and code of rights. . . . The failure of reform is not due to any lack of inspiration at the level of intention. It is due to a failure to bear in mind the real functioning of a society that out of excessive fidelity to tradition, cannot rid itself of a hierarchic theory of government, even though this is radically at odds with, on the one hand, the demands of advanced societies and, on the other, the evangelical principles that it repeatedly proclaims" (Duquoc, "Clerical Reform," in Alberigo, Jossua, and Komonchak, *The Reception of Vatican II*, 297–308, at 308).

56. See, for an early discussion of this issue, Philip Murnion, "The Parish Community: Theological Questions Arising from Attempts to Implement Vatican II," in *Proceedings of the Thirty-Sixth Annual Convention of the Catholic Theological Society of America*, ed. Luke Salm, FSC (New York: Catholic Theological Society of America, 1982), 39–55. Murnion notes that "Andrew Greeley has documented extensively the growing independence of Catholics who make up their own mind about doctrine and morality and who question the importance of teaching authority and liturgy. Father Greeley has also limned the profile of the communal Catholic, one who retains a Catholic identity that is culturally rooted but individually defined" (47). Murnion cites Andrew M. Greeley, *The Church in Crisis* (Chicago: Thomas More, 1979); and Greeley, *The Communal Catholic: A Personal Manifesto* (New York: Seabury, 1976). See also Michael Novak, "Diversity of Structures and Freedom within Structures of the Church," *Concilium*, vol. 1, *The Church and Mankind* (New York: Paulist Press, 1965), 103–13, at 112–13.

57. See Christian Smith et al., *Young Catholic America: Emerging Adults In, Out of, and Gone from the Church* (Oxford: Oxford University Press, 2014).

58. The only way that the pope can do this, given the worldwide scope of the Church and given the many other burdens of the pope's office, is through the

ministrations of the Curia. This means that blanket assertions such as the following by Karl Rahner, SJ, are really not appropriate, since they put forward a caricature (given that the Vatican is actually not very "gigantic" compared with the administration of other world bodies) that obscures the actual options: "It is becoming increasingly clear and more apparent in the Church's self-understanding that this supreme and permanent power of jurisdiction of the Pope for the whole Church is not simply identical with the whole gigantic administrative machinery which has developed historically and continues to exist and operate up to the present time in Rome" (Rahner, "Structural Change in the Church of the Future," in *Theological Investigations*, vol. 20, *Concern for the Church*, trans. Edward Quinn [London: Darton, Longman & Todd, 1981], 115–32, at 119).

59. See also *The Nature and Future of Episcopal Conferences*, ed. Hervé Legrand, Julio Manzanares, and Antonio García y García, trans. Thomas J. Green, Joseph A. Komonchak, and James H. Provost (Washington, DC: Catholic University of America Press, 1988); and, from a popular perspective, Xavier Rynne, *John Paul's Extraordinary Synod: A Collegial Achievement* (Wilmington, DE: Michael Glazier, 1986).

60. John W. O'Malley, SJ, *What Happened at Vatican II* (Cambridge, MA: Harvard University Press, 2008), 312.

61. Ibid. 300.

6

Presbyterorum Ordinis

David Vincent Meconi, SJ

Introduction

Since the conciliar decree *Presbyterorum Ordinis* ("On the Ministry and Life of Priests") was promulgated in 1965, the Roman Catholic theology of priesthood has been stamped by three towering papacies, a relative explosion of both official documents and theological speculation on the nature of the priesthood, as well as unforeseen challenges from wider society. Saint John Paul called for a resacralization of the Church's presentation of priesthood, Pope Emeritus Benedict stressed the cultic beauty of the priest's offering of the sacred liturgy, and Pope Francis has more recently called for his shepherds to "to smell like their sheep," ensuring the Church never again becomes "self-referential" but is always being propelled outward to society's margins.[1]

Yet, precisely at these margins, the Church has also been challenged by the wider world's aversion to any organizational structure based on hierarchy, to any appearance of judgmentalism and exclusivity, and to any commitment to objective truth claims, especially moral truths. Accordingly, post-conciliar Christianity has been forced to answer secular society's numerous calls to greater transparency and inclusion of all believers, despite creed or praxis. The hostile response that followed Pope Paul VI's issuing of *Humanae Vitae* in 1968, for example, is emblematic of this clash of cultures, and itself still has profound effects on how a priest prepares and thereafter relates to married couples, how he might preach on the sacrament of matrimony (if at all), and to a large degree how he approaches most divisions within his parish, if not his own rectory. The Church has also had to suffer the public shaming and consequent unraveling of the priesthood as a respectable office, embarrassingly razed by a decade-plus of shocking headlines. Furthermore, since Vatican II, today's priest labors in a Church whose more traditional demographics have often wandered elsewhere, where the once very clear distinction between cleric and lay is eroded, and where he is able to download his daily homily as he walks from his residence to morning Mass.

It was not until the final year of Vatican II that the two main documents on priesthood appeared. Whereas *Optatam Totius*, addressing the training of priestly candidates, was released on October 28, *Presbyterorum Ordinis* was finally made public on December 7, 1965.[2] This document, "On the Ministry and Life of Priests," was five years in the making, underwent no less than ten drafts, with more than 10,000 votes going into the finalized version. The purpose of this essay is to show the theological significance of *Presbyterorum Ordinis* (hereafter *PO*) as well as how it has contributed to post-conciliar understandings of the Church and the priesthood.

According to then Karol Wojtyła, *PO* was among the most important works of the council fathers, since "the doctrine concerning Christ's priesthood and man's share in it is at the very centre of the teaching of Vatican II and contains in a certain manner all that the Council wished to say about the Church, mankind and the world."[3] Other *periti* were clearly (and quite publicly) not so enamored with the decree. The great Dominican theologian, Yves Congar, for instance, did not try in the least to hide his hostility toward almost every aspect of *PO* when he admitted to a high-ranking prelate (within earshot of not a few) that "I myself am of this opinion and tell everyone that the text ought to be rejected since it is feeble, moralizing, paternalistic, without vision, inspiration or prophetic spirit! It contains no deep questioning, no biblical sources; it does not take up the real and burning questions of priests themselves."[4] Such irreconcilability would be characteristic of most of the time it took to form and write *PO*, itself the result of many years of internecine debates and disagreements.

This essay accordingly proceeds in three main sections. The first will be to provide the historical context out of which *PO* arose. Here we shall ask what were those composing the document thinking and why. What did the fathers at Vatican II see as the particular opportunities and challenges to the priesthood as the tumultuous twentieth century was drawing to a close? The second section examines closely the three chapters of *PO*. In this analysis we shall see how "On the Ministry and Life of Priests" sought to accomplish a twofold telos: to present the priest as a man who first recognizes the indispensable role of divine grace in his life, and then, in turn, to recognize (and thereby help increase) God's laboring in the lives of those entrusted to him. What emerges is a vision of the priesthood that is far from withdrawn or disassociated from daily life, but one that calls a priest to participate first in the eternal life of the Trinity and then in the everyday lives of the baptized. The third and final section will be an analysis of how *PO* has come to be used in major post-conciliar documents on the priesthood itself, namely in St. John Paul II's Apostolic Exhortation, *Pastores Dabo Vobis*, the *Catechism of the Catholic Church*, as well as in the *Directory for the Life and Ministry of Priests*.

I. Historical Context

On behalf of the Antepreparatory Commission for the Discipline of Clergy and Christian People, Vatican Secretary of State Cardinal Domenico Tardini (1888–1961) mailed out a questionnaire on the state of the priesthood to 2,549 bishops and 156 male religious superiors on June 18, 1959. From this international solicitation came the first schema, originally proposed as *De Clericis*, compiled intermittently between 1960 and 1962. In May of 1963 it was distributed on the council floor in order to be discussed with the aim of agreeing upon both working title and possible content. In the next round of discussion, the schema had been renamed *De Sacerdotibus*, and then eventually to *De Ministerio et Vita Presbyterorum*, by the time a draft was issued on November 20, 1964.

The Latin taxonomy is telling, revealing the very type of theologizing that transpired over the years of drafting *PO*: from addressing clerics, to emphasizing the sacerdotal ministry of some, to finally settling on the presbyter who is characterized through connection with others. The Latin terms denoting the more cultic and mediatorial image of the priest as the "giver of the sacred" were now officially replaced with a more ancient, biblically sanctioned Greek word signifying an "elder" who was recognized not by the sacred function he performs, but by his relationship to the people he guides.[5]

Having collated and schematized all the responses, the Commission for the Discipline of Clergy and Christian People transmitted twelve proposed headings to the council fathers on October 2, 1964. The anticipated themes, in order, were (1) the relationship between priest and laity, (2) the priest's conformation to the narrative of the Gospel, (3) various characteristics of priestly life, (4) priestly fraternity, (5) the importance of ongoing intellectual formation, (6) how pastoral activity should be configured to the particular culture, (7) the call for a more catholic vision and thus a care for ministry even outside one's own parish boundaries, (8) equitable distribution of material goods among all the clergy, (9) the overall purpose of such goods, (10) the purpose of ecclesiastical offices, (11) nondiscriminatory remuneration for priestly work, and (12) the establishment of a common endowment in each diocese.

Just about two weeks later (October 13), the public debate on these topics began in the council hall with François Marty (1904–1994), quondam Bishop of Reims (elevated to Archbishop of Paris shortly thereafter, in 1968) explaining that this set of themes would best help the council participants understand "the pastoral needs of the Church and the conditions of life and the apostolate of priests in today's world, in a positive rather than a negative way … for today's priests are not just fathers and masters of the laity, they are also brothers."[6] The schematic as well as the rhetorical emphases quickly focused on a priesthood that was not sharply situated above the people of God, but on a priesthood that admitted and cared for the relationality and humanity of the ordained—no longer exclusively over his flock, but presented now as one with all people on a common pilgrimage. The Tridentine need for a priesthood, timeless and essentially set apart, was quickly being replaced by this new stress on the commonality and collegiality of the Christian faithful.[7]

Regarding this important presentation of the priest, the fathers at Vatican II came from both sides of the aisles but in the end found a conciliatory middle. Eschewed were the propositions that the priest be understood first as an *alter Christus*; but also absent from the finalized decree was any mention of the various innovations then in vogue—for example, the worker-priest movement on the Continent, or the rumblings of (what would come to be known as) "liberation theology" from certain members of the Latin American Episcopal Conference (known as CELAM). Most significant, however, was the absence of the overly facile distinction between a priest who alone provides the things of heaven, and a laity whose mission is to "consecrate the world."[8] For the lines were no longer so binary, no longer so clear. In fact, the image of the Good Shepherd began to capture the extra-ecclesial nature of the contemporary priest: like Christ himself, one who "opposed a static mentality that wishes only to preserve the past . . . [but who] takes responsibility for those who do not enter the Church as well as those who have abandoned her, for the brothers and sisters separated from the Church and for all nonbelievers, to meet them and gain them for Christ."[9]

Throughout the first half of October 1964, debate on the content of the working schema of the document took place with healthy dialogue and oftentimes animated debate. While there was palpable unanimity about the importance of the Council's addressing the life of the priest directly, disagreements arose over both the brevity of the document and, more importantly, its content. The issue of the schema's Christocentricity, its alleged lack of Marian devotion, as well as the more visible and practical question of priestly celibacy ignited most of the discussion on the council floor. Was the proposed vision for the document drawing a sufficient enough conformity between Christ and the priest? With the question of mandatory celibacy alive in the West for some years now, would it be the right thing to address this often-divisive issue here?

By mid-October, debate over the schema had somewhat subsided, and those who were already in favor of it wanted to push for a final vote. This offered the last opportunity for discussion of any or all of the schemas, "a tactful way of allowing revision of a schema to take place without the appearance of a wholesale rejection of it."[10] But on October 19, only 930 fathers accepted the document before them for a final vote, while 1199 desired further input. Returned to the working commission, therefore, the newly entitled *De Ministerio et Vita Presbyterorum* appeared again on November 20, the final day before the third session of the Council would come to a close. Therefore, with the relative hush of the winter months before them, the committee emerged in late spring of 1965, having incorporated other desired themes into a new 165-page booklet (containing 446 proposals),[11] now officially entitled "On the Life and Ministry of Priests."

At the opening of the fourth session (September 14, 1965), eleven unfinished schemata remained, and those on the floor realized that they would now have to act swiftly and decisively. When the decree on priesthood came up for discussion, many quickly took up once again the question of clerical celibacy as integral to the priesthood in the West. A major proponent pushing this discussion was Brazil's Bishop Pedro Koop (1905–1988) who alarmingly argued that "married priests could exercise their conjugal, familiar, and socioeconomic experience in service of the ministry.... The fate of the Church in Latin America is in great danger. The choice is urgent: either we multiply the number of priests, or we can expect the fall of the Church in Latin America."[12] But not all agreed. The President of the Conference of Bishops of Latin America, Chile's Larraín Errázuris (1900–1966) cabled Pope Paul VI to assure him that not all from the Southern hemisphere agreed with Koop and that many bishops did not in fact desire to change the occidental discipline in support of celibacy. On October 11, therefore, the head-secretary of the council, Cardinal Eugène Tisserant (1884–1972) of the Roman Curia walked onto the council floor and read a missive from the Holy Father (to be released for the wider Church in L'Osservatore Romano that day), herewith forbidding any more discussion on the possibility of lifting the law of celibacy in the Latin rite.[13]

The last draft of Presbyterorum Ordinis ran 8,149 words in the Latin (standing as the fifth longest of the sixteen conciliar documents), and was approved with a vote of 2,390 for and only 4 against. Pope Paul VI promulgated the decree finally on December 7, 1965, the Feast of the great bishop of Milan, Saint Ambrose. PO's text caused mixed reactions in the years to follow. Let us now turn to the text to understand better its message and its call to the priest of the modern world.

II. The Theological Structure and Significance of Presbyterorum Ordinis

Sandwiched between a brief preface and conclusion, PO is divided into three main sections: (1) the priesthood in the ministry of the Church, (2) the ministry of priests, and (3) the life of priests. The overall aim of PO is to address the main issues the council fathers saw priests facing at the end of the twentieth century: their mission in the Church and in the world, their developing interaction with the People of God, their own need for spiritual sustenance as well as community, and even the more mundane admittance of financial and social support.

The Preface (PO §1) lays this all out: the proceeding decree is meant for all priests, but "especially those" secular priests who are directly "devoted to the care of souls." Whether diocesan or religious, all priests are made for the "service of Christ" (ad inserviendum Christo), introduced here as Teacher, Priest, and King (Magistro, Sacerdoti, et Regi). Although none of these dominical titles is elaborated upon here, they are all presented in terms of service, ordered to an incessant building up (indesinentera edificatur) of "the People of God, the Body of Christ and the Temple of the Holy Spirit." In this way, PO is clearly a Christocentric text, but a clear, ecclesial-pneumatic dimension is discernible throughout as well: for at nearly every mention of Christ the Priest and Teacher, the Holy Spirit and Church appear in tandem as well. The priest is first and foremost an extension of Christ's service to his people. He is ordained to serve in *persona Christi* to act as the one in whom the Holy Spirit labors, propelling the priest back into the Church, to the holy people of God from whom he originally came.

A very brief first section, "The Priesthood in the Ministry of the Church" (*PO* §§2–3), accordingly situates the priest as one sent into the Mystical Body on earth, with whom he shares the same anointing of all the baptized. As such, "there is no member who does not have a part in the mission of the whole Body; but each one ought to hallow Jesus in his heart, and in the spirit of prophecy bear witness to Jesus" (*PO* §2). Throughout, lines like this one stress the common faith of cleric and congregant alike, giving *PO* its unique theme. For example, when treating the Lord's intent in establishing ministers among his faithful (*instituit ministros . . . in societate fidelium*), *PO* first cites the 23rd Session of Trent on Holy Orders by defining the priest as one who is ordained "to offer sacrifice and forgive sins" (*Sacrificium offerendi et peccatare mittendi*).[14] But *PO* makes clear that this cultic expression of priesthood is a gift not intended for the priest himself, but for every man and woman, thus defining this sacerdotal role with its ultimate telos being *for all others* in the name of Christ (*pro hominibus nomine Christi*). Once again, we receive a widening of priestly service characteristic of Vatican II: the benefits of Holy Orders are meant not for the priest, nor only for those who bear the name Christian. Instead, the priest is to be a servant unto all men and women (*pro hominibus*) because he bears the name of Christ, not because they do. This ecclesial amplification runs throughout *PO*: priests are to be ministers not simply of God's people but "among the people" (*in gentibus*), seemingly regardless of creedal or denominational allegiance. The work of God is thus presented as greater than the work of God's visible Church, although that is where all pastoral work is ultimately directed.

Such work is presented in terms of glory. The glory of God is understood here not as slavishly placating some distant vassal, but rather holistically in terms of every aspect of human living. There are certainly echoes here of Irenaeus's much-celebrated definition of God's glory as "the human person fully alive,"[15] and this is to be the focus of ordained Catholic ministry: "The purpose, therefore, which priests pursue in their ministry and by their life is to procure the glory of God the Father in Christ. That glory consists in this— that men working freely and with a grateful spirit receive the work of God made perfect in Christ and then manifest it in their whole lives." Keeping in line with Vatican II's universal call to holiness,[16] the glory of Christ radiating through his faithful to the Father is to be realized in all aspects of human life, not just a glory realized in pious ceremonies or on Sunday mornings. A priest is therefore to dedicate all of his prayers and actions "to the increase of the glory of God and to man's progress in the divine life" (*PO* §2).

Here the distinctive character and charge of the priest is thus highlighted, and his sacred mediation is stressed. While *PO* never fails to emphasize that the priest is first one who comes from and now lives alongside others (*cum ceteris hominibus*), in his ordination, he is to give to them "the things that belong to God" (*quae sunt ad Deum*). These lines in the middle of PO §3 are the strongest language we receive for the distinctive role of the priest among the People of God. Here he is not simply one with them; he is also one ordained for them. The entire purpose of Holy Orders is meant to impart a life that is essentially not created: priests "cannot be ministers of Christ unless they be witnesses and dispensers of a life other than earthly life" (*Ministri Christi esse non possent nisi alius vitae quam terrenae testes essent et dispensatores; PO* §3). The ancient role of a priest as an agent of divinization beautifully captures the essential role of the ordained: the very work that most deeply identifies the priest is God's using him to impart God's own life.

Dispensing a "life other than earthly" is what the Church has always taught by Christian deification. Unfortunately, PO does not choose to elaborate on this central soteriological metaphor, but since Vatican II, it has nonetheless enjoyed a resurgence of theological study in theological circles.[17] The most official reflection of this *ressourcement* is surely found throughout the 1992 *Catechism*, especially where the Church invokes her best theologians to teach that

> the Word became flesh to make us "partakers of the divine nature" (2 Pet 1:4): "For this is why the Word became man, and the Son of God became the Son of man: so that [men and women], by entering into communion with the Word and thus receiving divine [adoption], might become a [child] of God" (St. Irenaeus, AH 3.19.1). "For the Son of God became man so that we might become God" (St. Athanasius, *On the Incarnation* §54.3). "The only-begotten Son of God, wanting to make us sharers in his divinity, assumed our nature, so that he, made man, might make men [and women] gods" (St. Thomas Aquinas, *Opusculum* §57.1–4).[18]

Life in Christ is not simply an ethical or a spiritual amelioration; it is becoming a new kind of human by receiving divine agency. It is appropriating a life and the attendant attributes of what is otherwise inaccessible to a mere creature—immortality, incorruptibility, mercy, eternal joy, and boundless charity. Of course, the aim of PO is not to elaborate finer theological teaching, but it is important to note that the traditional theology of humanity's becoming an adopted child, a divinized temple, another Christ, is at least linked explicitly to the priestly ministry. As much stress as PO wants to put on the commonality between priest and the lay faithful, it refuses to reduce the ministry of priesthood to being simply a psychologist, a social worker, or a teacher of anything reducibly created.

That said, however, the stress of PO is more in the direction of the priest's life being one not simply united to God, but also to God's people. Next, in §3, appear warnings that, even though the priest must never reduce his mission to the merely human, he must likewise refuse to distance himself from the

People of God (*non tamen ut separentur*) either. He must always grow in awareness of how his ministry is given both plausibility as well as power in proportion to his willingness to live in the world of his neighbor. The priest must fight against any human aloofness or clerical privilege. Taken from among men (cf. Heb 5:1), all priests of Christ must rather insist on living the life and conditions of his brothers and sisters (*sed neque hominibus inservire valerent si ab eorum vita condicionibus que alienire manerent; PO §3*).

This challenge for all things ecclesiastical to become immersed more in the concrete world of humanity was precisely what St. Pope John called for when he opened the Council: "The Church, we trust illuminated by the light of this Council, will grow in spiritual riches, and in so doing will also be strengthened with renewed powers [*novarum virium*] in order to meet the future without any apprehension. For by this process of being updated, through wise and mutual cooperation, the Church aims to convert [*convertant*] the minds of all people, families, and nations to things above."[19] *Aggiornamento* in the strategy of John XXIII was ultimately aimed at renewing the Church's credibility in order that the Gospel might become more convincing and concrete in the lives of all men and women. By becoming more "human," the Church thus aims to make people more "divine" by turning their minds to the things of heaven (*quae supra sunt, mentes convertant; PO §3*). In this way we see how *aggiornamento* is not simply the means by which the Church stays current; it is also an apologetic tool to win the minds of all men and women for Christ.

The second main section (*PO §§4–11*) on "The Ministry of Priests" examines the functions (mainly liturgical), the various relationships, as well as the best use and attraction of priestly vocations. A sensitivity to the many different situations any active priest finds himself in is obvious throughout. Accordingly, the main metaphor in this section is one of unity. The People of God are in need of unity, and only the Word of God can effect true communion (*coadunatur verbo Dei*) (*PO §4*). This ministry of unity has been entrusted to priests who must therefore show a special solicitude in making that divine word real and effective in the lives of others in the way they themselves live. This is particularly true in how clerics preach. They should always be searching for ways to make their words practically useful and fruitful in the lives of all, even in the lives of non-Christians (*uel coetibus non christianis*) in their local communities (*PO §4*).

From this description comes a beautiful definition of priests as men who have first received (*debitor essunt presbyteri*) and now owe what they been given, the truth of the Gospel, *to all* (*omnibus ergo ... ut cum eis communicant veritatem Evangelii; PO §4*). As such, preaching is stressed before the sacraments in which a homily occurs, as in the "Liturgy of the Word in the celebration of the Mass, in which the proclaiming of the death and resurrection of Christ is inseparably joined to the response of the people who hear" (*PO §4*). Notice, again, how all priestly ministry is directed toward the building up of God's faithful, as it is their response (*responsum populi audientis*) that is the telos of preaching. The fruitfulness of priestly ministry is found not in the sanctity of the minister himself (although that is never, of course, discounted), but in the holiness of the people he serves. This is why *PO* goes on to counsel that a homily should never rest in theological platitudes and abstract dogma, but should both admit the "very difficult circumstances of the modern world" and thereafter seek to use the homily to apply "the lasting truth of the Gospel to the particular circumstances of life" (*PO* §4).

As interactive and participatory as the ministry of the word is presented throughout *PO*, the Eucharist (to which Vatican II gave such wonderful theological attention) emerges as the sacrament providing all priestly activity with its force and meaning. While the other sacramental functions are listed— baptism, reconciliation, and anointing of the sick—only the Eucharist receives any sustained theological reflection. Yet even here the Eucharist is situated not just in the hands of the priest but in the hearts of the faithful: "Thus the Eucharistic Action, over which the priest presides, is the very heart of the congregation. So priests must instruct their people to offer to God the Father the Divine Victim in the Sacrifice of the Mass, and to join it to the offering of their own lives" (*PO* §5). The priesthood is once again represented as participating in both the divine life of God as well as in the very human lives of the people. The ordained minister must therefore be a pastor of hearts, able to teach the deepest mysteries of the Faith: namely, that God has become human and now continues his incarnation in the holy sacrifice of the Mass, but this is a sacrifice that the whole Mystical Body offers.[20] Consequently, priests and the special training they receive are to be ordered to teaching the faithful the theology of the Mass and their special role therein: "Priests likewise must instruct their people to participate in the celebrations of the sacred liturgy in such a way that they become proficient in genuine prayer [*sinceram orationem*]. . . . They must train the faithful to sing hymns and spiritual songs in their hearts to the Lord" (*PO* §5). This convergence of priestly office that is achieved *ex opere operato* and a priest's own personal prayer life (*ex opera operantis*) captures well the vision of *PO*: that a priest rely not simply on the sacramental objectivity of his public ministry, but become a mystic of the everyday, thereby openly offering his life as a prayer and song for all those seeking greater intimacy with Christ.

This emphasis on the heart is smoothly translated into a priestly preference for the poor (*PO* §6). Finding his vocation in the human condition, it thus follows that the priest must imitate Christ's own care for the marginalized and go where the Church is not often associated. The second subsection of "The Ministry of Priests" is entitled "Priests' Relationship with Others" (*PO* §§7–9), and takes up the more prosaic and practical issue of the presbytery's affiliations with bishops, one another, and the lay faithful. A great sensitivity to a priest's situation and cultural and age differences is incorporated and obvious in this section. What is striking, and what we witness throughout *PO*, is how the priest is called to let the various situations of his parishioners inform his way of life as well. Priests must therefore "listen to the laity, consider their wants in a fraternal spirit, recognize their experience and competence in the different areas of human activity, so that together with them they will be able to recognize the signs of the times" (*PO* §9). A final (and rather frail) word on the promotion and fostering of priestly vocations appears next (*PO* §§10–11), although a contemporary awareness of speaking in terms of vocations globally, as well as the importance of fraternal companionship, is evident.

The third main section, "The Life of Priests" (*PO* §§12–21) opens with the honest admittance that the Sacrament of Holy Orders is a reality that transcends natural human ability, and that the priest's availability (*docibiles*) is more important than his perfection. That is, God can (and must) use imperfect, sinful men (*indignos ministros*) to continue his Son's sacred mediation in this world. He thus calls "those who are more open to the power and direction of the Holy Spirit, and who can by reason of their close union with Christ and their holiness of life say with St. Paul: 'And yet I am alive; or rather, not I; it is Christ that lives in me' (Gal 2:20)" (*PO* §12). Christian perfection is thus once again explained not in terms of religion, but relationship: *PO* expresses the heart of the Faith not as one of fulfilling obligations or following rules, but as becoming so united to Christ that one's temptation to autonomy and absolute independence is obliterated. Highlighting Gal 2:20, *PO* thus upholds holiness as allowing Christ to take up residence within every baptized soul, and in the priest's in a special and unique way.

The decree goes on to illustrate this call to priestly holiness with the image of the Good Shepherd. The Good Shepherd is among the oldest and most popular depictions of Christ in the first years of Christianity, and it emerges here as the model by which priests should evaluate their own spiritual lives as well as their lives with others. Through various forms of asceticism, striving to remain "free of wantonness and lusts," through celebration of daily Mass and frequent penance, the true shepherd renounces "personal convenience" and seeks not what is useful to himself, but "to many, for their salvation" (*PO* §13). This means becoming, in a metaphor found in *Gaudium et Spes* §24, "a complete gift of themselves to the flock committed to them" (*PO* §14).

The great Christian paradox appears next: *PO* calls not for men who are strong to follow Christ but for men who are weak enough to know they need a savior. Human infirmity and imperfection allow those intent on holiness to see that they can never secure their own salvation, can never be the agents of their own felicity. In this context, the evangelical counsels are taken up: obedience (*PO* §15), celibacy (*PO* §16), and the "voluntary poverty" (*paupertatem voluntariam*) (*PO* §17) to which secular priests are at least invited to consider. This final factor of human living, the use and administration of material goods, is to be done in tandem "with the help of capable layman" (*peritis laicis; PO* §17), thus admitting not only that any one priest's personal gifts will be limited, but also that use of the Church's tangible commodities now demands a new collaboration and transparency.

The final division of this third main section, "Aids to the Life of the Priests" (*PO* §§18–21), reveals the most up-to-date insights about the concrete circumstances of priesthood. These paragraphs are rooted in the opening that everything throughout a priest's day is meant to help him "grow in union with Christ" (*unionem cum Christo*) and in all things (*in omnibus*); the priest is to search actively for God's providential will—spiritual reading, daily examination of conscience, regular celebration of Mass and the Sacrament of Reconciliation, and a desire for daily conversion in Christ (*PO* §18). Refusing to relegate God's activity to the overtly pious or ceremonial, however, *PO* goes on to state that a mature appreciation for human culture along with ongoing study (*cultura humana . . . studia*) is necessary for any healthy priests who are serious about communicating the Gospel to those in the world, and who are not afraid to learn from the world so as to "perfect their knowledge of divine things and human affairs and so prepare themselves to enter more opportunely into conversation with their contemporaries" (*PO* §19).

PO §§20–21 take up the practicality of payment in a way no magisterial document had in the past (evidenced by the conspicuous lack of footnotes in this short section). Since "the laborer is worthy of his hire" (Lk 10:16), various ideas for remuneration, the possibilities of the older use of benefices and endowments, as well as more modern ways of setting up common funds and systems of social assistance are all raised.

In the "Conclusion and Exhortation" (*PO* §22), the council fathers close by admitting that what prompts the writing of this decree is not only the unfailing joys of priestly life over the centuries, but also changing lifestyles (*hominum mores*) and the consequent changing of values (*quantumque ordo valorum in aestimatione hominum immutatur*) in the wider society (*PO* §22). The 1960s signaled changes that were only inchoately estimable on the council floor, but all sensed that a massive revolution was already upon them: "As a result, the ministers of the Church and sometimes the faithful themselves feel like strangers in this world, anxiously looking for the ways and words with which to communicate it" (*PO* §22). Loneliness is the final threat to the faith mentioned, and so *PO* closes with a comforting word on the unshakeable presence of Christ in his Church and in the souls of his faithful. Modernity has ushered in unforeseen types of ennui and spiritual torpor; never before have men and women been so instantly connected, but never have they felt so languidly alone. In combating this, the Church both calls and thanks her priests and reminds them in the final sentence of *PO* that the work entrusted to them does not arise out of their own power or talent, but that it comes from "him who is able to accomplish all things in a measure far beyond what we ask or conceive" (Eph 3:20).

III. Contemporary Contributions of *Presbyterorum Ordinis*

When Pope Paul VI turned to the significance of *PO* in his duly issued *Norms for Implementation of Our Council Decrees* on August 6, 1966, he quoted from *PO* §§7, 9–10, and 19–21 only.[21] What these sections have in common are in matters of administrative and disciplinary importance: the transferal of clergy, their ongoing study, and the questions of remuneration just examined. As such, the richer theology and the missionary nature of *PO* seems to have fallen quickly away from post-conciliar discourse. Examining the more formative works that have helped to determine contemporary views of the priesthood, in fact, reveals that the impact of *PO* has indeed been minimal at best. Rather, the discussions found at *Lumen Gentium* and *Optatum Totius* have more significantly shaped this discussion.

After its promulgation in December of 1965, the first real significant examination of priesthood would come just two years later in Pope Paul VI's encyclical, *Sacerdotalis Caelibatus*.[22] Reaffirming the West's belief that celibacy best conforms a man to Christ and thereby makes him a more viable and undivided witness of God's love for all, Paul VI here draws from *PO* in eighteen different instances, but quotes directly from the decree only three times. This distinction signals well the reception of *PO* after the council: there is agreement that its more up-to-date treatment of the priest's life and pastoral duties is timely and important, but there has not been much expressed reliance on the text itself. In *Sacerdotalis Caelibatus*, for instance, out of its 152 citations, *PO* appears with 15 "consult" (*confer*) prompts, citing the general sense of the priest as pastor and witness, but with only 3 actual quotes (from §5 and twice from §16). In this way, it is the overall message of what *PO* represents and not the direct wording of the document itself that becomes formative or pivotal in the years after Vatican II.

Between this 1967 public reaffirmation of priestly celibacy by Paul VI to the next significant papal document on priesthood in 1992 by John Paul II, the Congregation for Catholic Education issued nine documents pertaining to the formation and ministry of priests. With these many pages, the Holy See aimed to continue the content and contours of Vatican II's teaching on seminary and priestly life. Yet throughout these statements, we again see how little the text of *PO* is directly relied upon: rarely is the decree quoted, but it is usually referred to in the abstract.[23] This is in no way to imply a rupture between *PO* and subsequent teachings. In fact, quite the opposite is true: these documents capture Vatican II's theology of priesthood beautifully by presenting the priest (1) as one who comes from and ministers to a local people, (2) as one who must strive to pray and pastor and preach from the heart and from his own life's experience, and (3) as someone who has an emotional and physical life that cannot be ignored, but which must be integrated into the man's overall psychological and bodily health. What the documents in these intervening years do point to, however, is how the directives found throughout *PO* were already very much part of the Church's understanding and identification of her priests. For *PO* is minimally quoted and is never the focal point of any major statement or exhortation.

The next significant papal document on priesthood was John Paul II's long-awaited 1992 post-synodal Apostolic Exhortation, *Pastores Dabo Vobis*, and here *PO* fares a bit better. After the tumultuous years of the Council, many were looking for a clear and definitive statement on the objective holiness of the priestly call, of the Church's continued discipline of clerical celibacy— despite the "priest shortage" in the West—as well as for a better apologetic on why the Catholic Church must strive to keep the Sacrament of Holy Orders a male (*vir*) preserve. John Paul, they thought, would be just the one to produce such a multiplex document, and *Pastores Dabo Vobis* did not disappoint. This is a work of eighty-two massive sections (and with well over two hundred notes), filled with citations from Church Fathers, Medieval Doctors of the Church, as well as some of the best of contemporary theology. While John Paul II acknowledges *PO* thirty-one times in passing, he quotes from *PO* less than half of those times (at fourteen places throughout). Where he does use *PO*, John Paul does so to show the multivalent relationality involved in being a priest today: one who participates in the lives of bishops, other priests, and so, so many people. The pattern for this interdependence is the Trinity, and it is this sense of communion with God's people that allows a priest to flourish in his ministry.

Consequently, the nature and mission of the ministerial priesthood cannot be defined except through this multiple and rich interconnection of relationships that arise from the Blessed Trinity and are prolonged in the communion of the Church, as a sign and instrument of Christ, of communion with God, and of the unity of all humanity. In this context, the ecclesiology of communion becomes decisive for understanding the identity of the priest, his essential dignity, and his vocation and mission among the People of God and in the world (*Pastores Dabo Vobis* §12, citing *PO* §§7–8).

Communion more than consecration now defines the priest, who is called to allow his identity to flow from an "ecclesiology of communion" with both the People of God as well as the world.

In the same year (1992) as *Pastores Dabo Vobis* was issued, John Paul also approved and released the new *Catechism of the Catholic Church (CCC)*.[24] Here, *PO* is drawn from twenty-four times, twenty-two of those instances appearing in *Part Two: The Celebration of the Sacred Mystery*. Such a context makes it quite clear that the *Catechism* relegates a vast majority of its reliance on *PO* to the cultic enacting of ordained ministry: the priest is understood primarily as one who celebrates the sacraments for the people. That said, however, *PO*'s appearance in *Part Four: Christian Prayer* is most welcome. Outside the section on sacraments, therefore, the *CCC* relies on *PO* to maintain how a central responsibility of "ordained ministers" is to assist in forming the prayer lives of their own brothers and sisters. Referring to *PO* §§4–6, we learn that priests are first and foremost representative servants "of the Good Shepherd, they are ordained to lead the People of God to the living waters of prayer: the Word of God, the liturgy, the theological life (the life of faith, hope, and charity), and the *Today of God* in concrete situations" (*CCC* §2686). This *hodie Dei* is a jarring phrase, but it points to the "updating" *PO* hoped to inaugurate. God is to be found not only in religious practice and pious devotions, but in each moment of human existence. The priest therefore is not an archaic vessel of past tradition; rather, he is to be a man engaged in today's complex world who is so intimately familiar with the human condition that he is able to show seekers where God is active in the *concretis condicionibus* of their everyday lives (*CCC* §2686).

In 1994 John Paul again approved a document treating priesthood, this time under the auspices of the Congregation for the Clergy, then headed up by the Filipino Cardinal Jose Sanchez (Prefect, 1991–1996). In this *Directory for Life and Ministry of Priests*,[25] references to *PO* occur frequently, fifty-eight in all, but quoted directly only four times. This is a reoccurring pattern: *PO* is most often used in post-conciliar documents to provide a general framework or "feel" of the Church's sacerdology, but rarely is it explicitly quoted or analyzed textually. Also, similar to previous documents, the Directory uses mainly *PO* §2 to illustrate the participatory nature of the priesthood. For example, *PO* §2 is used twice in the following selection to express how Holy Orders not only configures the ordained priest to Christ himself, but also how it continues to connect the man to the holy people of God from whom he originally came:

> The Christological dimension, like the Trinitarian dimension, springs directly from the sacrament which ontologically configures the priest to Christ the Priest, Master, Sanctifier and Pastor of his People [here *PO* §2 is referenced at note 14]. The faithful who, maintaining their common priesthood, are chosen and become part of the ministerial priesthood are granted an indelible participation in the one and only priesthood of Christ. This is a participation in the public dimension of mediation and authority regarding the sanctification, teaching and guidance of all the People of God. On the one hand, the common priesthood of the faithful and the ministerial or hierarchical priesthood are necessarily ordered one for the other because each in its own way participates in the only priesthood of Christ and, on the other hand, they are essentially different [here *PO* §2 is referenced at note 15]. (*Directory* §6)

There is only one priest, Jesus Christ. All the baptized share in his priesthood, and that is the primal participation of the Christian. Yet from this ecclesia, some are called out into the hierarchical priesthood for a more expressed role in "sanctifying, teaching, and guiding" God's holy people. Both the ministerial as well as this hierarchical priesthood enjoy an "indelible participation" in Christ's one and only priesthood, the former through the office of Baptism, the latter through both Baptism and Holy Orders. While "essentially different" in their nature and purpose, both of these sacraments configure Christians to the person of Christ, now allowing his life to be identified with and recognizable in all.

More recently, the Congregation of the Clergy (now headed by Cardinal Dario Castrillon Hoyos) issued *The Priest, Pastor and Leader of the Parish Community*[26] on the Feast of John Vianney the Patron of Parish Priests, August 4, 2002. Here *PO* is referred to fourteen times, quoted directly three times. What is new here, however, is the fresh use of *PO* §§12–14 and the priest's call to be "a master of the spiritual life" (*Priest, Pastor and Leader* §10). This welcomed highlighting advances *PO* in a way that leaves behind the focus on §2 and the nature of the Christian priesthood, thereby turning to the priest himself and asking him to become a master of the human heart and an authentic guide for thirsty travelers. A priest's spirituality is thus always apostolic. For in understanding his own holiness, the priest must necessarily include others:

> The priest, however, is motivated to strive for holiness for a different reason: so as to be worthy of that new grace which has marked him so that he can represent the person of Christ, Head and Shepherd, and thereby become a living instrument in the work of salvation. (*Priest, Pastor and Leader* §10, referencing *PO* §12)

The document goes on to hold up the Eucharist and a healthy devotion to Mary as the means by which priestly holiness is best fostered. Here one can detect a slight shift in how *PO* is used. For, *Priest, Pastor and Leader* extracts a hitherto unmined jewel—namely, the priest as a "living instrument" whose salvation is bound up with the sanctification of the lives entrusted to him in such a way that he must become a "master" in all things human for them.

Perhaps aware that *PO* was not being fully utilized, this same Congregation of the Clergy held a major symposium in Rome to mark the decree's thirtieth anniversary in 1995. This gathering brought together the most focused and fertile thinking on *PO*; the collection of papers numbers sixty addresses of various lengths, but includes a major opening address by John Paul II, as well as unmatchable talks by then Cardinal Ratzinger and Monsignor Luigi Giussani.[27] Unfortunately this unique anthology on *PO* was published "in house" and therefore never widely promulgated, and thus hardly cited.[28] In my opinion, this is where the twenty-first century reception of *PO* will find its richest treasure. In holding priesthood up as a *cura animarum*, the Church simultaneously stresses both the ordained minister's participation in the divine life that he aims to bring to others, as well as the commonality of the *cor inquietum* he shares with those others. As a theology student seeking priestly ordination myself at the Jesuit University of Innsbruck in Austria, I grew very appreciative for the German word used for presbyter during my time there: *Seelsorger*, the one who cares (*sorgen*) for human souls (*Seelen*). This was a term, I came to learn, popularized by the Swiss theologian and Cardinal, Hans Urs von Balthasar, but nowhere in my years of study was it ever linked to the very salient passages of *PO*.[29] This is why the late Monsignor of Milan, Luigi Giussani, understands the future of the priesthood to be that of a pointer of life's purpose: "The priesthood upholds and expresses in the world the vision of life as purpose. For the priest, belonging to Christ as sent by the Father is the all consuming definition of one's own personality (Gal 2:20). Life and ministry are thus the response to a real, historic and existential event."[30] Stressing the priest as first and foremost a man of the heart has not only fertile ecumenical possibilities, but it also keeps the priesthood rooted in the soil of the human condition wherein a man is constantly reminded of his participation in the rest of humanity, and therefore of his own fallibility and need for salvation.

We have seen in these post-conciliar documents a pattern in their use of *PO*: the decree is held up as authoritative, but no one section or line has become a classical source (say, as *Lumen Gentium* §8 and *Gaudium et Spes* §24 have). If papal teaching has not used *PO* to its full extent, then we should not be surprised to see that secondary scholarship has been similarly sparse in its direct treatment of the text. As an early representative of this pattern, take a study issued under the auspices of the United States Catholic Conference in 1973.[31] Entitled *Spiritual Renewal of the American Priesthood*, this brief manual aims to update and inculturate a priestly spirituality within the context of North America in the years following the massive sea change brought about by Vatican II. There are very helpful chapters on topics such as "American Culture and Spirituality," "Personal Integration and Spirituality," as well as "Personal Relationships and Spirituality." Yet throughout these pages, *PO* is never quoted or even cited as an authoritative or helpful resource.

There is also a very fine set of essays compiled by Kenneth Whitehead in *After 40 Years: Vatican Council II's Diverse Legacy*.[32] While there are lengthy sections rightly dedicated to *Gaudium et Spes* and *Lumen Gentium*, there are also illuminative chapters on *Dei Verbum*, *Dignitatis Humanae*, and *Unitatis Redintegratio*. Given the intriguing title of Whitehead's collection, it would seem that *PO* did not leave a "diverse legacy" but instead has proven rather mainstream and relatively unifying. This plays out in Alan Schreck's *Vatican II: The Crisis and The Promise* as well.[33] Here, the only time Schreck relies openly on *PO* is not to tell us what it teaches, but rather to tell us that it does *not* address the ordination of women.[34]

This cursory canvassing of post-conciliar reception is certainly not exhaustive, and the documents of Vatican II will be finding their way into ecclesial and theological documents for centuries to come. What this study does find, however, is that *PO* has not been received as a watershed or as a significant turning-point in the life of the Church. Rather, *PO* points to the shifts in the priesthood that began well before the council. In this way, *PO* might best be read as a descriptive rather than a prescriptive text. It captures where all the council fathers knew the priesthood was going, and so instead of challenging needed clerical changes, it rather portrays contemporary pastoral practices.

To conclude, two remaining dimensions of *PO* need to be expressed. The first is its very human understanding of the ordained ministry. The greatest contribution *PO* made and will continue to make in ecclesiology is in its insistence that the ordained may never use his priesthood or his Christian piety to hide his humanity. Before the Church's minister is a priest configured to Christ, he is a man in need of salvation. This stressing of the priest's humanity is a change commensurate with the whole of Vatican II: the Church is not simply an otherworldly, Platonic, static reality, but she is also a pilgrim people stumbling as she goes. This is especially true for the Council's image of the priest. As Edward Hahnenberg states, in the pre-conciliar view, "it was clear what it meant to be a priest. A priest was a man set apart for the things of God. He was elevated above the community.... But Vatican II pushed this model off its pedestal."[35]

This admittance has fueled much contemporary theology, best crystallized perhaps by Pope Emeritus Benedict's admittance that the Gospel must never be exclusively thought of in terms of the divine. The Gospel message is for the whole human person and for the entirety of this created order. Heavenly agape and human eros can therefore never be pitted against each other as if they were enemies *in se*. Rather, agape sanctifies and universalizes eros in such a way that the human heart's desires become signals of God's own activity. Benedict therefore warns, "Were this antithesis (between eros and agape) to be taken to extremes, the essence of Christianity would be detached from vital relations fundamental to human existence, and would become a world apart, admirable perhaps, but decisively cut off from the complex fabric of human life."[36] Human life is "complex," and Vatican II was secure enough in her ability to teach the truth, that she opened the messy windows of the human condition and sought to serve Christ precisely there.

The second image *PO* offers the priesthood that is still fruitful for further reflection is the priest as the agent of supernatural life. As we have just seen, while *PO* does in fact stress the humanity both of the priest as well as the situations in which he ministers, he ministers not simply as human but as one who effects a life that is not his own. At *PO* §3, remember, we read that the Church's ordained "cannot be ministers of Christ unless they be witnesses and dispensers of a life other than earthly life." The priest's role as *deificator* is ancient, and a patristic recovery of the other-worldly fulfillment of all those made in the divine image and likeness. As Ratzinger noted in the 1995 Symposium:

> Happiness only exists in being open to the divine, that is to divinization. In this way the Council says with Augustine, the end of history is that mankind should become love: mankind will become adoration, living worship, the city of God, *civitas Dei*. In this way we realize the deep desire of all creation "that God be all in all" (1 Cor 15:28). Only in this perspective can we understand what worship and the sacraments are.[37]

As alluded to earlier, there is still much work to be done on this point, especially given the resurgence of studies on Christian deification in the past few years.

These two themes together show a possible way forward for *PO*: the ultimate call of the priest is to make his life the realization and effecting of Christ's own dominical reciprocity of *kenosis* and *theosis*. In the Son of God's emptying is the People of God's fulfillment. The mission of the ordained is hence to lay his life down in love so others may not only come to but become the only love that satisfies: Jesus's first *ordinandi* "were for that reason equally expropriated and called to join in Christ's sacrificial existence. And this expropriation means that their identity was emptied for the sake of the Eucharist."[38] The apostolic mission means becoming Eucharist for the world: becoming the Body of Christ in such a way that allows the one True Vine (cf., John 15) to bear fruit throughout every part of ourselves and in every part of his world.[39]

Admittedly, the reception of *PO* thus far has been relatively tepid, especially when compared to the Council's other groundbreaking documents. *PO* has not yet reached its ultimate potential in helping the Church formulate a fuller theology of the priesthood. However, there are still dimensions to be discovered and images to be elucidated. Further reception is needed, and perhaps with Pope Francis's very human understanding of the priest as the Good Shepherd, a further realization of PO will occur within the Church. Its theology of ministry is collaborative without ever reducing the priest to a mere communal leader. It offers a guide for greater fraternity among priests themselves, but also for greater lay involvement; it provides an honest awareness of a priest's psychological, emotional, and spiritual needs. A priest is called to participate passionately in the movements of his own human heart as well as in the divine life offered to him and to all by the Lord Jesus. As such, PO contains undeveloped insights into caring for a priest's humanity as well as his gift in bringing Christ's own life to the world.

NOTES

1. Pope Francis warns often against the Church's becoming self enclosed and thus perpetually self-referential. For example, during a homily for Pentecost, he warned how, "The older theologians used to say that the soul is a kind of sailboat, the Holy Spirit is the wind which fills its sails and drives it forward, and the gusts of wind are the gifts of the Spirit. Lacking his impulse and his grace, we do not go forward. The Holy Spirit draws us into the mystery of the living God and saves us from the threat of a Church which is gnostic and self-referential, closed in on herself; he impels us to open the doors and go forth to proclaim and bear witness to the good news of the Gospel, to communicate the joy of faith, the encounter with Christ"; section 3 of his 2013 Homily for Pentecost. http://m.vatican.va/content/francescomobile/en/homilies/2013/documents/papa-francesco_20130519_omelia-pentecoste.html.

2. For most of the historical data and activity on the council floor behind PO, I have relied throughout mainly on Decretum de Presbyterorum Ministerio et Via: Presbyterorum Ordinis, ed. Francisco Gil Hellín (Vatican City: Libreria Editrice Vaticana, 1996); see also John W. O'Malley, SJ, What Happened at Vatican II (Cambridge, MA: Harvard University Press, 2008); History of Vatican II, ed. Giuseppe Alberigo, with English edition by Joseph Komonchak, vol. 1, Announcing and Preparing Vatican Council II: Toward A New Era in Catholicism (Maryknoll, NY: Orbis Press, 1995), and vol. 4, Church as Communion: Third Period and Intersession, September 1964–September 1965 (Maryknoll, NY: Orbis Press, 2003); Karol Wojtyła, Sources of Renewal: The Implementation of Vatican II, trans. P. S. Falla (New York: Harper & Row, 1980); Religious Life and Priesthood: Perfectae Caritatis, Optatam Totius, Presbyterorum Ordinis, ed. Maryanne Confoy (Mahwah, NJ: Paulist Press, 2008).

3. Karol Wojtyła, Sources of Renewal: The Implementation of Vatican II, 225.

4. This is quoted as a conversation with Cardinal Suenens on October 14, 1964 and found at Alberigo and Komonchak, History of Vatican II, 4:354–55n108. For a scathing analysis (in which Congar calls PO médiocre), see his interview with Jean Puyo, a priest from the Diocese of Bordeaux (and chief editor of Journal de la Vie), in Jean Puyo interroge le Père Congar, ed. Jean Puyo (Paris: Le Centurion, 1975), 149.

5. In his invaluable reflections on the council, Joseph Ratzinger commented that this move from sacerdos to presbyter aimed to have ecumenical implications as well: "Luther's protest against the Catholic notion of priesthood was really based on the fact that in the Catholic view the priesthood was almost exclusively a sacrificial priesthood. In fact, even in patristic theology and especially in medieval theology, the old

association between *sacerdos* and *sacrificium*, between priest and sacrifice, had been emphasized again in contradiction to the view of the New Testament.... The schema on priestly life and ministry has now eliminated the one-sided emphasis on the idea of priesthood as sacrifice. It moved instead from the idea of the People of God meeting together, so that priesthood is seen fundamentally as service to faith" (*Theological Highlights of Vatican II* [New York: Paulist Press, 2nd ed., 2009], 249–50).

6. In Alberigo and Komonchak, *History of Vatican II*, 4:347.

7. For an extended analysis of the two theologies of priesthood present and integrated throughout *PO*, see the magisterial essay by Guy Mansini, OSB, and Lawrence J. Welch, "The Decree on the Ministry and Life of Priests, *Presbyterorum Ordinis*," in *Vatican II: Renewal within Tradition*, ed. Matthew L. Lamb and Matthew Levering (Oxford: Oxford University Press, 2008), 205–27.

8. According to Norman Tanner, Archbishop Marcel Lefebvre was concerned that Vatican II's renewal of the "priesthood of all the baptized" was obfuscating any illuminative theology of the ordained priesthood; cf. Alberigo and Komonchak, *History of Vatican II*, 4:352.

9. Pawel Latusek (1910–1973), Auxiliary Bishop of Gniezno, Poland, as quoted in Alberigo and Komonchak, *History of Vatican II*, 4:352.

10. Norman Tanner, in Alberigo and Komonchak, *History of Vatican II*, 4:355.

11. According to Mansini and Welch ("The Decree on the Ministry and Life of Priests, *Presbyterorum Ordinis*," 206), it was mainly *Lumen Gentium* §28 and *Lumen Gentium* §41 on priestly spirituality that were most importantly intertwined into this late draft.

12. Quoted in Henri Fesquet, *The Drama of Vatican II: The Ecumenical Council, June 1962–December 1965* (New York: Random House, 1967), 695.

13. At the final discussion, "more than one hundred bishops" continued to want inclusions on scripture's warranting of married bishops (citing 1 Tim 3:2–5 and Tit 1:6 supporting a married clergy), probably to have been included at *PO* §16 where celibacy is treated; cf. Confoy, *Religious Life and Priesthood*, 25.

14. Session 23 opened on July 15, 1563 and was dedicated to the sacrament of Holy Orders, *Doctrina de sacramento ordinis*, as in *Denzinger* §1763–1778, *Enchiridion Symbolorum*, ed. H. Denzinger (Fribourg: Herder Press, 1963), 412–16. One can see how this Tridentine theology provides the classic link between the Sacrament of Holy Orders and the priestly offering of sacrifice upon which *PO* is building.

15. This is a common rendering of St. Irenaeus of Lyons's (d. c. 200) phrase *homo vivens, gloria Dei; Adversus Haereses* [*AH*] 4.20.7 (*PG* 7/1.1037); see also the use of this quote in the *Catechism of the Catholic Church* §294 (hereafter [*CCC*]). http://www.vatican.va/archive/ccc_css/archive/catechism/p1s2c1p4.htm.

16. The locus classicus for this call has become *Lumen Gentium* §§39–40. http://www.vatican.va/archive/hist_councils/ii_vatican_council/documents/vat-ii_const_19641121_lumen-gentium_en.html.

17. The literature exploring the (lost) history of deification in the Christian tradition has exploded in the past few years. See, for example, A. N. Williams, *The Ground of Union: Deification in Aquinas and Palamas* (Oxford: Oxford University Press, 1999); Norman Russell, *The Doctrine of Deification in the Greek Patristic Tradition* (Oxford: Oxford University Press, 2004); *Theosis: Deification in Christian Theology*, ed. Stephen Finlan and Vladimir Kharlamov (Eugene, OR: Pickwick Publications, 2006); Daniel Keating, *Deification and Grace* (Naples, FL: Sapientia Press, 2007); Meconi, *The One Christ: St. Augustine's Theology of Deification* (Washington, DC: Catholic University of America Press, 2013).

18. *CCC* §460 slightly adjusted; http://www.vatican.va/archive/ccc_css/archive/catechism/p122a3p1.htm.

19. Pope John XXIII, *Gaudet Mater Ecclesia* §3 (my translation): Discourse on the Solemn Opening of the Second Vatican Council, October 11, 1962, https://w2.vatican.va/content/john-xxiii/la/speeches/1962/documents/hf_j-xxiii_spe_19621011_opening-council.html; see also John Paul II's Apostolic Constitution, *On the Publication of the Catechism of the Catholic Church Prepared Following the Second Vatican Ecumenical Council* (October 11, 1992). http://www.vatican.va/archive/ccc_css/archive/catechism/aposcons.htm.

20. This stress on the priesthood of all believers is today manifested in some beautifully translated lines in the recent 2011 English rendering of the Roman Missal, where the priest now prays over the Eucharistic oblation: "For them, we offer you this sacrifice of praise or they offer it for themselves and all who are dear to them," as in Eucharistic Prayer I, lines 8–10, Roman Missal (New Jersey: Catholic Book Publishing Corporation, 2011), 488.

21. The English appears as the Apostolic Letter of Pope Paul VI, issued in *Motu Proprio, Ecclesiae Sanctae: Norms for Implementation of Our Council Decrees* (Washington, DC: National Catholic Welfare Conference, 1966).

22. http://w2.vatican.va/content/paul-vi/en/encyclicals/documents/hf_p-vi_enc_24061967_sacerdotalis.html.

23. The most convenient way of finding these documents is at the website of the United States Catholic Bishops' Conference: http://www.usccb.org/beliefs-and-teachings/vocations/priesthood/priestly-formation/church-documents-for-priestly-formation.cfm. Note the nine issuances from the Holy Office here: nowhere in any of these is *PO* an essential part of the argument or teaching put forward. In some it does not appear at all, while in most it is simply referred to ("cf.") in order to support a theology of priesthood expressed elsewhere.

24. http://www.vatican.va/archive/ENG0015/_INDEX.HTM.

25. http://www.vatican.va/roman_curia/congregations/cclergy/documents/rc_con_cclergy_doc_31011994_directory_en.html.

26. http://www.vatican.va/roman_curia/congregations/cclergy/documents/rc_con_cclergy_doc_20020804_istruzione-presbitero_en.html.

27. Congregation for the Clergy, *Priesthood: A Greater Love: International Symposium on the Thirtieth Anniversary of the Promulgation of the Conciliar Decree Presbyterorum Ordinis*, ed. Anthony Bevilacqua et al. (Philadelphia: Archdiocese of Philadelphia, n.d.).

28. This collection of papers was originally entitled *Sacerdozio: Un amore piò grande*, and was translated as *Priesthood: A Greater Love*, by an unnamed seminary group under Philadelphia's Cardinal Bevilacqua; it was released simply by the Archdiocesan printer as A SYMPOSIUM ON THE THIRTIETH ANNIVERSARY OF THE PROMULGATION OF THE CONCILIAR DECREE *PREBYSTERORUM ORDINIS* (Archdiocese of Philadelphia, 1997).

29. This is a point made by Raymond Gawronski, SJ, "A Jesuit Spiritual Director: Spiritual Father, Friend of the Bridegroom," in *Seminary Theology II: Theology and Spiritual Direction in Dialogue*, ed. Deacon James Keating (Omaha: The Institute for Priestly Formation, 2011), 75–95, at 76.

30. Giussani, "The Priesthood Faced with the Radical Challenge of Contemporary Society," in Congregation for the Clergy, *Priesthood: A Greater Love*, 143–45, at 144.

31. Gerard T. Broccolo et al., eds., *Spiritual Renewal of the American Priesthood* (Washington, DC: United States Catholic Conference, 1973).

32. Kenneth D. Whitehead, ed., *After 40 Years: Vatican Council II's Diverse Legacy* (South Bend, IN: St. Augustine's Press, 2007).

33. Alan Schreck, *Vatican II: The Crisis and the Promise* (Cincinnati: St. Anthony Messenger Press, 2005).

34. Schreck, *Vatican II: The Crisis and the Promise*, 207; at the end of each chapter, Schreck provides "Favorite Quotes" from the conciliar documents; he cites two sentences from *PO* §3 and two from *PO* §4.

35. Edward P. Hahnenberg, *A Concise Guide to the Documents of Vatican II* (Cincinnati: St. Anthony Messenger Press, 2007), 88.

36. Pope Benedict XVI, *Deus Caritas Est* §7 (December 25, 2005). http://w2.vatican.va/content/benedict-xvi/en/encyclicals/documents/hf_ben-xvi_enc_20051225_deus-caritas-est.html.

37. Cardinal Joseph Ratzinger, "Life and Ministry of Priests," in Congregation for the Clergy, *Priesthood: A Greater Love*, 115–30, at 124; for more on Augustine's theology of the divinizing effect of liturgy, see my "Becoming Gods by Becoming God's: Augustine's Mystagogy of Identification," *Augustinian Studies* 39 (2008): 61–74.

38. Hans Urs von Balthasar, *Explorations in Theology*, vol. 4, *Spirit and Institution* (San Francisco: Ignatius Press, 1995), 365.

39. Cf. Augustine, *sermon 272*, in *Sermons of St. Augustine*, vol. III/7 (Sermons 230–272B), ed. Edmund Hill (Hyde Park, NY: New City Press, 1993), 300–01.

7

Optatam Totius

Robert Barron

Optatam Totius, Vatican II's document concerning the formation of priests, was approved by an overwhelming majority of the
Council fathers (2318 to 3), and promulgated by Pope Paul VI on
October 28, 1965. The massive support for this relatively brief statement would seem to indicate that its recommendations were rather
straightforward and uncontroversial. However, in the years following its publication, a crisis in the priesthood has unfolded, especially in the West. In the immediate wake of Vatican II, priests in
the United States and Western Europe left the active ministry in
droves, and in relation to the growing population of Catholics, the
number of priests worldwide has, over the past fifty years, dropped
dramatically.

There are, of course, many reasons for this decline—enormous
cultural shifts, the sexual revolution, loss of confidence in established institutions, the clergy sex-abuse scandal, etc.—but what
is particularly interesting for our purposes is that the crisis in
the priesthood has conduced, over the past fifty years, toward an
intense focus upon the priesthood and the training of priests.
Accordingly, the reception of *Optatam Totius* is complex and
includes, to mention just a few of the most prominent, the following
documents: *Ratio Fundamentalis Institutionis Sacerdotalis* from the
Sacred Congregation for Catholic Education, Paul VI's Encyclical
letter *Sacerdotalis Caelibatus*, *The Directory for the Ministry and the
Life of Priests* from the Congregation for the Clergy, John Paul II's
remarkable series of Holy Thursday letters to priests, as well as
his year-long Wednesday audience catechesis on the priesthood in
1993, and most importantly his Apostolic Exhortation *Pastores Dabo
Vobis*, Benedict XVI's letter proclaiming a year for priests, and, in
the American context, the *Program for Priestly Formation* (now in
its fifth edition) issued by the United States Conference of Catholic

Bishops. There is, obviously, an embarrassment of riches here, and in the context of this brief essay, we could never cover all of this material adequately. Thus, I have decided to concentrate on what I take to be the most important "moments" in the reception process, namely, *Pastores Dabo Vobis* and the *Program of Priestly Formation*. Drawing on my own experience as rector of the largest Catholic seminary in the United States, I should also like to include some of my own ruminations on how *Optatam Totius* might best be applied in the present ecclesial situation.

Overview of *Optatam Totius*

Before considering the reception of *Optatam Totius* over the past half-century, it would be useful to provide a brief overview of the document itself. The first significant observation that the Council Fathers make is that the duty of fostering vocations is incumbent upon the entire Church and is not the responsibility of priests and bishops alone.[1] Congruent with *Lumen Gentium*'s stress on the universal call to holiness and the priesthood of all believers, *Optatam Totius* wants to cultivate a culture of vocations throughout the life of the entire Christian community. John Paul II would echo this theme in *Pastores Dabo Vobis*, especially in his call for the family to be the "first seminary," and it would provide the theological foundation for the innumerable vocation societies that have flourished in the Church around the world since Vatican II.[2] *Optatam Totius* also calls upon priests themselves to recruit vocations through their "apostolic zeal" and the joyfulness of their lives. Though this might sound like something of a velleity, it has been shown over and over again in more recent years that priests are in fact among the happiest people.[3] Oddly, this state of affairs, though established with remarkable consistency, has not impressed itself on the popular consciousness. A common though demonstrably false perception is that priests are lonely, bored, and unhappy, and unfortunately for vocational recruitment, the general attitude seems more influential than the truth on the ground.

Continuing in the tradition established by the Council of Trent, *Optatam Totius* clearly affirms the importance of major seminaries for the formation of priests. In these "seed-beds"—and not in universities or mere houses of formation—seminarians should be shaped according to the mind of Christ, who is priest, prophet, and shepherd.[4] In using that famous triplet, *Optatam Totius* shows its indebtedness to the thought of John Henry Newman, who had borrowed and adapted the priest, prophet, king motif from the thought of John Calvin. It also demonstrates continuity with *Presbyterorum Ordinis*, which uses the same figure to articulate the nature of the priesthood.[5] In accord with both *Lumen Gentium* and *Presbyterorum Ordinis*, *Optatam Totius* maintains that the primary focus of the seminary should be training in the proclamation of the word of God. This emphasis is a function of a strict theologic: if faith is the door to the spiritual life, and if, furthermore, faith only comes from hearing, the first and most important pastoral task, the *primum officium*, is indeed the ministry of the Word. Hence, apprenticing to Christ in his prophetic mode is fundamental in the seminary.

Therefore, *Optatam Totius* calls for a revision of ecclesiastical studies in seminaries. Its first recommendation is that students be grounded in the humanities as well as in the physical sciences, so that they might be able to facilitate a dialogue between ancient faith and contemporary culture. It also calls for a keen promotion of the teaching of Latin, so that the treasures of the theological tradition might be unlocked more easily, and of Greek and Hebrew, so that the Bible might be more thoroughly understood. Further, it strongly promotes the study of philosophy, more specifically a consideration of the issues of "humanity, the world, and God."[6] And this investigation ought to be carried out, it argues, according to "that philosophical tradition that is of permanent value," meaning apparently the great *philosophia perennis* stretching from the ancients to the scholastics of the high Middle Ages. At the same time, it recommends that the intellectual formation of seminarians be supplemented by contemporary forms of thought, especially those that are dominant in their respective countries. The authors of *Optatam Totius* hope that the study of philosophy will help future priests understand the mysteries of the faith more profoundly but also sense the limitations of human knowledge.

In regard to theology, *Optatam Totius* stresses, first, the intimate link between doctrine and spirituality. The dogmas of the Church ought to be presented in such a way that they are not simply data for the mind but signposts on the spiritual itinerary. Secondly, it wants theology to inform a healthy and culturally engaged apologetics, so that future priests can defend the faith in a public setting. Thirdly, it wants Sacred Scripture to be taught in such a way that students appreciate the Bible as the "soul of theology."[7] This last suggestion, of course, is congruent with the renewal of Scriptural study called for by *Dei Verbum*. Dogmatic theology ought to be arranged so that Biblical themes come first and then the meditations of the church fathers, both East and West. It is not difficult to see the influence of the *ressourcement* tradition in this manner of laying out the starting points for dogmatics. Having taken in the Scriptural and patristic foundations, the seminarians are then to be instructed in the theology of St. Thomas: "Let the students learn, with the aid of speculative reason under the guidance of St. Thomas, to penetrate them (the mysteries of the faith) more deeply and see their connection."[8] We will return later to this vexed issue of the use of Thomas Aquinas in the intellectual formation of seminarians; for the moment, we will observe only that the formula used by *Optatam Totius*—"*Thoma magistro*" (with Thomas as master)—was meant to mollify both those who wanted Thomism strongly emphasized and those who felt that only the method and not necessarily the content of Aquinas's theology should be recommended.[9]

In line with the instincts of the liturgical movement and the strong Vatican II stress on the Sacred Liturgy, the document suggests that liturgy ought to be a privileged interpretive lens for the understanding of Christian dogma. This represented a significant shift from the relegation of liturgy to the arena of pastoral practice. One of the most important and seminal recommendations of *Optatam Totius* is that moral theology ought to be radically renewed: "Its scientific presentation ought to be more based on the teaching of Scripture."[10] This turning away from the rationalistic and purely deductive moral calculus of neo-scholastic moral theology has been slow in coming but has emerged in the last two decades as an extremely significant development.[11]

Finally, *Optatam Totius* insists that all of seminary formation be geared toward pastoral formation: "Therefore, all the methods used in training—spiritual, intellectual, and disciplinary—are to be coordinated by joint action towards this pastoral purpose."[12] In the sixth section of *Optatam Totius*, the council fathers specify the focus of this pastoral instruction: "The pastoral concern which should inspire the whole training of students also requires that they be instructed in matters especially concerning the sacred ministry: that is, in catechesis and preaching, in the liturgy and the administration of the sacraments, in works of charity, in the duty of helping those in error and unbelievers, and in all other pastoral tasks."[13] Relatedly, seminarians should be encouraged to cultivate those virtues that "favor dialogue with people," including "the capacity of listening to others, and of opening their hearts in a spirit of charity to the various circumstances of human need."[14] We will see how thoroughly this last point is developed, under the rubric of "human formation," by both John Paul II and the authors of the *Program for Priestly Formation*.

Reception

It is really quite remarkable how these suggestive but sketchy observations have inspired such a rich tradition of interpretation and reception. No one read this text with greater care than the man who was an active participant in the Council proceedings and who later became the pope most responsible for providing the Council with a definitive interpretation. In his 1992 Apostolic Exhortation *Pastores Dabo Vobis*, Karol Wojtyła, Pope John Paul II, offered a textured reading and application of *Optatam Totius*, which has provided the framework for thinking through seminary formation in the post-conciliar era.

In John Paul's document, we find the extremely influential schema of the "four pillars" of seminary education, namely, human, spiritual, intellectual, and pastoral.[15] The last three of these correspond rather clearly to *Optatam Totius*'s stress on forming seminarians who imitate Christ as priest, prophet, and shepherd. In fact, John Paul specially emphasizes the pastoral dimension, agreeing with *Optatam Totius* that all of seminary formation tends toward pastoral integration and repeating over and again throughout *Pastores Dabo Vobis* that the priest is meant to be configured to Christ as "head and shepherd of his people."[16] This seems to be John Paul's way of articulating the difference between the manner in which all the baptized participate in the kingly office of Christ and the manner in which ordained priests do so. While all the faithful exercise certain types of leadership within the context of the mystical body, ordained priests assume the principal responsibility of ordering the charisms within the community toward the upbuilding of the kingdom of God. The overall purpose of the seminary is to produce shepherds willing and able to give their lives in order to feed, protect, and direct their flocks.

What is new in John Paul's adaptation of *Optatam Totius* is the stress on human formation as a fourth pillar of priestly training. This has its roots in the earlier document's brief evocation of certain human qualities necessary for effective priestly ministry, but it also comes from John Paul's deep grounding in the thought of Thomas Aquinas, one of whose key principles is the tight relationship between nature and grace: *gratia supponit et perfecit naturam.*[17] Since God's grace works on and transfigures a nature that is receptive to it, corruptions in nature can effectively compromise the effectiveness of grace. This is why, in fact, John Paul goes so far as to say that human formation is the foundation for the other three. Another source for the pope's preoccupation with the human dimension of seminary formation is undoubtedly his training in the philosophical anthropology of the phenomenological movement. From his doctoral work on Max Scheler's ethics, through his trenchant study of moral agency in *The Acting Person*, to his meditations on sexuality in *Love and Responsibility*, Karol Wojtyła had long been interested in the nature of human choice and identity. Thus it is not surprising that this philosopher of human nature would want the seminarians of the world to be healthy and integrated human beings. Here John Paul echoes an adage attributed to Cardinal Albert Meyer of Chicago, a major player at Vatican II: "First we want to form gentlemen, then disciples, and finally priests." Employing an evocative trope, John Paul says that the humanity of the priest must function as a bridge between Christ and his people, a sort of Jacob's ladder on which the angels of God can ascend and descend.[18]

Now what are characteristic marks of an integrated humanity? A first, says John Paul, is the capacity to be a person of communion, which means the ability to relate to others sincerely, hospitably, and affably. It entails freedom from arrogance and self-regard and a willingness to reach out to those trapped in loneliness. Another dimension of a healthy humanity is what the pope calls "affective maturity," which amounts to an ordering of the emotions so as to make real love possible.[19] In his encyclical *Redemptor Hominis*, John Paul had specified that "man cannot live without love";[20] the affective maturity he discusses in *Pastores Dabo Vobis* is the condition of the possibility of exercising a true gift of self.[21] Essential to this emotional integration is a disciplining of the emotions in the direction of authentic love and the living out of the nuptial meaning of the body, which is to say, of the body's potential to become a vehicle of self-giving love for the sake of another.

The *Program for Priestly Formation* heartily embraces John Paul's vision for human formation and amplifies it. The American bishops speak of the movement from self-knowledge to self-acceptance and finally to self-gift.[22] In line with the recent stress in moral theology on virtue ethics, the *Program for Priestly Formation* emphasizes the cultivation of the classical cardinal virtues of prudence, justice, temperance, and courage, and it calls as well for "humility, constancy, sincerity, patience, good manners, truthfulness, and the keeping of one's word."[23] It also insists that a seminarian is "a man who respects, cares for and has vigilance over his body," for a physically unhealthy priest will not be able to carry the burdens of the priesthood.[24] Finally, it recommends that the seminarian cultivate a simple lifestyle and that he become "a good steward of material possessions."[25] John Paul II argued that the implementation of the Church's social teaching is an essential aspect of the "new evangelization," and central to that teaching is the conviction that the use of private property must always be for the common good. Priests and seminarians, above all, ought to witness to this healthy detachment.

One of the principal features of human formation—stressed by both John Paul II and the *Program for Priestly Formation*—is preparation for celibacy. Congruent with his customarily positive approach to the spiritual life, John Paul says that celibacy is the giving of "one's love and care to Jesus Christ and to his Church."[26] It is, above all, a mode of love and not a negation. Having said that, however, John Paul knows that the living out of celibate love depends upon a remarkable asceticism: "Freedom requires the person to be truly master of oneself, determined to fight and overcome the different forms of selfishness and individualism that threaten the life of each one, ready to open out to others, generous in dedication and service to one's neighbor."[27] A seminary must be the place where such asceticism is cultivated. The *Program for Priestly Formation* specifies that the physiological and psychological dimensions of celibacy must be presented but that, more importantly, the theological and spiritual rationale of the discipline must be brought forward, "so that it is made clear how it pertains to the logic of the ordained priesthood."[28] The scandals in the Church over the past twenty years have made painfully clear how necessary this training and discipline are.

After delineating the main features of human formation, John Paul turns to spiritual formation, the shaping of a candidate according to the priestly character of Jesus. An anthropology unhampered by the contemporary secularist ideology understands that the human being is naturally ordered to transcendence—to becoming, in Christian language, a son or daughter of God. This configuring to God takes on a special coloring in the context of priesthood, for the priest is called to friendship with Christ: "Those who are to take on the likeness of Christ the priest by sacred ordination should form the habit of drawing close to him as friends in every detail of their lives," precisely so that they can then draw others into that same intimacy.[29] The erstwhile disciples of John the Baptist asked Jesus, "Where do you stay?" and the Lord answered, "Come and see."[30] This conversation represents a permanent dynamic in Christian spiritual life, for the religious seeker is meant, finally, to come to the house of Jesus and to remain with the Lord, learning his mind, his ways, and his style of life. The seminary should be construed as a disciplined "staying" with Jesus so as to cultivate friendship with him.

What does this "remaining" with Jesus look like? John Paul explicitly cites *Optatam Totius*'s "triple path" of "faithful meditation on the word of God, active participation in the Church's holy mysteries, and the service of charity to the 'little ones.'"[31] One of the very best methods, he continues, for fostering the meditation on the Word is the classic practice of *lectio divina*, which involves both listening to the Word of God and responding to it prayerfully. In fact, he argues, this attention to Scripture is indispensable to the work of the new evangelization. Active participation in the mysteries is prayer in the fullest sense of the term. For the seminarian, this means the Liturgy of the Hours, prayed in its entirety, the frequent celebration of the Sacrament of Reconciliation, adoration of the Blessed Sacrament, the Rosary, and above all, the Eucharist on a daily basis. John Paul especially stresses the sacrament of penance for seminarians growing up in a culture that is fast losing a sense of sin and is marked by "subtle forms of self-justification."[32] The *Program for Priestly Formation* also recommends retreats and days of recollection, ascetical practice, obedience to one's superiors, simplicity of life, solitude, and spiritual direction at least once a month. Signaling its central importance, John Paul returns to a consideration of celibacy in this context of spiritual formation. He brings out the spousal profile of the discipline, showing how celibacy conforms a man to Christ who is bridegroom of his bride the Church. Just as a husband pledges exclusive fidelity to his wife, so the priest pledges exclusive fidelity in love to his bride. And just as a husband's chaste love brings forth children in the biological order, so the priest's chaste love brings forth new spiritual children for the Church.[33]

The third pillar that John Paul discusses is intellectual formation, the training of prophets. He notes first that this academic formation is tightly linked to the previous two pillars. On the one hand, the drive toward intellectual perception is deeply ingrained in human nature, and on the other, spirituality, which is tantamount to friendship with Jesus, naturally seeks understanding. Further, in our time, argues John Paul, theological and philosophical acuity is especially requisite for the successful exercise of the new evangelization. To a culture growing increasingly skeptical of religion in general and Catholicism in particular, we need priests who can sharply give reasons for the hope that is within them: "It strongly demands a high level of intellectual formation, such as will enable priests to proclaim, in a context like this, the changeless Gospel of Christ and to make it credible to the legitimate demands of human reason."[34]

Following *Optatam Totius* and his own instincts as a trained philosopher, John Paul observes that instruction in philosophy is crucial to the formation of seminarians. He subscribes to the standard justification for such study, namely, that there is a profound link between the kind of questions entertained by philosophers and those analyzed by theologians in the light of faith, but he adds a more contemporary rationale as well. Seminarians in the postmodern period are coming of age at a time when the very notion of objective truth is in doubt. Philosophy in its classical form should help convince future priests that there is a firm foundation for their own commitment and for their preaching: "If we are not certain about the truth, how can we put our whole life on the line, how can we have the strength to challenge others' way of living?"[35] John Paul's successor would speak famously of "the dictatorship of relativism," which has come to hold sway over much of the high culture in the West, and John Paul himself would bemoan the "culture of death" that flows precisely from this skepticism and indifferentism at the epistemological level.[36] In order to battle these poisonous states of affairs, he wants seminarians who are grounded in the *philosophia perennis* and who thereby embrace "the cult of truth," which is to say, a deep devotion to objective truth in both the metaphysical and moral orders.[37] The *Program for Priestly Formation* lays out this very concrete curriculum: "The philosophy program must include the study of logic, epistemology, philosophy of nature, metaphysics, natural theology, anthropology, and ethics." It further specifies that the thought of Thomas Aquinas in these areas should be "given the recognition that the Church accords it," noting *Optatam Totius*'s qualified endorsement of Thomism.[38]

Of course, one of the most remarkable developments in regard to the study of philosophy in a seminary context has been the emergence of programs of pre-theology throughout the Church. Since the majority of candidates approach seminary without the requisite formation in philosophy, the bishops of the United States and a number of other countries have implemented two-year programs that include a heavy dose of philosophy as well as courses in spirituality, basic religious studies, and the humanities.

But the intellectual formation of future priests is predicated principally on the study of theology or sacred doctrine. Taking a clear position on an issue much debated in the post-conciliar period, John Paul argues that authentic theology "proceeds from the faith and aims at leading to the faith."[39] He has no truck with the view that non-believers can practice theology in the proper sense of the term, though they might be engaging in religious study or sociology of religion. In this context, he cites Thomas Aquinas to the effect that faith is, as it were, the *habitus* of theology, the permanent principle of its operation. Thus, the theologian is first and foremost a believer, but a believer who stubbornly "asks himself questions about his own faith," seeking a deeper understanding.[40] John Paul wants these two aspects to remain intimately connected and intertwined in the hearts of seminarians. Since faith brings about a relationship with Jesus Christ in his mystical body, the Church, true theology must have both Christological and ecclesiological dimensions. The seminarian is meant to take on the mind of Christ and to think according to the intuitions and instincts of the Church (*sentire cum ecclesia*). Moreover, theology is meant to lead to spirituality and spirituality to theology in a mutually enhancing cycle. As St. Bonaventure put it, "Let no one think that it is enough for him to read if he lacks devotion, or to engage in speculation without spiritual joy, or to be active if he has no piety, or to have knowledge without charity."[41]

Theology, says John Paul, moves in two directions, the first toward the Word of God and the second toward the human person who receives that word. Concurring with the conciliar tradition, John Paul affirms that Sacred Scripture must be the soul of theology, informing all of its branches. But he also insists that theology must look carefully at the one who is called "to believe, to live, to communicate *to* others the Christian faith and outlook."[42]

This anthropological focus should be present as well in all aspects of theology, including dogmatics, morals, canon law, and pastoral theology. Theology has always been interested in the relationship between faith and reason, but this issue is of particular importance today, given the extreme valorization of scientific reason in the wider culture. Accordingly, John Paul urges that fundamental theology be given special emphasis in the seminary curriculum. Throughout his papacy, John Paul was preoccupied with the problem of the relationship between magisterial teaching and theological speculation. Ideally, the two work in concert, the former articulating the fundamentals of the apostolic faith and the latter teasing out the implications and applications of that faith for the present cultural situation. But in the postconciliar period, the two often appear as enemies, and theologians sometimes seem to present themselves as a second Magisterium. John Paul wants seminarians to be clear that a rival Magisterium would radically compromise the unity and missionary effectiveness of the Church.

A second major concern is the wedge that is sometimes driven between "high scientific standards in theology and its pastoral aim."[43] Especially when it is taught in a university setting, theology can become abstract, *wissenschaftlich*, and can come to lose its essential relationship to evangelization and pastoral praxis. John Paul wants seminarians trained according to serious "scientific" methodology, but he does not want them thereby to lose the feel for how theology must be applied in the pastoral setting.

A third area of interest today is the inculturation of the faith, often in cultures that are inimical to it. In accord with the Incarnational principle, the Church holds that the unchanging Word of God must become "flesh" in a wide variety of different cultures. Even as it avoids all forms of relativism and syncretism, the Church confirms that the Gospel takes on a variety of forms and colorations as it implants itself in the many cultures. John Paul wants seminarians to have a keen sensitivity to the tricky dynamics of this process.

Finally, reacting to some of the extreme activist interpretations of the faith that came to the fore in the post-conciliar period, John Paul holds strong against all forms of anti-intellectualism in the Church: "It is necessary to oppose firmly the tendency to play down the seriousness of studies and the commitment to them."[44] Especially now, he argues, when the Church is facing such a stern challenge from ideological secularism, sturdy intellectualism is desirable.

The fourth pillar that John Paul considers corresponds to the shepherding or kingly office of the priest. From one point of view, this training is one aspect among many, but in a larger sense, it is the organizing principle of the whole of seminary formation. John Paul enthusiastically cites *Optatam Totius* to the effect that "the whole training of the students should have as its object to make them true shepherds of souls after the example of our Lord Jesus Christ."[45] The study of theology ought to conduce, finally, to the pastoral task of preaching and catechizing; the study of worship and spirituality ought to lead, finally, to doing the work of salvation through the Eucharist and the other sacraments;

and human formation ought to make the candidate a suitable bridge between people and Christ. All of pastoral instruction is animated by and ordered to the pastoral charity of Christ himself, and seminary instruction in this area ought not be simply making a candidate familiar with various pastoral techniques, but rather a real apprenticeship to Christ, an initiation into "the sensitivity of being a shepherd."[46] What does this look like concretely? John Paul describes it as follows: "The conscious and mature assumption of responsibility, the interior habit of evaluating problems and establishing priorities and looking for solutions on the basis of honest motivations of faith and according to the theological demands inherent in pastoral work."[47] It is said that when, as Archbishop of Krakow, he was presented with a pastoral challenge, Karol Wojtyła would typically ask two questions: What does our faith say about this matter?[48] And whom can we get to help us? Such an approach was born of the cultivation of the pastoral *habitus* just described.

John Paul hopes that seminarians are sent for their pastoral internships, to parishes, where their priority should be the care for "the sick, immigrants, refugees and nomads," as well as those "sunk in inhuman poverty, blind violence, and unjust power."[49] Whatever power the seminarian exercises should be congruent with pastoral charity toward the weakest and most vulnerable. Of fundamental importance is that the seminarian develops his pastoral sensitivity in tandem with an awareness of the Church as mystery, communion, and mission. The work of the Church is, primarily, the work of the Holy Spirit, and the Church prospers only under the influence of the Spirit. When he loses sight of this, the seminarian or priest falls prey to a worldly activism. The Church is not a collection of individuals, but rather a mystical body, a communion. Cognizant of this, the seminarian can "carry out his pastoral work with a community spirit, in heartfelt cooperation with the different members of the Church: priests and bishop, diocesan and religious priests, priests and lay people."[50] A healthy pastoral attitude excludes any sort of individualist messianism. The priest does his work as a cell in a complex organism—under the bishop, in fellowship with his brother priests, in collaboration with laity and religious, and for the sake of the people of God. Lastly, the pastorally alert seminarian knows that the Church does not *have* a mission—the Church *is* a mission. Any pastoral field is a missionary field, especially in the fast-secularizing West, and the seminarian today has to be aware of the many tools available to him for proclamation and evangelization, including and especially the media of communication. The missionary attitude also involves a willingness on the part of the priest to go wherever his bishop sends him, even beyond the borders of his diocese or his country.

In its attempt to specify even further these recommendations in *Pastores Dabo Vobis*, the *Program for Priestly Formation* first discusses the proclamation of the Word, which *Presbyterorum Ordinis* famously teaches to be the *primum officium* of the priest.[51] The American bishops maintain that such proclamation is "aimed at the conversion of sinners."[52] Given the general cultural prejudice against being "negative" in spiritual matters, this might strike us as a bit surprising, but even the most casual acquaintance with the preaching of Jesus would indicate that the bishops are in line with deep Christian sensibilities. In his inaugural address in the Gospel of Mark, Jesus says, "The Kingdom of God is at hand. Repent, and believe the gospel" (Mk. 1:15). The assumption of the entire New Testament is that every human being has fallen into shadow and needs to turn to the light. Therefore, the matrix of every homily ought to be *metanoia*—turning around, conversion. Practically every Gospel presents a confrontation between Jesus and a sinner. Proclaimers of the Gospel ought, therefore, to consider a number of key questions: What are the dynamics of their conversation? How does Jesus move a given sinner to consider the offer of grace? What happens when that grace breaks through? More generally, the *Program for Priestly Formation* continues, the preacher ought to be able to affect the delicate balance between exegeting the Bible and interpreting the signs of the times. Preaching in fact is one of the privileged places where all four of the pillars come together naturally.

Next, the *Program for Priestly Formation* turns to a consideration of the sacramental ministry of the priest. Precisely because the priesthood is a type of spiritual fatherhood, it is connected intimately to the sacraments, which are the principle means by which Christ's life is communicated to his people. Baptism initiates the divine life; reconciliation restores it when it is lost; the Eucharist nourishes and sustains it; confirmation strengthens it; marriage and holy orders give it vocational focus; and the sacrament of the sick heals it and prepares it for transfiguration in a higher order. Therefore, a spiritual father has to be utterly at home with the theology and practice surrounding the sacraments. Eagerly following the lead of John Paul II, the American bishops insist that every seminarian should have "sustained contact with those who are privileged in God's eyes," which is to say "the poor, the marginalized, the sick, and the suffering."[53] They thereby cultivate the preferential option for the poor, and they are also prompted to understand the "social contexts and structures that can breed injustice."[54]

Drawing on years of experience since the Council, the American bishops recommend a number of venues for the pastoral training of seminarians. These include field education placements, pastoral quarters or sustained internships during the seminary years, clinical pastoral education, which usually takes place in a hospital setting, and diaconate internships. In all of these settings, the seminarian should be under the guidance of an experienced supervisor or spiritual father who provides practical feedback and clear direction. And all of these pastoral experiments should be followed by a focused and disciplined theological reflection that "provides an opportunity for personal synthesis, the clarification of motivations, and the development of directions for life and ministry."[55] Especially in these practical settings, the seminarians should develop leadership skills, including administration and the management of the physical and financial resources of a parish or institution. Increasingly, one hears from young priests the concern that they did not receive sufficient training in this regard while in seminary. To be sure, seminaries cannot do everything, but more needs to be done in this area, especially since the majority of young priests become pastors within a few years of ordination.

Application of Optatam Totius Today

What draws together *Optatam Totius, Pastores Dabo Vobis*, and the *Program for Priestly Formation* is a stress on evangelization. John Paul II's "new evangelization" is grounded firmly in the Vatican II documents, especially *Lumen Gentium, Gaudium et Spes, Presbyterorum Ordinis*, and *Optatam Totius*. Throughout his pontificate, John Paul emphasized the notion and unfolded its various aspects; and it is clearly the master idea behind both *Pastores Dabo Vobis* and the directives of the *Program for Priestly Formation*. Accordingly, the very best way to apply *Optatam Totius* in the situation of the early twenty-first century Church is to shape seminary programs for the purpose of new evangelization.

In the remainder of this chapter, I will lay out a number of qualities that ought to characterize priests of the new evangelization, and I will make at least some tentative suggestions as to how a seminary might inculcate them. First, an evangelizing priest must be deeply and personally in love with the Lord Jesus Christ. Christianity is not primarily a philosophy or an ideology or a program; it is, instead, a relationship with the person of the God-man. And evangelization is not the propagation of a set of ideas; it is the sharing of that relationship. Therefore, unless a person is already a friend of Jesus, he cannot offer friendship with the Lord to anyone else: *nemo dat quod non habet* (*no one gives what he doesn't have*). To be a true evangelist, the priest must not (to use the overworked cliché) just know about Jesus—he has to know Jesus. Therefore, the spiritual, pastoral, and academic programs of the seminary should help the student find the center and stay close to the fire. Kierkegaard said that a saint is someone whose life is about one thing.[56] He did not mean that the saint's life is monotonous; he meant that it is, in all of its variegation, focused on Christ alone. When a young man presents himself for admission to a Benedictine monastery, he is asked a simple question: "What do you seek?" If he is seeking anything other than God—security, the approval of others, escape from the world, etc.—he is encouraged to turn away. The spiritual program of the seminary ought to compel the student first of all to ask and answer that same question, and if the response is in the affirmative, it ought to move him through a series of exercises—contemplative prayer, Eucharistic adoration, *lectio divina*, the Liturgy of the Hours, mental prayer, the Mass, etc.—designed to order the whole of his life to Christ.

Secondly, priests of the new evangelization ought to know the story of Israel. The Good News (*euangelion*) that the first Christians shared concerned the resurrection of Jesus Christ from the dead, and that event represented the fulfillment of the promises made to the people of Israel. The first evangelists consistently read the risen Jesus through the lens of the history of salvation, *kata ta grapha* (according to the scriptures). They saw in Jesus's resurrection from the dead the establishment of Yahweh's kingship precisely through the human kingship of a son of David, and this king, they insisted, must reign as the ruler of the world. Hence the watchword of the early church was *Iesous Kyrios* (Jesus is Lord), a clear provocation in a culture that acknowledged Caesar as Lord. When Jesus is proclaimed in abstraction from Israel, therefore, he is diminished. In our cultural framework, he becomes a guru or a teacher of timeless spiritual truths, rather than the new king to whom final allegiance is owed. N. T. Wright has lamented that much of the Christology of the past two hundred years, both Protestant and Catholic, has been largely Marcionite in form, that is to say, formulated without substantive reference to the Jewishness of Jesus.[57] This means that seminarians who want to declare the kingship of Jesus must be immersed in Israel, and it implies that they must be men of the Bible. As *Optatam Totius* and its interpretive tradition have insisted, the Bible must take pride of place in the academic program of the seminary, and Scripture must be consistently invoked as the "soul" of theology. This Biblical orientation will guarantee that the future priests are filled with the ardor necessary for efficacious evangelization. As Aristotle observed in his *Rhetoric*, audiences finally listen only to an excited speaker. When the contemporary evangelist is convinced of the resurrection and furthermore appreciates the resurrection as the climax of the story of Israel, he will have the same excitement and enthusiasm evident in the first evangelists and in the authors of the New Testament.

One practical observation I would make in this context is that seminary formation in the Bible ought to put special stress on the canonical reading of the Scriptures. One unfortunate upshot of a strict application of the historical critical method is a tendency to break the Bible into its constitutive parts and to lose thereby a sense of its narrative integrity. Another way to put this is that an exclusive use of the historical critical method—given its preoccupation with discovering the intention of the human authors of the various biblical books—can obscure the purposes of the properly divine author of the entire Bible. Consequently, seminarians trained for the new evangelization should be keenly aware of how the various Biblical books relate to one another, echo one another, and contribute together to the telling of a great story, which culminates in the resurrection of Jesus Christ.

Thirdly, seminarians preparing for the new evangelization ought to be deeply and critically conversant with the contemporary culture. John Paul stressed that the new evangelization ought to be new in ardor, but he also insisted that it be new in expression. This means that seminarians concerned with announcing Jesus Christ to the world today have to know the culture well enough to formulate articulations of the faith that will be resonant with a contemporary audience. Here especially the study of philosophy is paramount. Again and again in today's Western cultural context, one hears echoes of Nietzsche's philosophy of the *Übermensch* and of Sartre's existentialism, by which I mean the valorization of self-creation and the setting aside of objective values, both epistemic and moral. It is crucially important that future evangelists understand this dynamic and have the intellectual resources to confront it. Another key theme in contemporary culture is an atheism born of the suspicion that God represents a threat to full human flourishing. This notion, with its roots in Feuerbach, Marx, and Freud, is born of a fundamental misconception of God as a supreme being alongside of other beings. A supreme being would indeed compete with other conditioned things in the measure that they would all occupy the same metaphysical space. But the God presented by classical Catholic philosophy is not one being among many—however supreme—but rather is the sheer act of being itself, *ipsum esse* in Aquinas's pithy formula. This distinction is pivotal, for it implies that God and creatures are not caught in a desperate zero-sum game, whereby the more God is glorified the more creatures are denigrated and vice versa. Rather, as St. Irenaeus has it, "The glory of God is a human being fully alive."[58]

Still another dominant philosophical motif in the contemporary West is what Charles Taylor calls "the disenchanted world," which is to say, the understanding of the universe as self-sufficient, self-contained, with no real reference to the supernatural.[59] The philosophical anthropology that corresponds to this metaphysics is, again to borrow Taylor's terminology, that of the "buffered self."[60] Along with many other postmodern philosophers, Taylor finds numerous warrants for the reintroduction of a keen sense of super-naturality and a concomitant embrace of the "porous self," a subjectivity open to transcendence.[61] Seminarians training to be new evangelists in our time have to be formed philosophically in such a way that they can spy and name these indicators of transcendence, what the Church Fathers called *semina verbi*. In regard to all of these issues, a knowledge of what *Optatam Totius* calls the *philosophia perennis* is indispensable.

I would make a final recommendation along more formational lines. Priests of the new evangelization should have the hearts of missionaries. Everyone knows the disturbing statistics dealing with the decline in church attendance in most Western countries. Even the most positive reading of the situation in the United States reveals that more than 75 percent of Catholics do not attend Mass regularly, which means that the overwhelming majority of Catholics are avoiding what Vatican II called "the source and summit of the Christian life."[62] This implies that the United States—indeed most Western countries—constitutes mission territory. Seminarians today should be deeply bothered by this situation and should burn with a passion to set it right. They cannot succumb to the indifference and religious relativism that dominates so much of the culture. And hence they must be immersed in the beauty of the Catholic tradition. Dietrich von Hilldebrand famously distinguished between the merely subjectively satisfying and the objectively valuable. The first is a function of one's private tastes and experiences, but the latter overthrows and transforms subjectivity, imposing itself with an undeniable authority. *The Divine Comedy, The Canterbury Tales*, Chartres Cathedral, the Sistine Ceiling, and the stories of Flannery O'Connor are not things that we like or do not like, according to our individual tastes. They are instances of the Good, objective values, to which subjectivity must accommodate itself. And the truly beautiful not only stops us in our tracks—or aesthetically arrests us, as Hans Urs von Balthasar says—but sends us on mission. If seminarians are to be true missionaries, therefore, they have to be connoisseurs of Catholic beauty, for it is especially the encounter with the objectively valuable that will convince them that their lives are not about them.

Conclusion

Sadly, the mass exodus of priests in the sixties and seventies of the last century was closely followed by the clergy sex abuse scandal, the worst crisis in the history of the American Church. The last several decades have been, it is fair to say, a bleak season for the priesthood. Yet within that period, very real rays of light have appeared, and among these are *Optatam Totius, Pastores Dabo Vobis*, the *Program of Priestly Formation*, and most remarkably, the heroic priesthood of John Paul II himself. One is reminded of the narrative told at the beginning of the first book of Samuel concerning Eli and his wicked sons, Hophni and Phineas. Eli was a sort of high priest, and his sons were priests. Hophni and Phineas were using their authority to abuse the people they were meant to serve, but when complaints were brought to their father, he did nothing. The result of this wickedness and indifference was disaster for Israel: the Philistines routed the Israelite army, killing 30,000 soldiers and making off with the Ark of the Covenant. When Eli heard the news of the death of his sons, he himself fell over dead. But in the wake of this calamity, Yahweh quietly stirred the heart of Hannah to beg for a son, and that child, Samuel, would come of age as one of the most powerful figures in Israelite history, setting the nation back on course and anointing David as King. God never gives up on his people, and he never tires of renewing the priesthood. The adoption of *Optatam Totius* and its rich implementation over the past fifty years represents one of the clearest signs of that renewal.

NOTES

1. *Optatam Totius*, in *Decrees of the Ecumenical Councils*, ed. Norman Tanner, SJ (Washington, DC: Georgetown University Press, 1990), no. 2, 2:948.

2. John Paul II, *Pastores Dabo Vobis (I Will Give You Shepherds: On the Formation of Priests in the Circumstances of the Present Day)* (Washington, DC: United States Conference of Catholic Bishops, 1992), no. 41.

3. See Stephen Rosetti, *The Joy of Priesthood* (Notre Dame: Ave Maria Press, 2005).

4. *Optatam Totius*, no. 4.

5. *Presbyterorum Ordinis*, no. 13, in Tanner, *Decrees of the Ecumenical Councils*, 2:1060.

6. *Optatam Totius*, nos. 14 and 15.

7. Ibid. no. 16.

8. Ibid. no. 16.

9. Ibid. no. 16.

10. Ibid. no. 16.

11. See, for example (among many), Servais Pinckaers, *The Sources of Christian Ethics* (Washington, DC: Catholic University Press, 1995).

12. *Optatam Totius*, no. 4.

13. Ibid. 19.

14. Ibid.

15. *Pastores Dabo Vobis*, nos. 43–59.

16. Ibid. no. 3.

17. See, among many other places, Thomas Aquinas, *Summa theologiae*, 1a, q. 1, a. 8, ad 2.

18. *Pastores Dabo Vobis*, no. 43.

19. Ibid.

20. *Redemptoris Hominis*, no. 10.

21. Ibid.

22. *Program for Priestly Formation*, 5th ed. (Washington, DC: United States Conference of Catholic Bishops, 2006), no. 80, 33.

23. Ibid. no. 76.

24. Ibid.

25. Ibid.

26. Ibid. no. 44.

27. Ibid.

28. Ibid. no. 79.

29. *Pastores Dabo Vobis*, no. 45.

30. Jn 1:35–39.

31. *Optatam Totius*, no. 8.

32. *Pastores Dabo Vobis*, no. 48.

33. Ibid. no. 50.

34. Ibid. no. 51.

35. Ibid. no. 52.

36. *Evangelium Vitae*, no. 12.

37. *Pastores Dabo Vobis*, no. 52.

38. *Program for Priestly Formation*, no. 156.

39. *Pastores Dabo Vobis*, no. 53.

40. Ibid.

41. Ibid.

42. Ibid. no. 54.

43. Ibid. no. 55.

44. Ibid. no. 56.

45. Ibid. no. 57.

46. Ibid. no. 58.

47. Ibid. no. 58.

48. See George Weigel, *Witness to Hope* (New York: HarperCollins, 1999).

49. *Pastores Dabo Vobis*, no. 58.

50. Ibid. no. 59.

51. *Presbyterorum Ordinis*, no. 4.

52. *Program of Priestly Formation*, no. 239.

53. Ibid.

54. Ibid.

55. Ibid.

56. See Soren Kierkegaard, *Purity of Heart is to Will One Thing* (San Francisco: Harper, 1964).

57. See N. T. Wright, *Jesus and the Victory of God* (Minneapolis: Fortress Press, 1996).

58. Irenaeus of Lyons, *Adversus haereses* 4.20.7.

59. Charles Taylor, *A Secular Age* (Cambridge: Harvard University Press, 2007).

60. Ibid., 27.

61. Ibid. 37.

62. *Lumen Gentium*, no. 11.

8

Perfectae Caritatis

Sara Butler, MSBT

No one could have guessed, in 1965, that religious life would be thrown into turmoil after the Second Vatican Council. Just the opposite: expectations ran high that the stripping away of outdated practices and attitudes would lead to significant renewal and greater flourishing. *Perfectae Caritatis*,[1] the Decree on the Up-to-Date (or Appropriate) Renewal of Religious Life, invited men and women Religious[2] to evaluate and renew their way of life in light of the demands of the Gospel, the inspiration of the founders, and the signs of the times, and most of them accepted the challenge with enthusiasm. Among the many observers who have attempted to account for the unexpected downward spiral,[3] few trace it simply to the influence of *Perfectae Caritatis*. Among the many factors at work, however, it is reasonable to ask how Religious have received *Perfectae Caritatis*.[4] Since the doctrinal foundations for the decree are found in *Lumen Gentium* chapters V ("The Universal Call to Holiness in the Church") and VI ("Religious"),[5] its reception has been closely tied to an interpretation of those chapters. The story of the Council's polarization over both procedure and content during the production of these chapters and of *Perfectae Caritatis* has been told,[6] but it is not well known. Still less well known are some accounts that indicate that what Religious commonly understand to be the Council's teaching—that *Lumen Gentium* excludes any comparison of vocations to holiness in terms of degrees—is actually the position rejected by the Council fathers. This essay will call attention to this misunderstanding and show that post-conciliar magisterial teaching on religious life consistently addressed and corrected it.

For Religious, *Lumen Gentium* chapter V raised such fundamental questions as these: If all the baptized are called to the same holiness, and if Baptism is the "state of perfection," what is the place and function of religious life?[7] What contribution is it supposed to make, and why should the Church's pastors have the authority to supervise religious institutes and intervene in their affairs? According to a study on religious life in the United States published in 1992,

> a significant percentage of religious no longer understand their role and function in the Church. This lack of role clarity can result in low-ered self-confidence, a sense of futility, greater propensity to leave religious life, and significant anxiety. The younger religious experience the least clarity, and among them, women religious experience less clarity than their male counterparts. Whatever clarity exists among men seems to emerge from the definitiveness of orders for priests and their definite role requirements as well as from the clarity of the lay vocation for brothers. Women religious are divided on the concept of consecrated life as distinct from or equal to the life of lay women. For both women and men religious, Vatican II substantially reinforced the role of the laity in the Church, but did not clarify for religious the unique contribution of their vocation.[8]

This comprehensive sociological study indicates that the reception of *Perfectae Caritatis* has been difficult, and it suggests that what Religious lost in terms of role clarity is related in some way to what the laity gained. Whether or not Religious should have understood things in this way, the fact is that many did.[9] The controversy over religious life at Vatican II was especially heated, and it now seems clear that many Religious received and accepted a flawed version of the Council's doctrine. In several cases, the resolution of the conciliar debates and the reasoning that supported it was misrepresented or simply not reported. As a result, they ignore or refuse the post-conciliar Magisterium on the grounds that it introduces a "restorationist" agenda alien to the Council's teaching.[10]

Four misconceptions about the Council's teaching that influenced the reception of *Perfectae Caritatis* are (1) that it deposed religious life from its previous position of prominence in the Church; (2) that it called into question the special character of religious life and the possibility of acknowledging any morally valuable difference between Christian vocations; (3) that it deliber-ately changed the traditional theology of the vows professed by Religious by re-ordering the evangelical counsels (chastity, poverty, and obedience instead of poverty, chastity, and obedience); and (4) that it opened the way to a re-definition of religious life by including societies of apostolic life[11] and secular institutes[12] in a chapter entitled "Religious."[13] As a result of (1) and (2), many Religious continue to raise questions about their identity, their "place" in the Church, and the value of their vocations. As a consequence of (3) and (4), many hold that the defining characteristic of religious life is religiously-motivated celibacy, and that the Church's pastors, through the instrumentality of the Congregation for Religious,[14] wrongly impose on contemporary Religious expectations that belong to a bygone era and an outdated ecclesiology. This essay will show that the Council did not, in *Lumen Gentium*, change the status of religious life, ~~and~~ but that it did, in the decree *Perfectae Caritatis*, provide for its "appropriate renewal."

Revisiting the Council's Teaching on Religious Life in *Lumen Gentium*

The first thing to notice is that *Perfectae Caritatis* does not stand alone. As a decree, it does not spell out doctrine but offers directions for implementing the doctrine that is spelled out elsewhere, namely, in chapters V and VI of *Lumen Gentium*. The interpretation of these and earlier chapters of *Lumen Gentium* has profoundly influenced the reception of *Perfectae Caritatis*, and it is possible today to observe how certain initial impressions, commentaries, and even translations (for English speakers) of these texts contributed to what became a veritable identity crisis for many Religious. The commentaries on these chapters of *Lumen Gentium* were most often written by the *periti*, or theologian "experts," who participated in the various commissions.[15] They had access to the drafts and explanations circulated among the Council Fathers, information about the discussion and debates, and their own memory of the course of events to go on. Their views, published in popular and journalistic accounts, generated some lasting impressions. To counteract misinterpretations of the Council's teaching being spread by "liberal reformers,"[16] Ralph M. Wiltgen, SVD, published *Religious Life Defined*, an English translation of the official commentary the Doctrinal Commission prepared for the Council fathers on the third and fourth drafts of *LG* VI.[17] In 1985, Paul Molinari, SJ, and Peter Gumpel, SJ, published a detailed account of the debate on *LG* V and VI that confirms Wiltgen's report and enlarges upon it in many respects.[18] Polarization on the nature and place of religious life did not end after the Council. Those who read *Lumen Gentium* with a hermeneutic of rupture and discontinuity were encouraged to embrace a new solidarity with the laity by eschewing as "elitist" any claims to a distinctive calling and by abandoning the external signs and traditions that set them apart. Those who read it with a hermeneutic of continuity and reform did not suffer the same disorientation and eventually profited from the vigorous call of *Perfectae Caritatis* to return to the sources (the Gospel and the charism of the founder) and its invitation to update by dispensing with traditions and customs that did not suit the times.[19]

The commentaries agree that during the drafting of *Lumen Gentium* members of the Doctrinal Commission and the Commission on Religious, along with their *periti*, engaged in an extended and acrimonious controversy behind the scenes and between the Sessions.[20] It began when the Council fathers sent the first draft of the *schema* on the Church, which included a short chapter on "The States of Life Devoted to Acquiring Evangelical Perfection," back to the Doctrinal Commission to be completely reorganized. When the second draft was published, the Commission of Religious was surprised to discover that the revised chapter on Religious had been inserted, without explanation, into an entirely new chapter on the universal call to holiness in the Church.[21]

Council fathers who were the superiors general of clerical institutes, members of the Commission on Religious, and bishops who were themselves Religious found this change unacceptable and insulting. Joining forces, they eventually gathered 679 signatures requesting a chapter devoted entirely to Religious and insisting on some amendments of a doctrinal nature. Pope Paul VI, getting word of their dissatisfaction, asked the members of the Doctrinal Commission to give their views diligent attention in the revision of the second draft.[22] This they did, but they left the treatment of religious life embedded, as part 2, in the chapter on the universal call to holiness.

The Council fathers were seriously divided, not only over the arrangement of the material (i.e., whether *Lumen Gentium* should have a separate chapter on Religious), but also over the doctrine itself.[23] According to the official summary from the Doctrinal Commission,[24] the fathers who favored a single chapter with two parts, the universal call to holiness and the religious life, were primarily concerned to correct the idea that the pursuit of holiness is the special prerogative and obligation of priests and Religious and that the Church's ascetical doctrine recognizes *"two classes of Christians,*[25] some with more and some with less perfection, depending upon the state in which they live."[26] Because they regarded the quest for holiness as the culminating point of *Lumen Gentium*, they thought it sufficient to mention religious life, in this context, as an expression of this quest. In their view, a separate chapter on Religious would only reinforce the mistake they wanted to correct. The fathers who favored a separate chapter agreed that all the baptized are called to holiness, but they wanted the importance of the religious state to be acknowledged, not only in its distinctive contribution to the Church's holiness, but more generally.[27] Some were concerned that failure to give Religious their own chapter would create the impression that the bishops did not value their vocation and the contributions men and women Religious make, for example, to the Church's missionary efforts.

Everyone knows that the Council eventually voted for a separate chapter on Religious—chapter VI in *Lumen Gentium*. Not everyone knows, however, that the Council voted in favor of the doctrine proposed by the second group of Council fathers (mostly Religious) rather than the first. Of the doctrinal issues in *Lumen Gentium* that affected the reception of *Perfectae Caritatis*, then, these four deserve special attention: the place of religious life in the Church's divine constitution, its difference from the baptismal vocation, its distinguishing characteristic, and the special obligations assumed by Religious.

1. *Religious Life and the Divine Constitution of the Church*

The text the Doctrinal Commission proposed for the second draft was intended to correct the popular notion that the Church was constructed as a three-tiered pyramid in which the laity occupies the bottom, Religious, the middle, and the clergy, the top tier. By divine institution, it said, the Church is composed of laypersons and clerics, and the religious state does not occupy an intermediate position between the two. Instead, some of the faithful from each of these states "are called by God to enjoy this special gift in the mystery of the Church, and are dedicated to his service."[28] According to Bishop André-Marie Charue, who advanced this proposal, Religious differ from "non-Religious" chiefly in their manner of seeking holiness, not because, as socially-organized, they have a place in the Church's constitution.[29]

The Council fathers who represented the interests of the Religious were unwilling to see the religious state reduced to a path to holiness chosen by some members of the Church as individuals or simply to a structure *in* the Church. In their view, there is another way to think about the Church's divine constitution. According to an intervention of twenty-five of them,

> The state of perfection[30] is *substantially of divine institution*: it stems from Christ's will, not by way of precept, but by way of counsel. The state of perfection creates a distinction in the Church, not on the basis of the Church as an hierarchical society, but on the basis of the Church as a spiritual society directed toward holiness. . . . The state of perfection is the perfect imitation of Christ which cannot be lacking to the Church.[31]

They went on to say that it is by Christ's will that there is in the Church "the twofold category of those who are called to practice the counsels effectively and totally, and of others who are not."[32] The Church, besides being a hierarchically ordered society, is also a spiritual society whose goal is the holiness of her members.[33] From this perspective, namely, that of her "life and holiness," those who profess the evangelical counsels differ from those who do not. Their service to the "perfection of charity" is essential to the holiness and witness of the Church. The religious state is not simply of human or ecclesiastical origin. Just as the evangelical counsels themselves have a divine origin, being Christ's gift to the whole Church, so too religious life takes its origin from the Lord's teaching and example. The institutes that comprise this state also have a "divine origin," moreover, because their founders act under divine inspiration, and the hierarchy recognizes the founder's charism as a gift of God to the Church. The Church's pastors not only mediate the foundation of religious institutes; they also have the obligation and authority to preserve and regulate the profession of the counsels for the sake of the Church's holiness and mission.[34]

To meet the objections of these Religious, the Council fathers added the word "hierarchical" to *LG*, no. 43. The approved text reads, "From the point of view of the divine and *hierarchical* structure of the Church, the religious state of life is not an intermediate one between the clerical and lay states."[35] By this qualification, they indicate that although the religious state does not belong to the Church's *hierarchical* constitution, it is not excluded from her *divine* constitution, considered under another formality.[36] This explanation is repeated at the end of *LG*, no. 4: "Thus, although the [religious] state constituted by the profession of the evangelical counsels does not belong to the *hierarchical* structure of the Church, nevertheless it belongs inseparably to her life and holiness."[37] These emendations significantly alter Bishop Charue's thesis[38] and provide the foundation for a new appreciation of the divine origin of religious life and its indispensable place in the Church.[39] In *LG*, no. 43, the Council explicitly affirms the divine origin of the evangelical counsels and the contribution Religious make not only to the Church's holiness but to her saving mission.

Those who failed to note the logic of these emendations saw only that the Council had removed religious life from its former place of prominence and relocated it in the Church's "life and holiness." This new location did not actually seem to distinguish the religious state from that of the rest of the baptized. If religious institutes have no clear "place" in the institution, many reasoned, there is no cause for the hierarchy to exercise authority over them in matters having to do with their way of life.

2. The Universal Call to Holiness

In *LG* V, "The Call to Holiness," the Council affirms that the Church is holy because she is Christ's Bride and Body and has been endowed with the Holy Spirit (*LG*, no. 39). It goes on to assert forcefully, with the intention of correcting a popular misunderstanding, that "all the Christian faithful of whatever rank or status are called to the fullness of Christian life and to the perfection of charity" (*LG*, no. 40).

The Doctrinal Commission wanted to emphasize sameness. Its "commentary" at the introduction of the new draft reads, "The perfection of holiness, which one must reach by following the commandment of charity, is open to all, and the *same holiness* is proposed for all states and walks of life."[40] A great number of fathers, including the group of 679, objected to this, and asked that the formulation be changed to acknowledge differences of degree and vocation. Their view prevailed. The Doctrinal Commission's "Relatio" sent to the Council fathers with the 1964 draft explains its response to the objection: "Therefore in the new text the affirmation of *one* holiness remains and the addition is not made as was done in the previous text, that holiness is also *the same*. Thus the new text recognizes implicitly that there is diversity according to various degrees and vocations."[41] For the Council, the call to holiness expressed in perfect charity is addressed to all (*LG*, nos. 39, 40), but Religious, in response to a divine call, pursue this holiness in a different way, namely, by the profession[42] of the evangelical counsels in a life-long gift of themselves to God in an institute approved by the Church (*LG*, nos. 43–44). In *LG* VI and also in *Perfectae Caritatis*, the Council does not hesitate to use comparative terms in describing religious life. Those who profess the evangelical counsels by vow or other sacred bond are said to be totally dedicated to God and his service "by a new and *special* title," and to be "*more* intimately consecrated to divine service" (*LG*, no. 44). They strive to follow Christ "more freely and imitate him *more* nearly" (*PC*, no. 1). Their special consecration is rooted in Baptism and provides an ampler manifestation of it" (*PC*, no. 5).[43]

By some mistake, the English translations of *LG*, no. 41 by the National Catholic Welfare Conference,[44] Abbott, and Flannery failed to notice that the Council fathers deliberately changed the earlier text to avoid saying that all are called to the *same* holiness. These translations report that "in the various types and duties of life, one *and the same* holiness is cultivated by all who are moved by the Spirit of God."[45] This small mistake, now corrected, went unnoticed for years. It seems to be at least partly responsible for the complaint that *Lumen Gentium* is inconsistent in asserting "sameness," on the one hand, and using comparative language, on the other. Many Religious formed in a democratic and egalitarian culture welcome this message of "sameness" and resist the hierarchy's attempts to oblige them to observe the essential elements of religious life,[46] in the mistaken belief that they contradict the Council's teaching.

The Council fathers were initially divided over whether religious life belonged to the Church's divine constitution and whether the holiness to which all the baptized are called admits of different degrees and vocations. They gave an affirmative answer to both. In both cases, however, the interventions, debates, and views promoted by some of the *periti* and journalists suggested the opposite.[47] It is not surprising, then, that many readers were unaware that the emendations made to the text of *Lumen Gentium* settled these debates in favor of the traditional teaching.[48] Two other closely related questions from the debates on *LG* V and VI affected the reception of *Perfectae Caritatis*, namely, the Council's decision to name chastity before poverty and obedience in listing the evangelical counsels[49] and to give *LG* VI the title "Religious," even though it addressed not only religious institutes but also secular institutes and societies of apostolic life.

3. The Re-Ordering of the Evangelical Counsels

LG V, "The Universal Call to Holiness," asserts early on that Christian holiness is often manifested by the practice of the counsels commonly called "evangelical," and that many Christians, impelled by the Holy Spirit, undertake to practice them, either "privately or in a form or state sanctioned by the Church" (*LG*, no. 39).[50] The transition from chapter V to chapter VI takes place in *LG*, no. 42. The text moves from the love of Christ who surrendered his life to save us, to the love that prompted the martyrs to follow him even to the shedding of their blood, and then to the love that prompts some of the faithful to observe the counsels, and in particular to embrace virginity or celibacy, "that precious gift of divine grace given to some by the Father (cf. Mt 19:11; 1 Cor 7:7) [so that they may] devote themselves to God alone more easily with an undivided heart (1 Cor 7:32–34)." The same article also relates the counsels of poverty (2 Corinthians 8:9) and obedience (Philippians 2:7–8) to the following of Christ.

When the decision was made to divide the chapter, the mention of the evangelical counsels was chosen as the point of transition. *LG* VI then proceeded to identify the counsels professed by Religious in the order already adopted, namely, *chastity*, poverty, and obedience. The Council kept this order for editorial convenience; doing so made it possible to move from one expression of holiness to another without a wholesale reorganization of the text. Was the reordering also theologically significant? No. As Elizabeth McDonough, OP, has noticed, the minutes explicitly assert that no one should conclude from this re-ordering that the Commission intended to propose a new doctrine, contradict the teaching of the Magisterium, or settle questions freely debated by theologians.[51]

One year later, the Council opened debate on the draft of *Perfectae Caritatis*. This text treated the counsels in the traditional order (poverty-chastity-obedience). At the request of 441 fathers, however, the order in *Perfectae Caritatis* (now, *PC*, nos. 12–14) was changed to match the presentation in *LG* VI. The report of the Doctrinal Commission once again indicates that the reason for listing chastity first was functional, not theological.[52] As it happened, however, since no explanation of the change was given in *PC* itself,[53] some theologians presumed to discover one. Without having seen the minutes of the Council, Molinari and Gumpel treat this re-ordering of the counsels as theologically important.[54] In their view, "it is not difficult to guess the reasons that led the Doctrinal Commission to abandon the traditional order and place virginity first."[55] They go on to identify the inversion as "a point of considerable importance for a true appreciation of the conciliar teaching."[56]

As McDonough points out, the unfounded speculation of Molinari and Gumpel has had serious implications for the reception of *Perfectae Caritatis*.[57] Chaste celibacy for the sake of the kingdom may be a condition for admission to the consecrated life,[58] but all three counsels, in their classical order, are essential to the form that is professed and lived in *religious* institutes. The classical order lists the evangelical counsels in relation to the value of the "goods" that are voluntarily renounced.[59] Poverty has to do only with the renunciation of material goods or "worldly" possessions. Chastity demands more because it involves the renunciation of goods that are both bodily and spiritual (sexual intimacy and marital and family relationships). Obedience is the most demanding because it requires the renunciation of a spiritual faculty, one's own will, to the direction of another. By this triple renunciation, Religious signify their intention to remove from their path all obstacles to the perfection of charity. Perpetual profession of the three evangelical counsels in a stable way of life approved by the Church is the means by which they make a complete gift of self, a "holocaust."[60] Members of religious institutes profess all three counsels, not just celibacy for the sake of the kingdom.[61]

Although some fathers and *periti* raised objections to the traditional order and to the theological explanation based on a progressive renunciation of "goods," the Council did not repudiate either of these in *Lumen Gentium* and *Perfectae Caritatis*.[62] Although these same fathers and *periti* vigorously promoted an alternative view,[63] the Council did not endorse it. Some Religious who accepted the theory that the new order of the vows had theological significance concluded that chaste celibacy is the defining characteristic of religious life, and that the poverty and obedience professed by Religious are no different from the virtues required of every disciple. In effect, McDonough asserts, they chose to redefine religious life as "a purely personal, cooperative endeavor recognized by the Church but with no reference to its prior communal or obediential aspects as understood for more than 1,500 years."[64] The consequences of this misunderstanding are intertwined with the next one.

4. Religious Life and the Other Forms of Consecrated Life

When the Council fathers decided to use the title "Religious" for *LG* VI, they used the term in a broad, generic sense.[65] *LG* V, in no. 42, had already referred to the Christian faithful who follow the Savior more closely by observing the evangelical counsels privately. *LG* VI went on to refer to "Religious," namely, those among the Christian faithful who are consecrated by vows or other sacred bonds to observe these counsels in various stable forms of living approved by the Church. Although most of these are members of religious institutes, some also belong to societies of apostolic life and secular institutes. It was not the Council's intention to define[66] or legislate for any of these, but several questions inevitably arose, for example, whether to focus on "consecration" or "profession of the evangelical counsels,"[67] since societies of apostolic life require common life but not profession of vows, and how to account for the inclusion in this chapter of secular institutes, since they neither require common life nor profess public vows. The Doctrinal Commission and the Commission on Religious agreed to use "Religious" as a general term, without further specification.[68] This decision, like the previous one, had an unanticipated consequence. Some Religious claim the right to abandon "elements" of the religious life they no longer intend to observe (e.g., common life, the exercise of religious authority by a superior and the corresponding obedience) on the grounds that they are not obligatory for members of other forms of the religious life (in the broad sense).

Perfectae Caritatis, Ecclesiae Sanctae, and the Reception of the Council's Teaching

The polarization that characterized the debates on *Lumen Gentium*'s chapter on Religious also affected the production of *Perfectae Caritatis*.[69] The division into two factions had an impact before the Decree was even finalized, and this influenced its eventual reception.[70] Exposure to the opposing views left many Religious either puzzled or persuaded that the Council was calling for a radical re-thinking of their vocation. Although *Perfectae Caritatis* itself supported and even strengthened the traditional theology of religious life, it was commonly interpreted and implemented in light of the positions advanced during the controversy over *Lumen Gentium*.

Whether or not *Perfectae Caritatis* takes its inspiration from the doctrine in *LG* VI, it highlights the ecclesial and Christological dimensions of religious life. In *PC*, nos. 1, 2, and 5, the Council situates religious life in its ecclesiological context. This way of life emerged in the Church's life "in keeping with the divine purpose" (*PC*, no. 1). By their ministries, Religious build up the Church as Christ's Body, and by their holiness they show forth the Church as his Bride. The more fervently they join themselves to Christ in a lifelong gift of themselves, the more the Church's life and mission flourish, so in addressing the life and discipline of Religious, the Council has in mind the greater good of the Church as a whole. The same articles of *Perfectae Caritatis* present the profession of the evangelical counsels in an explicitly Christological perspective. In response to God's call, Religious bind themselves to follow "Christ who, virginal and poor (cf. Mt. 8:20; Lk. 9:58), redeemed and sanctified men by obedience unto death on the Cross (cf. Phil. 2:8)" (*PC*, no. 1). All institutes are to take the following of Christ as set forth in the Gospels as their highest rule (*PC*, no. 2). Those who respond to this divine call oblige themselves to follow the counsels by vow, or similar bond, with the intention of handing their entire lives over to the service of God and of the Church.[71]

The decree *Perfectae Caritatis* was chiefly concerned with the renewal of religious institutes.[72] It directed Religious to undertake this by returning to the sources of Christian life and the original spirit of their founders; by adapting to the changed circumstances of modern life; by implementing the Church's biblical, liturgical, dogmatic, pastoral, ecumenical, missionary, and social agenda; and, above all, by fostering spiritual renewal in line with their purpose, namely, to follow Christ and attain union with God by the profession of the evangelical counsels (*PC*, no. 2).[73] It asked them to adapt their manner of praying, working, and governing themselves to their members' physical and psychological needs, the needs of the apostolate, and the demands of their culture and their social and economic circumstances (*PC*, no. 3). *PC* entrusted to the initiative of Religious themselves this invitation to wholesale renewal and reform; they were to keep in mind the principles it supplied (*PC*, no. 2) and the specific nature (e.g., contemplative, monastic, apostolic, secular) of their institutes (*PC*, nos. 7–11).

After the close of the Council, Pope Paul VI issued *Ecclesiae Sanctae* (1966), an apostolic letter that contained norms for the implementation of *Perfectae Caritatis*.[74] He directed every religious institute to convene a special general chapter to address the challenges posed by the decree and granted the chapter and the general council the right to experiment contrary to the norms of their constitutions,[75] provided the nature, purpose, and characteristics of the institute were kept intact. The period of experimentation was to continue until the next general chapter or the chapter immediately following it. *Ecclesiae Sanctae* set out several "criteria of suitable renewal"[76] and made specific recommendations, for example, about the Divine Office, mental prayer, mortification, poverty, and common life. All the members of each institute were to be consulted and to cooperate in the renewal process. The constitutions of each institute were to be revised; they were to include spiritual principles as well as juridical norms and to exclude whatever was obsolete; matters that might be subject to change were to be put in a directory. The revised constitutions and directories were to be submitted to the competent authority for approval.

This challenge undoubtedly opened many Religious to a deeper spiritual life, nourished by Scripture and the renewed liturgy and supported by spiritual direction; it called them to mature interdependence and required them to gain new skills for community living and communal discernment; it opened access to theological education and increased professionalism in ministry, and encouraged creativity and productivity. The profound self-examination this provoked led some Religious, however, to question the meaning and function of their vows and the value of their consecration. At the same time as they worked to accomplish the task set before them, they experienced the impact of the Council's teaching overall.[77] The "identity crisis" that followed has been especially severe for lay (as opposed to clerical) institutes of apostolic religious life. Their assessment of what should be changed or brought up to date and what should be discarded as obsolete was greatly influenced by what they understood the Council to have taught about religious life itself.

During the short interval between the promulgation of *Perfectae Caritatis* (1965) and Pope Paul VI's Apostolic Exhortation *Evangelica Testificatio* (1971), hundreds of sisters, brothers, and religious priests left their institutes. The exodus was at least partly due to the belief that the Council had changed the status of Religious by proclaiming that all the baptized are called to holiness. Many of those who left believed that if there was no special virtue attached to embracing the religious state, there was no reason to stay in it and no guilt or shame entailed in leaving it. Many who remained in religious life prepared to alter or dispense with whatever in their way of life underlined their difference from the rest of the baptized.[78] They felt obliged, in other words, to eschew any vestige of "elitism," that is, any suggestion that the vocation to the religious life made them part of a privileged class in the Church or gave them a claim to special regard. Those who embraced this view were inclined to eliminate as obsolete not only practices and traditions that were clearly outmoded but also those that distinguished them from the laity, for example, the religious habit; religious names and titles; religious domiciles; ascetical practices, devotions, and customs that were particular to the institute; and community life under the direction of a local superior.[79] For many women Religious in the United States, the challenge of adaptation and renewal was complicated by their appropriation of the feminist critique.[80] This had and continues to have repercussions on their relationship with their local Ordinaries and with the Holy See.[81]

Many Religious adopted changes such as these during the period (1966–1983) allowed for experimentation. They understood the Council to teach that all the baptized are called to "one and the same holiness," and that the religious state is essentially a movement or voluntary venture motivated by shared ideals and a common quest for God. Given these two assumptions, they came to think that religious life itself was open to radical redefinition, that it should be relatively independent of the hierarchy, and that Religious should consult their own experience as a norm rather than canonical criteria alien to it. On the assumption that consecrated celibacy for the sake of the kingdom was the defining characteristic of their way of life, and in order to respond to what they discerned to be urgent needs, some religious institutes allowed or adopted patterns of living (e.g., living alone) and working (e.g., individual ministries, even secular occupations and public offices) that are more appropriate to secular institutes than to religious institutes.[82] They redefined evangelical poverty, obedience, and common life in ways that compromised their witness, both individual and corporate, as Religious. Some changes were required for the sake of promoting adult relationships and respect for conscience. Others emerged as the unanticipated consequence of the professionalization of Church ministries, new patterns of ministry placement, a desire to serve the marginalized and abandoned, or an inability to maintain institutions due to loss of members. Some changes resulted from experimentation with small group living; others from the desire to retrieve the charism of the founder, the invitation to supply parochial services because of the clergy shortage, or the conviction that social justice could best be achieved by way of political action.

In 1983, the Sacred Congregation for Religious and Secular Institutes (SCRIS) prepared a document at the direction of Pope John Paul II, *Essential Elements in the Church's Teaching on Religious Life as Applied to Institutes Dedicated to the Works of the Apostolate.*[83] It marked the end of the period of experimentation. Some women Religious and their institutes found this summary to be at odds with the Council's call for appropriate renewal;[84] they met it with a deliberate strategy of "non-reception," which they justified by appeal to the directives of *Perfectae Caritatis* on the one hand, and by opposition, on feminist grounds, to control by "a resolutely patriarchal Vatican,"[85] on the other. The "non-reception" of *Essential Elements* and its specification of the obligations of Religious, as compared to men and women in other forms of consecrated life, was a decisive moment in their relationship with the Holy See.[86]

The Magisterium's Response to the Common Misconceptions

Magisterial documents that interpret the Council's teaching on religious life have poured forth in a steady stream since *Ecclesiae Sanctae.*[87] In 1971, in the Apostolic Exhortation *On the Renewal of the Religious Life according to the Teaching of the Second Vatican Council* (*Evangelica Testificatio*, no. 2),[88] Pope Paul VI expressed his grave concern that some Religious appealed "unjustly" to the Council "to cast doubt on the very principle of religious life."[89] Other documents followed encouraging collaboration with bishops,[90] urging involvement in integral human promotion while warning against engagement in partisan politics,[91] promoting contemplation,[92] laying down basic norms for apostolic Religious[93] and cloistered nuns,[94] exhorting to a covenant of spousal love,[95] calling for the witness of common life,[96] and more. The ninth General Assembly of the World Synod of Bishops (1994) took "The Consecrated Life and Its Role in the Church and in the World" as its topic, and Pope John Paul II gathered its fruits in a post-synodal Apostolic Exhortation, *Vita Consecrata*

(1996).[97] CICLSAL followed it up with *Starting Afresh from Christ* (2002),[98] and in 2008 issued an instruction on *The Service of Authority and Obedience*.[99]

In these documents, and in the 1983 Code of Canon Law, the Magisterium has addressed the four misconceptions identified in this essay, clarifying and deepening the Council's teaching in *Lumen Gentium* and *Perfectae Caritatis*. "Consecration" has emerged as a fundamental theological category. Identified as "the basis of religious life," it is a gift by which God sets certain members of the Christian faithful apart for "divine service" and offers them the grace to respond by "a profound and free self-surrender."[100] In the 1983 Code,[101] "Consecrated Life" functions as an umbrella category for religious institutes, secular institutes, diocesan hermits, and consecrated virgins.[102] The elements that comprise this vocation are identified in canon 573, §1:

> The life consecrated through the profession of the evangelical counsels is a stable form of living by which the faithful, following Christ more closely under the action of the Holy Spirit, are totally dedicated to God who is loved most of all, so that, having been dedicated by a new and special title to his honor, to the building up of the Church, and to the salvation of the world, they strive for the perfection of charity in the service of the kingdom of God and, having been made an outstanding sign in the Church, foretell the heavenly glory.

1. The Universal Call to Holiness and the Special Vocation to Consecrated Life

The Council taught that Christian holiness is "one," that is, the perfection of the love of God and neighbor, but, by omitting reference to "the same," it implicitly acknowledged differences of degree and vocation. Many Religious have relied on the flawed translation, "one and the same holiness," partly in the belief that it represents the Council's teaching (a simple mistake), but perhaps also from the desire to exclude odious comparisons and reject "a kind of spiritual elitism."[103] The idea that God issues everyone the same call, proposed at the Council in response to the Protestant critique, is also congenial to the feminist theory that difference is irreconcilable with equality and that rankings of any kind lead to abuse.[104] The analysis that excludes differences of degree and vocation, even if motivated by a praiseworthy humility, cannot be reconciled with the Catholic tradition that attributes the desire to do "more" to a divine call.[105]

In *Vita Consecrata*, nos. 30–34, Pope John Paul II distinguishes the universal or general call to holiness from the call to observe the evangelical counsels in the consecrated life:

> All those reborn in Christ are called to live out, with the strength which is the Spirit's gift, the chastity appropriate to their state of life, obedience to God and to the Church, and a reasonable detachment from material possessions: for all are called to holiness, which

consists in the perfection of love. *But Baptism in itself does not include the call to celibacy or virginity, the renunciation of possessions or obedience to a superior, in the form proper to the evangelical counsels.*[106]

The observance of the evangelical counsels incumbent on all the baptized, in other words, does not include the stricter observance that is voluntarily assumed by their profession, by vow or similar bond, for the whole of life, in a stable way of life approved by the Church. The profession made in the consecrated life is rooted in Baptism, but it presupposes "a particular gift of God *not given to everyone.*"[107] This way of life has always been considered to have an "objective superiority" (or "excellence"[108]) as "a way of showing forth the Church's holiness"[109] because those who embrace it reproduce—as nearly as possible and from a desire to be completely conformed to him—the poverty, chastity, and obedience of Jesus.[110] The comparison the Church makes, however, is between the ways of life, not the persons who espouse them. When the Church says that consecrated life possesses an "objective excellence," it does not mean that those who profess the counsels are holier than those who do not; it is a statement of fact regarding a manner of life that most closely approximates the example of the Lord.[111]

2. The Re-Ordering of the Evangelical Counsels and the Consecrated Life

All the baptized are called to "perfect charity," but not all are called to perfect continence in celibate chastity for the sake of the kingdom. The Council did not attribute theological significance to its decision to list chastity first among the evangelical counsels.[112] Still, the order does serve a certain purpose in that it identifies chastity as the "door" by which a person enters the consecrated life.[113] In practice, this means that married Christians who commit themselves to the observance of evangelical poverty and obedience and chastity according to their state of life, for example, in an ecclesial movement or other association of the faithful,[114] are not included in this category. Perfect continence observed in celibacy for the sake of the kingdom, then, is a distinguishing element of *consecrated* life.[115] Those who receive this gift and accept it go "beyond what is of precept in the matter of perfection" (*LG*, no. 42). Their choice, rooted in Baptism, entails an additional ecclesial consecration and always includes the observance, in some manner, of evangelical poverty and obedience. Those who observe all three counsels in religious life, however, assume a distinctive pattern of obligations.

3. Religious Life and the Other Forms of Consecrated Life

When Religious, in response to *Perfectae Caritatis*, undertook to adapt and renew their way of life, some, on the assumption that the Council had left the way open to do so, chose to redefine "common life" and the obligations of the vows of poverty and obedience.[116] For a time, some women Religious in institutes of apostolic life focused on their "lay" identity and questioned why they were subject to restrictions and disciplinary action when laywomen were not.[117] Some institutes of women Religious were surprised and offended when their revised constitutions failed to receive approval from SCRIS. According to *Essential Elements* and the 1983 Code of Canon Law, their modifications were ruled out.[118]

Consecrated life in religious institutes[119] is characterized not only by the public profession of poverty, chastity, and obedience but also by the common life, that is, life together with other members of one's (one) institute[120] according to an approved constitution, separated in some way from those who are not members, under the direction of a superior.[121] The manner of common life adopted by Religious differs greatly from one type of religious institute to another,[122] but it is a requirement for all Religious in the 1983 Code.[123] This obligation affects the interpretation of the counsels of poverty and obedience.[124] For Religious, vowed poverty entails more than choosing to "live simply" and to be financially dependent on the institute. Poverty is the vow of "common life," and it also entails actually living together under one roof and having equal access to the goods, facilities, and resources.[125] For Religious, vowed obedience entails not only sincerely seeking and following indications of God's will in consultation with other members of the institute, but also voluntarily submitting one's will to one's legitimate superior,[126] who governs according to the constitutions. The office-holder who, through the ministry of the Church, exercises personal authority,[127] is obliged to use that authority to safeguard the charism of the institute and the dignity of the members and to advance the mission entrusted to the institute. Obedience directs the members as they carry out their corporate apostolate in the name of the Church.[128] Their ministry is rooted in their consecration and must be expressed in accord with the founder's charism.[129]

4. Religious Life and the Divine Constitution of the Church

Finally, what is the place of consecrated life, and more specifically of religious life, in the constitution of the Church? The Council viewed the Church's divine constitution from two different perspectives. On the one hand, there is the divinely-established hierarchy according to which the Christian faithful are either lay people or clerics. In the Church, considered as a sacramentally-ordered institution, these are mutually-exclusive categories and, as *LG*, no. 43 says, Religious do not occupy some level or rank in between the two. On the other hand, the Church is first and foremost not an institution, but a communion, "a people made one with the unity of the Father, the Son and the Holy Spirit" (*LG*, no. 4). The ministerial priesthood was divinely instituted to serve that communion by teaching, sanctifying, and governing the rest of the baptized. In an analogous way, religious life exists, according to God's plan, to serve the Church's "life and holiness" (*LG*, no. 44). Religious life, from this perspective, is a constitutive element. It has a purpose beyond the sanctification of its members, namely, to foster the holiness of the whole Church.[130] By their state in life, Religious "give splendid and striking testimony that the world cannot be transformed and offered to God without the spirit of the beatitudes" (*LG*, no. 31). By the total dedication of their lives to the service of God and the Church, they remind the rest of the baptized of their vocation to the perfection of charity. Their consecration is at the root of their ministry and should color and qualify their corporate witness.

The Council fathers had not planned to address the place of religious life in the Church, but when some proposed to treat it only as an ascetical choice of individuals or groups, they responded by calling attention to its "divine origin" and claiming that it is a "divine gift," given not just to individuals or groups but to the Church as a whole (*LG*, no. 44). It does not belong to her sacramental constitution, but like the apostolic ministry it has been present from apostolic times and has taken shape in forms approved by the hierarchy. Religious life is a "divine gift," first, because it is a way of life lived and recommended by the Lord Jesus himself. It is a "divine gift," second, because the charisms that give rise to it come from the Holy Spirit. They are bestowed on the founders of religious institutes, but the authority of the Church intervenes by recognizing them and giving them public approval. This divine gift, then, is mediated by the Church's pastors.[131] By institutionalizing the founding charisms, the pastors make these gifts available to others. It is a divine gift, third, because God is the one who calls and who consecrates their members (*LG*, no. 44). An intervention on the part of the Church's pastors is required both for the recognition of a founder's gift and for the approval of an institute's constitutions. The pastors, moreover, have ongoing responsibility for regulating the profession of the evangelical counsels in the many expressions that the religious life takes (*LG*, nos. 43, 45).

Admittedly, the Council's teaching that religious life belongs to the Church's "life and holiness" did not clearly differentiate religious life from the life of the baptized, and there was no "name" for the divine constitution that it distinguished from its hierarchical constitution. In the 1960s, it was thought premature to call it the Church's "charismatic" dimension.[132] Today, however, this expression appears in magisterial statements, emerging perhaps from the need to locate the new ecclesial movements and other new forms of consecrated life. Since 1995, papal addresses have begun to refer to the "charismatic" and "hierarchical" aspects of the Church as complementary and "co-essential."[133]

Fifty years after *Perfectae Caritatis*, the Council's teaching is still disputed, but there is growing confidence that religious life is the Holy Spirit's gift, essential to the realization of God's plan for the Church; that it is established by the hierarchy's recognition of a founder's charism; that those called by God to enter it are invited to follow Jesus Christ "more closely" by the public profession of the evangelical counsels; and that by their consecration in a religious institute they freely accept a vocation to live wholly for the glory of God, the service of the rest of the baptized, and the realization of God's kingdom.

NOTES

1. *Vatican Council II: The Conciliar and Post-Conciliar Documents*, vol. 1, ed. Austin Flannery, OP (Collegeville, MN: Liturgical Press, 1996), 611–23. Texts of the Council documents will be cited from the Flannery translation unless otherwise noted.

2. In this essay, Religious with capital "R" will be used to designate men and women who are members of canonically established *religious* institutes. For other categories of consecrated life, see Elizabeth McDonough, OP, "Categories of Consecrated Life," *Review for Religious* 50, no. 2 (March–April 1991): 300–03.

3. The Center for Applied Research in the Apostolate (http://cara.georgetown.edu/frequently-requested-church-statistics) gives the following statistics, comparing the number of religious in the United States in 1965 to that in 2014: from 22,707 to 12,010 religious priests; from 179,954 sisters to 49,883; from 12,271 brothers to 4,318.

4. *Vatican Council II*, 350–423.

5. Conciliar and post-conciliar documents of the Magisterium will be cited as follows: *Perfectae Caritatis* = *PC; Lumen gentium* = *LG; Vita Consecrata* = *VC*; and *Essential Elements* = *EssEl*. Chapters will be identified by Roman numerals and sections by means of Arabic numerals prefaced by "no."

6. See Friedrich Wulf, "Introductory Remarks on Chapters V and VI" and "Decree on Appropriate Renewal of the Religious Life," in *Commentary on the Documents of Vatican II*, ed. Herbert Vorgrimler (New York: Herder & Herder, 1969), 1:253–60, and 2:301–32; Gregory Baum, OSA, *De Ecclesia: The Constitution on the Church* (Glen Rock, NJ: Paulist, 1965), 44–50; and Maryanne Confoy, SC, *Religious Life and Priesthood: Perfectae Caritatis, Optatum Totius, Presbyterorum Ordinis* (New York and Mahwah, NJ: Paulist Press, 2008), 177–206. The developments are recounted in historical sequence in *History of Vatican II*, ed. Giuseppe Alberigo, English version ed. Joseph A. Komonchak (Maryknoll, NY: Orbis, 1995–2000); see esp. 2:473–79, 3:365–66, and 4:46–49.

7. See Patricia Wittberg, SC, "The Collapse of an Ideology I and II," in *The Rise and Decline of Catholic Religious Orders: A Social Movement Perspective* (Albany: State University of New York Press, 1994), 223–56. In the glossary (279), the definition of the "universal call to holiness" explicitly excludes superiority: "Doctrine advanced by *Lumen Gentium* that all baptized Christians are called to a life of holiness, that the life of religious is not superior to the life of the laity." Whereas the first assertion is correct, the second does not represent the Council's teaching.

8. David Nygren, CM, and Miriam D. Ukeritis, CSJ, "The Religious Life Futures Project: Executive Summary," in *Review for Religious* 52, no. 1 (January–February 1993): 6–55, at 47–48.

9. For more on this, see my essay "Apostolic Religious Life: A Public, Ecclesial Vocation," in *Apostolic Religious Life in America Today: A Response to the Crisis*, ed. Richard Gribble, CSC (Washington, DC: The Catholic University of America Press, 2011), 41–66.

10. See, for example, Sandra M. Schneiders, IHM, *Prophets in Their Own Country: Women Religious Bearing Witness to the Gospel in a Troubled Church* (Maryknoll, NY: Orbis Press, 2011), 25f., 27, 46–47, 49, 56–57, 76, 124f.

11. Then known as "societies of common life," their members do not profess the evangelical counsels.

12. This way of life was quite new in the Church, having been approved by Pope Pius XII in 1947. Its members (lay and clerical) do not, as a rule, take public vows or live the common life.

13. Mary Judith O'Brien, RSM, and Mary Nika Schaumber, RSM, name three of the same questions in "Conclusion," in *The Foundations of Religious Life: Revisiting the Vision*, ed. Conference of Major Superiors of Women Religious (Notre Dame, IN: Ave Maria Press, 2009), 176–209, at 180.

14. Also called the Sacred Congregation for Religious and Secular Institutes (SCRIS) and, since 1988, the Congregation for Consecrated Life and Societies of Apostolic Life (CICLSAL).

15. For example, Wulf and Baum, n. 6 above.

16. William R. Burrows reports this in his foreword to *The Founding of the Catholic Church in Melanesia and Micronesia 1850–1875*, by Ralph M. Wiltgen, SVD, (Eugene, OR: Pickwick Publications, 2008), x. Except for the first chapter of *Religious Life Defined* (hereafter, *RLD*), Wiltgen lets the documents of the Doctrinal Commission speak for themselves. In his earlier book, *The Rhine Flows into the Tiber: The Unknown Council* (New York: Hawthorn Books, 1967), he gives details of the controversies over *Lumen Gentium* (103–9) and *Perfectae Caritatis* (212–22) from the perspective of many of the Religious—bishops and superiors general of clerical institutes—at the Council. Since the Religious achieved their goal by emending the texts, it is necessary to know these details.

17. *The Religious Life Defined: An Official Commentary on the Second Vatican Council Deliberations* (Techny, IL: Divine Word Publications, 1970). Wiltgen also provides a history of the earlier drafts, some explanatory notes, and the Latin texts of the last two drafts. Wiltgen's analysis is tied to the English translation in *The Documents of Vatican II*, ed. Walter M. Abbott, SJ (New York: Guild Press, 1966), so that is used here in reporting it.

18. *Chapter VI of the Dogmatic Constitution "Lumen Gentium" on Religious Life: The Doctrinal Content in the Light of the Official Documents*, trans. Mary Paul Ewen (Rome: Pontificia Università Gregoriana, 1987). But see Elizabeth McDonough, OP, " 'De Accommodata Renovatione: Between the Idea and the Reality . . .'—Occasion and Intent and Consequences of Vatican Council II," in Gribble, *Apostolic Religious Life*, 67–90, at 80. The serious mistake in their interpretation that McDonough discovered is discussed below.

19. See Pope Benedict XVI, "A Proper Hermeneutic for the Second Vatican Council," in *Vatican II: Renewal within Tradition*, ed. Matthew L. Lamb and Matthew Levering (Oxford: Oxford University Press, 2008), ix–xv. Not until the accounts of the debates on the Council floor and the minutes of the Doctrinal Commission became available in the *Acta Synodalia* did scholars have additional information for the interpretation of these chapters.

20. In the journalistic accounts, the Religious are depicted as "conservatives," bent on maintaining their privilege. Considerable resentment was expressed over the "exemption" of clerical orders from the supervision of the local ordinaries. At the time of the Council, one-third of the Council fathers were Religious, as were one-third of the world's priests, and most of the Church's missionary activity was entrusted to them. There were also two million women Religious, contemplative and active. See Wiltgen, *The Rhine*, 105f.

21. Wiltgen, *RLD*, 5–8. The draft chapter on the laity was divided (into II and IV) at the last minute, so some reports continue to refer to the chapter on the Call to Holiness as "Chapter IV."

22. He then lent support to this revision with his allocution *Magno Gaudio* (May 23, 1964), http://w2.vatican.va/content/paul-vi/en/speeches/1964.index.7.html.

23. Wiltgen, *RLD*, 18. Wiltgen provides a translation of both the general and the paragraph-by-paragraph commentary of the Doctrinal Commission. He had access only to these summaries, not council speeches or *modi*.

24. See *Acta Synodalia Sacrosancti Concilii Oecumenici Vaticani II* (Vatican City: Typis Polyglottis Vaticanis [1970–1980]): III/1, 329–33.

25. The Council fathers were concerned not only to affirm the Christian vocation of the laity but also to meet the Protestant objections to monasticism and the principle of vowed life.

26. Wiltgen, *RLD*, 55. Such was the view of seventy-nine fathers. See pp. 53–56 for the Commission's full account of the reasons for retaining a single chapter.

27. Ibid. 49–53, esp. 50. These Council fathers wanted to put the section on the universal call to holiness in the new chapter II, and to have a distinct chapter on Religious (ibid. 19).

28. More commonly, in fact, some men drawn to religious life are later called to the priesthood.

29. Charue spoke for the "European alliance" of bishops. In the apostolic constitution, *Provida Mater Ecclesia* (1947), no. 9 (http://w2.vatican.va/content/pius.../hf_p-xii_apc_19470202_provida-mater-ecclesia.html), Pope Pius XII spoke of religious life as "a state between that of the clergy and the laity."

30. Notice that this designation was not adopted by the Council fathers (Wiltgen, *RLD*, 33).

31. Ibid. 52–53 (=*Acta Synodalia* III/1, 331).

32. Ibid. 53.

33. Ibid. 62–63. This way of viewing the Church corresponds to the vision adopted in what is now *LG* II.

34. Ibid. 26–27. Molinari and Gumpel (*Chapter VI of the Dogmatic Constitution*, 12–30) add citations from the *Acta Synodalia* to their account.

35. Wiltgen, *RLD*, 35 (citing Abbott translation, 74); *Acta Synodalia* III/1, 316–17.

36. See the Doctrinal Commission's insertion at the end of *LG*, no. 13. The Church's members are diverse, it says, on two counts: by reason of their duties (distinguishing those in Holy Orders from the baptized) and by reason of their "situation and way of life" (distinguishing those who are in the religious state from those who are not).

37. My emphasis. No name was given to this alternative way of viewing the Church's divine constitution. According to Molinari and Gumpel, *Chapter VI of the Dogmatic Constitution*, 30–31, "charismatic" and "pneumatic" each presented some problems and neither had entered into common usage.

38. According to Molinari and Gumpel, *Chapter VI of the Dogmatic Constitution*, 31, "The Council in no way accepted the thesis proposed by [Mgr. Charue]."

39. Mary Prudence Allen, RSM, develops this theme in her chapter, "Communion in Community," in Conference of Major Superiors of Women Religious, *The Foundations of Religious Life*, 113–54. Allen refers to a valuable essay by Janusz A. Ihnatowicz, "Consecrated Life in the Ecclesiology of Vatican II," *Faith and Reason* 17 (1991): 167–87.

40. *Acta Synodalis* II/1. 280. See Molinari and Gumpel, *Chapter VI of the Dogmatic Constitution*, 46–47.

41. Wiltgen, *RLD*, 21f. (=*Acta Synodalia* III/1, 325–25). See also Molinari and Gumpel, *Chapter VI of the Dogmatic Constitution*, 47.

42. The minutes indicate that the Council fathers understood "profession" to include both vows and similar bonds.

43. Abbott translation (my emphasis).

44. See *Council Daybook: Vatican II, Session 3*, ed. Floyd Anderson (Washington, DC: National Catholic Welfare Conference, 1965), 326. This is the translation found on the Vatican website.

45. Abbott translation, 67 (my emphasis). Wiltgen (*RLD*, 22) calls attention to this mistake. The same mistake is found in Gregory Baum's widely used commentaries on the *Decree on the Renewal of Religious Life of Vatican Council II* (Glen Rock, NJ: Paulist, 1966), 15, and *De Ecclesia*, 145. The Latin text reads, "In variis vitae generibus et officiis una sanctitas excolitur ab omnibus, qui a Spiritu Dei agunter" (*Acta Synodalia* III/1, 295).

46. These were summarized in the 1983 document of the Sacred Congregation for Religious and Secular Institutes, "Essential Elements," http://www.vatican.va/roman_curia/congregations/ccscrlife/documents/rc_con_ccscrlife_doc_31051983_magisterium-on-religious-life_en.html. See below for discussion.

47. Molinari and Gumpel (*Chapter VI of the Dogmatic Constitution*, 46) comment, "Sadly, far too many translations of the conciliar texts, to say nothing of popularizations, have contributed to the widespread, but erroneous notion that Christian holiness is not only 'one' but also 'the same' for all, as if all Christians were called to the *same* holiness and to the *same* perfection of charity. . . . It is, in fact, this opinion which has contributed to the identity crisis affecting so many religious and priests. And yet it is an opinion patently opposed to the formal doctrine of the Council."

48. As Molinari and Gumpel (*Chapter VI of the Dogmatic Constitution*, 29–30) observe, these emendations do not stand out clearly because the Council fathers were obliged, by a previous vote, to work from the 1963 draft.

49. See McDonough, "*De Accommodata*," 79–84. I am indebted to McDonough for this very important insight into the history and ramifications of this question.

50. N.B. The distinction is not between "private" and "public" profession because they included secular institutes.

51. In "*De Accommodata*," 79n16, McDonough supplies the text from the *Acta Synodalia* III/3, 67–68.

52. McDonough, "*De Accommodata*," 80nn 17 and 18, with citation of text from *Acta Synodalia*, IV/4, 535.

53. Molinari and Gumpel (*Chapter VI of the Dogmatic Constitution*, 84) point out that the "Relatio" introducing *Perfectae Caritatis* (hereafter, *PC*) gave no reason for it.

54. See Molinari and Gumpel, *Chapter VI of the Dogmatic Constitution*, 82–84. McDonough (*De Accommodata*, 80) traces the influence of this view to their monograph.

55. According to Molinari and Gumpel (*Chapter VI of the Dogmatic Constitution*, 84), the counsel of virginity is "the most clearly attested in the New Testament," and the word "counsel" is used only in reference to it (1 Cor 7:25). Also, it seemed to them (86) that the Council deliberately shifted the emphasis from a theology of renunciation to the primacy of charity. In their view (88), "the love of the undivided heart for the person of Christ the Redeemer" expressed in consecrated virginity or celibacy also impels some of the faithful to embrace his poverty and obedience. And commitment to lifelong chastity for the sake of the kingdom renders visible and concrete the intention to make a total gift of self.

56. Ibid. 82.

57. McDonough (*De Accommodata*, 78). David L. Fleming, SJ, follows their view in "Understanding a Theology of Religious Life," in *Religious Life: Rebirth Through Conversion*, ed. Gerald A. Arbuckle, SM, and David L. Fleming, SJ (Staten Island, NY: Alba House, 1990), 21–50. McDonough (*De Accommodata*, 80) notes that John Manuel

Lozano, CMF, had proposed the same reading some years earlier in *Discipleship: Toward an Understanding of Religious Life* (Chicago: Claret Center for Resources in Spirituality, 1980).

58. After the Council, "Consecrated Life" replaced "Religious" as the umbrella concept; since then, "Religious" and "religious life" refer exclusively to those in religious institutes and their way of life.

59. Molinari and Gumpel (*Chapter VI of the Dogmatic Constitution*, 85) summarize this tradition. It is found in St. Thomas Aquinas, *Summa theologiae* II-II, Q. 186, a. 7, but dates back to the patristic era. St. Thomas's theology of religious life, in particular its ascetical interpretation of the counsels and its focus on the renunciation of goods, was subjected to a severe critique during the Council. See Wulf, *Commentary*, 2:309.

60. St. Thomas Aquinas, *Summa Theologica* II-II, Q. 186, a. 7 uses this expression, bringing forward the teaching of St. Gregory the Great.

61. Members of secular institutes do too, but with different consequences.

62. The early drafts of *Perfectae Caritatis* (see Latin texts in Molinari and Gumpel, *Chapter VI of the Dogmatic Constitution*, 82–83nn63, 64) kept this order.

63. They had reservations about the biblical foundation for the counsels of poverty and obedience as observed in the religious state.

64. McDonough, *De Accommodata*, 82–83. In her opinion, this had led to the re-definition of "the entire meaning and import of religious consecration by public, perpetual vow."

65. Wiltgen, *RLD*, 74, 76. In fact, their usage follows that of the 1917 Code of Canon Law, which included solitary ascetics in this category along with religious institutes. See Elizabeth McDonough, OP, *Religious in the 1983 Code: New Approaches to the New Law* (Chicago: Franciscan Herald Press, 1985), 44–45 and 58.

66. "Because strict 'definitions' are very difficult, especially when very many elements are still controverted, the Commission intentionally abstained from giving 'definitions,' both for the word 'laity' and for the word 'Religious'" (Wiltgen, *RLD*, 77; see also 34 and 81).

67. "Consecration," a broader category, includes those who do not make "profession" of vows (Wiltgen, *RLD*, 42).

68. Ibid. 74.

69. See Wiltgen, *The Rhine*, 212–22; Confoy, *Religious Life and Priesthood*, 184–206; and O'Brien and Schaumberg, "Conclusion," 183–85. According to the latter (183), the original draft was cut down from 200 to 19 articles, and modified by some 1400, or perhaps 14,000! (Confoy, 204) amendments.

70. See the quote from Francis Cardinal Spellman in Wiltgen, *The Rhine*, 217.

71. Wiltgen, *RLD*, 36: this is what identifies the religious state, according to the Doctrinal Commission.

72. See McDonough, "*De Accommodata*," 78. Its general principles also apply to societies of apostolic life and secular institutes (*PC* 1); secular institutes (*PC* 11) are not religious institutes.

73. *PC*, nos. 5–6 review the nature of the religious consecration; nos. 7–11 review the different kinds of institutes; nos. 12–14 review the evangelical counsels (beginning with chastity); and no. 15 deals with the ideal of common life.

74. See Paul VI, "Implementation of Certain Decrees of Vatican Council II [= *Ecclesiae Sanctae*]," *Review for Religious* 25, no. 6 (November 1966): 939–70; for the norms for the Decree on Religious Life, see 957–65. Several norms for the Decree on Bishops (*Christus Dominus*, nos. 22–40, http://www.vatican.va/archive/hist_councils/ ii_vatican_council/documents/vat-ii_decree_19651028_christus-dominus_en.html)

and the Decree on Missionary Activity (*Ad Gentes Divinitus*, nos. 10, 12, 16, 18, 21, and 40, http://www.vatican.va/archive/hist_councils/ii_vatican_council/documents/vat-ii_decree_19651207_ad-gentes_en.html) also pertain to religious institutes and their members.

75. They could also request permission of the Holy See to experiment contrary to the general law.

76. *Ecclesiae Sanctae*, Part II, no. 15.

77. As every account of the dismantling of religious life explains, this was also a time of unprecedented cultural change and upheaval. The Pastoral Constitution on the Church in the Modern World, *Gaudium et Spes* (http://www.vatican.va/archive/hist_councils/ii_vatican_council/documents/vat-ii_const_19651207_gaudium-et-spes_en.html), had a special appeal and relevance for Religious whose founders set out to address the social ills of their time.

78. Male Religious who were clerics did not draw the same conclusion, for they understood themselves largely in terms of the priesthood, and this remained distinct. For a review of issues they addressed, see Paul K. Hennessey, CFC, ed., *A Concert of Charisms: Ordained Ministry in Religious Life* (New York and Mahwah, NJ: Paulist Press, 1997).

79. See Sandra M. Schneiders, IHM, *New Wineskins: Re-Imagining Religious Life Today* (New York and Mahwah, NJ: Paulist Press, 1986), 89.

80. Sandra M. Schneiders, IHM, "Self-Determination and Self-Direction in Religious Communities," in *Women in the Church*, ed. Madonna Kohlbenschlag (Washington, DC: The Pastoral Press, 1988), 153–78, at 163.

81. See Anita M. Caspary, *Witness to Integrity: The Crisis of the Immaculate Heart Community of California* (Collegeville, MN: Liturgical Press, 2003) for an account of the "test case" that galvanized women Religious in the late 1960s. The experience of these Sisters shaped the response of many in the Conference of Major Superiors of Women, the predecessor of the Leadership Conference of Women Religious. Some women superiors eventually formed a separate organization, the Conference of Major Superiors of Women Religious. For background on this, see Lora Ann Quiñonez, CDP, and Mary Daniel Turner, SNDdeN, *The Transformation of American Catholic Sisters* (Philadelphia: Temple University Press, 1992); and Ann Carey, *Sisters in Crisis Revisited: From Unraveling to Reform and Renewal* (San Francisco: Ignatius Press, 2013).

82. For the distinction between the two forms, see David F. O'Connor, ST, "Two Forms of Consecrated Life: Religious and Secular Institutes," *Review for Religious* 45, no. 2 (March–April 1986): 205–19. Men as well as women religious made choices of this sort. See, for example, Joseph M. Becker, *The Re-Formed Jesuits* (San Francisco: Ignatius Press, 1992); or Peter McDonough, "From Aquinas to the Age of Aquarius," chap. 12 in *Men Astutely Trained: A History of the Jesuits in the American Century* (New York: Free Press, 1992), 356–89.

83. *Essential Elements* (http://www.vatican.va/roman_curia/congregations/ccscrlife/documents/rc_con_ccscrlife_doc_31051983_magisterium-on-religious-life_en.html) was sent to the US bishops in 1983 by Pope John Paul II as a companion piece to his Letter asking them to give pastoral assistance to religious institutes of apostolic life (http://w2.vatican.va/content/john-paul-ii/en/letters/1983/documents/hf_jp-ii_let_03041983_us-bishops.html). For its relationship to the 1983 Code, see Sharon Holland, IHM, "The Code and Essential Elements," *The Jurist* 44 (1984): 304–38; "A Canonical Analysis of *Essential Elements* in the Light of the 1983 Code of Canon Law," *The Jurist* 45 (1985): 438–50.

84. See the responses of US men and women religious and bishops to *Essential Elements* in Robert J. Daly et al., eds., *Religious Life in the U.S. Church: The New Dialogue* (New York: Paulist Press, 1984).

85. Schneiders, "Self-Determination," 163. In her opinion, the provisions of the law undermine the "rightful autonomy" regarding the manner of living the evangelical counsels, governance, and internal discipline promised religious institutes in canon 586; she traces the tension to "a clash between two incompatible ecclesiologies" (166).

86. Ibid. 168–71. Women religious were directly affected insofar as their revised constitutions did not receive approval for failure to incorporate provisions in the 1983 Code.

87. See Elizabeth McDonough, OP, "Canonical Counsel: Conciliar and Postconciliar Documents on Consecrated Life," *Review for Religious* 52, no. 2 (September–October 1993): 780–86. O'Brien and Schaumberg ("Conclusion," 183–208), review the chief documents from 1983 forward.

88. http://w2.vatican.va/content/paul-vi/en/apost_exhortations/documents/hf_p-vi_exh_19710629_evangelica-testificatio.html.

89. He mentions "the boldness of certain arbitrary transformations, an exaggerated distrust of the past ... and a mentality excessively preoccupied with hastily conforming to the profound changes which disturb Our times." By 1970, many members of two institutes of women Religious in the United States had left religious life over disputes with their local Ordinaries over their paths to renewal. See Ann Carey, *Sisters in Crisis Revisited*, 246–61.

90. SCRIS and Sacred Congregation of Bishops, *Directives for the Mutual Relations between Bishops and Religious in the Church* (*Mutuae relationes*), 1978 (http://www.vatican.va/roman_curia/congregations/ccscrlife/documents/rc_con_ccscrlife_doc_14051978_mutuae-relationes_en.html).

91. SCRIS, *Religious and Human Promotion*, 1978 (http://www.vatican.va/roman_curia/congregations/ccscrlife/documents/rc_con_ccscrlife_doc_12081980_religious-and-human-promotion_en.html).

92. SCRIS, *The Contemplative Dimension of Religious Life*, 1980 (http://www.vatican.va/roman_curia/congregations/ccscrlife/documents/rc_con_ccscrlife_doc_12081980_the-contemplative-dimension-of-religious-life_en.html).

93. This was the purpose of *Essential Elements*, 1983. See note 83.

94. CICLSAL, *Instruction on the Contemplative Life and on the Enclosure of Nuns* (*Verbi Sponsa*), 1999 (http://www.vatican.va/roman_curia/congregations/ccscrlife/documents/rc_con_ccscrlife_doc_13051999_verbi-sponsa_en.html).

95. Pope John Paul II, Apostolic Exhortation to Men and Women Religious in the Light of the Mystery of the Redemption (*Redemptionis donum*), 1984 (http://w2.vatican.va/content/john-paul-ii/en/apost_exhortations/documents/hf_jp-ii_exh_25031984_redemptionis-donum.html). The pope adds reflections on the spousal or covenantal character of religious consecration to the Christological themes stressed in *LG* VI and *Perfectae Caritatis*.

96. CICLSAL, *Fraternal Life in Community* (*Congregavit nos in unum Christi amor*), 1994 (http://www.vatican.va/roman_curia/congregations/ccscrlife/documents/rc_con_ccscrlife_doc_02021994_fraternal-life-in-community_en.html).

97. http://w2.vatican.va/content/john-paul-ii/en/apost_exhortations/documents/hf_jp-ii_exh_25031996_vita-consecrata.html.

98. http://www.vatican.va/roman_curia/congregations/ccscrlife/documents/rc_con_ccscrlife_doc_20020614_ripartire-da-cristo_en.html.

99. http://www.vatican.va/roman_curia/congregations/ccscrlife/documents/rc_con_ccscrlife_doc_20080511_autorita-obbedienza_en.html.

100. *EssEl*, no. 5.

101. http://www.vatican.va/archive/ENG1104/_INDEX.HTM.

102. For descriptions of each form as determined by the 1983 Code of Canon Law, see Elizabeth McDonough, OP, "Categories of Consecrated Life," *Review for Religious* 50, no. 2 (March–April 1991): 300–305. Canons 573–730 deal with institutes of consecrated life. Societies of apostolic life are dealt with in a separate section, canons 731–46.

103. See, for instance, Sandra M. Schneiders, IHM, *Buying the Field: Catholic Religious Life in Mission to the World* (New York: Paulist, 2013), 207: "If Religious are called to a response to the Gospel to which other Christians are not called we are once again involved in the kind of spiritual elitism, the two-tiered discipleship, that Vatican II disavowed when it taught that all Christians are called to one and the same holiness." (Schneiders acknowledges, however, that not every distinction entails hierarchical ranking.) What needs to be questioned is the assumption that different vocations necessarily derogate from the equal dignity of believers. See comments on the fallacy of "false alternatives" identified by Allen, "Communion," 138–39 and 220, n. 11; 221, n. 20; 225, nn. 96 and 97.

104. See Patricia Wittberg, SC, *From Piety to Professionalism, and Back? Transformation of Organized Religious Virtuosity* (Lanham, MD: Rowman & Littlefield, 2006). For sociologists, religious life is a "virtuoso" spirituality or vocation, that is, a vocation defined by the desire to do *more* and a willingness to renounce one's own comfort and ambition for the sake of a person or a cause. Wittberg (187) explains why Protestants found it alien.

105. Why should the call to follow Christ "more closely" than others by living in celibate chastity, giving up all one's possessions, and accepting direction from another as a mediation of God's will be regarded as an affront to those who do not feel called?

106. *Vita Consecrata* (hereafter, *VC*), no. 30 (my emphasis).

107. Ibid.

108. The English translation has "objective superiority," but in French, Italian, and Spanish the Latin "praestantia" is rendered "excellence," "eccellenza," and "excelencia."

109. *VC*, no. 32. See also nos. 18 and 105.

110. The Lord's "way of living in chastity, poverty, and obedience appears as the most radical way of living the Gospel on this earth, a way which may be called *divine*" (*VC*, no. 18). It is also a sign of life in the eschaton. Molinari and Gumpel (*Chapter VI of the Dogmatic Constitution*, 181) explain that *LG*, no. 46 excludes the claim the consecrated persons are better and holier because they belong to this state (on the one hand), but that it also rules out the idea that "any comparison between the various states of life in the Church is either useless or impossible" (on the other).

111. The Council's Christological explanation augments but does not replace the traditional one based on the renunciation of goods. See *EssEl*, nos. 15–16.

112. Thus, it did not teach that consecrated celibacy is "the defining characteristic of *religious* life," as Schneiders (*New Wineskins*, 114 [my emphasis]) asserts.

113. *VC*, no. 32. The pope cites canon 599 from the 1983 Code of Canon Law and the Council of Trent, Sess. 24, canon 10. See *Decrees of the Ecumenical Councils*, vol. 2: Trent to Vatican II, ed. Norman P. Tanner (London and Washington: Sheed & Ward and Georgetown University Press, 1990), 755. The Council identified celibate chastity as a "precious gift of divine grace given to some by the Father" (*LG*, no. 42).

114. *VC*, no. 62. See canon 298 from the 1983 Code of Canon Law and the encouragement given to such movements and associations by Pope John Paul II

in the Apostolic Exhortation *Christifideles Laici*, nos. 1 and 29 (http://w2.vatican.va/content/john-paul-ii/en/apost_exhortations/documents/hf_jp-ii_exh_30121988_christifideles-laici.html). Some lay members of such groups, often called "lay consecrated," also assume the obligation of chaste celibacy for the sake of the kingdom.

115. See *VC*, no. 62.

116. *VC*, no. 4 (my emphasis): "In recent years there has been felt the need to clarify *the specific identity of the various states of life*, their vocation and their particular mission in the Church."

117. This issue came up in response to their holding political office and their involvement in public theological dissent. Women religious are "lay persons," not clerics, but their consecration changes their canonical status. This is reflected in *LG*, no. 31, which distinguishes the Catholic laity not only from those "in holy orders" but also from those "who belong to a religious state approved by the Church."

118. See *Selected Issues in Religious Law*, ed. Patrick J. Cogan, SA (Canon Law Society of America: Bulletin on Issues of Religious Law 1985–1995, 1997) for examples.

119. See *EssEl*, nos. 9–10. Members of secular institutes retain their canonical identity as lay persons or clerics. Their form of consecration has a hidden and individual character, as contrasted with the public and communal witness of Religious. See Holland, "The Code," 310.

120. Canon 607: "§2. A religious institute is a society in which members, according to proper law, pronounce public vows, either perpetual or temporary which are to be renewed, however, when the period of time has elapsed, and lead a life of brothers or sisters in common. §3.The public witness to be rendered by religious to Christ and the Church entails a separation from the world proper to the character and purpose of each institute."

121. See Elizabeth McDonough, OP, "Common Life," *Review for Religious* 52, no. 2 (March–April 1993): 304–10. McDonough explains that a broad interpretation of common life (i.e., belonging to the same juridic person, with the same superior and constitution) was permitted in the 1917 Code because at that time the category "Religious" included solitary ascetics, but since it no longer does, Religious are now bound by the strict interpretation.

122. Consider the witness of very diverse forms such as cloistered monks and nuns and men and women in institutes of apostolic life.

123. See canons 607 §2 and 665 §1 and *EssEl*, nos. 18–22. *Fraternal Life in Community* identifies the ecclesiological dimension of common life as lived by Religious. Their communities bear witness to the Church as a sacrament of unity, express the mystery of ecclesial communion, and function as the place and subject of mission.

124. Religious aspire to acquire and live the virtues of poverty and obedience by freely undertaking to observe the vow as defined in canon law and in the particular law of their institute.

125. Common life should, however, be rooted in charity and find expression in communion in Christ; see canon 602.

126. See canon 601: "The evangelical counsel of obedience, undertaken in a spirit of faith and love in the following of Christ obedient unto death, requires the submission of the will to legitimate superiors, who stand in the place of God, when they command according to the proper constitutions." This traditionally includes an obligation to obey the Roman pontiff by virtue of the vow. Canon 970 in the 1983 Code corresponds to canon 499 §1 in the 1917 code. Religious institutes are now required to include this in their constitutions.

127. Some women religious have experimented with a collegial form for the ordinary government of their institute at its various levels, but SCRIS ruled that the superior must have "personal authority" so that religious obedience could be lived. See *EssEl*, no. 52.

128. This accounts for the limitations placed on the active involvement of Religious in politics; members of secular institutes are not restricted in the same way. See *Religious and Human Promotion*, no.11.

129. *EssEl*, no. 11; see canon 578.

130. *EssEl*, no. 7; *VC*, nos. 33, 34, 39.

131. Molinari and Gumpel, *Chapter VI of the Dogmatic Constitution*, 29–30; Wiltgen (*RLD*, 27) writes, "The link connecting the religious state with a divine origin, in other words, passes through the Church."

132. Molinari and Gumpel, *Chapter VI of the Dogmatic Constitution*, 30–31.

133. See "Message of Pope John Paul II for the World Congress of Ecclesial Movements and New Communities," May 27, 1998), §5 (w2.vatican.va/content/john-paul-ii/en/speeches/1998/may/documents/hf_jp-ii_spe_19980527_movimenti. html): "there is no conflict or opposition in the Church between the *institutional dimension* and the *charismatic dimension*, of which movements are a significant expression. Both are co-essential to the divine constitution of the Church founded by Jesus, because they both help to make the mystery of Christ and his saving work present in the world."

9

Apostolicam Actuositatem

Michele M. Schumacher

In his closing address of the Second Vatican Council on December 7, 1965, Pope Paul VI pointed to the fact that the council was devoted "principally, to the Church—her nature and composition, her ecumenical vocation, her apostolic and missionary activity.... But this introspection has not been an end in itself," he argues. Seeking "to find in herself, active and alive, the Holy Spirit, the word of Christ," so as in turn "to revitalize" in herself faith and charity, she has also sought to understand the modern world. "Never before perhaps, so much as on this occasion, has the Church felt the need to know, to draw near to, to understand, to penetrate, serve and evangelize the society in which she lives; and to get to grips with it, almost to run after it, in its rapid and continuous change."[1]

This "unceasing" desire of the council to understand the modern world has not, the pope admitted, gone without criticism. Indeed, "some," we are told, recognize "an alien way of thinking" therein "at the expense of the fidelity which is due to tradition, and this to the detriment of the religious orientation of the council itself."[2] Thus anticipating what Massimo Faggioli calls "the battle for [the] meaning" of Vatican II, "especially [the meaning accorded to] the relationship between tradition, *ressourcement*, and *aggiornamento*"—a battle that the Church historian recognized in 2012 as "far from over"[3]—Paul VI dismissed this negative critique of the council, by pointing to charity as "the principal religious feature of this council." It is charity, he proposes, that motivated "the religion of God who became man" to go out to meet "the religion (for such it is) of man who makes himself God."[4]

It is thus also charity which accounts, he suggested, for the Church's concern "not just with herself and with her relationship of union with God, but with man—man as he really is today: living man, man all wrapped up in himself, man who makes himself not only the center of his every interest but dares to claim that he is the principle and explanation of all reality."[5] After all, as the pope who closed the council put it straightforwardly, "The Catholic religion is for mankind."[6] Or, as he put it in his apostolic exhortation *Evangelii Nuntiandi* ten years later, the council's teaching "can be summed up in this objective: to ensure that the church of the twentieth century may emerge ever better equipped to proclaim the gospel to the people of this century"[7] (cf. *GS* 4).

From the perspective of this alliance between the Church and humankind—whom she serves by her proclamation and mediation of Christian salvation in word and in deed—it is not surprising that the council also stressed the "special and indispensible" (*AA* 1; cf. *LG* 30–37) role of the laity, who live and work "in the midst of the world and of secular affairs." As such we—the lay faithful—are uniquely situated to be "a leaven in the world" in view of making "all men partakers in redemption and salvation" (*AA* 2; cf. *LG* 31). The proclamation of the Gospel message by the lay faithful has a "peculiar efficacy because it is accomplished in the ordinary circumstances of the world" (*GS* 35). "At the forefront of the church's mission to evangelize all areas of human activity—including the workplace, the worlds of science and medicine, the world of politics and the diverse world of culture"—ours is the mission, as Pope John Paul II put it nearly twenty-five years after the council, of "testify[ing] how the Christian faith constitutes the only valid response ... to the problems and hopes that life poses to every person and society."[8]

Perhaps the most challenging of those problems since the council has been, as we shall see in the pages that follow, the threats to human life attributable not only to technological advances but also and most especially to the moral relativism that had developed out of the cultural context of secularism, which the council addressed. More dangerous than the threat of planetary destruction through nuclear warfare acknowledged in the closing message of the council[9] was—the popes implementing Vatican II were convinced—that of instrumentalizing human beings for the sake of scientific advancement. Such is the ironic danger to the person by a culture that had sacrificed its theocentric option in favor of an anthropocentric one. For, as the council put it straightforwardly, "Without a creator there can be no creature. ... Once God is forgotten, the creature is lost sight of as well" (*GS* 36).[10]

In the fifty years that followed the council, the Magisterium has continued to summon the lay faithful to exercise our common priesthood by way of a "sincere gift" (cf. *GS* 24) of ourselves to Christ in a manner that is inseparable from our gift of ourselves to our spouses and to our children (cf. *LG* 11) so as also to be witnesses to the culture at large (*AA* 11). Similarly, in our kingly mission, we have been called to govern creation *and ourselves* by respecting the natural order of creation and by bringing it (creation, including the creation whom we are as human persons) to its natural fulfillment in accord with God's purpose, rather than by manipulating it—as does the culture at large—according to our own wills. In so doing, we have been likewise called to be prophets to a world for whom freedom means aggressive self-affirmation and autonomy with regard to the Creator, and for whom responsibility means manipulating nature to our own ends. In short, we, the lay faithful, have been called to fulfill the original mission of Genesis—to "be fruitful and multiply, and fill the earth and subdue it" (1:28)—from the perspective of a *theocentric*, rather than from an *anthropocentric*, universe.

In the pages that follow, I will begin by presenting the particularly challenging states of affairs that have developed within the socio-cultural, political, and familial environment of the Western world following the council: the world in which we, the lay faithful, not only live, work, recreate, and raise our families, but simultaneously realize our mission of permeating the world with Gospel values according to our "distinctive task" of renewing the temporal order (cf. *AA* 7). This, more specifically, is a world wherein the cultural climate of secularism, which had profoundly preoccupied the council, is now threatening certain fundamental human values and human dignity—indeed, even human life itself—in the name of a fully autonomous understanding of human freedom. Secularism has, to be more specific, given birth to moral relativism.

To precisely this age and culture, which proposed freedom as the highest ideal, the post-conciliar Church acclaimed freedom—*authentic* freedom—as part of her message. As John Paul II put it in his first encyclical letter, the Church's "deep esteem for man, for his intellect, his will, his conscience and his freedom" has become "part of the content" of her "proclamation, being included not necessarily in words but by an attitude towards it. This attitude seems to fit the special needs of our times."[11] This state of affairs accounts, in turn, for the presentation by this same pope, in his 1981 post-synodal exhortation, *Familiaris Consortio*, of "the person" as "not at all a 'thing' or an 'object' to be used, but primarily [as] a responsible 'subject', one endowed with conscience and freedom, called to live responsibly in society and history, and oriented towards spiritual and religious values."[12]

In this way, the Magisterium of John Paul II called upon the laity to permeate the world with not only religious values, but also authentically human ones: values accorded to the human person in virtue of creation. It was, in fact, the very reality of creation that had been entirely forgotten or denied by a fundamentally secular culture. John Paul II thus insisted in his apostolic exhortation to the lay faithful that "every violation of the personal dignity of the human being is an offense against the Creator of the individual."[13] From this creational perspective, the saintly pope presented freedom as intrinsic to human nature, and thus as fundamentally orientated at the outset to the good of loving communion.

Such was the Church's response to the widespread opposition to her presentation of the meaning of authentic marital love as "inseparable"—as Pope Paul VI had taught in his highly controversial encyclical, *Humanae Vitae*—from its procreative meaning,[14] whence the ever-widening gap between magisterial teaching and the actual practice of the lay faithful. This breach, I will maintain, is not without consequences for our comprehension of the doctrine itself. After all, the inductive reasoning that allowed men and women throughout human history to recognize the "inseparable connection" between the two meanings of the conjugal act is no longer an effective means of drawing our contemporaries to this same conclusion. Instead, there is reason to believe that the prevalent use of the pill and other contraceptive devices has not only hindered pregnancy; it has also—along with secularism and the epistemological presuppositions that accompany it—obscured our minds and hearts from recognizing an objective world order that is not of our making: an order wherein is rooted the moral order.

In response, Pope John Paul II insisted upon the "inseparable" connection between human freedom and human life,[15] between the human body and the human soul,[16] between truth and freedom,[17] and between Christian faith and morals;[18] whence also his insistence upon faith in action. If, in fact, he was convinced that the world would be "humanized" through the family,[19] it was most especially by way of the *witness of love within the family*—and most especially the love between spouses, which John Paul II recognized as "the prime community of persons, source of every other community"[20]—that this witness was most especially significant. "Only if the truth about freedom and the communion of persons in marriage and in the family can regain its splendour, will the building of the civilization of love truly begin," he reasoned.[21] After all, he was convinced that *"the future of humanity passes by way of the family,"*[22] and it was in "saving the family" that the Church hoped to "save society itself."[23]

Picking up on the council's presentation of the family as "a school of deeper humanity" (*GS* 52),[24] and pointing to the family as "the basic cell of society" (cf. *AA* 11),[25] "that fundamental community in which the whole network of social relations is grounded, from the closest and most immediate to the most distant,"[26] John Paul II likewise pointed to the "primary concern" that must be "reserved for this community [of the family], especially in those times when human egoism, the anti-birth campaign, totalitarian politics, situations of poverty, material, cultural and moral misery, threaten to make these very springs of life dry up." Not surprisingly, then, he presented the *"lay faithful's duty to society"* as beginning *"primarily . . .* in marriage and in the family"[27] (cf. *AA* 11). Indeed, it was *"through the family"* that would come to pass—in the firm hope of the man whom Pope Francis would designate as "the pope of the family"[28]—*"the primary current of the civilization of love,* which finds therein its 'social foundations.' "[29] From the seat of St. Peter, there was thus reiterated the popular maxim as a truth to be heeded by all members of the Church, but most especially by the lay faithful: *charity*—which the council had presented as the "soul of the entire apostolate" (*AA* 3)—*begins at home.*

I. An Urgent Call to the Laity within the Cultural Climate of Secular Relativism

The lay faithful have, of course, always been called to partake of the Church's apostolate: "it is something that derives from the layman's very vocation as a

Christian" (AA 1). Just as "no member" of a living body "plays a purely passive part," but rather shares in the life and activity of the body, so too each and every member of Christ's mystical body is engaged for the good of the whole. "[A] member who does not work at the growth of the body to the extent of his possibilities must be considered useless both to the Church and to himself" (AA 8).

If, however, the lay members of Christ's faithful people have always shared in the threefold mission of Christ as priest, prophet, and king, by reason of their baptism,[30] "present circumstances" in the early 1960s required, the council argued, an "infinitely broader and more intense" engagement on their part.

> For the constant increase in population, the progress in science and technology, the shrinking of the gaps that have kept men apart have immensely enlarged the field of the lay apostolate, a field that is in great part open to the laity alone; they have in addition given rise to new problems which require from the laity an intelligent attention and examination. All the more urgent has this apostolate become, now that autonomy—as is only right—has been reached in numerous sectors of human life, sometimes with a certain relinquishing of moral and religious values, seriously jeopardizing the Christian life. (AA 1)

Twenty-three years later, in his 1988 apostolic and post-synodal exhortation, *Christifidelis Laici*, Pope John Paul II echoed the council (cf. AA 1) in pointing to "a particular urgency for the action of the lay faithful,"[31] in reason this time, however, of what he observed as "a new state of affairs ... both in the Church and in social, economic, political and cultural life."[32] Commenting on the Gospel parable of the "householder" who calls laborers into his vineyard at various times during the day (cf. Mt 20:1–16), John Paul II did not merely recall the comparison of St. Gregory the Great between the various times of the call and the various stages of a person's life.[33] Highlighting a concern that he shared with the synod fathers, he drew still another analogy from this Gospel scene: the urgency of the present time (1988) was such that the lay faithful were being called in this "third hour" (v. 3). Indeed, "if lack of commitment is always unacceptable, the present time [wherein the transcendent dimension had been more or less leveled in Western society to what is graspable to human reason and obtainable by human technology] renders it even more so. *It is not permissible for anyone to remain idle.*"[34]

To be sure, this urgency included the fact that there were still vast populations in which Christ was yet unknown, and this territory was "taking on such extensive and serious proportions ... that only a truly consolidated effort to assume responsibility by all members of the Church, both individuals and communities, can lead to the hope for a more fruitful response."[35] Beyond this already-urgent situation, however, and perhaps more disturbing still, was what John Paul II pointed to as "the ever-growing existence of *religious indifference* and *atheism*" especially "in its perhaps most widespread form of *secularism*,"[36] whence the de-Christianization of traditionally Christian cultures calling for re-evangelization.

Particularly worrisome for John Paul II was thus what his predecessor referred to as an "entirely self-explanatory" conception of the world "without any reference to God, who thus becomes unnecessary and is, as it were, an embarrassment." This worldview was further qualified by Paul VI as "a new form of atheism," "a man-centered atheism, which is not abstract or metaphysical but pragmatic, based on a pre-ordained plan, and militant."[37] Hence, although the human being is often exalted by contemporary Western culture, even to the point of "idolatry," he or she is no longer recognized, John Paul II continued in *Christifideles Laici*, "as the living image of God (cf. Gen 1:26)."[38] There inevitably follow gross violations of human dignity, or what Paul VI called "the inhuman propensities of this [atheistic form of] humanism": the proclamation of pleasure "as the supreme good; the desire for power and domination; discrimination of every kind."[39]

This already tragic situation inciting a concerted effort from the lay faithful to proclaim the message of Christian salvation was, when combined "with new prospects opened up by scientific and technological progress," even more threatening to human dignity, as John Paul II pointed out in his 1995 encyclical *Evangelium Vitae*.[40] Citing the council's condemnation of "whatever is opposed to life itself . . ., whatever violates the integrity of the human person . . . 3, whatever insults human dignity" (*GS* 27),[41] and pointing beyond the "concentration camps, violence, torture, terrorism, and discrimination" that bore mention in his first encyclical,[42] he drew attention to "a new cultural climate . . . that gives crimes against life *a new and—if possible—even more sinister character*." Although, to be more specific, his previous encyclical found him preoccupied with the threat of human self-destruction,[43] nearly twenty years later he mourned more intensely *the loss of conscience* in the modern world. "Broad sectors of public opinion justify certain crimes against life in the name of the rights of individual freedom," he explained, "and on this basis they claim not only exemption from punishment but even authorization by the state, so that these things can be done with total freedom and indeed with the free assistance of health-care systems."[44] In short, modern secularism had given birth—it bears repeating from our introduction—to moral relativism.

One hardly needs more than a moment's reflection to enumerate the various threats against human life that he might have had in mind, and these have since only broadened in scope and depth. Beyond the legalizing of abortion in numerous countries shortly after the council, the rise of pornography due to the internet, and the continued trafficking of human organs and human persons (including those of the unborn in the recent Planned Parenthood scandal), we have since come to witness the expansive rise of legalized euthanasia and every imaginable form of manipulating human reproduction from surrogate mothering and in vitro fertilization to frozen embryo transfer, test-tube babies, research on human embryos, and human cloning. In addition to these terrible crimes against humanity, gender ideology has become mandatory curriculum in public schools in many Western countries, marriage has been redefined, adoption has been granted to same-sex couples throughout the world, and the United States has engaged in a terrible battle over the mandating of contraceptive coverage without a conscience clause.

Again, as these numerous examples serve to illustrate, no less "grave and disturbing" than the tragic sacrifice of so many human lives is the fact that human consciences were, he observed in 1995, "finding it increasingly difficult to distinguish between good and evil in what concerns the basic value of human life,"[45] even to the extent that "an anti-life mentality" has become socially and culturally prevalent.[46] This in turn was linked to a profoundly individualistic understanding of human freedom: an understanding of freedom as self-designating and wholly autonomous, rather than as teleologically oriented toward what Pope Francis would refer to some thirty years later as the "essentials": "what is most beautiful, most grand, most appealing and at the same time most necessary,"[47] that is to say, what is proper to the transcendent realm.

When, moreover, freedom is detached from objective truth, it is impossible, as John Paul II noted in *Evangelium Vitae*, to lay a rational basis for universal, personal rights, and society is given over to "the mercy of the unrestrained will of individuals or the oppressive totalitarianism of public authority."[48] The holy pope thus pointed to the astonishing contradiction between a world community acclaiming the idea of universal human rights—"rights inherent in every person and prior to any Constitution and State legislation"—and "a tragic repudiation of them in practice."[49] Replacing the criterion of personal dignity and the accompanying requirements of "respect, generosity and service" was thus "the criterion of efficiency, functionality and usefulness," which meant that persons were no longer considered "for what they 'are,' but for what they 'have, do and produce,'" whence "the supremacy of the strong over the weak."[50]

Ours had become "a civilization of production and of use, a civilization of 'things' and not of 'persons,' a civilization in which persons are used in the same way as things are used. In the context of a civilization of use, woman can become an object for man, children a hindrance to parents, the family an institution obstructing the freedom of its members."[51] It follows, John Paul II reasoned, that the human being is "no longer capable of posing the question of the truest meaning of his own existence, nor can he assimilate with genuine freedom these crucial moments of his own history," such as the moment of birth or death. Rather, he or she is preoccupied "with 'doing,' and using all kinds of technology," of busying him- or herself "with programming, controlling and dominating birth and death."[52] Hence, for example, the desire of many contemporary women to be "liberated" of their life-giving capacity, in virtue of which they are, as Joseph Ratzinger notes, "creative in the truest sense of the word," so as to "produce" instead: namely, in a manner valued by a "masculine society of technicians, of salesmen, of politicians who seek profit and power," and who "instrumentalize everything for their own ends."[53]

This "great drama" of a culture that has come to value productivity over life itself "can leave nobody indifferent," John Paul II insisted in his first encyclical, for the human person, who has become obsessed with profit and efficiency, pays for this obsession with the currency of human life. In contrast to the responsible dominion that he or she is called to exercise over the visible world in virtue of creation (cf. Gen 1:28)—a domination which ought to consist "in the priority of ethics over technology, in the primacy of the person over things, and in the superiority of spirit over matter"—he or she becomes, as he put it, "the slave of things, the slave of economic systems, the slave of production, the slave of his own products."[54] It is thus not surprising that still more recently (in 2004) the Pontifical Council for Peace and Justice presented "*the truth itself of the being who is man*" as "the first of the great challenges facing humanity today."[55]

II. The Church's Response to the Crisis of Secularism: Promoting Faith in the Creator

Guided by hope that the God of life would be victorious in preserving human life against the threat that man is to himself, John Paul II called upon all the lay faithful—who, after all, had the specific task of transforming culture in accord with this hope—to share the Second Vatican Council's own esteem for the created and temporal orders. These, the council taught, were to be valued not as realities to be renounced or repudiated for the Gospel's sake, but rather—and far more positively—as expressions of the Creator's infinite goodness: "not merely helps to man's last end," but realities possessing "a value of their own, placed in them by God, whether considered individually or as parts of the integral temporal structure" (*AA* 7).

In this way the council had invited the faithful to correct a secular worldview that not only had denied the transcendent realm—so as to reduce everything to the *hic et nunc*—but also had lost its appreciation for the intrinsic goodness of the temporal order. Ours had become what Charles Taylor calls a "disenchanted"[56] world: a world that was no longer recognized as inhabited by grace, of course, but also a world wherein the divine immanence was no longer apparent in the natural realm. Not only was St. Augustine's timeless notion of God as "nearer to me than I am to myself"[57] no longer timely, but nature itself—far "from being '*mater*' (mother)"—was "reduced," in the mind of John Paul II's contemporaries as he observed, "to being 'matter,' and is subjected to every kind of manipulation."[58] Nature had, in other words, been epistemologically evacuated of that dynamic inner force whereby it is propelled to its proper (even defining) fulfillment.[59] As Joseph Ratzinger observed already in 1966, the scientific discoveries and technological advances of the modern era had led to a perception not only of human action, but even of the world itself, from—it bears repeating—an essentially "functional point of view": not from the "viewpoint of contemplation and wonder," but from a utilitarian framework that "measures, weighs and acts." Religious mystery had thus vanished from the modern, secular worldview, "because this mystery cannot be methodologically examined."[60]

If then the world was still regarded by a secular society as invested with value, this value was thought to belong to it only insofar as it had been manipulated by the human intellect or by the human will, if not by human action. In no way was it thought to belong to it in virtue of creation, still less by reason of a divine pronouncement (cf. Gen 1:31).[61] Indeed, as John Paul II put it in an interview on the occasion of the fifteenth anniversary of his pontificate, a world "that is self-sufficient, that is transparent to human knowledge, that is ever more free of mysteries thanks to scientific research, that is ever more an inexhaustible mine of raw materials for man" does not need God. His place has been usurped by *the demi-god* of modern technology," who alone is charged to render men happy.[62]

In contrast to this profoundly secular worldview and in view of encouraging a culture of life—a culture recognizing life as a gift to be received, treasured, and fostered—John Paul II called upon the Christian faithful to assume a "contemplative outlook": an outlook arising "from faith in the God of life, who has created every individual as a 'wonder' (cf. Ps 139:14)." Such, he continued in his 1995 encyclical *Evangelium Vitae*, "is the outlook of those who see life in its deeper meaning, who grasp its utter gratuitousness, its beauty and its invitation to freedom and responsibility. It is the outlook of those who do not presume to take possession of reality but instead accept it as a gift, discovering in all things the reflection of the Creator and seeing in every person his living image (cf. Gen 1:27; Ps 8:5)."[63] In short, this is a view of the world and of life as intrinsically endowed with meaning: meaning—and thus also with purpose and orientation—that is not simply granted to them (to the world and to human existence in particular) by the human person or by the human community. Rather this meaning is theirs in virtue of their creation by an all-knowing and all-loving God.

As the above passage from John Paul II makes clear, it was not only a renewed vision of the world, as willed by God—and thus also as loved by him (cf. Gen 1:31) and as orientated by him to the good of human persons (cf. vv. 27–30)—that this pope was calling for. Even more fundamentally, he was concerned with renewing the anthropological implications of this creational perspective, that is to say, the vision of the human person as created and thus as endowed with a "proper and primordial nature." This, more specifically, is "the 'nature of the human person,' which is *the person him*[or her-]*self in the unity of soul and body*, in the unity of his [or her] spiritual and biological inclinations and of all the other specific characteristics." As such, he or she is also ordered to "authentic fulfillment, a fulfillment which . . . can take place always and only in human nature."[64]

In direct opposition to this metaphysical anthropology, John Paul II observed that much of contemporary Western culture regarded the human person as "a freedom which is self-designing,"[65] or "self-defining," a "phenomenon creative of itself and its values. Indeed, when all is said and done man would not even have a nature; he would be his own personal life project. Man would be nothing more than his own freedom!"[66] In other words, the human being is regarded by secular culture as ultimately responsible for his or her own life and destiny and even for his or her own nature.

While the human person is thus reduced to his or her own freedom, the latter is reduced to an autonomous power "whose only reference point" is, as Ratzinger observed in 1991, what the individual conceives as "his own [subjective] good."[67] As differing from what Servais Pinckaers calls "freedom for excellence"—that is to say, freedom "rooted in the soul's spontaneous inclinations to the true and the good"[68]—this fundamentally subjective conception of freedom is, Ratzinger continues, "no longer seen positively as a striving for the good, which reason uncovers with help from the community and tradition, but is defined rather as an emancipation from all conditions that prevent each one from following his own reason,"[69] whence its designation "freedom of indifference."[70]

Lost is what John Paul II points to in 1993 as the "essential bond between Truth, the Good and Freedom."[71] He thus set out in this important encyclical, *Veritatis Splendor*, to correct the current tendency of "detaching human freedom from its essential and constitutive relationship to truth."[72] In so doing, John Paul II appealed to natural law, which cannot be reduced, he insisted, to "norms on the biological level."[73] Nor, on the other hand, does it "allow for any division between freedom and nature."[74] On the contrary, it is freedom's rootedness in a nature not of its own making that enables it to seek the good of the human person and the human community, rather than its destruction.

John Paul II invites the faithful to pose, along with the rich young man of the Gospel, the fundamental question of "our time" and of "every time": the question, "What good must I do to have eternal life?" (cf. Mt 19:16). This is a question, John Paul II observed, "not so much about rules to be followed," but rather *"about the full meaning of life."* As such, it is *"an essential and unavoidable question for the life of every man,"* and not simply of an elect few. It is a question reflecting "the aspiration at the heart of every human decision and action, the quiet searching and interior prompting which sets freedom in motion."[75] This, in other words, is a question that directs freedom to its natural goal: goodness and truth.

In precisely this way, John Paul II adopted what he designated in his first encyclical as a *"missionary* attitude": an attitude which "always begins with a feeling of deep esteem for 'what is in man,' for what man has himself worked out in the depths of his spirit concerning the most profound and important problems." As such, it is an attitude respecting everything that is natural to the human person in virtue of his or her creation: an attitude—it bears repeating from our general introduction—of "deep esteem for man, for his intellect, his will, his conscience and his freedom." Secondly, it is an attitude respecting "everything that has been brought about in him by the Spirit, which 'blows where it wills' "[76]: an attitude of humble recognition of the divine order of redemption at work, at least potentially, in the heart of every man.

In adopting this attitude, John Paul II also adopts the attitude of Christ in his dialogue with the rich young man (cf. Mt 19:16–26). The pontiff observes more specifically that far from constraining the young man's freedom by way of obligation or constraint, Christ appeals instead "to the absolute good which attracts us and beckons us," as the "echo of a call from God, who is the origin and goal of man's life."[77] Similarly—that is to say, in imitation of Christ—John Paul II sought to stir human hearts in an effort to reawaken within them the yearning for this perfect and eternal good: for, that is to say, God himself (cf. Mk 10:18; Lk 18:19).[78] After all, it is this yearning, he was convinced, that reveals a fundamental anthropological truth: a truth challenging the primacy that had been granted to human freedom in much secular thought about love. This truth concerns, more specifically, the meaning and thus also the purpose of human freedom; for, as he observed in his prepontifical work *Love and Responsibility*, "freedom exists for the sake of love, because it is by way of love that human beings share most fully in the good." Indeed, Wojtyła defined love itself as willfully "limit[ing] one's freedom on behalf of another.... Love commits freedom and imbues it with that to which the will is naturally attracted—goodness." That is why, he suggested, we can experience that the human being "longs for love more than for freedom." In short, "freedom is the means and love the end."[79]

It is from this creational perspective that human nature could once again be recognized as purposefully organized in its "spiritual and biological inclinations" in view of its specific end: as, that is to say, intended by the Creator and as willfully appropriated by the human person, who is called to "direct and regulate his [or her] life and actions and ... make use of his [or her] own body," in accord with those purposes.[80] Precisely because the human person is characterized by reason, God provides for him or her "differently from the way in which he provides for beings which are not persons," John Paul II explained in light of the constant teaching of the tradition. "He cares for man not 'from without,' through the laws of physical nature, but 'from within,' through reason, which by its natural knowledge of God's eternal law is consequently able to show man the right direction to take in his free actions."[81]

Such, in short, was a vision of human persons that rectified the all-too-often utilitarian or functional one of the culture at large: a vision particularly suited to the lay vocation of "engaging in temporal affairs and directing them according to God's will" (*GS* 31)[82] and of likewise being "free and responsible collaborators of God the Creator"[83] in the important mission of transmitting human life. In this way, significance was also granted to human freedom. Indeed, as John Paul II put it, *"the Council treats human freedom very seriously and appeals to the inner imperative of the conscience in order to demonstrate that the answer, given by man to God and to His world through faith, is closely connected with this personal dignity."*[84]

III. The Church's Commitment to Truth and the Problematic Gap between Doctrine and Practice

Pointing to the moral significance of human freedom and the exercise of conscience did not mean—as is made explicit in the context[85]—that the Church, under the leadership of John Paul II, was willing to alter her doctrine in an effort to keep up with the times. Nor was she willing to alter moral norms in accord with the popular opinion, wrongly presented in terms of the *"sensus fidelium"* (cf. *LG* 25). To be sure, John Paul II fully granted to the laity, "by reason of their specific role of interpreting the history of the world in the light of Christ," the task of "illuminat[ing] and organiz[ing] temporal realities according to the plan of God, Creator and Redeemer." At the same time and within the same context, however, he clarified that the "supernatural sense of faith" accorded to the laity by the council was not to be understood as consisting "solely or necessarily in the consensus of the faithful,"[86] nor in the practice of the masses.[87] "Following Christ, the Church seeks the truth," John Paul explained, "which is not always the same as the majority opinion." It furthermore belongs to the "task of the apostolic ministry," he insisted, "to ensure that the Church remains in the truth of Christ,"[88] and thus also in the truth concerning the human person, created in the image of God, and in the truth about human love.[89]

In short, there could be no question, as far as John Paul II was concerned, of a purely subjective morality: of substituting personal "experience" or even personal convictions for Gospel truth. Similarly, the conciliar ideal of *aggiornomento* could not be invoked to allow the world, with its ever-current trend toward moral relativism, to influence Church teaching. Instead, the Church must always foster "the essential good of man," John Paul II argued, and thus the truth rather than *"an appearance of truth."* Hence, *"when the true doctrine is unpopular, it is not right to seek easy popularity,"*[90] John Paul II insisted with reference to the controversial encyclical on the regulation of human birth, *Humanae Vitae.* In fact, "it comes as no surprise to the Church," we read in that encyclical, "that she, no less than her divine Founder, is destined to be a 'sign of contradiction,'" which in no way absolves her of "the duty imposed on her of proclaiming humbly but firmly the entire moral law, both natural and evangelical."[91]

Meanwhile, dissenters from *Humanae Vitae,* such as Todd A. Salzman and Michael G. Lawler, raised the question in 2008: "How can anyone claim that the Church believes that artificial contraception is morally wrong when some 89 percent of the communion-Church does not believe that claim?"[92] In this way, they echo the concern of sociologist Andrew Greeley in his observation, some thirty years earlier (in 1977), of the huge gap between magisterial teaching and actual practice. Pointing to an apostasy rate in the United States that had doubled in fifteen years, as well as a substantial decline in church attendance, a one-third decrease in financial contributions to the Church, and the departure of thousands of priests and nuns from ministry, he attributed "virtually all of this decline" to "a single problem—[the Church's position on] birth control."[93]

In light of what he recognized as a church "in an organized shambles" at that time, it is not surprising that Greeley predicted a disaster was ahead. "The dynamics at work in American Catholicism at the present time are such," he argued in 1977, "that it is relatively easy to imagine the 'worst case' eventuality and relatively difficult to imagine the quite modest 'best case' eventuality. The birth control encyclical not only canceled out the [positive] effects of the Vatican Council"[94]—as measured by "mass attendance, communion reception, confession, daily prayer, accepting the church's right to teach, Catholic activism and approval of one's son becoming a priest"[95]—"it also set into motion forces which have caused grave losses to the Catholic church and which will be very difficult to reverse in the next fifteen years [1978–1992]."[96]

In contrast to this devastating prediction, however, he happily reported five years ahead of schedule—in 1987—that American Catholics "have survived the turbulence of the years since the Second Vatican Council with their basic affiliation to the church relatively unchanged," despite a still-mounting rejection of Church doctrine. Although, to be more specific, nine out of ten American Catholics in 1987 rejected the Church's teaching on birth control, divorce, and abortion, and four out of five disagreed that premarital sex was always wrong, this massive dissent had not—contrary to his own prediction ten years earlier—been accompanied by a massive exodus from the Church.[97] They tend to "stay in the church, reject some sexual teachings, and protest with diminished financial support, a combination of responses which suggests a sophisticated (if not orthodox) response, hardly what one would expect from men and women who have been confused by false teachers."[98] Greeley concludes quite simply that the lay faithful are not looking to the teaching Magisterium to "enlighten" them on matters of sexual morality.[99]

"How can Catholics justify continued reception of the sacraments while at the same time rejecting certain doctrines which the teaching authority presently deems of paramount importance?" he asks. "My research suggests," the Chicago priest explained, "that they do so by an appeal from church leaders, who they think do not understand, to God, who they think does understand."[100] Greeley concludes by recognizing "no reason to think that clear, forceful, and insistent repetition of teaching will change the mind of the American laity."[101]

Recent statistics reveal, moreover, that this trend has hardly declined. In response to the "notification" by the Congregation for the Doctrine of the Faith that many of the proposals in Margaret Farley's book *Just Love*[102] are "in direct contradiction with Catholic teaching," Lisa Cahill argues that US Catholics widely support these same proposals. Reporting in 2012, Cahill notes that 98 percent of Catholic women are currently using or have used artificial birth control, and that 64 percent of US Catholics favor the legal recognition of gay unions, more than the national average.[103] This current majority approval of gay unions represents, moreover, a significant increase since 1986, when Greeley reported that "two-thirds of American Catholics continue to accept the Church's teaching" on this subsequently controversial subject.[104] Hence, while Farley's book was written to ease the alleged suffering of Catholics and Christians of other denominations "due to teaching that may be observed in the breach, but is still part of the official self-definition of their faith traditions," Cahill concludes that this goal may soon be obsolete. "Fear of nonacceptance by people in second marriages or gay relationships should decline quickly, if recent statistics tell the truth."[105]

While Cahill thus seemed to join Greeley in making light of the gap between orthodoxy and orthopraxy—after all, American Catholics apparently did[106]—the German theologian Dietmar Mieth considered it in 1987 as nothing less than "a crisis": "not ... a crisis of morals in the sense that people really do not know what the right thing is and what they ought to do. Instead, we are dealing with a moral conflict within the church that, as it were, is not being carried on in an open, dialogical, and communicative manner because it thwarts practical, lived convictions within the church in certain areas."[107] By this "thwarting practical lived convictions," he obviously meant, in the context, allowing the laity to exercise their prophetic mission in the Church in such a way that they were "free" to thwart magisterial teaching, namely by "an appeal"—to return to Greeley's provocative comment—"to God, who they think does understand [human weakness, presumably]."[108] Or, as Mieth puts it, when the pope substitutes his "personal conscience" for the "responsibility of conscience" (*Gewissensverantwortung*) of married couples, "the disrespected conscience [of the faithful] responds with its emancipation."[109] Such is apparently what the Scottish Dominican Fergus Kerr dolefully identifies as "a silent schism."[110]

IV. Epistemological Error and Moral Evil

As this "silent schism" exemplifies, in question is the conviction of Paul VI that "our contemporaries are particularly capable of seeing that this teaching [namely, that of the 'inseparable connection ... between the unitive significance and the procreative significance ... inherent to the marriage act'] is in harmony with human reason."[111] Whether or not that conviction was accurate in 1968 when the encyclical was first issued, "the majority of Catholics in the West now find the basic principle of the inseparability of the unitive and procreative dimensions of sexual activity simply unintelligible"[112]—even "unbelievable"[113]—Kerr observed in 2008; "and yet the teaching of the Catholic Church rests on that principle."[114]

Let us be honest with ourselves, however. We are not talking about some obscure principle of astrophysics. The so-called unintelligible principle of *Humanae Vitae* might be summed up quite simply as this: sex = strengthened conjugal unity + babies. Of course we all know—as did Paul VI—that not every "act of insemination (intercourse) is of itself procreative," as Richard McCormick nonetheless deems necessary to point out in his accusation that the Magisterium still ascribes to "Aristotelian biology." Thanks to the discovery of the ovum in 1827, we now know by deduction what men and women throughout human history knew by induction: that, the American Jesuit continues, "the vast majority" of conjugal acts do not lead to conception.[115] It is, in fact, precisely this knowledge that has incited Catholic doctors and scientists to determine, with an amazing precision, a woman's (relatively limited)[116] period of fertility, and they have used this precision to help couples to both achieve and avoid pregnancy, without recourse to contraception.[117] They have moreover done this—determined fertility with precision—in response to the Council's mandate, which (contra McCormick) is taken up directly in *Humanae Vitae*.[118]

Meanwhile, however, we are witnessing not only an outright denial—or what Mary Eberstadt calls the "will to disbelieve"[119]—among many Westerners of the obvious connection between the sexual revolution (and the extensive use of the pill) and the terrible loss of respect for human dignity and human life referred to in the first part of this article, but also an apparent blindness regarding the connection between the two meanings of the married act: and this despite (if not due to!) widely-pervasive (even mandatory) sexual education programs in most Western nations. If not for a similar "will to disbelieve," how—I can hardly help but ask—is it possible that the epistemological association between sex and procreation could practically disappear from the mental register of two generations of Catholics since *Humanae Vitae* was issued?

On the other hand, should we be surprised that a breach in practice with respect to the Church's moral doctrine—and an apparently very large one at that, if the statistics cited by dissenters are accurate, not to mention those who present themselves as Catholic[120]—might be linked to a breach in the most obvious epistemological conclusions? Might it not be the case, more specifically, that widespread contraceptive use has practically hindered the inductive reasoning that allows us to draw an obvious conclusion, namely that sexual intercourse leads to babies? Take the case of Judith Schwartz, writing in a popular women's magazine in 1993, who identifies herself as belonging to the first generation "to define a good girl not as someone who abstains from sex but as someone who 'takes precautions.'" Schwartz—one such "good girl" who "conscientiously" avoids "being in a state of potential motherhood"—attributes to this contraceptive "diligence" and "hygiene" her inability to draw the logical connection between sex and pregnancy. "That it takes egg and sperm to make a baby is among the more obvious facts that women live with," she admits; "yet somehow we don't *live* with it. As daughters of the sexual revolution, we've been surrounded all our lives by the images and temptations of recreational sex. Consequently," she observes, "basic, species-preserving, reproductive sex occupies a separate, wholly unexplored territory in our mind."[121]

Because, as this example serves to illustrate, we have effectively manipulated our own human nature by manipulating the human (especially female) body in accord with our own contorted intentions—those of, for example, reproductive "freedom"[122] or sexual liberation[123]—it is not surprising that our conceptions of our nature's purposes, or ends, have also changed. When, however, human nature is altered by the human will and intelligence in a way that is arguably in conflict with its (nature's) purposes, it cannot be brought to the witness stand to testify against itself. To do so—to question nature's purpose according to the assumption that it must be "assumed into the human sphere and be regulated within it [presumably by way of technological and scientific domination, as differing from virtuous abstinence],"[124] as the "majority" of the famous papal birth control commission put it one year before *Humanae Vitae* was issued in its rebuttal to the so-called minority report[125]—is to divide the human being into "parts, organs, functions" that are "conceived as contra-distinct from him [or her]."[126]

This division, in turn, serves the subordination of man's "parts" to his or her spiritual nature "almost as are plants and animals" in reason of "cultural values," as the minority papal commission report put it in that same year.[127] Implied in this thinking is thus a radical spiritualization of human nature and a reduction of the human body "to raw material for human activity and for its power," as Pope John Paul II observed nearly thirty years later. Hence, this "nature needs to be profoundly transformed, and indeed overcome by freedom, inasmuch as it represents a limitation and denial of freedom." Far beyond the admission of a corporal-spiritual division into human nature, and far more dangerously, is thus the usurpation of the Creator's prerogative by giving to human knowledge and volition the task of establishing ontological truth rather than that of discovering and confirming it. "Indeed," it bears repeating, "when all is said and done man would not even have a nature," as John Paul II put it; "he would be his own personal life-project."[128]

It is altogether fitting that the "Majority Report" rebuttal should grant to human persons "the responsibility . . . for humanizing the gifts of nature and using them to bring the life of man to greater perfection."[129] What is questionable, however, is to cater—as this commission did—to "a certain change in the mind of contemporary man," such that "he feels . . . more conformed to his rational nature, created by God with liberty and responsibility, when he uses his skill to intervene in the biological processes of nature [as differing from the exercise of virtuous abstinence on fertile days when children are not desired] . . . than if he would abandon himself to chance [as differing from divine providence]."[130] It is thus not surprising that the minority commission voiced concern that sufficient place be accorded "in human life for the action of the Holy Spirit and for his mission of healing sin."[131] As for Paul VI, he sought to defend "conjugal morals in their integral wholeness" and thus also "the dignity of man and wife" by encouraging them "not to abdicate" from their "own responsibility in order to rely on technical means."[132]

In his own extensive reflection upon "the questions raised by *Humanae Vitae*" and his attempt "to look for an answer to them,"[133] John Paul II pointed, once again,[134] to "a hidden and at the same time rather explicit tendency" in contemporary, especially Western, civilization to determine progress "with the measure of 'things,' that is, of material goods." In contrast, he recognized *Humanae Vitae* as making "a resolute appeal to measure man's progress with the measure of the 'person,' that is, of that which is a good of man as man," of that "which corresponds to his essential dignity" (cf. *GS* 35).[135] Such, he explained more specifically (in the final of his 130 general audience addresses that compose his theology of the body), is a good that is measured "by ethics [or virtue] and not only of 'technology.'"[136]

The doctrine of *Humanae Vitae* was thus recognized by John Paul II as inscribed within the goal, proper to the council, of "recapturing the ultimate meaning of life and its fundamental values" in view of renewing Western civilization. "Only an awareness of the primacy of these [ethical] values"—which John Paul II identified as "the values of the human person as such"—"enables man to use the immense possibilities given him by science in such a way as to bring about the true advancement of the human person in his or her whole truth, in his or her freedom and dignity. Science is called to ally itself with wisdom."[137]

From this perspective, "the problem" addressed by *Humanae Vitae* "lies in maintaining *the adequate relationship* between that which is defined as *'domination . . . of the forces of nature'* (*HV* 2) and *'self-mastery'* (*HV* 21)." Whereas, to be more specific, our contemporaries tend to transfer "the methods proper to the first sphere to those of the second"[138]—to regulate, in other words, the properly human sphere by means of science and technology—the dominion that the human person is called to exercise over himself belongs more properly to the order of ethics, by, that is to say, a positive modification of his own actions. "It is *not* merely a question of a certain *'technique,'*" John Paul II explained in his theology of the body, "but of *ethics* in the strict sense of the term as the *morality of a certain behavior*."[139]

In short, the point of contention that underlies much of the controversy surrounding *Humanae Vitae* from its inception until the present day is due, John Paul II recognized, to two fundamentally opposed anthropological and ethical perspectives: perspectives differentiated according to whether one seeks to control nature *to one's own ends*—as in the Baconian project at the origin of modern science[140]—or whether instead one seeks, by the exercise of virtue, to control one's own self—that is to say, one's impulses, dispositions, and behavior—*to God's end or purpose* for marriage, family and the human person as such.

V. The Inseparable Connection Between Faith and Morality: Witnessing in Act

Citing Rosemary Radford Ruether, Lisa Cahill holds that "while the celibate cultivates sexual self-control and asceticism, that ethic should not dominate the sexuality of wives and husbands."[141] In this way, she apparently echoes Uta Ranke-Heinemann's insistence that "the [magisterium's opposition to the] pill is only a new occasion to make all of marriage more ascetical and sexless, to turn lay people into monks and celibates,"[142] and to turn the conjugal act into "a kind of celibate act."[143]

Of course, the point is well made by Josef Pieper that "heresy and hyperasceticism are and always have been close neighbors." In fact, "complete asensuality, unfeelingly advers[ity] to all sexual pleasure" is actually regarded by the Church's common doctor, St. Thomas Aquinas, as an "imperfection" and even "a moral defect [*vitium*]," Pieper explains.[144] As for the virtue of chastity, its purpose is hardly to "poison eros," as Friedrich Nietzsche would have it. Nor are the Church's "commandments and prohibitions" to be seen as a means of "turn[ing] to bitterness the most precious thing in life": of "blow[ing] the whistle just when the joy, which is the Creator's gift, offers us a happiness which is ... [a] foretaste of the Divine," as Pope Benedict might well have summarized a common objection to the Church's moral teaching.[145] On the contrary, the prescriptions of *Humanae Vitae* hold firm to the conviction of St. Thomas that "nature has introduced pleasure into the operations that are necessary for man's life":[146] whether that of the individual or that of the species, and procreation is "a very great good [*bonum excellens*]"[147] indeed.

It is presumably for this reason—that "the exceeding pleasure" (*abundantia delectationis*) of the conjugal act is "not opposed to the mean of virtue" so long as it is in "conformity with right reason"[148]—that Michel Labourdette teaches that the virtue of chastity ought "not only to 'moderate' [pleasure], but also seek at times to obtain it. Chastity should also incite desire."[149] Similarly, Cahill has reason to affirm that "the sexual union of spouses needs at least as much to be encouraged, occasioned, and sustained, as to be mastered, limited, and scheduled."[150] In short, "chastity is not *in se* a virtue of renunciation or of abstinence; it is primarily—like all the others—a *virtue of exercise*." Just as the virtue of temperance with regard to food and drink, for example, is practiced "every time that one eats and drinks," and not primarily when one is fasting, so too chastity is "not only practiced in celibacy." On the contrary, it is exercised *primarily* within the context of marriage and the marital act, Labourdette continues; and it attains "its human and Christian perfection in keeping to its correct measure [*sa juste mesure*]."[151]

Because, moreover, this "right measure" in matters of sexuality is determined by responsible parenthood, Labourdette reasons, it is justifiable "to intervene [namely, by articificial means, he holds] so that the fecundity of the act does not depend upon chance [*hasard*], nor simply upon biological rhythm, but that it be willed in a *responsible manner*, which takes into consideration the whole of human finality." Still more specifically, this means regulating fecundity "according to ends which are no longer animal but human."[152] In this way Labourdette repeats almost verbatim the proposition that he helped draft in the majority rebuttal of the papal birth commission in 1966: and this despite considerable scientific progress that had been made in the interim in determining the window of a couple's fertility.[153]

If the proposition of Labourdette is to be faulted, however, it is not on account of an ignorance of science,[154] and certainly not on account of his insistence upon "responsibility," or even justice, toward one's spouse and one's (potential and/or actual) children. Rather, it is his reduction of the virtue of "chastity" (and thus also the corresponding, or governing, notions of "responsibility" and "justice") to the meaning that has been assigned to them by our secular culture: namely that of taking (contraceptive) "precautions" against pregnancy when it is deemed imprudent or undesirable. In so doing, he considerably departs from his own Thomistic tradition, which regards the virtue of chastity as controlling one's *passions*—and not one's *fertility*, as Labourdette and many dissenters of *Humanae Vitae* would have it—in accord with reason: in this case, the *"ratio"* (or ordering principle) of responsible parenthood (and we might add the *"ratio,"* forgotten by Labourdette, of justice toward one's spouse, whose personal dignity requires that he or she always be treated as a subject and never as simply an object of desire).[155]

In the words of St. Thomas, "chastity takes its name from the fact that reason *chastises* concupiscence, which, like a child needs curbing"[156]: *not*, it bears repeating, because "the free act of reason … is incompatible with the aforementioned pleasure,"[157] but because the ordering principles of responsible parenting and justice toward one's spouse and even toward the human species might be diverted by self-indulging lust. In fact, lust—Pieper's translator calls it "unchastity"—is said by the German Thomist (with reference to the master)[158] to actually "destroy the structure of the person" by corrupting the virtue of prudence, by blinding the spirit, and by splitting the power of decision. Lustful surrender and the soul's willful abandonment "to the world of sensuality"—not in the Manichaean manner, but by a will-to-pleasure that is contrary to the spirit of genuine *eros*,[159] which necessarily seeks the transcendent good—"paralyzes the primordial powers of the moral person: the ability to perceive, in silence, the call of reality, and to make, in the retreat of this silence, the decision appropriate to the concrete situation of concrete action."[160] The virtue of chastity, in contrast, prepares the human person for contemplation of reality better than any other virtue, Pieper explains.[161]

It follows that while it is the domain of justice "to establish the order of reason in all human affairs"—including, as Labourdette points out, the order in marital and familial relations—it belongs to the virtue of temperance, and in particular to its sub-category of chastity (the virtue ironically invoked by Labourdette in his argument against the doctrine of *Humanae Vitae*) "to safeguard this good, inasmuch as they *moderate* the passions, lest they lead man away from reason's good."[162] In fact, by disciplining the sexual urge, chastity is said by Pieper to actually "realize the order of reason."[163] Hence, without resorting to a sort of Manichaeism, which qualifies the pleasures of the flesh as intrinsically evil, St. Thomas argues that it is at times "praiseworthy, and even necessary for the sake of an end *to abstain* from such pleasures"[164] as result from the conjugal act: even when that means foregoing the "very great good" (*bonum excellens*)[165] of procreation or the accompanying good of promoting conjugal unity (which might obviously be fostered by other means). Similarly, in the words of Pope Benedict, "*eros* needs to be disciplined and purified if it is to provide not just fleeting pleasure, but a certain foretaste of the pinnacle of our existence, of that beatitude for which our whole being yearns."[166]

In this way Pope Benedict joins St. Thomas in calling for a certain ascetical practice—as in the practice of periodic abstinence (Natural Family Planning), for example—in favor of promoting what he qualifies as an *authentically* erotic love: one that is indeed "ecstasy," but "not in the sense of a moment of intoxication." What he has in mind, rather, is "a journey, an ongoing exodus [*ex-stasis*] out of the closed inward-looking self towards its liberation through self-giving, and thus towards authentic self-discovery and indeed the discovery of God."[167] In the proposition drawn from Labourdette's treatise on chastity, in contrast, we are confronted once again with the underlying question that has been emphasized throughout these pages: that of whether Christians are still capable, or even willing, to acknowledge "basic [moral] truths" that might be addressed to their consciences—as in the pastoral proposition of Dietmar Mieth—"in consideration of the facts and a morally correct argumentation."[168] Instead, there is good reason to believe that the current cultural climate of secularism and the prevalent practice of "love making" without regard for its two-fold meaning (of procreation and conjugal unity, which presupposes that one's spouse is not reduced to a simple "object" of one's desires) has clouded minds and hearts from recognizing an objective world order upon which a moral order might be based. Lost, along with the notion of God himself, is "the idea," as Ratzinger put it, "that another will, the will of the Creator, calls us and that our being is right when our will is in harmony with his will."[169]

The way out of this relativist quandary is hardly, of course, to revert to authoritative statements coming from the Magisterium—statements that are sadly perceived as subjecting married love to "the voyeuristic sphere of a clerical bedroom police force," as Ranke-Heinemann would have it.[170] Indeed, as Mieth correctly insists, "Arguments resting on authority, or the constancy of a doctrine, or on the establishing of historical rules of thumb as timeless precepts are not sufficient"[171] to a modern mindset. Nor, he argued, can the Church hope to promote healthy moral lives among the faithful by simply preaching a doctrine of "prohibitive commands," as he claimed was the case when he wrote in 1986. What is needed instead, he suggested, is an experiential approach to Christian morality. Recognizing that "the agreement" between the Catholic (dissenting) majority and magisterial teaching "is greater ... on the level of human values and basic attitudes, or basic models of behavior ... than at the level of normative application," [172] he pointed to the fact that "human beings discover their 'nature' precisely in dealing with this realm of responsibility and creativity."[173] In short, "Christians ... would rather learn, for example, how faithful love can be positively lived than to hear what, when, where, how often, and with whom one may or may not do this or that."[174]

Ironically, we are not far from John Paul II's own conviction that the most profound desires of the human heart actually reveal the nature of the human person to him- or herself, along with nature's imperatives. "Does man not sense, together with concupiscence, a deep need to preserve the dignity of the reciprocal relations that find their expression in the body thanks to its masculinity and femininity?" he rightly asked. "Does he not feel the need to impregnate them with everything that is noble and beautiful? Does he not feel the need to confer on them the supreme value, which is love?"[175] Pointing in this way to the attractive—even compelling—nature of a conjugal love that is true both to the demands of the Gospel message (cf. Mt 5:27–28; 10:39; 16:25) and to human freedom itself, it is puzzling that his teaching has not been more widely embraced, despite a continually growing appeal, especially among youth, for popularized versions of his theology of the body.

If, on the other hand, this teaching is to be effectively received at the level of the domestic church in view of reversing the terrible abominations against human life and human dignity and—more positively—of fostering a civilization of love, as was the profound hope of the saintly pontiff, then it is not enough for the current and subsequent magisteria to simply repeat his teaching. Nor does it suffice that this doctrine be preached from the pulpit; nor even that there be an ongoing dialogue between the Church and contemporary world culture, as the council judged essential to the success of the Church's mission. If, rather, this teaching is to be appreciated for what it is—a profound affirmation of the essential dignity and responsibility of the human person, who is called by the Creator to be both an object of love (the beloved) and a loving subject (the lover)—then we, the lay faithful, must live these truths in such a way as to radiate their truth in the world, to the world, and for the world. Such is the need, as Mieth likewise observes, "to place the attractiveness of values and positive models of human basic attitudes *together* in the foreground."[176] In short, *The Gospel of Life*—the name that John Paul II gave to the eleventh of his fourteen encyclical letters—must not only be preached. It must also be *experienced*, so as also to be *witnessed*.

Of course, it bears repeating that not everyone would agree that the Church's sexual moral teaching can be equated with Christ's word, or the truth of the Gospel. "An opinion is frequently heard," John Paul II admitted, "which questions the intrinsic and unbreakable bond between faith and morality, as if membership in the church and her internal unit were to be decided on the basis of faith alone, while in the sphere of morality a pluralism of opinions and of kinds of behavior could be tolerated, these being left to the judgment of the individual subjective conscience or to the diversity of social and cultural contexts."[177] To those of such a mindset, he granted that being moral does *not* mean simply "disposing oneself to hear a teaching and obediently accepting a commandment." Nor, however, does this fact lessen its demands. Because *"the essential and primordial foundation of Christian morality"* is, as the saintly pope saw and taught it, the *"sequela Christi,"* this morality "more radically . . . involves holding fast to the very person of Jesus, partaking of his life and his destiny, sharing in his free and loving obedience to the will of the Father."[178]

Or, as Pope Francis put it more recently,

Christian morality is not a form of stoicism, or self-denial, or merely a practical philosophy or a catalogue of sins and faults. Before all else, the Gospel invites us to respond to the God of love who saves us, to see God in others and to go forth from ourselves to seek the good of others. Under no circumstance can this invitation be obscured! All of the virtues are at the service of this response of love. If this invitation does not radiate forcefully and attractively, the edifice of the Church's moral teaching risks becoming a house of cards, and this is our greatest risk. It would mean that it is not the Gospel which is being preached, but certain doctrinal or moral points based on specific ideological options. The message will run the risk of losing its freshness and will cease to have "the fragrance of the Gospel."[179]

In short, there "cannot be," as John Paul II taught in terms resonating with conciliar teaching[180] (and even with the reasoning of recent dissenters)[181] "two parallel lives":

On the one hand, the so-called "spiritual" life, with its values and demands; and on the other, the so-called "secular" life, that is life in a family, at work, in social relationships, in the responsibilities of public life and in culture.... In fact, every area of the lay faithful's lives, as different as they are, enters into the plan of God who desires that these very areas be the "places in time" where the love of Christ is revealed and realized for both the glory of the Father and service of others.[182]

Such, Pope Francis suggests, is the joy of the Gospel: *Evangelii Gaudium*. Such also is liturgy: "the participation of the People of God in the 'work of God'."[183] In fact, "the celebration which gives meaning to every other form of prayer and worship is found," John Paul II teaches, "in *the family's actual daily life together*, if [that is to say] it is a life of love and self-giving."[184]

NOTES

1. Pope Paul VI, Discourse to the Last General Council Meeting of the Second Vatican Council, December 7, 1965, in *Closing Speeches, Vatican Council II* (Boston: St. Paul Editions), 5–14, here 8–9. Also available online: http://w2.vatican.va/content/paul-vi/en/speeches/1965/documents/hf_p-vi_spe_19651207_epilogo-concilio.html.

2. Ibid. 9.

3. Massimo Faggioli, *Vatican II: The Battle for Meaning* (Mahwah, NJ: Paulist Press, 2012), 18.

4. Pope Paul VI, Discourse to the Last General Council Meeting of the Second Vatican Council, 9, 10.

5. Ibid. 9–10.

6. Ibid. 10, 11, 13.

7. Paul IV, Apostolic Exhortation on "Evangelization in the Modern World," *Evangelii Nuntiandi* (December 8, 1975), no. 1, http://w2.vatican.va/content/paul-vi/en/apost_exhortations/documents/hf_p-vi_exh_19751208_evangelii-nuntiandi.html. See also the words of Pope Francis: "I prefer a Church which is bruised, hurting and dirty because it has been out on the streets, rather than a Church which is unhealthy from being confined and from clinging to its own security" (Apostolic Exhortation on the Joy of the Gospel, *Evangelii Gaudium* [November 24, 2013], no. 49, http://w2.vatican.va/content/francesco/en/apost_exhortations/documents/papa-francesco_esortazione-ap_20131124_evangelii-gaudium.html). See also ibid. no. 180.

8. John Paul II's *Ad Limina* Address, "The Laity, Their Life and Mission," in *Origins: CNS Documentary Service* 28, no. 5 (June 18, 1998), 78–80, at 79. Cf. John Paul II, Post-Synodal Apostolic Exhortation on the Vocation and the Mission of the Lay Faithful in the Church and in the World, *Christifideles Laici* (December 30, 1988),

no. 34, http://w2.vatican.va/content/john-paul-ii/en/apost_exhortations/documents/
hf_jp-ii_exh_30121988_christifideles-laici.html.

9. In his address to women on December 8, 1965, we read these telling words: "Our technology runs the risk of becoming inhuman. Reconcile men with life and above all, we beseech you, watch carefully over the future of our race. Hold back the hand of man who, in a moment of folly, might attempt to destroy human civilization." (Cf. the council's message to women on December 7, 1965, in *Closing Speeches, Vatican Council II*, 29).

10. Cf. John Paul II, Apostolic Exhortation, "On the Role of the Family in the Modern World," *Familiaris Consortio* (November 22, 1981), no. 30; available at: http://w2.vatican.va/content/john-paul-ii/en/apost_exhortations/documents/hf_jp-ii_exh_19811122_familiaris-consortio.html; and John Paul II, Encyclical Letter "On the Gospel of Life," *Evangelium Vitae* (March 25, 1995), no. 96, http://w2.vatican.va/content/john-paul-ii/en/encyclicals/documents/hf_jp-ii_enc_25031995_evangelium-vitae.html.

11. John Paul II, Encyclical letter "On the Redeemer of Man," *Redemptoris Hominis* (March 4, 1979), no. 12, http://w2.vatican.va/content/john-paul-ii/en/encyclicals/documents/hf_jp-ii_enc_04031979_redemptor-hominis.html.

12. John Paul II, *Familaris Consortio*, no. 5.

13. John Paul II, *Christifideles Laici*, no. 37.

14. See Paul VI, Encyclical letter "On Human Life," *Humanae Vitae* (July 25, 1968), no. 12, http://w2.vatican.va/content/paul-vi/en/encyclicals/documents/hf_p-vi_enc_25071968_humanae-vitae.html.

15. See, for example, John Paul II, *Evangelium Vitae* no. 96.

16. See, for example, John Paul II, Encyclical letter "On the Splendor of Truth," *Veritatis Splendor* (August 6, 1993), no. 49, http://w2.vatican.va/content/john-paul-ii/en/encyclicals/documents/hf_jp-ii_enc_06081993_veritatis-splendor.html.

17. See, for example, John Paul II, *Veritatis Splendor*, no. 96, 99.

18. See, for example, John Paul II, *Veritatis Splendor*, no. 110.

19. The family, John Paul II reasoned, is *"the centre and the heart of the civilization of love,"* which would lead to the "humanization of the world" (Letter to Families, *Gratissimam Sane* [February 2, 1994], no. 12, https://w2.vatican.va/content/john-paul-ii/en/letters/1994/documents/hf_jp-ii_let_02021994_families.html).

20. John Paul II, *Christifideles Laici*, no. 52.

21. John Paul II, *Gratissimam Sane*, no. 13.

22. John Paul II, *Familiaris Consortio*, no. 86.

23. John Paul II, *Christifidelis Laici*, no. 40.

24. Cf. John Paul II, *Familiaris Consortio*, no. 21.

25. John Paul II, *Christifidelis Laici*, no. 40.

26. John Paul II, *Gratissimam Sane*, no. 2.

27. Ibid. (original emphasis).

28. See his homily during the mass and canonization of John Paul II and John XXIII on the Second Sunday of Easter, April 27, 2014. Available online at: http://w2.vatican.va/content/francesco/en/homilies/2014/documents/papa-francesco_20140427_omelia-canonizzazioni.html.

29. John Paul II, *Gratissimam Sane*, no. 15.

30. See *The Catechism of the Catholic Church*, nos. 873, 900, 901, 904, http://www.vatican.va/archive/ccc_css/archive/catechism/p123a9p4.htm; the Pontifical Council for Justice and Peace, *Compendium of the Social Doctrine of the Church* (London and New York: Burns & Oates, 2005), no. 542, 272–73 (also available at: http://www.vatican.va/roman_curia/pontifical_councils/justpeace/documents/rc_pc_justpeace_

doc_20060526_compendio-dott-soc_en.html); and John Paul II, *Ad Limina* Address, "The Laity, Their Life and Mission," 79.

31. John Paul II, *Christifideles Laici*, no. 3. For details on the synod, see George Weigel, *Witness to Hope* (New York: Harper Perennial, 2005), 552–55. Originally published by First Cliff Street Books, New York, 1999.

32. John Paul II, *Christifideles Laici*, no. 3.

33. Cf. ibid. nos. 45, 48, and 58.

34. Ibid. no. 3.

35. Ibid. no. 35.

36. Ibid. no. 4 (original emphasis); cf. Paul VI, Apostolic Exhortation, *Evangelii Nuntiandi*, no. 51. See also John Paul II, *Crossing the Threshold of Hope*, ed. Vittorio Messori (New York: Alfred A. Knopf, 1994), 112–13.

37. Paul VI, *Evangelii Nuntiandi*, no. 55. See also Karol Wojtyła, *Sources of Renewal: The Implementation of Vatican II*, trans. P. S. Falla (San Francisco: Harper & Row, 1980), 49–51. The original Polish edition was published in 1972.

38. John Paul II, *Christifideles Laici*, no. 5.

39. Paul VI, *Evangelii Nuntiandi*, no. 55.

40. John Paul II, *Evangelium Vitae*, no. 4. Cf. Paul VI, *Evangelii Nuntiandi*, no. 14.

41. Cf. John Paul II, *Evangelium Vitae*, no. 3.

42. John Paul II, *Redemptoris Hominis*, no. 17.

43. See ibid. no. 15. Cf. the council's message to women on December 7, 1965, in: *Closing Speeches, Vatican Council II*, 29.

44. John Paul II, *Evangelium Vitae*, no. 4.

45. John Paul II, *Evangelium Vitae*, no. 4.

46. John Paul II, *Familiaris Consortio*, no. 30.

47. Pope Francis, Apostolic Exhortation "On the Joy of the Gospel," *Evangelii Gaudium* (February 2, 1994), no. 35, http://w2.vatican.va/content/francesco/en/apost_exhortations/documents/papa-francesco_esortazione-ap_20131124_evangelii-gaudium.html.

48. John Paul II, *Evangelium Vitae*, no. 96. In short, "all too often freedom is confused with the instinct for individual or collective interest or with the instinct for combat and domination, whatever be the ideological colors with which they are covered" (John Paul II, *Redemptoris Hominis*, no. 16).

49. John Paul II, *Evangelium Vitae*, no. 18; see also no. 69; and Joseph Ratzinger, "The Problem of Threats to Human Life," in *The Essential Pope Benedict XVI: His Central Writings and Speeches*, ed. John F. Thornton and Susan B. Varenne (New York: HarperCollins, 2007), 381–92, at 382–83 (originally published in the April 8, 1991 issue of *L'Osservatore Romano*).

50. John Paul II, *Evangelium Vitae*, no. 23.

51. John Paul II, *Gratissimam Sane*, no. 13. Cf. John Paul II, *Christifideles Laici*, no. 5.

52. John Paul II, *Evangelium Vitae*, no. 33.

53. Joseph Ratzinger with Vittorio Messori, *The Ratzinger Report*, trans. Salvator Attanasio and Graham Harrison (San Francisco: Ignatius Press, 1985), 98–99.

54. John Paul II, *Redemptoris Hominis*, no. 16.

55. The Pontifical Council for Justice and Peace, *Compendium of the Social Doctrine of the Church*, no. 16 (original emphasis).

56. See Charles Taylor, *A Secular Age* (Cambridge, MA: Harvard University Press, 2007).

57. "Interior intimo meo et superior summo meo [deeper than my inmost understanding and higher than the topmost height that I could reach]" (Augustine of Hippo,

Confessions III, 6: Aureli Augustini, Confessionum, Bibliothèque Augustinienne, vol. 13, trans. Eugène Tréhorel and Guilhem Bouissou, ed. M. Skutella [Paris: Études augustiniennes, 1992]). Cf. Pope Benedict XVI, Encyclical letter on "God is Love," *Deus Caritas Est* (December 25, 2005), no. 17, http://w2.vatican.va/content/benedict-xvi/fr/encyclicals/documents/hf_ben-xvi_enc_20051225_deus-caritas-est.html.

58. John Paul II, *Evangelium Vitae*, no. 22.

59. See Kenneth Schmitz, *At the Center of the Human Drama: The Philosophical Anthropology of Karol Wojtyła/Pope John Paul II* (Washington, DC: The Catholic University Press of America, 1993), 132–34; and "Modernity Meets Tradition: The Philosophical Originality of Karol Wojtyła," *Crisis*, April 1, 1994, 30–36.

60. Joseph Ratzinger, *Theological Highlights of Vatican II*, with introduction by Thomas P. Rausch, trans. Henry Traub, Gerard C. Thormann, and Werner Barzel (New York: Paulist Press, 1966), 232. We are not far from the recent encyclical letter of Pope Francis, "On Care for Our Common Home," *Laudato Si'* (May 24, 2015), http://w2.vatican.va/content/francesco/en/encyclicals/documents/papa-francesco_20150524_enciclica-laudato-si.html.

61. On the typically modern presentation of nature as it has been presented by modern feminism, see Michele M. Schumacher, "The 'Nature' of Nature in Feminism: From Dualism to Unity," in *Women in Christ: Towards a New Feminism*, ed. Michele M. Schumacher (Eerdmans: Grand Rapids, MI, 2004), 17–51.

62. John Paul II, *Crossing the Threshold of Hope*, 55. Similarly, Ratzinger referred in 1991 to the cultural tendency "to 'see through' things and to control them," a tendency that "essentially knows no limits" (*Turning Point for Europe?*, trans. Brian McNeil [San Francisco: Ignatius Press, 1994], 37).

63. John Paul II, *Evangelium Vitae*, no. 83. Cf. Pope Francis, *Laudato Si'*, no. 215.

64. John Paul II, *Veritatis Splendor*, no. 50 (original emphasis).

65. Ibid.

66. Ibid. no. 46. Similarly, Joseph Ratzinger observes that "gradually, even the most difficult object of nature—man—must become scientifically comprehensible, that is, subordinate to the knowledge of the natural sciences" (*Turning Point for Europe?*, 37).

67. Joseph Ratzinger, "The Problem of Threats to Human Life," 382.

68. Servais Pinckaers, *The Sources of Christian Ethics*, 3rd ed., trans. Mary Thomas Noble (Washington, DC: The Catholic University of America Press, 1995), 332. For the Catholic tradition following St. Thomas Aquinas, "the natural inclinations to goodness, happiness, being and truth were," Pinckaers explains, "the very source of freedom. They formed the will and intellect, whose union produced free will" (245).

69. Joseph Ratzinger, "The Problem of Threats to Human Life," 382.

70. Ibid. Cf. Servais Pinckaers, *The Sources of Christian Ethics*, esp. 240–53, 327–53; and Servais Pinckaers, *Morality: The Catholic View*, preface by Alasdair MacIntyre and trans. Michael Sherwin (South Bend, IN: St. Augustine's Press, 2001), 65–81.

71. John Paul II, *Veritatis Splendor*, no. 84.

72. Ibid. no. 4.

73. Ibid. no. 50. See also Karol Wojtyła, *Love and Responsibility*, trans. J. T. Willetts (San Francisco: Ignatius Press, 1993), 56–57. The Polish original was published in 1960.

74. John Paul II, *Veritatis Splendor*, no. 50. Similarly, he points out that natural law receives its name "not because it refers to the nature of irrational beings [so as to be identified with inclinations of a sub-rational nature], but because the reason which promulgates it is proper to human nature" (no. 42).

75. John Paul II, *Veritatis Splendor*, no. 8. Despite in fact the common tendency of interpreting the call of this particular Gospel scene as destined for those who have been chosen for the evangelical councils (see, for example, the *Catechism of the Catholic Church*, nos. 915–16, 918), this call is *"meant for everyone,"* John Paul II teaches (*Veritatis Splendor*, no. 18; emphasis his): not only because "every believer is called to be a follower of Christ (cf. Acts 6:1)" (no. 19), but also because it is "the new, specific form of the commandment of love of God" (no. 18). Similarly, the previous invitation to "go, sell your possessions and give the money to the poor" is said to "bring out the full meaning of the commandment of love for neighbour" (no. 19).

76. John Paul II, *Redemptoris Hominis*, no. 12.

77. John Paul II, *Veritatis Splendor*, no. 7.

78. Cf. ibid. no. 9.

79. Karol Wojtyła, *Love and Responsibility*, 136; cf. Servais Pinckaers, *L'Evangile et la morale* (Paris/Fribourg: Cerf/Editions Universitaires Fribourg, 1990), 168. "This," Wojtyła continues, "is what gives freedom its real entitlement to one of the highest places in the moral order, in the hierarchy of man's wholesome longings and desires" (*Love and Responsibility*, 135–36).

80. John Paul II, *Veritatis Splendor*, no. 50. Hence, for example, "In order to perfect himself in his specific order, the person must do good and avoid evil, be concerned for the transmission and preservation of life, refine and develop the riches of the material world, cultivate social life, seek truth, practice good and contemplate beauty" (no. 51).

81. Ibid. no. 43. Cf. St. Thomas Aquinas, *Summa theologiae*, I-II, q. 94.

82. This citation also occurs in the *Catechism of the Catholic Church*, no. 898. See also John Paul II, *Familaris Consortio*, no. 5.

83. Paul VI, *Humanae Vitae*, no. 1.

84. John Paul II, *Crossing the Threshold of Hope*, 190 (original emphasis). Cf. *DH* 1–3.

85. *"Is it true that the Church has come to a standstill and that the world is moving away from it?"* John Paul II asks. In reply, he argues that abandoning the truth about the human person "does not represent a step forward, and cannot be considered a measure of 'ethical progress'" (*Crossing the Threshold of Hope*, 173–74; emphasis his).

86. John Paul II, *Familiaris Consortio*, no. 5.

87. Such is what Georges Cottier signals as the confusion between the "normal" with the "normative." See Georges Cottier, *Défis éthiques* (Saint-Maurice: Éditions Saint-Augustin, 1996), 90ff. As a case in point, Todd A. Salzman and Michael G. Lawler maintain that for "people with a permanent homosexual orientation who do not choose that orientation ... a homosexual orientation *is* normative" (*The Sexual Person: Toward a Renewed Catholic Anthropology* [Washington, DC: Georgetown University Press, 2008], 108). "*Homosexual* and *heterosexual* are *further* specifications of *sexual* orientation, and this further specification constitutions what is normative for homosexual or heterosexual persons" (109).

88. John Paul II, *Familiaris Consortio*, no. 5. Pope Francis recently has reiterated this teaching in an address before the International Theological Commission. See http://www.catholicherald.co.uk/news/2013/12/09/sensus-fidelium-doesnt-mean-majority-opinion-francis-tells-theologians/.

89. See, for example, John Paul II, *Gratissimam Sane*, no. 11.

90. John Paul II, *Crossing the Threshold of Hope*, 173 (original emphasis). See also John Paul II, *Gratissimam Sane*, no. 12.

91. Paul VI, *Humanae Vitae*, no. 18. Similarly: "Since the Church did not make either of these laws, she cannot be their arbiter—only their guardian and interpreter.

It could never be right for her to declare lawful what is in fact unlawful, since that, by its very nature, is always opposed to the true good of man" (no. 18).

92. Salzman and Lawler, *The Sexual Person*, 263. For statistical reference, see George H. Gallup, Jr., *Religion in America 1996* (Princeton, NJ: Princeton Religion Research Center, 1996), 44. The authors point to a similar discord between doctrine and practice with regard to cohabitation before marriage.

93. Andrew Greeley, *The American Catholic: A Social Portrait* (New York: Basic Books, 1977), 149.

94. Ibid. 148.

95. Ibid. 131. Greeley goes on to argue that "if it had not been for the positive dynamic introduced by the Council, the deterioration analyzed in this chapter would have been even worse." Or, to put it more positively, "if the Vatican Council had been the sole force at work from 1963 to 1974, the proportion above the mean on Catholic activism would have risen seven points (from 45 to 52 percent)." In contrast, if "the encyclical *Humanae Vitae* had been the sole force, that same proportion would have declined twenty-one points (from 45 to 24 percent). What actually happened was that the two forces operated simultaneously. The larger negative force of the encyclical masked the smaller positive force of the Council, but the Council had the effect of attenuating the larger negative influence of the encyclical by about one-third" (139–41).

96. Ibid. 148.

97. See Andrew Greeley, "The Lay Reaction," in *The Church in Anguish: Has the Vatican Betrayed Vatican II?*, ed. Hans Küng and Leondard Swidler (San Francisco: Harper & Row, 1987), 284–88, at 285. The original German edition was published one year earlier: *Katholische Kirche—Wohin? Wider den Verrat am Konzil* (Munich: R. Piper GmbH & Co. KG, 1986). Already in the late 1960s, Greeley reported, "37 percent of the pill users were receiving monthly communion, as opposed to 18 percent of the rhythm users and 15 percent of the no birth control group" (*The American Catholic*, 142).

98. Andrew Greeley, "The Lay Reaction," 285.

99. "But the point is that the continued, persistent, and vehement proclamations of the Vatican had no effect at all on the attitudes of American Catholics" (ibid. 287). Cf. Uta Ranke-Heinemann, *Eunuchs for the Kingdom of Heaven: Women, Sexuality, and the Catholic Church* (New York: Doubleday, 1990), 297.

100. Andrew Greeley, "The Lay Reaction," 286.

101. Ibid. 287.

102. Margaret Farley, *Just Love: A Framework for Sexual Ethics* (New York: Continuum, 2006).

103. Lisa Cahill, "Vatican Dogma v Margaret Farley's Just Love," *theguardian.com*, June 18, 2012, http://www.theguardian.com/commentisfree/2012/jun/18/vatican-dogma-v-magaret-farley-just-love. Similarly, Richard J. Fehring and Elizabeth McGraw report that "Catholics constitute one of the largest groups of women who procure abortion, use contraception at a higher percentage than the general US population, and use sterilization as the number one method of contraception" ("Spiritual Responses to the Regulation of Birth (A Historical Comparison)," *Life and Learning* 12 [2002]: 265–86, at 281). See also Richard Fehring and Andrea Schlidt, "Trends in Contraceptive Use among Catholics in the United States: 1988–1995," *Linacre Quarterly* 68 (May 2001): 170–85; and Stanley K. Henshaw and Kathryn Kost, "Abortion Patients in 1994–1995: Characteristics and Contraceptive Use," *Family Planning Perspectives* 28, no. 4 (1996): 140–47, http://www.guttmacher.org/pubs/journals/2814096.pdf.

104. Andrew Greeley, "The Lay Reaction," 286.

105. Lisa Cahill, "Vatican Dogma v Margaret Farley's Just Love."

106. Charles E. Curran puts it frankly, when he notes that "people can make the decision to disagree in theory and in practice with church teaching and still consider themselves good, loyal Roman Catholics" ("Destructive Tensions in Moral Theology," in Küng and Swidler, *The Church in Anguish: Has the Vatican Betrayed Vatican II?*, 273–78, at 277).

107. Dietmar Mieth, "Moral Doctrine at the Cost of Morality? The Roman Documents of Recent Decades and the Lived Convictions of Christians," in Küng and Swidler, *The Church in Anguish: Has the Vatican Betrayed Vatican II?*, 125–43, at 125. See also Curran, "Destructive Tensions in Moral Theology," 277–78. To be sure, John Paul II was well aware of these criticisms; see his *Gratissiman Sane*, no. 12.

108. Andrew Greeley, "The Lay Reaction," 286.

109. Mieth maintains more specifically that in his doctrinal decisions (*Lehrentscheidungen*), Paul VI chose to "substitute" his "personal conscience" for the "responsibility of conscience" (*Gewissensverantwortung*) of married people. See Dietmar Mieth, "Geburtenregelung–bis 'Humanae vitae' (1968). Elemente der Lehrtradition," in *Lehramt und Sexualmoral*, ed. Peter Hünermann (Düsseldorf: Patmos, 1990), 27–47, at 46.

110. Fergus Kerr, *Twentieth-Century Theologians: From Neoscholasticism to Nuptial Mysticism* (Malden, MA and Oxford: Blackwell Publishing, 2007), 219.

111. Pope Paul VI, *Humanae Vitae*, no. 12.

112. Fergus Kerr, *Twentieth-Century Theologians*, 214.

113. Ibid. 216.

114. Ibid. 214. In the words of Paul VI in *Humanae Vitae*, "The Church, calling men back to the observance of the norms of the natural law, as interpreted by its constant doctrine, teaches that each and every marriage act [*quilibet matrimonii usus*] must remain open to the transmission of life. That teaching, often set forth by the magisterium, is founded upon the inseparable connection, willed by God and unable to be broken by man on his own initiative, between the two meanings of the conjugal act: the unitive meaning and the procreative meaning" (nos. 11–12). Cf. *Catechism of the Catholic Church*, nos. 2366, 2369, http://www.vatican.va/archive/ccc_css/archive/catechism/p3s2c2a6.htm.

115. See Richard A. McCormick, "'*Humanae Vitae*' 25 Years Later," *America*, July 17, 1993, http://americamagazine.org/issue/100/humanae-vitae-25-years-later.

116. Given the lifespan of sperm (five days) and the lifespan of the ovum (24 hours), pregnancy is only possible during the five days preceding ovulation (during which sperm might be kept alive in a woman's very clear mucus) and the actual day of ovulation, and doctors and scientists have become very precise in determining those days based on signs from a woman's body: her body temperature, the opening of her cervix, and the presence and character of her cervical mucus.

117. Notable is the Paul VI Institute in Omaha, NE, which has created the Creighton Model FertilityCare System and NaProTechnology. See their website at: http://www.popepaulvi.com/.

118. See Paul VI, *Humanae Vitae*, no. 24.

119. Such is the title she gives to the first chapter of her book, *Adam and Eve after the Pill: Paradoxes of the Sexual Revolution* (San Francisco: Ignatius Press, 2012). See also http://www.firstthings.com/article/2009/02/002-the-will-to-disbelieve.

120. Fehring and Schlidt, for example, report, "On a percent basis, more Catholic women are using some form of contraception than woman as a whole . . . in all age and

ethnic groups" ("Trends in Contraceptive Use among Catholics in the United States: 1988–1995," 172).

121. Judith D. Schwartz, "How Birth Control Has Changed Women's Sexuality," *Glamour* March 1993, 236.

122. Angela Franks has good reason to argue that the popular notion of "free choice in reproduction extends only one way, namely, to the choice against children" ("The Gift of Female Fertility: Church Teaching on Contraception," in *Women, Sex, and the Church: A Case for Catholic Teaching*, ed. Erika Bachiochi [Boston: Pauline Books and Media, 2010], 97–119, at 101).

123. Franks fittingly sums up the conviction of many sadly misled women when she writes, "I am imprisoned by my body, especially by my fertility, and I need to control it, bend it to my will, in order to be free" (ibid. 105).

124. "The Birth Control Report. III: The Argument for Reform," *The Tablet*, May 6, 1967, 510–13, at 512, http://archive.thetablet.co.uk/article/6th-may-1967/22/the-birth-control-report. Also published in Latin by Jean-Marie Paupert, ed., *Contrôle des naissance et théologie* (Paris: éditions du Seuil, 1967), 156–62. This "report" is, in fact, a rebuttal to the so-called "minority" report cited below (under the title: "The Birth Control Report. II: The Conservative Case").

125. The reports were, as Michael Waldstein reports, "intentionally leaked to the press." See his introduction to *Man and Woman He Created Them: A Theology of the Body*, by John Paul II, trans. Michael Waldstein (Boston: Pauline Books & Media, 2006), 100. For more information on the report and its context within the controversy surrounding *Humanae Vitae*, see George Wiegel, *Witness to Hope*, 206–10; Janet E. Smith, *Humanae Vitae: A Generation Later* (Washington, DC: The Catholic University of America Press, 1991), 11–35; and Richard J. Fehring, and Elizabeth McGraw, "Spiritual Responses to the Regulation of Birth (A Historical Comparison)," *Life and Learning* 12 (2002): 265–86, http://uffl.org/vol12/fehring12.pdf. The original "majority" report was "Birth Control Report. I: The Majority View," *The Tablet*, April 22, 1967, 449–55, at 449, http://archive.thetablet.co.uk/article/22nd-april-1967/21/the-birth-control-report. The report was also published under the title "Majority Papal Commission Report," in *The Catholic Case for Contraception*, ed. Daniel Callahan (London: The Macmillan Company/Collier-Macmillan Limited, 1969), 149–73 (credit is given there to the *National Catholic Reporter*, April 19, 1967); and in Latin by Paupert, *Contrôle des naissance et théologie*, 179–89. See also the so-called "final report to the pope," dated May 26, 1966: "The Papal Commission on Birth Control," *The Tablet*, September 21, 1968, 947–51, http://archive.thetablet.co.uk/article/21st-september-1968/21/the-papal-commission-on-birth-control.

126. "The Birth Control Report. II: The Conservative Case," *The Tablet*, April 29, 1967, 478–85, at 482, http://archive.thetablet.co.uk/article/29th-april-1967/22/the-birth-control-report-ii-the-conservative-case-. Also published, under the title "Minority Papal Commission Report," in Callahan, *The Catholic Case for Contraception*, 174–211, here at 194 (credit here is given to the *National Catholic Reporter*, April 19, 1967). The Latin text is available in Paupert, *Contrôle des naissance et théologie*, 163–78.

127. "The Birth Control Report. II: The Conservative Case," 482.

128. John Paul II, *Veritatis Splendor*, no. 46.

129. "The Birth Control Report, III: The Argument for Reform," 511. Cf. Paul VI, *Humanae Vitae*, no. 16.

130. "The Birth Control Report, III: The Argument for Reform," 512. Similarly, he feels himself free, as the Minority Papal Commission summarized the argument of its opponents, to "frustrate his own biological, sexual function, even, when voluntarily

aroused, because it is subject to reason for the bettering of the human condition" ("The Birth Control Report. II: The Conservative Case," 483) ("Minority Papal Commission Report," 200).

131. "The Birth Control Report. II: The Conservative Case," 483 ("Minority Papal Commission Report," 201).

132. Paul VI, *Humanae Vitae*, no. 18.

133. John Paul II, General Audience of November 28, 1984, in *Man and Woman He Created Them*, 663.

134. Cf. John Paul II, *Gratissimam Sane*, no. 13; *Christifideles Laici*, no. 5.

135. John Paul II, General Audience of November 28, 1984, in *Man and Woman He Created Them*, 662. Hence, the Church's promotion of "responsible parenthood," or "the morally right regulation of fertility" was to be understood in light of the precise question, "*What is the true good of human persons and what corresponds to the true dignity of the person?*" (John Paul II, General Audience of September 5, 1984, in *Man and Woman He Created Them*, 637 [original emphasis]).

136. John Paul II, General Audience of November 28, 1984, in *Man and Woman He Created Them*, 662.

137. John Paul II, *Familiaris Consortio*, no. 8; cf. *GS* 15.

138. John Paul II, General Audience of August 22, 1984, in *Man and Woman He Created Them*, 630–31.

139. John Paul II, General Audience of August 29, 1984, in *Man and Woman He Created Them*, 635 (original emphasis). He explains more specifically, "Although the 'periodic' character of continence is . . . applied to the so-called 'natural rhythms' (*HV* 16), still, *continence* itself is a definite and permanent moral attitude, *it is a virtue*, and thus the whole mode of behavior guided by it becomes virtuous" (635).

140. "Among all the reasons," given by the majority commission, "for the moral legitimacy of contraception, the *foremost* reason, the reason that is *most of all* ('*maxime*') a reason," Michael Waldstein explains, "is not the population explosion, not a personalist understanding of sexual intercourse, but the duty of humanizing nature. Humanizing is achieved," as the report put it, "through 'tremendous progress in the control of matter by technical means' " (Waldstein, introduction to *Man and Woman He Created Them*, by John Paul II, 101). See "The Birth Control Report. III: The Argument for Reform," 511. This vision accords with that of Francis Bacon, who recognized the idea of a teleological conception of nature—one in which nature is understood as ordered at the outset to certain ends that define it as such—as being "as sterile as a virgin consecrated to God, who produces nothing" ("*sterilis et tamquam virgo Deo consecrate, quae nihil parit*") (Francis Bacon, *De dignitate et augmentis scientiarum* III, 5. In, *The Works of Lord Bacon*, vol. 2 [London: Wiliam Ball, 1984], 340). On the Baconian project of manipulating nature according to the human will, see Waldstein, introduction, 36–44; and Michael Allen Gillepsie, *The Theological Origins of Modernity* (Chicago: University of Chicago Press, 2008), 37–42. The central question of modernity, as Gillepsie understands it, is more specifically the problematic relation between human freedom and natural necessity. See, for example, ibid. 262–63. Still more generally, see Louis Dupré, *Passage to Modernity: An Essay in the Hermeneutics of Nature and Culture* (New Haven and London: Yale University Press, 1993).

141. Lisa Sowle Cahill, *Sex, Gender and Christian Ethics*, 204.

142. Ranke-Heinemann, *Eunuchs for the Kingdom of Heaven*, 296; see also chap. 10, "Lay People into Monks."

143. Ibid. 297.

144. Josef Pieper, *The Four Cardinal Virtues* (Notre Dame, IN: Notre Dame University Press, 166), 154; cf. Aquinas, *ST* II-II, q. 142, a. 1; q. 152, a. 2, ad. 2; q. 153, a. 3, ad. 3.

145. Cf. Benedict XVI, *Deus Caritas Est*, no. 3.

146. Aquinas, *ST* II-II, q. 142, a. 1.

147. Ibid. q. 153, a. 2.

148. Ibid. ad. 2.

149. Michel Labourdette, *Cours de théologie morale* (Plans sur Bex: Parole et Silence, 2012), 2:904.

150. Lisa Sowle Cahill, *Sex, Gender and Christian Ethics* (Cambridge and New York: Cambridge University Press, 1996), 204.

151. Labourdette, *Cours de théologie morale*, 2:905. Cf. Aquinas, *ST* II-II, q. 142, a. 1.

152. Michel Labourdette, *Cours de théologie morale*, 2:944 (original emphasis).

153. See "The Birth Control Report. III: The Argument for Reform," 512. It is perhaps important to note, as is mentioned in the foreword to his *Cours de théologie morale*, II, that he finished writing his course in the 1980s.

154. On the contrary, he has good reason to argue, "If nature itself has determined that the great majority of its acts [approximately one in two-hundred, he specifies] cannot be fecund, one cannot hold that the nature of each one [act] is to be fertile, nor to be ordained directly [*prochainement*] to fertility. There is, *for nature itself*, an intermediary justifying end" (Labourdette, *Cours de théologie morale*, 2:944) namely that of conjugal unity. "The problem, then," as far as Labourdette is concerned, "is that of the two-hundredth coitus. Should it be left entirely to chance?" he asks (943).

155. Pieper enumerates three implications of the "order of reason" in the sexual domain: "First, that the immanent purpose of sexual power be not perverted but fulfilled (in marriage, with its threefold 'good'); second, that the inner structure of the moral person be kept intact; and, third, that justice between men be not infringed" (*Four Cardinal Virtues*, 158).

156. Aquinas, *ST* II-II, q. 151, a. 1.

157. Ibid. *ST* II-II, q. 153, a. 2, ad. 2.

158. See ibid. q. 153, a. 5, ad. 1; q. 15, a. 3; q. 53, a. 6, ad. 2; q. 180, a. 2, ad. 3; q. 155, a. 1, ad. 2.

159. Hence it is "not contrary to virtue, if the act of reason be sometimes interrupted for something that is done in accordance with reason," as in the case, Thomas reasons, of one seeking sleep (ibid. q. 153, a. 2, ad. 2).

160. Pieper, *Four Cardinal Virtues*, 159–60.

161. See ibid. 160.

162. Aquinas, *ST* II-II, q. 123, a. 12 (emphasis added).

163. Cf. Pieper, *The Four Cardinal Virtues*, 158.

164. Aquinas, *ST* II-II, q. 142, a. 1.

165. Ibid. q. 153, a. 2.

166. Benedict XVI, *Deus Caritas Est*, no. 4.

167. Ibid. no. 6.

168. Mieth, "Moral Doctrine at the Cost of Morality?," 127.

169. Joseph Ratzinger, *A Turning Point for Europe*, 34. In short, morality has lost, Ratzinger observes, "its evidential character" (33).

170. Ranke-Heinemann, *Eunuchs for the Kingdom of Heaven*, 297.

171. Ibid. 135.

172. Mieth, "Moral Doctrine at the Cost of Morality?," 142.

173. Ibid. 135.

174. Ibid. 142. Mieth admits that the magisterial teaching of John Paul II presented a "personal understanding of nature" (132).

175. John Paul II, General Audience of October 29, 1980, in *Man and Woman He Created Them*, 313.

176. Mieth, "Moral Doctrine at the Cost of Morality," 142 (original emphasis).

177. John Paul II, *Veritatis Splendor*, no. 4.

178. Ibid. no. 19 (original emphasis).

179. Pope Francis, *Evangelii Gaudium*, no. 39.

180. See *AA* 4; *LG* 36; and the *Catechism of the Catholic Church*, no. 912.

181. See Cathleen Kaveny, "The Big Chill: *Humanae Vitae* Dissenters Need to Find Voice," *Commonweal*, October 10, 2013, https://www.commonwealmagazine.org/big-chill.

182. John Paul II, *Christifideles Laici*, no. 59. Cf. Pope Francis, *Evangelii Gaudium*, no. 180.

183. *The Catechism of the Catholic Church*, no. 1069, http://www.vatican.va/archive/ccc_css/archive/catechism/p2.htm.

184. John Paul II, *Evangelium Vitae*, no. 93 (original emphasis). On the liturgical dimension of conjugal life and of the "language of the body" in marriage, see John Paul II, *Man and Woman He Created Them*, 610–15.

10

Ad Gentes

Ralph Martin

The Purpose of the Council

The overall purpose of Vatican II as expressed by the Council itself and post-conciliar popes could be stated as "renewal for the sake of evangelization":

> Although by the power of the Holy Spirit the Church will remain the faithful spouse of her Lord and will never cease to be the sign of salvation on earth, still she is very well aware that among her members, both clerical and lay, some have been unfaithful to the Spirit of God during the course of many centuries. ... Led by the Holy Spirit, Mother Church unceasingly exhorts her sons to purify and renew themselves so that the sign of Christ can shine more brightly on the face of the Church. (*Gaudium et Spes*, no. 43)[1]

When Pope John XXIII stated the reasons for convoking Vatican II, he made it clear that his hope was that the work of the Council would result in an *"aggiornamento"* that would enable the Church to communicate the Gospel more effectively to the modern world. The post-Vatican II popes have shared this understanding of the desired outcome of the Council.

Pope Paul VI issued his influential Apostolic Exhortation, *Evangelii Nuntiandi* (On Evangelization in the Modern World) "on this tenth anniversary of the closing of the Second Vatican Council, the objectives of which are definitely summed up in this single one: to make the Church of the twentieth century ever better fitted for proclaiming the Gospel to the people of the twentieth century."[2] Paul VI hoped that this document would help provide "a fresh forward impulse, capable of creating within a Church still more firmly rooted in the undying power and strength of Pentecost a new period of evangelization."[3]

Pope John Paul II chose the occasion of the twenty-fifth anniversary of the conclusion of the Second Vatican Council, in 1990, to issue the most important recent magisterial document on evangelization, the encyclical *Redemptoris Missio* (Mission of the Redeemer), a document that draws liberally from the insights that Paul VI articulated in *Evangelii Nuntiandi*. In this important encyclical the Pope made it clear that this "new evangelization" has its roots in the documents of the Second Vatican Council:

> The Second Vatican Council sought to renew the Church's life and activity in the light of the needs of the contemporary world. The Council emphasized the Church's "missionary nature." ... Twenty-five years after the conclusion of the Council and the publication of the Decree on Missionary Activity *Ad Gentes*, fifteen years after the Apostolic Exhortation *Evangelii Nuntiandi* issued by Pope Paul VI, and in continuity with the magisterial teaching of my predecessors, I wish to invite the Church to renew her missionary commitment.[4]

In the document intended to orient the Church as she entered the third millennium, *Novo Millennio Ineunte* (At the Beginning of a New Millennium), John Paul II again repeated his understanding of the twofold purpose of the Council:

> From the beginning of my pontificate, my thoughts had been on this Holy Year 2000 as an important appointment. I thought of its celebration as a providential opportunity during which the Church, thirty-five years after the Second Vatican Ecumenical Council, would examine how far she had renewed herself in order to be able to take up her evangelizing mission with fresh enthusiasm.[5]

Ad Gentes

Ad Gentes Divinitus (The Decree on the Church's Missionary Activity)[6] was intended, in the overall evangelization optic of Vatican II, to reinforce and inspire the ongoing traditional missionary activity of the Church, construed as bringing the Gospel and planting the Church in regions where the Gospel may not have been preached nor the Church established to the point of self-sufficiency. While not being among the most intensely debated and controversial texts of Vatican II (unlike the debates over collegiality and papal primacy that took place in connection with *Lumen Gentium* [Constitution on the Church], or those in connection with *Dignitatis Humanae* [Declaration on Religious Liberty], or those in connection with *Nostra Aetate* [Declaration on the Relations of the Church to Non-Christian Religions]), neither was it one that "sailed through" such as *Inter Mirifica* (Decree on the Means of Social Communication) or *Gravissimus Educationis* (Declaration on Christian Education).[7] Despite its rocky journey, it ended up being approved by the biggest majority of any Council document with 2,394 yes votes and only 5 no votes.[8]

Initial drafts were criticized for not taking more fully into account the mission theology of *LG*, which broadened the conception of mission from the "missions" to mission as a constituent part of the Church's identity and the responsibility of all the baptized. When time was running out and a revised text was not yet in view, the proposal was made to simply settle for a list of propositions and not a full-fledged document. The proposal was rejected and a group of distinguished theologians, including Yves Congar and Joseph Ratzinger, worked to produce the final draft that was overwhelmingly accepted.

The final text incorporated the broader understanding of mission articulated in *LG*—all of us are called to mission by virtue of baptism—as well as strongly affirming the continuing importance of traditional missionary work. Some of the significant theological foundations that *AG* articulated for the mission of the Church were that the mission flowed from the Trinity itself and was essential to the Church's nature, and that all the baptized were called, simply by virtue of baptism, to participate in the mission. Thus an important distinction was made between the traditional missionary work of the Church (missions) and the fundamental mission of the Church itself and all the baptized. Both are strongly affirmed in the document:

> Having been divinely sent to the nations that she might be "the universal sacrament of salvation" (*LG* 48), the Church, in obedience to the command of her founder (Mt 16:15) and because it is demanded by her own essential universality, strives to preach the Gospel to all men. (*AG* 1)

> The Church on earth is by its very nature missionary since, according to the plan of the Father, it has its origin in the mission of the Son and the Holy Spirit (*LG* 1). (*AG* 2)

> The special undertakings in which preachers of the Gospel, sent by the Church, and going into the whole world carry out the work of preaching the Gospel and implanting the Church among people who do not yet believe in Christ are generally called "missions." (*AG* 13)

The primary means by which the mission is carried out, affirmed numerous times in *AG*, is by the preaching of the Gospel. The goal of this preaching is to lead people to the sure salvation found in Christ and the Church. What can we say of the reception of this missionary decree in terms of its effectiveness in deepening the missionary impulse of the Church?[9]

What Actually Happened? Its Reception

In the immediate aftermath of Vatican II, rather than seeing the missionary work of the Church invigorated, a rather calamitous collapse took place.

Theological currents that had already been present before and during the Council, which questioned the value of traditional missionary work, grew in strength, despite the strong affirmations of AG and LG. Magisterial responses to this doctrinal confusion consisted primarily in reaffirming the command that Jesus gave us to evangelize and describing in sometimes eloquent ways, how Jesus fulfills the human person. Despite regular mentions of "salvation," the teaching of Vatican II that it is possible to be saved without hearing the Gospel or explicitly joining the Church (LG 16; AG 7; GS 22), raised a cloud of doubt about the urgency of evangelization, which magisterial attempts to deal with the confusion did little to effectively address.[10]

The era of colonialism was quickly drawing to an end, and severe critiques of the entwining of missionary work with colonialism impacted many missionaries and shook their confidence. Theological theories that argued for the possibility of people being saved without hearing the Gospel grew in popularity and ubiquity. Possibility very quickly morphed into probability and then virtual certainty. Affirmations of the need to respect the values of existing cultures and the discovery and affirmation of the "seeds of truth" that already existed in them took the focus off the enduring need for conversion. The positive statements about the Jewish religion in Vatican II ushered in an intense time of dialogue that explored common values, attempted to definitively put an end to anti-Semitism in Catholic theology and life, and sometimes issued in claims that the Jews were no longer called to conversion to Christ but had a "separate covenant" that was sufficiently salvific. There seemed to be an extreme reluctance to directly say that all human beings are called to conversion to Christ, including his own people, which further allowed doubt to grow.[11] And the rise of "liberation theology" called for an emphasis on "development" and improving the political and economic situation and structures of peoples in a way that led many to neglect the fundamental mission of the Church of direct evangelization ordered toward faith, repentance, and conversion.[12]

As Stephen Bevans notes, despite the frequent magisterial calls for the central role that proclamation should have in the mission of the Church, there is a great reluctance to accept this among many missionaries. Questions about the salvific value of other religions, concerns about "imposing" Western culture, theological speculation about how possible salvation is without hearing the Gospel, have all contributed to what Bevans notes is "much hesitation among missionaries and mission theologians about such a central role [for proclamation]."[13] Bevans points out that for the first few years after Vatican II the numbers of missionaries continued to rise, but after 1968 a steady and often precipitous decline set in that has still not been reversed:[14]

> Gone was any certainty of the superiority of the more firmly established "sending churches," and gone was the certainty of the superiority of Western culture. ... And, perhaps more radically, with Vatican II's acknowledgement of the possibility of salvation outside of explicit faith in Christ and membership in the Church (LG 16 and 9; NA 2; AG 9 and 11), many Catholics—including missionaries—no longer

saw missionary activity as an urgent need. If people could be saved by following their own consciences in the context of their own religions, why try to convert them?[15]

The collapse of missionary work, though, was part of a larger collapse that saw tens of thousands priests and nuns abandoning their vocations amid increasingly radical proposals for continuing change in the moral, doctrinal, and disciplinary beliefs and practices of the Church. Some of the theologians who played a major role as theological advisors during Vatican II were quite public in their opinions that Vatican II did not go far enough and that further change was necessary. Conferences with the theme of "Toward Vatican III" were held by esteemed Catholic institutions. Pope Paul VI's decision to uphold the traditional Catholic teaching on the immorality of contraception in 1968 was met by open rebellion by priests and only lukewarm "pro forma" support by many Bishops, further encouraging the lay-faithful to pick and choose from among the Church's teachings what "in conscience" they felt good about.

Besides the confusion within the Church and the apparent inability of many in Church leadership to discern what was in harmony with Church teaching and what was not,[16] or the inability to make the hard decisions that public opinion would not react kindly to, there was the upheaval in the wider culture. 1968 is often noted by cultural historians as a major turning point in the rejection of tradition and authority in the culture at large, with the student riots and anti-war demonstrations, the assassination of Martin Luther King and the preceding assassination of John F. Kennedy, and a musical and drug culture that celebrated what traditionally had been seen as immoral behavior. The youth culture's turn against traditional Christian values—symbolized and epitomized by the "sexual revolution"—gathered force over the years and eventually influenced the whole culture.

During John Paul II's pontificate, Cardinal Joseph Ratzinger described the actual situation in rather stark terms, using the biblically resonant phrase "mass apostasy":

> We are witnessing a sort of mass apostasy; the number of baptized persons is decreasing drastically.... And an undeniable advance of secularism, as we have already pointed out, is also ascertainable, with different features, in the United States. In short, in the Western world the almost complete identity that once existed between European and American culture and Christian culture is dissolving. All this is true. And the number of people in the West who feel that they are really members of the Church will decline further in the near future. We do not know what might happen in fifty years time—such futurology remains impossible—but for the near future we see the process of secularization continuing; we see the faith diminishing; we see the separation between the commonly accepted culture and Christian faith and culture.[17]

We will now consider the papal response to this missionary collapse. The post-conciliar magisterial documents on evangelization provide not only an authoritative witness to the lack of reception of *AG* but also authoritative diagnoses of the theological currents undermining evangelization and serious, though largely ineffective, attempts to respond to the confusion.

The Papal Response to the Missionary Collapse

Pope Paul VI: Evangelii Nuntiandi

Regarding the situation prior to the 1974 Synod on Evangelization, Francis Cardinal George provides a helpful summary:

> Taken out of the context of faith, valid questions spawned ideologies that destroyed mission, as missionaries and missiologists sometimes substituted a radical commitment to the world for the commitment of faith. In trying to rethink mission in the modern world, some opted to do so on the world's terms by emptying proclamation of its content and making missiology almost a secular science. With that development went a rejection of *Ad gentes* in practice and often in theory.[18]

After the Synod, in an attempt to respond to the undermining of evangelization in general and traditional missionary work in particular, Pope Paul VI in 1975 published his enduringly helpful Apostolic Exhortation, *Evangelii Nuntiandi*. Subsequent popes, including Pope Francis, cite it frequently. In the document the Pope strongly reaffirmed the traditional importance of missionary work and the wider emphasis of Vatican II that all of us are called to mission. Pope Paul VI directly addressed some of the major sources of confusion that he identified as weakening the missionary zeal of the Church. He writes to encourage the brethren "in their mission as evangelizers, in order that, in this time of uncertainty and confusion, they may accomplish this task with ever increasing love, zeal and joy" (*EN* 1). He asks, "In our day, what has happened to that hidden energy of the Good News ... to what extent and in what way is that evangelical force capable of really transforming the people of this century ... does the Church or does she not ... after the Council and because of the Council ... find herself better equipped to proclaim the Gospel and to put it into people's hearts with conviction, freedom of spirit and effectiveness?" (*EN* 4).

The implicit answer to these questions is "no," and Paul VI devotes the rest of his Apostolic Exhortation to addressing what he thinks are the causes that have made the post-conciliar period a time of waning zeal and evangelization, a time of "uncertainty and confusion." He addresses both doctrinal and spiritual factors and has strong and clear words as he addresses them.

In addressing the strong influence of liberation theology, he asserts that Christian liberation is indeed liberation "from everything that oppresses man but which is above all liberation from sin and the Evil one" (*EN* 9). In addressing those who claim that a silent witness is all that is necessary, he affirms, "There can be no true evangelization if the name, the teaching, the life, the promises, the kingdom and the mystery of Jesus of Nazareth the Son of God are not proclaimed" (*EN* 22). In addressing those who say that salvation is equally possible in any religion, he makes the strong assertion, to be developed later in some theological depth in *Dominus Iesus*, that

> neither respect and esteem for these religions nor the complexity of the questions raised is an invitation to the Church to withhold from these non-Christians the proclamation of Jesus Christ.... Our religion effectively establishes with God an authentic and living relationship which the other religions do not succeed in doing, even though they have, as it were, their arms stretched out towards heaven.... Let us state this fact with joy at a time when there are not lacking those who think and even say that ardor and the apostolic spirit are exhausted, and that the time of the missions is now past. (*EN* 53)

In commenting on the lack of fervor when it came to evangelization, Paul VI traces this in part to two misconceptions. One misconception, he says, is that to proclaim the Gospel is to impose truth on people. This misconception was later addressed at length in the *Doctrinal Note on Some Aspects of Evangelization*, but which was addressed directly in 1975 by Paul VI as well, who distinguishes proposing the Gospel from imposing the Gospel. This distinction has been taken up and repeated by each succeeding pope.

The second misconception expresses itself like this: "Why proclaim the Gospel when the whole world is saved by uprightness of heart? We know likewise that the world and history are filled with 'seeds of the Word'; is it not therefore an illusion to claim to bring the Gospel where it already exists in the seeds that the Lord Himself has sown?" (*EN* 80). To this, Paul VI responds, "God can accomplish this salvation in whomsoever He wishes by ways which He alone knows [*AG* 7] ... even though we do not preach the Gospel to them; but as for us, can we gain salvation if through negligence or fear or shame—what St. Paul called 'blushing for the Gospel' (Rom 1:16)—or as a result of false ideas, we fail to preach it?" (*EN* 80).

With little exaggeration it has been said that according to *EN* the only class of people certainly not saved are Catholics who fail to preach the Gospel!

While Paul VI's words are quite striking, since he does not convincingly make a case for why evangelization is necessary if people can be saved without hearing the Gospel, the rhetorical threat of Catholics not being saved if they do not evangelize seems to have made little impact. We will need to return to what the Council actually teaches about the possibility of being saved without hearing the Gospel, as I believe this is "the" issue that needs to be clarified if evangelization is to flourish. I will attempt to show that the answer to the confusion that has persistently undermined evangelization lies in a careful reading of Vatican II, particularly the last three sentences of *LG* 16, which have virtually been ignored.

John Paul II: Redemptoris Missio

The papal efforts to reestablish conviction about the need for evangelization and recover the teaching of *AG* took a further major step with the publication of *Redemptoris Missio* (Mission of the Redeemer), the encyclical of John Paul II. He purposely published it on the twenty-fifth anniversary of the closing of Vatican II and the promulgation of *AG*, and the fifteenth anniversary of *EN*, to underline its continuity with the conciliar and previous post-conciliar papal teaching on evangelization.[19] As an encyclical it remains the most authoritative post-conciliar document on mission. Pope Francis's inspiring document on evangelization, *Gaudium Evangelii* (Joy of the Gospel), which does not primarily address doctrinal confusion or the post-Vatican II missionary collapse, is an Apostolic Exhortation.

Pope John Paul opens the encyclical with a summary of the purpose of Vatican II as regards mission:

> The Second Vatican Council sought to renew the Church's life and activity in the light of the needs of the contemporary world. The Council emphasized the Church's "missionary nature," basing it in a dynamic way on the Trinitarian mission itself. The missionary thrust therefore belongs to the very nature of the Christian life. (*RM* 1)

But then the Pope immediately addresses the fact that rather than seeing a post-Vatican II resurgence of missionary activity, just the opposite has occurred:

> Nevertheless, in this "new springtime" of Christianity there is an undeniable negative tendency, and the present document is meant to help overcome it. Missionary activity specifically directed "to the nations" [*ad gentes*] appears to be waning.... Difficulties both internal and external have weakened the Church's missionary thrust towards non-Christians, a fact which must arouse concern among all who believe in Christ. For in the Church's history, missionary drive has always been a sign of vitality, just as its lessening is a sign of a crisis of faith.... I also have other reasons and aims: to respond to the many requests for a document of this kind; to clear up doubts and ambiguities regarding missionary activity *ad gentes*, and to confirm in their commitment those exemplary brothers and sisters dedicated to missionary activity and all those who assist them. (*RM* 2)

This diagnosis is a very grave one even though it is stated in serene tones. What can be a more serious problem for the Church to confront than a crisis of faith? The Pope then identifies certain theological theories, which he believes are undermining motivation to evangelize:

> Some people wonder: Is missionary work among non-Christians still relevant? Has it not been replaced by inter-religious dialogue? Is not human development an adequate goal for the Church's mission? Does not respect for conscience and for freedom exclude all efforts at conversion? Is it not possible to attain salvation in any religion? Why then should there be missionary activity? (RM 4)

Remarkably, fifteen years after Pope Paul VI attempted to address the same theological questions, the same questions persist, and John Paul II addressed them once again.

His responses to them are along the same lines of Paul VI's responses, although at greater length, with more detailed theological argumentation.[20] He reaffirmed the uniqueness of Christ's identity and role in the redemption of the world (RM 5); rejected theological currents that would separate the message from the messenger, Christ from the Spirit's work, the Kingdom from the Church, or the Logos from the person of Jesus—all major themes in contemporary theology (RM 13–19). He stated once again that the Church is not imposing when it carries out missionary work or violating human freedom, but rather proposing (RM 8), and he made clear that the Kingdom cannot be reduced to simply temporal improvements (RM 20). He reaffirmed that indeed it is possible for people to be saved, who, through no fault of their own, have not heard the Gospel but have come into a mysterious contact with Christ's redemptive work through the power of the Holy Spirit and respond to it positively (RM 9–10).

John Paul then asked the question:

> God offers mankind this newness of life, "Can one reject Christ and everything that he has brought about in the history of mankind?" Of course one can. Man is free. He can say "no" to God. He can say "no" to Christ. But the fundamental question remains: Is it legitimate to do this? And what would make it legitimate? (RM 7)

Notably, there is no clear statement of the consequences of saying "no" to God or to Christ. And yet this is a key element of the preaching of Jesus and the Apostles.[21] This silence on the consequences of not responding positively to the Gospel is generally characteristic of the post-conciliar efforts to clear up theological confusion pertaining to mission. It is a continuation of the conciliar strategy of emphasizing the positive and winning people by a positive presentation of the beauty of the faith and the goodness of life in Christ. I think we must say that up until now the strategy does not seem to be successful.

After John Paul II addresses the main theological confusions, he sums up the reasons for carrying out mission:

> To the question, "why mission?" we reply with the Church's faith and experience that true liberation consists in opening oneself to the love of Christ. In him, and only in him, are we set free from all alienation

and doubt, from slavery to the power of sin and death.... Why mission? Because to us, as to St. Paul, "this grace was given, to preach to the Gentiles the unsearchable riches of Christ" (Eph. 3:8). (*RM* 11)

This is a very rich encyclical, and we have only highlighted the theological obstacles that John Paul II identifies as undermining the purpose of Vatican II and *AG*, and indicated the lines of his responses. Other features of the encyclical that we can only note as enduringly important are his basic definition of "new evangelization" as contrasted to mission *ad gentes* and ordinary pastoral care (*RM* 33); his challenging definition of the purpose of evangelization, namely, conversion and discipleship (*RM* 46); his extended theological explication of the work of the Holy Spirit, and his frequent comments on the apostolic preaching and the experience of the early church as recounted in the Acts of the Apostles (*RM*, chapter 2); and his very important treatment of "missionary spirituality," where he brings out the importance of the contemplative and charismatic dimensions of the Spirit's working in the apostles and the early church and its relevance for mission today (*RM*, chapter 8).

Dominus Iesus

Ten years after *RM* and thirty-five years after the Council and *AG*, the Congregation for the Doctrine of the Faith published *Dominus Iesus* (*DI*) (On the Unicity and Salvific Universality of Jesus Christ and the Church) on August 6, 2000—the Feast of the Transfiguration and the anniversary of the death of Blessed Pope Paul VI. It was a document intended to deal definitively with an issue that the Council and previous popes thought had already been dealt with.

As Cardinal George puts it in his commentary on *AG*,

> It all seems clear enough. Yet the crisis in mission and in interreligious dialogue occasioned another document, *Dominus Iesus*, which repeats what the council had already said clearly in *Ad gentes*, namely, Christianity's claim to absolute validity.[22]

The main purpose of the document was to directly address the theological currents that relativize Christ and the Church and undermine mission, currents that despite the previous magisterial efforts to address them had grown in strength and ubiquity even in Pontifical Universities. These currents that had already been addressed by Paul VI in *EN* and John Paul II in *RM* now were to receive what was intended to be a definitive theological refutation.

DI repeats the positive affirmations about the world religions found in Vatican II, affirms the importance of continuing inter-religious dialogue, but strongly reaffirms the necessity of evangelization:

> Equality, which is a presupposition of inter-religious dialogue, refers to the equal personal dignity of the parties in dialogue, not to doctrinal

content, nor even less to the position of Jesus Christ—who is God himself made man—in relation to the founders of the other religions. Indeed, the Church, guided by charity and respect for freedom, must be primarily committed to proclaiming to all people the truth definitively revealed by the Lord, and to announcing the necessity of conversion to Jesus Christ and of adherence to the Church through Baptism and the other sacraments, in order to participate fully in communion with God the Father, Son and Holy Spirit. (*DI* 22)

And *DI* clearly identifies the relativistic theories that threaten mission:

The Church's constant missionary proclamation is endangered today by relativistic theories which seek to justify religious pluralism, not only *de facto* but also *de jure* (or in principle). As a consequence, it is held that certain truths have been superseded: for example, the definitive and complete character of the revelation of Jesus Christ, the nature of Christian faith as compared with that of belief in other religions, the inspired nature of the books of Sacred Scripture, the personal unity between the Eternal Word and Jesus of Nazareth, the unity of the economy of the incarnate Word and the Holy Spirit, the unicity and salvific universality of the mystery of Jesus Christ, the universal salvific mediation of the Church, the inseparability—while recognizing the distinction—of the kingdom of God, the kingdom of Christ and the Church, and the subsistence of the one Church of Christ in the Catholic Church. (*DI* 4)

While recognizing the limits of human language to encompass the mystery of God, *DI* strongly affirms that a full, adequate, and totally reliable revelation is really communicated to us in the words and deeds of Jesus, since they have the Divine person as their subject. (*DI* 6)

Perhaps the clearest statement of both the positive value yet radical limitations of non-Christian religions is contained in *DI* 7, which begins by quoting the *Catechism*:

"Faith is first of all a personal adherence of man to God. At the same time, and inseparably, it is a free assent to the whole truth that God has revealed." (Catechism of the Catholic Church [*CCC* 150]) Faith therefore, as "a gift of God" and as "a supernatural virtue infused by him" (*CCC* 153), involves a dual adherence: to God who reveals and to the truth which he reveals out of the trust which we have in him who speaks.... For this reason, the distinction between theological faith and belief, in the other religions, must be firmly held. If faith is the acceptance in grace of revealed truth, which "makes it possible to penetrate the mystery in a way that allows us to understand it coherently" (John Paul II, Encyclical Letter *Fides et Ratio*, 13), then belief in the other religions, is that sum of experience and thought that constitutes the human treasury of wisdom

and religious aspiration, which man in his search for truth has conceived and acted upon in his relationship to God and the Absolute
(*Fides et Ratio*, 31–32).

Another significant statement is found in *DI* 22:

> If it is true that the followers of other religions can receive divine
> grace, it is also certain that objectively speaking they are in a gravely
> deficient situation in comparison with those who, in the Church, have
> the fullness of the means of salvation (Pius XII, *Mystici Corporis, DS*
> 3821).

At the same time, *DI* generously acknowledges the work of the Holy Spirit
in individuals in the various non-Christian religions, which could bring them
to a saving contact with Christ and the Church without that knowledge being
explicit (*DI* 21).[23]

DI was met with a mixed reaction. Some applauded it for its clear and
strong stands on the uniqueness of Christ and the Church. Others attacked
it for its negative judgments on non-Christian religions and what was considered an ecumenically insensitive reaffirmation of the unique claims of the
Catholic Church.[24] One thing that is clear, though, is that the confusion about
the grounds for mission has continued.

In 2007 the Congregation for the Doctrine of the Faith published its
Doctrinal Note on Some Aspects of Evangelization.[25] Section 3 of the *Doctrinal
Note* speaks, yet again, of the "growing confusion" which is undermining
evangelization:

> There is today, however, a growing confusion which leads many to
> leave the missionary command of the Lord unheard and ineffective (cf.
> Mt 28:19). . . . It is enough, so they say, to help people to become more
> human or more faithful to their own religion; it is enough to build
> communities which strive for justice, freedom, peace and solidarity.
> Furthermore, some maintain that Christ should not be proclaimed
> to those who do not know him, nor should joining the Church be
> promoted, since it would also be possible to be saved without explicit
> knowledge of Christ and without formal incorporation in the Church.
> (*Doctrinal Note* 3)

While the *Doctrinal Note* addresses in a thorough manner the question of
whether preaching the Gospel is an imposition on people's freedom, it does
not thoroughly address the doctrinal confusion lurking around the truth of
it being possible for people to be saved without hearing the Gospel and the
common temptation to presume such people are saved. This omission—not
only in the *Doctrinal Note*, but in all the post-conciliar magisterial documents
intended to restore conviction about the need to evangelize—I submit is the
reason why the confusion persists, and unless addressed, will continue to
persist.

Why the Continuing Confusion?

Why, more than fifty years after the close of Vatican II, and after all the post-conciliar documents intending to resolve doctrinal confusion concerning the need to evangelize, does confusion still exist? I think the principal reason is that the primary cause of the indifference to evangelization has not been clearly enough identified and responded to. I think the primary cause of the undermining of mission is a theological and popular culture of universalism, which has come to hold as "gospel truth" that virtually everyone will be saved except perhaps for a very few especially evil people. With that as the common understanding, even sometimes among very orthodox and spiritual Catholics, why evangelize indeed?

In a 1991 essay that appeared in the journal *Theological Studies*, John Sachs, a Jesuit theologian at Boston College, expresses what he claims is the current Catholic theological consensus:

> We have seen that there is a clear consensus among Catholic theologians today in their treatment of the notion of apocatastasis and the problem of hell.... It may not be said that even one person is already or will in fact be damned. All that may and must be believed is that the salvation of the world is a reality already begun and established in Christ. Such a faith expresses itself most consistently in the hope that because of the gracious love of God whose power far surpasses human sin, all men and women will in fact freely and finally surrender to God in love and be saved.
>
> When Balthasar speaks of the duty to hope for the salvation of all, he is articulating the broad consensus of current theologians and the best of the Catholic tradition. Like other theologians, notably Rahner, he intentionally pushes his position to the limit, insisting that such a hope is not merely possible but well founded. I have tried to show that the presumption that human freedom entails a capacity to reject God definitively and eternally seems questionable. And, although this presumption enjoys the weight of the authority of Scripture and tradition, it would seem incorrect to consider this possibility as an object of faith in the same sense that the ability of human freedom in grace to choose God is an object of faith.[26]

I think there are certain texts in the documents of Vatican II, which have been neglected, that could provide an important key to finally resolving the confusion. The words of John Paul II remain true:

> What a treasure there is, dear brothers and sisters, in the guidelines offered to us by the Second Vatican Council.... With the passing of the years, the Council documents have lost nothing of their value or brilliance. They need to be read correctly, to be widely known and taken to heart as important and normative texts of the magisterium within the

Church's Tradition ... [so as to understand] the great grace bestowed on the Church in the twentieth century: there we find a sure compass by which to take our bearings in the century now beginning.[27]

And while the Council and the post-conciliar documents on evangelization followed the overall conciliar strategy of "emphasizing the positive," they never intended to deny or withhold their proper due to other elements of the message that are essential for the faithful and effective transmission of the faith.

As we have seen, the reasons given for evangelization in the major post-conciliar documents such as *Evangelii Nuntiandi* (*EN*) and *Redemptoris Missio* (*RM*) are predominantly positive, speaking of how Christianity can enrich or fulfill the human person. Avery Dulles describes this pastoral strategy:

> Neither Vatican II nor the present pope [John Paul II] bases the urgency of missionary proclamation on the peril that the non-evangelized will incur damnation; rather they stress the self-communicative character of love for Christ, which gives joy and meaning to human existence (*RM* 10–11; cf. 2 Cor 5:14).[28]

Richard John Neuhaus studied the reasons given for evangelization in *RM* and came up with six, none of which speak of the eternal consequences of rejecting the good news, or the fact that those who have never heard the good news are not to be presumed saved. He claims that a study of Benedict XVI's writings both as Pope and before would be in harmony with these reasons and this approach as well.[29]

This, of course, is in stark contrast to the traditional focus on the eternal consequences that rest on accepting or rejecting the Gospel that motivated almost two thousand years of mission. This emphasis also stands in stark contrast to the stress placed on the eternal consequences of accepting or rejecting the Gospel, characteristic of the previous modern papal encyclicals devoted to the missionary task of the Church, published prior to 1960.[30]

Pope Francis, in his very inspiring and valuable Apostolic Exhortation *Evangelii Gaudium* (The Joy of the Gospel), nevertheless follows in the same line as the preceding post-conciliar papal teaching on evangelization, emphasizing the positive benefit of following Jesus, but remaining silent on the consequences of not following: "We know well that with Jesus life becomes richer and that with him it is easier to find meaning in everything. This is why we evangelize" (*EG* 266).

When Christian conversion is presented as an "enrichment," it is very easy to view it as "optional," since in the background of most peoples' minds there is the belief that virtually everybody will be saved because God is so merciful—which is also, according to John Sachs, the consensus of Catholic theologians. And even when the magisterial documents speak of salvation from sin and the devil, they do so in a way that does not clearly explain what sin and the devil are, and why we need to be saved from them. While most of the post-conciliar magisterial effort to establish evangelization and the intent of *AG* to a central place in the life of Catholics has focused on talking about the positive features of being a Christian, less attention has been placed on the necessity of a personal response to the grace of God, and virtually no attention has been focused on the consequences of not responding—namely, eternal separation from God. I submit that all three elements need to take their rightful place in order for evangelization to flourish and the intent of *AG* to be realized, as they do in the preaching of Jesus and the apostles. Even apart from effectiveness, it is a matter of faithfulness to transmitting what Jesus has asked us to transmit, without adding anything, or taking anything away.[31]

When *Dominus Iesus* and the subsequent *Doctrinal Note on Evangelization* were issued, many thought that the most serious doctrinal confusions affecting evangelization were definitively refuted. But these documents only addressed one part of the problem. These documents firmly restate the absolute uniqueness and necessity of Christ and the Church for salvation. There is only one savior for the whole world, and no one is saved except through Jesus Christ and some manner of link with the Church, however implicit it may be. Both Rahner and Balthasar, the theologians mentioned by Sachs as providing the theological underpinnings for what he thinks is the well-founded hope that everyone will be saved, agree with this central truth: no one is saved apart from Christ. The problem is that they do not acknowledge unambiguously the authoritative teaching of Christ, as carried forward in the tradition and rearticulated in *LG* 16, that "very often" human beings are not living their lives in a way that will lead them to salvation, and there is a real probability of many being lost unless they are addressed with a call to repentance, faith, and baptism, and positively respond to such a call—an effective renewed evangelization. These documents deal with the issues raised by a theology of religious pluralism and a certain relativism, but they do not deal with the problem of a *de facto* or even theoretical universalism, which agrees with everything these documents assert, but still assumes that virtually no one will be lost.

Fortunately, there is an important text in the documents of Vatican II that gives us a key as to how such a balanced communication of all three elements can be undertaken. The most important text of Vatican II that explores the possibility of being saved without hearing the Gospel is *LG* 16. The two other main conciliar references to this possibility are in *AG* 7 and *GS* 22, both of which depend on *LG* 16.

So, what does *LG* 16 tell us? Even though *LG* 16 only consists of ten sentences, it is packed with carefully constructed phrases with significant theological import, and very important footnotes.[32] The text first explains how "those who have not yet received the Gospel are related to the People of God in various ways." A footnote here references a text from St. Thomas, *Summa theologiae* III, q. 8, a. 3, ad 1 ("Those who are unbaptized, though not actually in the Church, are in the Church potentially. And this potentiality is rooted in two things—first and principally, in the power of Christ, which is sufficient for the salvation of the whole human race; secondly, in free-will").

It is clear that this "relatedness" is not actually salvific, but potentially salvific.[33] Special mention is made first of the Jews, then of the Muslims and then of unspecified other religions and peoples, "those who in shadows and images seek the unknown God" (*LG* 16). Buddhists and Hindus are specifically mentioned in *Nostra Aetate*, but the text here does not mention them by name, since it is not intending to limit its teaching to just the religions it names. The text then affirms God's universal salvific will, citing 1 Tim 2:4 as a basis for its exploration of how salvation for those who do not know the Gospel might be possible. We will designate this first section of *LG* 16 (the first four sentences) as *LG* 16a, although it will not be the focus of our analysis. Later on in the text, which we will cite below, a fourth group of those who have not heard the Gospel is added, those who "have not yet arrived at an explicit knowledge of God." We will include here the three sentences of *LG* 16 that treat of how salvation for all four of these categories of non-Christians might be possible:

> Those who, through no fault of their own, do not know the Gospel of Christ or his Church, but who nevertheless seek God with a sincere heart, and moved by grace, try in their actions to do his will as they know it through the dictates of their conscience—those too may achieve eternal salvation. Nor shall divine providence deny the assistance necessary for salvation to those who, without any fault of theirs, have not yet arrived at an explicit knowledge of God, and who, not without grace, strive to lead a good life. Whatever good or truth is found amongst them is considered by the Church to be a preparation for the Gospel[34] and given by him who enlightens all men that they may at length have life.

We will designate the above three sentences of *LG* 16 as *LG* 16b. And finally, consider the last three sentences, which are virtually ignored in theological treatments of this topic:

> But very often [*at saepius*],[35] deceived by the Evil One, men have become vain in their reasonings, have exchanged the truth of God for a lie and served the world rather than the Creator (cf. Rom. 1:21, 25). Or else, living and dying in this world without God, they are exposed to ultimate despair. Hence to procure the glory of God and the salvation of all these, the Church, mindful of the Lord's command, "preach the Gospel to every creature" (Mk. 16:16) takes zealous care to foster the missions.

We will designate these concluding three sentences of *LG* 16 as *LG* 16c.[36]

We have already commented on two of the three footnotes attached to *LG* 16. The third footnote is particularly relevant to our topic, but given the space limitations of this chapter, I can only indicate briefly what it refers to. It references the *Letter of the Holy Office to the Archbishop of Boston*[37] in relationship to the Fr. Feeney case. Fr. Feeney held to a very strict interpretation of the theological axiom *Extra Ecclesiam Nulla Salus* (Outside of the Church there is no salvation) and believed that unless someone died as an explicit Catholic they could not be saved. The *Letter* reaffirms the possibility of being saved without explicit faith and even talks about implicit or unconscious desire; however, its definition of these is quite important. The *Letter* says that not any kind of implicit faith or desire is sufficient for salvation but only that which includes supernatural faith and supernatural charity—which involves a personal response to the God who gives light and a surrender of one's life to the One who reveals himself, and the conformity of one's life to what is revealed.[38]

The Council here is teaching that under certain very specific conditions salvation is possible for non-Christians. What are these conditions?

1. That non-Christians be not culpable for their ignorance of the Gospel.
2. That non-Christians seek God with a sincere heart.
3. That non-Christians try to live their life in conformity with what they know of God's will. This is commonly spoken of as following the natural law or the light of conscience. It is important to note, as the Council does, in order to avoid a Pelagian interpretation, that this is possible only because people are "moved by grace."
4. That non-Christians welcome or receive whatever "good or truth" they live amidst—referring possibly to elements of their non-Christian religions or cultures that may refract to some degree that light that enlightens every man (Jn 1:9). These positive elements are intended to be "preparation for the Gospel." One could understand this to mean either a preparation for the actual hearing of the Gospel or preparation for, perhaps, some communication of God by interior illumination.

The Related Council Texts

The two other Council texts we cited must now be considered. GS 22, when speaking of our incorporation into the death and resurrection of Christ, which gives us hope for our resurrection, has this to say about non-Christians:

> All this holds true not for Christians only but also for all men of good will in whose hearts grace is active invisibly. For since Christ died for all, and since all men are in fact called to one and the same destiny, which is divine, we must hold that the Holy Spirit offers to all the possibility of being made partners, in a way known to God, in the paschal mystery.

LG 16 is cited in a footnote as a foundation for this statement. Being "men of good will" is another way of stating a condition that is more fully explicated in LG 16b. GS 22 does not try to explain how this possibility of salvation is offered and what response to it must be made for it to be effective. Joseph Ratzinger, in his commentary on GS, thinks that the explicit mention of the

Holy Spirit in *GS* 22 as the means by which the Paschal Mystery is made present adds an important element to *LG* 16, which he thinks could be interpreted in too Pelagian a manner, laying too much stress on what man must do to be saved, even though the role of grace is mentioned.[39] I do not share this concern because of the explicit mention of grace in *LG*b.

Finally, *AG* 7 must be considered:

> The reason for missionary activity lies in the will of God, "who wishes all men to be saved and to come to the knowledge of the truth. For there is one God and one Mediator between God and men, himself a man, Jesus Christ, who gave himself as a ransom for all" (1 Tim. 2:4–5), "neither is their salvation in any other" (Acts 4:12). Everyone, therefore, ought to be converted to Christ, who is known through the preaching of the Church, and they ought, by baptism, to become incorporated into him, and into the Church which is his body. Christ himself explicitly asserted the necessity of faith and baptism (cf. Mk. 16:16; Jn. 3:5), and thereby affirmed at the same time the necessity of the Church, which men enter through baptism as through a door. Hence those cannot be saved, who, knowing that the Catholic Church was founded through Jesus Christ, by God, as something necessary, still refuse to enter it, or to remain in it [*LG* 14 is referenced here]. So, although in ways known to himself God can lead those who, through no fault of their own, are ignorant of the Gospel to that faith without which it is impossible to please him (Heb. 11:6), the Church, nevertheless, still has the obligation and also the sacred right to evangelize. And so, today as always, missionary activity retains its full force and necessity.

The obvious intent of this text is to reaffirm the continuing importance of missionary activity. It would appear, though, that relative to the world's population, the numbers of those who know the Catholic Church is founded by Christ and is necessary for salvation but refuse to enter her are relatively small. Correspondingly, for the vast majority, salvation must then be possible without hearing the Gospel. While emphasizing that it is the will of God that missionary activity be carried out is certainly, in itself, a theoretically compelling reason, for many people failing to explain why missionary activity is still important given that people can be saved without it, and the presumption that usually accompanies this belief, leaves the exhortation much weaker in its effect than it could be.

What *LG* 16 reminds us of, not only by its reference to the *Letter of the Holy Office to the Archbishop of Boston* in its very specific definition of what is required for non-explicit salvation to take place, but also in *LG* 16c's explicit citation of Romans 1, is that none of us live in a neutral environment. The wounds of original sin, the reality of personal sin, the reality of the devil, and of a world culture impelling us on paths that lead to destruction are at work today as they always have been. Even with all the helps we have as Catholics, some of us sometimes choose the darkness rather than the light. How much easier is it to be swept away by a culture of blasphemy and immorality without the help of Christ and the Church? What *LG* 16c importantly tells us is that "very often" human beings may not be inculpably ignorant of the Gospel, or may not be seriously seeking God, or may not be trying to live in accordance with the light of conscience, may not be responding positively to the impulses of the Spirit, the work of grace. Therefore, for the sake of their salvation, it is urgent that we preach the Gospel, and call people who are on the broad way that leads to destruction to the narrow way of Jesus and His Church, that leads to life. What *LG* 16c reminds us of is that Christianity is not a game or an optional enrichment exercise but a matter truly of life and death, salvation and damnation. The implication is that if we truly love people we will not only be concerned about their earthly well-being, but will be concerned about the salvation of their souls, about their faith, their repentance, their fidelity to Christ.[40]

Unless we squarely face the bad news—original sin and personal sin have severe consequences—it is impossible to really appreciate the good news (God is rich in mercy, out of the great love with which he loved us we are saved by grace through faith).[41]

Following the often ignored but extremely important sentences of *LG* 16c, we find one of the most stirring calls to evangelization contained in the Council documents: "By her proclamation of the Gospel, she draws her hearers to receive and profess the faith, she prepares them for baptism, snatches them from the slavery of error, and she incorporates them into Christ so that in love for him they grow to full maturity . . . for the glory of God, the confusion of the devil and the happiness of man" (*LG* 17). The new "missionary age" called for by *AG* and hoped for by post-conciliar popes has not yet fully dawned, but perhaps, as the full teaching of Vatican II on salvation is recovered, and our continued prayers for a "new Pentecost" are heard, we will yet see it burst forth.

NOTES

1. The translation I will be using for all Vatican II documents is that of Austin Flannery, ed., *Vatican Council II: The Conciliar and Post Conciliar Documents*, vol. I (Northport, NY: Costello Publishing, 1992).

2. Paul VI, Apostolic Exhortation, *Evangelii Nuntiandi* (hereafter *EN*) (On Evangelization in the Modern World), December 8, 1975 (Boston: Pauline Books and Media, 1976), 2. The numbers after references to papal documents and the documents of Vatican II refer to the numbered sections of such documents, not page numbers. All subsequent documents will be abbreviated similarly.

3. *EN* 2.

4. John Paul II, Encyclical Letter, *Redemptoris Missio* (hereafter *RM*) (Mission of the Redeemer), December 7, 1990 (Boston: Pauline Books and Media, 1991), 2.

5. John Paul II, Apostolic Letter, *Novo Millennio Ineunte* (hereafter *NMI*) (At the Beginning of a New Millennium), January 6, 2001 (Boston: Pauline Books and Media, 2001), 2.

6. Henceforth references to the Vatican II documents will be abbreviated by the standard initials of their Latin titles, e.g. *Ad Gentes Divinitus, AG; Lumen Gentes, LG*, etc.

7. Besides the material relevant to *AG* in *Acta Synodalia*, and the major histories of the documents of Vatican II such as the five-volume *History of Vatican II*, ed. Giuseppe Alberigo and Joseph Komonchak (New York: Orbis, 1995–2003) and the six-volume *Commentary on the Documents of Vatican II*, ed. Herbert Vorgrimler (New York: Herder & Herder, 1967–1969), there are shorter treatments in Xavier Rynne, *Vatican Council II: An Authoritative One-Volume Version of the Four Historic Books* (New York: Farrar, Straus and Giroux, 1968), 511–20; *Evangelization and Religious Freedom*, ed. Stephen B. Bevans and Jeffrey Gros (New York/Mahwah: Paulist Press, 2009), 3–148; William R. Burrows, "Decree on the Church's Missionary Activity," in *Vatican II and Its Documents: An American Reappraisal*, ed. Timothy E. O'Connell (Wilmington, DE: Michael Glazier, 1986), 180–96. It is surprising to note that many notable books devoted to assessing Vatican II pay very little attention to *AG*: Richard R. Gaillardetz and Catherine E. Clifford, *Keys to the Council: Unlocking the Teaching of Vatican II* (Collegeville, MN: Liturgical Press, 2012); Marc Cardinal Ouellet, *The Relevance and Future of the Second Vatican Council: Interviews with Fr. Geoffroy de la Tousche*, trans. Michael Donley and Joseph Fessio (San Francisco: Ignatius Press, 2013); *Vatican II: Did Anything Happen?*, ed. David G. Schultenover (New York: Continuum, 2008); Massimo Faggioli, *Vatican II: The Battle for Meaning* (New York and Mahwah, NJ: Paulist Press, 2012); Augustino Marchetto, *The Second Vatican Ecumenical Council: A Counterpoint for the History of the Council*, trans. Kenneth D. Whitehead (Scranton, PA: University of Scranton Press, 2010). For an informal memoir of the development of *AG* by a bishop who was involved in the process, see Donal Lamont, "*Ad Gentes*: A Missionary Bishop Remembers," in *Vatican II Revisited by Those Who Were There*, ed. Alberic Stacpoole (Minneapolis, MN: Winston Press, 1986), 270–82. For a brief overview of the theological issues already percolating regarding mission before the Council, the development of the final document and a review of its main points, see Edward Hahnenberg, *A Concise Guide to the Documents of Vatican II* (Cincinnati: St. Anthony Messenger Press, 2007), 133–40.

8. See *Evangelization and Religious Freedom*, ed. Stephen B. Bevans and Jeffrey Gros (New York and Mahwah, NJ: Paulist Press, 2009), 28.

9. On August 6, 1966, Pope Paul VI published *Motu Proprio*, "Apostolic Letter *Ecclesiae Sanctae*," which established guidelines for implementing various conciliar decrees including guidelines for *AG*. The guidelines are mainly of an administrative, educational, and financial nature, desiring to gain the support of the whole Church for missions and give greater input to the Vatican office coordinating missions on the part of the worldwide Church.

10. See Robert J. Schreiter, "Changes in Roman Catholic Attitudes toward Proselytism and Mission," in *New Directions in Mission and Evangelization 2: Theological Foundation*, ed. James A. Scherer and Stephen B. Bevans (New York: Orbis, 1994), 114, 118–19. Schreiter, a well-known Catholic missiologist, describes the crisis that followed Vatican II as it affected the worldwide missionary effort of the Church, attributing it in part to the general questioning of certainties that took place after the Council, and most specifically to "the most profound questioning of the missionary movement, both in its principles and its practice, that the Catholic Church had ever undergone." He cites the shift from a conversion-oriented understanding of mission to an understanding that now included dialogue, inculturation, respect for non-Christian religions, and sensitivity to Western imposition of culture in the name of the Gospel as

all contributing to the crisis. But he singles out the question about how necessary it is, really, for someone to become a Christian and a member of the Church in order to be saved. "To be sure, the Council documents continue to speak of the necessity of the church and membership in the church as the visible sign of the fullness of salvation to which we might attain here on earth. But in almost the same breath, speaking of the church as pilgrim and provisional necessarily opened up the question of just how necessary the church was—really—to salvation. Might not conversion to a better life along the lines one's life had already taken be a better task for the missionary rather than insisting upon formal membership in the church? And what was to come into greater evidence in the succeeding period was that the boundaries of church itself, once so dear and secure, were now beginning to appear considerably vaguer." For a broader, ecumenical view of the history of missionary work and contemporary thinking, see *Mission in the Twenty-First Century*, ed. Andrew Walls and Cathy Ross (Maryknoll, NY: Orbis Books, 2008).

11. In the United States, the *Covenant and Mission* report seemed to deny the need for Jews to encounter Christ, and the resulting controversy led to the Doctrinal Committee of the US Bishops finally affirming that, indeed, Jews too were invited to life in Christ. For an overview of the drift toward universalism and the reactions of various Church bodies to the drift, see Gerald H. Anderson, "Theology of Religions and Missiology: A Time of Testing," in *The Good News of the Kingdom: Mission Theology for the Third Millennium*, ed. Charles Van Engen et al. (Maryknoll, NY: Orbis Books, 1993), 200–208: "Today if a Christian theologian says that the Jewish people do not need the Gospel, the same theologian very likely will also deny that people of other faiths need the Gospel, and we end up with a theological relativism that rejects the Christian mission to all people of other faiths. Mission to the Jewish people is the litmus test of an adequate theology of religions for missiology" (206). An Italian missionary, Fr. Anthony Furioli, MCCF, writing in the *African Ecclesial Review* 34 (June 1992): 170–82, describes the theological atmosphere that undermines evangelization: "Some theologians today ask themselves: '*Is mission still necessary as it was in the past? Can it still be considered essential in this day and age?*' . . . They base this above all on *AG* 7 which states that God in ways known only to Himself can speak to those ignorant of Jesus Christ and the Christian faith. They say that Vatican II has great respect for great religions like Hinduism, Buddhism, Islam, etc. . . . and conclude by saying, '*Let these good and honest people live in holy peace*'" (171).

12. A lot of the energies of the Congregation for the Doctrine of the Faith during this time were taken up with formulating responses to Marxist-inspired liberation theology, which, until the collapse of communism in 1989, seemed to be sweeping Latin America and spreading to other continents as well. One trenchant comment on this era: "While the Catholic Church was opting for the poor, the poor were opting for the evangelicals and Pentecostals."

13. Stephen B. Bevans and Jeffrey Gros, *Evangelization and Religious Freedom* (New York and Mahwah, NJ: Paulist Press, 2009), 100.

14. For the statistics that map the shocking decline of the Church in Europe, see Peter Hunermann, "Evangelization of Europe? Observations on a Church in Peril," in *Mission in the Third Millennium*, ed. Robert J Schreiter (Maryknoll, NY: Orbis Books, 2001), 57–80. For the statistics that map the American decline, see Sherry Weddell, *Forming Intentional Disciples: The Path to Knowing and Following Jesus* (Huntington, IN: Our Sunday Visitor Publishing, 2012), 15–47. See also Ralph Martin, "The Post-Christendom Sacramental Crisis: The Wisdom of Thomas Aquinas," *Nova et Vetera*

(English Edition) 11, no. 1 (2013): 59–77. See also Ralph Martin, *The Urgency of the New Evangelization* (Huntington, IN: Our Sunday Visitor, 2013), 11–21.

15. Bevans and Gros, *Evangelization and Religious Freedom*, 59.

16. When in the early 1980s the Ad Hoc *Committee to Oversee the Use of the Catechism* of the US Bishops reported on its evaluation of catechetical texts in use and found a great majority of them to be doctrinally deficient, despite many of them having the *imprimatur*, there was a strange silence about responsibility and competence, and not a word of repentance for the millions of souls that were misled. Fortunately the promise to do better in the future has been largely fulfilled.

17. Joseph Ratzinger, *New Outpourings of the Holy Spirit*, trans. Michael J. Miller and Henry Taylor (San Francisco: Ignatius Press, 2007), 115.

18. Francis Cardinal George, "The Decree on the Church's Missionary Activity," in *Vatican II: Renewal Within Tradition*, ed. Matthew L. Lamb and Matthew Levering (New York: Oxford University Press, 2008), 300.

19. While not primarily focused on the question of mission, the Extraordinary Synod of 1985, which gave some very solid guidelines for the proper interpretation of the Council, was another important step in restoring a measure of balance to the whirlwind of theological confusion. The final "Message to the People of God" and "The Final Report" may be found in a number of places including in Xavier Rynne, *John Paul's Extraordinary Synod: A Collegial Achievement* (Wilmington, DE: Michael Glazier, 1986), 107–32. See also Hermann J. Pottmeyer, "A New Phase in the Reception of Vatican II: Twenty Years of Interpretation of the Council," in *The Reception of Vatican II*, trans. Matthew J. O'Connell, ed. Giuseppe Alberigo et al. (Washington, DC: The Catholic University of America Press, 1987), 27–43. For a somewhat detailed account of both the traditionalist and progressive criticism of the Council, see Daniel Menozzi, "Opposition to the Council (1966–84)," in Alberigo et al., *The Reception of Vatican II*, 325–48. For a complex analysis of the cultural and philosophical post-conciliar period, see Giuseppe Alberigo, "The Christian Situation after Vatican II: Phenomenology and History of the Postconciliar Period," in Alberigo et al., *The Reception of Vatican II*, 1–24.

20. For an overview of the development of missiology from Vatican II to *RM*, see Thomas Stransky, "From Vatican II to *Redemptoris Missio*," in *The Good News of the Kingdom: Mission Theology for the Third Millennium*, 137–47. For a book-length overview, see Francis Anekwe Oborji, *Concepts of Mission: The Evolution of Contemporary Missiology* (Maryknoll, NY: Orbis Books, 2006). Oborji identifies proclamation as the common thread of Vatican II and post-Vatican II magisterial mission theology. "Proclamation could be called the unifying term of all previous and contemporary missionary paradigms and theories studied in this book" (206). See also William Richey Hogg, "Vatican II's Ad Gentes: A Twenty Year Retrospective," *International Bulletin of Missionary Research* 9, no. 4 (October 1985): 146–54.

21. I have devoted a whole chapter of my book *The Urgency of the New Evangelization* to the topic of what Jesus and the Apostles actually asked us to tell people. Besides the positive message of God's mercy being offered, there is also in the New Testament an emphasis on the need for a personal response, and a clear statement of the consequences of responding positively—forgiveness of sins, eternal life—or negatively—condemnation, perishing, hell.

22. George, "The Decree on the Church's Missionary Activity," 303.

23. For a balanced interpretation of what Vatican II actually teaches about salvation and the non-Christian religions, see the numerous articles and books published by Gavin D'Costa on this subject. His most recent published essay is "Vatican II on

Muslims and Jews: The Council's Teachings on Other Religions," in *The Second Vatican Council: Celebrating its Achievements and the Future*, ed. Gavin D'Costa and Emma Jane Harris (London: Bloomsbury, 2013), 105–20. See also Mikka Ruokanen, *The Catholic Doctrine of Non-Christian Religions: According to the Second Vatican Council* (Leiden: E. J. Brill, 1992), 144–45. Note also the comments of Ratzinger in relationship to the final draft of *AG*: "Here, again, closer reflection will once more demonstrate that not all the ideas characteristic of modern theology are derived from Scripture. This idea is, if anything, alien to the biblical-thought world or even antipathetic to its spirit. The prevailing optimism, which understands the world religions as in some way salvific agencies, is simply irreconcilable with the biblical assessment of these religions. It is remarkable how sharply the Council now reacted to these modern views. During the debate on the parallel passages on the text on the Church, it had seemed more amenable" (Joseph Ratzinger, *Theological Highlights of Vatican II*, trans. by Henry Traub, Gerard C. Thormann, and Werner Barzel [New York: Paulist Press, 1966], 173). In an examination of all the writings of Congar on the question of the relationship of non-Christian religions to salvation, Thomas Potvin sums up Congar's position: "Congar's evaluation of Non-Christian or Non-biblical Religions, which a vast majority of the world's inhabitants follow, is somewhat negative. To put it summarily, he does not recognize them as authentic instruments of that gratuitous salvation of humankind which the Triune God desires and realizes according to his universal plan of salvation. On the other hand, Congar is of the opinion that followers of such religions can, under circumstances we shall mention later, benefit from salvation, but not specifically through—to use a technical term—the 'instrumentality' of their religion, be it one of the world's major and universally esteemed religions, such as Buddhism, Hinduism or Taoism" (Thomas Raymond Potvin, "Yves Congar on *Missio ad Gentes*," *Science et Esprit* 55, no. 2 [2003]: 139). Furthermore, he says, "In his eyes the latter [structures of non-Christian religions] are not exempt from the debilitating influence of the Adversary, nor are they free from serious limitations in teaching and practice, and they may serve to impede their adherents embracing the Gospel of God. Furthermore, they are properly speaking, the fruit of human inventiveness, representing the project of humans, rather than the positive and specific project of the Triune God which Christ Jesus has revealed to us" (160). See also a typical article among the many Congar wrote on the topic: Yves Congar, "The Necessity of the Mission 'Ad Gentes,'" *Studia Missionalia* 51 (2002): 157–65.

24. Gerald O'Collins's casual statement (*Living Vatican II: The 21st Council for the 21st Century* [New York and Mahwah, NJ: Paulist Press, 2006], 15) that *AG* 7 contradicts *DI* 7 is without foundation. This misreading of magisterial documents is characteristic; see also Gerald O'Collins, "John Paul II on Christ, the Holy Spirit, and World Religions," in *Irish Theological Quarterly* 72 (2007): 323–37. In his book *Salvation for All: God's Other Peoples* (New York: Oxford University Press, 2008), O'Collins devotes a great deal of effort to assembling and assessing the Biblical testimony of God's promise of universal salvation and draws conclusions on this basis that seem not well founded, since the methodology he adopted was to consider just the "positive" passages and not the "negative." In his introduction, he states, "But my purpose is not to survey equally and appraise both the 'negative' and the 'positive' witness; to do that would call for a book twice the length of this one" (v). This remarkable "methodology" is similar to what we will see in people claiming to state the teaching of *LG* 16 while ignoring its last three sentences.

25. Published December 3, 2007, available at www.vatican.va under documents of the Congregation for the Doctrine of the Faith, http://www.vatican.va/roman_curia/

congregations/cfaith/documents/rc_con_cfaith_doc_20071203_nota-evangelizzazi-one_en.html. In a tepid address given by Pope Benedict XVI on the occasion of the fortieth anniversary of *AG*, he simply reaffirms the solid theology of *AG*, speaks of the mission *ad gentes* as sometimes seeming to be "slowing down," and reaffirms the need to push on anyway (Benedict XVI, "Proclaiming and Living the Gospel: The Duty of All," *L'Osservatore Romano*, English Weekly Edition, N. 12–22, March 2006, 4).

26. John R. Sachs, "Current Eschatology: Universal Salvation and the Problem of Hell," *Theological Studies* 52 (1991): 252–53. While I was in Rome recently, a well-known theologian who teaches at a Pontifical University was teaching a group of American priests in Rome for a sabbatical theological updating, very much along the lines of the universalist consensus that Sachs claims. In a book prepared to update wider audiences theologically, John Fuellenbach, *Throw Fire* (Manila: Logos Publishing, 1998), 191, this same theologian offers this as a discussion question: "How convinced am I that God's saving will is meant for all, and that God will most probably save all human beings effectively?" My own in-depth assessment of the contribution that Rahner and Balthasar make to the collapse of missionary zeal is contained in Ralph Martin, *Will Many Be Saved? What Vatican II Actually Teaches and Its Implications for the New Evangelization* (Grand Rapids, MI: Eerdmans, 2012), 93–128, 129–90.

27. *NMI* 57.

28. Avery Dulles, "The Church as Locus of Salvation," in *The Thought of John Paul II: A Collection of Essays and Studies*, ed. John M. McDermott (Rome: Editrice Pontificia Universita Gregoriana, 1993), 176.

29. Richard John Neuhaus, "Reviving the Missionary Mandate," in *The New Evangelization: Overcoming the Obstacles*, ed. Steven Boguslawski and Ralph Martin (New York and Mahwah, NJ: Paulist Press, 2008), 34–42. The many very fine Pastoral Letters published by a number of American Bishops in recent years on the New Evangelization mostly follow in the same line: a positive presentation of life in Christ with virtually no mention of the eternal consequences of rejecting the new life. One such example is the very fine "Pastoral Letter on the New Evangelization," by Archbishop Donald W. Wuerl, in *Disciples of the Lord: Sharing the Vision*, published on August 23, 2010, and available on the Archdiocese of Washington, DC website: http://adw.org/wp-content/uploads/2014/02/Disciples-of-the-Lord.pdf (accessed May 2, 2011).

30. For an account of the pre-1960, twentieth-century mission encyclicals, see Martin, *Will Many Be Saved?*, 193–95. See also William Richey Hogg, "Some Background Considerations for *Ad gentes*," *International Review of Mission* 56, no. 223 (July 1967): 281–90.

31. See Ralph Martin, "The Pastoral Strategy of Vatican II: Time for an Adjustment?," in D'Costa and Harris, *The Second Vatican Council*, 137–63. Even in the traditional "mission territories," mission seems to have collapsed into pastoral care or human development in many places. In reviewing contemporary mission maga-zines published by missionary orders and Pontifical Mission Societies, almost all the "mission reports" seem to be focused on human development and the construction of buildings, with scarcely ever a mention of conversion.

32. The full Latin text of *LG* 16 with an English translation is available on the Vatican website, www.vatican.va, under Vatican II documents, http://www.vatican.va/archive/hist_councils/ii_vatican_council/documents/vat-ii_const_19641121_lumen-gentium_lt.html.

33. A recent doctoral dissertation analyzes philosophically the text of *GS* 22, which states, "For, by his incarnation, he, the Son of God, has in a certain way united

himself with each man." See Caroline Farey, "A Metaphysical Investigation of the Anthropological Implications of the Phrase: 'Ipse enim, Filius Dei, incarnatione sua cum omni homine quodammodo se univit' (For, by his incarnation, he, the Son of God has in a certain way united himself with each man—*Gaudium et spes*, 22)," PhD diss., Pontificia Universitas Lateranensis, 2008, 162–72. Here too it is clear that the nature of the union is not salvific. Her analysis of "in a certain way" shows the multitude of meanings that could be intended, as well as those which clearly are not. While the dissertation is done in the faculty of philosophy, it draws heavily on Patristic and Scholastic theological sources. Her conclusions mirror Aquinas's understanding of a union that brings with it "potential."

34. The following footnote is inserted here as backing for this text: "See Eusebius of Caesarea, *Praeparatio Evangelica*, I, 1: PG 21, 28 AB." Joseph Ratzinger ("La Mission d'Après Les Autres Textes Conciliaires," in *Vatican II: L'Activité Missionnaire de l'Église* [Paris: Cerf, 1967], 129n11) indicates that this reference to Eusebius does not really support the point being made, but, of course, the point can be supported in other ways: "The reason for this allusion is not very clear, since in this work Eusebius, in treating of the non-Christian religions, has another emphasis than our text: Eusebius underlines the aberrations of the pagan myths and the insufficiency of Greek philosophy; he shows that Christians are right in neglecting these in order to turn to the sacred writings of the Hebrews which constitute the true 'preparation for the gospel.'" ("La raison de cette allusion n'est pas très claire, car dans cet ouvrage l'orientation d'Eusèbe, par rapport aux religions non chrétiennes, est tout autre que dans notre texte: Eusèbe signale les égarements des mythes païens et l'insuffisance de la philosophie grecque; il montre que les chrétiens voint juste en les négligeant pour se tourner vers les livres saints des Hébreux qui constituent las véritable 'préparation évangélique.'") The *Sources Chrétiennes* translation of this text, *La Préparation Évangélique: Livre I*, trans. Jean Sirinelli and Édouard des Places (Paris: Cerf, 1974), 97–105, shows that Euesbius, in the chapter cited, only mentions the non-Christian religions and philosophies as being in dire need of conversion. He speaks of them as representing a piety that is "lying and aberrant" (*mensongère et aberrante*) and cites the Scripture that speaks of "exterminating all the gods of the nations" and making them "prostrate before Him."

35. The Walter Abbott translation that appeared in 1966 translates the Latin phrase as "but rather often." The commonly used Flannery translation of the Council documents translates the Latin *at saepius* as "very often." This is the translation we will be using. Other English translations use "but often" (the translation of the National Catholic Welfare Conference, the precursor of the National Council of Catholic Bishops, which is contained in *The Sixteen Documents of Vatican II: Introductions by Douglas G. Bushman* [Boston: Pauline Books and Media, 1999]). The Vatican website (http://www.vatican.va/archive/hist_councils/ii_vatican_council/documents/vat-ii_const_19641121_lumen-gentium_en.html) translation also uses "but often." The English translation (by Clarence Gallagher) of *Lumen Gentium* in Norman Tanner's two-volume collection of the *Decrees of the Ecumenical Councils* (Washington, DC: Georgetown University Press, 1990) uses "more often, however." The French translation of the text that Congar collaborated on translates *at saepius* as "mais trop souvent" (*L'Église de Vatican II*, Tome I, Texte Latin et Traduction, P.-Th. Camelot [Paris: Cerf, 1966]). The Vatican website translation uses "bien souvent," http://www.vatican.va/archive/hist_councils/ii_vatican_council/documents/vat-ii_const_19641121_lumen-gentium_fr.html. The Italian translation on the Vatican website is "ma molto spesso." http://www.vatican.va/archive/hist_councils/ii_vatican_council/documents/vat-ii_

const_19641121_lumen-gentium_it.html. The Spanish translation on the Vatican website is "pero con mucha frecuencia," http://www.vatican.va/archive/hist_councils/ii_vatican_council/documents/vat-ii_const_19641121_lumen-gentium_sp.html.

36. It is remarkable how little the entirety of this text is considered even when the theological matter it deals with is the main subject under analysis. Theologians such as Karl Rahner, among many others, focus on *LG*a and *LG*b but completely ignore the crucial *LG*c. One of the few theologians to notice the import of *LG*c is Alan Schreck, *Vatican II: The Crisis and the Promise* (Cincinnati: Servant, 2005), 219–39.

37. *Letter of the Holy Office to the Archbishop of Boston.* The entire text of the letter in its original Latin along with an English translation was first published in *The American Ecclesiastical Review* in October 1952 (127): 307–15. It is also available in Neuner/Dupuis, 854–57, and Denzinger 3866–72.

38. For a fuller treatment of what this *Letter* contains and the background that led to it and its implications for understanding salvation, see Martin, *Will Many Be Saved?*, 40–53.

39. Joseph Ratzinger, "Pastoral Constitution on the Church in the Modern World," in *Commentary on the Documents of Vatican II*, ed. Herbert Vorgrimler, trans. W. J. O'Hara (London: Burns & Oates; New York: Herder and Herder, 1969), 5:161–63.

40. As one commentator put it, "The trouble with the Council's approach to mission is that although it stresses that Catholics must seek to convert unbelievers, it gives no adequate reason for doing so. It does give Christ's command to evangelize as a reason, but it gives no proper explanation of why that command is given, or of the good that the commandment is supposed to promote. This, of course, means that the command is unlikely to be followed; and it has in fact been largely disregarded since the Council. This lack of an explanation of the reason for evangelization is a departure from Catholic tradition, which has presented evangelization as an activity that should be undertaken in order to save the souls of unbelievers" (John Lamont, "What Was Wrong with Vatican II," *New Blackfriars* 99, no. 1013 [January 2007]: 89). See also Ralph Martin, "The Pastoral Strategy of Vatican II: Time for an Adjustment?" *Josephinum Journal of Theology* 19, no. 1 (Winter/Spring 2012): 70–90. Stephen Bullivant (*Faith and Unbelief* [New York and Mahwah, NJ: Paulist Press, 2014], 125), after a very sympathetic treatment of atheism and the possibility of salvation, eventually comes to the conclusion: "According to the Gospels, Jesus himself testifies to this link between evangelization and salvation. Hence, from the previously quoted coda to Mark's Gospel: 'Go into all the world and proclaim the good news to the whole creation. The one who believes and is baptized will be saved; but the one who does not believe will be condemned' (16:15–16). This statement alone, quite apart from any hopes to the contrary—however well-grounded—ought to give us pause. As was argued at the end of Chapter 4, while hope may indeed be justified, presumption is not. And as unfashionable and unpalatable as it might seem to say so, it is this that is the best and most urgent rationale for evangelizing today's unbelievers."

41. As one friend put it, "Before you can preach the Good News, you have to preach the bad news, because if you don't, they'll think that the Good News is not news at all."

11

Unitatis Redintegratio

Matthew J. Ramage

Introduction

It is nearly impossible to overestimate the impact of the decree *Unitatis Redintegratio* on the life of the Church over the past fifty years. A watershed moment in Christian history, the proclamation of this document catalyzed innumerable endeavors in the field of ecumenism, which have made an indelible stamp on the Church's identity. As John Paul II wrote thirty years after the Council, with the proclamation of this document the Church committed herself "irrevocably" to the venture of seeking to re-establish full visible unity among all Christians.[1]

Over the past five decades, the Church's ecumenical journey has proven to be a work ever in progress, marked both by bright spots and blemishes, milestones and setbacks. The goal of this chapter is to capture some of these highlights and trace the post-conciliar legacy of *Unitatis Redintegratio* (*UR*), pointing to areas in which its teaching has been fruitfully received as well as calling attention to aspects of the document that still await full reception as we approach the five-hundredth anniversary of the Reformation and anticipate further ecumenical prospects with the Christian East.

Unitatis Redintegratio in Retrospect: A Survey of Key Figures, Literature, and Events

Given the extraordinary scope of *UR*'s post-conciliar legacy, it is impossible to treat every significant outcome of the decree here in a single chapter. We will therefore have to content ourselves with a survey of what this author has judged to be the ecumenical highlights inspired by *UR* over the last fifty years. While the below treatment is as chronological as possible, the discussion is subdivided principally by author or subject. After this survey, highlights from particular dialogues and prospects for the future will be explored in greater depth.

John XXIII

Though properly speaking Angelo Roncalli's contribution to *UR* was not one of reception but rather inspiration, one would be remiss not to observe that the future Pope John XXIII's life was arguably the most significant of all currents that paved the way for *UR*'s reception. As early as 1925, then-Archbishop Roncalli concerned himself with problems dividing the Eastern and Western Church during his tenure as papal ambassador to Bulgaria, a legacy he further advanced after his 1934 transfer to Istanbul where he would serve as apostolic delegate to Turkey and Greece. In his first public address as pope in 1958, John made it clear that concern for the reunion of Christians would be one of the hallmarks of his papacy. Shortly thereafter, his 1959 encyclical *Ad Petri Cathedram* recognized among the separated brethren "an intense desire for unity of some kind" and acknowledged that "almost all those who are adorned with the name of Christian even though separated from Us and from one another have sought to forge bonds of unity by means of many congresses and by establishing councils."[2] Expressing continuity with the prior teaching of Popes Pius XI and Pius XII, John references the former's *Mortalium Animos* in making it clear that the unity sought through such endeavors "must be solid, firm and sure, not transient, uncertain, or unstable."[3] Yet even in its confirmation of the Church's prior measures, John's encyclical exudes a fresh perspective as he approvingly cites the dictum "in essentials, unity; in doubtful matters, liberty; in all things, charity."[4]

Having announced his intention to call the Second Vatican Council in 1959, a year later John enshrined his commitment to ecumenism with the unprecedented move of creating the Secretariat for Promoting Christian Unity.[5] Then, in his opening speech at the Council, the pontiff identified the promotion of Christian unity as one of its main goals.[6] The means to this end, John elaborates, were to consist in "the medicine of mercy rather than that of severity." This is by no means to say that John envisioned a nebulous union akin to that condemned by his predecessors. On the contrary, for John the greatest concern of the Council was to guard and teach the sacred deposit of Christian doctrine more efficaciously. "The substance of the ancient doctrine of the deposit of faith is one thing, and the way in which it is presented is another": this was John's architectonic principle that would enable the Church to go about her business of renewal, developing fresh approaches to the ecumenical question while remaining firmly in continuity with the tradition.[7]

Johannes Willebrands

Though little known outside of ecumenical circles, arguably the most important figure in the early days of *UR* was Johannes Cardinal Willebrands, who had an incalculable effect on both the preparation and reception of the decree.[8] So high was his esteem for the document that Willebrands believed it fulfilled John XXIII's prayer for something like a "new Pentecost" to take place at Vatican II.[9] A pioneer of ecumenism before the Council, then-Monsignor Willebrands coordinated the *Conférence catholique pour les questions œcuméniques*, a group which promoted exchanges and collaboration among the pioneers of Catholic ecumenism in the decade immediately preceding Vatican II. From 1960 to 1969 he served as secretary of the Secretariat for Promoting Christian Unity under Cardinal Bea until he became its president after Bea's death. Between 1965 and 1970, Willebrands established and co-chaired the Joint Working Group between the Roman Catholic Church and World Council of Churches (WCC) and began international bilateral dialogues with the Lutheran World Federation, Anglican Communion, and World Methodist Conference. The revolutionary dimension of this work is apparent when one recalls that, as late as 1957, Giovanni Battista Montini himself—who as Pope Paul VI would solemnly approve *UR*—had taught that the Catholic Church could not participate in such ecumenical meetings.[10]

Particularly noteworthy is Cardinal Willebrands's 1970 speech presented in Cambridge on the different complementary "types" (*typoi*) of Church life. Willebrands argues that within the larger unity of the Church there is room for diversity in theology, liturgy, spirituality, and canonical discipline.[11] In keeping with *UR*'s solemn declaration that the Churches of the East have the power to govern themselves according to the disciplines proper to them, he maintains that full communion between churches of different types "does not of itself demand unity of organization but does require oneness and coherence in the faith professed."[12] Elaborating further, the cardinal observes that such a state of affairs would enrich the Church:

> We will become able to realize a diversity containing nothing which destroys unity or is incompatible with it.... The typology would explain and show as legitimate the diverse traditions, theological statements and methods, spirituality, and the form of church life, even if one's own tradition lacks certain elements proper to the other, which however are reconcilable with what Christ has given. This would enrich both diversity in unity and the catholicity and unity of the Church of Christ.[13]

The last line of this quote reflects more than a mere intimation of *UR*. Indeed, the decree itself laments that "the divisions among Christians prevent the Church from attaining the fullness of catholicity proper to her."[14] Echoing *LG*'s conviction that the presence of different rites within the Church causes her catholicity to shine forth more resplendent, Willebrands goes so far as to say that "the Church needs a variety of *typoi* to manifest the full catholic and apostolic character of the one and holy church."[15]

Willebrands's understanding of the *typoi* may be traced back to Paul VI himself, as revealed in a conversation between the pontiff, then-Msgr.

Willebrands, and Dr. Lukas Vischer, WCC observer at Vatican II. In his official report to the WCC composed shortly after his audience with Pope Paul, Vischer noted Paul's emphasis upon the importance of the "typology" of the Churches, insisting "that every tradition should maintain its characteristic features." If united to Rome, the Anglican Communion thus would not have to give up their *Book of Common Prayer.* Lutherans, meanwhile, could "develop their particular traditions" with respect to the Bible. In connection with the Orthodox, the pope also emphasized the importance of Eastern liturgical traditions in the church.

At the end of the above conversation, Pope Paul turned to Msgr. Willebrands and asked him if he agreed. The latter nodded and added that "this idea of typology should first be lived out within the Roman Catholic Church."[16] Indeed, on the subject of Eastern Churches, *UR* makes it clear that "a certain diversity in customs and observances only adds to [the Church's] splendor."[17] It is worth noting, however, that Willebrands and Pope Paul have extended the general commendation of unity within diversity in the Church. Whereas this expression typically describes the diversity one finds in the various traditions of East and West, here the authors seem to assert something positive about the diversity that exists within the divided Western Church.

Paul VI

After considering the theology of the *typoi* as articulated by Johannes Willebrands and Paul VI, one would be remiss not to underscore a few of the latter's hallmark contributions to the Church's ecumenical path. The most foundational of all perhaps goes without saying, but it should not be forgotten that it was Paul who continued the Council after John's death and who oversaw the publication of the majority of the conciliar documents, including *UR.* Over the course of the Council, Paul made a number of historical initiatives to foster Christian unity. He became the first pope in a millennium to visit the Christian East, joining Ecumenical Patriarch Athenagoras I in Jerusalem in 1964. In 1967 the two exchanged visits in Istanbul and in Rome, and at the end of this visit published a joint declaration in which they adopted *UR*'s language of referring to one another as "sister Churches."[18] Perhaps most significantly, their first meeting in Jerusalem led to a 1965 joint declaration in which the two resolved to "remove both from memory and from the midst of the Church the sentences of excommunication" from the Great Schism of 1054.[19] Read aloud simultaneously at the Second Vatican Council in Rome and at a special ceremony in Istanbul, the declaration did not end the schism; it did, however, provide an invaluable impetus for the five decades of Catholic-Orthodox ecumenism that followed.

In addition to his ongoing dialogue with Athenagoras, Pope Paul made great strides with the Oriental Orthodox, a family of six churches with no administrative center. Sometimes called non-Chalcedonian, pre-Chalcedonian, or Ancient Eastern Churches, these churches are distinguished from the broader Orthodox Church in that they never accepted the

Christological teachings of the Council of Chalcedon (451). Given their unique theological position, it is not surprising that in the past the Oriental Orthodox themselves were erroneously labeled as monophysites.[20] In 1971, Paul VI and Mar Ignatius Jacoub III of the Syrian Orthodox Church issued a common declaration clarifying this matter, declaring that they "are in agreement that there is no difference in the faith they profess concerning the mystery of the Word of God made flesh and become really man, even if over the centuries difficulties have arisen out of the different theological expressions by which this faith was expressed."[21] In 1973 Paul signed a similar declaration with the Coptic Orthodox Church in the person of Shenouda III, Pope of Alexandria and Patriarch of the See of St. Mark. The most significant feature of the declaration is its joint confession of faith, yet it also explicitly recognizes a broader shared heritage with many convergences in the theology, spirituality, and liturgy of the two churches.[22]

While impressive, Paul VI's advances with the Christian East were by no means his only area of achievement in the ecumenical arena. As discussed above, it was under the leadership of Paul and Willebrands that the Joint Working Group between the Roman Catholic Church and WCC was established and members of the Catholic Church were first sent to its plenary assembly. As an expression of his ecumenical commitment, Paul himself visited the headquarters of the WCC in Geneva in 1969. It was also during Paul's tenure that the Catholic Church began bilateral dialogues with the Lutheran World Federation (1967), Anglican Communion (1970), and a number of other communities.[23] In 1966 he became the first pope in history to officially receive an Anglican Archbishop of Canterbury at the Vatican.[24] On this occasion the two leaders signed a common declaration in which they resolved to forget past sins and to inaugurate "a serious dialogue which, founded on the Gospels and on the ancient common traditions, may lead to that unity in truth, for which Christ prayed."[25] Within just two years, the dialogue initiated by Archbishop Ramsey and Paul would produce the Malta Report, the first joint agreement of its kind since the Reformation. Among the noteworthy elements of this report, one should recall its citation of UR to the effect that "among the Western Communions separated from the Roman See the Churches of the Anglican Communion 'hold a special place.'"[26] It insists that divergences between these communities since the sixteenth century "have arisen not so much from the substance of this inheritance as from our separate ways of receiving it."[27]

John Paul II

The numerous advances made during the pontificate of John Paul II defy any attempt to summarize succinctly. At this point only a few essential highlights will be surveyed, leaving the extensive work accomplished concurrently by the Pontifical Council for Promoting Christian Unity (PCPCU) to be treated in a section below.

Already in 1985 John Paul had shown how dear to his heart was the reunion of East and West. In his encyclical *Slavorum Apostoli*, the pontiff pointed to Sts. Cyril and Methodius as "the authentic precursors of ecumenism, inasmuch as they wished to eliminate effectively or to reduce any divisions, real or only apparent, between the individual communities belonging to the same Church."[28] Their lives are an invitation to restore the unity that was "gravely damaged" within a couple centuries of their lifetimes. They are invoked as "champions and also the patrons of the ecumenical endeavor of the sister Churches of East and West."[29]

The year 1995 was particularly momentous in the ecumenical world as John Paul II published two important documents in the same month, the Apostolic Letter *Orientale Lumen* and the Encyclical *Ut Unum Sint*. The latter cites *UR* extensively, reminding Christians that the commitment to ecumenism enshrined by Vatican II is irrevocable.[30] The pontiff adds that, contrary to the perception of many, ecumenism "is not just some sort of 'appendix' which is added to the Church's traditional activity," but rather an organic part of her life and work which "must pervade all that she is and does."[31] Concern for reunion extends to the whole Christian community according to the ability of each member.[32]

John Paul strikes a healthy balance in his approach to differences between the Catholic Church and the communities with whom she is in dialogue. On the one hand, he endorses *Gaudium et Spes* in affirming that what unites Christians is much greater than anything dividing them.[33] He acknowledges that both sides are to blame for the lack of unity among Catholics and other Christians, and that dialogue can help us to see that former arguments were "really over two different ways of looking at the same reality."[34] On the other hand, the pontiff remains adamant that true unity "can be attained only by the adherence of all to the content of revealed faith in its entirety" and that "compromise is in contradiction with God who is Truth."[35] As *UR* indicates, the "courageous journey towards unity" requires that we avoid "both false irenicism and indifference to the Church's ordinances."[36] Thus his understanding of the "hierarchy of truths" discussed in *UR* correctly steers partners in dialogue away from settling upon a lowest common denominator. Instead it focuses discussion first on that which is essential for the reestablishment of unity.[37]

Finally, one would be remiss not to recall John Paul's efforts to ensure a sound interpretation of the Council's programmatic affirmation that the Church of Christ "subsists in the Catholic Church, which is governed by the Successor of Peter and by the Bishops in communion with him."[38] While the Catholic Church is bound or "linked" (*coniunctam*) to all Christians through a sacramental bond established in baptism, the Church continues to exist fully only in the Catholic Church.[39] Accordingly, some Christian traditions stand in closer proximity than others to the fullness that resides in the Catholic Church. Reprising the language used in *Lumen Gentium* and employed throughout *UR*, John Paul distinguishes "ecclesiastical communities" (Protestants) from

"Churches" (Orthodox) and observes that between the latter and the Catholic Church there exists an objectively more intimate union. Orthodox communities are recognized as "churches" by virtue of their possession of true sacraments and apostolic succession.[40] This critically important qualification has enabled the Church to pursue the ecumenical journey along two distinct fronts with much greater clarity over the past decades.

It is striking that John Paul's *Orientale Lumen* should be published the same month as his encyclical on Christian unity. The pontiff's ecumenical ardor is obvious in this Apostolic Letter as he speaks of a "passionate longing that the full manifestation of the Church's catholicity be restored" and prays that we may be granted "a full taste of the divinely revealed and undivided heritage of the universal Church."[41] John Paul impresses upon the faithful a cry of urgency for reunion for many reasons, not least of which is for the sake of a more fruitful "new evangelization."[42] He also calls the West to a greater appreciation of the spiritual and theological patrimony of the East. The theology of divinization profoundly reminds man of how great his calling is, while apophaticism powerfully underscores the need to constantly recall "the humble acceptance of the creature's limits before the infinite transcendence of a God who never ceases to reveal himself as God."[43] The inexpressibility of the divine reality and the mystery of man's call to share in the divine nature are both reflected in Eastern liturgy, which "everyone knows" is celebrated with great love.[44]

Finally, in addition to his writing, attention should also be paid to the many great acts and events in the life of John Paul that have had an incalculable impact on the face of ecumenism. One in particular offers a powerful illustration of this pope's humility and power to change hearts. John Paul was the first pontiff to visit Greece in more than 1,200 years, and his 2001 stay began in a climate of hostility. He was not greeted by any representatives from the Greek Orthodox Church, and after his brief meeting with the Primate of Greece, the latter publicly read a list of "thirteen offences" committed by Catholics against the Orthodox, complaining that no pardons had ever been asked by Catholics for their past crimes—in particular the 1204 sack of Constantinople by Latin Christians. However, John Paul's response to Archbishop Christodoulos forever changed the course of ecumenism. He spoke of the need for a "purification of memory" and begged forgiveness for past sins of the Church—in particular the events that had unfolded in Constantinople.[45] The pope's words met with applause, and following the speech John Paul and Christodoulos issued a common declaration before the bema of St. Paul atop the Areopagus.[46] The statement condemns all recourse to "violence, proselytism and fanaticism in the name of religion," echoing a similar condemnation from John Paul's 1987 joint declaration with Ecumenical Patriarch Dimitrios I.

Directory for the Application of Principles and Norms on Ecumenism

As will be discussed further below, the PCPCU witnessed prodigious ecumenical developments over the course of John Paul's pontificate. However, the pontiff's 1993 approval of the *Directory* deserves special mention here. The document represents a revised edition of the Ecumenical Directory called for by Vatican II and published in two parts in 1967 and 1970. In the course of its sweeping theological and practical considerations, the document cites *UR* over sixty times. It begins by summarizing Catholic doctrinal principles undergirding her ecumenical practices, after which it proposes means to direct ecumenical efforts at various levels and elaborates practical principles for such matters as ecumenical formation, communion in the spiritual life, and cooperation in the world.

The *Directory* treats numerous concrete situations such as mixed marriages and the sharing of sacraments. In particular, the basis for the document's many practical considerations can be found in the *Code of Canon Law* revised in 1983 and the *Code of Canons of the Eastern Churches* promulgated in 1990. Here it is made clear that Catholics may receive sacraments "only from a minister in whose Church these sacraments are valid."[47] A norm of great ecumenical importance, the document nevertheless indicates that "in certain circumstances, by way of exception, and under certain conditions, access to these sacraments may be permitted, or even commended, for Christians of other Churches and ecclesial communities."[48] These concessions and stipulations represent great progress in the ecumenical arena. They manifest a sober recognition of lingering obstacles to full communion, while at the same time pointing toward the goal of ecumenism and calling attention to the unacceptability of a Church that remains divided.

Reflecting the opening paragraphs of *UR*, the *Directory* exhorts Christians not to rest satisfied with present forms of communion seeing as "they do not correspond to the will of Christ, and weaken his Church in the exercise of its mission."[49] By its very nature, the unity of Christ's body "requires full visible communion of all Christians" which in turn "is the ultimate goal of the ecumenical movement."[50] In line with *UR*, it adds that this quest "by no means requires the sacrifice of the rich diversity of spirituality, discipline, liturgical rites and elaborations of revealed truth that has grown up among Christians in the measure that this diversity remains faithful to the apostolic Tradition."[51] Catholics are to "give value" to these elements, mentioning by name those found "in the mystical tradition of the Christian East and the spiritual treasures of the monastic life, in the worship and piety of Anglicans, in the evangelical prayer and the diverse forms of Protestant spirituality." This appreciation should not remain purely theoretical but also be accompanied by practical knowledge of other spiritual traditions gained through "sharing prayer and participating in some form of public worship or in devotional acts of other Christians."[52] In addition to spiritual sharing, Christians are encouraged to collaborate in social and charitable initiatives whenever possible.[53]

Benedict XVI (Prior to Papal Election)

Over the more than fifty years spanning his work as a *peritus* at Vatican II to the end of his pontificate, Joseph Ratzinger has arguably contributed more than any other individual to the advancement of ecumenism in the past century. In this section the works of Ratzinger prior to his papal election will be considered, leaving the words and events of his pontificate for further below.

To get a glimpse of then-Father Ratzinger's ecumenical perspective, there is no better place to begin than with his journal of the Council, published in English under the title *Theological Highlights of Vatican II*. The first important text here contains Ratzinger's reply to Council observer Edmund Schlink, whose ecclesiology reflected "the conviction that none of the 'existing churches' is *the* Church of Jesus Christ but rather that they are various concretizations of the one Church which does not exist as such."[54] Responding that Catholics cannot share Schlink's conviction despite areas of agreement on other points, Ratzinger makes it clear that "there is the Church, which they identify with the historic continuity of the Catholic Church." And yet he then adds,

> The Catholic cannot demand that all the other Churches are disbanded and their members be individually incorporated into Catholicism. However, he can hope that the hour will come when "the Churches" that exist outside "the Church" will enter into its unity. But they must remain in existence as Churches, with only those modifications which such a unity necessarily requires.[55]

According to Ratzinger, the Catholic Church "has no right to *absorb* the other Churches." Rather, "A basic unity—of Churches that remain Churches, yet become one Church—must replace the idea of conversion, even though conversion retains its meaningfulness for those in conscience motivated to seek it."[56] The divisions that have arisen in Christianity stem largely from the reality that unity had been curtailed in favor of uniformity, thus precluding the presence of an enriching diversity which "should have had a legitimate existence within the Church."[57] Uniformity and unity are not identical for Ratzinger and the tradition that has followed: "Above all, [this] means that a real multiplicity of Churches must be made alive again within the framework of Catholic unity."[58]

Another important dimension of Ratzinger's ecumenical perspective comes across in letters he exchanged with Orthodox and Lutheran bishops. Published in the volume *Pilgrim Fellowship of Faith*, Cardinal Ratzinger's 2001 letter to Metropolitan Damaskinos of Switzerland makes a bold move in favor of union in arguing that "we ought not really to be asking, 'Can we legitimately communicate with one another?' but rather, 'Can we legitimately refuse Communion to one another?' "[59] In this same book, Ratzinger proceeds to insist that true division in the Church exists when there is a split in the confession of faith and the administration of the sacraments, whereas "all other differences do not ultimately count . . . they do not divide us in the heart of the Church."[60] From this basic understanding, the task then remains "to distinguish purely human divisions from the real theological divides." Purely human elements "like to give themselves the importance of something essential," and thus a "high proportion of church schisms" stem from "the silent divinization of what is our own, which is the everlasting temptation for man." Ecumenism demands of us the maturity to free ourselves from these distortions and to be comfortable with a certain variety which "by no means needs to disappear, because it does not detract from the nature of the Church."[61]

As he relates in the 1997 interview book *Salt of the Earth*, Ratzinger does not hope for "an absolute unity of Christians within history" for the very reason that "fragmentation continues to occur at the very same time that efforts toward unity are taking place."[62] New sects are constantly forming, ruptures within the various Christian communities are widening, and in the Catholic Church herself he sees ruptures so deep "that one sometimes really has the feeling that two Churches are living side by side in one Church."[63] Echoing the language mentioned above, Ratzinger thus counsels that what is most important in ecumenism "is that all of us constantly recall the essentials, that everyone try ... to jump over his own shadow and to grasp the real core in faith." Great confessional unions will not come quickly, and in any case "it is much more important that we accept each other with great inner respect, indeed, with love, that we recognize each other as Christians, and that in the essential things we try to bear a common witness to the world."[64]

The "Ratzinger Formula"

In the ecumenical endeavor to discern the "definite content" or "common center" of the Christian faith, a pivotal principle first proposed by Ratzinger in 1976 has attracted considerable attention among high-ranking prelates.[65] Called the "Ratzinger formula" by Cardinal Kasper, the proposal seeks to identify reasonable expectations for reunion on the part of Catholics and their respective dialogue partners.[66] After describing the maximum demands that Catholics would wish to impose on the Orthodox and Protestants and vice versa, he hones in on the question of Roman primacy. Acknowledging that Catholics will not be able to convince Orthodox to accept the full scope of the 1870 definition and that Catholics cannot declare the definition erroneous, Ratzinger maintains, "Nor is it possible, on the other hand, for [the Catholic] to regard as the only possible form and, consequently, as binding on all Christians the form this primacy has taken in the nineteenth and twentieth centuries."[67] The principle or "formula" to follow, then, is that "Rome must not require more from the East with respect to the doctrine of primacy than had been formulated and was lived in the first millennium."[68] What, concretely, this would look like Ratzinger proceeds to explain:

> Reunion could take place in this context if, on the one hand, the East would cease to oppose as heretical the developments that took place in the West in the second millennium and would accept the Catholic Church as legitimate and orthodox in the form she had acquired in the course of that development, while, on the other hand, the West would recognize the Church of the East as orthodox and legitimate in the form she has always had.[69]

Referencing the words of Patriarch Athenagoras in his historic 1967 meeting with Paul VI, Ratzinger states that "Rome need not ask for more" than that the Orthodox acknowledge the pope as successor of St. Peter and as the "one [who] also presides in charity." This affirmation expresses "the essential content of the doctrine of primacy as it was known in the first millennium."[70]

Benedict XVI (Post-Papal Election)

In his very first address as pope, Benedict announced that the work of ecumenism would be not just a priority but *the* priority of his pontificate: "Peter's current Successor takes on as his primary task the duty to work tirelessly to rebuild the full and visible unity of all Christ's followers. This is his ambition, his impelling duty." Fully aware that "good intentions do not suffice for this," the newly elected pontiff emphasized that "concrete gestures that enter hearts and stir consciences are essential, inspiring in everyone that inner conversion that is the prerequisite for all ecumenical progress."[71]

Benedict's 2006 visit to Turkey constitutes one such gesture. Following a turbulent response to his Regensburg address just a couple of months earlier, in this country Benedict managed to kill two birds with a single stone as he was able to make headway both with Muslim and Orthodox leaders.[72] However, Benedict's initial intent for the trip was to join Patriarch Bartholomew I in commemorating the Feast of Saint Andrew and to sign a common declaration with him.[73] On this visit the two were able to do this as well as to pray together as "brothers" before relics of Saint John Chrysostom and Saint Gregory Nazianzen.[74] Two years later, the patriarch joined Benedict for a mass in St. Peter's Basilica during which the two recited the Creed together in Greek without the Filioque. When one witnesses gestures such of these in the life of Pope Benedict, it comes as no surprise when he says, "The place where we are, if you will, closest to home, and where there is also the most hope of reunion, is Orthodoxy."[75]

Warm relations with the Anglican Communion are also a hallmark of Benedict's ecumenical legacy. As early as 2006, Benedict had received Archbishop of Canterbury Rowan Williams in Rome during which time the two issued a common declaration praising the "significant elements of shared faith" discovered through Anglican-Catholic dialogue.[76] During his own 2010 trip to the United Kingdom, Benedict became the first pope to enter Westminster Abbey. That a pope would venture to do this and that the Church of England would welcome him is an eminent sign of healing following five centuries after the latter's split with Rome over the issue of papal primacy. This welcome is all the more remarkable given that the purpose of Benedict's visit was to beatify John Henry Cardinal Newman, an Anglican convert to Catholicism. Further, in what at first glance could well appear as a slap in the face to the Anglican Church, in 2009 the pontiff had established three "personal ordinariates." Crafted in response to groups of Anglicans who petitioned "repeatedly and insistently to be received into full Catholic communion," the purpose of these structures is to accommodate clergy and groups of believers who desire union with Rome while maintaining the liturgical, spiritual, and pastoral traditions of the Anglican Communion.[77] It is remarkable that such a move, which easily could have been perceived as poaching, was in fact supported by Rowan Williams, who saw in it "further recognition of the substantial overlap in faith, doctrine and spirituality between the Catholic Church and the Anglican tradition." Such a step would never have been possible without the four decades of bilateral dialogue preceding it. Thus the initiative represents "one consequence of ecumenical dialogue between the Catholic Church and the Anglican Communion."[78]

Finally, Benedict XVI's efforts toward reunion with the Society of St. Pius X (SSPX) were both generous and bold, even if not the success for which the pontiff hoped. An endeavor outside the typical scope of ecumenism, the quest to bring the SSPX back into the fold was a priority for Benedict. Part of the pontiff's strategy was his 2007 provision which extended permission for celebration of the Roman liturgy in use prior to the reform of 1970. This liturgy is considered by Benedict "an extraordinary expression of the same *lex orandi* of the Church," and thus the two expressions of the mass "in no way lead to a division in the Church's *lex credendi*."[79] Further hoping to pave the way for reunion, in 2009 Benedict made the bold decision to rescind the 1988 excommunication of the leaders of the SSPX.[80] However, after an embroiled response to the announcement, the pontiff soon clarified his deep regret that the limits of this provision were not better explained. The excommunication and its remission "affects individuals, not institutions." The disciplinary level on which "the individuals were freed from the burden of conscience constituted by the most serious of ecclesiastical penalties" must be distinguished from the doctrinal level and the "danger of schism" that arose from Archbishop Lefebvre having illicitly ordained four bishops without a pontifical mandate.[81] Unfortunately and despite repeated efforts to do so, by the end of his pontificate Benedict was unable to succeed in achieving union with the SSPX at large.

Highlights from Particular Dialogues and Prospects for the Future

Having surveyed key figures and events of the past half century of ecumenism, at this point selected dialogues will be surveyed in more specificity. There are a number of excellent resources available that offer a comprehensive overview of the ecumenical scene since Vatican II. There is neither need nor space to examine all of them here.[82] The brief remarks that follow will limit themselves principally to achievements the Catholic Church has attained in international dialogue with Lutherans, Anglicans, and a number of churches in the East, as it is here that the most visible developments have taken place.[83]

Lutheran World Federation

As an indication of how important outside observers were at Vatican II, it was Lutheran Professor George Lindbeck who in 1964 first proposed the idea of a worldwide dialogue with the Catholic Church.[84] Within just four years, the International Lutheran-Roman Catholic Commission on Unity had produced its first common document and over the course of the past five decades has issued several more.[85]

Unquestionably the most significant milestone of the Lutheran-Catholic dialogue, the 1999 Joint Declaration on the Doctrine of Justification is singular due to its high level of official reception. Unlike other documents produced by dialogues which have more the character of non-binding "study documents," the declaration was solemnly signed by both churches and has even entered into the body of reference texts used in theological education.[86] Thus Jared Wicks, SJ, writes that its signing is to be placed alongside the foundation of the WCC, the promulgation of UR, and the publication of Faith and Order's 1982 *Baptism, Eucharist, and Ministry* as one of the four great ecumenical moments of the past century.[87] Nullifying past condemnations, this document is described by Cardinal Kasper as granting us "substantial agreement" and a "common witness to the essence of the Gospel." Repeating an idea visible in Ratzinger's thought discussed above, Kasper observes that differences in the way Catholics and Lutherans continue to conceive of justification need not be divisive, but rather it is possible to accept "a differentiated agreement, a reconciled diversity."[88]

With this agreement in place, Wicks observes that the "most urgent" issue now to be faced concerns "Christian moral practice, e.g. of sexuality of marriage, as the fruit of justification."[89] That is to say, in the present state the discussion must turn to what "living righteously" means in practice—a question which necessarily entails the effort to elucidate the Gospel's binding positive and negative norms and to establish an authoritative "moral corpus" from the tradition.[90]

Thus as they continue to consider the post-justification behavior of Christians, Catholics and Lutherans today find themselves in a new phase of ecumenism. In preparation to commemorate the five-hundredth anniversary of the Reformation, in 2013 the PCPCU and the Lutheran World Federation jointly issued the work *From Conflict to Communion: Lutheran-Catholic Common Commemoration of the Reformation in 2017*. The publication offers a joint history of the Lutheran Reformation and the Catholic response while reviewing Luther's theology in light of five decades of Lutheran-Catholic dialogue. As of this volume's writing, it is too early to tell precisely what joint commemorations will take place between Lutherans and Catholics in 2017.

Anglican/Episcopalian

According to Charles Morerod, "the most striking result" of the movement toward Church unity has been accomplished in the Anglican-Catholic dialogue.[91] The fruits produced by the Anglican Roman Catholic International Commission (ARCIC) are enormous, as this body has issued some fifteen common documents over the past several decades.[92] As in the case of the current Lutheran-Catholic dialogue, so too Catholics and Anglicans today are focusing their attention on moral issues, particularly in regards to human sexuality. ARCIC-III met in Brazil in 2013 to discuss the Church as communion and how to discern sound ethical teaching. Official results from this meeting are still forthcoming.[93] Granting the weighty issues involved in this sphere, the commission expressed confidence that remaining differences do not concern the essential shape of the faith and cannot be compared to all that we hold in common.[94]

Existing in parallel with ARCIC, the International Anglican-Roman Catholic Commission for Unity and Mission (IARCCUM) also has been meeting since 2001. Following the Anglican Communion's authorization of a rite of blessing for same-sex couples and ordaining a bishop living openly in a same-sex relationship, IARCCUM had to put its work on a temporary hiatus to allow for moral discernment.[95] However, in 2007 the commission was able to issue its first agreed statement, *Growing Together in Unity and Mission*. The work has been described as corresponding to "a new genre of ecumenical document."[96] Like the recent works *Harvesting the Fruits* by Cardinal Kasper and *Celebrating a Century of Ecumenism* by John Radano, it offers a review and synthesis of the fruits of past dialogue, in this case with an eye to elements Anglican and Catholic authorities might officially identify as areas of shared faith.

At the time of this chapter's composition in 2014, the Church of England has just officially approved the ordination of female bishops. The full ecumenical implications of this move remain to be seen, but suffice it to say that the decision will not likely move the Catholic and Anglican communions any closer toward reunification.

Oriental Orthodox

Building on the various bilateral dialogues begun during Paul VI's pontificate and the common declarations signed by our most recent pontiffs, in 2003 the Catholic Church formally began dialogue with the Oriental Orthodox churches together as a family.[97] At its sixth meeting in 2009, the joint commission finalized its first document, *Nature, Constitution and Mission of the Church*. To say this is a milestone seems an understatement, since it represents the first joint text co-produced by these churches since the Council of Ephesus in the year 431. Despite this agreement, there remain a number of obstacles to union with the Oriental Orthodox. As Donna Geernaert observes, the greatest difficulty is that member churches of this group are diverse and do not know each other very well. Some still do not recognize Catholic baptism, and others (Africans) do not allow mixed marriages.[98]

One of the most recent developments in the ongoing journey toward reunion with this group was the historic visit of Tawadros II, Pope of

Alexandria, to Pope Francis in 2013. Marking the fortieth anniversary of Pope Shenouda III's meeting with his predecessor Paul VI, Francis thanked the Coptic patriarch for the charity shown to the new Coptic Catholic Patriarch, for whose installation Tawadros was present. Repeating a theme that has already emerged many times in his pontificate, Francis spoke to Tawadros of an "ecumenism of suffering" wherein the sharing of daily sufferings in radicalized Islamic society represents an effective instrument of unity for Christians as they strive for mutual forgiveness, reconciliation, and peace.[99] The pontiff likewise spoke of an "ecumenism of martyrdom" and an "ecumenism of blood" to Catholicos Karekin II, Patriarch of the Armenian Apostolic Church, during his visit to the Vatican in 2014. "As in the ancient Church, the blood of the martyrs became the seed of new Christians," said Francis, "so in our day the blood of many Christians has become the seed of unity."[100]

Assyrian Church of the East

With origins tracing back to Mesopotamia, the Assyrian Church of the East is distinguished from the Oriental Orthodox in that it not only rejected the Council of Chalcedon but even the Council of Ephesus prior to it. For this reason, this church has been referred to as Nestorian, though most scholars today would agree that this is not fair to the Assyrians.[101] In a similar manner as we have seen in the case of Oriental Orthodox, in 1994 John Paul II and Patriarch Mar Dinkha, Head of the Assyrian Church of the East, signed a common Christological declaration. The document affirms that the two churches are "united today in the confession of the same faith in the Son of God who became man so that we might become children of God by his grace."[102]

The most significant moment in ecumenical relations with the Assyrian Church of the East came in 2001 when the CDF and PCPCU officially recognized the validity of the Anaphora of Addai and Mari. Indeed, Robert Taft, SJ, goes so far as to label this "the most remarkable Catholic magisterial document since Vatican II."[103] This anaphora is notable because it lacks a recitation of the Institution Narrative. Despite this, the Catholic Church determined it to be valid based on three major arguments. First, its validity was never questioned, dating back as it does to the very early Church and used "with the clear intention of celebrating the Eucharist in full continuity with the Last Supper and according to the intention of the Church." Second, with a reference to UR 15, the document states that the Assyrian Church of the East is "built upon orthodox faith and apostolic succession" and has "preserved full Eucharistic faith in the presence of our Lord." Finally, it recognizes that the words of Eucharistic Institution "are indeed present in the Anaphora of Addai and Mari, not in a coherent narrative way and *ad litteram*, but rather in a dispersed euchological way, that is, integrated in successive prayers of thanksgiving, praise and intercession."[104]

Unfortunately, there has been considerable tension between the Catholic Church and the Assyrian Holy Synod since 2005 when the latter suspended

Mar Bawai Soro, the bishop in California who had been in charge of ecumenical relations. In May 2008 he was received into the Chaldean Catholic eparchy in San Diego along with many clergy and lay faithful.[105] Having once almost finalized an agreed statement on the sacraments, this dialogue has not met since 2004.

Orthodox Churches of the Byzantine Tradition

Ecumenical dialogue with the Orthodox Church (as distinct from Oriental Orthodox discussed above) began with a 1975 agreement between Catholics and Orthodox that a real theological dialogue should take place. More than a decade after dialogue was initiated between the Catholic Church, Lutherans, and Anglicans, in 1979 Catholics and Orthodox formed a joint international commission, which has since met more than a dozen times and issued several key works.[106]

One of the most significant complicating factors in the quest for reunion of East and West regards the former's longstanding grievances over the phenomenon of "uniatism." The 1993 Balamand document *Uniatism: Method of Union of the Past, and Present Search for Full Communion* is worthy of mention as it specifically addresses this phenomenon wherein certain Eastern churches are joined to Rome within the Catholic communion.[107] The document hinges on two balancing affirmations. On the one hand, it rejects uniatism as a method or model for the unity being sought by Catholics and Orthodox today. On the other, it makes it clear that Oriental Catholic Churches "have the right to exist and to act in answer to the spiritual needs of their faithful." In doing so, the commission reiterates a principle taught by Ratzinger above: while individuals remain free and even obliged to follow their conscience, in the search for re-establishing unity "there is no question of conversion of people from one Church to the other in order to ensure their salvation."[108] Both the pope and the Patriarch of Constantinople supported this articulation. However, as a sign of the frequent gulf that exists between dialogue commissions and the faithful of the various churches, the Orthodox Church in Greece condemned the Balamand statement and Romania's Greek Catholic bishops rejected it out of hand, while it was only in Ukraine that it gained bilateral support.[109] The question of uniatism would be discussed again at the commission's meeting in Baltimore in the year 2000, and in 2007 the Ravenna Document revealed that the issue required still further consideration "in the near future."

The other milestone that must be mentioned here is the 2007 Ravenna document *Ecclesiological and Canonical Consequences of the Sacramental Nature of the Church: Ecclesial Communion, Conciliarity and Authority*, which yielded an important agreement that would serve as the basis for future discussion on the universal role of the bishop of Rome. The Ravenna meeting was initially compromised when the Russian Orthodox delegation walked out of the meeting as soon as it began over a dispute with the Ecumenical Patriarch of

Constantinople. Eventually this particular disagreement was settled, and the Ravenna document was later approved by the patriarchate of Moscow.[110]

At Ravenna the churches affirmed that "councils are the principal way in which communion among bishops is exercised," and that as a consequence a local Church cannot modify the Creed.[111] The ecumenicity of conciliar decisions "is recognized through a process of reception" whose nature it proceeds to spell out.[112] Seeing as a regional synod or council has no authority over any other ecclesiastical region, naturally the document observes that councils held after the Great Schism in the West yet regarded as ecumenical only contributed to the estrangement of Catholics and Orthodox.[113]

Further, the Ravenna document reveals agreement on the existence of an order (*taxis*) among local Churches, which does not thereby imply inequality in their ecclesial nature.[114] It maintains that conciliarity at the universal level in an ecumenical council "implies an active role of the bishop of Rome, as *protos* of the bishops of the major sees, in the consensus of the assembled bishops."[115] The bishop of Rome is first, but he cannot do anything without the consent of all. Primacy and conciliarity are interdependent and complementary realities in the Church.

The Ravenna meeting concluded with a clear awareness that the precise role of the bishop of Rome in the communion of all the Churches needs to be studied in greater depth.[116] The following statement captures the essence of Ravenna's consensus:

> Both sides agree that this canonical *taxis* was recognized by all in the era of the undivided Church. Further, they agree that Rome, as the Church that "presides in love" according to the phrase of St Ignatius of Antioch, occupied the first place in the *taxis*, and that the bishop of Rome was therefore the *protos* among the patriarchs. They disagree, however, on the interpretation of the historical evidence from this era regarding the prerogatives of the bishop of Rome as *protos*, a matter that was already understood in different ways in the first millennium.[117]

After this breakthrough at Ravenna, a sub-commission met in Crete in 2008 to draft the working document "The Role of the Bishop of Rome in the Communion of the Church in the First Millennium." Discussed at the commission's 2009 plenary meeting in Paphos, it remained unfinished and was intended to be the subject again at the Vienna meeting of 2010. However, at Vienna the Russian delegation once again arrived wielding a crucial objection. Successfully blocking the Crete text, the Russians maintained that it lacked a sufficiently clear statement that the jurisdiction of the bishop of Rome did not extend to the East in the first millennium.[118] This dialogue poses a particularly delicate situation at the present point of time due to the crisis in Ukraine and consequent tensions with the Russian Orthodox Church.[119]

Though distinct from the international Orthodox-Catholic dialogue, the work of the North American Orthodox-Catholic Consultation deserves special mention for the many joint documents it has published. These include responses to the international commission's various statements as well as such works as *Apostolicity as God's Gift in the Life of the Church* (1986), *An Agreed Statement on Conciliarity and Primacy in the Church* (1989), *The Filioque: A Church Dividing Issue?: An Agreed Statement* (2003), and *Steps Towards a Reunited Church* (2010).[120] The consultation acknowledges two substantive issues which still divide its churches, one theological (concerning the origin of the Holy Spirit) and one ecclesiological (the ecclesiological issue of primacy).[121]

On the subject of the Filioque, the churches of this regional consultation have resolved to "refrain from labeling as heretical the traditions of the other side on the subject of the procession of the Holy Spirit."[122] Thus they envision a reunion in which the churches "recognize each other as authentic embodiments of the one Church of Christ, founded on the apostles."[123] Concerning the question of primacy, they recommend that close attention be paid to the principle of subsidiarity according to which "higher" levels of episcopal authority would be expected to act only when "lower" levels are unable to guarantee union in faith.[124] In this light, the bishop of Rome's relationship with the Eastern Churches "would have to be substantially different from the relationship now accepted in the Latin Church." Like the international commission, this regional consultation recognizes the papal "primacy of honor." Thus the pope of a reunited Church would be expected to mediate disputes among primates who themselves would have the right to appeal to him for doctrinal guidance.[125]

Pope Francis

Francis, who for ten years was a leader in the Argentine ecumenical movement and served as Ordinary for the Eastern-rite faithful in that country, is poised to make something more concrete come of the shared understanding of the Church detailed above. Early in his pontificate, he has already spoken numerous times to the effect that "[the Eastern] vision of the Church and of synodality is marvelous" and that the Western Church needs renewal through an infusion of "fresh air from the East."[126] In his first major document, the apostolic exhortation *Evangelii Gaudium*, Francis explicitly expressed his commitment to ecumenism, and on the subject of synodality expressly stated his desire to continue the discussion begun at Ravenna on how to exercise the Petrine primacy.[127]

Other, perhaps more subtle actions—such as his citation of ecumenical Patriarch Bartholomew in his encyclical *Laudato Si'*—demonstrate that Francis has an ecumenical heart.[128] That Francis prefers above all the modest title "Bishop of Rome"—and that he proclaimed St. Gregory of Narek doctor of the Church—are also indications of his desire to heal past wounds with the East and strive more earnestly toward a common vision of the Church. Then there are the overt maneuvers, such as the two common declarations signed between Francis and Bartholomew in the year 2014 and his most recent achievement, a landmark 2016 joint declaration with Patriarch Kirill of Moscow and All Russia.[129] In making these moves, Francis is standing on the shoulders of the ecumenical giants whom we have discussed in this chapter. A reality Francis would not deny, the growing prospect for unity under his leadership has been made possible by the many sacrifices and achievements of his predecessors from both sides of the aisle.

Conclusion

In commemorating the anniversary of *Unitatis Redintegratio*, we can look back with gratitude to the abundant fruits it has produced over the five decades of ecumenism touched upon in this chapter. By way of conclusion, at this point it will be helpful to add a few more words regarding the present state of ecumenism with an eye to what lies on the ecumenical horizon.[130]

As Cardinal Kasper puts it in his work *Harvesting the Fruits*, the various dialogues and milestones in the recent history of ecumenism have enabled Christians to identify convergences in our traditions and to cooperate with one another in the world. Many of the classical disputes that stood at the root of our divisions have been resolved through a new consensus on fundamental points of doctrine. The polemical and apologetic tone of the past has largely been replaced by an emphasis on what we hold in common rather than on what divides us.[131]

At the same time, this ongoing quest for the truth has shown more clearly remaining differences in our traditions and areas that must be addressed in this next phase of the ecumenical journey. The original euphoria of the ecumenical movement has faded, but one might argue that the naïve optimism of the past has given way to a new sobriety.[132] As we have seen in this chapter, the Catholic Church's vision of unity today is not one that imagines other Christians dismantling their churches and converting to Catholicism, but rather searches for a communion in essentials, which respects diversity wherever it is consonant with the core of the Christian faith. As Popes Francis and Benedict have both clearly stated, what is to be hoped for in the ecumenical movement is a unity *through* multiplicity and diversity.[133]

Several potentially significant events lie immediately ahead on the ecumenical horizon. On the Western side, there is the anniversary of the Reformation to be officially commemorated by Catholics and Lutherans together in 2017. As mentioned above, currently the central topic of debate in dialogue with Lutherans and Anglicans concerns the ethical sphere and in particular matters regarding human sexuality.[134] On the Eastern front, Pope Francis has already set a date with Patriarch Bartholomew I of Constantinople to celebrate the anniversary of the Council of Nicea in 2025.[135] While other problems such as the Filioque remain stumbling blocks, here the core question clearly concerns the precise role to be played by the bishop of Rome in a reunited Church.

In the end, whether the immense undertakings of the official ecclesial institutions are to have any practical effect will depend upon the reception of their work in the Church at large. As Ratzinger has well said, "Unity can grow only if particular communities live out their faith with unity as their goal."[136] This task cannot be accomplished by commissions but needs the prayerful support of the whole Church. Thus the movement called spiritual ecumenism is referred to in *UR* as "the soul of the ecumenical movement."[137] As John Paul put it, this movement requires a change of heart on the part of all Christians along with a commitment to holiness of life and public and private prayer for the unity of Christians.[138] Ratzinger's diagnosis from a few decades ago probably still holds true today: reunion "is fundamentally possible, but the spiritual preparation is not yet sufficiently far advanced."[139]

For our recent pontiffs, a frenetic and superficial chase after unity divorced from the spiritual life and afraid to confront real sources of division is not authentic ecumenism. Though we must not adopt a passive posture in matters of Christian unity, it is always important to remember that unity is a gift of the Holy Spirit and thus something we cannot make ourselves.[140] The goal of ecumenism remains full, visible communion among all Christians; yet, in the above examination of lingering problems dividing our traditions, it remains to be seen whether and to what extent we will achieve this goal in history. However, at the close of his pontificate Benedict XVI showed that we have cause to rejoice in that the true Second Vatican Council has at last begun to appear "with all its spiritual force."[141] Pope Francis for his part has such confidence in the future of ecumenism that he would proclaim these words from within the Holy Sepulcher: "We need to believe that, just as the stone before the tomb was cast aside, so too every obstacle to our full communion will also be removed. This will be a grace of resurrection, of which we can have a foretaste even today."[142]

NOTES

1. John Paul II, *Ut Unum Sint*, 3; cf. 77: "The ultimate goal of the ecumenical movement is to re-establish full visible unity among all the baptized," http://w2.vatican.va/content/john-paul-ii/en/encyclicals/documents/hf_jp-ii_enc_25051995_ut-unum-sint.html.

2. John XXIII, *Ad Petri Cathedram*, 64, http://w2.vatican.va/content/john-xxiii/en/encyclicals/documents/hf_j-xxiii_enc_29061959_ad-petri.html.

3. Ibid. 66; cf. 110, 131.

4. Ibid. 72.

5. As a conciliar preparatory commission, the Secretariat was ultimately responsible for preparing *Unitatis Redintegratio*, *Nostra Aetate*, *Dignitatis Humanae*, and, together with the doctrinal commission, *Dei Verbum*. After the Council, Paul VI confirmed the Secretariat as a permanent dicastery of the Holy See, and it continued under the presidency of Augustin Cardinal Bea until his death in 1968. Johannes Cardinal Willebrands, whose ecumenical work will be discussed below, succeeded Bea in 1969. John Paul II's 1988 *Pastor Bonus* renamed the Secretariat the Pontifical Council for Promoting Christian Unity, the name it bears still today.

6. "Pope John's Opening Speech to the Council," in Walter M. Abbott, *The Documents of Vatican II* (New York: Guild Press, 1966), 717. That fostering Christian unity would be one of the Council's principal aims was reiterated in the very first paragraph of *Sacrosanctum Concilium*, the first constitution it promulgated.

7. Ibid. 715.

8. The majority of the historical highlights immediately below are summarized clearly and succinctly in Jared Wicks, SJ, "Cardinal Willebrands's Contributions to Catholic Ecumenical Theology," *Pro Ecclesia* 20, no. 1 (2011): 6–27. An earlier version of Wicks's paper can also be found in an important volume containing papers from the two 2009 symposia held in honor of the cardinal to commemorate the centenary of his birth: Adelbert Denaux, Peter de Mey, and J. G. M. Willebrands, *The Ecumenical Legacy of Johannes Cardinal Willebrands* (Leuven: Peeters, 2012).

9. Wicks, "Cardinal Willebrands's Contributions," 9.

10. Giovanni Battista Montini, "Discorso nel santuario di S. Antonio Abate," in *Discorsi e scritti milanesi* (1954–1963), 3 vols. (Rome: Istituto Paolo VI/Studium, 1997). Translation in Charles Morerod, OP, "The Decree on Ecumenism, *Unitatis Redintegratio*," in *Vatican II: Renewal within Tradition*, ed. Matthew Lamb and Matthew Levering (New York: Oxford University Press, 2008), 313. In this connection, now-Bishop Charles Morerod, OP, recalls that the First Vatican Council in 1870 had a far less positive view of the divisions that exist within Christianity, referring to them as "heresies, condemned by the fathers of Trent, which rejected the divine magisterium of the church and allowed religious questions to be a matter for the judgment of each individual." Observing that said groups "have gradually collapsed into a multiplicity of sects, either at variance or in agreement with one another," the Council lamented that "by this means a good many people have had all faith in Christ destroyed" (Morerod, "The Decree on Ecumenism," 311; First Vatican Council, *Dei Filius*, 5, https://www.ewtn.com/library/COUNCILS/V1.HTM). For further attempts to stem the tide of indifferentism, which was a danger perceived to be inherent within the ecumenical gatherings of the time, see Pius XI, *Mortalium Animos*, 6–8, http://w2.vatican.va/content/pius-xi/en/encyclicals/documents/hf_p-xi_enc_19280106_mortalium-animos.html.

11. Wicks, "Cardinal Willebrands's Contributions," 12.

12. Ibid. 14; *UR* 16. Here Wicks is summarizing from Willebrands's 1972 address at Lambeth Palace entitled "Prospects for Anglican-Roman Catholic Relations," given in *Information Service*, no. 101 (1990/II-III): 100–105.

13. Wicks, "Cardinal Willebrands's Contributions," 12–13. Wicks is citing a 1965 address given by Willebrands in Strasbourg entitled "Inhalt, Ziel, und Aufgabenbereich möglicher Kontakte und Zusammenarbeit zwischen römisch-katholischer Kirche und Lutherischem Weltbund," published in *Mandatum Unitatis: Beiträge zur Ökumene* (Paderborn: Bonifatius, 1989), 26.

14. *UR* 4; cf. *Ut Unum Sint* (*UUS*), 28, http://w2.vatican.va/content/john-paul-ii/en/encyclicals/documents/hf_jp-ii_enc_25051995_ut-unum-sint.html. In light of this deficiency, the decree adds, "It is hardly surprising if sometimes one tradition has come nearer than the other to an apt appreciation of certain aspects of the revealed mystery or has expressed them in a clearer manner. As a result, these various theological formulations are often to be considered as complementary rather than conflicting" (*UR* 17). Echoing *UR* but putting it more starkly, Cardinal Kasper acknowledges that the Catholic Church herself is "wounded" by the divisions of Christianity, and that "ecumenism is no one-way street" requiring the "exchange of gifts" called for by John Paul II. The cardinal goes even further in suggesting that the Catholic Church has

much to gain from ecumenism since "several aspects of being Church are better real-ized in the other Churches" (Kasper, *Current Problems*, II).

15. Wicks, "Cardinal Willebrands's Contributions," 13–14; cf. *LG* 23. This text is drawn from Willebrands's address "Prospects for Anglican-Roman Catholic Relations," cited above.

16. Lukas Vischer, "Report on a private audience with Pope Paul VI, 14 November 1964," in *Paolo VI e l'ecumeniso: colloquio internazionale di studio: Brescia, 25-26-27 settembre 1998* (Brescia: Istituto Paolo VI, 2001), 261.

17. *UR* 16.

18. Common Declaration of His Holiness Pope Paul VI and the Ecumenical Patriarch Athenagoras I (October 28, 1967); cf. *UR* 14 and *UUS* 57. This expression that appears in *UR* is itself ancient. On the history and proper interpretation of the expression, see Congregation for the Doctrine of the Faith, *Note on the Expression "Sister Churches"* (June 30, 2000), http://www.vatican.va/roman_curia/congregations/cfaith/documents/rc_con_cfaith_doc_20000630_chiese-sorelle_en.html. As Cardinal Ratzinger observes in the document's preface, the CDF is responding here to an "eccle-siology of sister churches" whose exponents "think that in fact the one Church of Christ does not exist, but may be re-established through the reconciliation of the two sister Churches." It also has in its sights an "improper" application of the expression to the relationship between the Catholic Church and the Anglican Communion. Though Paul VI is said to have referred to the Anglican Communion as a sister church in his ecumenical dealings, this was never officially taught by the pontiff.

19. Joint Catholic-Orthodox Declaration of His Holiness Pope Paul VI and the Ecumenical Patriarch Athenagoras I (December 7, 1965), 4.B, https://w2.vatican.va/content/paul-vi/en/speeches/1965/documents/hf_p-vi_spe_19651207_common-declaration.html. See also John Paul II, *UUS* 17, 41, 52.

20. The Oriental Orthodox do not speak of Christ as one person in two natures but instead refer to "the one incarnate nature of the Word of God" in accordance with the formulation of St. Cyril of Alexandria. At the same time, however, these com-munities reject the monophysitism of Eutyches who held that Christ's humanity was absorbed into his divine nature. See the discussion in Ronald Roberson, CSP, "Oriental-Orthodox-Catholic International Dialogue," in *Celebrating a Century of Ecumenism: Exploring the Achievements of International Dialogue*, ed. John Radano (Grand Rapids, MI: Eerdmans, 2012), 304. On the subject of ecumenical progress in this area, Cardinal Kasper writes, "It was recognized that when speaking of one per-son and two natures, the starting point was a different philosophical conception, but with the same meaning as far as the matter itself is concerned. This understanding has enabled maintaining the common faith in Jesus Christ as true God and true man, without imposing on the other one's own respective formula; thus, the formulations of the Council of Chalcedon were not forced upon the Ancient Oriental Churches" (*Current Problems*, III).

21. Common Declaration of His Holiness Pope Paul VI and His Holiness Mar Ignatius Jacoub III (October 27, 1971), https://w2.vatican.va/content/paul-vi/en/speeches/1971/october/documents/hf_p-vi_spe_19711027_dichiarazione-comune.html. The Syrian Orthodox Church, also known as the "Jacobite" Church, includes the Malankara Syrian Orthodox Church in India. Today the latter is distinct from the Malankara Orthodox Syrian Church in India, which was dependent on the Syrian Orthodox patriarchate until the twentieth century when there was a split in the community.

22. Common Declaration of His Holiness Pope Paul VI and His Holiness the Pope of Alexandria Shenouda III (May 10, 1973), https://w2.vatican.va/content/paul-vi/en/speeches/1973/may/documents/hf_p-vi_spe_19730510_dichiarazione-comune.html.

23. Due to the constraints of this chapter, not all of these can be discussed in detail. However, in addition to the dialogues mentioned here, it should be noted that bilateral dialogues with the following communities began during the pontificate of Paul VI: Methodist (1967); Reformed (1970); Pentecostal (1972); Evangelical (1977); Christian Church (1977).

24. Paul put his own fisherman's ring on Archbishop Michael Ramsey as a symbolic acknowledgment of his episcopal ministry. It should be noted that an earlier, private visit had been made by then-Archbishop of Canterbury Francis Fisher to John XXIII in Rome as early as 1960. See René Girault, "The Reception of Ecumenism," in *The Reception of Vatican II*, ed. Giuseppe Alberigo and Joseph A. Komonchak (Washington, DC: Catholic University of America Press, 1987), 141.

25. Common Declaration of His Holiness Paul VI and His Grace Michael Ramsey, Archbishop of Canterbury (March 24, 1966).

26. Anglican-Roman Catholic Preparatory Commission, *The Malta Report* (January 2, 1968), 2; cf. *UR* 13.

27. Anglican-Roman Catholic Preparatory Commission, *The Malta Report* 4.

28. John Paul II, *Slavorum Apostoli* (*SA*), 14, http://w2.vatican.va/content/john-paul-ii/en/encyclicals/documents/hf_jp-ii_enc_19850602_slavorum-apostoli.html.

29. *SA* 27.

30. *UUS* 3.

31. *UUS* 20.

32. *UUS* 19; cf. *UR* 5. Perhaps neglected at times, in this connection the following conciliar teaching is worth recalling: "It is especially the duty of bishops to seek out men and both request and promote dialogue with them" (*Christus Dominus*, 13), http://www.vatican.va/archive/hist_councils/ii_vatican_council/documents/vat-ii_decree_19651028_christus-dominus_en.html.

33. *UUS* 20; *Gaudium et Spes* (*GS*), 92: "For the bonds which unite the faithful are mightier than anything dividing them. Hence, let there be unity in what is necessary; freedom in what is unsettled, and charity in any case," http://www.vatican.va/archive/hist_councils/ii_vatican_council/documents/vat-ii_const_19651207_gaudium-et-spes_en.html.

34. *UUS* 11, 38; cf. *UR* 3.

35. *UUS* 18. More recently, Pope Francis and Patriarch Bartholomew I have likewise affirmed that theological dialogue "does not seek a theological lowest common denominator on which to reach a compromise, but is rather about deepening one's grasp of the whole truth that Christ has given to his Church" (Common Declaration of Pope Francis and Patriarch Bartholomew I [May 25, 2014], 4), https://w2.vatican.va/content/francesco/en/speeches/2014/may/documents/papa-francesco_20140525_terra-santa-dichiarazione-congiunta.html.

36. *UR* 4, 11. Cardinal Kasper would later add, referencing *UR*: "The Catholic Church takes the other Churches seriously precisely in that she does not even out the differences nor does she consider these differences as being of 'equal value', but she respects the other Churches in the otherness which they claim for themselves. In that sense she speaks with them '*par cum pari*', on a parity level, 'on an equal footing'" (*Current Problems*, 12); cf. *UR* 9.

37. *UUS* 37; *UR* 11. When John Paul II visited Switzerland in 1984, the former general secretary of the WCC suggested a common document on this notion, which was eventually produced by the WCC-Catholic Church Joint Working Group in 1990 under the title *The Notion of the "Hierarchy of Truths": An Ecumenical Interpretation* (file:/// C:/Users/mramage/Downloads/06%20Sixth%20Report%20Joint%20Working%20 Group.pdf). It is suggested that the expression "hierarchy of truths" came to John XXIII from Edmund Schlink, a German Protestant observer at the Council. See Morerod, "The Decree on Ecumenism," 337n59.

38. Second Vatican Council, *Lumen Gentium* (*LG*), 8, http://www.vatican.va/ archive/hist_councils/ii_vatican_council/documents/vat-ii_const_19641121_lumen-gentium_en.html; *UR* 4; *UUS* 10, 86. Cardinal Kasper would later write of the expression *subsistit in*: "The decisive element of the Second Vatican Council's ecumenical approach is the fact that the Council no longer identifies the Church of Jesus Christ simply with the Roman Catholic Church, as had Pope Pius XII as lately as in the Encyclical *Mystici corporis* (1943)" (*Current Problems*, II).

39. *LG* 15; *UUS* 74; *UR* 22; *GS* 92. See also the important clarification of the teaching conveyed with *subsistit in* crafted by the CDF in *Dominus Iesus*, 16–17, http:// www.vatican.va/roman_curia/congregations/cfaith/documents/rc_con_cfaith_doc_ 20000806_dominus-iesus_en.html.

40. *UR* 15. See also the articulation of this difference in Joseph Ratzinger, *Theological Highlights of Vatican II* (New York: Paulist Press, 1966), 116, and, later, in Benedict XVI, *Light of the World* (San Francisco: Ignatius Press, 2010), 94–95.

41. John Paul II, *Orientale Lumen* (*OL*), 1, https://w2.vatican.va/content/john-paul-ii/en/apost_letters/1995/documents/hf_jp-ii_apl_19950502_orientale-lumen.html.

42. *OL* 3.

43. *OL* 16.

44. *OL* 6; *UR* 15.

45. John Paul II, Address to His Beatitude Christodoulos, Archbishop of Athens and Primate of Greece (May 4, 2001), 2, https://w2.vatican.va/content/john-paul-ii/en/speeches/2001/may/documents/hf_jp-ii_spe_20010504_archbishop-athens.html. See also the International Theological Commission's 1999 *Memory and Reconciliation: The Church and the Faults of the Past*, especially 5.2, http://www. vatican.va/roman_curia/congregations/cfaith/cti_documents/rc_con_cfaith_doc_ 20000307_memory-reconc-itc_en.html.

46. Common Declaration of John Paul II and His Beatitude Christodoulos, Archbishop of Athens and Primate of Greece (May 4, 2001), 2, https://w2.vatican.va/ content/john-paul-ii/en/speeches/2001/may/documents/hf_jp-ii_spe_20010504_ archbishop-athens.html. On the subject of common declarations, it should be noted that, like his predecessor Paul VI, John Paul issued a series of such documents jointly with patriarchs of Oriental Orthodox churches. The first, signed with Moran Mar Ignatius Zakka I, Patriarch of Antioch and All the East and Supreme head of the Universal Syrian Orthodox Church (1984), acknowledged that past schisms "in no way affect or touch the substance of their faith." Other common declarations were signed with Supreme Patriarch and Catholicos Karekin I of All Armenians (1996) and Catholicos Aram I of Cilicia of the Armenians (1997).

47. PCPCU, *Directory for the Application of Principles and Norms on Ecumenism*, 132, http://www.vatican.va/roman_curia/pontifical_councils/chrstuni/documents/rc_ pc_chrstuni_doc_25031993_principles-and-norms-on-ecumenism_en.html.

48. PCPCU, *Directory*, 129; cf. *CIC*, can. 844, 4, http://www.vatican.va/archive/ ENG1104/_INDEX.HTM; and *CCEO*, can. 671, 4, http://www.intratext.com/X/

ENG1199.HTM. Of course, this exception is not granted simply under any conditions whatsoever. The person must "be unable to have recourse for the sacrament desired to a minister of his or her own Church or ecclesial community, ask for the sacrament of his or her own initiative, manifest Catholic faith in this sacrament, and be properly disposed" (PCPCU, *Directory*, 131).

49. PCPCU, *Directory*, 16.

50. Ibid. 20.

51. Ibid; cf. *UR* 4, 15–16.

52. Ibid. 63.

53. Ibid. 64.

54. Ratzinger, *Theological Highlights*, 110.

55. Ibid. 114–15.

56. Ibid. 115. That Ratzinger sees this principle applying to Protestant communities as well can be seen in his insisting that "the Catholic does not insist on the dissolution of the Protestant confessions and the demolishing of their churches but hopes, rather, that they will be strengthened in their confessions and in their ecclesial reality" (Ratzinger, *Principles of Catholic* Theology [San Francisco: Ignatius Press, 1987], 202).

57. Joseph Ratzinger, *Theological Highlights*, 112–13.

58. Ibid. 113.

59. Joseph Ratzinger, *Pilgrim Fellowship of Faith: The Church as Communion* (San Francisco: Ignatius Press, 2005), 232. In the same vein the author writes that, despite the difficulties that separate Christians, we must learn that the issue of unity is "of so high a rank that it can be sacrificed only to safeguard what is most fundamental, not where the way to it is obstructed by formulations and practices that, however important they may be, do not destroy community in the faith of the Fathers and in the basic form of the Church as they saw her." We should, he continues, "inquire always not just about the defensibility of union, of mutual recognition, but even more urgently about the defensibility of remaining separate, for it is not unity that requires justification but the absence of it" (Ratzinger, *Principles*, 199–200).

60. Ratzinger, *Pilgrim Fellowship*, 255.

61. Ibid.

62. Joseph Ratzinger, *Salt of the Earth* (San Francisco: Ignatius Press, 1997), 242.

63. Ibid. 243. On the confusion that results in various places from the constant creation of new ruptures and sects, see Benedict XVI, *Ecclesia in Medio Oriente*, 11–18, http://w2.vatican.va/content/benedict-xvi/en/apost_exhortations/documents/hf_ben-xvi_exh_20120914_ecclesia-in-medio-oriente.html; and *Africae Munus*, 89–91, http://w2.vatican.va/content/benedict-xvi/en/apost_exhortations/documents/hf_ben-xvi_exh_20111119_africae-munus.html.

64. Ibid. On the distinction between essentials and non-essentials, see also Ratzinger, "What Unites and Divides Denominations? Ecumenical Reflections," in *Joseph Ratzinger in Communio*, vol. 1 (Grand Rapids, MI: Eerdmans, 2010). Ratzinger hopes that all will learn to "distinguish between essential and non-essential and so find the way to a diversified, pluriform unity" (7).

65. Ratzinger, *Principles*, 203; cf. 218–19.

66. Kasper, *Current Problems*, III.

67. Ratzinger, *Principles*, 198.

68. Ibid. 199.

69. Ibid.

70. Ibid. For a more recent attempt to sketch what this reunion would look like, see the 2010 North American Orthodox-Catholic Dialogue, *Steps Towards a Reunited*

Church, discussed below (http://www.usccb.org/beliefs-and-teachings/ecumenical-and-interreligious/ecumenical/orthodox/steps-towards-reunited-church.cfm).

71. Benedict XVI, First Message at the End of the Eucharistic Celebration with the Members of the College of Cardinals in the Sistine Chapel (April 20, 2005), 5, https://w2.vatican.va/content/benedict-xvi/en/messages/pont-messages/2005/documents/hf_ben-xvi_mes_20050420_missa-pro-ecclesia.html.

72. While outside the scope of this chapter on ecumenism, the respect paid by Benedict to the Muslim faith should be noted. Removing his slippers, Benedict not only entered Istanbul's Sultan Ahmed Mosque, but prayed facing Mecca alongside the mufti of Istanbul. Notwithstanding the violence provoked in the Muslim world following his Regensburg Address, a few years later Benedict was able to report, "After all the awful things that happened, about which I can only feel sadness . . . this controversy led to the development of a truly vigorous dialogue" (*Light of the World*, 98).

73. Common Declaration of Pope Benedict XVI and the Ecumenical Patriarch Bartholomew I (November 30, 2006), http://w2.vatican.va/content/benedict-xvi/en/speeches/2006/november/documents/hf_ben-xvi_spe_20061130_dichiarazione-comune.html.

74. The relics had been taken to Rome in 1204 after the sack of Constantinople during the Fourth Crusade. In a great ecumenical gesture, John Paul II returned them to Istanbul shortly before his death. For other ecumenical moments in which Rome restored ancient treasures to the Orthodox, see Roberson, "Oriental-Orthodox-Catholic International Dialogue," 254.

75. Benedict XVI, *Light of the World*, 86.

76. Common Declaration of Pope Benedict XVI and the Archbishop of Canterbury His Grace Rowan Williams (November 23, 2006), http://w2.vatican.va/content/benedict-xvi/en/speeches/2006/november/documents/hf_ben-xvi_spe_20061123_common-decl.html.

77. Benedict XVI, *Anglicanorum Coetibus,* 5.III, http://w2.vatican.va/content/benedict-xvi/en/apost_constitutions/documents/hf_ben-xvi_apc_20091104_anglicanorum-coetibus.html. For further explanation of his decision to create the ordinariates, see Benedict XVI, *Light of the World*, 96–97.

78. Joint Statement by the Archbishop of Westminster and the Archbishop of Canterbury (October 20, 2009), http://www.anglicannews.org/news/2009/10/joint-statement-by-the-archbishop-of-westminster-and-the-archbishop-of-canterbury.aspx.

79. Benedict XVI, *Summorum Pontificum,* art. 1, http://w2.vatican.va/content/benedict-xvi/en/motu_proprio/documents/hf_ben-xvi_motu-proprio_20070707_summorum-pontificum.html.

80. Congregation for Bishops, Decree Remitting the Excommunication "Latae Sententiae" of the Bishops of the Society of St. Pius X (January 21, 2009), http://www.vatican.va/roman_curia/congregations/cbishops/documents/rc_con_cbishops_doc_20090121_remissione-scomunica_en.html.

81. Benedict XVI, *Letter to the Bishops of the Catholic Church Concerning the Remission of the Excommunication of the Four Bishops Consecrated by Archbishop Lefebvre* (March 10, 2009), https://w2.vatican.va/content/benedict-xvi/en/letters/2009/documents/hf_ben-xvi_let_20090310_remissione-scomunica.html.

82. For a more comprehensive overview of the ecumenical landscape among the various Christian communities, the following resources are recommended: Brian Cope and Michael Kinnamon, eds., *Ecumenical Movement: An Anthology of Key Texts and Voices* (Grand Rapids: Eerdmans, 1997); Jeffrey Gros, FSC, *Growth in Agreement II: Reports and Agreed Statements of Ecumenical Conversations on a World Level, 1982–1998*

(Grand Rapids: Eerdmans, 2001); Jeffrey Gros, *Growth in Agreement III: International Dialogue Texts and Agreed Statements, 1998–2005* (Grand Rapids: Eerdmans, 2008). As the writing of this chapter, the most up-to-date print resource is Radano, *Celebrating a Century of Ecumenism*, with its various essays, some of which are cited here. The United States Conference of Catholic Bishops website (http://www.usccb.org/beliefs-and-teachings/ecumenical-and-interreligious/) is also rich with up-to-date ecumenical resources including results from regional dialogues within North America. Finally, there is the official website of the PCPCU whose resources are mentioned in the footnote below.

83. The website for the PCPCU (http://www.vatican.va/roman_curia/pontifical_councils/chrstuni/) provides a comprehensive database of texts from a host of dialogues in which the Church has been engaged, including: the World Council of Churches, Orthodox Churches of the Byzantine Tradition, Oriental Orthodox Churches, Old Catholic Churches of the Union of Utrecht, Assyrian Church of the East, Anglican Communion, Lutheran World Federation, World Methodist Council, Mennonite World Conference, World Alliance of Reformed Churches, Baptist World Alliance, Christian Church, Pentecostal Churches, and World Evangelical Alliance. On a more informal level and with no official reports, the Church has also been in dialogue with Seventh Day Adventists, the Salvation Army, and non-denominational Christians. It is also worth mentioning that Mormon representatives were invited to attend an ecumenical prayer service with the pope for the first time during Benedict's visit to the United States in 2008.

84. Jared Wicks, SJ, "Lutheran-Roman Catholic World-Level Dialogue: Selected Remarks," in Radano, *Celebrating a Century of Ecumenism*, 57.

85. The documents are as follows: Phase I (1967–1972): *Malta Report: The Gospel and the Church* (1972); Phase II (1973–1984): *The Eucharist* (1978); *All Under One Christ* (1980); *Ways to Community* (1980); *The Ministry in the Church* (1981); *Martin Luther—Witness to Christ* (1983); *Facing Unity—Models, Forms, and Phases of Catholic-Lutheran Church Fellowship* (1984); Phase III (1986–1993): *Joint Declaration on the Doctrine of Justification* (1999); Phase IV (1995–2006): *The Apostolicity of the Church* (2006). This list is compiled from the PCPCU website: http://www.vatican.va/roman_curia/pontifical_councils/chrstuni/index.htm; and Cardinal Walter Kasper, *Harvesting the Fruits: Basic Aspects of Christian Faith in Ecumenical Dialogue* (London: Bloomsbury, 2013), xi–xii. Wicks has compiled a list that also includes results of regional dialogues in the United States and elsewhere in his "Lutheran-Roman Catholic World-Level Dialogue," 73–76. Interestingly, it was the observer Lindbeck who also acknowledged that some kind of infallible authority would be indispensable if Christian unity matters (Morerod, "A Thomistic Contribution to Ecumenism," in *Wisdom and Holiness, Science and Scholarship, Essays in Honor of Matthew L. Lamb*, ed. Michael Dauphinais and Matthew Levering [Sapientia Press, Naples, FL, 2007], 260).

86. Wicks, "Lutheran-Roman Catholic World-Level Dialogue," 59. As an indication of how wide an influence this agreement has or could have, the Lutheran World Federation represents 70.5 million Lutherans in 79 countries. Additionally, in 2006 the World Methodist Council, which represents 80 million people worldwide, voted unanimously to sign the agreement.

87. Ibid. 59–60.

88. Kasper, *Current Problems*, IV.

89. Wicks, "Lutheran-Roman Catholic World-Level Dialogue," 61.

90. Ibid. 66.

91. Morerod, "The Decree on Ecumenism," 330.

92. The documents are as follows: Preparatory Commission (1967–1968): *Malta Report of the Preparatory Commission* (1968); ARCIC-I (1970–1981): *Windsor Statement: Eucharistic Doctrine* (1971); *Ministry and Ordination* (1973); *Authority in the Church I* (1976); *Eucharistic Doctrine: Elucidation* (1979); *Ministry and Ordination: Elucidation* (1979); *Authority in the Church I: Elucidation* (1981); *Authority in the Church II* (1981); *Preface, Introduction, and Conclusion to the Final Report* (1982); *Clarifications of Certain Aspects of the Agreed Statements on Eucharist and Ministry* (1994); ARCIC-II (1983–2005): *Salvation and the Church* (1987); *Church as Communion* (1991); *Life in Christ: Morals, Communion, and the Church* (1994); *The Gift of Authority: Authority in the Church III* (1999); *Mary: Grace and Hope in Christ* (2005). Links to these documents can be found on the PCPCU website: http://www.vatican. va/roman_curia/pontifical_councils/chrstuni/sub-index/index_anglican-comm.htm. A helpful breakdown of most of them is found in Kasper, *Harvesting the Fruits*, xii–xiv.

93. Currently the Episcopal Church in the United States is unable to participate in ARCIC-III, as the Archbishop of Canterbury determined that certain of its teachings were inconsistent with beliefs of the Anglican Communion at large. However, the national dialogue between Catholics and Anglicans in America continues to meet and study similar topics.

94. See the discussion in Geernaert, "Achievements of ARCIC and IARCCUM," in Radano, *Celebrating a Century of Ecumenism*, 128–29.

95. As Benedict XVI observes on this topic, "We must recognize the fact that Protestantism has taken steps that have led it farther away from us, rather than closer to us; women's ordination and the acceptance of homosexual partnerships are just two of many similar examples. There are also other ethical positions, other instances of conformism with the spirit of the present age, that make the dialogue more difficult" (*Light of the World*, 93–94). See also Kasper, *Harvesting the Fruits*, 203 on "the crucial question of theological anthropology" which he considers "the root of Western church divisions." In his 2004 address to the PCPCU entitled "The Church's Future: Ecumenism, Evangelization," Kasper further speaks of "an ethical liberalism that creates further dissent, either within these communities themselves or between them and the Catholic Church," http://www.vatican.va/roman_curia/pontifical_councils/ chrstuni/documents/rc_pc_chrstuni_doc_20041121_kasper-ecumenismo_en.html.

96. Donna Geernaert, SC, "Achievements of ARCIC and IARCCUM," 135–36.

97. Not to be confused with Orthodox Churches of the Byzantine tradition, the six churches in this family include the Armenian Apostolic Church, Coptic Orthodox Church, Syrian Orthodox Church; Malankara Orthodox Syrian Church; Ethiopian Orthodox Church; and Eritrean Orthodox Church, which has functioned independently since the nation's independence from Ethiopia in 1993. For particular results, see Radano, *Celebrating a Century of Ecumenism*, xxiii; and Roberson, "Oriental-Orthodox-Catholic International Dialogue," 304ff. For more on the nature of the division between the Catholic Church and Oriental Orthodox churches in relation to the Council of Chalcedon's Christology, see the discussion of Oriental Churches above.

98. Roberson, "Oriental-Orthodox-Catholic International Dialogue," 310.

99. Francis, Address to Pope Tawadros, Pope of Alexandria and Patriarch of the See of St. Mark (May 10, 2013), https://w2.vatican.va/content/francesco/en/speeches/ 2013/may/documents/papa-francesco_20130510_tawadros.html.

100. Francis, Address to Catholicos Karekin II, Patriarch of the Armenian Apostolic Church (May 8, 2014), https://w2.vatican.va/content/francesco/en/ speeches/2014/may/documents/papa-francesco_20140508_patriarca-armeni.html. Francis used this same expression during the 2014 his ecumenical celebration with

Ecumenical Patriarch Bartholomaios in the Holy Sepulcher, adding, "Those who kill, persecute Christians out of hatred, do not ask if they are Orthodox or Catholics: they are Christians. The blood of Christians is the same" (May 25, 2014), https://w2.vatican.va/content/francesco/en/speeches/2014/may/documents/papa-francesco_20140525_terra-santa-celebrazione-ecumenica.html.

101. See Roberson, "Oriental-Orthodox-Catholic International Dialogue," 311ff.

102. Common Christological Declaration between the Catholic Church and the Assyrian Church of the East (November 11, 1994), http://www.vatican.va/roman_curia/pontifical_councils/chrstuni/documents/rc_pc_chrstuni_doc_11111994_assyrian-church_en.html. In the years that followed, a warm relationship also developed between the Assyrians and their Catholic counterpart, the Chaldean Catholic Church. In 1996 the primates pledged to form a joint commission that would elaborate a common catechism, oversee the foundation of a seminary in the United States, and develop common pastoral programs. In 1997 they issued the Joint Synodal Decree for Promoting Unity recognizing one another's diverse practices as legitimate.

103. See Taft's article "Mass Without the Consecration? The Historic Agreement on the Eucharist between the Catholic Church and the Assyrian Church of the East Promulgated 26 October 2001," *Centro Pro Unione Semi-Annual Bulletin* 63 (Spring 2003): 15–27.

104. PCPCU, Guidelines for Admission to the Eucharist between the Chaldean Church and the Assyrian Church of the East (July 20, 2001), http://www.vatican.va/roman_curia/pontifical_councils/chrstuni/documents/rc_pc_chrstuni_doc_20011025_chiesa-caldea-assira_en.html.

105. Roberson, "Oriental-Orthodox-Catholic International Dialogue," 313.

106. The documents are as follows: Munich (1982): *The Mystery of the Church and the Eucharist in the Light of the Mystery of the Holy Trinity*; Bari (1987): *Faith, Sacraments and the Unity of the Church*; Valamo (1988): *The Sacrament of Order in the Sacramental Structure of the Church, with Particular Reference to the Importance of the Apostolic Succession for the Sanctification and Unity of the People of God*; Balamand (1993): *Uniatism: Method of Union of the Past, and Present Search for Full Communion*; Ravenna (2007): *Ecclesiological and Canonical Consequences of the Sacramental Nature of the Church. Ecclesial Communion, Conciliarity and Authority*. These documents are all available on the PCPCU website: http://www.vatican.va/roman_curia/pontifical_councils/chrstuni/sub-index/index_orthodox-ch.htm. Space constraints do not allow here for a full discussion of the progress made at joint commission meetings which took place between the publication of these works and laid the groundwork for them.

107. Roberson, "Oriental-Orthodox-Catholic International Dialogue," 252. Depending on the author, a "uniate" church may refer either to an Eastern church that has never broken communion with the Holy See or to one that went into schism and subsequently sought reconciliation.

108. Joint International Commission for Theological Dialogue between the Roman Catholic Church and the Orthodox Church, *Uniatism: Method of Union of the Past, and Present Search for Full Communion*, 15.

109. Roberson, "Oriental-Orthodox-Catholic International Dialogue," 253.

110. For more on this drama, see ibid. 257–60; and Sandro Magister, "Papal Primacy. Russia Heads the Resistance Against Rome," October 6, 2010, http://chiesa.espresso.repubblica.it/articolo/1345026?eng=y.

111. Joint International Commission for Theological Dialogue between the Roman Catholic Church and the Orthodox Church, *Ecclesiological and Canonical Consequences of the Sacramental Nature of the Church: Ecclesial Communion, Conciliarity and Authority*,

9, 33, http://www.vatican.va/roman_curia/pontifical_councils/chrstuni/ch_ortho-dox_docs/rc_pc_chrstuni_doc_20071013_documento-ravenna_en.html.

112. Ibid. 37.

113. Ibid. 27, 39.

114. Ibid. 42.

115. Ibid.

116. Ibid. 45.

117. Ibid. 41.

118. While it does not represent the commission's definitive position, an unofficial version of the initial Crete document has been made available by Sandro Magister and at least hints at the direction the dialogue had been going: http://chiesa.espresso. repubblica.it/articolo/1341814?eng=y.

119. Pope Benedict and Patriarch Kirill of Moscow demonstrated affection for one another and acknowledged a common ethical vision of witness to Christ in the midst of a rampantly secularized world; see Bendedict XVI, *Light of the World*, 87–88. On the subject of a potential meeting between the two, however, Benedict had said, "Nevertheless, opinion in Russia has to be prepared for a meeting of this kind. There is still a certain fear of the Catholic Church" (91). Indeed, as sources such as George Weigel's open letter to Kirill (http://www.firstthings.com/web-exclusives/2014/06/an-open-letter-to-the-patriarch-of-moscow) demonstrate, tensions are currently running high in the case of ecumenical relations with the Russian Orthodox Church.

120. A complete listing of these works is found on the USCCB Ecumenical and Interreligious Affairs office website: http://www.usccb.org/beliefs-and-teachings/ecumenical-and-interreligious/ecumenical/ecumenical-documents-and-news-releases.cfm#CP_JUMP_112270.

121. Indeed, the role played by the bishop of Rome in the worldwide Catholic communion is described here as the "root obstacle" preventing full communion between Catholics and Orthodox. See the North American Orthodox-Catholic Consultation's *Steps Towards a Reunited Church*, 2.

122. North American Orthodox-Catholic Consultation, *The Filioque: A Church Dividing Issue?*, IV, http://www.usccb.org/beliefs-and-teachings/ecumenical-and-interreligious/ecumenical/orthodox/filioque-church-dividing-issue-english.cfm. It may surprise some Catholics to learn that the consultation recommends "that the Catholic Church, as a consequence of the normative and irrevocable dogmatic value of the Creed of 381, use the original Greek text alone in making translations of that Creed for catechetical and liturgical use" (IV).

123. North American Orthodox-Catholic Consultation, *Steps Towards a Reunited Church*, 6.a.

124. Ibid. 6.g.

125. Ibid. 7.e.

126. Francis, interview with Corriere della Sera, March 5, 2014; in-flight press conference, July 28, 2013.

127. Francis, *Evangelii Gaudium*, 244–46; interview with *America Magazine*, September 30, 2013, http://americamagazine.org/pope-interview.

128. Francis, *Laudato Si'*, 7–9, http://w2.vatican.va/content/francesco/en/encyclicals/documents/papa-francesco_20150524_enciclica-laudato-si.html.

129. Common Declaration of Pope Francis and Patriarch Bartholomew I (May 25, 2014); Ecumenical Blessing and Signing of Common Declaration (November 30, 2014); Joint Declaration of Pope Francis and Patriarch Kirill of Moscow and All Russia (February 12, 2016), https://w2.vatican.va/content/francesco/en/speeches/

2016/february/documents/papa-francesco_20160212_dichiarazione-comune-kirill.
html. Although the document concentrates primarily on the need for solidarity in
today's troubled times, it is significant that Francis and Kirill also tackled the subject
of uniatism. After reiterating their mutual understanding that their mission "entails
mutual respect for members of the Christian communities and excludes any form of
proselytism," Francis and Kirill add, "It is today clear that the past method of 'uniatism,' understood as the union of one community to the other, separating it from its
Church, is not the way to re–establish unity. Nonetheless, the ecclesial communities
which emerged in these historical circumstances have the right to exist and to undertake all that is necessary to meet the spiritual needs of their faithful, while seeking
to live in peace with their neighbours. Orthodox and Greek Catholics are in need of
reconciliation and of mutually acceptable forms of co–existence" (Joint Declaration of
Pope Francis and Patriarch Kirill of Moscow and All Russia, 24–25).

130. An excellent resource to consult on the past and current state of ecumenical
affairs is the paper of John Crossin, OSFS, entitled "The Decree on Ecumenism and
Its Effects: Past, Present, and Future." I would like to thank Fr. Crossin for sharing
this text from which several important sources were drawn in this chapter. The paper
is available at http://www.shu.edu/academics/artsci/catholic-studies-department/
upload/The-Decree-on-Ecumenism-and-Its-Effects5-Crossin7.pdf.

131. Kasper, *Harvesting the Fruits*, 196–97.

132. Ibid. 2–3. Some would argue that the ecumenical movement has fallen into
a crisis of stagnation, as Cardinal Kasper observes in the introduction to his *Current
Problems in Ecumenical Theology*. As of this chapter's composition, an important new
book is due out on this subject: Michael Kinnamon, *Can a Renewal Movement Be
Renewed?: Questions for the Future of Ecumenism* (Grand Rapids, MI: Eerdmans, 2014).

133. Both popes refer to Oscar Cullmann as the authority from whom they origi-
nally derived this idea. See Joseph Ratzinger, *Church, Ecumenism, and Politics* (San
Francisco: Ignatius Press, 2008), 135–37; and *Pilgrim Fellowship of Faith*, 258. For the
current pontiff's articulation, see Francis and Abraham Skorka, *On Heaven and Earth:
Pope Francis on Faith, Family, and the Church in the Twenty-First Century* (New York:
Image, 2013), 217.

134. Although this author has not seen his summons taken up sufficiently in
practice, Charles Morerod, OP, has called attention to the necessity of addressing the
contradictory philosophical presuppositions that undergird the respective traditions
of Protestantism and Catholicism. This "semi-unconscious substratum" most significantly concerns how the nature of man's relationship with God is conceived. Like the
moral issues that are now on the docket for ecumenical debate, this dimension of our
divisions has largely been ignored over the course of doctrinal debates. As Morerod
puts it, however, "It is not enough to compare positions of two Christian confessions
on a particular point. Each point must be situated within the context of two complex
systems" (*Ecumenism and Philosophy: Philosophical Questions for a Renewal of Dialogue*
[Ann Arbor, MI: Sapientia Press, 2006], 166). The following might best encapsulate
Morerod's main point: "I would like to suggest, daringly, that not only the cause of
unity, but also the very intention of the Reformers, would be better served if it were
disengaged from certain philosophical presuppositions which have been partially conditioning it for almost half a millennium, and which limit its fruition" (171). This charitable critique of Protestantism aligns well with Benedict XVI's Regensburg Address,
in which he calls attention to the problematic process of de-hellenization initiated by
the Reformers.

135. The precise nature of the meeting between Francis and Bartholomew has yet to be determined. It should also be noted that the Orthodox have their own synod slated for 2016 whose results could have a potentially significant impact on the future of ecumenical relations between East and West.

136. Ratzinger, *Church, Ecumenism, and Politics*, 88; cf. 89, 134.

137. *UR* 8. Kasper has written an important little work called *A Handbook of Spiritual Ecumenism* (Hyde Park, NY: New City Press, 2007), which is a resource for ordinary faithful interested in or already involved in ecumenism. The USCCB has also recently made a short video series entitled *On the Path to Christian Unity* available on its website: http://www.usccb.org/beliefs-and-teachings/ecumenical-and-interreligious/on-the-path-toward-christian-unity.cfm.

138. *UUS* 21.

139. Ratzinger, *Principles of Catholic Theology*, 199.

140. See Ratzinger, *Church, Ecumenism, and Politics*, 88, 108, 121.

141. Benedict XVI, Address to the Parish Priests and Clergy of Rome (February 14, 2013), http://w2.vatican.va/content/benedict-xvi/en/speeches/2013/february/documents/hf_ben-xvi_spe_20130214_clero-roma.html.

142. Francis, Ecumenical Celebration on the Occasion of the 50th Anniversary of the Meeting between Pope Paul VI and Patriarch Athenagoras in Jerusalem (May 25, 2014), https://w2.vatican.va/content/francesco/en/speeches/2014/may/documents/papa-francesco_20140525_terra-santa-celebrazione-ecumenica.html.

12

Orientalium Ecclesiarum

Adam A. J. DeVille

Introduction

Orientalium Ecclesiarum (henceforth: *OE*), the decree on the
Catholic Eastern Churches (Flannery's translation[1]), was promulgated on November 21, 1964, the very same day as two other closely
linked documents: *Lumen Gentium* (*LG*), on the Church; and
Unitatis Redintegratio (*UR*), on the search for Christian unity. All
three of these documents, different though they are in some ways,
including their status or authority, can and should be examined
together, for they treat overlapping ecumenical and ecclesiological
questions. Though the primary focus of this essay is on *OE*, the
other aforementioned two texts will necessarily be given some secondary scrutiny here, especially *LG*, which is arguably the most
important of all the conciliar texts and has undeniably had a major
impact (not all of it positive) on the incomplete realization of the
vision of *OE*. Such a reading of these three texts in tandem is in fact
prescribed by *OE* itself.[2] I proceed in four parts:

(I) a close, critical reading of *OE* itself in the context of the council of 1964;

(II) a re-reading or "re-reception"[3] of the document in 2015 in the
light of a half-century of changes in Eastern Catholic life,
some of them inspired or encouraged by later Roman magisterial documents, including in particular the 1990 *Code of
Canons of the Eastern Churches*, the 1993 *Ecumenical Directory*,
the 1995 encyclical *Ut Unum Sint* and apostolic letter *Orientale
Lumen*, and the 1996 Instruction for Applying the Liturgical
Prescriptions of the Code of Canons of the Eastern Churches;

(III) an examination of the theological literature to see what Eastern Christians themselves have been saying and writing in the last fifty years in response to *OE*;

(IV) a description of various desiderata Eastern Christians—and here I deliberately include Eastern Orthodox alongside Eastern Catholics—are still hoping to see achieved as we enter the second half-century after Vatican II.

I. The Decree: Context

To understand what a far-reaching and broad-minded decree *OE* was and is, it is necessary for a moment to consider—albeit too briefly and baldly—the history[4] of straitened and strained relations between the Catholic Church and the Christian East, especially since the Counter-Reformation.[5] After increasing conflict and estrangement in the latter years of the first millennium, and after the mutual excommunications in July 1054 between the papal legate and ecumenical patriarch in Constantinople (which was never intended as "church-dividing"), relations between East and West continued on a sharp downward decline after the Fourth Crusade in 1204.[6] As the empire in the East was about to disappear in the first half of the fifteenth century, East and West met in the last council of union, first in Ferrara and then later in Florence, to unite in the face of Turkish Islam. Though the conciliar fathers agreed on the terms of union, the whole thing would soon collapse in failure when their people, especially in the East, revolted and refused to "receive" the council. It was to be the last meeting attempting such wholesale reunification.[7]

After the failure of Florence, the Reformation further shattered Christian unity in the West. The Catholic Church at this point—as the eminent historian Robert Taft has put it—changed tactics, and <u>instead</u> of wholescale unity with the entire East (as at Florence, where decrees were signed with Chalcedonian and non-Chalcedonian Orthodox alike) <u>instead</u> began receiving smaller groups of Orthodox Christians into communion through various negotiations.[8] Arguably the prototype for this new method of unity was the one that remains today the most controverted: Orthodox Christians from what is now Ukraine (especially those in Galicia), who journeyed to Rome and negotiated terms in the Union of Brest.[9] Thus was born what has come to be known as "uniatism."

A "uniate" was originally a neutral or even positive Slavic neologism[10] for "one who seeks unity," but it has since been turned into a pejorative by many Orthodox, who view it as a synonym for "one who betrays Orthodoxy by submitting to papal jurisdiction."[11] Today, officially, the Catholic and Orthodox Church both agree that the term should, if only as a matter of courtesy, be dropped, since it has come to be seen as offensive by many Eastern Catholics. Moreover, there is also an official agreement since 1993 that the method of "uniatism," that is, of Catholics receiving individual churches or groups of Orthodox into full communion, must be abandoned.[12]

After Brest, similar ventures would follow with other Eastern Christian groups, all pursued with three ideas firmly in mind on the Roman side: an "ecumenism of return,"[13] which conceived of unity as a unilateral process of one "side" repenting and "returning" to the other; a "soteriological exclusivism," by which it was held that the Latin Church alone had the sacramental and liturgical means for salvation, making not just communion with her, but active imitation *of* her singular Latin practices and beliefs, necessary for all wishing to be saved; and a "pyramidal ecclesiology," in which the only possible model of the Church and of Christian unity was an undifferentiated hierarchical structure with the pope on top and everyone subservient to him.

In this context, relations between Catholics and Orthodox, and between Latin and Eastern Catholics, shrank to a rather narrow level as each side remained rather fearful and suspicious of the other at least up until Pope Leo XIII's 1894 encyclical *Orientalium Dignitas*,[14] which marked something of a spirit of openness in theory. It elaborated thirteen proposals having to do with sacramental discipline and patriarchal jurisdiction, and also mentioned the establishment of special colleges in Rome where Melkite, Armenian, and other Eastern Christians could study—a process that would be carried on by Pope Benedict XV, who founded the illustrious Pontifical Oriental Institute in 1917, from which now several generations of the world's leading scholars, Catholic and Orthodox alike, have graduated.[15]

Notwithstanding these modest advances, few of which trickled down to dioceses or parishes, Eastern Catholics largely remained with no natural allies, being often regarded by many of their Western brethren as insufficiently Latin and therefore suspect as Catholic, and by their Eastern brethren as insufficiently Orthodox and therefore suspect as quasi-Latins seeking to "trick" the Orthodox into Roman submission. Whatever generosity popes from Leo XIII on manifested was not often matched by other Curial offices or most of the rest of the Catholic hierarchy, especially many American bishops after large numbers of Eastern Catholics began immigrating here in the late nineteenth century.

Thus Eastern Catholics often came under pressure to rid themselves of distinctive liturgical practices (such as using the original version of the Nicene Creed without, of course, the Filioque),[16] and distinctive disciplines such as a married priesthood.[17] Even where they were not ordered outright, many Eastern Catholics adopted Latin practices out of a certain "subaltern" mentality or inferiority complex, particularly evident in Eastern Catholics living near large Latin majorities in places such as the Polish-Lithuanian Commonwealth and later North America. Singular Latin practices—e.g., the Rosary, or Stations of the Cross, or confessional booths at the back of the church—came increasingly to be found in Eastern Catholic parishes. This process, today known as Latinization,[18] was born out of "the mentality and convictions of the times, according to which a certain subordination of the non-Latin liturgies was perceived toward the Latin-rite liturgy, which was considered 'ritus praestantior.'"[19]

In addition to liturgical and sacramental innovations and degradations, there was also a gradual loss of the freedom of self-governance on the part of the Eastern Catholic Churches. Eastern Catholics came in some instances to be micromanaged by the Latin Church's dicasteries in Rome, for example, having their bishops appointed by Rome rather than elected by their own synods; or having their patriarchs treated in sometimes humiliating fashion as subordinates to Latin cardinals or even archbishops.[20] Over time, then, most Eastern Catholics went from seeing themselves as "sister churches" capable of self-government and having equally legitimate, venerable, and apostolic traditions of theology, canon law, spirituality, *and* liturgy, to being little more than "rites," that is, a bunch of quaint "ethnics" permitted to differ from the Latin West only to the extent of having an "exotic" liturgy. In other words, the vision of "union *with*" the pope of Rome was replaced by the reality of submission *to* him and his Curia.

The Decree: Contents

In this context just sketched, then, the six sections of *OE*, and the changes called for in each of them, are little less than revolutionary. Though this document was small in size compared to some other conciliar texts, and the numbers of Catholics it concerned then or since represents a tiny percentage of the total Catholic population in the world,[21] the decree has loomed large in shaping Eastern Catholic life since 1964, as discussed below. Moreover, it must be noted here that the tiny numbers of Eastern Catholics at Vatican II had an enormously outsized influence not just on the drafting of *OE*, but on many other texts and issues, including liturgics and the restoration of the diaconate.[22] In what follows, we look at each of *OE*'s sections in order.

"PARTICULAR CHURCHES OR RITES" Appropriately enough, the decree begins with nomenclature. It evidences a certain ambivalence and awkwardness in referring to Eastern Catholics as being combined "into different groups, which are held together by their hierarchy, and so form particular churches or rites" (no. 2). As we will see in the post-conciliar period, this ambivalent language of "rite" would be dropped as far from the equivalent of a "church." Such a vision would take decades after *OE* to develop, though *OE* itself goes some way toward that very development when it insists upon equality of all Catholics, recognizing that "these individual churches both Eastern and Western, while they differ somewhat among themselves in what is called 'rite,' namely in liturgy, in ecclesiastical discipline, and in spiritual tradition, are nonetheless all equally entrusted to the pastoral guidance of the Roman Pontiff." More strongly still, the paragraph ends by flatly insisting that "these churches are of equal rank so that none of them is superior to the others because of its rite. They have the same rights and obligations, even with regard to the preaching of the gospel in the whole world."[23] As we shall see later, this vision of complete equality remains in some ways yet to be fully achieved, but it was a very promising start.

"PRESERVATION OF THE SPIRITUAL HERITAGE" That search for autonomy features clearly in the next two sections. Here in the second section is an acknowledgement that gifts of the East are gifts of the whole Church. Here we see a move toward recognizing that "Catholic" includes more than just the Latin or West-Roman tradition. Catholicity properly understood includes the Armenian, Alexandrian, Antiochene (West Syrian), Chaldean (East Syrian), and Byzantine traditions alongside the Latin. Moreover, the decree states clearly that "the churches of the East like those of the West have the right and duty to govern themselves according to their own special disciplines" (no. 5), thus leading up to the next section.

"THE EASTERN PATRIARCHS" The document then treats Eastern patriarchs (nos. 7–11). By all accounts, then and since, this remains the weakest and most problematic part of the decree, clearly a product—as many commentators have put it—of Latins offering *their* "papalized" vision of an Eastern patriarchal office. This section of *OE* clashes with key sections of *Lumen Gentium*, especially the latter's wholesale incorporation of the definition of papal primacy and jurisdiction as defined at Vatican I (cf. nos. 22–25). A half-century after the council, Catholics both East and West still struggle to come up with a coherent way of reconciling patriarchal jurisdiction with papal. Nevertheless, the decree did go some way toward recognizing the antiquity of the patriarchal office (no. 7), the equality of rank with other primates (no. 8), and the importance that patriarchal "rights and privileges" (no. 9, where it is used twice) be not only preserved, but strengthened and even adapted today to fit new needs.[24]

"SACRAMENTAL DISCIPLINE" AND "DIVINE WORSHIP" These two sections begin at once with a practical pastoral issue which was then—and still, sadly, today is—a difficulty for Eastern Catholics with children in Roman Catholic schools: the sequence of, and age necessary for, the sacraments of initiation. Historically, of course, all Christians, East *and* West observed the original order of baptism-anointing-eucharist *even for infants*, there being no coherent reason to baptize infants but not to commune them.[25] Later on, the sacraments came to be separated in the West and conferred much later chronologically in order to allow the bishop to remain the minister of these mysteries.[26] In time and under the pressure of Latinization, many Eastern Catholics abandoned their tradition, separated the sacraments, and forced their children to wait for some supposed "age of reason" before having their "first communion" and later still their "confirmation."[27] Some even went so far as to suggest that chrismating and communing infants was borderline sacrilege and must be forbidden.[28] *OE* is quite clear in calling a halt to such nonsense and insisting on a recovery of the ancient order of initiation (nos. 12–13)[29] before going on, moreover, to call for a recovery of Vespers (no. 15) on Saturdays and the eve of feasts and a restoration of the permanent diaconate (no. 17) and minor orders. The section ends with a call to find a common paschalion, that is, an agreement on how to calculate the date of Easter.

"RELATIONS WITH THE SEPARATED BRETHREN" This final section begins with an exhortation for Eastern Catholics to do all they can to facilitate unity with the Orthodox in light of the principles articulated in *Unitatis Redintegratio* (*OE* 24). ONCE AGAIN, AS NOTED AT THE OUTSET OF THIS CHAPTER, THIS FINAL SECTION OF *OE* NEEDS TO BE READ ALONGSIDE NOT JUST *UR*, BUT ALSO *LUMEN GENTIUM*, WHERE THE LATTER'S TREATMENT OF THE PAPACY REMAINS THE BIGGEST STUMBLING BLOCK TO IMPROVED "RELATIONS WITH THE SEPARATED BRETHREN" AND ULTIMATELY FULL CHRISTIAN UNITY.

This section also treats the delicate matter of *communicatio in sacris*, allowing an unprecedented generosity: Orthodox and Catholics can approach each other's priests for the sacraments of "Penance, the Eucharist, and the Anointing of the Sick" (no. 27). The decree is self-conscious about what a change and even risk this represents, and so notes that "this more relaxed regulation concerning . . . *communicatio in sacris* . . . is entrusted to the watchfulness and control of local ordinaries" (no. 29). We shall discuss this in more detail below.

II. Post-Conciliar Teaching

This openness to sacramental sharing just noted would be seen in postconciliar legislation and documentation, beginning with the draft version of the 1967 *Ecumenical Directory*, which was toned down in the version published in 1970, and retains that more "conservative" approach in the updated version of 1993.[30] It retains the permissions given in *OE*, but adds restrictions including the note that "Eastern Churches, on the basis of their own ecclesiological understanding, may have more restrictive disciplines in this matter, which others should respect" (no. 122) and more strongly still "a Catholic who legitimately wishes to communicate with Eastern Christians must respect the Eastern discipline as much as possible and refrain from communicating if that Church restricts sacramental communion to its own members to the exclusion of others" (no. 124). Today, officially, most Orthodox Churches do indeed have restrictions and officially most say they will refuse the Eucharist (and other sacraments or even quasi-sacramental rites in some cases) to Catholics, who should not even approach in the first place—though as I have documented elsewhere, this is far from a unanimous belief or practice.[31]

After these heady gains at the council, the post-conciliar period got down to the hard work of translating many of the loftier exhortations and idealistic visions into liturgical, pastoral, and canonical "legislation." The several versions of the Ecumenical Directory accomplished some of this, though with a wide focus on all non-Catholics, not just the East. Documents that focused exclusively on the East would take more time, and most of them do not appear until the last decade of the century. Let us turn to some of those major documents now in chronological order. Each of these would not have been possible without *Orientalium Ecclesiarum*.

1990 Code of Canons of Eastern Churches (CCEO)

This new code of Eastern canon law,[32,33] which was in the works for more than a half-century, began where *OE* had left off: at the conclusion of *OE*, and at the opening of the apostolic constitution by which Pope John Paul II promulgated the CCEO, one finds the same provisional language shaped by the same ecumenical hope and longing for unity (see Table 12.1):[34]

The CCEO would for the most part carry out the various practical directives of *OE* on such matters as the sacraments of initiation, the ordination of married men, the importance of the Divine Office being celebrated alongside the Divine Liturgy, and the other matters noted above. Though not perfect, it managed to update old canons, introduce some new ones, and call for each Eastern Catholic Church *sui iuris* to introduce its own *ius speciale* to supplement, where necessary alter, and in general apply the universal norms of the CCEO, which was of necessity going to be very broad and general in legislating for nearly two-dozen diverse Eastern Catholic Churches.[35]

On one issue, however, the CCEO would be less than successful at translating the conciliar visions and hopes into law, and in failing to do so be roundly criticized by Eastern Christians. That issue is already hinted at in the passage quoted above: what constitutes the "supreme authority of the Church"? The default position in the CCEO was clear: the Supreme Pontiff is that authority.[36] As noted above, the CCEO merely repeats Latin ecclesiology on this point and unhelpfully offers no kind of integration of Eastern ecclesiology.[37]

1995: "Encyclical of the Month Club"

We have touched already on the 1993 version of the *Ecumenical Directory* and so proceed on to the pivotal year of 1995[38] when there was a flurry of major documents from Pope John Paul II, including his encyclical on Christian unity,

Table 12.1

Orientalium Ecclesiarum (1964)	Sacri Canones (1990)
"All these directives of law are laid down in view of the present situation until such time as the Catholic Church and the separated Eastern Churches come together into complete unity" (no. 30).	"The laws of the Code . . . [shall] be in force until abrogated or changed by the supreme authority of the Church for a just cause, of which causes full communion of all of the Eastern Churches with the Catholic Church is indeed the most serious."

Ut Unum Sint, and then his apostolic letter *Orientale Lumen*, both issued in May 1995.[39] Both were indebted to *OE*. The former was a landmark, as I have shown elsewhere, in calling for Christians, especially those in the East, to help the pope come up with ways to reconfigure his office so that it could again be an instrument of unity. *OE*, and Vatican II in general, did not make such an explicit call to deal with the papacy in particular terms. But, more generally, *OE*, and especially UR (see the opening sentence), *did* make clear that the Catholic Church was irrevocably committed to the cause of unity—as Pope John XXIII had also made clear in calling for the council in 1959 and again in his opening address in October 1962. And as popes, beginning with Paul VI in 1967, quickly realized, the biggest stumbling block to Christian unity was precisely the papacy.

In both documents the pope recognizes that the ecumenical partner closest to the Catholic Church is precisely the Orthodox Church. *Orientale Lumen* (*OL*) was consciously issued on the centenary of Pope Leo's *Orientalium Dignitas*, discussed above. Though addressed to the whole Christian East, its primary focus was on Eastern Catholics, who were encouraged and exhorted to continue the work of *OE* and the other reforms set in motion by Vatican II. It was also secondarily addressed to Roman Catholics, who were challenged repeatedly and pointedly to know and appreciate Eastern monastic, liturgical, sacramental, and iconographical traditions (inter alia) in some detail, and thus grow in love (a word used dozens of times) for the Christian East.

The overriding importance of *OL* comes in four ways. First, there are several places in which the pope (as he was often wont to do over his twenty-seven years in office) openly and humbly confesses where the Catholic Church has not treated the East with generosity, charity, fairness, and justice (nos. 17 and 28).

Second, he recognized legitimate diversity in theological methods, abandoning once and for all any notion in which the particularity of Latin theology was seen as the exhaustive supplier of genuinely Catholic theology. Here again *OE*'s flat insistence of the equality of all Catholics is brought forward and underscored. Thus the pope writes,

> In the study of revealed truth East and West have used different methods and approaches in understanding and confessing divine things. It is hardly surprising, then, if sometimes one tradition has come nearer to a full appreciation of some aspects of a mystery of revelation than the other, or has expressed them better. In such cases, these various theological formulations are often to be considered complementary rather than conflicting. (no. 5)

Third, one sees his insistence that the Christian East, Orthodox but especially Catholic, must now and forever be seen not as some extraneous, exotic other, but as part and parcel of the Catholic Church qua Catholic. In other words, it is time to move beyond the old notions of "Greek East" and "Latin West," which were problematic insofar as they reified identities into homogenous ideologies to be used against the other.[40] Moreover, such geographical circumscriptions overlooked the Syriac Christian tradition.

Fourth and perhaps most significant is his insistence that "the Church of Christ is one. *If* divisions exist, that is one thing; they must be overcome, but *the Church is one, the Church of Christ between East and West can only be one*, one and united" (no. 20 [my emphasis]). This can be read in two ways: descriptively and proleptically. It can be a simple description of the evils of division and the undeniable importance of unity.

Or it can—and I would argue should—be taken as a proleptic description: after raising a doubt ("*if* divisions exist") he goes on stoutly to insist that the Church *is* one; East and West can *only* be one. All three strongly suggest that the pope was not (or at least not totally) envisioning East-West unity as a development yet to be achieved in the future (though plainly in other places, here as elsewhere, he does view it as something yet to be attained), but as something we *already* experience right now. Of course, Vatican II recognized this in *UR, OE*, and *LG* when it referred to degrees of imperfect communion, which all Christians already enjoy.

But I think what the pope is doing here goes beyond that. Without making it explicit, he is recognizing that after the 1965 lifting of the excommunications[41] by Pope Paul VI and Patriarch Athenagoras on the same day, there is, at the very least canonically, no division between East and West: de facto we are divided, and everybody knows that; but de iure we are not, because since 1965 we are no longer excommunicated. But what are we, and where?

The sentences hurled by cardinal and patriarch against each other in July 1054 were only between two cantankerous and bigoted[42] churchmen and their entourages, and never intended to go beyond that;[43] moreover, there is very good reason to believe that Cardinal Humbert, acting as papal legate, had no authority in the first place, for the pope was by that point dead,[44] and thus legatine authority, in the terms of Latin canon law, would have ceased with the pope's death. Here I turn to one of the most singular and forthright of the pope's Orthodox interlocutors, David Bentley Hart, who in response to the pope recognized that while *OL* is a "hymn of love to Eastern Christianity," it also ineluctably raises a series of acute questions:

> When and where can we really locate the schism? Not only in time and space, that is, but within dogmatic and canonical norms? We are divided, we know, but how, when, and by what authority? And, while it is a social and cultural and political fact that we are divided, what is its theological rationale? Can the failure of communion between two patriarchs or bishops—a frequent event in the early church—create a real division of sacramentally united communions from one another? . . . And if communion has never truly wholly ceased, how can we actually identify the moment, the cause, or in fact the possibility of that division?
>
> And this, I think, may be the real question that a discussion of papal jurisdiction must ultimately broach, the least obvious or

expected question of all: not how can we possibly discover the doctrinal and theological resources that would enable or justify reunion, but how can we possibly discover the doctrinal and theological resources that could justify or indeed make certain our division. This is not a moral question—how do we dare to remain disunited?—but purely a canonical one: are we sure that we are?[45]

Hart's question remains an open and crucial one.

1996 Liturgical Instruction

Let us turn now to the 1996 "Instruction for Applying the Liturgical Prescriptions of the Code of Canons of the Eastern Churches," issued by the Oriental Congregation in 1996. The instruction is a very lengthy document that treats liturgical history and theology in considerable detail before offering detailed prescriptions on practical matters pertaining to all seven sacraments—from how and when initiation should be celebrated to the type of bread to be used in the Eucharist and the type of vestments clerics can and should wear. Additionally, it offers welcome counsel to recover authentic Eastern art, especially genuine Byzantine iconography, which had in some Eastern Catholic (especially East-Slavic) parishes been replaced with odd hybrids influenced, inter alia, by the Italian Renaissance.

It would be a category mistake, however, to see this document as merely some kind of compendium of rubrics or a "handbook" for uncertain clerics on how to celebrate divine service. The length, the detail, and the richness of the vision combine to offer *all* Catholics an entire liturgical catechesis of great winsomeness. In this document we see here enacted a vision of liturgy precisely as *theologia prima*, in David Fagerberg's terms.[46] Moreover, I would argue that it would be a mistake to see that the vision here pertains only to Eastern Catholics. Roman Catholics, still struggling to "repristinate" their liturgical traditions after infelicities of the reform process of the last half-century, could also benefit from the instruction's liturgical catechesis and comprehensive vision of liturgy and life.

The vision offered is of course directed primarily at Eastern Catholics, who until Vatican II (and only incompletely in most places since the council) had not recovered such deeply catechetical and poetic riches as Vespers and Matins, which the East prescribes (as does, of course, the Western traditions[47]) on the eve and mornings of feasts respectively *alongside* the Divine Liturgy.[48] Moreover, other gems of poetry and piety such as the deeply Mariological Akathist hymn were also lost, as were important and deeply ascetical celebrations of the Liturgy of the Pre-Sanctified Gifts during Lent.[49]

In sum, all the practical suggestions and prescriptions aim to continue and deepen the process of recovery of authentic Eastern traditions and practices for which OE had called. But it is clear, a half-century after the council, and two decades after the Instruction, that on liturgy a great deal of work remains to be done. And for those still setting about to do that work today, the Instruction ends on a wise note, arguing for a pastorally sensitive approach in places by clarifying that "the insistence on the full recuperation of Tradition does not mean to function to the detriment of changes necessary for the sensibility of the contemporary culture" (no. 124). In other words, merely because something was done in, say, Constantinople in 1017, or Lviv in 1780, or Thessaloniki in 1910, does not mean that it must be slavishly copied in a parish in Toronto, Pittsburgh, or Melbourne in 2015. The instruction's vision of tradition, then, is of a healthy and living phenomenon that can and in some cases should change, rather than remain a static object in a museum of antiquities.

III. Earlier Theological Analysis of *OE* and Vatican II

We turn now to a brief and selective but representative survey of some literature from respected Orthodox, Eastern Catholic, and Roman Catholic canonists, liturgists, and church historians from 1986 to 2014.

The canonist George Gallaro was recently elevated to the episcopate as bishop of the Italo-Albanian Eparchy of Piano de Sicilia in Italy after a long career working at times for Melkite, Ukrainian Catholic, and Ruthenian (Byzantine) Catholic universities, seminaries, and tribunals. In 1986 he wrote a *plaidoyer*: "*Orientalium Ecclesiarum* Deserves More Attention."[50] There, a little more than two decades after *OE* was published, Gallaro takes the view that *OE* was and remains limited, "temporary," still "evolving," and "provisional" in everything it suggested,[51] though on balance he sees it as a good thing[52] "animated with good intentions."[53] He argues that the decree's usefulness is limited by confusion over vague and ill-defined terms, chiefly the exhortation to return to authentic "Eastern tradition." What constitutes authentic Eastern tradition? Gallaro cautions that any attempt to encourage such a return cannot consist simply in a mindless return to the past, but must take account of lived communities of faith in very different contexts in the late twentieth century.

Noting some other problems discussed in this essay above—including the poorly conceived discussion in *OE* about patriarchates—Gallaro argues that the biggest weakness of *OE* was its view of "Roman primacy. . . . The West cannot envision the primacy except in the form of jurisdiction, and communion as submission. Ideas on this topic are only slowly evolving."[54] Since 1986, however, ideas have evolved considerably,[55] though their implementation has not.

The well-known Byzantine liturgical historian Robert Taft wrote a brief article in 1991, a pivotal year for many Eastern Catholics with the collapse of the Soviet Union.[56] Taft also shared many of the criticisms of Gallaro and others, especially that *OE* "remained perforce a *Latin* document *about the East*."[57] But like Gallaro, Taft also saw that *OE*'s "scant thirty paragraphs contain several progressive elements remarkable for their openness and breadth of vision."[58] And any fault with the document, and especially its ongoing post-conciliar implementation, cannot be attributed solely to "Roman foot-dragging [or] to ill-will." Instead one must frankly recognize that "Eastern Catholic Churches do not always show themselves mature enough to shoulder the autonomy they claim."[59] Taft concluded that "in sum, progress has been made, though a few issues remain intractable, often because no solution that would not cause more problems than it solves is available."[60]

1995 saw the publication of the so-called Zoghby initiative, named after the Melkite archbishop who promoted a formula for full communion between the Melkite Greek Catholic Church and the Greek Orthodox patriarchate of Antioch.[61] Though ultimately it went nowhere, it was a hopeful initiative that testified to the deep levels of existing eucharistic sharing among the two increasingly persecuted Christian minorities, especially in Syria and Lebanon.[62]

In 1996 the late Roman Catholic canonist and liturgist Frederick McManus published an early analysis of the 1990 CCEO.[63] McManus's article acknowledges the debts owed by the CCEO to *OE* before reviewing the former in some detail. He concludes that there are things in the CCEO that offer "a fresh and positive perspective," especially in its ecumenical vision, but that "the Eastern code is somewhat deficient in seizing upon some of the conciliar insights of 1962–1965."[64] Chief of the deficiencies is, once again, an inadequate treatment of papal primacy vis-à-vis the Eastern patriarchates.[65]

The Ukrainian Catholic church historian Taras Khomych wrote an article in 2006 that treats the history of Eastern Catholics ("uniates") and briefly looks at what has changed thanks to Vatican II.[66] Once again Khomych's essay concludes by noting Catholics (Roman and Eastern) have yet to come up with a credible "ecclesiology much more compatible with that of the Orthodox Churches."[67]

2006 also saw the publication of *The Church in the Making* by the Roman Catholic ecclesiologist Richard Gaillardetz.[68] Though focused primarily on *Lumen Gentium* and *Christus Dominus*, Gaillardetz does spend a little time on *OE* and its aftermath, concluding that the document occasioned some gains in Eastern Catholic life but that even in 2006 "the situation facing the Eastern Catholic churches is still fraught with difficulties," not least their on-going disdain from the Orthodox and the ongoing attempts to treat them "as little more than exotic ornamentation superimposed upon a church that still sees itself in predominantly Western categories."[69] In other words—in a conclusion becoming common by now—Gaillardetz notes that the question of jurisdiction, including that of Eastern bishops vis-à-vis the bishop of Rome, and the "synodal election" of those bishops themselves, all continue to vex East-West relations even within the Catholic Church.[70]

Far and away the most significant response to *OE* from Catholic and Orthodox scholars came on its fiftieth anniversary in the fall of 2014. The Metropolitan Andrey Sheptytsky Institute of Eastern Christian Studies organized a two-day conference at the University of Toronto, inviting Eastern Orthodox, Eastern Catholic, and Roman Catholic scholars to speak on various aspects of *OE* and its aftermath, especially liturgy, relations between churches, the search for unity, and the fate of Eastern Catholics in Eastern Europe and the Middle East.[71] Much of the analysis offered in Toronto repeated themes noted above: gratitude for major advances, but sober recognition of what work remains to be accomplished in liturgical reform but above all in ecclesiological and ecumenical reforms pertaining to episcopal, patriarchal, and papal jurisdiction.

IV. Desiderata in the Next Fifty Years

Let us conclude, then, by taking up some of the unfulfilled hopes and reforms, especially those pertaining to questions of papal and patriarchal authority. In what follows, we take the six sections of *Orientalium Ecclesiarum* in order, and in so doing we can see that work still remains to be done in order to more fully realize the vision of the council. Much good and hard work—pastoral and theological—has been done in the last two decades especially, but much work also remains to be done.

"Particular Churches or Rites"

In some ways, the challenge here is two-fold in both directions: the Latin Church needs to more fully understand her own particularity and to restrain her tendencies to act as *more* than a particular Church.[72] At the same time, Eastern Catholics need to stop acting as *less* than equal particular churches and to assert their "rights" as fully as possible for the good of the *entire* Church catholic.

Thus Eastern Catholics need to continue the recovery of their own authentic and specific traditions by, for example, having Eastern Catholic synods elect bishops throughout the world and thus refuse to be penned into some supposed "historic homeland."[73] It could equally be done by presbyteral ordination of qualified married men anywhere an Eastern Catholic bishop has need, and thus once and for all eradicating unjust attempts to prohibit married clergy in North America in particular.[74] It could also be done by Eastern Catholics setting up ecclesial communities and structures wherever they are needed, stressing the greater priority of evangelization over the lesser propriety of respecting "national" borders or the incoherent claims of some Orthodox Christians to having an exclusive rule over their "canonical territory," a term to which no Eastern Christian in today's highly mobile and much-changed world has been able to give any coherent definition.

None of this is a call for Eastern Catholics to be unpleasantly intransigent or willfully contumacious: it is a call for them to implement the vision described in *OE* as noted above. There is, then, a conciliar mandate for the continued assertion of Eastern Catholic rights and freedoms in the fullness of the Catholic Church. There is, moreover, an ecumenical mandate also: for the failure of Eastern Catholics to live as fully as possible is a scandal (in the Pauline sense of *skandalon* or stumbling block to unity) to the Eastern Orthodox who, seeing the fate that has often befallen their Eastern brethren—Latinizations, loss of independent self-governance, and the other things noted above—are rightly wary of any further *rapprochement* with Rome.[75]

Preservation of the Spiritual Heritage

On this score, if one defines "spiritual heritage" to include liturgy, spirituality, and iconography, then many Eastern Catholics have made considerable strides since Vatican II in preserving what was theirs and "re-pristinating" it in light of the conciliar mandate and directions. But demographic and economic factors are against them, at least in North America, where virtually every Eastern Catholic (and Orthodox) church has been in steep numeric decline for several decades.[76] (The same cannot be said for Eastern Catholics in the "homelands" such as Ukraine, where the church is flourishing.) The causes of decline in North America especially differ considerably for Eastern Christians, who have seen their churches shrivel largely because of a failure to pass on the faith and culture to the next generation due to an excessive preoccupation with ethnic identity and preservation of language—an issue that most Western churches, Catholic and Protestant, deracinated as they largely are, do not face today.

The situation of the Ukrainian Greco-Catholic Church (UGCC) is instructive here: when her early members arrived in North America in the late nineteenth century, and again in three more subsequent "waves" of immigration (after the First, Second, and Cold wars), the emphasis, as one often finds in immigrant communities, especially those fleeing poverty and persecution, was on preservation of language and ethnicity, not propagation of the faith, which was assumed to be handed on with the language and ethnicity, but often, sadly, was not. The situation was compounded in the case of Ukrainian Catholics who, for most of the twentieth century, in Ukraine and around the world, were the repository of a nationalist hope for an autonomous nation-state in Europe, which was not realized until 1991. Until then, the UGCC often functioned as a "surrogate state" concerned primarily with preserving its linguistic and ethnic heritage. As a result, the last large wave of immigration right after the Second World War has largely died off, and parishes have been closing across the continent for over a decade now because that generation often neglected to pass on the faith to their children and grandchildren, who were alienated from the liturgy and life of the UGCC by no longer speaking or understanding the Ukrainian language.

The Eastern Patriarchs

Here we see a greatly unfulfilled challenge and much work that lies ahead. As Ukrainian Catholics in particular are painfully aware, "patriarchs" and "patriarchates" are often treated as playthings subject to the ever-changing winds of Moscow-Rome relations.[77] *OE* says that new patriarchates can be established today either by the pope or by ecumenical council. But *OE* is incapable of giving a justification to this approach, which was the practice neither in the first millennium nor in most of the second. The struggle remains for both Eastern and Roman Catholics to overcome the remnants of a Latinized ecclesiology that has never understood patriarchates and has no practical working experience of them as viable and autonomous institutions in the Church not subject to papal, especially curial, micro-management.[78]

Moreover, those ancient patriarchates that still exist—the Melkite, for example—are often not respected as they should be, but instead subject to micromanagement from curial officials in Rome, who still act as though every patriarchate in the world is geographically circumscribed but that the Roman patriarchate knows no such limits. As the Melkite Catholic bishop Nicholas Samra has recently put it in reference to his own patriarchate, Rome treats the "patriarchal territory" of the Melkite Church according to "the lines of the Ottoman Empire."[79] And as he further noted, it has no problem ignoring Eastern canon law and proper juridical procedure to install Latin bishops over Eastern ones whenever and wherever it chooses.[80]

An additional, and arguably the most serious, issue the council did not address at all was the fact that Rome itself is a patriarchate, and needs to learn anew to act like one. The council's doctrine of "collegiality" (developed in *Lumen Gentium*) has remained an under-developed and unfulfilled desideratum. Pope Paul VI tried to move the Roman Church toward more collegial or conciliar governance by creating a so-called synod of bishops. The problem, however, as Eastern Christians know, is that any synod properly so called must have legislative authority and electoral power. This current synod has neither— it is purely consultative and advisory. In fact, the late UGCC Metropolitan Maxim Hermaniuk of Canada once dismissed the Roman synods as no more than "international study days of the Catholic bishops," noting that the bishops just talked and talked and talked, but could never act—they had no power, and they were hamstrung by the curia, which, Hermaniuk maintained, was the real problem in the Church.[81] The development of a patriarchal mentality, and practical institutions to that end, *within the Latin Church*, would help *all* the Catholic churches. I have written elsewhere at length and in considerable detail on what this would look like, and will not repeat that here.[82]

"Sacramental Discipline" and "Divine Worship"

Here, with gratitude, one must note the enormous progress made, as witnessed not just in landmark documents such as the 1996 Instruction, reviewed above, but at the popular and parochial level. Many, perhaps most, Eastern Catholic parishes today have restored the discipline and proper order of the sacraments of initiation. Many have sought, often with some controversy and pastoral difficulty, to root out Latinizations. Many, and likely most, today have returned to the use of the Nicene Creed based on the original text, i.e., *sans filioque*. Many have attempted to restore what was lost in their churches—e.g., authentic iconography—and in their liturgical life (e.g., music).

But much work remains to be done. To cite the three most obvious examples of work in progress:

- Many parishes still have Saturday night anticipatory "Masses" when the tradition clearly requires Vespers.

- Hardly any parishes celebrate Vespers on the eve of feasts, or Matins on the morning of feasts.
- Very few parishes celebrate the full cycle of Lenten services, especially the beautiful and moving Forgiveness Vespers, Canon of St. Andrew of Crete, and the Liturgy of Pre-Sanctified Gifts.

OE also called for a common date for the celebration of Easter or Pascha, but this remains unfulfilled in 2015, though Pope Francis has recently suggested the one solution that would most likely break the impasse.[83]

"Relations with the Separated Brethren"

OE, as noted above, permits *communicatio in sacris* with the Orthodox in some circumstances, especially the sacraments of Penance, Eucharist, and Anointing. Orthodox Christians can approach Catholic priests for those sacraments, and Catholics can approach Orthodox priests for the same sacraments if circumstances require it. Here one must record the fact that Catholic generosity in this regard is very rarely matched, officially, with Orthodox generosity, which in North America at least officially (de jure though not always de facto) refuses all sacramental sharing with anybody not fully Orthodox.

There are, however, certain more generous exceptions to this, including Lev Gillet, a beloved spiritual guide who wrote under the nom de plume "A Monk of the Eastern Church."[84] Gillet and numerous other Orthodox thinkers, including Olivier Clément, Antoine Arjakovsky, David Bentley Hart, Nikos Nissiotis, Catholicos Aram of Cilicia, and Michael Plekon, have shown another way. They have argued for a change in the rule that prohibits our sharing the Eucharist now.[85]

That rule insists that Catholics and Orthodox have to find complete and total unity of faith first before we can share the Eucharist, and the last challenge to such unity is the developed Catholic doctrine of the papacy—as my book shows only too well. But this "traditional" or "official" argument has long since failed to cohere for at least two reasons. First, the idea that we have to have some kind of perfect doctrinal accord, a complete unity of dogmatic understanding, is to hold ourselves to an artificial, unhistorical, and wholly unnecessary standard. Nobody in the first millennium, and arguably for much of the second, would have thought such a standard necessary or indeed possible. Doctrinal disagreements in the early Church were not always ipso facto causes for breaking communion. That is still the case today in the Orthodox world, where communion is regularly—absurdly—broken over territorial disputes in which no doctrine is involved.[86]

This takes us to the second reason: even those churches (as among the family of Oriental or non-Chalcedonian Orthodox, as well as the Byzantine Orthodox) who, on paper, *are* in full doctrinal accord and agreement with one another only rarely share the Eucharist together, thus putting the lie to the claim that doctrinal accord always precedes eucharistic hospitality.[87] Here the criticism advanced by the Orthodox scholar Andrew Louth must be carefully noted. Louth warns against the Orthodox tendency to wax "eloquent about our wonderful eucharistic ecclesiology," when "in practice not only is there little trace of any kind of 'eucharistic' ecclesiology, there is often enough little trace of the *communio* or *koinonia*. . . . *Koinonia* implies at least communication, and there is often little of that between patriarchates, especially between the patriarchates of Constantinople and Moscow."[88]

Let us instead insist that the sine qua non for eucharistic sharing remains common recitation of the Nicene Creed together. If Orthodox and Catholic bishops can do that—and they can—then what else is necessary? Why insist on more? Why erect artificially high, if not impossible, barriers to unity? Can we not adopt the solution of the Council of Jerusalem and simply say to each other, "It has seemed good to the Holy Spirit and to us to lay upon you no greater burden than these necessary things" (Acts 15:28)?

In the years ahead, then, it seems to me the best way to commemorate the good work done at Vatican II, and to hasten the completion of the work remaining undone, is for all of us to apply, as widely and frequently as we can, the "life-giving bread and saving chalice" so that Christ's eucharistic Body can heal His mystical body, the Church. Let us insist on sharing the Eucharist together. To those who would interrogate people at the chalice by demanding to know first "Are you Catholic or Orthodox?" let us reply in the fashion of the Ukrainian Catholic theologian Andriy Chriovsky, when confronted with an unhelpful binary: "Yes." In doing so, may we advance to the centenary of *Orientalium Ecclesiarum* in 2064, fully healed of the divisions that Vatican II tried so hard to overcome.

NOTES

1. The Vatican website: www.vatican.va in 2015 translates the title "Decree on the Catholic Churches of the Eastern Rite," which is problematic in two ways to be discussed in my text.

2. In paragraph 24, discussing the search for unity between Eastern Catholics and Eastern Orthodox, it is said that the former "have the special duty of fostering the unity of all Christians . . . according to the principles laid down in the decree of this holy council, 'On Ecumenism.'"

3. By "re-reception" I have in mind something like the process described by Denis Edwards, "The Holy Spirit as the Gift: Pneumatology and Catholic Re-reception of the Petrine Ministry in the Theology of Walter Kasper," in *Receptive Ecumenism and the Call to Catholic Learning*, ed. Paul D. Murray (Oxford: Oxford University Press, 2008), 197–210.

4. I cover some of this dolorous history in "The Search for Unity," *Our Sunday Visitor*, May 25, 2014, https://www.osv.com/OSVNewsweekly/Article/TabId/535/ArtMID/13567/ArticleID/14703/The-search-for-unity.aspx.

5. For the history of estrangement up to the eve of the Reformation, see Henry Chadwick's magisterial *East and West: The Making of a Rift in the Church: From Apostolic Times until the Council of Florence* (Oxford: Oxford University Press, 2005).

6. The Crusades are and remain perhaps the most vexatiously (and often deliberately or tendentiously) misunderstood of all events in Christian history. Reliable treatments are to be found in Rodney Stark, *God's Battalions: The Case for the Crusades* (New York: HarperOne, 2010); and especially any of the works by Jonathan Riley-Smith, perhaps starting with his short recent study, *The Crusades, Christianity, and Islam* (New York: Columbia University Press, 2011).

7. For many decades, the standard study in English of the council was that of the Jesuit Joseph Gill, whose 1959 book was recently reissued: *The Council of Florence* (Cambridge: Cambridge University Press, 2011). Gill's work, however, will need to be re-read in light of the critical scholarship of Christiaan Kappes in, for example, "Mark of Ephesus, the Council of Florence, and the Roman Papacy," in *Primacy in the Church: The Office of Primacy and the Authority of Councils*, vol. 1, ed. J. Chryssavgis (Crestwood, NY: SVS Press, 31 Jan 2016), 109–150, whose recent publications on Florence, and especially the controverted figure of Mark of Ephesus, are upending the traditional images held by both Catholic apologists for the council and Orthodox apologists for the supposed intransigence of Mark.

8. For details on many of these groups, including those not covered here, see Robert Taft's invaluable essay, "The Problem of 'Uniatism' and the 'Healing of Memories': Anamnesis, not Amnesia," *Logos: A Journal of Eastern Christian Studies* 41–42 (2000–2001): 155–96, esp. 164–67.

9. The best treatment of this remains Boris Gudziak's *Crisis and Reform: The Kyivan Metropolitanate, the Patriarchate of Constantinople, and the Genesis of the Union of Brest* (Cambridge, MA: Harvard University Press, 2001).

10. The etymological history may be found in Christian Cannuyer, "Uniatisme," *Catholicisme: hier, aujourd'hui, demain* 15 (2000): 455–83. Some of the wider history is noted below, but see also Ernst C. Suttner, *Church Unity: Union or Uniatism? Catholic-Orthodox Ecumenical Perspectives* (Rome: Dhamaram Publications, 1991).

11. The typical Orthodox reaction to "uniatism" conveniently overlooks Orthodoxy's own "uniate" communities—groups of disaffected Roman Catholics and other Western Christians who have come into communion with Orthodoxy but have been allowed to use various jerry-rigged Western liturgies since the nineteenth century. For more on the history of such communities, see Taras Khomych, "Eastern Catholic Churches and the Question of 'Uniatism': Problems of the Past, Challenges of the Present, and Hopes for the Future," *Louvain Studies* 31 (2006): 214–37, esp. 230–31. For more on the liturgical problems created by having Western-rite communities in an otherwise Byzantine Orthodox context, see Jack Turner, "Western-Rite Orthodoxy as a Canonical Problem," *Logos: A Journal of Eastern Christian Studies* 51 (2010): 229–48.

12. On this, see the still somewhat controversial 1993 Balamand statement of the official international Orthodox-Catholic dialogue: http://www.vatican.va/roman_curia/pontifical_councils/chrstuni/ch_orthodox_docs/rc_pc_chrstuni_doc_19930624_lebanon_en.html.

13. *Unitatis Redintegratio* moves sharply away from this model, as does *Orientalium Ecclesiarum*. It was clearly articulated in paragraph 10 of Pope Pius XI's unfortunate *Mortalium Animos* in 1928. But in 2005, it was repudiated by Pope Benedict XVI, who in a speech at an ecumenical meeting in Germany said "unity does not mean what could be called ecumenism of the return: that is, to deny and to reject one's own faith history. Absolutely not! It does not mean uniformity in all expressions of theology and spirituality, in liturgical forms and in disciplines." http://w2.vatican.va/content/benedict-xvi/en/speeches/2005/august/documents/hf_ben-xvi_spe_20050819_ecumenical-meeting.html.

14. http://www.papalencyclicals.net/Leo13/l13orient.htm.

15. The current Ecumenical Patriarch Bartholomew is an alumnus of the Pontifical Oriental Institute.

16. See A. E. Siecienski's superlative study, *The Filioque: History of a Doctrinal Controversy* (Oxford and New York: Oxford University Press, 2010).

17. See my forthcoming book which traces Roman harassment of this practice from 1929 onward and the untold damage done by it.

18. A balanced analysis of this by a Ukrainian Catholic may be found in Peter Galadza, "Liturgical Latinization and Kievan Ecumenism: Losing the Koine of Koinonia," *Logos: A Journal of Eastern Christian Studies* 35 (1994): 173–94.

19. General Instruction, paragraph 24. The phrase *"ritus praestantior"* is attributed to Pope Benedict XIV (r.1740–58), but Maria Teresa Fattori's recent scholarship has shown him to be much more of a scholar with pastoral solicitude for the East than some have previously thought: "Benedict XIV and his Sacramental Policy on the Eastern Churches," *Logos: A Journal of Eastern Christian Studies* 53 (2012): 221–57.

20. This was an issue early in the conciliar sessions, with liturgical processions into St. Peter's being an occasion for controversy when the Eastern patriarchs were insultingly (so some of them felt) placed *behind* the Roman cardinals.

21. It is hard to get precise figures, but it is said that today Eastern Catholics of all traditions perhaps number around 20 million compared to nearly 1.4 billion Roman Catholics.

22. On Eastern, especially Melkite, influence, see the invaluable Maximos IV, *L'Eglise Grecque Melkite au Councile* (Beyrouth: Dar al-Kalima, 1967). This work was recently translated into English, and is also available at https://melkite.org/faith/faith-worship/introduction. Patriarch Maximos IV was a figure of towering influence at Vatican II, and on him see, inter alia, Gerasimos T. Murphy, *Maximos IV at Vatican II: A Quest for Autonomy* (Newton, MA: Sophia Press, 2011). Other Eastern Catholics played a role at the council, and *The Second Vatican Council Diaries of Met. Maxim Hermaniuk (1960–1965)*, trans. Jaroslav Z. Skira (Leuven: Peeters, 2012) offers us some insights into the one-time leader of the Ukrainian Catholic delegation at the council.

23. This latter point seems banal: of course the Gospel should be preached in the whole world! But it has often been remarked by Eastern Catholic clergy and theologians I know—though I have never been able to find documentary evidence of it—that Eastern Catholics outside their "homelands" were explicitly "forbidden" by the Latin Church from evangelizing, which was allegedly restricted to Latin missionary efforts alone.

24. The eminent Orthodox observer at the council, Alexander Schmemann, noted that the patriarchal office was read through a highly papal lens, thus distorting it somewhat: Alexander Schmemann, "A Response," in *The Documents of Vatican II: Introductions and Commentaries by Catholic Bishops and Experts; Responses by Protestant and Orthodox Scholars*, ed. Walter M. Abbott, trans. Joseph Gallagher (Piscataway, NJ: New Century, 1966). Schmemann's point is amplified and extended by the Orthodox canonist Patrick Viscuso in "Orthodox-Catholic Unity and the Revised Code of Eastern Canon Law," *Journal of Ecumenical Studies* 27 (1990): 108–15.

25. In other words, all the arguments against paedocommunion are equally arguments against infant baptism!

26. In the East, priests have long been the primary and ordinary ministers of baptism, chrismation, and communion.

27. I have first-hand evidence and experience, even in the last decade, of Eastern Catholic sacraments of initiation being ignored by Roman Catholic schools *and bishops* who attempted, sacrilegiously, to "confirm" such students for a second time.

28. See Mark Morozowich's valuable historical research in "Eastern Catholic Infant Communion: Has Catholic Dogmatic Teaching Prohibited It?," *Logos: A Journal of Eastern Christian Studies* 49 (2008): 71–90. His evidence enables him to offer an unequivocal "No!" to the question in his title.

29. The struggle over the order of initiation remains for the Latin Church, sadly, which seems—as news stories even in 2015 make clear—to flail about trying to find workable solutions. It is sad that the recovery of the *universal* order of baptism-anointing-eucharist encouraged in *OE* for the East was not also encouraged for the West. A superb new study by the Catholic-trained Orthodox liturgical scholar Nicholas Denysenko offers promising ways forward: *Chrismation: A Primer for Catholics* (Collegeville, MN: Liturgical Press, 2014).

30. See here for the text in its current iteration: http://www.vatican.va/roman_curia/pontifical_councils/chrstuni/documents/rc_pc_chrstuni_doc_25031993_principles-and-norms-on-ecumenism_en.html.

31. I count as friends several Orthodox priests who have invited me to receive the Eucharist in their parishes, and I have heard from Catholic friends who have similarly been invited even by Orthodox bishops. Moreover, it is an open secret that among Melkite Greek Catholics and Orthodox in Syria and Lebanon (and among many of their "diaspora" parishes in North America), where inter-marriage is very widespread, that one week a family receives at the wife's Orthodox parish, and the next week that same family again receives the Eucharist en masse at the husband's Melkite parish *in the full knowledge of their Catholic and Orthodox pastors and hierarchs*. On a scholarly level, there is far from Orthodox unanimity on this issue of restricting the Eucharist only to Orthodox, as I noted in my review of Antoine Arjakovsky's *Church, Culture, Identity*, in *Logos: A Journal of Eastern Christian Studies* 49 (2008): 322–24.

32. An overview of the development and first ten years of the CCEO's existence and implementation may be found in David Motiuk, "The Code of Canons of the Eastern Churches: Some Ten Years Later," *Studia Canonica* 36 (2002): 189–224.

33. The apostolic constitution mentioned in the note below gives a potted history of the six-decade-long process of composing the CCEO. I give more details and scholarly references in my *Orthodoxy and the Roman Papacy: Ut Unum Sint and the Prospects of East-West Unity* (Notre Dame: University of Notre Dame Press, 2011), 188–90.

34. *Sacri Canones* is the apostolic constitution of Pope John Paul II promulgating the CCEO on October 18, 1990. Text here: http://w2.vatican.va/content/john-paul-ii/la/apost_constitutions/documents/hf_jp-ii_apc_19901018_sacri-canones.html#*.

35. The diversity and complexity of the East can sometimes be maddening to sort out. The best place to begin is with Ron Roberson's *The Eastern Churches: A Brief Survey*, now in its seventh edition and no longer updated in print but online instead, as here: http://www.cnewa.org/default.aspx?ID=123&pagetypeID=9&pageno=1.

36. See canons 42–54.

37. I have addressed this issue to some extent elsewhere (see my *Orthodoxy and the Roman Papacy*, 71–77), and will do so again in the fourth and final section of this essay.

38. The phrase is not mine but comes from the late priest Richard John Neuhaus, "That They May Be One," *First Things*, October 1995, http://www.firstthings.com/article/1995/10/001-that-they-may-be-one.

39. I analyze *Ut Unum Sint* in *Orthodoxy and the Roman Papacy*, 1–16. 1995 was also the year of another major encyclical, *Evangelium Vitae*.

40. On this, see two recent and invaluable collections, the first edited by George E. Demacopoulos and Aristotle Papanikolaou, *Orthodox Constructions of the West* (New York: Fordham University Press, 2013); the second is edited by Andrii Krawchuk and Thomas Bremer, *Eastern Orthodox Encounters of Identity and Otherness: Values, Self-Reflection, Dialogue* (New York: Palgrave, 2014).

41. I treat the mutual lifting of excommunications, and the subsequent role of "memory" and "oblivion," in my "The Principles of Accommodation and Forgetting in the 21st Century," in *Primacy and Conciliarity in the Church*, ed. John Chryssavgis (Crestwood, NY: St. Vladimir's Press, 2016).

42. "Neither Cardinal Humbert nor Patriarch Michael could be described as learned in theology or in church history" (Chadwick, *East and West*, 210).

43. "Humbert's curse lay only on Patriarch Michael, Leo of Ochrid, and their immediate supporters, *not upon the whole eastern church*" (ibid. 212 [my emphasis]). "The exchanges between Humbert and Michael were personal to themselves" (218). In proof of this, note that East and West were still commemorating each other liturgically (in, e.g., the Byzantine diptychs) and sharing the Eucharist until well into the thirteenth century in many places, and for centuries beyond that in more remote places such as the Greek Islands, as Kallistos Ware has documented in his *Eustratios Argenti: A Study of the Greek Church under Turkish Rule* (Oxford: Oxford University Press, 1964).

44. Chadwick, *East and West*, 206.

45. David Bentley Hart, "The Myth of Schism," in *Ecumenism Today: The Universal Church in the 21st Century*, ed. F. A. Murphy and C. Asprey (Aldershot and Burlington, VT: Ashgate, 2008), 106.

46. David Fagerberg, *Theologia Prima: What is Liturgical Theology?* (Chicago and Mundelein, IL: Hillenbrand, 2012). Fagerberg came out of a Lutheran background to become Roman Catholic, but his liturgical theology is deeply immersed in the East, especially the premier Orthodox liturgical theologian of the last century, Alexander Schmemann.

47. See Robert Taft, *The Liturgy Of The Hours In East And West*, 2nd rev. ed. (Collegeville, MN: Liturgical Press, 1993).

48. I wrote plaintive requests for their return in diocesan and other "popular" venues in Canada and the US over the years to no avail: "Why Cracker-Jack Christianity Will Rot the Teeth Out of Your Head," *Progress* 18 (July 2004): 14; "Whatever Happened to Matins and Vespers?," *The New Star* 45 (October 2009): 16–17; and "When Sects Put Us to Shame: The Enfeeblement of the Church," *Catholic Insight* 11 (2003): 36–39.

49. The definitive study is Stefanos Alexopoulos, *The Presanctified Liturgy in the Byzantine Rite: A Comparative Analysis of Its Origins, Evolution, and Structural Components* (Leuven and Walpole, MA: Peeters, 2009).

50. George Gallaro, "*Orientalium Ecclesiarum* Deserves More Attention," *Nicolaus* 2 (1986): 293–301.

51. Ibid. 294.

52. Ibid. 296: "Despite all the defects . . . it is animated by a sincere, although not always efficacious, desire of leading . . . the Eastern Churches back to the authentic Eastern tradition."

53. Ibid. 301.

54. Ibid. 296.

55. For extensive details on that evolution, see my book *Orthodoxy and the Roman Papacy*.

56. Robert Taft, "Eastern Catholic Churches (Orientalium Ecclesiarum)," in *Modern Catholicism: Vatican II and After*, ed. Adrian Hastings (New York: Oxford, 1991), 135–40.

57. Ibid. 135.

58. Ibid. 136.

59. Ibid. 137.

60. Ibid.

61. For a lengthy treatment of this, see S. M. Aboueid, *Archbishop Elias Zoghby and Orthodox-Catholic Reconciliation: An Exposition in Light of Contemporary Ecumenical Thought* (Fairfax, VA: Eastern Christian Publications, 2007).

62. For analysis, see G. Hachem, "Un projet de communion ecclésiale dans le patriarcat d'Antioche entre les Églises grec-orthodoxe et melkite-catholique," *Irenikon* 72 (1999): 453–78.

63. Frederick McManus, "The Code of Canons of the Eastern Catholic Churches," *The Jurist* 53 (1993): 22–61.

64. Ibid. 56.

65. Cf. McManus's overall approach with that of David Motiuk's article, "The Code of Canons of the Eastern Churches." Motiuk is a Ukrainian Catholic canonist and bishop.

66. Taras Khomych, "Eastern Catholic Churches and the Question of 'Uniatism': Problems of the Past, Challenges of the Present, and Hopes for the Future," *Louvain Studies* 31 (2006): 214–37.

67. Ibid. 233.

68. Richard Gaillardetz, *The Church in the Making: Lumen Gentium, Christus Dominus, Orientalium Ecclesiarum* (Mahwah, NJ: Paulist Press, 2006).

69. Ibid. 115.

70. Ibid. 165.

71. The papers have not been published, which makes detailed comments here rather difficult. For those who have the time, the Sheptytsky Institute's YouTube channel has video recordings of all the lectures and discussion: https://www.youtube.com/playlist?list=PLX95n5cXR7cWnrg2iR_VCi_9-GEP_Hi3c.

72. On this point, John Faris's article is invaluable: "The Latin Church *Sui Iuris*," *The Jurist* 62 (2002): 280–93.

73. The current practice, based on spurious arguments, claims that, e.g., the Ukrainian Greco-Catholic synod is empowered to elect new bishops in and for Ukraine only according to its 1991 borders. The dozens of Ukrainian Catholic bishops in dioceses in Western Europe, the United Kingdom, North and South America, and Australia were all appointed by Rome.

74. The history of that legislation is analyzed by several scholars in my forthcoming book *Married Catholic Priests*, University of Notre Dame Press, forthcoming, 2018.

75. The late Ukrainian Orthodox archbishop of Chicago, Vsevelod Majdansky, who was close to and supportive of Ukrainian Catholics, argued at length about the scandal of the latter's treatment at the hands of Rome, and insisted that until and unless Rome could, at length, demonstrate a record of treating Eastern Catholics as autonomous equals, as legitimate sister churches, the Orthodox would never trust Rome enough to enter into communion with her again. See his several essays on this point in his *We Are All Brothers* (Fairfax, VA: Eastern Christian Publications, 1999).

76. Eastern Christians are notoriously bad at numbers- and record-keeping, and their small size often means that larger surveys—the recent Pew Survey for example—fail to pick them up because they are statistically insignificant. Trying to get a sense of current demographics is thus a fraught business, but what records we have clearly indicate massive decline. Some—but only some—recent data may be found in Alexei Krindatch, *Atlas of American Orthodox Churches* (Brookline, MA: Holy Cross Press, 2011).

77. On this, see the notoriously blunt "Interview with Jesuit Fr. Robert Taft of the Pontifical Oriental Institute," conducted by John Allen and published in the *National Catholic Reporter*, February 4, 2004, http://www.natcath.org/mainpage/specialdocuments/taft.htm.

78. See my "On the Patriarchate of the West," *Ecumenical Trends* 35 (2006): 1–7. In *Orthodoxy and the Roman Papacy* (47–106), I analyze patriarchates in the light of both Roman Catholic and Eastern Christian history, theology, and canon law.

79. Nicholas Samra, "Eastern Catholicism in the Middle East," YouTube video, posted October 23, 2014, https://www.youtube.com/watch?v=nQZKDqXcOE0&list=PLX95n5cXR7cWnrg2iR_VCi_9-GEP_Hi3c&index=6. Samra later in that lecture details some very recent and very disturbing meddling by Roman curial officials in Melkite affairs beyond anything that can be justified.

80. Note the alarming story told by Samra at the above video lecture, starting at 22:40.

81. Hermaniuk is quoted in Patrick Granfield, *The Limits of the Papacy* (Dublin: Darton, Longman, and Todd, 1980), 95. Further thoughts of Hermaniuk are recorded by Andriy Chirovsky in his "Editorial," *Logos: A Journal of Eastern Christian Studies* 46 (2005): 289–300.

82. See my *Orthodoxy and the Roman Papacy*, esp. 117–59.

83. See my analysis: "Pope Francis and the Absurdly Vexed Calendar Question," *Catholic World Report*, June 25, 2015, http://www.catholicworldreport.com/Blog/3981/pope_francis_and_the_absurdly_vexed_calendar_question.aspx.

84. For more on him, see the biography written by Elisabeth Behr-Sigel, *Un moine de l'Église d'Orient: Le Père Lev Gillet, un libre croyant universaliste, évangélique et mystique* (Paris: Cerf, 1993). In addition, see the volume Peter Galadza and I worked on: *Unité en division: les lettres de Lev Gillet ("un moine de l' Église d'Orient") à Andrei Cheptytsky 1921–1929* (Paris: Parole et Silence, 2009).

85. For someone who comes close to this view but pulls back slightly, see the Romanian Orthodox theologian Radu Bordeianu, *Dumitru Staniloae: An Ecumenical Ecclesiology* (London and New York: T&T Clark, 2011).

86. As I write this in late June 2015, news emerged that the Orthodox patriarchate of Jerusalem has broken communion with the Orthodox patriarchate of Antioch over a dispute as to whose "territory" Qatar is.

87. Perhaps even more absurdly, the late primate of the UGCC, Metropolitan Andrey Sheptytsky, at his presbyteral ordination in the Byzantine rite was forbidden from giving the Eucharist to his own parents, who remained Polish Roman Catholics forced to commune from the reserved sacrament in a nearby Latin tabernacle and brought to Sheptytsky's ordination liturgy!

88. Andrew Louth, "Receptive Ecumenism and Catholic Learning—An Orthodox Perspective," in Murray, *Receptive Ecumenism*, 366.

13

Inter Mirifica

Daniella Zsupan-Jerome

Among the first documents promulgated by the Second Vatican Council was the Decree on the Mass Media (*Inter Mirifica*). This document is a short text often critiqued for its lack of theological depth, its abstract delivery, and its lack of a realistic and nuanced understanding of the media and mass communication.[1] In terms of its reception, *Inter Mirifica* is famous for passing while holding the highest number of "no" votes in the penultimate round of approval by the Council Fathers. Despite this rocky beginning, for the more appreciative observer the document is still a solid start, lending importance to social communication as a topic worthy of conciliar attention, and thus theological reflection and pastoral priority. While this short decree is indeed one with room to grow, its treatment of social communication put the topic on the conciliar table, and on the broader table of the thought of the Church. In our day and time, this has become an important legacy and a solid starting point for thinking about communication in our digital culture. If and when the case needs to be made about the theological and pastoral relevance of communication, *Inter Mirifica* as a conciliar decree offers an indisputable starting point.

In our digital culture, making the case for the relevance of communication outside of ecclesial or theological contexts is almost a given: so important is social communication today that it is in fact integral to our way of experiencing the world. This integral role of social communication is well beyond the instrumental awareness of our dependence on ever-smaller, ever-more advanced gadgets. Beyond these instruments, we are experiencing a cultural shift, one in which our way of thinking, knowing, and relating is rapidly changing in light of innovation in communication technologies. We can properly speak of living in a digital culture, in which communication is in large part the animating force of the shape our world is taking.

This important cultural shift is not lost on the Church. Pastoral planning meetings buzz with the urgency of how to engage in social media, how to get the attention of digital natives, or how to establish a digital presence for the parish or ministry. Theologians likewise ponder anew concepts like presence, encounter, authenticity, authority, and community in light of our experience of digital communication. In this cultural context, *Inter Mirifica* and the subsequent social communication documents have the potential for re-emerging like the Church's best-kept secret: an existing magisterial corpus on communication to mine in light of the urgent questions, opportunities, and challenges presented by digital culture today. In the flow of digital culture, this corpus offers a foothold for pastoral and theological work. For those especially overwhelmed, this also offers the comforting realization that the Church had thought systematically about social communication well before the advent of the World Wide Web, and has continued to do so through Web 1.0 and 2.0, social and mobile media, to our experience today of wearable bio-responsive gadgets and the Internet of things. For theologians, this corpus also holds a creative call: something to build upon, to dialogue with, and to continue to interpret in our day and time. In the context of all this, *Inter Mirifica* is more than a document: it is a symbol of the Church's roots for dialogue to grow between faith and digital culture today.

The theological and cultural critiques originally voiced against *Inter Mirifica* are not to be dismissed. In some ways, this original critique was a generative force toward better articulation of the Church's thought on social communication, such that we find in the 1971 document *Communio et Progressio*, or in St. John Paul II's considerable thought on the matter through a cultural lens in documents like *Redemptoris Missio* (1990) or *The Rapid Development* (2005). While *Inter Mirifica* was written with definite room to grow, it is its symbolic role that has become invaluable today. Its legacy is one of de facto legitimating social communication as an important topic for the Church, and generating a social communication tradition that continues to affirm this. The challenge for our digital context is not necessarily to invent a new response but rather to claim this existing legacy, to build on it for our day and time and to integrate and implement its moral imperatives in pastoral contexts. In this, there remains room to grow, especially around integrating a comprehensive approach to social communication into the pastoral formation programs of the Church.

The task of this chapter is to examine the reception of *Inter Mirifica* since its promulgation in 1963. The reception of the document is discernible in the discussion it has generated both in subsequent ecclesial documents and in the theological work of the Church. This chapter considers both of these below. In addition to these, pastoral implementation of the practical directives of *Inter Mirifica* also merits examination, especially around comprehensive pastoral formation in social communication that the document envisions. Echoing commentators who often point to room to grow regarding this pastoral area, this chapter also envisions a constructive approach forward to round out this general critique.

Reception in Later Documents

Inter Mirifica was a self-aware document: it recognized its limitation in terms of the lack of comprehensive analysis in what it offered. The Council Fathers themselves articulated this as part of their deliberations as they integrated a call for further work into the document itself.[2] As a result, instead of an exhaustive analysis, *Inter Mirifica* set up a generative structure for the work to continue. It called for the creation of a more comprehensive document on social communication, a curial agency to engage in pastoral thought and visioning around this topic, and an annual World Communications Day to reflect on the topic.[3] Each of these has contributed to the corpus of ecclesial documents on social communication, forming a "social communication tradition" available for the Church today.[4]

The first and most significant document composed in light of *Inter Mirifica* is *Communio et Progressio* (1971), the pastoral instruction created explicitly in response to *Inter Mirifica*'s call for a more comprehensive examination. Franz-Josef Eilers points to *Communio et Progressio* as the highlight of the entire social communication tradition, and as a document on social communication read and respected well beyond just Roman Catholic ecclesial circles.[5] In 187 paragraphs, *Communio et Progressio* elaborates on the theological foundations of communication (6–18), on the reality of communication in human society (19–100), and on communication in, with, and by the Church (101–34, 162–87). The order of these sections is revelatory, putting the Church clearly in dialogue with society, rather than the more prescriptive approach that was met with critique during the drafting of *Inter Mirifica*. *Communio et Progressio* also highlights particular media, including print, cinema, radio, television, and theater (135–61). This reclaims an approach also originally intended for *Inter Mirifica* itself but which was later eliminated in the final version of the conciliar decree.

For the work of pastoral theology, the most notable aspect of *Communio et Progressio* is its articulation of theological foundations in paragraphs 6–18. Although this brief section is far from exhaustive, it offers three salient elements that continue to animate theological reflection around this topic today: the metaphor of Christ as the Perfect Communicator, the supreme expression of communication as a gift of self in love, and communion as the ultimate end of any communicative act. Each of these will be considered in greater detail further below. These elements root communication deeply in theology, and provide a stable Christological framework for communication even as particular communications media may change or evolve over time. We can equally ask about a handwritten letter, a telephone call, an email, or one's activity on Snapchat or Instagram whether it is an authentic expression of giving of oneself in love, whether it leads to communion, and whether it reveals

Christ's own communication in any fashion. In fact, examining the possibilities and challenges for this Christological framework remains a salient theological project for our digital context, some decades later.

Highlighting Snapchat or Instagram as examples above may quickly date this chapter to the mid-2010s, a challenge that is part and parcel of engaging with the topic of social communication in general. Even though *Communio et Progressio* was an all-out effort for a comprehensive document, its very topic is its Achilles heel in terms of contemporary relevance. By the late 1980s it had become dated, largely because of the rapid innovations in communication technology, including the advent of the personal computer. In 1992, the Pontifical Commission (now Council) for Social Communication published a twentieth anniversary document to *Communio et Progressio*, the pastoral instruction *Aetatis Novae*, in order to update conversation on the topic of social communication. In this sense, *Aetatis Novae* remains closely related to *Communio et Progressio*, and is a document that continues the magisterial response to the call of *Inter Mirifica* to think further on this topic. This close connection between these three documents is also reflected in method and structure: all three begin with a theological vision, make cultural observations, then offer pastoral directives in light of these.

In addition to following in line with *Inter Mirifica* and *Communio et Progressio*, *Aetatis Novae* demonstrates the influence of St. John Paul II, particularly his assessment of the influence of media not just as a set of instruments but as a comprehensive cultural reality. As Eilers notes, this cultural lens was already discernible in Auxiliary Bishop Karol Wojtyła's contribution to the discussion of *Inter Mirifica* at the Second Vatican Council, and it is a lens he would develop and emphasize throughout his papacy, whether on the new evangelization, on the culture of life, or other hallmark elements of his thought.[6] *Aetatis Novae* draws from several of his documents, including *Sollicitudo Rei Socialis* (1988), *Christifideles Laici* (1989), *Redemptoris Missio* (1990), and *Centesimus Annus* (1991), when reflecting on the culture of communication and the Church's possibilities to engage with it, especially from the approaches of morality and ethics, social justice, or pastoral work. Articulating this culture-based approach when it comes to social communication was prophetic: in our digital context decades later, it is all the more evident that communication has engendered a cultural shift and needs to be engaged comprehensively as a reality that is shaping how people think, relate and experience the world. As *Aetatis Novae* noted, "Much that men and women know and think about life is conditioned by the media; to a considerable extent, human experience itself is an experience of media" (*AN* 2). Highlighting communication as a total cultural reality reflects growth in the Church's thought on social communication, from the critiqued lack of depth in *Inter Mirifica* to elaboration and emphasis in these latter two documents. In addition, given that this comprehensive reality that has become all the more fluid in our present digital context, building on this approach is not only desirable but necessary.

Following *Aetatis Novae*, the Pontifical Council for Social Communication generated a number of shorter documents to continue the conversation on social communication called for by *Inter Mirifica*. These include *100 Years of Cinema* (1996), *Ethics in Advertising* (1997), *Ethics in Communications* (2000), and the sibling documents *Ethics in Internet* (2002) and The *Church and Internet* (2002). In addition to these, a significant legacy of *Inter Mirifica* is the World Communications Day Messages, published annually since 1967 around the late January feast of St. Francis de Sales.[7] Each of these is a brief papal reflection on some aspect of social communication relevant to our world today, ranging in topics from particular media, particular aspects of culture or society, particular categories of people, particular theological or pastoral concepts, or particular opportunities or challenges. Since the last documents of the Pontifical Council in 2002, the Messages are unequivocally the platform where the conversation around social communication has continued in the documents of the Church today. Because of their format, they have some distinct advantages for resonating with digital culture: they are brief and focus generally on one pastoral point. Because they are messages, they do not need to summarize the existing tradition in the fashion of longer documents, or articulate basic foundations each time they address a topic. Instead, assuming and building on all this rich background, they can generally focus and reflect specifically on a theme in a way that a longer document often does not. As a result, the World Communications Day Messages are brief and focused, usually around ten paragraphs each, a length definitely palatable even for digital culture and our shortened attention spans.

In addition to his thought dialoging with social communication in *Aetatis Novae*, St. John Paul II picked up the topic elsewhere, most notably in his 2005 apostolic letter *The Rapid Development*. *The Rapid Development* is addressed "to those responsible for communications," which by 2005 was becoming an increasingly fluid and broad category. The apostolic letter begins citing *Inter Mirifica* and affirming the progress on the topic of social communication since its promulgation forty years previously; in this, the apostolic letter is situating itself in the social communication corpus generated by the conciliar decree. In fourteen paragraphs, the apostolic letter presents a substantial invitation into the theology of communication, naming themes that are worthwhile to ruminate on well beyond their brief presentation in the document. Along these lines, the letter echoes many themes of *Communio et Progressio*, such as the Incarnation and the trajectory of communication to communion, but also lends additional emphasis to Trinitarian theology, the Eucharist, and the work of the Holy Spirit. Throughout it all, St. John Paul II remains characteristically cultural in his approach, and he calls for pastoral renewal within the Church, especially focusing on formation, participation, and dialogue toward this (11). In addition to presenting this pastoral vision, St. John Paul II's closing words are poignant, echoing the Scriptural words he made famous: "do not be afraid":

To those working in communication, especially to believers involved in this important field of society, I extend the invitation which, from the beginning of my ministry as Pastor of the Universal Church, I have wished to express to the entire world "Do not be afraid!"

Do not be afraid of new technologies! These rank "among the marvelous things"—*inter mirifica*—which God has placed at our disposal to discover, to use and to make known the truth, also the truth about our dignity and about our destiny as his children, heirs of his eternal Kingdom.

Do not be afraid of being opposed by the world! Jesus has assured us, "I have conquered the world!" (Jn 16:33)

Do not be afraid even of your own weakness and inadequacy! The Divine Master has said, "I am with you always, until the end of the world" (Mt 28:20). Communicate the message of Christ's hope, grace and love, keeping always alive, in this passing world, the eternal perspective of heaven, a perspective which no communications medium can ever directly communicate, "What eye has not seen, and ear has not heard, and what has not entered the human heart, what God has prepared for those who love him." (1 Cor 2:9)

Composing this apostolic letter near the end of his life, his urgency is palpable here: he is striving to encourage and empower the Church toward authentic communication. His words are also pastorally sensitive, as he addresses the fear and sense of being overwhelmed many pastoral leaders and ministers may feel when faced with the rapidly changing landscape of the "world of communication" (3). In addition to offering theological foundations, dialogue with culture and pastoral visioning, these words of sincere encouragement are perhaps the most heartfelt reception of *Inter Mirifica* in a subsequent ecclesial document. They are seeking to motivate and empower the Church in a context where the need and urgency is clear, but the way forward is instead unclear and overwhelming in a rapidly changing and technologically driven culture.

Theological Analysis

Building on the Church's own continued magisterial reflection, *Inter Mirifica* received some attention from theologians, particularly among those interested in social and pastoral communication. The classic study on the document is Enrico Baragli's *L'Inter mirifica; introduzione, storia, discussione, commento, documentazione* (1969),[8] which is a comprehensive treatment of *Inter Mirifica*, including the text of the document itself with extensive commentary and background. By virtue of being a conciliar document, *Inter Mirifica* has also been noted in most commemorative anthologies on the documents of the Second Vatican Council, as well as in a smaller number of collections on the social communication documents of the Church.[9]

Theological discussion sparked by *Inter Mirifica* is generally focused on communication, and for theological depth, it is usually coupled with its daughter-document, *Communio et Progressio*. Because *Inter Mirifica* was published among the first documents of the Council, commentators note that it lacked the benefit of the Council's own development of thought, such as what becomes distilled in documents like *Gaudium et Spes*.[10] *Communio et Progressio*, on the other hand, had the opportunity to reflect on social communication in light of the Council; the document itself acknowledges this as it names *Gaudium et Spes, Unitatis Redintegratio, Dignitatis Humanae, Ad Gentes*, and *Christus Dominus* along with *Inter Mirifica* as notable sources (*CP* 2). As such, for greater theological depth, *Communio et Progressio* is generally coupled with theological work done on *Inter Mirifica*. *Inter Mirifica/Communio et Progressio* offer an essential starting point for articulating a theology of communication, as well as for envisioning the ecclesiological role of communication. When it comes to pastoral and practical work, both of these are theological prerequisites. Along these lines, this chapter turns to examining each of these below, before offering a concluding call for integrating social communication into pastoral and ministerial formation.

Articulating a Theology of Communication

As noted, the theological depth of *Inter Mirifica* is lacking in articulation, which is remedied to a great extent by *Communio et Progressio*. Nonetheless, *Inter Mifirica* does plant some important seeds, especially when recognizing the theological "bookends" it presents to frame its practical directives aimed at the moral order and the common good. These "bookends" are references to God the Creator in paragraphs 1–2, and Christ in eschatological glory in paragraph 24.

In the opening paragraphs of the document, the human creativity that has brought about the technological innovations of our time is set in its ultimate context, as a reflection of the work of God the Creator: "the genius of humankind, especially in our times has produced marvelous technical inventions from creation, with God's help" (*IM* 1). After further describing the pervasive reality of mass communication in highly positive terms, paragraph 2 names God the Creator again: "[The means of social communication] contribute greatly to relaxation, the enrichment of people's minds, and the spread of consolation of the kingdom of God. But the church also knows that they can be used in ways which are damaging and contrary to the Creator's design" (*IM* 2). From this point, the document launches its teaching and directives, primarily around the moral use of the media, in society and in the Church.

Beginning with the Creator and the Creator's design, *Inter Mirifica* implies a fundamental theological point: human creativity, when authentic in its expression, finds both its source and ultimate telos in God. Whatever marvels our human genius can bring into existence, these are concrete expressions of our identity *in imago Dei*, particularly reflecting the Creator through our own acts of creativity. Recalling the pre-eminence of the Creator's design in paragraph 2, we are reminded that whatever creative works emerge from our human genius, they need to find their proper place in the divine order, so as to merit the constructive and positive appraisal articulated in the opening paragraphs of the document. Human creativity is only marvelous if it submits itself under the greater context of God's design. Technological innovation is indeed impressive: it is mind-blowing to consider how much and how quickly our reality has been shaped by it in the matter of mere decades. When the human person places him and herself, without God, at the source of this exponential innovation, we are left with a distorted view of our own power, finitude, and obligation to one another. The results can be disastrous. Here, we are back in the Garden of Eden, back at the Tower of Babel, back at the Golden Calf, and at any other moment in salvation history when humankind has taken matters into its own hands. On the other hand, situating technological innovation in the Creator's design leads these to truly merit being called marvelous.

If our beginning point with technological innovation is God's own creativity and divine plan, then the end-goal of these equally transcends us. The final paragraph of *Inter Mirifica* closes with an image of Christ in eschatological glory: "Rather will the media, like salt and light, add savor to the earth and light to the world.... The name of the Lord will thus be glorified by these modern inventions as it was in former times by the masterpieces of art; as the apostle said: 'Jesus Christ is the same yesterday, today, and forever' (Heb 13:8)" (*IM* 24). The reference to salt and light recalls Matthew 5:13–16, and its extended metaphor in the context of the Sermon on the Mount. The closing chapter of the Letter to the Hebrews likewise lists a number of social and moral directives before arriving at the here-quoted phrase. Through comparison of format, both of these references help to underscore the value of *Inter Mirifica*, which too is made up largely of directives about social and moral deeds.

The reference to Christ in glory is also eschatological. The phrase "Jesus Christ is the same yesterday, today and forever" is infused with liturgical meaning, especially as it is uttered in the context of the preparation of the Paschal Candle at the Easter Vigil: "Christ yesterday and today, the beginning and the end, the alpha and the omega. All time belongs to him and all ages. To him be glory and power, through every age and forever."[11] Evoking the image of the lit Paschal Candle processed in to offer the light of Christ for the Church, the symbolism of light here echoes the reference to salt and light earlier in the paragraph. The image also communicates Christ's final sovereignty, as alpha and omega, and as rightful recipient of all glory and power. It is an image rooting us in the Paschal Mystery, as the ultimate context of Christian identity and activity. The means of social communication and their moral use are therefore oriented toward Christ in glory, the Paschal Christ, and Christ who is the Light of the World, and Christ the King who reigns eternal. Oriented toward this, one must reflect on how our means and ways of communication can reveal this powerful reality as well as guide and invite us toward it.

Beginning and ending with God are the theological bookends of social communication offered in *Inter Mirifica*. *Communio et Progressio* builds upon these to elaborate on what theological points arise in between them. As noted above, paragraphs 6–18 in Part I of *Communio et Progressio* contain the pillars for continuing to construct a theology of communication, namely: the metaphor of Christ the Perfect Communicator, communication as a gift of self in love, and the trajectory of communication as leading ultimately to communion. When considering the bookends offered in *Inter Mirifica*, the eschatological image of Christ in glory could be regarded as an especially generative source for the development of these pillars.

Ordering all of our ways and means of social communication to the final glory of Christ raises the practical question of how to engage in communication worthy and revelatory of this telos. It also raises the theological question of what we can know and imitate about Christ's own ways and means of communication. This salient question casts a wide net: it has the potential to embrace Christological reflection on the Christ as the Word, as well as reflection on concrete moments of Christ communicating: preaching, telling parables, writing in the dirt, staying silent, and so forth. Perhaps as a fruit of such theological reflection, in *Communio et Progressio* we are presented with the metaphor of Christ the Perfect Communicator:

> Through His "incarnation," He utterly identified Himself with those who were to receive His communication and He gave His message not only in words but in the whole manner of His life. He spoke from within, that is to say, from out of the press of His people. He preached the Divine message without fear or compromise. He adjusted to His people's way of talking and to their patterns of thought. And He spoke out of the predicament of their time. (*CP* 11)

The metaphor of Christ the Perfect Communicator reveals communication that is contextual, seeking mutuality and encounter, and totally engaged and engaging. In thinking about conforming our ways and means of social communication to that of Christ, one point for imitation is being fully embedded in the reality of our time while boldly and courageously inviting us all beyond it. Communication done in the image and likeness of Christ is therefore engaged and committed to encounter, all the while inviting hope, joy, and dynamic movement toward Divine Mystery.

Building further on Christ's own communication, *Communio et Progressio* offers a theological definition of communication that includes the salient phrase "giving of self in love":

> Communication is more than the expression of ideas and the indication of emotion. At its most profound level it is the giving of self in love. Christ's communication was, in fact, spirit and life. In the institution of the Holy Eucharist, Christ gave us the most perfect and most intimate form of communion between God and man possible

in this life, and, out of this, the deepest possible unity between men.
Further, Christ communicated to us His life-giving Spirit, who brings
all men together in unity. The Church is Christ's Mystical Body, the
hidden completion of Christ Glorified who "fills the whole creation."
As a result we move, within the Church and with the help of the word
and the sacraments, towards the hope of that last unity where "God
will be all in all." (*CP* 11)

Here, we discover a theological articulation of what is only alluded to in
Inter Mirifica's bookend of Christ in glory. The theology of communication
is held in the context of the theology of communion. Communication as an
act of giving oneself in love is communication oriented toward communion,
an orientation we can discover in Christ's own example from the moment of
the Incarnation, through his ministry, his death on the cross, and his resurrection and the gift of the Spirit. This gift of self in love comes to us in each
sacramental celebration, especially the Eucharist, and calls us to do likewise.
Receiving Holy Communion, we are called into communion with Christ, the
Church and all of Creation. Our acts of communication, when they are gifts
of ourselves offered in love, pave the way into this mystery. Ordering our ways
and means of social communication to Christ in glory means a call to self-
giving love expressed through communication.

Communio et Progressio cements this connection between communication
and communion as it names communion as the goal of social communication:

So, "among the wonderful technical inventions" which foster communication among human beings, Christians find means that have been
devised under God's Providence for the encouragement of social relations during their pilgrimage on earth. These means, in fact, serve to
build new relationships and to fashion a new language which permits
men to know themselves better and to understand one another more
easily. By this, men are led to a mutual understanding and shared
ambition. And this, in turn, inclines them to justice and peace, to
good will and active charity, to mutual help, to love and, in the end, to
communion. The tools of communication, then, provide some of the
most effective means for the cultivation of that charity among men
which is at once the cause and the expression of fellowship. (*CP* 12)

Envisioning communication as an act of self-giving love will generate the
possibility of relationships, growth into mutuality, and collaboration—all heralds of Christ in glory. When it comes to social communication, "Christ is yesterday, today, and forever" is expressed in ways and means of communication
that bring people together in justice and peace, good will and active charity,
mutual help and love. In contrast to these, communication that is divisive,
violent, unjust, lacking in truth, and lacking in charity distances us from communion and from the image of Christ in glory. Our ways and means of social
communication thus have a kind of sacramental potential in this regard: as at

once the cause and expression of fellowship, they can become efficacious signs of communion when performed or used authentically as gifts of self in love.

As gleaned from *Inter Mirifica* and *Communio et Progressio*, a theology of communication begins and ends in God, and thus must reflect the Creator as well as Christ in eschatological glory. Between these, the theology of communication reveals Christ the Perfect Communicator, who was fully Incarnate and who also heralds the Reign of God. Christ's self-communication can be summed up as a gift of self in love, a dynamic of revelation manifest from the Incarnation through the descent of the Holy Spirit at Pentecost. The ultimate end of Christ's loving self-gift was communion—of humankind to God and to one another in all of Creation. The sacramental language of the Church continues to reflect this reality. Social communication is also called into this reality, to serve as a sign of communion in its authentic expression. Building on these foundations, the role of communication in the life of the Church also merits analysis.

Communication and the Church

Another theological question emerging from *Inter Mirifica/Communio et Progressio* is the definition and role of communication in the reality of the Church. For theologians like Avery Dulles, there is such a close connection between the theology of communication and ecclesiology that the Church can in fact be equated with communication, and all that the Church does can be framed as a communicative act.[12] This close connection between communication and Church is also consistent with the magisterial understanding of evangelization as constitutive of the Church, which highlights any development in communication not only relevant for a specific sector of church communicators but for the Church as a whole. [13] *Inter Mirifica* itself points toward this connection between Church, communication and evangelization when it states, "The Catholic Church was founded by Christ our Lord to bring salvation to everybody and consequently is duty bound to preach the gospel. It believes that its task involves using the media to proclaim the good news of salvation as well as teaching people how to use them properly" (*IM* 3). According to the later document *Evangelii Nuntiandi*, evangelization as a proclamation of the Good News is the Church's "deepest identity" (14). Evangelization is also a fundamentally communicative posture and act, a basic ecclesial disposition to share the Good News, to hand on the content of faith, or to make present the Word in our day and time. In light of such an ecclesiological emphasis based on the centrality of evangelization, the role of communication is thus essential to the Church.

In our digital context, this comprehensive understanding of the Church as communication is a salient approach to the equally comprehensive reality of communication in digital culture as a whole, and is fertile ground for further theological thought on communication. At the same time, one challenge of this comprehensive approach is that while it is theologically sophisticated, it can be pastorally overwhelming. If in the Church all is communication, then it becomes difficult to distinguish the particular role of communication in ministry, or to discern concrete steps for implementation. Though distinguishing the particular role of communication can be difficult, this is not to imply that it is impossible: careful theological reflection is needed here to guide concrete pastoral implementation toward what it means to communicate well in a Church where communication is constitutive of communal identity and mission.

To balance the comprehensive view of the Church as communication, another approach to Church and communication is to narrow communication to the work of very specific media, such as the press, publishing, film, television, radio, and the internet. If the first approach was overly theological at the expense of the practical, then this second approach is predominantly practical and instrumental. When observing the curial structures in the Church that are concerned with communication, this instrumental approach as centered around key media remains in effect, and likely for its practical benefit and task of effectively communicating the news, teachings, and celebrations of the Church to a global community. However, a challenge for this instrumental approach is that in our digital culture, instrumentality is no longer sufficient for comprehending the impact of communication technologies on life and society as a whole. From the tenor of the ecclesial documents noted above, it is evident that this broader cultural approach is both desirable and increasingly necessary. While evangelization calls us to take a step back and reflect on the realities of culture and context, this second instrumental approach does readily not lend itself to such.

A third approach to Church and communication, then, is an emphasis on social communication as a cultural reality in and outside of the Church. In this sense, the role of communication in the Church is as a pastoral context, and one that has gained much relevance in the digital age. Social communication was a term introduced into the Church's vocabulary by *Inter Mirifica*, a legacy that Eilers highlights as a laudable achievement for its emphasis not on instruments (media) but on the human and social reality of communication.[14] Even as media change, social communication is about people, and in our digital context, this emphasis on the human person becomes increasingly important. In the World Communications Day Messages reflecting specifically on our digital context, this is an evident theme; both Benedict XVI and Francis have emphasized encounter and human connection in this regard.[15] Because social communication is a person-centered reality, it is also worthy of pastoral attention in the life of the Church, which is a truth already articulated at the deliberations of *Inter Mirifica* during the Council; in fact, it was this pastoral emphasis that justified the presence of the topic on the conciliar agenda.[16] Recognizing the topic as social communication rather than as media or technology retains the emphasis on persons, community, and ultimately culture as these are shaped, challenged, or benefitted by the media and communication technology available to them. For this reason, when considering the reality of digital communication, approaching this as a cultural reality remains consistent with this person-centered approach that lends itself to pastoral implications. Additionally and equally relevant is the nature of digital culture itself, which is a reality no longer contained within specific gadgets, but, as Antonio Spadaro points out, is an ambiance that surrounds us.[17] Living in a context in which digital communication shapes our thinking and behavior on a cultural level, social communication remains a salient term for both theological thought and pastoral praxis.

Pastoral Practice and Future Directions

This chapter casts *Inter Mirifica* as a document with room to grow. The above overview of the subsequent social communication documents and theological reflection reveals some of the growth that has emerged from the foundations of this document, or from the topic of social communication that it has emphasized for the theological and pastoral work of the Church. As St. John Paul II noted in 2005 in *The Rapid Development*, "The Christian community has taken significant steps in the use of the means of communication for religious information, for evangelization and catechesis, for the formation of pastoral workers in this area, and for the education to a mature responsibility of the users and the recipients of the various communications media" (2). At the same time, there still remains room for growth, particularly in the area of pastoral training and formation.

The call for pastoral training and formation for social communication is a regular theme in the documents surveyed above. Beginning with *Inter Mirifica*, it is a theme noted with consistent emphasis and increasing urgency. *Inter Mirifica* 15 calls for the training of priests, religious, and laity "at once"; *Communio et Progressio* refers to it as the Church's "most urgent task" (107); and *Aetatis Novae* reiterates that education and training for pastoral workers and priests should be an "integral part of formation"(18). Despite the consistent call, implementing this training has been a challenge. The 1986 document of the Congregation for Catholic Education, entitled *Guide to the Training of Future Priests Concerning the Instruments of Social Communication*, describes in its introduction this inadequacy in no uncertain terms:

> Given the wide diversity of local situations it is understandable that formation work and its fruits in this regard have not been equal everywhere. Formation in the means of social communication is relatively new, lacking at times both suitable experience and prepared teachers, such that the whole formation work seems in many cases difficult, poorly organized and inadequate. There are at times organizational and technical delays and dearths which contrast with the rapid evolution that is actually going on in communication systems and techniques involving the entire cultural, social and spiritual universe of the human person.

Despite of the consistent call for pastoral formation since *Inter Mirifica*, it is evident that by 1986 this had not yet been implemented in a total and comprehensive fashion. Three decades later, in our present time, this challenge not only endures but is made more complex by the advent of digital culture. In light of this ongoing challenge, the *Guide* presented a way forward in 1986, which still offers a foundation for envisioning pastoral formation today.[18] At the same time, in this area there is room to grow, particularly around the reality of social communication in a digital culture for priests, religious, and laity alike. As a still-developing area in the reception of *Inter Mirifica*, work in pastoral training and formation for social communication remains a worthwhile task.

One enduring challenge for implementing comprehensive training and formation programs is the fluid and quickly changing nature of digital culture. This dynamism is also exponential; changes in technological innovation seem to emerge faster and faster in our time. In this rapidly changing context, it is difficult to pin down what exactly the cultural context is that such training and formation is aiming toward. As a result, training and formation efforts grasp at the moment and can default to skill building and instrumental competency instead. At the same time, the social communication tradition highlighted above offers a number of solid conceptual starting points that remain consistently relevant even as times change and can open the way toward a more comprehensive approach. These include communication as theological, social, self-giving, and spiritual. This chapter concludes by briefly examining each of these in turn.

Approaching communication as theological, social, self-giving, and spiritual is an effort to align social communication training and formation with the fourfold approach to ministerial formation as outlined in documents such as *Pastores Dabo Vobis* (1992): intellectual, human, pastoral and spiritual.[19] This alignment is intentional and is seeking to demonstrate that social communication formation is not only a particular skill or competency that can be contained in one area, but rather a general ministerial disposition that engages all four pillars of a comprehensive formation program. Along these lines, the following convergences are fruitful starting points.

Communication as Theological and Intellectual Formation

As consistently demonstrated by the social communication documents, communication is fundamentally rooted in theological soil. Communication is at the heart of Trinitarian theology, the Incarnation, revelation, ecclesiology, and evangelization. Because of this, social communication formation delves deeply into the theology of communication especially around these essential concepts, and it seeks a deeper understanding of human communication in light of these divine mysteries. Human communication is made theologically meaningful through such an inquiry, and gaining such a theological framework offers flexibility for pastoral implementation. If one's pastoral approach to communication is deeply rooted in theological reflection on the Trinity, the Incarnation, and the Church, then the rapidly changing reality of communication technologies becomes less overwhelming and more of a dynamic partner in dialogue with some firmly rooted theological foundations.

Communication as Social and Human Formation

Examining the theology of communication reveals that one essential aspect of authentic human communication is that it is relational: it is the human person's fundamental outward movement to engage with another. Recalling the importance of the term "social communication" from above, communication remains a relational act of the human person whether done by word, text, or tweet. *Communio et Progressio*'s trajectory from communication to communion moves this relational act to its theological and spiritual end. As social communication is fundamentally relational, it has significance for human formation in ministerial programs. The question of "how can I truly encounter another, relate authentically with another, build community and communion with another" is a question both for human formation and social communication training. While human formation helps to hone this awareness, social communication training also points to its practical expression in contexts of communication.

Communication as Self-Giving and Pastoral Formation

Insofar as communication is relational, it is also in its most authentic form a gesture of self-gift, offered in love. This disposition is also distilled from theological reflection on communication, as self-giving love defines the communication dynamic of the inner life of the Trinity as well as the total revelatory movement of God from the Incarnation to the Paschal Mystery and Pentecost. Loving self-gift is constitutive of God's self-communication, and this is made especially evident in Christ, who is the fullness of revelation (*DV* 7). Pastoral formation as articulated in *Pastores Dabo Vobis* echoes this closely: "[Seminarians] should be trained to undertake the ministry of the shepherd, that they may know how to represent Christ to humanity, Christ who 'did not come to have service done to him but to serve others and to give his life as a ransom for the lives of many' (Mk 10:45; Jn 1 3:12–17), and that they may win over many by becoming the servants of all (1 Cor. 9:19)" (57). In this, effective social communication is at the service of pastoral work—it is a disposition of loving self-gift that underscores the ministry of the shepherd and represents Christ especially through communicative acts. Or, social communication training and formation has an integrally pastoral aspect to it that asks how one can be of service to and represent Christ in and through communication.

Communication as Spiritual and Spiritual Formation

Spiritual formation seeks to foster an ever-deepening relationship with God to serve as the indispensable foundation of work in ministry. When it comes to social communication formation, the role of the Holy Spirit and one's capacity to walk in step with the Spirit is likewise indispensable; for effective pastoral communication, a robust spirituality is needed. As Eilers recalls, the role of the Holy Spirit is central to communication, revealing this role most explicitly at Pentecost as the moment when the Church gains her ability to communicate the Gospel and when her evangelizing mission is born.[20] Formation for communication thus prepares the minister to serve out of this Pentecost moment and to continue to respond to the Holy Spirit in and through communicative acts. Both social communication formation and spiritual formation ask the same question in this regard: how can I learn to discern the movement of God's Spirit and follow in step with the Spirit in life and in professional ministry?

These four convergences above are merely a starting point in developing a comprehensive vision for pastoral training and formation in social communication, one that integrates both the four pillars of ministerial formation and the complexity of social communication seriously and brings these into intentional dialogue. Developing this dialogue further is one salient direction for room to grow for the continued reception of *Inter Mirifica* more than fifty years after its promulgation.

NOTES

1. For a detailed description of the concerns about *Inter Mirifica* within the conciliar deliberation process itself, see Karlheinz Schmidthus "Decree on the Instruments of Social Communication," in *Commentary on the Documents of Vatican II*, ed. Herbert Vorgrimler (New York: Herder and Herder, 1967), 92–95. For a summary of critical responses to *Inter Mirifica* once it was promulgated, see Norman Tanner, *The Church and the World: Gaudium et Spes and Inter Mirifica* (New York and Mahwah, NJ: Paulist, 2005), 110–13.

2. See, for instance, the position stated by Cardinal Godfrey of Westminster, summarized in Xavier Rynne, *Letters from Vatican City: Vatican Council II (First Session) Background and Debates* (New York: Farrar, Strauss & Company, 1963), 180.

3. See *Inter Mirifica*, 18–19, 32.

4. For a systematic study of the social communication documents, see Franz-Josef Eilers, *Communicating Church: Social Communication Documents: An Introduction* (Manila: Logos/Divine Word, 2011), and Daniella Zsupan-Jerome, *Connected Toward Communion: The Church and Social Communication in the Digital Age* (Collegeville, MN: Liturgical Press, 2014).

5. Franz-Josef Eilers, SVD, "'Inter Mirifica' After 40 Years" (unpublished manuscript, accessed August 6, 2015), http://www.freinademetzcenter.org/pdf/Inter%20Mirifica%20after%2040%20Years.pdf.

6. Franz-Josef Eilers, SVD, "Church and Social Communication: 40 Years of *Inter Mirifica* and Beyond," *Ad Veritatem* 5, no. 1 (2005): 1, http://www.fabc.org/offices/osc/docs/pdf/Inter%20Mirifica%2040%20Years%20and%20Beyond.pdf.

7. See complete list of World Communications Day Messages at http://www.pccs.it/gmcs/index_eng.htm.

8. Enrico Baragli, *L'Inter mirifica; introduzione, storia, discussione, commento, documentazione* (Rome: Studio Romano della Comunicazione Sociale, 1969).

9. See chapters on *Inter Mirifica* by Avery Dulles, Andre Ruszkowski, and Robert White in *Vatican II: Assessment and Perspectives: Twenty Five Years After (1962–1987)*, ed. Rene Latourelle (New York and Mahwah, NJ: Paulist, 1989), 3:528–611; Mathijs Lamberigts in Giuseppe Alberigo and Joseph A. Komonchak, in *History of Vatican II* (Maryknoll: Orbis, 1997), 3:267–79; Richard John Neuhaus in *Vatican II: Renewal Within Tradition*, ed. Matthew Levering and Matthew Lamb (New York: Oxford, 2008), 351–56. See also note 4 above.

10. Walther Kampe, "Communicating with the World: The Decree *Inter Mirifica*," in *Vatican II Revisited by Those Who Were There*, ed. Alberic Stacpoole (London: Geoffrey Chapman, 1986), 200.

11. "The Blessing of the Fire and Preparation of the Candle," in *The Roman Missal*, 3rd typical ed., trans. The International Commission on English in the Liturgy (Washington, DC: United States Catholic Conference of Bishops, 2011), 344–45.

12. See Avery Dulles, "The Church Is Communications," *IDOC Internazionale* 27 (June 1971): 68–82; "Vatican II and Communications," in Latourelle, *Vatican II*, 3: 528–47.

13. See, for instance, *Evangelii Nuntiandi*, 14–15.

14. Franz-Josef Eilers, *Communicating Church: Social Communication Documents* (Manila: Logos/Divine Word, 2011), 136.

15. See Benedict XVI, "Social Networks: Portals of Truth and Faith, New Spaces for Evangelization," Message for the 47th World Communications Day, January 24, 2013; and Francis, "Communications at the Service of an Authentic Culture of Encounter," Message for the 48th World Communications Day, January 24, 2014.

16. See the summary of Cardinal Cento's remarks in Xavier Rynne, *Letters from Vatican City: Vatican Council II (First Session) Background and Debates* (New York: Farrar, Strauss & Company, 1963), 176.

17. Antonio Spadaro, *Cybertheology: Thinking Christianity in the Era of the Internet* (New York: Fordham, 2014), vii.

18. For a more detailed dialogue between the Guide and the challenge of pastoral formation today, see Zsupan-Jerome, "Articulating Ministerial Formation," in *Connected Toward Communion*, 67–80.

19. See John Paul II, *Pastores Dabo Vobis* (1992), paragraphs 43–59.

20. Franz-Josef Eilers, *Communicating in Ministry and Mission* (Manila: Logos/Divine Word, 2009), 33–46.

PART THREE

The Declarations

14

Dignitatis Humanae

Nicholas J. Healy, Jr.

> *The extent and depth of the teaching of the Second Vatican Council call for a renewed commitment to deeper study in order to reveal clearly the Council's continuity with tradition, especially in points of doctrine which, perhaps because they are new, have not yet been well understood by some sections of the Church.*
>
> John Paul II[1]

The reception and interpretation of the Declaration on Religious Freedom, *Dignitatis Humanae*, began with the solemn ceremonies of December 8, 1965 marking the end of the Second Vatican Council. Speaking on behalf of Pope Paul VI and the Council fathers, Cardinal Lienart of Lille delivered the following "Message to Rulers":

> At this solemn moment, we, the fathers of the twenty-first Ecumenical Council of the Catholic Church ... address ourselves respectfully and confidently ... to all those who hold temporal power. We proclaim publically: We do honor to your authority and your sovereignty, we respect your office, we recognize your just laws, we esteem those who make them and those who apply them. But we have a sacrosanct word to speak to you and it is this: Only God is great. God alone is the beginning and the end. God alone is the source of your authority and the foundation of your laws. Your task is to be in the world the promoters of order and peace among men. But never forget this: It is God, the living and true God, who is the Father of men and women. And it is Christ, His eternal Son, who came to make this known to us and to teach us that

we are all brothers and sisters. He it is who is the great artisan of order and peace on earth.... In your earthly and temporal city, God constructs mysteriously His spiritual and eternal city, His Church. And what does this Church ask of you after close to two thousand years of experiences of all kinds in her relations with you today? She tells you in one of the major documents of this Council. She asks of you only freedom, the freedom to believe and preach her faith, the freedom to love her God and serve Him, the freedom to bring to mankind her message of life.[2]

The "major document" that Cardinal Lienart refers to, *Dignitatis Humanae*, had been formally approved the preceding day with 2308 Council fathers voting in favor and 70 against. Although approved by an overwhelming majority and commended by Paul VI as "one of the greatest documents"[3] of the Council, the Declaration on Religious Freedom was the most controversial text of Vatican II. A significant minority of Council fathers harbored reservations on the grounds that *Dignitatis Humanae* seemed to depart from established Catholic doctrine on the duties of the state toward the Catholic religion. Within the majority that supported an affirmation of religious freedom, there were deep disagreements about the ground of religious freedom and the relationship between freedom and truth.

In the fifty years since the Council, *Dignitatis Humanae* (hereafter *DH*) has become a cornerstone of the social doctrine of the Catholic Church. In the words of John Paul II, "The Church in our time attaches great importance to all that is stated by the Second Vatican Council in its Declaration on Religious Freedom."[4] "Religious freedom," he writes, "is at the basis of all other freedoms and is inseparably tied to them all."[5] *DH* also has continued to generate controversy and debate. Behind Archbishop Marcel Lefebvre's schismatic act of consecrating bishops without papal mandate was a conviction that *DH* represented a departure from Catholic doctrine and a capitulation to the heresy of modernism. Among the supporters of religious freedom, the disagreements that accompanied the drafting of *DH* have served as a fault line for differing accounts of the nature, foundation, and scope of the right to religious freedom.[6]

There are several reasons why a relatively short document with a "very modest scope"[7] has been the source of intense controversy and debate. First, as Avery Dulles notes, *DH* is "the only document of Vatican II that explicitly claims to be a development of doctrine."[8] The stated aim of the document was to "search the sacred tradition and teaching of the Church from which to draw forth new things that are always in harmony with the old" and "to develop the teaching of the more recent popes on the inviolable rights of the human person" (*DH* 1).[9] Commenting on this aspect of *DH* John Courtney Murray writes,

[The Declaration on Religious Freedom] was the most controversial document of the whole Council, largely because it raised with sharp emphasis the issue that lay continually below the surface of all the conciliar debates—the issue of the development of doctrine. The notion of development, not the notion of religious freedom, was the real sticking point for many of those who opposed the Declaration even to the end.[10]

The question of how to understand the nature of this development and thus the teaching of *DH* in the context of the Catholic tradition as a whole remains an open question.

A second reason why *DH* has generated such interest and debate is the central importance of the question of freedom for the Church's encounter with modernity. "The era we call modern times," writes Joseph Ratzinger, "has been determined from the beginning by the theme of freedom; the striving for new forms of freedom."[11] Both *Gaudium et Spes* and *DH* acknowledge the legitimacy of this aspiration for freedom, "for authentic freedom is an exceptional sign of the image of God in man."[12] At the same time, the Council fathers recognized the need for a critical discernment of the modern idea of freedom in light of the truth of human nature and the Christian mystery of redemption in Christ. In the years since the Council, the question of human freedom and especially the relationship between freedom and truth has gained a new prominence as the "crucial issue" of our time.[13]

My aim in what follows is to explore the teaching of *DH* on religious freedom in light of some of the main interpretive issues that have informed the reception of the document. My essay is divided in three parts: Part I will summarize the teaching of *DH* and introduce three basic issues or disputed questions. Part II will present the reception and interpretation of *DH* by the teaching office of the Church. Popes Paul VI, John Paul II, and Benedict XVI all participated in the conciliar debates on the question of religious freedom. Each of these popes emphasized the fundamental importance of the right to religious freedom and sought to implement and develop the teaching of *DH*. Part III will consider the current state of the question by way of presenting some of the key figures and positions that have shaped and guided the interpretation of the document.

I. The Teaching of *Dignitatis Humanae*—The Key Interpretive Issues

The Declaration on Religious Freedom, subtitled "On the Right of the Person and of Communities to Social and Civil Freedom in Religious Matters," consists of two sections preceded by a brief preface. Chapter 1 presents the general idea of religious freedom and reflects on the foundation and scope of this right. Chapter 2 develops the idea of religious freedom in light of Christian revelation, emphasizing the essential freedom of the act of faith and the freedom of the Church to proclaim the Gospel.

The point of departure for *DH* is the fact that "men and women of our time are becoming more conscious every day of the dignity of the human person. Increasing numbers demand that in acting they enjoy and make use of their own counsel and a responsible freedom, not impelled by coercion but moved by a sense of duty. They also demand that juridical limits be set to the public power, in order that the rightful freedom of persons and associations not be excessively restricted" (*DH* 1). The aim of *DH* is to discern and deepen this new awareness of human dignity in light of God's revelation in Christ which has been entrusted to the Church: "Carefully attending to these desires of men's hearts, and proposing to declare to what degree they are in conformity with truth and justice, this Vatican Council searches the sacred tradition and teaching of the Church, from which it draws forth new things that are always in harmony with the old" (*DH* 1).

To ensure the harmony of new and old, the preface includes an affirmation of the truth of revelation and an acknowledgment that the "one true religion subsists in the Catholic and apostolic Church" (*DH* 1). All men and women are called to seek this truth and to hold fast to it once it is known. Thus in "develop[ing] the teaching of the recent popes on the inviolable rights of the human person," *DH* "leaves intact [*integram*] the traditional Catholic teaching on the moral duty individuals and society have toward the true religion and the one Church of Christ" (*DH* 1).

Part 1, entitled "The General Principle of Religious Freedom," begins with an affirmation of the right to religious freedom. The key text reads as follows:

> This Vatican Council declares that the human person has a right to religious freedom. Such freedom consists in this, that all men should be immune from coercion on the part of individuals, social groups or any human power, so that no one is forced to act against his conscience in religious matters, nor impeded from acting according to his conscience, both in private and in public, whether alone or in association with others, within due limits. In addition, this Council declares that the right to religious freedom truly has its foundation in the very dignity of the human person. (*DH* 2)

DH proceeds to unfold the meaning and ground of the right to religious freedom by situating the right in the context of the "obligation to seek the truth, especially the truth concerning religion" (*DH* 2). In order to satisfy this obligation in a way that is in keeping with their own nature and dignity, human persons must "enjoy psychological freedom as well as immunity from external coercion" (*DH* 2). It follows that the right to religious freedom "persists even for those who do not satisfy their obligation to seek the truth and to hold fast to it; the exercise of this right is not to be impeded, provided that just public order is preserved" (*DH* 3).

Secondary arguments in support of the right to religious freedom include a reflection on the mediation of conscience and the social nature of the human person, who seeks truth through free inquiry, dialogue, and communication. *DH* also notes that religious acts "transcend the earthly and temporal order of things" (*DH* 3). Accordingly, political authority would "exceed its limits if it presumes either to direct or impede religious acts" (*DH* 3).

The right to religious freedom belongs to individuals and religious communities, which have "the right not to be impeded ... in erecting buildings or in acquiring and making use of any necessary goods" or "prevented from publicly teaching about or witnessing to their faith in speech or in writing" (*DH* 4). Regarding the delicate question of the civil recognition or the "establishment" of the Catholic religion, *DH* teaches that "if, in light of a people's particular circumstances, special civil recognition is granted to one religious community in the juridical order of the state, it is necessary at the same time that the right to freedom in religious matters be acknowledged and observed for all citizens and religious communities" (*DH* 6).

In order to avoid arbitrary abuses under the pretext of religious freedom, *DH* introduces the limiting principle of "just public order" (*DH* 2; *DH* 3). The concept of a just public order includes the effective protection of the rights of all citizens, safeguarding public peace and responsibility for the proper guardianship of public morality. As a general rule, "man's freedom should be acknowledged as far as possible, and should not be restricted except when and insofar as necessary" (*DH* 7).

The second chapter of *DH* is premised on the idea that the Church's teaching on religious freedom "has its roots in divine revelation":

> Although revelation does not expressly affirm the right to immunity from external coercion in religious matters, it nonetheless brings to light the dignity of the human person in all its fullness. It manifests the respect Christ showed for the freedom with which man is to fulfill his duty of believing the word of God. (*DH* 9)

The true dignity of the human person is disclosed by "the respect Christ showed for the freedom with which man is to fulfill his duty of believing the word of God" (*DH* 9). "The act of faith is of its very nature a voluntary act" (*DH* 10). The nature of the act of faith precludes "every kind of coercion on the part of men" (*DH* 10).

A "fundamental principle" for the relationship between the Church and civil society is the idea that the Church should "enjoy as much freedom in acting as the care of man's salvation may demand" (*DH* 13). There is, then, a "harmony" between religious freedom and the freedom of the Church.

DH concludes with an exhortation for "all men and women to consider carefully how necessary religious freedom is, especially in the present condition of the human family . . . [in which] men and women of different cultures and religions are being bound to one another with closer ties, and there is a growing consciousness of the responsibility proper to each person" (*DH* 15).

Most of the discussion of *DH* has revolved around three basic interpretive issues. The first and most basic question is how to understand the nature and foundation of the right to religious freedom. *DH* affirms that "the right to religious freedom has its foundation in the very dignity of the human person" (*DH* 2). What is the sense and foundation of human dignity in this context? *DH* also grounds the right to religious freedom in the obligation to seek the truth, especially the truth about God. Does the person's relation to God and to truth inform the meaning of human dignity and the content of the right to immunity from coercion? In his book *John Paul II and the Legacy of Dignitatis Humanae*, Hermínio Rico frames this question as follows:

> The basic issue at [the] level of the foundation of the right to religious freedom has to do with the kind of definitive answer to the following question: Where does human dignity ultimately rest in the person? . . . [Does it rest in] the freedom inherent in every person? . . . Or is it the person's relationship with transcendent truth?[14]

As suggested by Rico, the underlying question involves the relationship between human freedom and truth. One line of interpretation—represented by Rico, John Courtney Murray, Pietro Pavan, and Martin Rhonheimer (among others)—views the right to religious freedom as a formally juridical concept that abstracts from the question of truth. In the words of Rhonheimer, "The Declaration on Religious Freedom in fact dissolves, on the doctrinal level, the link between truth and the right to religious freedom."[15] "Religious freedom," writes Pavan, "does not concern . . . the person's relation to truth."[16] Other commentators such as Philippe André-Vincent and David L. Schindler consider the connection between freedom and truth as foundational for human dignity and as informing the right to religious freedom.[17] In the eyes of André-Vincent and Schindler, the crowning achievement of *DH* is a deeper understanding of the intrinsic and inseparable unity of truth and freedom.

The second interpretive issue involves the "due limits" to religious freedom. This question in turn presupposes an account of the nature and purpose of political authority. Consider, for example, two very different proposals regarding the responsibility of the state:

> The civil power also, and not only each of the citizens, has the duty of accepting the revelation proposed by the Church itself. Likewise, in its legislation, it must conform itself to the precepts of the natural law and take a strict account of the positive laws, both divine and ecclesiastical, intended to lead men to supernatural beatitude. . . . It devolves seriously upon the civil power to exclude from legislation, government, and public activity everything it would judge to be capable of impeding the Church from attaining its eternal end.[18]

> Religious acts, in which men and women privately and publicly order themselves toward God out of a personal, intimate conviction, transcend the temporal and earthly order of things. In performing these acts, therefore, man is not subject to the civil power, whose competence, on account of its end, is restricted to the earthly and temporal order, and whose legislative power extends only to external actions. The public power, therefore, since it cannot pass judgment on interior religious acts, likewise cannot coerce or impede the public exercise of religion, provided that the demands of public order are preserved. . . .

The public power completely exceeds its limits if it involves itself in any way in the governing of minds or the care of souls.[19]

The first text, taken from the preparatory schema *De Ecclesia*, which was drafted under the direction of Cardinal Ottaviani, presupposes the traditional Catholic view that the purpose of political authority is to care for the temporal common good. Responsibility for the common good includes an acknowledgment of the truth of the Catholic religion and allows the suppression of public manifestations of false religions. The second text, taken from an earlier draft of *DH* (*textus emendatus*), suggests the total incompetence of the state in religious matters. Instead of the traditional idea of responsibility for the common good, the *textus emendatus* presents the purpose of political authority in terms of "protecting, cultivating, and defending the natural rights of all citizens."[20]

The final text of *DH* differs from both of these earlier drafts. *DH* describes the purpose or "proper end" of political authority as "the care of the temporal common good" (*DH* 3). At the same time, *DH* develops the idea of the common good in light of a new awareness of the dignity and freedom of human persons. In terms of the disputed question of the state's responsibility for the truth and practice of religion, *DH* acknowledges the transcendent nature of religious acts. Accordingly, political authority "would be said to exceed its limit if it presumes either to direct or to impede religious acts" (*DH* 3). At the same time, care for the common good requires that political authority should "acknowledge and show favor to the religious life of its citizens" (*DH* 3). In what sense is this responsibility grounded in the state's recognition of the truth of human nature and/or the truth of religion?

In addition to acknowledging and favoring the religious life of its citizens, "civil society has the right to protect itself against abuses that could be committed under the pretext of religious freedom" (*DH* 7). As noted above, the limiting criterion for the right to religious freedom is "just public order," which includes care for "public peace" and "the proper guardianship of public morality" (*DH* 7). What is the relationship between the "temporal common good" and a "just public order"? Under what conditions could the right to religious freedom be limited in the name of upholding a just public order?

The third interpretive issue, which presupposes and implicates the preceding questions, concerns the development of doctrine. Can the teaching of *DH* be interpreted as an authentic development rather than a reversal or contradiction of earlier teaching by popes Gregory XVI, Pius XI, and Leo XIII? Most commentators agree that *DH* represents a shift or novelty with respect to the teaching and practice of these nineteenth-century popes. Does the novelty of *DH* represent an authentic development or a rupture with the preceding tradition? Thomas Pink summarizes the dilemma as follows:

In the nineteenth century, in encyclicals from Gregory XVI's *Mirari Vos* in 1832 to Leo XIII's *Libertas* in 1888, the Catholic Church taught that the state should not only recognize Catholic Christianity as the

true religion, but should use its coercive power to restrict the public practice of, and proselytization by, false religions—including
Protestantism. Yet in its declaration on religious freedom, *Dignitatis
Humanae*, the Second Vatican Council declared that the state should
not use coercion to restrict religion—not even on behalf of the true
faith. Such coercion would be a violation of people's right to religious
liberty. This looks like a clear change in Catholic doctrine.[21]

Despite their obvious differences, "traditionalist" theologians such as
Marcel Lefebvre and Michael Davies and "progressive" theologians such as
Charles Curran, Richard McCormick, and John T. Noonan share a common
assumption: *DH* represents a break with or contradiction of earlier papal
teaching.[22] The former argue that the teaching of *DH* is erroneous, while revi-
sionist theologians often adduce the example of *DH* to support other possible
changes in Catholic doctrine.

Other interpreters such as John Courtney Murray, Basile Valuet, Avery
Dulles, Brian Harrison, Russell Hittinger, Martin Rhonheimer, and David
Schindler interpret *DH* as a genuine development of doctrine, although each
will explain the nature of this development differently.[23] Is the novelty of *DH*
on the level of prudential policy or doctrine?[24] What kind of hermeneutic is
appropriate for the interpretation of a conciliar text?

II. The Reception and Interpretation of *Dignitatis Humanae*
by the Teaching Office of the Church

Pope Paul VI

Pope Paul VI closely followed the conciliar debate on religious freedom and
the drafting of *DH*. Following the debate at the start of the fourth session
in September of 1965, he met with Bishop Émile De Smedt of the Pontifical
Council for Promoting Christian Unity, which was responsible for revising
the text in light of oral and written interventions. Gilles Routhier summarizes
the content of the meeting as recorded in a handwritten note of De Smedt
entitled "Instructions de Paul VI pour la révision du texte": "To emphasize
the obligation of seeking the truth; to present the traditional teaching of the
ecclesiastical magisterium; to avoid basing religious freedom solely on freedom of conscience; to state the doctrine in such a way that the lay state would
not think itself dispensed from its obligations to the Church."[25] All of these
concerns were addressed in the final revisions to the document and these concerns informed Paul VI's subsequent interpretation of *DH*.

According to Luigi Mistò, the fundamental contribution of Pope Paul VI
to the reception of *DH* consists in "the affirmation of the dignity of the human
person, whose true greatness is proposed in the light of Revelation."[26] A recur-
ring theme in Paul VI's reflections on *DH* is the importance of the human
being's relation to God as the enabling ground of freedom:

The Council has made its own the great expectation of the modern civil world by acknowledging this primary, extremely noble natural prerogative: human freedom. Two points deserve mention. The first concerns the basic and supreme reason for human freedom: once again it is human dignity. Note how the Council expressed itself: "True freedom in a human being is the greatest sign of the divine image. In fact, God decided to allow people to follow their own counsel, so that they would spontaneously seek and reach him, freely accepting their Creator." Remove this deliberately free and morally binding relationship with God from human beings and one would take away the most cogent reason for human freedom. The second point that should be mentioned is the following: a person's relationship with God must neither be forced nor prevented where religion is concerned; this is the basic reason behind the Council's Declaration on Religious Liberty in the area of civil coexistence.[27]

The Council has spoken of freedom, referring to it many times. Freedom is a wonderful word.... None of you will want to confuse freedom with ideological and religious indifference, nor with individualism set up as a system.[28]

Another important aspect of Paul VI's reception of *DH* is the revision of "concordats" governing the relationship between the Church and various states.[29] To take just one representative example, an agreement with Spain signed on July 28, 1976 and ratified on August 28, 1976 notes that "the Second Vatican Council which has established as its fundamental principles, to which relations between the political community and the Church must conform, the mutual independence of both parties ... a healthy collaboration ... religious freedom as a right of the human person."[30] Prior this agreement, Spain had already changed the provision of Article 6 of the Charter of 13 July 1945 (*Feuro de los Españoles*): "No one shall be disturbed for his religious beliefs nor the private exercise of his religion. There is no authorization for external ceremonies or manifestations other than those of the Catholic religion." With Vatican approval, this formula was changed to: "The state guarantees the protection of religious liberty, which shall be guaranteed by the effective juridical provision which will safeguard morals and public order."[31]

John Paul II (1978–2005)

The first non-Italian pope in over four hundred and fifty years brought to Rome a new awareness of the threat to human dignity posed by totalitarian regimes. For John Paul II, the twofold theme of human dignity and religious freedom was the centerpiece of the political and spiritual struggle between the Church and atheistic communism. After the fall of communism, John Paul II continued to reflect on the importance of human dignity and religious freedom in light of new challenges within Western liberal societies.

Four points stand out in John Paul II's extensive commentary on *DH*.[32] The first point is an emphasis on religious freedom as the foundation of the structure of human rights. The idea that religious freedom is the first and most basic freedom resounds like a refrain throughout his corpus.

> Religious freedom, an essential requirement of the dignity of every person, is a cornerstone of the structure of human rights, and for this reason an irreplaceable factor in the good of individuals and of the whole of society, as well as of the personal fulfillment of each individual. It follows that the freedom of individuals and communities to profess and practice their religion is an essential element for peaceful human coexistence.... The civil and social right to religious freedom, inasmuch as it touches the most intimate sphere of the spirit, is a point of reference of the other fundamental rights and in some way becomes a measure of them ... religious freedom in so far as it touches the most intimate sphere of the spirit, sustains and is as it were the *raison d'être* of other freedoms.[33]

> The right to religious freedom is "not merely one human right among others," but "rather [it] is the most fundamental, since the dignity of every person has its first source in his essential relationship with God the Creator and Father, in whose image and likeness he was created."[34]

In short, "in any consideration of fundamental human rights, a primary place must always be accorded to religious freedom."[35]

The second characteristic of John Paul II's approach to religious freedom is a concern to ground the right to religious freedom in an adequate philosophical and theological anthropology. The teaching of *Gaudium et Spes* that "Jesus Christ, in revealing the mystery of the Father's love, fully reveals man to himself" is both a reference point and guiding principle for John Paul II. In his first encyclical letter, *Redemptor Hominis*, John Paul II unfolds the significance of this Christocentric anthropology for the meaning of religious freedom:

> The Declaration on Religious Freedom shows us convincingly that, when Christ and, after him, his Apostles proclaimed the truth that comes not from men but from God ("My teaching is not mine, but his who sent me," that is the Father's), they preserved, while acting with their full force of spirit, a deep esteem for man, for his intellect, his will, his conscience and his freedom. Thus the human person's dignity itself becomes part of the content of that proclamation, being included not necessarily in words but by an attitude towards it. This attitude seems to fit the special needs of our times. Since man's true freedom is not found in everything that the various systems and individuals see and propagate as freedom, the Church, because of her divine mission, becomes all the more the guardian of this freedom, which is the condition and basis for the human person's true

dignity.... Today also, even after two thousand years, we see Christ as the one who brings man freedom based on truth, frees man from what curtails, diminishes and as it were breaks off this freedom at its root, in man's soul, his heart and his conscience.[36]

In summary, the foundation of human dignity and thus the full measure of human freedom is the human person's relation to God: "The freedom of the individual finds its basis in man's transcendent dignity: a dignity given to him by God the Creator and Father, in whose image and likeness he was created."[37] This leads to the third aspect of John Paul II's interpretation of *DH*: the intrinsic unity of freedom and truth.

Already during the Council, the relationship between freedom and truth emerged as a chief concern of Bishop Karol Wojtyła. In his words, *"non datur libertas sine veritate"* ("there is no freedom without truth").[38] The unity of freedom and truth became a key theme of his pontificate. In *Veritatis Splendor*, he criticizes currents of thought that tend to dissolve the essential bond between freedom and truth. Helping man to rediscover this bond "represents one of the specific requirements of the Church's mission."[39] Freedom is "never freedom 'from' the truth but always freedom 'in' the truth."[40] The right to religious freedom is an inner requirement of the human person's responsibility for the truth. Reciprocally, truth itself calls for a free and personal adherence. As *DH* affirms, "In no other way does truth impose itself than by the strength of truth itself, entering the mind at once gently and with power" (*DH* 1).

The fourth and final aspect of John Paul II's approach to religious freedom consists in his repentance for past actions by members of the Church. In a section devoted to the "freedom of the Church," *DH* acknowledged that in "the life of the people of God as it has made its pilgrim way through the vicissitudes of human history, there have at times appeared ways of acting less in keeping with the spirit of the Gospel, or even opposed to it" (*DH* 12). John Paul II goes further in examining the historical record and calling attention to the "the sinfulness of her children, recalling all those times in history when they departed from the spirit of Christ and the Gospel."[41]

Another painful chapter of history to which the sons and daughters of the Church must return with a spirit of repentance is that of the acquiescence given, especially in certain centuries, to intolerance and even the use of violence in the service of truth. It is true that an accurate historical judgment cannot prescind from careful study of the cultural conditioning of the times, as a result of which many people may have held in good faith that an authentic witness to the truth could include suppressing the opinions of others or at least paying no attention to them. Many factors frequently converged to create assumptions which justified intolerance and fostered an emotional climate from which only great spirits, truly free and filled with God, were in some way able to break free. Yet the consideration of mitigating factors does not exonerate the Church from the obligation to express profound regret for the weaknesses of so many of her sons and daughters who sullied her face, preventing her from fully mirroring the image of her crucified Lord, the supreme witness of patient love and of humble meekness. From these painful moments of the past a lesson can be drawn for the future, leading all Christians to adhere fully to the sublime principle stated by the Council: "The truth cannot impose itself except by virtue of its own truth, as it wins over the mind with both gentleness and power."[42]

Benedict XVI (2005–2012)

The first year of Benedict XVI's papacy coincided with the fortieth anniversary of the conclusion of Vatican II. In an important address to the curia in December of 2005, Benedict XVI noted the anniversary and posed a series of questions: "What has been the result of the Council? Was it well received? What, in the acceptance of the Council, was good and what was inadequate or mistaken? What still remains to be done?" And finally, "Why has the implementation of the Council, in large parts of the Church, thus far been so difficult?"[43] Benedict provided a partial answer to this last question by contrasting "a hermeneutic of discontinuity and rupture" with "a hermeneutic of reform." The former risks "ending in a split between the pre-conciliar Church and the post-conciliar Church. It asserts that the texts of the Council as such do not yet express the true spirit of the Council."[44] The hermeneutic of reform includes elements of continuity and discontinuity held together within the unity of the one subject— the Church: "She is a subject which increases in time and develops, yet always remaining the same, the one subject of the journeying People of God."[45]

In a fascinating passage, Pope Benedict proceeds to offer a reason why a hermeneutic of discontinuity can seem convincing:

> In the great dispute about man which marks the modern epoch, the Council had to focus in particular on the theme of anthropology. It had to question the relationship between the Church and her faith on the one hand, and man and the contemporary world on the other.... The question becomes even clearer if, instead of the generic term "contemporary world," we opt for another that is more precise: the Council had to determine in a new way the relationship between the Church and the modern era.[46]

Given the scale of the problem as well as the history of mutual mistrust, the task of re-thinking the relationship between the Church and the modern era was "extremely demanding ... [requiring] a synthesis of fidelity and dynamic."[47]

This hermeneutical principle guides Pope Benedict's interpretation of DH. While acknowledging the discontinuity between the 1864 "Syllabus of

Errors" and *DH*'s affirmation of religious liberty, Benedict discerns a deeper continuity within the shared faith of the Church. At the heart of this continuity is a renewed understanding of the freedom proper to faith and the essential unity of truth and freedom. Freedom is not merely an empty form, an ability to do what one wants. In the words of Ratzinger, freedom means "full membership, being at home ... participation in being itself."[48] "Freedom," he says, "is identical with ontological dignity, which of course makes sense only if ontological dignity is really 'dignified': the gift of love and being given in love."[49] Reciprocally, truth includes freedom as essential to its own fullness:

> The truth cannot unfold except in an otherness open to God, who wishes to reveal his own otherness in and through my human brothers and sisters. Hence it is not fitting to state in an exclusive way: "I possess the truth." The truth is not possessed by anyone; it is always a gift which calls us to undertake a journey of ever closer assimilation to truth. Truth can only be known and experienced in freedom; for this reason we cannot impose truth on others; truth is disclosed only in an encounter of love.[50]

Following in the footsteps of his predecessor John Paul II, Pope Benedict XVI emphasizes that religious freedom cannot be conceived simply in negative terms as immunity from coercion. The Council's affirmation of religious freedom presupposes a positive understanding of freedom grounded in the transcendent dignity of the human person who is created in love and called to live in communion with the truth.

> The right to religious freedom is rooted in the very dignity of the human person, whose transcendent nature must not be ignored or overlooked.... The transcendent dignity of the person is an essential value of Judeo-Christian wisdom, yet thanks to the use of reason, it can be recognized by all. This dignity, understood as a capacity to transcend one's own materiality and to seek truth, must be acknowledged as a universal *good*, indispensable for the building of a society directed to human fulfilment.
>
> Openness to truth and perfect goodness, openness to God, is rooted in human nature; it confers full dignity on each individual and is the guarantee of full mutual respect between persons. Religious freedom should be understood, then, not merely as immunity from coercion, but even more fundamentally as an ability to order one's own choices in accordance with truth.[51]

III. Signposts for the Interpretation of *Dignitatis Humanae*

"The debate on religious liberty," writes Joseph Ratzinger, "will in later years be considered one of the most important events of the Council already rich enough in important events."[52] The debate continued after the conclusion of the Council. As John Courtney Murray predicted, *DH* was both "an end and a beginning."[53] The document left open the task of systematically elaborating the philosophical and theological foundations and the implications of the right to religious freedom. Rather than attempt a survey of the vast number of articles and books on the significance of *DH*, my aim in this concluding section is to introduce some of the central figures or schools of interpretation that inform the current state of the question.

Marcel Lefebvre—Dignitatis Humanae as a Departure from Catholic Tradition

> We are forced to choose. Naturally, in our time of liberalism many people cannot understand that we can defend opinions that can seem "outdated," "antiquated," "medieval," etc. But the doctrine of the Church is the doctrine of the Church. When the popes condemned liberty of thought, liberty of conscience, liberty of religions, they explained why they condemned them. Leo XIII wrote long encyclicals on the subject. One only has to read them; the same applies for Pope Pius IX and Pope Gregory XVI. Again, all of this is based on the Church's fundamental principles, on the fact that the Church is truth, the only truth. This is the way it is; you either believe it or you don't, of course, but when you believe, then you have to draw the consequences. That is why, personally, I do not believe that the declarations of the Council on liberty of conscience, liberty of thought, and liberty of religions can be compatible with what the popes taught in the past. Therefore we have to choose.[54]

In order to appreciate Archbishop Marcel Lefebvre's fundamental opposition to *DH*, it is necessary to know the standard Catholic teaching on the relationship between the Church and the state prior to Vatican II.[55] Lefebvre sums up preconciliar teaching as follows:

> This body of doctrine can be summarized as the union of the temporal and spiritual powers and the indirect subordination of the temporal power to the spiritual. As a consequence, the care of religion (*cura religionis*) of the State—that is, its duty to recognize and favor the true religion and its members—results both from the proper end of the State, which is the temporal common good of society, and from its "ministerial" function with regard to the spiritual power. Consequently, indifferentism on the part of the State and the juridical order of civil society was condemned as such with remarkable persistence.[56]

According to this view, the state as such has a duty to honor God and recognize the truth of the Catholic religion. Civil authority also has a duty to protect the true religion and to suppress the public manifestations of false religions. Under particular circumstances, civil authority may tolerate other forms of worship as required by the common good, but may never give positive approval of error. In short, error has no rights.

In the eyes of Lefebvre, the right to religious freedom cannot be reconciled with the traditional doctrine of the Church sketched above. One of the principal mistakes of *DH*, he argues, is a "confusion between the ontological dignity of man and his operative dignity."[57] Ontological dignity "consists in the nobility of a nature endowed with intelligence and free will [and] called by it to know God."[58] "The ontological dignity of the human person is the same in everyone and can never be lost."[59] Operational dignity, by contrast, "is the result of the exercise of his faculties, essentially intelligence and will."[60] David Schindler explains the significance of this distinction:

> Lefebvre's problem with the teaching of *Dignitatis humanae*, in sum, is that it roots the right to religious freedom not in this operative dignity of man, which consists in "the actual adherence of the person to the truth," but rather in the ontological dignity of man, which "refers only to his free will" made in the image of God. In the view of the Declaration, "any man, regardless of his subjective dispositions (truth or error, good or bad faith), is inviolable in the actions by which he operates his relation to God." But, according to Lefebvre, this is false: "when man cleaves to error or moral evil, he loses his operative dignity, which therefore cannot be the basis for anything at all."[61]

Schindler proceeds to uncover one of the main weaknesses in Lefebvre's interpretation of *DH*: his failure to grasp the original unity between freedom and truth:

> The Declaration thus takes over the essential concerns of both Murray (*freedom, rights*) and Lefebvre (*truth, duty*), while nevertheless *transforming the basic terms in which their respective arguments are articulated*. The Declaration is able to affirm an original unity between freedom and truth, such that it is right to say both that the truth alone frees and that the truth alone really does free, because of the Declaration's (implicitly) presupposed ancient-medieval view regarding the spirituality of the free-intelligent human act and the transcendentality of truth, both of which imply relation to the Creator. All persons have the right to seek the truth, ultimately about God, *in freedom, because all persons share in the spiritual nature of the human act ordered to the transcendental nature of truth, and are (thereby) obliged to seek the truth about God*. This means that there can be no entry into truth, rightly understood, no legitimate promotion of the person's movement toward truth, that does not presuppose and demand respect for the interior self-determining, hence free, activity proper to

the spiritual nature of the person. [Lefebvre's criticism of *DH* is] in the end warranted only if the ancient-medieval tradition's idea of the spirituality of the free-intelligent human act and of the transcendentality of truth is false.[62]

Referring to the conciliar debates on religious freedom, Lefebvre notes that a number of Council fathers opposed the early drafts of the Declaration and that "this opposition forced Paul VI to insert a few clauses favorable to the thesis of Tradition—favorable, that is, to the obligation to submit oneself to the truth and the faith."[63] Instead of uncovering the significance of these passages on the obligation to seek the truth, Lefebvre concludes that "the text became contradictory."[64]

It is well known how Lefebvre's opposition to *DH* eventually led to a loss of full communion with the Catholic Church. John Paul II, Benedict XVI, and Francis have all sought to heal this wound.

John Courtney Murray and the Juridical Approach to Religious Freedom

John Courtney Murray played a crucial role in the drafting and the interpretation of *Dignitatis Humanae*, despite his untimely death in August of 1967.[65] In the widely read *Documents of Vatican II*, edited by Walter Abbott, Murray introduced, translated, and annotated the Declaration on Religious Freedom. During the Council and in the months immediately following, he published several commentaries on the text.[66] As Jeffrey Gros observes, "It is sometimes difficult to distinguish evaluating the declaration and evaluating the work of one of its drafters, John Courtney Murray."[67]

Murray's approach to religious freedom is characterized by two interlocking claims. First, the right to religious freedom involves a "negative" understanding of freedom—a "freedom from" as distinct from "freedom for." In Murray's own formulation, religious freedom is "an immunity; its content is negative." "In its juridical sense as a human right," he writes, "religious freedom is a functional or instrumental concept. Precisely by reason of its negative content it serves to make possible and easy the practice of religious values."[68]

Secondly, the state is deemed to be totally incompetent in religious matters:

Inherent, therefore, in the notion of religious freedom is the notion of government incompetence in matters religious. This latter notion, however, has to be exactly understood. The constitutional provision for religious freedom is a self-denying ordinance on the part of government. That is to say, government denies to itself the competence to be a judge of religious belief and action.[69]

In an essay entitled "This Matter of Religious Freedom," published in the journal *America* soon after the close of the third session, Murray summarizes his juridical approach as follows:

The advocates of religious freedom were divided among themselves.... To understand the division, one would have to note the difference in methodology and focus of argument between the first two drafts of the Declaration and the third draft. The first two drafts followed a line of argument common among French-speaking theologians. The argument began, not in the order of historical fact, but in the order of universal truth. The truth is that each man is called by God to share the divine life. This call is mediated to man by conscience, and man's response to it is the free act of faith. The essential dignity of man is located in his personal freedom of conscience, whereby he is truly a moral agent, acting on his own irreducible responsibility before God. Thus religious freedom was conceived to be formally and in the first instance an ethical and theological notion; the effort then was made to conclude, by inference to the juridical notion of religious freedom, man's right to the free exercise of religion in society. The trouble was that this structure of argument seemed vulnerable to the advocates as well as to the adversaries of religious freedom. It is not obvious that the inference from freedom of conscience to the free exercise of religion as a human right is valid. Nevertheless, many French-speaking theologians and bishops considered their view to be richer and more profound. They were therefore displeased by the third draft Declaration, which relinquished their line of argument in favor of a line more common among English and Italian-speaking theorists. This line, as I have indicated, addresses the problem where it concretely exists—in the legal and political order. It considers religious freedom to be formally and in the first instance a juridical notion.[70]

As Murray notes, a number of French bishops were displeased by the third draft of *DH* that Murray had authored. Their concern was summed up in the intervention of Bishop Ancel, speaking on behalf of more than a hundred French bishops:

Several times the request has been made that the ontological foundation of religious freedom be set forth. For the argument stemming simply from the dignity of the human person seems to some to be insufficient. Moreover, the connection that exists between the obligation to seek the truth and religious freedom itself has not yet been made clear. To be sure, we have often heard that man has an obligation to seek the truth; likewise, we have heard that religious freedom presents no obstacle to this obligation; but at no time, unless I am mistaken, has the positive connection between these two been made clear. Thus, in a few words, I would like to indicate what this ontological foundation is, and in this way to show the necessary connection that exists between the obligation to seek the objective truth and religious freedom itself. My proposition is as follows: the very obligation to seek the truth itself constitutes the ontological foundation of religious freedom, as set forth in our text. For in fact every man, because he is a human being, endowed with reason and free will, is bound to seek the objective truth, and to hold fast to it and order his whole life according to its demands. All those who seek truth and justice with their whole heart, even non-believers, can agree with us on this principle. On the other hand, because it has its foundation not in any subjective disposition, but in the very nature of man, this principle has a strictly universal validity. Ultimately, this principle is explicitly affirmed by Scripture in countless ways and in different forms. Nevertheless, in order for man to be able to satisfy this obligation in the way God wills, that is, in a way consistent with his nature, he must enjoy not only psychological freedom but also immunity from all coercion. Not only is there no opposition between religious freedom and the obligation to seek the truth, therefore, but religious freedom in fact has its foundation in this obligation itself, and the obligation to seek the truth in turn requires religious freedom.[71]

The final document incorporates this suggestion of Ancel, which was echoed by Wojtyła and Pope Paul VI. Murray's claim that "the doctrinal line that was installed in the third schema [i.e. a formally juridical approach] ... remained intact through the subsequent three revisions of the texts"[72] is open to challenge.

In several of the commentaries that he wrote immediately following the Council, Murray expressed a certain dissatisfaction with the final version of *Dignitatis Humanae*. He especially objected to what he called "the prominence given to man's moral obligation to seek the truth, as somehow the ultimate foundation of the right to religious freedom."[73] He goes on to argue that the duty to seek the truth does not deserve a place in the structure of a demonstration of the right to religious freedom. Why? Because it fails to yield the crucial political conclusion that governments should not hinder individuals or religious communities from public worship. "The classic Catholic government, for instance," Murray writes, "or the contemporary communist government, for another instance, does not greatly bother about man's duty to search for truth. They simply maintain that they already have the truth; that they represent the truth ... that consequently they are empowered to repress public manifestations of error."[74] There is a crucial presupposition in Murray's reasoning that needs to be brought to light: truth is indifferent to freedom. This is why a Catholic state in possession of the truth would no longer be concerned with the freedom of its citizens.

For understandable reasons, Murray's conception of religious freedom has largely set the terms for the interpretation of *DH*. More recently, a number of commentators have questioned whether his juridical approach provides the most adequate framework for the Council's teaching.

The Ontological Unity of Truth and Freedom

In his 1976 book *La Liberté religieuse: Droit fondamental*, Dominican Father Philippe André-Vincent summarized the teaching of *DH* as follows:

> the mother-idea [of *DH*] appears with the foundation of the right to religious freedom: the ontological bond of the person with truth, a natural bond grounding a natural obligation to search for the truth and to adhere to it, grounding at the same time a right to the freedom necessary to realize that obligation. The ontological bond of freedom to truth is the mother-idea of the Declaration.[75]

In a major new study "Freedom, Truth, and Human Dignity: An Interpretation of *Dignitatis Humanae* on the Right to Religious Freedom," David L. Schindler develops a similar thesis regarding the ontological unity of truth and freedom. In dialogue with John Courtney Murray and Karol Wojtyła, Schindler uncovers the significance of the changes introduced into the final text as a result of the conciliar debate. Schindler's core thesis is summed up in the following passage:

> With the conciliar affirmation of religious freedom, the Church has signaled a new awareness of the importance of freedom in addition to, or even despite, her traditional emphasis on truth. On the contrary, with this conciliar teaching, rightly understood, the Church rather signals a development in her understanding of the inherent unity of truth with freedom and freedom with truth. While still affirming that the truth alone frees, she now affirms at the same time, in a more explicit way, that truth itself presupposes freedom, and that truth really does free.[76]

In support of this thesis, Schindler's argument unfolds in the following steps:

(1) There is an originally given, intrinsic relation between freedom and truth.
(2) This is best conceived in light of the ancient-medieval understanding of the spiritual nature of the human being and human act (*anima forma corporis*), and the transcendental nature of truth, as recovered in distinct ways by Pinckaers (freedom) and Pieper (spirit, knowledge, and truth, especially in relation to God).
(3) The Declaration's teaching regarding the right to religious freedom presupposes and (implicitly) takes over this earlier teaching, in terms of the human person as subject of rights. The Declaration does not develop this understanding of the person in a thematic way. Its intention, rather, is to arrive at an adequate notion of a right, and this involves attending in a particular way to the subjectivity of the person, which it affirms while simultaneously securing the intrinsic link between that subjectivity and the order

of truth, especially religious truth. But this process evidently involves the Declaration in drawing out more fully and explicitly the interiority tradi- tionally understood to be proper to the human act, an interiority fraught with an originally given true relation to the world (all that exists) and to God. Human subjectivity or interiority, in other words, is first positively, not 'negatively' (or 'indifferently'), related to the world and to God, and is necessarily presupposed by this relation.

(4) The Declaration thus ties the meaning of rights to a human subjectivity understood to be originally 'truthed' by the world and, implicitly and more profoundly, by relation to the Creator. The right to religious freedom is an immunity from coercion only inside, and by virtue of, this naturally given positive relation to God and others. On the Declaration's view, what is primary in the self's relation to the other is a positive letting be. On the juridical view, by contrast, what is primary is the self's negative immunity from constraint or intrusiveness by the other.

(5) This position affirmed by the Declaration, even if not developed in an integrated fashion, exposes the root problem of the prevalent 'juridical' interpretation, which holds that the right to religious freedom is primar- ily negative. This negative sense is indeed essential to the right's proper meaning as conceived by the Declaration, but is understood to take its inner dynamic from within the human being's original true and positive relation to God and to other human creatures.

(6) The pontificates of John Paul II and Benedict XVI confirm the foregoing interpretation of religious freedom in *Dignitatis Humanae*, while develop- ing in a more integrated way the notion of the person undergirding this interpretation. They develop further the relationality to truth and God implied in the medieval conceptions of the spiritual, interior-subjective nature of the human act, and of this act's original-transcendental ordering toward and by the world. John Paul II and Benedict XVI, in other words, affirm the modern emphasis on the subjective dimension of the person, by way of taking over and drawing out the further meaning already implicit in the medievals' objective notions of the human spirit and truth.[77]

Schindler shows how this development in the Church's understanding of the mutual inherence of freedom and truth implies new developments also in the understanding of the relationship between state and society, the state's responsibility for religion, and the relationship between church and state, as well as in the nature and meaning of rights. In terms of the importance of *DH* for the Church's encounter with modernity, Schindler concludes,

> The Church is to embrace from her depths the principle of subjec- tive rights that is arguably the central concern of the modern social- political order. She is nonetheless called at the same time, in light of the prevalent juridical-liberal understanding of subjective rights, to transform these rights from the inside out, by reconfiguring the original meaning of subjectivity to include positive reference to the

anteriorly given truth and goodness of others under God. Indeed, it is just the radical and comprehensive nature of the Church's embrace of the principle of a subjective right that itself establishes the demand for a profound transformation of the prevalent liberal-juridical understanding of such a right. It is not the case that rights can be adequately treated first as simply "negative" immunities, the foundations of which can vary without affecting the original mean-ing of immunity. On the contrary, on the Council's reading, the meaning of rights as immunities takes its original form from inside the human subject's positive "obligatory" objective ordering toward God and others. The Church's embrace of rights, in a word, can be properly understood only when tied to, and situated within, her com-prehensive Christological and anthropological mission to the con-temporary world: within the call to form a "civilization of love" open finally to the God revealed in Jesus Christ. This, it seems to me, is the comprehensive burden of the teaching of the Council on the right to religious freedom.[78]

Conclusion

In the apostolic constitution Humanae Salutis, which officially convoked the Second Vatican Council, Pope John XXIII indicated the basic concern of the upcoming Council:

> Today the Church is witnessing a crisis underway within society. While humanity is at the threshold of a new age, tasks of immense seriousness and breadth await the Church, as in the most tragic peri-ods of her history. It is a question in fact of bringing the modern world into contact with the perennial life-giving energies of the Gospel, a world which exalts itself with its technical and scientific conquests, but also bears the effects of a temporal order that some have wanted to reorganize by excluding God.[79]

At the heart of this task of bringing the modern world into contact with the Gospel is the question of human freedom. John Courtney Murray sug-gested that with the promulgation of DH "a second great argument will be set afoot—now on the theological meaning of Christian freedom."[80] The argu-ment about human freedom has continued to unfold in ways that may have surprised Murray. One significant development is the rediscovery of freedom at the very heart of truth. Religious freedom, writes John Paul II, "is the most fundamental of rights in relation to a person's primary duty; that is to say the duty to draw closer to God in light of the truth with the movement of spirit which is love."[81] By upholding the transcendent dignity of the human person and the right to religious freedom, DH provides a sure foundation for the Church to propose anew her vision of the human family as created in love and destined for eternal life in communion with God.

NOTES

1. John Paul II, "Ecclesia Dei," (July 2, 1988) http://www.vatican.va/roman_curia/pontifical_commissions/ecclsdei/documents/hf_jp-ii_motu-proprio_02071988_ecclesia-dei_en.html.

2. *Acta Apostolicae Sedis* [hereafter *AAS*] (Vatican City: Typis Polyglottis Vaticanis, 1966), 58:10–11.

3. 58, 74; cited in Luigi Mistò, "Paul VI and *Dignitatis humanae*: Theory and Practice," in *Religious Liberty: Paul VI and Dignitatis humanae*, ed. John T. Ford (Brescia: Publicazzioni dell'Istituto Paolo VI, 1995), 13.

4. John Paul II, *Redemptor Hominis*, 12, http://w2.vatican.va/content/john-paul-ii/en/encyclicals/documents/hf_jp-ii_enc_04031979_redemptor-hominis.html.

5. John Paul II, "Message to the Secretary General of the United Nations," December 2, 1978, https://w2.vatican.va/content/john-paul-ii/en/letters/1978/documents/hf_jp-ii_let_19781202_waldheim.html.

6. For a summary account of the redaction history of *DH*, see Nicholas J. Healy, "The Drafting of *Dignitatis Humanae*," in *Freedom, Truth, and Human Dignity: The Second Vatican Council's Declaration on Religious Liberty*, ed. David L. Schindler and Nicholas J. Healy, Jr. (Grand Rapids, MI: Eerdmans, 2015).

7. John Courtney Murray, "The Declaration on Religious Freedom," in *Bridging the Sacred and the Secular: Selected Writings of John Courtney Murray*, ed. J. Leon Hooper (Washington, DC: Georgetown University Press, 1994), 187.

8. Avery Dulles, "*Dignitatis Humanae* and the Development of Catholic Doctrine," in *Catholicism and Religious Freedom: Contemporary Reflections on Vatican II's Declaration on Religious Liberty*, ed. Kenneth L. Grasso and Robert P. Hunt (Lanham, MD: Rowman and Littlefield, 2006), 43.

9. Citations of *Dignitatis Humanae* are from the translation by Patrick Brannan and Michael Camacho in Schindler and Healy, *Freedom, Truth, and Human Dignity*, 1–37.

10. John Courtney Murray, "Introduction to *Dignitatis Humanae*," in *The Documents of Vatican II*, ed. Walter M. Abbott (New York: America Press, 1966), 673.

11. Joseph Ratzinger, *Truth and Tolerance: Christian Belief and World Religions*, trans. Henry Taylor (San Francisco: Ignatius Press, 2004), 236.

12. *Gaudium et Spes*, 17, http://www.vatican.va/archive/hist_councils/ii_vatican_council/documents/vat-ii_const_19651207_gaudium-et-spes_en.html.

13. Cf. John Paul II, *Veritatis Splendor*, 30–32, http://w2.vatican.va/content/john-paul-ii/en/encyclicals/documents/hf_jp-ii_enc_06081993_veritatis-splendor.html.

14. Hermínio Rico, *John Paul II and the Legacy of* Dignitatis Humanae (Washington, DC: Georgetown University Press, 2002), 142.

15. Martin Rhonheimer, *The Common Good of Constitutional Democracy*, ed. William F. Murphy (Washington, DC: Catholic University of America Press, 2013), 387–88.

16. Pietro Pavan, "The Declaration on Religious Freedom," in *Commentary on the Documents of Vatican II*, ed. Herbert Vorgrimler (New York: Herder and Herder, 1968), 4:63.

17. Cf. Philippe André-Vincent, *La liberté religieuse: Droit fondamental* (Paris: Téqui, 1976); David L. Schindler, "Freedom, Truth, and Human Dignity: An Interpretation of *Dignitatis Humanae* on the Right to Religious Freedom," in Schindler and Healy, *Freedom, Truth, and Human Dignity*, 39–209.

18. Draft of a Dogmatic Constitution on the Church, *De Ecclesia*, in *Acta et Documenta Concilio Oecumenico Vaticano II Apparando. Series secunda* (Praeparatio) (Vatican City: Typis Polyglottis Vaticanis, 1964–1969), II/4:658–59.

19. Draft of a Declaration on Religious Freedom, *Textus emendatus*, in *Acta Synodalia Sacrosancti Concilii Vaticani II*, 34 vols. [hereafter cited as *AS*] (Vatican City: Typis Polyglottis Vaticanis, 1970–1999), III/8:432.

20. Ibid.

21. Thomas Pink, "Conscience and Coercion," *First Things* (August/September 2012): 45–51, at 45.

22. Cf. Marcel Lefebvre, *Religious Liberty Questioned* (Kansas City, MO: Angelus Press, 2002); Michael Davies, *The Second Vatican Council and Religious Liberty* (Long Prairie, MN: Neumann Press, 1992); Charles Curran, *Catholic Moral Theology in Dialogue* (Notre Dame, IN: Fides Pub, 1972); Richard A. McCormick, *The Critical Calling* (Washington, DC: Georgetown University Press, 1989); John T. Noonan, *A Church That Can and Cannot Change: The Development of Catholic Moral Teaching* (Notre Dame, IN: University of Notre Dame Press, 2005).

23. Cf. Basile Valuet, *La liberté religieuse et la tradition catholique: Un cas de développement doctrinal homogène dans le magistère authentique*, 3 vols. (Le Barroux: Abbaye Sainte-Madeleine, 1998); Avery Dulles, "*Dignitatis Humanae* and the Development of Catholic Doctrine"; Brian W. Harrison, *Religious Liberty and Contraception* (Melbourne: John XXIII Fellowship, 1988); F. Russell Hittinger, "The Declaration on Religious Freedom, *Dignitatis Humanae*," in *Vatican II: Renewal within Tradition*, ed. Matthew L. Lamb and Matthew Levering (New York: Oxford University Press, 2008), 359–82; Martin Rhonheimer, "Benedict XVI's 'Hermeneutic of Reform' and Religious Freedom," in *The Common Good of Constitutional Democracy*, ed. William F. Murphy (Washington, DC: Catholic University of America Press, 2013); David L. Schindler, *Freedom, Truth and Human Dignity*.

24. Brian Harrison, for example, has developed the thesis that *DH* shifted policy, not doctrine. Cf. Harrison, "What Does *Dignitatis Humanae* Mean? A Reply to Arnold Guminski," in *Religious Freedom: Did Vatican II Contradict Traditional Catholic Doctrine? A Debate* (South Bend, IN: St. Augustine's Press, 2013), 87:

> My basic position is that the big difference between the Church's stance on religious liberty before and after Vatican II lies not in her old and new doctrinal teachings respectively; for these, though certainly not identical, are quite compatible, thanks largely to their very general (non-specific) content. Rather, it lies in the Church's very different pre- and postconciliar prudential judgments as to how much restriction on false and immoral propaganda is in fact required by a just public order, given the dramatic social and political changes of recent centuries.

In a recent series of articles, Thomas Pink has developed a relatively novel interpretation of *DH* on the basis of distinction between a "jurisdiction-centered view" and a "person-centered view" of religious freedom. In terms of the development of doctrine, Pink's conclusion is similar to the thesis of Harrison:

> And that was certainly not because the Catholic Church opposed religious coercion as such. Rather, religious coercion might be legitimate, but only on the authority of the Church. The Church was the only body with the right to coerce on behalf of religious truth: to issue directives, and to back those directives up by the threat of punishments. The state could act only as the Church's agent. It had no authority of its own in this matter. We can now see how *Dignitatis Humanae* does not change doctrine after all. Religious coercion by the state is now morally wrong, and a violation of people's rights, not because religious coercion by any authority is wrong, but because the

Church no longer authorizes it. The Church is now refusing to license the state to act as her coercive agent, and it is from that policy change, and not from any change in underlying doctrine, that the wrongfulness of religious coercion by the state follows. ("Conscience and Coercion," *First Things* [2012]: 45–51, at 46)

See also, Thomas Pink, "The Interpretation of *Dignitatis Humanae*: A Reply to Martin Rhonheimer," *Nova et Vetera* 11 (2013): 77–121.

25. Gilles Routhier, "Finishing the Work Begun: The Trying Experience of the Fourth Period," in *History of Vatican II*, ed. Giuseppe Alberigo (Maryknoll, NY: Orbis, 2006), 5:111n239.

26. Mistò, "Paul VI and *Dignitatis humanae*: Theory and Practice," 14.

27. *Insegnamenti di Paolo VI* 9 (1971): 704–5; cited in Mistò, "Paul VI and *Dignitatis humanae*," 18.

28. *Insegnamenti di Paolo VI* 7 (1969): 1001; cited in Mistò, "Paul VI and *Dignitatis humanae*," 22.

29. Luigi Mistò provides a table with a synopsis of the thirty-one agreements signed between the Vatican and various governments between the end of 1965 and August 6, 1978. See also Roland Minnerath, *L'Église et les États Concordataires, 1846–1981* (Paris: Éditions du Cerf, 1983).

30. Mistò, "Paul VI and *Dignitatis humanae*," 27–28.

31. Cf. Michael Davies, "*Dignitatis Humanae* and Spain," in *The Second Vatican Council and Religious Liberty* (Long Prairie, MN: Neumann Press, 1992).

32. For a bibliography of John Paul II's writings and pronouncements on the theme of religious freedom, see Rico, *John Paul II and the Legacy of Dignitatis Humanae*, 246–51. See also, Avery Dulles, "John Paul II on Religious Freedom: Themes from Vatican II," *The Thomist* 65 (2001): 161–78; Jaroslaw Kupczak, "John Paul II and the Legacy of *Dignitatis Humanae*," *The Thomist* 67 (2003): 662–65.

33. John Paul II, "Message for the 1988 World Day of Peace," December 8, 1987, http://w2.vatican.va/content/john-paul-ii/en/messages/peace/documents/hf_jp-ii_mes_19871208_xxi-world-day-for-peace.html.

34. John Paul II, "Message for the 1991 World Day of Peace," December 8, 1990, https://w2.vatican.va/content/john-paul-ii/en/messages/peace/documents/hf_jp-ii_mes_08121990_xxiv-world-day-for-peace.html.

35. John Paul II, "Address to the Word Jurist Association of the World Peace through Law Center," May 9, 1992, http://w2.vatican.va/content/john-paul-ii/en/speeches/1992/may/documents/hf_jp-ii_spe_19920509_giuristi.html.

36. John Paul II, *Redemptor Hominis*, 12.

37. John Paul II, "Message for the 1991 World Day of Peace," December 8, 1990.

38. AS III/2, 251. See also Karol Wojtyła, *Love and Responsibility*, trans. Grzegorz Ignatik (Boston: Pauline Books, 2013), 96f.

39. John Paul II, *Veritatis Splendor*, 64, http://w2.vatican.va/content/john-paul-ii/en/encyclicals/documents/hf_jp-ii_enc_06081993_veritatis-splendor.html.

40. Ibid.

41. John Paul II, *Tertio Millenio Adveniente*, 33.

42. Ibid. 35.

43. Benedict XVI, "Address to the Roman Curia," December 22, 2005, http://w2.vatican.va/content/benedict-xvi/en/speeches/2005/december/documents/hf_ben_xvi_spe_20051222_roman-curia.html.

44. Ibid.

45. Ibid.

46. Ibid.

47. Ibid.

48. Joseph Ratzinger, *Church, Ecumenism, & Politics: New Endeavors in Ecclesiology*, trans. Michael J. Miller et al. (San Francisco: Ignatius Press, 2008), 186–87.

49. Ibid.

50. Benedict XVI, Post-synodal Apostolic Exhortation, *Ecclesia in Medio Oriente*, 27, http://w2.vatican.va/content/benedict-xvi/en/apost_exhortations/documents/hf_ben-xvi_exh_20120914_ecclesia-in-medio-oriente.html.

51. Benedict XVI, "Message for the Celebration of the World Day of Peace," January 1, 2011, http://w2.vatican.va/content/benedict-xvi/en/messages/peace/documents/hf_ben-xvi_mes_20101208_xliv-world-day-peace.html.

52. Joseph Ratzinger, *Theological Highlights of Vatican II* (New York: Paulist Press, 1966), 95.

53. Cf. *Religious Liberty: An End and a Beginning*, ed. John Courtney Murray (New York: Macmillan, 1966).

54. Marcel Lefebvre, press conference, September 15, 1976; cited in the "Foreword" to *Religious Liberty Questioned*, trans. Jaime Pazat de Lys (Kansas City, Missouri: Angelus Press, 2002), v–xi, at xi.

55. Cf. Gregory XVI, *Mirari Vos* (1832), http://www.papalencyclicals.net/Greg16/g16mirar.htm; Pius IX, *Quanta Cura* (1864), http://www.papalencyclicals.net/Pius09/p9quanta.htm; Leo XIII, *Immortale Dei* (1885), http://www.papalencyclicals.net/Leo13/l13sta.htm; Leo XIII, *Libertas Praestantissimun* (1888), http://www.papalencyclicals.net/Leo13/l13liber.htm.

56. Lefebvre, *Religious Liberty*, 2.

57. Ibid. 3.

58. Ibid. 19.

59. Ibid.

60. Ibid. 20.

61. David Schindler, *Freedom, Truth, and Human Dignity*, 81.

62. Ibid. 83.

63. Lefebvre, *Religious Liberty*, 3.

64. Ibid. xiv.

65. Cf. Joseph Komonchak, "The American Contribution to *Dignitatis Humanae*: The Role of John Courtney Murray, SJ," *U.S. Catholic Historian* 24 (2006): 1–20; Dominique Gonnet, *La liberté religieuse à Vatican II: La contribution de John Courtney Murray, S.J.* (Paris: Éditions du Cerf, 1994).

66. According to J. Leon Hooper, Murray wrote thirty-eight articles on the issue of religious freedom before 1962, then another thirty during and after the Council. See esp. John Courtney Murray, "On Religious Liberty," *America* 109 (1963): 704–6; "The Problem of Religious Freedom," *Theological Studies* 25 (1964): 503–75; "The Declaration on Religious Freedom: A Moment in Its Legislative History," in *Religious Liberty: An End and a Beginning*, ed. John Courtney Murray (New York: The Macmillan Company, 1966), 15–42; "The Issue of Church and State at Vatican Council II," *Theological Studies* 27 (1966): 580–606.

67. Jeffrey Gros and Stephen B. Bevans, *Evangelization and Religious Freedom:* "Ad gentes," "Dignitatis humanae" (New York: Paulist Press, 2008), 224.

68. John Courtney Murray, "The Declaration on Religious Freedom: A Moment in Its Legislative History," in *Religious Liberty: An End and A Beginning*, ed. John Courtney Murray (New York: Macmillan, 1966), 19.

69. Ibid. 36–37.

70. John Courtney Murray, "This Matter of Religious Freedom," *America* 112 (1965): 40–43.

71. *AS* IV/2:16–20.

72. John Courtney Murray, "The Declaration on Religious Freedom: A Moment in its Legislative History," 42.

73. John Courtney Murray, "The Declaration on Religious Freedom," in *Vatican II: An Interfaith Appraisal*, ed. J. H. Miller (Notre Dame, IN: University of Notre Dame Press, 1966), 570.

74. Ibid.

75. Philippe André-Vincent, *La liberté religieuse: Droit fondamental* (Paris: Téqui, 1976), 203–4.

76. Schindler, *Freedom, Truth, and Human Dignity*, 43.

77. Ibid. 103–5.

78. Ibid. 161.

79. *AAS* 54 (1962), 6.

80. John Courtney Murray, "Introduction to *Dignitatis Humanae*," in *The Documents of Vatican II*, ed. Walter M. Abbott (New York: America Press, 1966), 673.

81. John Paul II, "To Participants in the 5th International Colloquium on Juridical Studies" (March 10, 1984), https://w2.vatican.va/content/john-paul-ii/it/speeches/1984/march/documents/hf_jp-ii_spe_19840310_colloquio-giuridico.html.

15

Gravissimum Educationis

Paige E. Hochschild

Gravissimum Educationis is a brief document, a *declaration* in magisterial genre, revised in its final form in the waning days of a long council.[1] The length of the declaration, however, is not proportionate to the importance of education for the council fathers, who always intended to produce a significant teaching on this topic. The complexity of the subject of education and the challenge of applying general principles to diverse institutions in different parts of the world ultimately resulted in a less ambitious document. Instead, the council fathers left behind a clear mandate for further development by relevant Congregations, in light of the expected revision of the Code of Canon Law. *Gravissimum Educationis* (*GE*) draws deeply from the Catholic encyclical tradition, and its signal accomplishment is the articulation of the centrality of education in a democratic age, in conjunction with the council's clear mission to "safeguard and propose" with more effective teaching the "sacred deposit of Christian *doctrina*."[2] Appropriately, the content of the declaration becomes both clearer and richer when it is read in conversation with the ecclesiology of *Lumen Gentium*, the Church-world relationship of *Gaudium et Spes*, and the liberties and obligations of the Catholic faithful asserted in *Dignitatis Humanae*.

The Content of the Document

Gravissimum Educationis offers a clear example of the pattern of the council to speak, when possible, to "the world" on the one hand, and to "her own" on the other.[3] The integrity of the order of natural goods and the order of sacramental grace are carefully differentiated but nevertheless inseparable. The idea that education is founded in "universal rights" as well as duty and obligation to the "common good" is consistent with earlier magisterial writings.[4] However, while the right to education is vested first in the family and the Church, a stronger emphasis is placed on the individual as a bearer of rights, both as a matter of personal dignity, and in light of redemption in Jesus Christ. Distinctive aspects of Christian education, including religious and moral education, are referred to the "formation of the human person in the pursuit of his ultimate end and of the good of [society]" (1): this is the summary aim of *all* education.

The document opens by acknowledging the importance of education in a time in which there is greater access to knowledge, greater social mobility, a higher degree of participation in political process, and more leisure—which, in turn, may foster scientific inquiry and technological advance. The *Introduction* to the document affirms the contemporary pattern of the promoting of education, while alluding to new problems of experimentation in "method" as well as the absence of education in which "love and truth are developed together." *Gravissimum Educationis* thus proposes a holistic approach to education, founded on a Christian humanism, in light of the unchanging purpose and mission of the Church: to proclaim Christ to all, for the salvation and restoration of all things and people (2).[5] The first part of the document provides social and historical context; the document then lays out principles and particular concerns, differentiating education in general from Christian formation in particular; finally, it considers those who educate primarily (parents) and secondarily (the Church; schools and their teachers; institutions of higher education and their faculties).

The "universal right to an education" (1) is conditioned by cultural situations, differences of ability, traditional practices, and the demands of local associations. Young people have the right to a sense of "moral values" (*valores*), as essential for the mature exercise of responsible freedom. Despite the concern in the introduction about experimentation in method, the document urges the use of all recent advances in psychology and in the "arts and science of teaching."[6]

"Christian education" adds the cultivation of the gift of faith given in baptism to the formation of moral values. This obligation particularly falls to pastors and the catechetical-liturgical functions of the Church. Both the moral and the sacramental formation of the conscience are necessary to fulfill the highest personal end of education: conformity of the child of God to Jesus Christ (2). Those who are formed through Christian education serve the growth and health of the Church, and they bear witness as salt and light to the world of the "hope that is in them."[7]

Consistent with magisterial writings on education and the family since the pontificate of Leo XIII, parents are held to a serious obligation as the "primary and principle educators" of their children (3). Parents are responsible for creating an atmosphere in the home of "love and respect for God and man"; the family should be a school of virtue precisely through ordering persons to the common good of society. The family is therefore by its very nature not self-sufficient. It serves the whole community and depends upon the assistance of the whole community: in its ordering to the common good, the family learns its frailty as well as its missional end. "Civil society" promotes its own proper good through education, and this is a legitimate "common temporal good." The principle of subsidiarity requires that the state first and foremost protect the "duties and rights" of parents. In addition (*demum*), the Church has a duty to educate her children, both for the "complete perfection" of persons, and for "the good of earthly society and the building of a world that is more human." Schools are recognized as having "special importance" in intellectual as well as human formation; they are also civic centers in which common cultural and religious work may unite a community. As soon as the document speaks of particular institutional forms, such as the family, it is clear that education falls within strongly overlapping spheres of interest—the civil and the ecclesiastical. *Gravissimum Educationis* sees the family as the institution that bears the greatest burden of Church-state tension.

Paragraph 6 on the "duties and rights" of parents effectively prefaces the second half of the document: first, moral and religious formation is shown to be necessary in *all* school environments (7), and second, schools and institutions of higher learning that share in the Church's mission of education are treated with particular attention to their mission and constitution ("educational instruments" [8–12]). In restating the duty of parents, the institutional questions are contextualized in the good of society as a whole: we will argue later that the assumption that university-aged children are autonomous individuals poses a challenge to the incorporation of a sense of the common good in mission statements in higher education. If parents have a primary duty to educate, the state should not put in place a "school monopoly." This sounds like an oft-repeated defense of the place of Catholic schools in modern states, present in magisterial texts since the nineteenth century. However, in light of the document's acknowledgement of properly civic ends for education, this comment is undoubtedly addressed to new situations.[8] Consonant with the pastoral tone of the Council's constitutions, *GE* makes this argument in an urgent and yet positive fashion, on the basis of the Church's vision of the human person: insofar as revelation plumbs the depths of humanity more completely, a Christian education will be more authentically "human." Accordingly, the state must protect the rights of children to models of education that include moral and religious formation, which should in turn better foster in students a sense of their "civic duties and rights." Education is clearly seen to be a powerful social force, and the document asks that states observe subsidiarity, respecting the ability of parents to choose how to educate their children, if necessary through granting public subsidies.[9]

The Church is obligated to assist families where Catholic schooling is not the norm. In line with the council's teaching on religious liberty, "civil authorities" are urged as well to assist by seeing that children are formed according to the moral and religious principles of their own traditions. The Catholic school retains pride of place in the education and formation of Catholic citizens in "leading an exemplary apostolic life" (8). Again, the effect is twofold: fulfilling the mission of the Church for her people, and fostering "dialogue between the Church and mankind, to the benefit of both." The importance of well-trained teachers is highlighted, according to usual standards; they must also be singular witnesses to Christ. Teaching is described as an apostolate, a "true service," and a "vocation" (5). Teachers must see themselves as assisting parents; parents in turn are to support Catholic schools "to the best of their ability." Pastors and "all the faithful" are explicitly tasked with helping schools to achieve their mission; this is especially true with regard to those who are poor, without family, or not of the Catholic faith. At more than one point, Religious men and women are praised for their singular sacrifices in making the work of Catholic schooling possible.

Finally, *GE* addresses higher education. Catholic colleges and universities are urged to pursue the truth in liberty "of scientific inquiry" and, after the model of the doctors of the Church, especially St. Thomas Aquinas, realize more deeply "the harmony of faith and science" (10). These institutions should be excellent and accessible; the study of sacred theology should be open to laypeople (through a faculty or chair of theology at every Catholic university); "special attention" should be paid to scientific research; moreover, there should be energetic pastoral attention given to students, through chaplaincies and university centers, particularly at non-Catholic institutions. The application of these exhortations has been extensively if inconclusively discussed, largely under the rubric of juridical versus missional character, from the late 1960s until the promulgation of the Apostolic Constitution *Ex Corde Ecclesiae* on August 15, 1990.

Article 11 is addressed to faculties of "sacred sciences," as well as "ecclesiastical faculties." This distinction occurs in Pius XI's *Deus Scientiarum Dominus* (1931), where the latter term (*ecclesiasticae facultates*) has multiple referents.[10] In *GE*, "theological faculties" is the broader term employed, and these faculties are tasked with the study of revelation, the "legacy of Christian wisdom," dialogue with "separated brethren" and the theological formation of priests (11). "Ecclesiastical faculties" are urged to update their laws for the sake of excellence and conversation between theology and other disciplines. *Sapientia Christiana*, promulgated in 1979, governs ecclesiastical universities and faculties, which clarified the nature of certain institutions; however, it does not remove the ambiguity of the section heading in *GE* insofar as it addresses higher theological instruction in general.[11]

The document from Vatican II concludes: "co-operation is the order of the day" (12).[12] Co-operation and co-ordination is hoped for between the Church and the state, between Catholic schools and other schools, between Catholic and non-Catholic faculty, and among the faculty from disciplines within the university. This is a significant theme in recent documents on a Christian approach to education. For Catholic institutions in particular, intellectual conversation across the disciplines is to be a hallmark, in pursuit of the furtherance of culture and community. But Catholic institutions should particularly seek the common good in conjunction with the academy at large, given the special role of teachers in furthering the "solitary goal" of the Church: "to serve" like Christ by being a "witness to the truth."[13]

Catholic Schools and Catholic Colleges and Universities after *Gravissimum Educationis*: "The Consequences of Uniqueness"

The second half of *GE* is devoted to Catholic schools of various kinds, including primary and secondary schools, professional and technical schools, colleges, universities, and faculties of "sacred sciences" (ecclesiastical faculties). Schools and universities receive some detailed application of the general principles from the first half of the document, but on the whole these paragraphs reveal the clear concession of the council fathers to the difficulty of applying general principles to a multitude of institutions worldwide. Much more work was demanded and expected after the council. *Sapientia Christiana* was promulgated in 1979 to govern ecclesiastical faculties, along with many more documents on priestly formation for those faculties and institutions committed to this task.[14] *Ex Corde Ecclesiae* was promulgated in 1990 after many years of controversy and collaboration, to govern Catholic universities and colleges. There have been several very fine documents on Catholic education produced by the Congregation for Catholic Education since the council; these require consideration, given their explicit aim of taking up the unfinished work of *GE* in the context of the experience of post-conciliar Catholicism.

The following documents from the Congregation are relevant: *The Catholic School* (1977) develops an outline and sense of mission for the Catholic school in a contemporary context; *Lay Catholics in Schools: Witnesses to the Faith* (1982) discusses the service and formation of lay teachers, praising it as complementary to the work of religious brothers and sisters; *The Religious Dimension of Education in a Catholic School* (1988) engages the anthropology of *Gaudium et Spes* and applies this to curriculum in great detail; finally, *The Catholic School on the Threshold of the Third Millennium* (1997) is a retrospective look at principles from the council, taking stock of challenges new and old.[15]

Beginning with the 1997 document, the mixed tone of hopefulness and profound anxiety is striking.[16] It opens with wide-ranging critique:

> On the threshold of the third millennium education faces new challenges which are the result of a new socio-political and cultural context. First and foremost, we have a crisis of values which, in highly developed societies in particular, assumes the form, often exalted by the media, of subjectivism, moral relativism and nihilism. The extreme pluralism pervading contemporary society leads to behavior patterns which are at times so opposed to one another as to undermine any idea of community identity. Rapid structural changes, profound technical innovations and the globalization of the economy affect human life more and more throughout the world. Rather than

prospects of development for all, we witness the widening of the gap between rich and poor, as well as massive migration from underdeveloped to highly-developed countries. The phenomena of multiculturalism and an increasingly multi-ethnic and multi-religious society is at the same time an enrichment and a source of further problems. To this we must add, in countries of long-standing evangelization, a growing marginalization of the Christian faith as a reference point and a source of light for an effective and convincing interpretation of existence.[17]

The late eighteenth century was a significant period of national interest in the control and reform of education, often with noble intent. The resulting systems of primary and secondary education in Europeans countries vary in their balance between basic schooling and practical orientation. The experience in the United States is historically very unique, in general as well as for Catholic immigrants. After initially settling in Maryland, Catholics were generally unwelcome in the New World; this feeling increased with renewed waves of immigration during the nineteenth century, and priests and religious orders were crucial for providing not only education but a sense of cultural rootedness for their respective communities.[18] The common schools that arose in Massachusetts from the work of a group of professional educators, in the 1830s and '40s, were intended to replace the local, ad hoc system of community and parish-based schools with a Lancasterian model (graded classes with monitoring of large groups) and standardized curriculum and training.[19] Consolidation, centralization, and "scientific" pedagogy were watchwords for uniform quality; for Catholics, they seemed to conceal clear secularizing tendencies, and even Protestant-nationalist tendencies, geared toward producing a unified citizenry. Compulsory attendance laws were passed in Massachusetts in 1852.

The third Plenary Council of Baltimore (1884) responded to a strong push for Catholics to participate in "common schooling" (public education), by requiring that every parish in the country open its own school within two years. This was not a practical expectation; nevertheless, there were 13,292 Catholic schools in the United States by 1966, and while they adapted many of the practices of the common (public) schools, they were marked by local differences and community character.[20] There was a clear understanding that parish schools should form good Catholics *and* good American citizens. They were seen to constitute the center of the local community, in conjunction with the parish church. Catholics were expected to support their schools, financially and otherwise. Nevertheless, fewer than half of all American Catholic children attended them.[21] Given these general observations, the common description of the shift from before the council to after as a radical shift from inward-looking provincialism to an outward-looking service mentality, seems strained.[22] Changes at the neighborhood level in the United States during the 1960s and '70s are more effectively explained by sociological factors common to all urban and rural communities.

Nevertheless, with the mainstreaming of Catholics in American society, new rationales are needed for the existence of Catholic schools, if they are more than simply another form of private schooling. The documents produced by the Congregation since 1977 look at the council in contemporary context as a genuine opportunity for articulating the role of Catholic schools, both in the life of the local Church, and in service to the common good. The clear hope is that the school will serve as a locus for community, an ambitious center of human formation: committed to intellectual excellence and human flourishing, in conjunction with the family and the parish, in order to build a Church that is an embodied sign of hope, ready to renew contemporary culture and promote the deeper humanity of the Gospel. However, the "signs of the times" are interpreted in these documents with increasing concern, as proposing unforeseen obstacles to education, arising within family life and parish life, derived from the effects of technology and mass media, and in conjunction with practical problems such as the cost of education and qualifications of teachers. As one peruses the Congregation's deeply insightful documents, the challenges seem insurmountable—indeed, it is rarely clear *how* the vision of the council for education, as touching upon the very essence of the Church's mission, might be accomplished.

The documents taken together propose three fruitful challenges to Catholic schools, of particular relevance to the situation in North America: the formation and character of teachers, the content and pedagogy behind school curriculum, and the challenge of Catholic identity.

Teacher formation is thought to overemphasize method and pedagogical technique. These are important, but less so than excellence in particular subject areas and depth of holistic formation of the person of the teacher.[23] "Holistic formation" is above all a matter of faith formation and pastoral provision for the care of Catholic schoolteachers.[24] The Catholic teacher should have a noble sense of *vocation*: they share in a crucial aspect of the work of the Church (the *prophetic* dimension of Christ's ministry), and they exercise this vocation "for personal sanctification and the exercise of an apostolic mission."[25] They should exemplify in their teaching and in the witness of their lives a deep synthesis of "faith, culture and life."[26] Above all, teachers should see themselves as students of truth alongside their own students: this implies that the *habits* of inquiry proper to the posture of a disciple are just as essential as the mastery of material. Teachers should be images and examples of Mary listening at Jesus's feet, receiving the Teacher in the receptive inquisitiveness of faith.[27]

The *content and pedagogy of curriculum* suggests a deeper, albeit related, challenge for Catholic education. At the heart of a holistic *education* there is an expectation of a broadly humanistic curriculum, with a dominant goal of avoiding the reduction of learning to "useful" outcomes.[28] The content of the curriculum must speak to the "deepest human needs" rather than the rapidly shifting values of the "present day." Moreover, the acknowledged tendency of parents to see education as a means to the ends of personal success and material sufficiency contributes to a "production mentality" in learning outcomes.

The presence of a humanities curriculum is proposed in order to counterbalance these two tendencies.

More than one document echoes the curricular specifics offered in earlier encyclicals by Pope Pius XI and Pope Pius XII: Catholic education should above all be based in *history*, attentive to the truth and development of human culture over time, in the context of the whole scope of "human grandeur" and misery.[29] Historical study should take account of the philosophical heritage of the Catholic intellectual tradition, and engage critical skills of judgment, development of literary sensibility (in order to understand the "mysteries of the human spirit") as well as aesthetic appreciation. A healthy philosophical and theological anthropology is emphasized much more in the documents produced under the pontificate of John Paul II, as a necessary presupposition of good pedagogy.[30] However, sound anthropology should also be an object of study, in conversation with contemporary social sciences: attention should be given to the consequences of embodiment, the spiritual nature of the person, the proper scope of human freedom (including "true" and "false autonomy"), the emotions, creativity, and the rights and duties that accompany natural sociality.[31] Above all else, education must include mature ethical formation, practically and theoretically, so that older youth can engage their culture critically. Good ethical education, in a Catholic context, will be *essentially* connected to sacramental life, particularly the sacraments of Confession and Eucharist, and they will furthermore be ordered to vocational discernment (to marriage, consecrated life, or holy orders).[32] Finally, religious education may take the form of catechesis at a certain age, but this should be intelligently distinct from genuine religious-theological education. Theological study should build on and be integrally related to the humanities curriculum, and include Scripture study, salvation history, history of the Church, sacramental theology, and ecclesiology.

These two challenges combined—the professional and spiritual formation of teachers, and the advocacy of a basically classical curriculum, with an emphasis on historical and theological study—suggest that radical alternatives are hoped for from the professional guild.[33] A provocative idea recurs in all of these documents: learning above all must seek to be integrated. What this might look like is not always clear, but the humanistic curriculum envisioned is presumably a part of the answer. The documents after *GE* state unequivocally that every discipline has a proper autonomy.[34] No area of study is "subservient" to faith, to be reshaped in light of a narrow apologetics. Nevertheless, the unity of human knowledge, in all of its scientific and cultural scope, is an essential presupposition of holistic and truly human education. The search for meaning and the desire for truth must shape one another.[35] The student's developing sense that there are great questions to be asked, and that there are worthy answers to be found, serves to unify more deeply a sense of the conversation between "faith and culture," because human persons are by nature protagonists of culture, and also the "subject of religion."[36] The mutual enrichment of reason and creativity on the one hand, and reason and faith on the other, should be the signal attainment of the "integration of knowledge," in a cultural context that generally assumes the foreignness of faith.

Catholic identity in the Catholic school poses the third and final challenge. While schools assume a juridical intimacy with the local bishop, the implications of this for identity and "Catholic character" in shifting circumstances are not clear. The term "identity" expresses an identifiable ecclesial personality, which confers an instrumental "structure" of pastoral ministry.[37] At the same time, it is "by reason of its educational activity" that a school is said to be a properly "ecclesial entity." Ecclesial personality should be fostered by "all those who make up the educating community." While the juridical relationship with the bishop is an unambiguous marker of catholicity, in all of these documents, from *GE* to *The Catholic School on the Threshold of the Third Millennium*, the content of "identity" can never be reduced to this juridical relationship; rather, it arises from the synthesis of faith and life, and the synthesis of faith and culture, that should be the hallmark of Catholic pedagogy. "In the Catholic school's educational project there is no separation between time for learning and time for formation, between acquiring notions and growing in wisdom."[38]

The Catholic school should be distinctive by virtue of its deeply human atmosphere: it should be obviously "different," and its teachers should seek to be icons of Christ, completing the work of baptism.[39] The Catholic school should be adequate in its facilities, but also *proudly not luxurious*.[40] A sense of unity should be visible and unique, marked by the presence of Mary and love of the pope.[41] The school should be seen as a place of community, and not merely an institution; pastoral care and evangelization should occur within this framework. Closely related to the dimension of pastoral care, religious education should not be marginalized as one subject matter among many; instead, a grand intellectual vision of the whole curriculum should place theological learning at the center, in a way that respects the integrity of the disciplines, yet pushes all areas of study to greater excellence and inquisitiveness.[42] And finally, Catholic identity should be a matter of witness to the world: not simply witness by the *individual*, empowered through full participation in the life of the Church, but rather one of *corporate* witness by the Church, in which schools are said to be "central."[43] Service to the community should arise from a deep sense of evangelical witness and obligation to the common good.

In brief, the mark of Catholic identity is also the mark of success: to produce students who together have the "courage to follow the consequences of uniqueness."[44] A deep sense of identity, based in a sure confidence that Jesus Christ is at the heart of human flourishing, and the source of salvific unity, might be the unrealized hope of the council for Catholic schooling.

The reasons for critical concern in these documents are often refreshingly, if disturbingly, specific. Concern is directed at the field of education itself: very often, through no fault of their own, teachers find themselves shouldering responsibility for wider social problems; at other times, however, the documents imply that teacher formation has become forgetful of the centrality of the child, through abandoning excellence in a particular discipline over and above technique; moreover, faith formation is said to be inadequate for teachers intending to teach in Catholic schools. Schools themselves are directly blamed for a kind of embarrassment about Catholic character, seen in a lack of vision with respect to moral and intellectual greatness, as well as a tendency to embrace models of secular "neutrality."[45]

Governments are charged with the obligation to support, as a matter of justice, diverse educational institutions. Financial obstacles are identified, such as increasing inaccessibility of Catholic education to all but the wealthy, as well as the lack of just pay for lay teachers. Some religious orders are chastised for leaving behind schools, when education has been judged to be secondary to their revised apostolate: this, it seems to the Congregation, is decisive proof that the genuinely apostolic character of education as human formation has been separated from mere schooling.[46]

Concern is directed toward young people who, as students, often "shun effort," are "incapable of self-sacrifice and perseverance and who lack authentic models to guide them."[47] The document diagnoses the prevalence of "indifference," non-practicing Catholic families, and a weak, apathetic, or absent religious and moral formation.[48] The result in the school is seen in "a certain degree of pedagogical tiredness, which intensifies the ever increasing difficulty of conciliating the role of the teacher with that of the educator in today's context."[49] Carefully but clearly a root problem is diagnosed throughout the document of 1997: the family has failed in its duty to educate (5–6). The school community is urged to help parents remember their "primary role" as educators, and not simply "delegate it."[50] Pope John Paul II's *Letter to Families* is clearly influential in this document, although the charge of responsibility laid upon parents is far from new. The added element is found in the personalist account of love in relation to the common good: if children are the gift of domestic society, giving the family its uniquely sacrificial form, the failed duty of the family is particularly grave.[51]

The Catholic School on the Threshold offers two principles essential for recovering and renewing the purpose and mission of the Catholic school in the world today. First, a sense of *courage* in how the Catholic is called to be *in the world*, for the sake of mission and cultural renewal, is required. The Church-world relationship in *Gaudium et Spes* is recalled: "It is not merely a question of adaptation, but of missionary thrust, the fundamental duty to evangelize, to go towards men and women wherever they are, so that they may receive the gift of salvation."[52] Second, institutional renewal through a revitalized sense of Catholic "identity" is more essential than ever.[53] The Catholic school is said to be at the "heart of the Church"; it does not provide a service, nor does it have a merely ancillary function. It does the work of Jesus Christ.

Ex Corde Ecclesiae: The Fate of Gravissimum Educationis in American Higher Education

The 1983 Code of Canon Law honors the ecclesiological vision of *Lumen Gentium* and the missional dynamic of the Church in *Gaudium et Spes* when it organizes *all* forms of education under the teaching ministry of the Church. *Ex Corde Ecclesiae* comes late to the conversation; however, it is a reactive document, the fruit of an attempt to take account of two decades of institutional experience and integrate them with the canons of the Code and the general principles of *GE* as interpreted within the context of the whole council.[54]

New circumstances make the late hour of promulgation perhaps unfortunate: the proliferation of Catholic institutions by the 1990s, particularly in the United States, has been noted; the membership and demographics of religious orders have undergone a seismic post-conciliar shift, with inevitable outcomes for sponsored educational institutions; cultural and social-religious upheavals in the second half of the twentieth century have produced a generation of young people unaccustomed to war or personal poverty (in the wealthy West, at any rate). Most Catholic colleges and universities in the United States have redefined their mission through administrative reorganization, with majority lay boards as a buffer against ecclesiastical interference.[55] The concerns of popes a century ago seem archaic when the "separation of Church and state" has become a household phrase. Nevertheless, the eagerness of Catholic universities to rely on federal funding in conjunction with the rising profile (and cost) of university education, arguably transfers an older form of Church-state tension to the individual student or family. For good or ill, the American experience has been formative of the Church's thinking about the mission of Catholic universities in a contemporary age, given a uniquely American preoccupation with autonomy. *Ex Corde Ecclesiae* must therefore be read in its proper historical and religious context, as a specific response to a new series of situations and unresolved tensions.

The absence of a tradition of post-conciliar reflection on Catholic higher education comparable to what exists on Catholic primary and secondary schooling is genuinely problematic. Institutions themselves have led the way, sometimes compelled by a competitive educational marketplace, in choosing to invest in "institutional vision."[56] At times, these discussions are colored by hostility or indifference, reflecting the tensions of different generations of lived Catholicism. Certain norms in *Ex Corde* have received disproportionate attention, while general principles of education familiar from *GE* and previous teaching, reflecting the Catholic vision of the human person and the nature and mission of the Church, remain hard to articulate.[57] There is evidence that students and families—those who actually constitute the education "marketplace"—are eager to hear articulations of this vision.[58]

The final part of this essay focuses on higher education in the United States, identifying three challenges for Catholic universities and colleges arising from the general principles of *GE*. First, there is inadequate discussion of mission precisely in a time of rapid cultural change. Nearly exclusive institutional concern with autonomy and the acceptance of new legal languages describing the purported "wall" of separation between Church and state make it difficult to re-imagine the shared common good to which both state and Church are ordered, as per *Gaudium et Spes*.[59] Second, an analogous problem exists internal to the Church, in the tendency to frame questions of governance and authority as primarily about power and economics. This raises important questions about canon law, the laity, and the theological foundation of episcopal authority; however, these questions cannot be addressed adequately in the absence of a revived theology of the lay apostolate as developed in *Lumen Gentium* and *Apostolicam Actuositatem*.[60] The Council proclaims a deep, pastoral and missional interdependence of clergy and laity within the mystical body of Christ. A dynamic and more functional unity may be essential for the Catholic university to succeed in fulfilling the greatness of its mission. Third, a substantive vision of excellence in education, attained through research and the ongoing integration of knowledge, holistic attention to the student, and genuine conversation between faith and culture, is clearly expected as much from universities as from Catholic schools. It is not clear, however, whether universities have fared much better than Catholic schools in articulating this vision at the level of pedagogy.

I. The Catholic University: For the Human Person and for the Common Good?

The first challenge raises the fundamental question of the purpose of a university. A liberal arts college might say that it exists as a *cosmos* writ small, with a pedagogy ordered to knowledge for its own sake, for the sake of formation of the whole person in preparation for a mature, adult life. In the twentieth century, many institutions in North America have shifted from a collegiate style of education to a loosely German, research-university model. Motivations for this change are often presented as neutral or unambiguously good: institutional excellence, efficiency of delivery, greater access for a larger number of students, the desirability of funding, and realistic job preparation. Understandably utilitarian calculations and the dominance of programs of professional training make the liberal arts, wisdom-oriented thesis seem implausible—even if it should be true. Excellence in education is associated with technical facility and research (especially the quantity thereof, and the correlation of funding dollars), rather than teaching and the moral development of the student. Increased access has arguably balkanized higher education, with significantly higher prestige and money invested in relatively few elite institutions. Many colleges and universities split their classroom time between professional preparation and very basic forms of learning (for example, teaching writing or literature at a level that not long ago would have been standard for secondary-level work). This seems imprudent given the shocking cost of a university degree; it also fails to consider the significant role of community colleges, and the importance of associations responsible for formation in skills of art, craft, and manufacturing.

Catholic universities and colleges need not have a singular form and mission. On the other hand, the challenge of finding any single account of the end of Catholic education suggests that Catholic institutions share in a broader cultural crisis concerning the purpose of education, the goal of personal development and the common good of society. *Gravissimum Educationis* describes "principles" for education: the goods of social progress, cultural enrichment

and above all the formation of the human person "in the pursuit of his ultimate end ... and the good of (society)" (1). The Christian and moral dimension of education, according to *GE*, is simply non-negotiable in light of the full
dignity of the human person revealed in Jesus Christ (2). Post-conciliar documents about Catholic schools signal awareness of ongoing cultural changes,
and new challenges posed at the intersection of family life, parish, school, and
the broader community. They reveal frustration with the unwillingness of governments to support religious-affiliated institutions, and even more with the
failure of families to take responsibility for the spiritual well-being and moral
formation of their children. Schools, it is argued, cannot fulfill their intended
end if they become the sole custodian of the more ambitious, pastoral dimensions of education. The clarity and success of the mission of Catholic schooling becomes intelligible only in light of an ecclesial and political vision of the
common good. The cry for a more richly developed and lived vision, incipient
and in development from the pontificate of Leo XIII to that of Pius XII, recurs
in post-conciliar documents on Catholic schools. The absence of a comparable
reflection upon the role and mission of Catholic universities is striking.

Gravissimum Educationis offers two practical principles developed at
length in *Ex Corde*: first, education presupposes a *liberty of individual disciplines* as necessary for a "deeper realization of the harmony of faith and science" and for intellectual excellence; second, the importance of *pastoral care*
for university students marks the age of these students as a uniquely difficult
one (10). A gentle critique of the modern university is evident in the link of liberty to the harmony of faith and knowledge. Intellectual freedom is contained
within (and not limited by) the supposition of a substantive unity of truth: this
unity can never be complete; rather, it reflects a confidence in the coherence
of both nature and human reason rightly understood. A renegotiated place for
faith at the banquet of scientific learning is essential to intellectual freedom,
because it potentially expands a scope of investigation and reminds the scien-
tist of the spiritual dimension of persons and culture. No magisterial document suggests that the institutional presence of faith entails an interference
with, or a disfiguring of, particular disciplines exercised in accord with their
own principles.[61] Faith testifies to the integrity of mystery, and the coherence
of mystery with truth, even as faith demands an understanding that satisfies
human rationality. Freedom of inquiry that institutionally and intellectually
excludes faith potentially abandons the responsibility of the Catholic university to articulate an ancient and compelling vision of the unity of the sciences
as they touch upon the whole of human life and culture.

The second principle, that of the obligation of pastoral care, is closely
related to the first, since it requires universities to be devoted to the whole good
of the student as well as to the common good of Church and society. Education
as care of the soul is an ancient idea, and in a modern context it should appear
minimally as an attempt at integration between classroom learning and lived
experience outside of the classroom. Beyond the campus, this should involve
a genuine service of education, bringing together the life of the mind with the

life of faith in a variety of professional and social contexts. Universities should be fearless about their mission to form students, and unashamed of the call of *GE* that full human formation takes as its exemplar the person of Jesus Christ.

Attention to intellectual excellence and disciplinary integrity is well documented in the sources we have considered. In the United States, the era of the Council hardly marks these as novel concerns: for example, Thomas J. Shahan, the fourth rector of the Catholic University of America (1909–1928), oversaw considerable growth and academic investment.[62] The influence of Christopher Dawson and other theorists of liberal arts education was salutary in curricular development at the University of Notre Dame through the 1950s. Institutional commitment to scientific inquiry within the disciplines, integrating conversations with philosophy and theology, is clearly intended to be the hallmark of a Catholic form of excellence. However, narratives about institutional freedom and excellence in the 1960s, while understandable in their unique cultural milieu, are wholly inadequate to the content of the Catholic intellectual tradition. *Ex Corde, Fides et Ratio*, and multiple addresses of Pope Benedict XVI to academics deploy a language that fearlessly associates Christian faith with "enlightenment."[63] These sources strongly reject intellectual autonomy as neutral indeterminacy; in this, the warnings of *Gaudium et Spes* 36 and 41, and *Dignitatis Humanae* 1–3 are taken with appropriate seriousness.[64]

An ambitious, ongoing task is thus to be expected of Catholic universities in the modern world. At the time of the Council, an important period of cultural assimilation and intellectual self-critique in American higher education generated much good fruit; however, the rapid pace of secularization, combined with the unusual salience of Christianity in the public square, made the understandable desire for mainstream respectability uniquely dangerous. Philip Gleason notes the climax of this desire as concurrent with the final years of the Council: in 1964, John D. Donovan argued that pre-1950 Catholic higher education was no longer "structurally feasible." Catholic intellectuals, sensitive to charges of "siege mentality" and un-American "ghettoism," were ready for new models.[65] By 1965, after a series of conflicts over academic freedom, the institutional combination of "Catholic" with "intellectual" was derided as oxymoronic by a prominent public Catholic, John Cogley, religion editor at the *New York Times* (in 1965–1967) and former editor of *Commonweal*.[66] It was widely agreed that standards of real excellence were simply not to be found within the Catholic intellectual tradition.

Catholic universities and colleges in the United States have always been diverse in their character and governance. While generalizations are therefore descriptively limited, many of the older schools were founded by religious orders fleeing persecution or motivated by missionary service. The desire for substantive freedom arises from the conviction that such freedom is absolutely necessary for the work of the Gospel. The kind of academic freedom that became the rallying cry of the 1960s, however, was oddly lacking in content; by some accounts, it stood for nothing less than an epistemologically idealist absolutism.[67] Freedom as autonomy is a potentially dangerous political abstraction, a merely "terrestrial humanism" that violates human dignity and problematizes the very idea of the common good with its attendant obligations. While tensions in the 1960s between religious orders and the Roman Curia suggest that even terrestrial humanism can be useful, the lack of a rich and necessary connection between freedom as autonomy and academic excellence remains troubling. The tendency after the 1960s toward greater disciplinary specialization and research (and not teaching) as the marks of excellence would create new obstacles to the articulation of mission for the sake of the good of the student.

Gravissimum Educationis treats universities and colleges as a distinct but analogous species of "school." It is appropriate to challenge Catholic universities to consider questions of freedom and governance in the context of a larger discussion of their contribution to the renewal of the common good, as well as the mission of the Church. If the Catholic university is essentially related to the nature and mission of the Church, individual right will be both supported by and subordinated to the mission of the Church in the world. The acceptance of the strong authority of institutions external to the university has proved useful and even necessary. However, the thinness of the kind of excellence promoted by the call for autonomy has come to be easily shaped by these same institutions—agencies for assessment, departments for federal and state funding, and disciplinary professional groups—rather than by the university itself.[68] The rising costs of secondary education make the original mission of many institutions to privilege the underprivileged, and to educate in a way that respects cultural diversity, impossible. One might ask a provocative question: do we really *need* Catholic universities if standards for its excellence—or simply its survival—are extrinsic to its own traditions and mission? While Catholic universities would benefit from taking this question seriously, unfortunately the burden of its being unanswered continues to rest upon the shoulders of the heavily indebted student.

II. The Catholic University: A Civil Entity or a Canonical-Juridical Person?

The question of the canonical status of universities, colleges, or faculties that are called "Catholic" may be a pressing issue for mission. Canon 808 of the 1983 Code states that, even if a school is de facto Catholic, the ability to call itself such flows from its relationship to the visible Church: "no university is to bear the title or name of Catholic university without the consent of competent ecclesiastical authority." The competence of relevant authority is contextualized within the over-arching duty of the Church to teach as an apostolic and missionary person, whose finality is vested in Jesus Christ's own commands. This duty is given material form in the founding and governing (*moderandi*) of institutions.[69] The distinction between "title" and "name" (*nomen*) implies that public self-description as Catholic is relevant, even if the adjective "Catholic" is not part of the name of a school. Moreover, whether official consent is sought or tacit permission is thought to exist at a particular time, the right to teach as a Catholic institution is nevertheless derivative rather than self-originating. *Gravissimum Educationis* is wholly consistent with earlier documents in asserting that this right is public and political in character, and not restricted to merely religious education.

Many Catholic colleges in the United States came into existence during the first half of the nineteenth century due to episcopal initiative or patronage.[70] Other schools were founded by some "association of the faithful" or as an apostolic work of a religious order or prelature. Historical and structural pluralism of institutions of higher education makes a single model of dependence undesirable and impractical. This was clearly acknowledged by the bishops in preliminary sessions for the drafting of *GE*, who also hoped for clearer standards for identity, professional qualifications, and governance.[71] The difference between North American and continental European degree structures posed further challenges to the possibility of unified standards as a basis for identity. By the 1960s, European bishops still frequently treated university faculty with the same criteria as they would ecclesiastical faculties, making appeal to *Deus Scientiarum Dominus* (1931), a document only later said to apply narrowly to ecclesiastical faculties.[72]

By the time of the publication of the 1983 Code, the matter of the relationship of Catholic universities and colleges in the United States to both the local and the curial hierarchy had been largely reframed. Two stories serve to illustrate a dramatic shift in approach to this question: one concerning the independence of Jesuit schools, and the other surrounding the publication of the document, *The Catholic University in the Modern World* in 1972.[73]

The Society of Jesus sought membership in the IFCU (International Federation of Catholic Universities), and the Superior General set in motion a correspondence with the Prefect of the Sacred Congregation of Seminaries and Universities, petitioning for "official recognition" as a first step.[74] By this time, Jesuit universities were enjoying significant growth and internal diversity in the United States, and the demand for greater academic freedom was more likely directed against authority internal to the order.[75] Georgetown University, granted a pontifical charter in 1833, was included in the list of institutions for which official recognition was sought. The Superior General argued for recognition on the basis of the particular Catholicity of Jesuit schools, the "vigilance of the Society's superiors," and the involvement of the American hierarchy in the everyday life of these schools.[76] In response, the Congregation proposed "canonical erection" as the usual mode of recognition. When the Superior General bristled at this, the Congregation pointed to the example of the Catholic University of America as evidence that canonical erection hardly entailed lesser intellectual status, nor was the objection plausible of "fear of persecution."[77] Canon 1376 of the 1917 Code was interpreted as enjoining "unity of direction" and moral and educational purpose, and *not* merely Catholic orthodoxy. The Congregation clearly implied that this unity of direction was not present in the wide range of Jesuit institutions—although it was not made clear how canonical erection would provide this unity.

Canon 1376 also required that any Catholic university have its statutes approved by the Apostolic See, even if it were sponsored by a religious order. The Congregation proposed this route as an alternative, first asking the Superior General to review all non-approved statutes of Jesuit schools. The list of institutions provided by the Congregation included only non-canonically erected schools, seventeen of which were in the United States; Georgetown was therefore not included on this list, even though its statutes had not been reviewed and approved. Where the Jesuits remained primarily interested in membership in the IFCU, the Congregation had clearly moved the conversation into new territory entirely. In a letter dated June 15, 1959, the Superior General demurred in strong terms, saying that these Jesuit institutions were "of a private character, with regard to their governance," owing their erection "to the state, always with the approval of the local ordinary and the Sacred Congregation of Religious." Moreover, by virtue of civil erection, these schools were able to confer degrees comparable to those of state universities, and that this was adequate for the fulfilling of their mission.[78]

Several important issues are raised by this exchange, the goal of which—membership in the IFCU—was eventually abandoned. While the Congregation for Seminaries and Universities claimed authority over all universities, there was a lack of clarity about the form and extent of this authority due in part to poor translation of European institutional criteria: were some of these schools even universities at all, as opposed to loosely constituted colleges, effectively closer to a lyceum? This in turn skewed the question of competence and erection: did a university have to be canonically erected *already* for the Congregation to claim competence over them? Or, did the act of petitioning for "recognition" confirm an already existing relationship? It should be noted that the closing exchange in this dialogue set the terms for future discussion of North American Catholic universities and colleges. The appeal to civil erection as an alternative to canonical erection, evidenced in the degrees granted, would serve as a crucial basis for a strong claim of autonomy. Civil erection reframed the question of authority in conjunction with the distinctive status of religious institutes, since religious can claim a prudential space within canon law between their vowed submission to the relevant superior and their relationship with various curial offices. On a merely practical level, the necessity of reporting to multiple curial bodies created a space for bureaucratic maneuvering.[79]

The second and related narrative concerns the 1967 meeting of the IFCU at Land O'Lakes, Wisconsin, which generated an important statement under the leadership of Fr. Theodore Hesburgh, CSC. The IFCU by this time had a more distant relationship with the Congregation; nevertheless, Cardinal Pizzardo objected to the election of Hesburgh as its president. This objection was overruled by Hesburgh's friend, now-Pope Paul VI.[80] The statement produced at Land O'Lakes would be adopted by the IFCU and provide a template for the 1972 document approved in Kinshasa. This in turn was described as a "magna carta" for Catholic universities of all kinds, everywhere. It opens with a description of four attributes which, if present, would indicate that an institution was de facto Catholic, "whether canonically erected or not."[81] These attributes, and their presence in *Ex Corde*, are striking given the initial refusal of American university representatives to help Rome draw up flexible but substantive characteristics of Catholic universities. At a World Congress in Rome in 1969, many of these same representatives argued that the situation in America was so foreign and internally varied, that this would be impossible and undesirable.[82]

American university leaders, from 1969 to 1972, steadfastly refused to open up matters of university structure, governance, and life for discussion with Rome; instead, they focused on the question of juridical status and the authoritative relationship appropriate between Catholic universities and the Congregation (or the local Bishop). In light of this, it is remarkable that from the Declaration *Cum Dubium* (1959) to the 1972 document, all parties assume the inclusion of canonically erected and non-canonical under a single over-arching category of Catholic university—loosely consistent with pre-Conciliar practice.[83] This may explain the observation of Prefect Cardinal Garrone that the real matter under discussion was not in fact *whether* there exists some kind of dependence, or relationship, between universities and ecclesiastical authority—it is simply already there, given their self-description as Catholic—but rather the *implications* of having two very different kinds of institutions with analogous relationships to ecclesiastical authority.[84] No party wished to argue that any institution was more or less "Catholic" simply by virtue of its declared juridical status. Nevertheless, the understandable preoccupation with autonomy and freedom, combined with the focus on juridical status, tended to restrict the discussion to matters of governance in the abstract. The four attributes in the 1972 document should have been the more substantive object of study.

After this document was approved, all seemed well in Catholic higher education in the United States. The Congregation followed up in 1974 with a request to the presidents of Catholic universities and colleges, asking simply, How is the implementation of this document going? Cardinal Garrone alluded to the need for investing in the *ongoing* task of "defining or identifying" the Catholic university.[85] The only coordinated response amounted to a single effort: campus ministry. There was no evidence of extended discussion about curriculum, pedagogy, or mission, nor was there any significant conversation with the local hierarchy. In fact, the very idea of some kind of common mission in American Catholic higher education was rejected, on the grounds that the 1972 document legitimated merely individualistic interpretations of general principles of Catholicity. The American hierarchy appeared to accept this. The consensus by the mid-1970s was that Catholic colleges and universities simply had to be "legally independent" in order to receive financial benefits from civil authorities, but that this need not prevent institutions from serving the Gospel. The argument made in 1969, that institutional diversity was an obstacle to a single canonical language for describing the "dependence" of universities in relation to ecclesial authority, now became an argument against any genuine unity of vision in education.

This seems a clear failure in light of *GE*. It is remarkable that *Gaudium et Spes* was frequently appealed to, along with the "spirit" of the Council, as definitive grounds for maximal autonomy. The expectation of genuine intellectual, academic freedom, evident in *Ex Corde* as much as in the documents on Catholic schools, was not controversial; nevertheless, the false steps of certain curial figures, such as Pizzardo and Ottaviano, were used as decisive proof that the interests of Rome and of universities were strongly at odds with one another. After much collaborative goodwill through the 1970s, Cardinal Garrone was dismissed as a "conservative," once again attacking "academic freedom in Catholic universities."[86] *Gaudium et Spes* was said to urge "cooperation" and "mutual support" in precisely the way imagined by a few powerful and increasingly wealthy American universities. The Vatican was accused of continuing conversations at the level of mere juridical authority, with the result that it presumably wanted universities to function as a subordinate, unthinking "arm of the Church." Nevertheless, a 1974 letter from the secretary of the ACCU to Rome states that all universities meeting certain conditions are clearly Catholic, whether canonically erected or not: once again, the absence of juridical clarity was thought to be a decisive argument in favor of autonomy.[87]

Missing from this picture of general hostility is any sense of the Church-world relationship present in the actual text of *Gaudium et Spes*. The inability to embrace language of ecclesial unity in strong but non-juridical terms, as determined by the mission of the Church, reveals a remarkable failure of imagination. Academic freedom need not be opposed to the task of forming the whole student for wisdom, for the sake of discerning critically the "signs of the times," in order to "sacralize" the culture. The goodness and "integrity" of the secular realm was said to be a novel invention of *Gaudium et Spes*—despite its explicit affirmation in magisterial documents since the nineteenth century, as well as being a fundamental metaphysical principle in the tradition. Language of "openness" signaled a new negotiation and opposition between the orders of nature and grace, in the following three respects.

INTELLECTUALLY: The language of this second narrative invokes a sense of autonomy that is explicitly repudiated by *Gaudium et Spes* 36. The integrity and "independence" of the secular flows from the goodness of creation. The intelligibility, "stability, truth . . . and order" in things is proper to them, grounding the efficacy of scientific inquiry. On the other hand, this intelligibility fades as the dependence of things upon the Creator is "forgotten." David Burrell, CSC, acknowledges the importance of academic freedom as part of the "academic administrator's" arsenal; however, writing as an academic theologian, he repudiates this language as inadequate to the complexity of the dual allegiances that he has to *both* academic and ecclesial communities. The academic is, at it were, a public person, and not simply one of the baptized; she must consider her "role *within*" the Church, and the responsibility to the body of Christ that this entails.[88] Recent history of the supposedly grave mediocrity of Catholic education does not provide grounds for assuming that Catholicity and ecclesial unity are at odds with academic excellence by the standards of the professional guilds.[89] It is arguably the task of the Catholic university to demonstrate that the opposite is in fact the case.

ECCLESIOLOGICALLY: The move from clerical to lay boards of trustees was required by accreditation, for the sake of eligibility for federal funding. There were also many voices defending this move as a realization of the Council's call for "lay leadership."[90] While this cannot be cynically dismissed as mere opportunism, the new lay constitution of many boards was used as an argument *against* greater ecclesial unity, or more visible relationships of oversight with local hierarchy. This was said to be obviously inimical to the freedom particular to the lay state.[91] This assumes too much about the laity as a monolithic entity, and arguably *uses* the laity as part of a basically clerical battle between university leaders within a local church and curial bodies. *Lumen Gentium* does not see the integrity of the lay state as opposed to the proper function and pastoral oversight of the hierarchy.[92] The dominance of the images of "mystery" and "body" in the opening part of the Constitution on the Church underlie a strong, missional ambition of total unity of God's people. The hostile tone and distinctly Americanist flavor of the discussions through the 1970s precluded discussion about procedures or visible structures for a greater professional unity of purpose between the hierarchy and the laity.

Gravissimum Educationis identifies education as a central part of the mission of the Church, as well as a uniquely lay apostolate. The appeal to freedom, made with aggressive self-evidence, may speak refreshingly to centuries of experience between religious orders and the Curia. For the laity, however, in a time a rapid cultural change, the loss of visible, cultural ties to the everyday life of the Church poses an immediate challenge to the forging of Catholic identity. For this reason, the supposition that the local hierarchy is a merely "external" accessory to the life of the university—explicitly repudiated by *Ex Corde*—is unhelpful.[93] The 1972 document (par. 59) provided the option favored by most American university leaders: a negative relationship, in which the bishop only intervenes in dire situations.

Unity is recognized as important by all parties. When Fr. Hesburgh offered the image of the university as the place where the Church "does its thinking," he clearly understood the university to be setting the terms of unity, from a place of internally guaranteed authority.[94] Accordingly, the usefulness of bishops is judged by academic standards: "competent ecclesiastical authority" is willfully misunderstood to mean "competent" in the sense proper to American jurisprudence (intellectual fitness), or in a sense that would be determined, for example, by an academic theologian (scientific competence).[95] Either way, there is no possible analogy between the teaching of the academic and the teaching role of the bishop; nor could a bishop enter into the conversation within a university, given the external nature of his own qualifications.

All kinds of Catholic universities were discussed during the Council as *part* of the Church, and thus essential instruments in the work of the Church in the modern world. Evangelization is described (in *Lumen Gentium* and *Gaudium et Spes*) in respectful terms appropriate to modern persons in light of their education and cultural situation. Cultural renewal is seen as a particular patrimony attendant to the Catholic intellectual tradition. Evangelization and cultural renewal are closely related to education at all levels, although it cannot be reduced to either of these. Language of authority and the Magisterium discussed in the preparatory committee on education, was instead contextualized ecclesiologically in *Lumen Gentium*. Language about the need for theology, especially biblical studies, to be done "in" the Church, in communion with the Magisterium, was contextualized in the Constitution on Revelation (*Dei Verbum*). In those two documents, the dignity of the work of the laity is increased rather than decreased by their deeper reconstitution as the body of Christ, the Church.

POLITICALLY-LEGALLY: Unique circumstances and a distinct American heritage may reasonably inform concerns about freedom and autonomy. It is not clear what new situation was feared during the 1970s. Civil incorporation was eagerly interpreted by American university leaders as an alternative to ecclesial personality; there is no clear argument in support of this. The existence of fine institutions that grant degrees with both civil and canonical effects continues to argue against concerns about freedom and excellence. To be sure, there is a tradition older than the continental Reformation of appealing to either the local or the imperial secular authority for safeguard against ecclesiastical muscling. Given the series of court cases in the 1970s challenging institutions that might offer a "pervasively sectarian" educational atmosphere, the assuring of widespread public approval through legal recourse seems short-sighted. *Ex Corde* asks that universities serve a common *institutional* purpose of evangelization and renewal, through their excellence; they are also tasked with being a witness to the academic guilds of an authentically Christian presence.[96] There should be ongoing reflection across the disciplines of how this might occur, in a way that does not violate scientific integrity or institutional funding.

The Catholic University: Educating for Excellence?

Morey and Piderit frame their study of institutions of Catholic higher education with two criteria—uniqueness and inheritability.[97] Current issues in higher education highlight the challenge of uniqueness in a profession that is self-regulating. *Gravissimum Educationis* calls colleges and universities to an excellence that embodies a harmony of "dependence" upon the Church and the "pursuit of individual subjects according to their own principles, methods and liberty of scientific inquiry" (10). *Gravissimum Educationis* also calls for a rich presence of theological study, particularly in conversation with philosophical and scientific disciplines. The document suggests that, while Catholic education should be accessible, a large number of institutions might not be desirable if the plurality itself would compromise either quality or Catholicity. Finally, the document urges many forms of collaboration between the hierarchy and the university for the sake of the pastoral care of students and other members of the university community.

The new Code and *Ex Corde* together try to respond decisively to any lingering questions about *dependence*. Less attention has been directed at the broad and ambitious vision of educating the whole human person in light of their full dignity as rational persons and children of God. The 1994 document issued by the Congregation for Catholic Education, the Pontifical Council for the Laity and the Pontifical Council for Culture, seeks to integrate the vision of education developed in *Ex Corde* with a sense of the university's participation in the cultural and pastoral mission of the Church, as per *Gravissimum Educationis*.[98] Particular exhortations resonate with earlier documents on Catholic schools: faith should not be present in a university or college as though artificially added from without; professors should not "change" what they teach so much as allow their disciplines to open up to the kinds of "big questions" that make the integration of knowledge across the disciplines more likely. A conversation between faith and the various disciplines should be constant, particularly in light of the poorly understood Catholic confidence in the harmony of science and religion. The pastoral care of faculty as well as students should be a signal concern of the bishop and local pastors. Student life should make it easy for students to actually live out their faith; campus ministry should be active and diverse, offering multiple spiritual formational styles to students. Service should be genuinely sacrificial, a fruit of evangelical obligation, and not an added line on a curriculum vitae. Above all, education should be mindful of and directed toward the whole person; professional preparation is an acceptable dimension of university education, but it is not its original purpose. While educators must be mindful of the understandable anxiety of students about financial and professional competence, they must direct students to the accessibility and beauty of truth, as the real and ennobling goal of education. Catholic universities, as much as Catholic schools, have struggled to enact these noble ideas in a practical and systematic way.

In a 2008 address that was originally intended for Rome's La Sapienza University, but cancelled due to faculty protests, Pope Benedict XVI argued that truth is a matter of *theoria*, of a seeing that is only satisfied by possession. If human reason is made for the truth, the possession of all truth is immediately a good for persons: it is transformative of the mind and its disposition, making the knower good. Institutional education, whether Catholic or not, must be grounded in an authentic and humble commitment to truth if its desired end is the good of the student as a person. The modern Catholic university is uniquely positioned to educate in this way. Should it choose to be fearlessly committed to excellence, unashamed of its ecclesial mission to sacralize the culture, and convinced of the capacity of human persons for truth and for fellowship with God, only then will the Catholic university fulfill the vision of the council fathers who produced *Gravissimum Educationis*. Benedict XVI's 2008 speech, rejected before it could be heard, is nothing less than a hopeful entreaty to fulfill this vision—from the heart of a professional educator, who waits for another St. Dominic.

NOTES

1. http://www.vatican.va/archive/hist_councils/ii_vatican_council/documents/vat-ii_decl_19651028_gravissimum-educationis_en.html.

2. Pope John XXIII's opening speech to the council (October 11, 1962), *Gaudet Mater Ecclesiae*: "Ut sacrum christianae doctrinae depositum efficaciore ratione custodiatur atque proponatur" (http://w2.vatican.va/content/john-xxiii/la/speeches/1962/documents/hf_j-xxiii_spe_19621011_opening-council.html).

3. *Gravissimum Educationis* 4; 7. All references to magisterial documents are to paragraph or article numbers, as denoted within the text.

4. Particularly, Pope Pius XI's *Divini Illius Magistri* 12 and 28 (Rome: Libreria Editrice Vaticana, 1929); this encyclical is the most influential source for *Gravissimum Educationis*. Pope Leo XIII's social encyclicals, *Aeterni Patris* (1879), *Sapientiae Christianae* (1890), *Rerum Novarum* (1891), *Militantis Ecclesiae* (1897), and *Affari Vos* (1897) treat education as a proper work of the Church as well as of the state (all available at http://w2.vatican.va/content/leo-xiii/en/encyclicals.index.html#encyclicals). See the *Acta Apostolicae Sedis* at http://www.vatican.va/archive/aas/index_it.htm for Pope Pius XI's *Studiorum Ducem* (*AAS* 15, 1923), 309–26, and *Mit Brennender Sorge* (*AAS* 29, 1937), 145–67. For examples of Pope Pius XII's talks to students and educators, cf., *Allocution to the Minor Seminaries of France* (*AAS* 49, 1957), 296–300; *Allocution to Secondary Students in Rome* (*AAS* 49, 1957), 281–287.

5. This resonates with the basic and fruitful tension of the council, as articulated in Pope John XXIII's opening speech (cf. n. 2, above, noting the use here of *custodire*), given its stated purpose "to hand on Catholic teaching which, regardless of difficulties and controversies, remains the common patrimony of humanity . . . not as though we only guard this precious treasure; but swiftly and fearlessly do the work which our age demands, as the Church has done these twenty centuries" ("non detortam tradere vult doctrinam catholicam, quae, licet inter difficultates et contentiones, veluti patrimonium commune hominum. . . . Attamen nostrum non est pretiosum hunc thesaurum solum custodire, quasi uni antiquitati studeamus; sed alacres sine timore, operi, quod nostra exigit aetas . . . quod Ecclesia a viginti fere saeculis fecit").

6. In *Gravissimum Educationis* 1, the entreaty for a "positive and prudent sexual education" has been frequently commented upon. The location of this sentence may account for the common interpretation that this be public and institutional; however, the guidelines published by the Pontifical Council for the Family on December 8, 1995 clarify that sexual education is primarily a task for the family, in which the model of sacrifice and "joy in chastity" must be lived as well as taught (73). The guidelines acknowledge the place of school programs, but only with reservations: "Other educators can assist in this task, but they can only take the place of parents for serious reasons of physical or moral incapacity" (23). The argument offered is not a matter of general rights, as though "parents are capable of satisfying every requirement of the whole process of raising children" (23); rather, this task is appropriate to the family because it is there that children must learn the "true values of the human person and

Christian love, taking a clear position that surpasses ethical utilitarianism" (http://www.vatican.va/roman_curia/pontifical_councils/family/documents/rc_pc_family_doc_08121995_human-sexuality_en.html).

7. Cf. *Lumen Gentium*, 9.

8. According to Pohlschneider, the council fathers were mindful of the decreasing number of Catholic schools, and therefore of the increasing number of Catholics educated in secular institutions; the document acknowledges this with a pastoral tone (*Gravissimum Educationis*, 7; Johannes Pohlschneider in Herbert Vorgrimler, ed., *Commentary on the Documents of Vatican II* [Montréal: Palm, 1967], 4: 13). Paragraph 3 states, "In addition, therefore, to the rights of parents and others to whom the parents entrust a share in the work of education, certain rights and duties belong indeed to civil society, whose role is to direct what is required for the common temporal good." This role includes protecting parental rights, assisting parents and communities unable to educate their children, and building schools. While Pohlschneider speaks of the educational rights of "the State" (*Commentary*, 23), the context of the paragraph in question is the family's need of help from the *whole community* (*societas*); moreover, the subject in this paragraph is not the state, but "civil society" (*societas civilis*). The term "state" (*cives*) does not occur until paragraph 6, which concerns "the duties and rights of parents." It is not clear whether this ambiguity is deliberate, but given that education is identified as an issue pertaining differently to the state and the Church, it is unhelpful. For early documents addressing the dual ends of education, see Pius IX's 1849 encyclical *Nostis et Nobiscum*, 29–31 (https://www.ewtn.com/library/encyc/p9nostis.htm) and Pius XI on the Church and the German Reich, *Mit Brennender Sorge* (*AAS* 29, 1937), pars. 5, 16, 31, 39.

9. *Codex Iuris Canonici*, c. 797 (Rome: Libreria Editrice Vaticana, 1983). The first paragraph of *Gravissimum Educationis* 6 echoes *Divini Illius Magistri* 48: distributive justice is observed in the non-violation of the conscience of parents.

10. http://w2.vatican.va/content/pius-xi/la/apost_constitutions/documents/hf_p-xi_apc_19310524_deus-scientiarum-dominus.html.

11. The 1983 Code distinguishes (based on *Sapientia Christiana* 2–8; cf. http://w2.vatican.va/content/john-paul-ii/en/apost_constitutions/documents/hf_jp-ii_apc_15041979_sapientia-christiana.html) between Catholic universities on the one hand, and ecclesiastical universities on the other. Independent faculties, institutes or schools granted charters by the Holy See to grant ecclesiastical (or canonical) degrees according to the European system, are grouped with ecclesiastical universities (cf. Book III, Chapters II and III). All "ecclesiastical" institutions are de facto pontifical; the latter term otherwise indicates an honorific conferred on a Catholic university by the Pope, with juridical effects (e.g. Catholic University of America, Washington, DC; Saint Paul University, Ottawa). The distinguishing marks of juridical persons in the Church is clearly a subject for ongoing development and clarification. It is worth noting that the original draft of *Gravissimum Educationis* treated universities Catholic and ecclesiastical *together*, in the second of three parts; cf. "Schema Constitutionis, De Scholis Catholicis et de Studiis Academicis," in *Schemata Constitutionum et Decretorum ex Quibus Argumenta in Concilio Disceptanda Seligentur* IV (Rome: Typis Polyglottis Vaticanis, 1972), 277–345.

12. Cf. *Gaudium et Spes*, 52, 73, 76, 85, and 89 (at http://www.vatican.va/archive/hist_councils/ii_vatican_council/documents/vat-ii_const_19651207_gaudium-et-spes_en.html).

13. *Gaudium et Spes*, 3.

14. Significant curricular development has been proposed by the Congregation for Catholic Education since 1979; on ecclesiastical faculties, see John M. Huels,

"The Juridic Status of Catholic Faculties of Theology: Overview of the Universal Law," *Studia Canonica* 37 (2003): 301–22; Oscar Eone Eone, "Facultés et Universités Écclesiastiques et Universités Catholiques: Convergences et Divergences," *Seminarium* 44 (2004): 479–511.

    15.   http://www.vatican.va/roman_curia/congregations/ccatheduc/documents/ rc_con_ccatheduc_doc_19770319_catholic-school_en.html;   http://www.vatican. va/roman_curia/congregations/ccatheduc/documents/rc_con_ccatheduc_doc_ 19821015_lay-catholics_en.html; http://www.vatican.va/roman_curia/congregations/ ccatheduc/documents/rc_con_ccatheduc_doc_19880407_catholic-school_en.html; http://www.vatican.va/roman_curia/congregations/ccatheduc/documents/rc_con_ ccatheduc_doc_27041998_school2000_en.html.

    16. The United States Conference of Catholic Bishops (USCCB) responded to this document with its own in 2005, "Renewing our Commitment to Catholic Elementary and Secondary Schools in the Third Millennium" (at http://www.usccb.org/beliefs- and-teachings/how-we-teach/catholic-education/upload/renewing-our-commitment- 2005.pdf). While more pragmatic in tone and content, it offers striking statistical observations about the United States, above all of decreasing numbers of Catholic schools in cities, by contrast with suburban areas; 95 percent of teachers and admin- istrators are laypeople (in 2005); since 1990, the total cost of educating a student has risen by 13 percent; average tuition has doubled.

    17. *The Catholic School on the Threshold of the Third Millennium* 1; http://www.vati- can.va/roman_curia/congregations/ccatheduc/documents/rc_con_ccatheduc_doc_ 27041998_school2000_en.html.

    18. Timothy Walch, *Parish School: American Catholic Parochial Education from Colonial Times to the Present* (New York: Crossroads Publishing Company, 1996), 23–37.

    19. Horace Mann, *The Common School Journal* (Boston: Marsh, Capen, Lyon and Webb, 1839), 1:113–14; Joseph Murphy et al., *Pathways to Privatization in Education* (Santa Barbara, CA: Greenwood Publishing Group, 1998), 158.

    20. R. M. Jacobs, "U.S. Catholic Schools and the Religious Who Served in Them: Contributions in the First Six Decades of the 20th Century," *Catholic Education: A Journal of Inquiry and Practice* 2, no. 1 (1998): 15–34.

    21. Walch, *Parish School*, 4.

    22. See, for example, as a characteristic account, Stephen J. Denig and Anthony J. Dosen, CM, "The Mission of the Catholic School in the Pre-Vatican II Era (1810– 1962) and the Post-Vatican II Era (1965–1995): Insights and Observations for the New Millennium," *Catholic Education: A Journal of Inquiry and Practice* 13, no. 2 (2009): 141: "It was a transition from viewing all ministry as inward (i.e. clergy supporting the Catholic community proper) to viewing ministry as outward (i.e. clergy and laity col- laborating in providing ministry to the wider world." In the pre-Vatican II era, schools were marked by "catechizing Catholic youth and preserving them from Protestant pros- elytizing"; by contrast, after the Council, Catholic schools "realized they now had a mission to serve . . . the wider world." The doors were now open to non-Catholics, "not in order to proselytize, but to empower the poor." These statements are at most partially accurate, revealing anxiety about the cultural integrity of communities prior to urban flight in the United States. The authors admit that this narrative of total change restricts religious formation (after Vatican II) mainly to catechesis, and the Church-world mode of interaction to "social justice and service." Magisterial documents after *Gravissimum Educationis* all agree on the non-proselytizing character of the Catholic school, but with these careful conditions: (1) Catholic schools must be committed to the basically religious character of holistic formation (*The Catholic School*, 12, 17, 18); (2) the role of

schools in the "saving mission of the Church" can never be compromised (9); and (3) pedagogy should assume that education involves awakening the religious dimension of the human person (described in *The Religious Dimension of Education* [1988] as a kind of "pre-evangelization" [http://www.vatican.va/roman_curia/congregations/ccatheduc/documents/rc_con_ccatheduc_doc_19880407_catholic-school_en.html]).

23. *The Catholic School*, 39 (http://www.vatican.va/roman_curia/congregations/ccatheduc/documents/rc_con_ccatheduc _doc_19770319_catholic-school_en.html).

24. *The Catholic School*, 78.

25. *The Catholic School*, 6; *Lay Catholics in Schools: Witnesses to Faith*, The Sacred Congregation for Catholic Education, 1982, 61, http://www.vatican.va/roman_curia/congregations/ccatheduc/documents/rc_con_ccatheduc_doc_19821015_lay-catholics_en.html.

26. *Lay Catholics in Schools*, 30.

27. *The Catholic School*, 6.

28. *The Catholic School* (29) argues that the overall effect of the standardizing of curriculum across many communities and kinds of schools results in "depersonalization" and a "mass production mentality" appropriate to a technological culture of shallow memory.

29. *The Religious Dimension*, 58.

30. Cf. *The Religious Dimension*, 105–6, where the *whole person* is said to be the subject of education—the intellect, will and emotions—which in turn makes it possible for the relationship between teacher and student to be one of genuine charity. "The teacher's love ... gives value" to the things studied. The teacher's love for the student, as a whole person, in turn ennobles the relationship and circumscribes its pastoral character; accordingly, the teachers should understand that "we love persons" and not "formulas."

31. *The Religious Dimension*, 53, 55.

32. *The Religious Dimension*, 83.

33. Most dioceses in the United States have required the adopting of standard curriculum, test-indexed standards, and teacher certification. While appropriate credentials are reasonably expected, this practice can exclude gifted young teachers who choose to focus on subject matter rather than pedagogical method in undergraduate study; see *Lay Catholics in Schools*, 64, where "pluralistic" centers of teacher formation are critiqued for lack of "synthesis," and where a different vision of the "human person" may be operative. Article 65 suggests, surprisingly, that teachers could pursue a course of religious formation under the guidance of ecclesiastical faculties; it is not clear how this would mitigate the tendency of curriculum to become either "irreligious" or "fragmented and insufficient" (*The Religious Dimension*, 55). In response to the call for renewed parental responsibility, the rise of homeschooling and the interest of parents and charter schools in "classical curriculum" is noteworthy. For example, see Craig N. Horning, "The Intersection of Religious Charter Schools and Urban Catholic Education: a Literature Review," *Catholic Education: A Journal of Inquiry and Practice* 16, no. 2 (2013): 364–87; cf. G. M. Wilhelm and M. W. Firmin, "Historical and Contemporary Developments in Home School Education," *Journal of Research on Christian Education* 18 (2009): 303–15.

34. See, for example, *The Religious Dimension*, 53: faith cannot be "identified with any one culture"; rather, it must inspire "every culture."

35. *The Religious Dimension*, 51.

36. *The Catholic School on the Threshold of the Third Millennium*, 37: "These premises indicate the duties and the content of the Catholic school. Its task is fundamentally

a synthesis of culture and faith, and a synthesis of faith and life: the first is reached by integrating all the different aspects of human knowledge through the subjects taught, in the light of the Gospel; the second in the growth of the virtues characteristic of the Christian" (http://www.vatican.va/roman_curia/congregations/ccatheduc/documents/rc_con_ccatheduc_doc_27041998_school2000_en.html). On the contemporary sense of faith and education, for a common position, see Peter Conn, "The Great Accreditation Farce," *Chronicle of Higher Education*, June 30, 2014 (http://chronicle.com/article/The-Great-Accreditation-Farce/147425/).

37. *The Catholic School on the Threshold*, 11.

38. *The Catholic School on the Threshold*, 14.

39. *The Catholic School*, 47; cf. *The Catholic School on the Threshold*, 14: "All of this demands an atmosphere characterized by the search for truth, in which competent, convinced and coherent educators, teachers of learning and of life, may be a reflection, albeit imperfect but still vivid, of the one Teacher. In this perspective, in the Christian educational project all subjects collaborate, each with its own specific content, to the formation of mature personalities."

40. *The Religious Dimension*, 29.

41. *The Religious Dimension*, 44.

42. *The Catholic School*, 50, 55.

43. *The Catholic School*, 18.

44. *The Catholic School*, 66.

45. "Pedagogy and the sciences of education themselves have appeared to devote greater attention to the study of phenomenology and didactics than to the essence of education as such, centered on deeply meaningful values and vision. The fragmentation of education, the generic character of the values frequently invoked and which obtain ample and easy consensus at the price of a dangerous obscuring of their content, tend to make the school step back into a supposed neutrality, which enervates its educating potential and reflects negatively on the formation of the pupils. There is a tendency to forget that education always presupposes and involves a definite concept of man and life" (*The Catholic School on the Threshold*, 10).

46. *The Catholic School on the Threshold*, 13.

47. *The Catholic School on the Threshold*, 6.

48. *The Religious Dimension of Education* (1988) (http://www.vatican.va/roman_curia/congregations/ccatheduc/documents/rc_con_ccatheduc_doc_19880407_catholic-school_en.html) likewise diagnoses the "signs of the times" with a critical eye, noting the formation of young people by a rapidly shifting media culture with the result of shallow intellectual and spiritual commitments, a surprising degree of worldliness combined with poor moral formation, common experience of loneliness, depression and family discord, drug use and the "cult of the body" (10), and finally the dominance of criteria of practical utility and technological and economic progress.

49. *The Catholic School on the Threshold*, 6.

50. *The Catholic School on the Threshold*, 20.

51. Cf. *Gratissimam Sane* (1994), 13–14 (https://w2.vatican.va/content/john-paul-ii/en/letters/1994/documents/hf_jp-ii_let_02021994_families.html).

52. *The Catholic School on the Threshold*, 3.

53. *The Catholic School on the Threshold*, 11.

54. http://w2.vatican.va/content/john-paul-ii/en/apost_constitutions/documents/hf_jp-ii_apc_15081990_ex-corde-ecclesiae.html.

55. D. J. O'Brien, *From the Heart of the American Church: Catholic Higher Education and American Culture* (Maryknoll, NY: Orbis Books, 1994); P. Steinfels, "Catholic

Identity: Emerging Consensus," in *Catholic Education at the Turn of the New Century*, ed. J. M. O'Keefe (New York: Garland, 1997), 199–203; J. T. Burtchaell, *The Dying of the Light: The Disengagement of Colleges and Universities from their Christian Churches* (Grand Rapids, MI: Eerdmans, 1998); M. K. Hellwig, "Higher Education and the Catholic Church: Some Underlying Assumptions," in *Current Issues in Catholic Higher Education* 20, no. 2 (April, 2000): 27–39.

56. Robert Abelman and Amy Dalessandro, "An Assessment of the Institutional Vision of Catholic Colleges and Universities," *Catholic Education: A Journal of Inquiry and Practice* 12, no. 2 (2013): 223.

57. From the section entitled "General Norms," attention has been directed by American institutions to mission and identity (cf. Arts. 2.3; 4.1), enacting pastoral care for students (cf. Art. 6.1), and the proportion of Catholic vs. non-Catholic teachers (cf. Art. 4.4). Given that the document has the tone of an exhortation, albeit promulgated with the force of law, it is regrettable that institutions rarely have the resources to undertake institutional discussion of large parts of the document, which clearly intends to offer a teaching parallel to the post-conciliar tradition of teaching on Catholic Schools.

58. On documents for institutional vision, see C. C. Morphew and M. Hartley, "Mission Statements: A Thematic Analysis of Rhetoric Across Institutional Type," *Journal of Higher Education* 77, no. 3 (2006): 456–71; R. B. Young, "Colleges on the Cross Roads: A Study of Mission Statements of Catholic Colleges and Universities," *Current Issues in Catholic Higher Education* 21, no. 2 (2001): 65–81. M. M. Morey and J. J. Piderit point to students and parents as the crucial audience for clear articulation of mission; cf. *Catholic Higher Education: A Culture in Crisis* (Oxford: Oxford University Press, 2006), 117–18. This book has become a standard text for study of Catholic institutional mission, although its data is limited by almost exclusive dependence upon surveys of administrators. The author thanks the faculty of the 2014–2015 *Catholic Intellectual Tradition Seminar* (Mount St. Mary's University, MD) for intelligent observations about this book.

59. Cf. *GS* 42; 43; 60; 67; 73–76 (http://www.vatican.va/archive/hist_councils/ii_vatican_council/documents/vat-ii_const_19651207_gaudium-et-spes_en.html).

60. Cf. *LG* 1–17; 30–38 (http://www.vatican.va/archive/hist_councils/ii_vatican_council/documents/vat-ii_const_19641121_lumen-gentium_en.html); *AA* (http://www.vatican.va/archive/hist_councils/ii_vatican_council/documents/vat-ii_decree_19651118_apostolicam-actuositatem_en.html); cf. as one example of a recognized need for theological reflection, Yves Congar's *Lay People in the Church: A Study for a Theology of the Laity*, trans. Donald Attwater (Westminster MD: Newman Press, 1957).

61. See, for example, *Fides et Ratio* 9; 45 (http://w2.vatican.va/content/john-paul-ii/en/encyclicals/documents/hf_jp-ii_enc_14091998_fides-et-ratio.html#-1).

62. Philip Gleason, *Contending with Modernity: Catholic Higher Education in the Twentieth Century* (Oxford: Oxford University Press, 1995), 94. Gleason discusses the debates of Catholic educators in the 1930s on the "liberal arts" and how "Catholic liberal arts" might compare to new curriculum put in place by Robert M. Hutchins at the University of Chicago (247). At a 1937 meeting of the National Catholic Education Association's Midwest Region, Hutchins in turn criticized Catholic educators of imitating the worst tendencies of secular colleges ("athleticism, collegialism, vocationalism, and anti-intellectualism"), rather than cultivating their own best tendencies ("dedication to research, to high academic standards, and to inculcating good work habits").

63. Cf. *Fides et Ratio*, 45 and 77 (http://w2.vatican.va/content/john-paul-ii/en/encyclicals/documents/hf_jp-ii_enc_14091998_fides-et-ratio.html); *La Sapienza*

Lecture of January 18, 2008 (http://w2.vatican.va/content/benedict-xvi/en/speeches/2008/january/documents/hf_ben-xvi_spe_20080117_la-sapienza.html); see also Joseph Cardinal Ratzinger, *Principles of Catholic Theology* (San Francisco: Ignatius, 1987), 315–64.

64. Accreditation serves to enforce uniform quality and excellence; its criteria merit critical examination over time, given a diversity of institutional models. The most significant shift in Catholic institutions during the 1960s was the requirement that members of governing boards be disinterested, and therefore *not* drawn from the university itself (e.g. deans or professors). They should also represent a broad public interest, and strong *autonomy* is said to be necessary for this; cf. Commission on Higher Education, Middle States Association of Colleges and Schools, *Characteristics of Excellence in Higher Education: Standards for Accreditation* (Philadelphia: Middle States Commission on Higher Education, 1982).

65. John Tracy Ellis, "American Catholics and the Intellectual Life," *Thought* 30 (1955): 351–88; Thomas O'Dea, *American Catholic Dilemma* (New York: Sheed and Ward, 1958).

66. John Cogley, "The Future of an Illusion," *Commonweal*, June 2, 1967, 310–16; John D. Donovan, *The Academic Man in the Catholic College* (New York: Sheed and Ward, 1964); Philip Gleason, "What Made Identity a Problem?," in *The Challenge and Promise of a Catholic University*, ed. Theodore M. Hesburgh (Notre Dame: University of Notre Dame Press, 1994), 97. The specific event in 1965 that occasioned the harshest declarations was the faculty-union-administration battle at St. John's University in Queens, NY; this resulted in some administrative restructuring as well as lay membership on the board. The press release from October 15, 1965 states, "The University is clearly prepared to undertake the necessary catharsis needed to achieve the specifically identified objective—academic excellence." See Anthony J. Dosen, *Catholic Higher Education in the 1960s: Issues of Identity, Issues of Governance* (Charlotte, NC: IAP, 2009), 172.

67. Kenneth Garcia, *Academic Freedom and the Telos of the Catholic University* (New York: Palgrave Macmillan, 2009), 40. Garcia cites John Courtney Murray as representative of a balance between intellectual freedom and social-cultural embeddedness: rather than shut out the world, Murray said, the "Catholic intellectual's task was to analyze and understand it.... To seek and love and liberate the truth that is at the heart of every error" (70).

68. It should be observed that the conversation about Catholic higher education in the United States from the years of the Council until the promulgation of the Code in 1983 occurred mostly between a few (clerical) academic leaders and the Curia. This conversation did not "permeate campus life" until the publication of *Ex Corde*; cf. Sandra M. Estanek, *Understanding Student Affairs at Catholic Colleges and Universities: A Comprehensive Resource* (Franklin, WI: Sheed and Ward, 2002), vii.

69. Canon 807. Compare 1376.1 from the 1917 Code (http://www.intratext.com/X/LAT0813.HTM): "The canonical constitution of a Catholic university or faculty is reserved to the Apostolic See."

70. Most colleges founded in the first half of the nineteenth century were founded by bishops; e.g., Georgetown, which was handed over by Bp. John Carroll to the Jesuits only after their restoration. See Philip Gleason, "The American Background of *Ex Corde Ecclesiae*," in *Catholic Universities in Church and Society: A Dialogue on Ex Corde Ecclesiae*, ed. John P. Langan (Georgetown: Georgetown University Press, 1993), 7.

71. Gleason, "The American Background of *Ex Corde Ecclesiae*,", 8–10.

72. http://w2.vatican.va/content/pius-xi/la/apost_constitutions/documents/hf_p-xi_apc_19310524_deus-scientiarum-dominus.html. For this reason Cardinal Pizzardo,

presiding over the Sacred Congregation of Seminaries and Universities, advised against treating universities in detail in any Vatican II document. His words offer an example of the very different European perspective when he reckons that "besides ecclesiastical universities (according to the Apostolic Constitution *Deus Scientiarum Dominus*) there can be counted today about eighty which are called Catholic universities ... forty in North America" (*Acta et Documenta Concilio Oecumenico Vaticano II Apparando*, series 2, vol. 2 [Vatican City: Typis Polyglottis Vaticanis, 1965], Par. 2, 803 [translation in Conn, *Catholic Universities in the United States and Ecclesiastical Authority*, 76]).

73. Found in Alice Gallin, ed., *American Catholic Higher Education* (Notre Dame: University of Notre Dame Press, 1992).

74. The IFCU was founded by papal decree in 1948; a regional branch in North America (the Association of Catholic Colleges and Universities) currently includes more than 90 percent of accredited Catholic colleges and universities. It exists to "help member institutions strengthen their stated Catholic mission and to foster collaboration among Catholic colleges and universities," according to their webpage.

75. The Jesuit Educational Association had imposed co-ordination among Jesuit universities since 1934, but it was eventually pushed aside in favor of ad hoc consultative bodies of university presidents (cf. Gleason, "The American Background of *Ex Corde Ecclesiae*.").

76. The correspondence initiated in 1958 is preserved in the Historical Archive of the Society of Jesus in Rome; it is translated in part by James Jerome Conn, SJ, in *Catholic Universities in the United States and Ecclesiastical Authority* (Rome: Gregoriana, 1991), 62–72.

77. Conn, *Catholic Universities in the United States and Ecclesiastical Authority*, 63.

78. Conn, *Catholic Universities in the United States and Ecclesiastical Authority*, 66n55: "Queste Università, do caratere privato, quanto all direzione, devono allo Stato la loro erezione—approbante semper Ordinario loci et S. Congregatione de Religiosis—e dalla medesima autorità civile ricevono l'autorizzazione di concedere gradi academici che vengono riconosciuti come quelli delle Università Statali" (from Jean-Baptiste Janssens to Giuseppe Pizzardo).

79. The Declaration *Cum Dubium Ortum*, issued on November 17, 1959 by the Sacred Congregation of Seminaries and Universities (*Acta Apostolicae Sedis* 51 [1959], 920), clarifies that any university "entrusted to the secular clergy or a religious family is dependent upon the Sacred Congregation of Seminaries and Universities." The use of the term "dependent" suggests that relationship to the relevant ecclesial authority is necessary to the "essence" of the institution. The Declaration gives broad scope to "dependence," and includes the qualification "in any way [*quomodocumque*] subject"; however, Conn argues (*Catholic Universities* 69) that "curial practice with respect to non-canonically erected universities is not sufficiently definitive." In the end, the offer made in 1961 to canonically erect all existing Jesuit institutions in a single stroke was rejected; this may have been due to questions about guaranteeing ownership of ecclesiastical properties.

80. There is much literature on the Land O'Lakes statement and its relationship to the 1972 IFCU document, the 1980 statement from the USCCB, *Catholic Higher Education and the Pastoral Mission of the Church*, and *Ex Corde Ecclesiae* (http://w2.vatican.va/content/john-paul-ii/en/apost_constitutions/documents/hf_jp-ii_apc_15081990_ex-corde-ecclesiae.html). See "Land O'Lakes Statement: The Nature of the Contemporary Catholic University," in *The Catholic University: A Modern Appraisal*, ed. Neil G. McCluskey (Notre Dame: University of Notre Dame Press, 1970). The event of

the Land O' Lakes meeting is described expansively by Fr. Hesburgh in his autobiography, *God, Country, Notre Dame*, with Jerry Reedy (New York: Doubleday, 1990), 227–45. On the relevance of Hesburgh's friendship with Pope Paul VI, his "ace in the hole," see Michael O'Brien, *Hesburgh: A Biography* (Washington, DC: Catholic University of America Press, 1998), 281.

81. These attributes are largely incorporated into *Ex Corde Ecclesiae*, summarized from the opening paragraph of the 1972 document: (1) Christian inspiration that is institutional and not merely individual; (2) reflection on human knowledge in light of the faith, and contributing to the same; (3) fidelity to Christianity as it comes through the Church; and (4) institutional service to the People of God and the human family. Cf. *Ex Corde*, 13.

82. See McCluskey, *The Catholic University: A Modern Appraisal*, 347. It is clear at this time, with a new Prefect at the head of the Congregation, that the desire for some common norms is both well-intentioned and necessary in preparation for drafting the new Code of Canon Law.

83. "Declaration *Cum dubium ortum*," from the Sacred Congregation of Seminaries and Universities (*Acta Apostolicae Sedis* 51 [1959], 920).

84. "Observations of the Sacred Congregation for Catholic Education on the Project of the Document Prepared by the Council and the Committee of the International Federation of Catholic Universities (IFCU) during the Meeting Held at Grottaferrata-Rome (February 3–5, 1972)," May 20, 1972 (ACCUA Archives; cf. also http://cathol-ichighereducation.org/documents/Vatican%20Docs%20on%20Edu/The%20Problems%20of%20Updating%20Catholic%20Universities_%20S.Con.%20pro%20Insti.%20Cath._%20Rome,%2010,%20May%201972.pdf).

85. Cardinal Gabriel-Marie to the Presidents of Catholic Colleges and Universities, Association of Catholic Colleges and Universities Archives (October 21, 1974).

86. Hesburgh and Reedy, *God, Country, Notre Dame*, 234.

87. "A Summary of Some Responses to Cardinal Garrone's Letter to American Catholic Colleges of Oct. 7 [sic], 1974, prepared by College and University Department, NCEA," Association of Catholic Colleges and Universities Archives (October 1975).

88. David Burrell, CSC, "Beyond 'Dissent' and 'Academic Freedom,'" in *Universities: Catholic and American, Responsible and Free*, ed. Alice Gallin (Washington, DC: ACCU, 1987), 52. Burrell is speaking particularly as a theologian and Holy Cross priest; he is also a respected philosopher. The question of the *mandatum* granted to theologians, as per Canon 812, clarified the language of mission vs. mandate deployed in Pius XII's dealings with lay groups. This was discussed during the drafting of *Apostolicam Actuositatem* at the Council; bishops wanted to see more theological content in the *mandatum*, rather than merely juridical relationship, precisely in order to raise up the dignity of a particular work as ecclesial. In the end, they avoided the topic as beyond the scope of their committee. They did conclude that the *mandatum* describes a relationship of particular unity with the local bishop (entailing both care and solicitude), and that it could not be merely individual. *Ex Corde* interprets the *mandatum* as individual, but not merely juridical, expressing the expectation that Catholic theologians, deputized by their *institutions* to teach, will to the best of their knowledge teach in accord with established Catholic doctrine. The moral rather than juridical character of the *mandatum* allows for freedom of inquiry, while it should inform the *desire* of the individual teacher in light of the ecclesial mission of his or her institution; see Robert P. Deeley, *The Mandate for Those who Teach Theology in Institutes of Higher Studies* (Rome: Patrizio Graziani, 1986), 46; 170. This was rejected by American academic clerics when preliminary

drafts of the new code were circulated, and subsequently minimized through inter-pretation; cf. Richard P. McBrien, "Newness in Fidelity," *Notre Dame Magazine* 12, no. 2 (1983): 41; see also Conn on McBrien's idea of internal vs. external teaching authority of the hierarchy (*Catholic Universities in the United States and Ecclesiastical Authority*, 307). One could argue that the issue of the theologians' *mandatum* is too prominent in recent discussions about Catholic identity, with the net effect of reserving Catholic mission to a small portion of the faculty.

89. By contrast, see Pio Card. Laghi, Eduardo Card. Pironio, and Paul Card. Poupard, *The Presence of the Church in the University and in University Culture*, May 22, 1994, http://www.vatican.va/roman_curia/pontifical_councils/cultr/documents/rc_pc_cultr_doc_22051994_presence_en.html: "[The Catholic university] only achieves its full identity when, at one and the same time, it gives proof of being rigorously serious as a member of the international community of knowledge and expresses its Catholic identity through an explicit link with the Church, at both local and universal levels."

90. See, for example, Charles L. Currie, SJ, "Finding New Structures: Responsive Governance for a New Age," *Conversations on Jesuit Higher Education* 45 (April 2014): 19–21. This has been linked to revision of the relationship between religious orders and their sponsored institution; cf. Thomas C. Hunt, *Handbook of Research on Catholic Higher Education* (Charlotte, NC: Information Age Publishing, 2003), 122.

91. Hesburgh and Reedy, *God, Country, Notre Dame*, 171, 236. In a letter from Hesburgh to Cardinal Garrone (March 30, 1970), he argues that any kind of "sub-ordination" to the Church is simply contrary to lay presence on a board of trustees. Fordham president Joseph A. O'Hare said that we live in a "post-clerical age" (Conn, *Catholic Universities in the United States and Ecclesiastical Authority*, 308); the implica-tion for the university is that its very essence is to be "independence of ecclesiasti-cal authorities." The university is not part of the Church, as it clearly falls outside of canon law and therefore ecclesiastical authority; however, the "Church is present in the university."

92. See *Lumen Gentium*, paragraphs 10–14, 30–32.

93. *Ex Corde Ecclesiae* 5.1.

94. This is cited frequently even today; cf. Anthony J. Dosen's account of the inter-view in which this phrase was first employed by Hesburgh, in *Catholic Higher Education in the 1960s: Issues of Identity, Issues of Governance* (Charlotte NC: Information Age Publishing, 2009), 118.

95. See, for example, in the volume containing notes on the Kinshasa meeting of the IFCU, R. J. Henle, SJ, "Regional Report for North America," *Catholicorum Universitatum Internationalis Federatio* (Paris: n.p., 1968), 224.

96. *Ex Corde*, 13; *Lumen Gentium*, 37.

97. Melanie M. Morey and John J. Piderit, *Catholic Higher Education: a Culture in Crisis* (Oxford: Oxford University Press, 2006), 83.

98. *The Presence of the Church in the University and in University Culture*.

16

Nostra Aetate

Gavin D'Costa

Introduction

The *Declaration on the Relationship of the Church to Non-Christian Religions (Nostra Aetate = NA)*, promulgated on October 28, 1965, was heralded as a dramatic change of attitude by the Catholic Church toward the world religions. Elsewhere, I have treated the doctrinal aspect of this claim, arguing that there was a development of doctrine that took place as well as innovation, but no formal conciliar or papal magisterial doctrinal discontinuity. There were radical elements of discontinuity in terms of social and pastoral strategy toward other religions. In this sense, Vatican II was deeply significant and its impact long lasting.[1] These different levels of discontinuity within doctrinal continuity were in keeping with Pope John XXIII's call to the Council at its opening: to seek to freshly implement doctrinal teachings in the modern world.[2] The doctrinal backbone regarding other religions is found in the *Dogmatic Constitution on the Church (Lumen Gentium = LG)* 16, and the development and working out of this is found in *NA* 1–4.

In this chapter I address three tasks simultaneously. First, I summarize the key achievements of *LG* 16 and *NA* 1–4. Second, I look at the reception of three aspects of teachings found in *LG* and *NA* related to (a) dogmatic questions; (b) issues related to Judaism; and (c) issues related to Islam. I do not attend to Hinduism and Buddhism, the only two other religions explicitly named in *NA* apart from Judaism and Islam, because the Council paid less detailed attention to the latter, and the reception regarding Judaism and Islam has been in the forefront in the English-speaking world.[3] I limit myself to the English-speaking world. I give limited attention to the reception of *NA* by non-Christian communities, although this is an important area of reception. I selectively examine "reception" in terms of Catholic theologians and the different offices of the ecclesial Magisterium. These two receptive traditions constantly inter-act, sometimes in friction, but often in creative tension. Thirdly, I indicate areas that seem most promising for future exploration, related to the trajecto-ries of ongoing reception of NA. These three foci will help the reader see the contours of a hugely colorful and complex map.

Before proceeding, it will be helpful to briefly indicate how the Holy See institutionally supports the importance of NA and has ensured, how-ever imperfectly, NA's continuing reception and implementation within the Catholic world. During the Council the Secretariat for non-Christians was formed. It was renamed in 1988: the Pontifical Council for Interreligious Dialogue (PCID) and was given a special secretary for relations to Islam.[4] In 2006 the PCID was briefly "merged" by placing the leadership of the Council under the auspices of the Pontifical Council for Culture. This move, initiated by Pope Benedict XVI, was interpreted by some as a demotion of status.

Others interpreted this as signaling a shift in the understanding of "reli-gion" away from a purely "spiritual" notion to a more holistic socio-political view. In 2007 the original status of the PCID was restored, following some of the repercussions of Pope Benedict's infamous Regensburg speech. A separate dicastery was required to handle the high level media issues related to the growth of Islam and its high profile in Europe and the Middle East. The PCID runs a journal, Pro Dialogo, keeps a Directory of Catholic interfaith organizations, and seeks to further its founding aims (1) to promote respect, mutual understanding, and collaboration between Catholics and the followers of others religious traditions; (2) to encourage the study of religions; and (3) to promote the formation of persons dedicated to dialogue. The PCID has also developed many consultations on key questions as they arise, sometimes work-ing with the World Council of Churches, investigating for example, the thorny question of interfaith prayer.[5] Pope John Paul II's interfaith prayer meeting in 1986 (and again in 1993 and 2002) had a high profile, but the concern about what this meeting projected to a wider public caused Pope Benedict's modifi-cation of the ceremony in 2011.[6] Pope Francis's "Abrahamic" prayer meeting with Presidents Peres of Israel and Abbas of Palestine in 2014 indicated a new and interesting direction on interfaith prayer.

There is one area where the PCID is possibly vulnerable. In being the sole dicastery related to good interreligious relations, the profile of mission in relation to dialogue has been obscured. This was partially addressed in 1984 by the Secretariat, and more urgently in 1991 with the Congregation for the Evangelization of Peoples (CEP). However, non-Christians have their main contact with the PCID, not the CEP, so the continued misperception from out-side the Church, and often within, is that mission and evangelization are not central to the Catholic Church. Some argue that the splitting of the Pontifical Commission for Religious Relations with the Jews (PCRRJ), founded in 1974, from the PCID is also problematic, but there are historical and theological fac-tors for this division grounded in Christianity's Jewish roots.

A. Brief Summary of *NA*'s Teachings on a Key Dogmatic Issue, Its Reception, and Future Trajectories

The Salvation Question

LG 14–16 is crucial to understanding the dogmatic framework within which *NA* operates. This hermeneutic rule was formalized at the 1984 Bishop's Synod and stated that Dogmatic Constitutions should be employed to properly interpret Decrees and Declarations.[7] Surprisingly, some important commentaries and scholarly articles on *NA* did not address *LG* in explicating *NA*, which inevitably skewed the reception process, not least regarding certain doctrinal questions. One such question has been the salvific status or otherwise of non-Christian religions. The Council did not formally address this question. It reiterated the accepted pre-Conciliar position that salvation was possible for invincibly ignorant non-Catholics under certain conditions.[8] How this was possible and whether it was despite or through non-Christian religions was not a concern of the Fathers. That was far too technical a question and one that was unresolved among theologians.

Nevertheless, it became a central concern in the reception of *NA* for the simple reason that the positive attitude found in *NA* toward the world religions along with *LG* 16's acknowledgement that salvation was possible outside the visible Church raised the question, How was this salvation possible: through or despite the religions? For instance, of the non-theistic religions, *NA* acknowledged that which is "true and holy," along with "spiritual and moral good things, as well as the socio-cultural values" (*NA* 2). Regarding Islam, it affirmed far more, especially its central monotheistic truth: "they worship the one God" (*NA* 3). About Judaism, *NA* affirmed a "spiritual" unity through a joint "faith and election" (*NA* 4). The Council was concerned to be positive. However, this led some theologians to argue that these positive comments endorsed the view that the religions provided the salvific means for those who lived within them.[9] The balancing claims in the Council against this view ranged from the insistence on always bearing witness to the Christian faith (*NA* 2; and *AG* [*Ad Gentes* = *AG*] 6, 8, 11); to the significant damage done to humans through sin and the power of Satan (*LG* 16); to the truth of the Catholic Church (*LG* 1, 8, 14–16) as the path founded by God for all persons (*AG* 7, 10); and to the claim that other religions were *praeparatio evangelicae* (*LG* 2, 9, 16, 17; *AG* 3, 9, 11, 15), a preparation for the Gospel of salvation.

There have been different interpretations of the Council on this point among theologians and a slow process of clarification by the Magisterium in response to these debates. The reception of the Council on this question roughly developed along three different avenues. Karl Rahner's theology of the "anonymous Christian" and "anonymous Christianity" deeply influenced readings and interpretation of the Council.[10] Ironically, Rahner, a Jesuit, was clear that the Council did not formally address this question, but he also felt his own *theologoumenon* was not explicitly ruled out by the Council.[11] This indicates that reception can be predicated on many other factors than the text itself, such as the status of a particular theologian and the cultural zeitgeist. Rahner argued that non-Christian religions should be viewed analogously to Israel before Christ, as a legitimate path to salvation until such time that their adherents discovered the historical and existential truth of the Gospel, whereupon Christianity became for Judaism, or that particular Jew, the absolute means to salvation. Rahner's "analogy" defended Israel's sui generis character, but also allowed for many provisional salvific, or what Rahner called "lawful," religions. Rahner viewed other religions as salvific means included in God's plan, but he also maintained that salvific grace was always causally dependent upon Christ. Hence the term anonymous Christian and Christianity: indicating Christ's final and efficient causal saving action working in individuals and in their religions, such that the true telos of all humans was the Catholic Church. Subsequently, this "inclusivist" approach (for it "included" other religions within Christianity's economy of salvation) was often associated as the one formally taught by the Roman Catholic Church, as it seemed to explain different elements found in the Council: the positive significance of other religions, the necessity of mission, and Christ and his Church as the means of salvation.[12] However, Rahner's approach on this matter, from the slim evidence of debates on the floor of the Council, was in fact viewed with caution by key Council Fathers, who felt it undermined the mission and the importance of the Church.[13]

Jacques Dupuis, SJ, developed Rahner's position, drawing heavily upon Pope John Paul II's reception and development of Council teachings on these matters.[14] Dupuis noted two specific points of development. First, the Pope clarified that grace operates through cultures and religions, not only through the interior conscience and soul of the human person. A number of theologians had argued that conscience, not the religions, mediated grace.[15] Conscience was unambiguously affirmed in LG 16; and the status of the religions was contested after the Council. Dupuis saw this as an advance from the Council. Second, the Pope taught that the Holy Spirit was at work in these cultures and religions. Religions could not just be attributed to human searching and grasping after the truth. Dupuis saw in these two developments of teaching papal approval of the Rahnerian position. However, Dupuis also developed Rahner's position in positing that other religions must be included positively and enduringly within God's salvific plan. This follows if they were used by the Holy Spirit to positively form children of God. He argued that the causality of the Church in salvation should be understood in terms of moral and final causality, through its prayers for non-Christians, and not in terms of efficient causality.[16]

For Dupuis, as with Rahner, there is no question about Christ's efficient and final saving causality. His significant difference from Rahner was related to the role of the Church. Dupuis called himself a "pluralist-inclusivist,"[17] indicating that he was developing Rahner's position, with his unique anchoring in Christology, but with a new angle on ecclesiology regarding the source of all salvation. Dupuis saw his position as drawing out what was implicit in the Council and made explicit in the post-Conciliar magisterium. As we will note in a moment, the Magisterium, acting through the Congregation for the Doctrine of the Faith, saw Dupuis's position as open to problematic interpretations.

A second line of reception opened up, sometimes harshly reacting against the above. Hans Urs von Balthasar had vigorously objected to Rahner's notion of anonymous Christianity and did not think the Council endorsed Rahner's trajectory.[18] Balthasar, along with the majority of Catholic theologians at the time, and along with magisterial teaching up until that period, viewed the religions (apart from Israel) as human striving. The history of Israel and its covenant pointing to Christ for its consummation mark a special salvation history. In contrast, the history of religions, in all its complexity, partook of general revelation, or what was sometimes called primitive revelation. God never left Himself without witness, but He also had chosen a particular path preparing for Christ, His unique self-revelation. Balthasar and many other theologians thus read the Council through this more traditional lens, which was termed "exclusivist," as it affirmed the sole and unique truth of Catholic Christianity.[19] Unlike some Protestant forms of "exclusivism," which hold all non-Christians to be damned, Catholics could not reach this conclusion given the teachings of the Council. The truth of Christ's revelation is central to this form of "exclusivism," not the exclusion of non-Catholics from salvation.

This second exclusivist trajectory of reception was thus far more cautious about the status of the religions. Ralph Martin has argued against Rahner's claim that LG 16 was the greatest achievement of the Council in endorsing "salvation optimism."[20] Martin argues for "salvation pessimism" from a close reading of the last sentence of LG 16 and the tradition.[21] Similarly, in contrast to the first tradition of reception, Ilaria Morali interprets Pope John Paul II's teachings in sharp contrast to Dupuis. She argues that if all conciliar teachings are kept in tension, the acknowledgement of grace and the Holy Spirit working in other religions does not indicate their salvific efficacy in an objective manner, nor does it detract from their objective error and shortcomings.[22] This point was reiterated by the Magisterium through the Congregation for the Doctrine of the Faith.

For theologians working within this second trajectory of reception, the important question is not related to the salvific efficacy of other religions. This is not possible, as these religions do not preach Christ, who is God's self-revelation. The question instead is to explain how invincibly ignorant non-Christians may be saved if they die without any knowledge of Christ, and for some, without any knowledge of God (non-theists). If salvation in its fullest sense of justification and beatific vision is possible for those who die as invincibly ignorant non-Christians, does this mean that justification is possible without explicit knowledge of the triune God? If yes, then salvation requires no faith and knowledge of Christ and the trinity. Curiously, this links up with another vexed issue: the salvation of unbaptized infants. Interestingly, before the Council, this "solution" had been utilized by some theologians who saw non-Christians as analogous to unbaptized infants.[23]

In 2007 the International Theological Commission (ITC) has given guidance on this matter.[24] It suggested that such infants may be saved through the prayers of the Church, invoking the causality and efficacy of the Church and Christ. While this causality issue is important, the analogy has a crucial weakness. It erases the meaning of the non-Christian religion and the free will of those in other religions. The analogy is more helpful in its explanation of the causality of the Church and Christ in the plan of salvation, which is so central to addressing the situation of non-Christians.

On the other hand, if the answer to the question, whether justification is possible without explicit knowledge of the triune God, is no, then other problems arise. If the non-Christian must come to some explicit knowledge of the Gospel to attain full justification, this requirement need not negate the potential value of the non-Christian religion, but it does give an objective "limit" to what can be attained within that religion. The limit regards the objective truth of who God is: trinity, with the Son incarnate in the historical Jesus. Anything short of this is not the full and clear truth that is the deposit of faith. However, it opens up the question as to how full justification can be attained without faith in God's trinity at the time of death. Some theologians have pointed to a post-mortem solution to resolve the tensions.[25] This would properly allow for the maturation of the truth, goodness, and holiness present in the non-Christian religions to come to full fruition, so that explicit faith in Christ and the triune God become possible as a condition of the beatific vision. That this maturation is also required, although in a different sense, for Catholics who must undergo purgatorial purification before entry into the beatific vision, indicates that the matter is complex and moves between the subjective and objective levels in a way that is not entirely transparent in this life. Some theologians understandably feel uncomfortable by the speculative and potentially individualist cast in this solution, but they also see a purgatorial solution in a more communal fashion, bringing all humanity to its completion.[26]

If the question has been framed correctly, either a "no" or a "yes" answer will require further explanation for how salvation and justification is *received*. That it is *given* through the Paschal Mystery of Christ's death for all women and men, as taught in *Gaudium et Spes* (= GS) 22 and reiterated in the post-Conciliar magisterium, seems clear. How it is received by those who die as invincibly ignorant non-Christians is the important, unresolved issue.

The final trajectory of the Council's reception is a radical development from Rahner's inclusivism, unsupported by Rahner. This position removed Christ's salvific causality entirely and emphasizes the non-Christian religions as genuinely independent means of salvation through God's, not Christ's, causality. The Church obviously plays no role. This allowed for a plurality of salvific means. Theologians like Paul Knitter,[27] once a disciple of Rahner, argued that the Council supported this radical view in its positive teachings about other religions. Knitter argues that NA indicated that the religions contained genuine objective means of truth and grace: "God," for instance, in the case of Islam; and "God" and "faith and covenant," in the case of Judaism.[28] Some theologians further argue that the post-conciliar magisterium began a U-turn after the Council because of their "conservative" instincts.[29] This minority reception tradition was dubbed "pluralism" in its affirmation of plural religions as salvifically efficacious in their own right. Pluralism was seen by its advocates as rejecting paternalism and religious imperialism. Pluralism was also attractive to some Asian Catholics keen on seeking an Indian identity breaking away from the European cast of Latin Catholicism. This allows such Indian theologians to give greater affirmation to Hinduism and Buddhism than had taken place at the Council.[30]

The papal magisterium has reacted consistently since the Council in rejecting "pluralism," with Pope Benedict XVI being most vocal on this point given the ravages of "relativism" in late European modernity. "Pluralism" was seen as a species of "indifferentism" that was consistently condemned prior to the Council. The inclusivist reception trajectory provides an interesting testing of the borderlands regarding the unfolding of the Council's legacy. The Dupuis "case," sitting on the cusp of inclusivism and pluralism, indicates the complexity of reception and its interaction with the Magisterium. Dupuis's main work was investigated by the Congregation for the Doctrine of the Faith resulting in a *Notification* on his book in 2001.[31] While not finding Dupuis guilty of error, his work was found to be susceptible to misunderstandings in six areas. The *Notification* helps chart the limits of theological exploration by indicating positions that are erroneous within the six areas. The two key areas for us regard the trinitarian action of God's saving economy and the role of the Church in that economy. On the first, the *Notification* maintains the sole and universal salvific mediation of Christ's work, such that it is contrary "to the Catholic faith to hold that the salvific action of the Holy Spirit extends beyond the one universal salvific economy of the Incarnate Word" (5). On the second, it affirms the role of the Church in that economy so that all peoples are called to become part of the Church, as she is the "sign and instrument" (6) of salvation for everyone. The *Notification* then clarifies (8) the question about other religions as means of salvation:

> It is therefore legitimate to maintain that the Holy Spirit accomplishes salvation in non-Christians also through those elements of truth and goodness present in the various religions; however, to hold that these religions, considered as such, are ways of salvation, has no foundation in Catholic theology, also because they contain omissions, insufficiencies and errors [note: Cf. SECOND VATICAN COUNCIL, *Lumen gentium*, 16; *Nostra aetate*, 2; *Ad gentes*, 9; PAUL VI, *Evangelii nuntiandi*, 53; JOHN PAUL II, *Redemptoris missio*, 55; CONGREGATION FOR THE DOCTRINE OF THE FAITH, Declaration *Dominus Iesus*, 8] regarding fundamental truths about God, man and the world. . . . Furthermore, the fact that the elements of truth and goodness present in the various world religions may prepare peoples and cultures to receive the salvific event of Jesus Christ does not imply that the sacred texts of these religions can be considered as complementary to the Old Testament, which is the immediate preparation for the Christ event.

The religions, despite all that is positively said about them, cannot be considered as "ways of salvation." The religions cannot be considered on a par with Israel, whose history is sui generis, thus blocking a kind of Rahnerian analogy that is often pursued. Finally, all religions in differing degrees (given Israel's difference) may act as a preparation (*praeparatio evangelicae*), but "preparation" is a preliminary instruction to the Gospel and not the Gospel itself. This is because at the level of revelation, the truth of God is trinity, which establishes a genuine difference and an objective inadequacy in the non-Christian religions. This point was made differently in *DI* (*Dominus Iesus* = *DI*) 21–22, published a year earlier, with a phrase that had caused some (possibly unnecessary) offense: "If it is true that the followers of other religions can receive divine grace, it is also certain that objectively speaking they are in a *gravely deficient* situation in comparison with those who, in the Church, have the fullness of the means of salvation."[32] The same point is formally taught by Pope John Paul II: God, who desires to call all peoples to himself in Christ and to communicate to them the fullness of his revelation and love, "does not fail to make himself present in many ways, not only to individuals, but also to entire peoples through their spiritual riches, of which their religions are the main and essential expression even when they contain 'gaps, insufficiencies and errors.' "[33] The *Notification* thus underwrites John Paul II's developments of teachings arising from the Council, but indicates that these do not lead to contradicting already-established teachings. The second paragraph cited from the Notification resists the analogy of Israel being applied to other religions, something that Dupuis does, following Rahner. We see a clear rejection of pluralism and some forms of inclusivism and a continuing conversation with "inclusivist pluralism."

A tentative conclusion is in order. After the Council, the major lines of reception by theologians and the Magisterium would indicate (a) that pluralist theologies are incompatible with the Catholic faith; (b) that certain sorts of inclusivism are problematic when they grant other religions salvific status in any objective sense that makes them comparable or convergent with Catholicism; (c) that Catholic exclusivist approaches certainly keep the Council's teachings intact; (d) that in the light of the post-Conciliar magisterium's affirmation of religious cultures and the activity of the Holy Spirit within them, those exclusivists who view other religions purely as "human action" need to acknowledge the development of teaching on this matter.

Consequently, it is possible to identify four areas for further dogmatic research. First, the varying meanings of *praeparatio evangelicae*—a term frequently used in the Council and subsequently—must be investigated to illuminate possible models and their limitations when conceptualizing the status of non-Christian religions. Second, the manner in which original sin has damaged the human search for God (so as to clarify whether salvation optimism can ever be justified) is required, but also to clarify the action of the cross over sinful humanity, now and in the eschaton. The sea change from salvific pessimism to salvific optimism within modern European and Anglo-American Catholic culture went undetected at the Council, although it was present as a constant cultural condition in the reception of the Council texts. Third, the need to explicate a profound theology of mission, which hardly began at the Council, is called for. In some respects, the New Evangelization has focused on re-evangelization and only tangentially addressed the "necessity" of the evangelization to all peoples. Fourth, a fuller theology of justification is required to clarify precisely how invincibly ignorant non-Christians enter into the beatific vision.

B. Brief Summary of NA's Teachings on the Jewish People, Its Reception, and Future Trajectories

The Council's Teaching on Deicide and on Covenant

Christian attitudes to the Jewish people have been mainly negative, predicated on two points: the Jewish people rejected Christ—indeed they killed him, and thus forfeited their covenant; and that since that time they have continued in this obstinacy. The Council addressed and rejected both these points. Once again, LG 16 is vital in setting the scene. LG 16 frames the matter of the religions in terms of "those who have not yet accepted the Gospel" and who are "related [ordinantur] to the Church in various ways." The footnote to this opening sentence, note 18, has been long neglected in explicating the Council's vision.[34] Then follows an almost verbatim quote from the Latin Vulgate Bible of Romans 9:4–5 and 11:28–29, highlighting the themes that would most acutely feature in the reception of the Council. It states that the Jewish people are those "to whom the testaments and promises were given," ensuring their "election." The closing sentence of this single Latin sentence affirms, "God never goes back on his gifts and his calling." The covenant with the Jews is not revoked by God. What precisely are the implications of this Pauline scriptural teaching? This would be *the* key issue of reception after the Council.[35]

NA's initial draft was solely concerned to rebut the deicide charge against "the Jews" and the terrible tradition of contempt that followed. The *Tridentine Catechisms* had already stated that sin per se, not the Jews per se, was to blame for the death of Christ, and that Catholics shared in this condition of sin; indeed they were more culpable than the Jewish crowds at the crucifixion.[36] However, the dark days of the Holocaust had exposed the depths of anti-Semitism within Christian culture and in neo-pagan Nazism. The intense struggle at the Council over the "deicide" charge and the passage of NA is well documented.[37] The final vote was an unambiguous victory over what Jules Isaac, the Jewish historian, had called "the teaching of contempt."[38] NA also explicated Romans 11, reiterating LG 16: that the "Jews still remain very dear to God, whose gift and call are without regret." NA affirmed a deep spiritual patrimony, through Abraham, Moses, and the prophets, and the Church's dependence on this ancient root onto which the gentile church had been grafted (Rom 11:17–24).

Adam Gregerman, a Jewish commentator, rightly notes that "it was only after some time that the brief remarks in *Nostra Aetate* about God's continuing covenant with the Jews, not the rejection of the deicide charge, took center stage."[39] One might add that Catholic re-readings of Romans 9–11 is one major legacy of the Council. But first, let me briefly register some Jewish "reception" to the teachings and how that reception has prompted Catholic theologians and the ecclesial magisterium.

Jewish Reception of the Council and Some Catholics Responses

ANTI-SEMITISM

Given the internal diversity of modern Judaism, there were varied and complex Jewish reactions.[40] There was affirmation of all that was taught and generally a warm reception. However, some Jews had concerns about what was not said. One line of questioning, still present, asks why there is no clear acknowledgement of the Catholic Church's role in anti-Semitism, let alone any apology or repentance for its sins against the Jews. Since the Council, this concern has settled around three issues: the institutional level of Catholic anti-Semitism such that the Catholic Church itself should acknowledge its guilt and failings and seek repentance as a Church; the level of anti-Semitism in certain popes, particularly Pius XII, should be acknowledged; and the possibility of New Testament anti-Semitism must be faced. This latter is most forcefully expressed by Catholic theologians.[41] There are historical and theological issues at stake in this reception history.

European and the American Bishops' conferences have made formal statements that address ecclesial complicity and silence, but have localized these through their national churches expressing repentance. For example, in 1995, the Bishops of the Netherlands acknowledged "a tradition of theological and ecclesiastical anti-Judaism," which they firmly reject.[42] In 1997 the French bishops acknowledged that "too many of the Church's pastors committed an offense, by their silence [and such a silence] was a sin. . . . We recognize that the Church of France [shares] with the Christian people the responsibility for failing to lend their aid" to the Jewish people. This section finishes: "We beg God's pardon, and we call upon the Jewish people to hear our words of repentance."[43] Given the differences between local churches, this organic process seems appropriate, but this leaves untouched the need for a central magisterial response on behalf of the entire church.

Pope John Paul II returned to these issues constantly.[44] Speaking through the important PCRRJ document, *We Remember: A Reflection on the Shoah* (1988),[45] the Pope distanced the Catholic Church from all three issues being contested, while admitting that many Catholics, at all levels, had acted sinfully. The Pope asked for pardon from God and from the Jewish people for sins against the Jewish people:

> "In the Christian world—I do not say on the part of the Church as such—erroneous and unjust interpretations of the New Testament regarding the Jewish people and their alleged culpability have

circulated for too long, engendering feelings of hostility toward this people." Such interpretations of the New Testament have been totally and definitively rejected by the Second Vatican Council (section 3). . . .[46]

The Pope also attributes anti-Semitism to neo-paganism:

The Shoah was the work of a thoroughly modern neo-pagan regime. Its anti-Semitism had its roots outside of Christianity and, in pursuing its aims, it did not hesitate to oppose the Church and persecute her members also. (section 4)[47]

The sinfulness of "the Church" and whether Christianity itself is guilty of anti-Semitism are problematic, since they are not susceptible to purely historical analysis but also bear upon doctrinal issues. There has been much theological discussion about the notion of the "Church as such" being sinful, given the teaching that she is made up of sinners, but nonetheless spotless—in so much as the Church represents Christ.[48] Can the Church as "spotless" (in its objective sacraments, its *de fide* teachings, and in both thus being Christ's presence here on earth) actually be sinful or wrong? This would amount to arguing there is a higher truth than revelation if that which the Church formally proclaimed as revelation could be said to be wrong. In this specific case it would require one to show that the Magisterium solemnly and formally taught anti-Semitism was a Christian duty. Here we would have a clear case of the Church "as such" sinning, in so much as its formal exercise of the Magisterium would be compromised. While there is no denying there are "theological and ecclesiastical traditions" of anti-Semitism, there is no clear evidence that the Magisterium has formally taught and proclaimed anti-Semitism.

Likewise, on the other question, if New Testament scripture itself was seen to be objectively wrong, rather than interpreted incorrectly, then the primary source of authority in Catholic ecclesiology collapses. This does not require that questions are repressed or not asked regarding the New Testament's teachings, but one must also recognize that the interpretation of the New Testament is by the rule of faith, notwithstanding the importance of historical criticism. If anti-Semitism within Christian culture can be critiqued through the recovery of scripture, which is what happened at Vatican II, then the notion of Christian culture being intrinsically anti-Semitic is problematized. Admittedly, these matters also have to be decided through sifting historical evidence, and the historical issues are far from resolved. These matters are also dependent on particular ecclesiological models, none of which go unquestioned by theologians. The legacy of the Council asks for a humble and honest inspection of these issues. The depths of anti-Semitism within Christian culture should never be underestimated.

COVENANT AND COVENANTS The second area touched upon in Jewish reception raises the question that many Catholic theologians have been grappling with: what is the significance of attesting that God has remained faithful to his covenant(s)?[49] Does this testify to God's fidelity and love of his people, whatever they may do? Does it mean that modern-day Judaism enjoys a valid covenant with God? Does Paul's view entail a repudiation of "supersessionist" and "abrogationist" positions (that the Old Testament and Israel are now superseded and invalid), while still affirming a "fulfilment" position (that these earlier covenants find their fulfilment in Christ and are not invalid or abrogated), so that the Jewish patrimony must be fully inculturated into the gentile church?[50] Furthermore, will this "fulfilment" take place through conversion now, or only at the end times? Regarding reception, one cannot predict what will unfold as the Council's teachings are received in the practices of Catholics, especially those closely working with Jews. I will outline and briefly comment on some lines of reception—and only future history will hopefully witness these issues becoming resolved and new ones requiring attention.

The receptions by Catholic theologians are varied. They all believe they are faithful to the Council, but their interpretations are not all compatible. The Magisterium has sometimes entered public discussion to clarify the Church's teachings, and this has helped steer the debate. Senior cardinals as individual teachers have not always agreed on issues. This is to be expected. This was true on the Council floor—and will always be the case. Such differences indicate healthy debate. Key to this debate have been the post-Conciliar teachings emanating from the PCRRJ,[51] the Pontifical Biblical Commissions (PBC),[52] and most especially Pope John Paul II's pontificate in which he regularly addressed Jewish people, sometimes in their synagogues and also in the Holy Land.[53] For pedagogic purposes I will outline five "types" of response.

First, some theologians and biblical scholars argued that St. Paul in Romans had not envisaged that the covenant with the Jews at the time of his writing was actually valid, but rather that Israel's "no" to Christ had a divine purpose. At the end times the Jewish people would accept Jesus as messiah. God had never been unfaithful to his covenant, but those Jews who failed to follow Christ were unfaithful to the covenant. Many argued that the Council was simply stating the resolved position of the Church on this matter.[54] The more conservative wing within this reception tradition holds a supersessionist or abrogationist viewpoint: that the covenant tradition was continued through Christ, so the Church, both Jewish and Gentile, was the continuation of the covenants that had been forfeited by Israel's "no" to Christ. But Israel's final "coming in" at the end times would re-graft them into their covenant to which they had been unfaithful. This position also allowed that God had never changed his mind or gone back on his promises. This reading has come under some pressure from PCRRJ directives, which indicated that Jews today have a "spiritual fecundity" because of their adherence to the Old Testament revelation: "We must remind ourselves how the permanence of Israel is accompanied by a continuous spiritual fecundity, in the rabbinical period, in the Middle Ages and in modern times, taking its start from a patrimony which we long shared."[55] There is of course a world of difference between "spiritual fecundity" and the notion of the Jewish people being in a "valid covenant," but there is also a world of difference between "spiritual fecundity" and the idea of a people whose spiritual identity will only be regained at the end times.

Second, some theologians held that the Council simply did not speak of Jews after the time of Christ but was reflecting only on biblical Israel. These theologians note that in the Council *aula*, the question of contemporary Jewry's theological status had not been present and that Rabbinic Judaism constitutes a new branch in Second-Temple Israel. The textual challenge to this position hangs on the subtle shifts in the Latin translation of the Greek New Testament by which some Catholics argue that the Council intended to affirm the covenantal status of contemporary Judaism. "*Nostra Aetate* rendered a Greek verbless relative clause in Romans 9:4–5 in the present tense: 'theirs is the sonship and the glory and the covenants and the law and the worship and the promises; theirs are the fathers and from them is the Christ according to the flesh.' "[56] The deeper challenge to this position came after the Council in various statements from the PCRRJ that read *NA* 4 as requiring attention to the "spiritual fecundity" of contemporary Judaism.

Third, and returning to the question of "covenant," we find a more sophisticated version of the first model in Rahner's anonymous Christian theory, where Israel's "legitimate validity" exists only until such time as a Jew is confronted with the historical and existential truth of Christ. If they reject the Gospel, their religion became "invalid" *for* them, but not for Jews who have not rejected Christ. Rahner's position is a development from the more conservative reading above, where from the literal moment of Christ's resurrection, Israel becomes invalid in not following Christ. This position hovers between supersessionism and fulfilment.

Fourth, there is a position within which I understand the post-conciliar magisterium to operate.[57] Since God's people are initially forged through the promises and covenants of the Old Testament, then by virtue of that Testament being central to Judaism, Judaism partakes of those covenants. Judaism's fidelity to the covenant(s), rather than God's fidelity which is unquestioned, is hermeneutically complicated by three factors. First, the Jewish understandings of the covenant(s) must be taken seriously, but cannot be determinative for Christian theology. Second, Christian theology's view of the "covenant(s)" is required to make the determinative judgment as to whether this or that form of Judaism is "covenantal" (Christologically understood). The relationship (or hermeneutical gap) between the first and second positions requires considerable discussion. Indeed, it has led to many unresolved lacuna, such as when the PBC argues that Christians must attend to the self-understanding of the Jewish people in terms of their scriptural exegesis and that their reading is a legitimate and possible one. But it then fails to resolve the theological question of how to address incompatible mutually exclusive exegetical outcomes. Such readings may be possible, but does "legitimacy" entail truth or simply that they are not hermeneutically irresponsible readings? The latter is acceptable; the former more problematic. Once more, a Jewish voice warns at a cheap solution here, which could easily lead to relativism.

Catholics and Jews should spend more time plumbing the meaning of the claim that "the Jewish reading of the Bible is a possible one." If this

Jewish reading that is void of any Christology or Christian doctrine is possibly correct, how can a Christian not see it as separate from the good news of Christian Scriptures—i.e., Marcionism or some form of supersessionism? Is it possible for the Jewish reading to be (objectively) correct for Jews but of necessity objectively incorrect for faithful Christians? This is the kind of relativism that for good reason the Church usually rejects. On the level of mutual recognition and good relations, this idea is welcome, but it is not . . . theologically coherent.[58]

There is also a third hermeneutical problem: there is no unitary voice within "Judaism." This is highlighted in understanding the Mosaic covenant and the *halakha* (religious practices) deriving from it. Some progressive Jewish movements have dispensed with *halakha* altogether, while some Orthodox Jews view it as a defining norm.[59] Since Jews are not agreed on what is normative religious Judaism, can a non-Jewish group who claims to be spiritually Semite offer decisive answers? All three questions require considerable attention before the debate can move forward. This task is politically fraught, but theologically necessary.

Apart from Judaism's status, the reality of a shared covenantal history also requires the gentile parts of the Church to recover its Jewish roots and heritage. As John Paul II put it, the "Jewish religion is not 'extrinsic' to us, but in a certain way is 'intrinsic' to us."[60] This is an interesting, demanding, and only more recently discovered legacy of the Council. It is demanding, because for years Judaism has been treated as a blind and cursed figure, external to Catholicism. Now, in this internalizing affirmation of "Judaism" (but whose Judaism?), there is a new danger of failing to take seriously the otherness and diversity of Judaism. Nevertheless, there is a clear need to study and learn from the prayers and piety of Judaism down through the ages, the scriptural exegetical methods and discussions of the rabbis, the debates about the *halakha*, and most controversially, learning from and welcoming Jews who remain Jews while following Jesus. These latter groups, especially for this essay, the Hebrew Catholics (who are Roman Catholics), but also those Protestant, such as Hebrew Christians, Jews for Jesus (who are independent groups with a more Protestant orientation), and the more complex independent Messianic Jews, have been greatly undervalued. They often suffer suspicion from gentile Christians and religious Jews who feel betrayed. In the light of the Council, one might argue there is a special vocation and message in Hebrew Catholics, who bring with them their Jewish patrimony while becoming united to Christ's body in the Catholic Church. Friedman, a prophetic Jewish founder of the Hebrew Catholics, challenged missionary work to the Jews precisely because traditional mission required the rejection of Jewish identity and thus, the destruction of God's chosen people. He argued that only Hebrew Catholics offered a special witness to Israel that had not yet come to Christ.[61] How is the universal church listening to and learning from this local Jewish-Catholic community? The prophetic value of these customs and prayers within Catholicism get inadequate theological attention. It may even be that only communities like the Hebrew Catholics can offer real witness to the Jewish people.

The fifth reception position has moved toward a "two covenant" model. By "two covenant," I indicate the view that the Jews are in a valid covenant and will be saved in that covenant precisely because it is valid. Some argue that this salvation is nevertheless through Christ, and other more radical theologians argue that Jewish salvation is from God, not Christ. Here, the Jewish covenant represents the reality of two covenants and two salvific traditions.[62] The first particular covenant is made to Israel and the Jews; and the second universal covenant, predicated upon the first, is made to the gentiles.[63] This latter position of two covenants and two paths of salvation has been criticised in *DI* 21 and explicitly by Cardinal Koch in a talk to Catholics and Jews.[64]

Cardinal Kasper's comments on *DI* not applying to the Jewish people, while causing some ambiguity, were not in keeping with the readings offered by Cardinals Ratzinger and Dulles.[65] Cardinal Koch, who followed Kasper, has made it clear that there cannot be two covenants, only one; only one people of God, not two; that there cannot be two salvific paths, only one; that the New Testament is not a substitution but a fulfilment of the Old.[66] The fullness of the legacy of the Council will slowly be worked out, but now uniquely also in conversation with the Jewish peoples.

Mission to the Jews and the Letter to the Romans

Finally, there is the reception that revolves around Romans 11:25–27, which has been called the *Sonderweg* (special way) position.[67] In this model, Israel's salvation will come only at the end times when Christ returns, and only then will all Jews accept him. This happens independently of the Church's missionary endeavor. Israel will not, and cannot, be saved before then. Israel's continued existence is a mystery for the Church, but one that remains a sign of God's special way for the Jewish people. This position can be held while negating or affirming an active covenant in present day Judaism, or/and affirming a "spiritual fecundity." In one sense, logically, all three positions might be bolted on to the *Sonderweg* position. Admittedly, the *Sonderweg* position is contested on biblical grounds, although mainly among Protestant scholars, especially in the claim that missionary activity with the goal of conversion is inappropriate in relation to the Jews.[68]

At the Council, some fathers held the *Sonderweg* position, and in recent Catholic circles it would appear to be held by senior cardinals such as Ratzinger (including while Pope Benedict), Kasper, and Koch (the past and present heads of the PCRRJ). All three Cardinals have argued that witness to Jews by Catholics is legitimate, only when done with deep respect and reverence for the Jewish religion, as are individual conversions by Jews to the Catholic Church. Koch makes a point of emphasizing that the Catholic Church "neither has nor supports any specific institutional work directed towards Jews."[69] This does not account for groups like Hebrew Catholics or for the earlier charism of the founding of the Sisters of Our Lady of Sion (founded by the Jewish Catholic, Theodore Ratisbonne, for mission to the Jewish people). Koch's comment overlooks that there is no institutional work directed toward Hindus or Buddhists per se. Does this indicate a "special way" regarding those religions?

This ambivalence can also be seen in a number of areas. For example, consider the changes to the Good Friday prayers (where the conversion of the Jews is foregrounded, backgrounded, and also occluded in the various differing formulations).[70] It can be seen in the controversy over the United States Conference of Bishops website document, *Reflections on Covenant and Mission* (2002).[71] This was formally criticized and corrected, for it appeared to negate any mission toward the Jews. The correction, "A Note on Ambiguities Contained in Reflections on Covenant and Mission" (2009),[72] was subsequently corrected after widespread protests from American Jewish groups who "could not continue to converse with Catholics" if "proclamation" was part of dialogue.[73]

The question of mission to the Jewish people remains unresolved, but requires clarity, especially given the Council's universal call to mission in *Ad Gentes*; *LG* 16's clear placing of Judaism within the orbit of mission; the Council's teaching on fulfilment; and the fact that all religions in *LG* 16 were viewed as *praeparatio evangelicae*. While the actual question of "mission" to the Jewish people may be resolved on pragmatic and psychological grounds (to many Jews, mission toward them is reminiscent of extinguishing the Jewish people—and this point cannot be taken lightly), the theological grounds require clarification: is the *Sonderweg* interpretation gaining a semi-magisterial status; and what of the universal causality of Christ's saving grace?[74] The Hebrew Catholics present a remarkable resolution to this problem that is only slowly emerging: only Catholics who have remained Jews can convince Jews/Israel that they are not called to deny the promises made to them by God if they follow Jesus. Koch is acutely aware of the difficulties on this matter: "That the Jews are participants in God's salvation is theologically unquestionable, but how that can be possible without confessing Christ explicitly, is and remains an unfathomable divine mystery."[75] This is akin to the problem we have already identified in the section A, showing there is a relationship between particular and general questions.

There are many other issues that have not been touched on in this section, perhaps most significantly the following: the shared monotheism of Israel and the Church, and the Jewish view of the trinity; the State of Israel and its relations with the Vatican; and the united call by both Jewish and Catholic leaders for cooperation between the two religions to preserve common values and the public role of religion. Much exciting work remains to be done in all these areas so that the fruits of the Council will be realized and nurtured.

C. Brief Summary of *NA*'s Teachings on the Muslim People, Its Reception, and Future Trajectories

Christian attitudes to Islam have been mainly negative because Islam apparently denies central truths claimed by Christians—and vice versa. It may be possible to say that the Council's teaching represents an "absolutely new beginning."[76] Reference to Islam at the Council arose through hostile Arab-Muslim reaction to the news of a sympathetic statement regarding the Jews and from Eastern Uniate Catholic communities. Pope Paul VI is reported to have instructed Cardinal Bea to ensure that every time the Jews were mentioned, Muslims should be too, so that no charges of partisanship could be made against the Church.[77] LG 16's framing of the issues in the context of invincible ignorance and mission has been addressed above. After the special place of the Jewish people, the Muslims are mentioned. Two themes are addressed in the single Latin sentence, both of which form the legacy of the Council on Islam. The first affirms of Muslims, "along with us they worship the one merciful God," who is creator and judge. The second indicates Abraham as a shared type in "faith" (fiedem Abrahae). NA 3 explicates these, adding more characteristics to the God who is worshiped in both religions: a God who speaks to humanity, is merciful, a lawgiver, and who invites submission to His inscrutable ways. On Abraham, NA says he is the model of submission. NA adds four further new themes: (1) that Jesus is respected as a "prophet," even though he is not acknowledged as divine, and that the Virgin Mary is honored; (2) that Muslims pursue a moral life; (3) that their prayer, almsgiving, and fasting is testimony to their search for God; (4) the two communities should move forward from their "dissensions and enmities" to work together for social justice and moral causes.[78]

All six themes arising from the Council have been developed in creative and cooperative ways.[79] The raft of positive statements pastorally moved the Church into new waters. The Secretariat for non-Christians was given a special remit regarding Islam, which was enhanced in the PCID.[80] In 1969, the Secretariat for Non-Christian Religions published a remarkable document, Guidelines for Dialogue between Christians and Muslims, which was revised and expanded in 1981 by Maurice Borrmans after international consultation.[81] Borrman's recent theological reflections on Islam indicate the necessarily slow and complex future trajectory on these issues.[82] Muslims in institutional groups have continuously collaborated with the PCID.[83] Muslim leaders took a particularly galvanizing initiative in their publication of A Common Word between Us and You (2007), marking the anniversary of the thirty-eight Muslim scholars' Open Letter (2006) to Pope Benedict XVI after his Regensburg speech (2006).[84] These two actions prompted the Vatican to inaugurate further institutional resources to develop good relations with Muslims. During the pontificates of John Paul II, Benedict XVI, and Pope Francis, an entirely new theme has arisen to add to the six already outlined: the need for Muslims to grant freedom of worship to Christians.

Before examining theological issues, a brief word is in order on Muslim receptions of the Council. Many Muslims have welcomed the positive appreciation of Muslim piety, beliefs, and morality, and many Muslim individuals and communities have begun to work together with Catholics at local, national, and international levels. Such cooperation creates alliances that generate good will and mutual appreciation. However, some Muslims were critical of the Council on three particular issues.[85] First, given the importance of the Qur'an and the prophet Muhammad, they regretted that no mention was made of either. It seemed that an empty shell of Islam was being affirmed. Second, some Muslims (and some Catholics) also felt concerned that Islam is never mentioned by name, but only "Muslims." I argue elsewhere that this latter is a misperception, in part due to translation issues.[86] Third, some felt that the five pillars of Islam were not mentioned, but only three (prayer, fasting, almsgiving). Islam, as Islam sees itself, was minimized. In what follows I shall focus primarily on the first issue, partly because of its importance to Muslims but also because key theological issues are involved. The second two points emphasize the importance of a question that has been asked since the Council: if Muslim piety was affirmed, if the true God is, worshipped in Islam, then surely this piety and true belief must be either through or despite the Qur'an and Muhammad. Which was it?

The Qur'an and Muhammad

The question above (can Muslim piety directed to the God who Christians worship be understood to happen through or despite Islam) was answered "despite" by some theologians in their reception of the Council. Miikka Ruokanen, for example, made a strong case that the "God" of Islam affirmed by the Council could be known through natural reason. That God is knowable through reason was the teaching of Vatican I (Denzinger 3004).[87] Ruokanen further argues that the main Catholic tradition sees salvation history begin through Israel and continue through that specific covenant.[88] Catholic theology always allowed for the operation of God through conscience and nature, and *DV* (*Dei Verbum* = *DV*) does not indicate a shift away from this paradigm. This answer kept with the affirmation of the true God's action in Muslim faith and piety but avoids affirming that this theism is other than a form of natural religion. This technically leaves open the questions about Muhammad and the Qur'an, and even allows for them to be seen as transmitters of this natural religion available to all.

While many Catholic commentaries do not follow Ruokanen's line, there is an interesting irony here. While Ruokanen's position has been criticized as unnecessarily restrictive, it actually coheres best with the Muslim view of revelation. Most Muslims see "revelation" as a truth given to all peoples that has been distorted and misinterpreted by some people. Jews and Christians are both special "people of the book" (see Qur'an 3:64–71), but Jews and Christians are also responsible for distorting and misinterpreting this original truth in their current, corrupted scriptures.[89] Muslims believe that the recitations given to Muhammad reiterate these primal truths. Muhammad does not come with a new revelation or a development of what had been previously given. In this sense, there is a fundamental difference in the understanding of "revelation": one is static (not pejoratively meant); the Christian's is progressive (that develops and moves to new levels).[90] This difference means that the interpretation given by Ruokanen is probably most accurately related to Muslims, even if some Catholics want to say more.

Alternative receptions of the Council teaching on this issue point to three factors that would indicate that God is not just known through conscience and nature in regard to Islam. God is depicted as having "spoken" (*homines allocutum*) (*NA* 3), which indicates his special communication to Islam. Abraham, a biblical type, is mentioned in both *LG* 16 and *NA* 3, which indicates the shared biblical traditions, and, some argue,[91] may even point toward a participation in special revelation. The significance of Abraham as a common patriarch to all three traditions (Jewish, Christian, and Muslim) has been important. Tom Michel, SJ, argues that in the Pauline view, since Abraham is seen to have had faith in "Christ" and was thus saved by that faith, we may be able to understand how Muslims relate to the true God, by analogy with Israel, pre-Christ. On this basis, Michel argues that Islam may be understood as a salvific faith.[92] Also, since *NA* gives such detailed attention to Muslim practices and beliefs, it is clearly indicating that this knowledge of God comes through the religion.

However, what is far from clarified is whether this knowledge of God may be understood as "supernatural." On the one hand, there is the more mainline position that argues that the Muslim understanding of God is akin to that of *praeparatio evangelicae*, although not of the same status as that of Israel, given Israel's special standing in salvation history. More progressive positions argue that this knowledge of God is of the true saving God as it is the God of the Old Testament and, in part, the God of the New. One Council father claimed that the virgin birth, accepted in Islam, meant that Muslims shared a greater patrimony with the Church than did Israel.[93]

Given the significance of Christ as the culmination of Israel's history, we can see that discussions within Jewish-Christian and Muslim-Christian dialogues revolve around this central Christological issue. With both religions, the question of the relationship between the one God and the trinitarian God is seminal for moving forward. Some Catholics have been involved in trying to show that the potential "clash" between these beliefs has hardly begun to be theorized adequately. This is because the Muslim rejection of the incarnation as *shirk* (sinfully associating the created with the uncreated) is safeguarded against by the Chalcedonian definition. The difference between the divine and human natures in Christ means that there is no mixing or confusing of the divine and human nature in the incarnation. Further, the Muslim rejection of the trinity is possibly predicated on a rejection of crude tritheism.[94] It is in these areas that the most important long-term contributions might come, for if it could be shown clearly that the incarnation does not offend against *shirk* and the trinity is not three gods, but that both doctrines are a substantive defense and elaboration of monotheism, then Muslims may find less offense in these doctrines.[95] However, whether Muslims could entirely drop their objections, given the Qur'anic critique, is also finally dependent on methods of Qur'anic exegesis.[96] Let me move now to the Qur'an and Muhammad, remembering that these matters are interrelated.

After the Council, slow and cautious steps were made regarding the Qur'an and Muhammad. The caution indicates the serious asymmetries that require careful negotiation. Historically, the Qur'an was viewed as "anti-scripture," containing as it did much that contradicted Christian truth. Its teachings on Christians, Jesus, the trinity, and the cross seem incompatible with Christianity. Even while the precise interpretation of the Qur'an on each of these four issues is contested and the Muslim exegetical traditions are varied, it is clear that Muslims have seen Christians as corrupting their own scriptures and divinizing Christ, who was a human prophet. Nevertheless, there were some minor traditions of positive appreciation of Islam in the Latin West and more so among some Eastern Christians. The Qur'an also contained much that was palatable to Christians, affirming a common belief in one transcendent God, who is a lawgiver, a judge, and merciful.[97] This dual quality (affirming Christian truths while denying Christian truths) is precisely what makes it so difficult to speak "clearly" about the Qur'an. But the Council had begun tentatively and indirectly to indicate ways forward: the God of Muslims had "spoken" to humans, which may refer to a shared belief in God's communication; the mention of the biblical Abraham indicates a shared scriptural tradition. The Council had also made the important step of allowing for the possibility of invincible ignorance so that Qur'anic and Muslim "denials" of truths of the Catholic faith need not be viewed as heresy or apostasy, as was previously the case. Rather, one might now begin to focus on what was held in common to build bridges into the future. Inevitably, balancing these different insights was susceptible to a diversity of reception.[98]

On the one hand, some Catholics argued that if Muslims worshipped the same God, historically this was through, not despite, the Qur'an. For every Muslim, the Qur'an is central in guiding prayer, devotion, piety and reverence for God. Hence, it was argued, some formal recognition of the Qur'an must follow the Council's indirect acknowledgements. One such scholar in the forefront of this stream of reception is Robert Caspar, a White Father. Caspar was one of the *periti* involved in advising on the drafting of *LG* 16 and the actual drafting of *NA* 3.

The other was Georges Anawati, OP. Lest one think that a *peritus* at the Council has special interpretative authority, Caspar's interpretations are sometimes questioned, although not by name, by Anawati.[99] Caspar's involvement in the *Groupe de Recherche Islamo-Chrétien* (GRIC), a distinguished group of ecumenical theologians, moved to a nuanced position of acknowledging that Catholics could affirm the Qur'an as transmitting "a" Word of God. They argued this on the basis of their own careful Christian reading of the Qur'an, as well as experiencing the deep spirituality of so many Muslims who are formed by the Qur'an.[100]

Caspar is honest in registering conflicting religious truths held by the two communities, but he highlights the human element involved in all scripture, and thus suggests that the truth of God is beyond these limited human expressions.[101] Caspar's position is echoed in Hans Küng and Jacques Dupuis. Dupuis writes about the Christian recognition of revealed truth in the Qur'an, despite its overall incompatibility with Christian truth: "This does not prevent the divine truth it contains from being the word of God uttered through the prophet. Seen in its historical context, Muhammad's monotheistic message indeed appears as divine revelation mediated by the prophet. This revelation is not perfect or complete; but it is no less real for all that."[102] In Dupuis's statement, we also see Muhammad's "prophethood" acknowledged as a corollary to this positive affirmation of the Qur'an. Küng unpacks this logic as the inevitable consequence of the Council's teachings.[103]

Caspar's move takes us close to the type of pluralism earlier identified as problematic. His solution may also be difficult for Muslims in interfaith dialogue as he reads the Qur'an purely from a Christian standpoint, disallowing its divine authority. The disallowing is permissible hermeneutically, but can hardly be advanced as furthering better relationships with Muslims in requiring *them* to abandon an important doctrinal tenet of their faith. Caspar's position is also helpful in showing how interfaith dialogue and inculturation are related. Caspar's position encourages Christians to take the text of the Qur'an more seriously so as to deepen their own attention to God. This would be an inculturation of the Qur'an. The work of Giulio Bassetti-Sani, OFM, actually goes one step further and attempts to read the Qur'an as being compatible with Christian orthodoxy. He argues that if the Qur'an is from God, then it must be compatible with Christian truth.[104] This is analogous to the move which argues that since the Old Testament is the Word of God, it must be in conformity with the New. However, this would be to appropriate a scripture that is not intrinsic to one's self-definition.

Caspar's more qualified reading of the Qur'an is significantly distinct from taking Muslim readings of the Qur'an as legitimate. He also operates with certain hermeneutic rules that have not been accepted by most Muslim commentators. So is Caspar departing from interreligious dialogue in his Christian affirmation of the Qur'an and now disengaging from Muslims in his affirmative claims about the Qur'an? Further, is such inculturation as Caspar and Bassetti-Sani perform a cause of scandal to Muslims? Some would argue that there is "scandal" and offense given to Muslims where, for example, in the tensions in Malaysia, some Muslims strongly object to Christians using the Arabic proper name *Allah* in Christian literature and liturgy. Catholics respond that this is equally their language and that they have used this term in their liturgy for hundreds of years. This complex, tensive energy between inculturation and interreligious dialogue will inevitably continue, as it requires the prudential judgment of local communities in each instance, rather than an overarching theoretical resolution. For instance, the PCID *Guidelines* explicitly dissuade Christian readings of the Qur'an in interfaith situations, for Christians have "no right to impose [their] methods and conclusions upon their Muslim friends" (49), and "we show our respect for the faith of others when we avoid any suggestion of incorporating them into our way or of trying to take them over" (109). The latter sentiment may well seem contrary to inculturation. As with the case of Hebrew Catholics, this approach discourages the contrary directive of the Council to take up and purify all that is good and true, wherever it is found in cultures (AG 21–22; GS 58).

In contrast to the first group of scholars above, there are other Catholic scholars of Islam such as the Dominicans Jacques Jomier and George Anawati, and the Jesuits, Christian Troll, Felix Körner, Edmond Farahian, Christiaan van Nispen, and Samir Khalil Samir,[105] who strongly resist an over-easy affirmation of Islam. They develop their response to the Council precisely because of their concern to dialogue with Islam as it understands itself, and not purely with a concern for a Christian reading of Islam. While they all acknowledge, with the Council, the many truths to be found within the Islamic tradition and thus also found in the Qur'an, they express reservations about affirming the Qur'an as "revelation" or a "Word of God," because of the different meanings given to these terms within the two traditions. It would be misleading to Christians to use these terms, for it would imply that the Qur'an is objectively the truthful word of God—without it having to be judged according to *the* Word of God given in Christ. Likewise, for these scholars, to see Muhammad as a "prophet" (Küng and Dupuis) is to misuse language and impose new conceptualities that belong to neither religion to secure short-term and fragile agreement. This focus on the fundamental incompatibilities between the two religious traditions deriving from *their own* interpretative traditions of scripture and/or Christology drives the basic approach of what is probably the majority receptive tradition among Catholic theologians and Islamists.

What of the papal magisterium? Pope John Paul II is the first Pope to approvingly and reverently cite the Qur'an in speeches to Muslims.[106] He always cites a parallel text in Christian scripture. This might indicate that the criteria by which Christians must discern what is true or false in the Qur'an is by the only method they have: testing it by Christian scripture. I have chosen a quote to illustrate my point because here the Pope also resolves one way of dealing with the Abrahamic issue, an image consistently invoked in his speeches. He resolves it, for the time being, by leaving it unresolved. He acknowledges that Muslims see their faith as deriving from Abraham. In this respect he stays with the Council's ambiguity, even if some theologians have marched down bold and interesting Abrahamic avenues, which indicate the many paths that require further research on this matter. [107]

> Faith in God, professed by the spiritual descendants of Abraham—Christians, Muslims and Jews—when it is lived sincerely, when it penetrates life, is a certain foundation of the dignity, brotherhood and freedom of men and a principle of uprightness for moral conduct and life in society. And there is more: as a result of this faith in God the Creator and transcendent, one man finds himself at the summit of creation. He was created, the Bible teaches, "in the image and likeness of God" (Gen 1:27); for the Qur'an, the sacred book of the Muslims, although man is made of dust, "God breathed into him his spirit and endowed him with hearing, sight and heart," that is, intelligence (Surah 32.8).[108]

Some writers see in his citations of the Qur'an an important step forward, but it is difficult to judge the full implications. Positively, it shows the Magisterium moving a step forward from the Council in acknowledging that the Qur'an contains both natural and divine truths: here an insight in theological anthropology; and also the commonality of Abraham, who is part of sacred salvific history. The divine truths contained in both scriptures relate to Mary's virginity cited in another speech.[109] These quotations show a positive regard and reverence for the holy book of Muslims, which is an important step forward from pre-Conciliar days.

However, one must also mention the Pope's "private" comments on revelation in his book, *Crossing the Threshold of Faith*. He writes,

> Whoever knows the Old and New Testaments, and then reads the Koran, clearly sees the *process by which it completely reduces Divine Revelation*. It is impossible not to note the movement away from what God has said about Himself, first in the Old Testament through the Prophets, and then finally in the New Testament through His Son. In Islam all the richness of God's self revelation, which constitutes the heritage of the Old and New Testaments, has definitely been set aside.[110]

He is simply drawing attention to the different understandings of revelation in the two communities. In Islam, the Qur'an restates what has always been taught but been corrupted by Jews and Christians. In Christianity there is a genuinely progressive history of revelation starting at creation, then through Israel, culminating in Christ. In reading the positive statements on the Qur'an by the Pope, we must not assume that radical differences of what constitutes "revelation" can be bypassed. The Pope could not explore these complex issues in his public utterances.

However, as a philosopher thinking aloud, his contextualizing insight reminds us of deeper problems behind apparently affirmative words. Understandably, there was much consternation about this book by Muslims. This is a real problem for the Catholic Church. If any high-level teacher indicates public critical comments, many see this as a backward step in interreligious dialogue, rather than working through to a maturity where one might be analytically honest about an other's religion.

One might argue that the proper reception of the Council's teachings on Islam (and Judaism) is also related to something entirely other than the Council's teachings: one's paradigmatic understanding of "religion." In Caspar, Dupuis, Küng, and like-minded thinkers, there is perhaps what George Lindbeck has called an experiential-expressivist approach to religion. This focuses on the reality beyond language, which is usually affirmed as a shared reality, which generates new forms of language. This means that experiential arguments are often given greater prominence in discussing matters. However, in the more conservative mainline group of Jomier, Anawati, Troll, and others, there is an emphasis on what Lindbeck calls the cultural-linguistic approach, whereby we understand language, signs, and performative traditions as shaping and forming our experience. Here, there is no reality so easily identified "behind" and beyond language, a non-signed reality, invoked by the

experiential-expressivist. Lindbeck had already seen a *tendency* toward pluralism within experiential-expressivist and a more conservative tendency among
cultural-linguistic types.[111] To be sure, the latter do not deny a reality beyond
signs, but emphasize only the limitations of thought and action within signs;
while the former do not always minimize signs, they do often emphasize the
divine reality beyond our grasp. Pope Benedict's move to assimilate the PCID
into the Council for Culture may have had this concern in mind: religions are
socio-cultural configurations of power.

This issue underlies the discussion about a whole series of keywords in
Islamic and Catholic dialogue: God, Abraham, revelation, salvation, and judgment, to name a few. One of the great achievements and challenges of the
Council was to suggest that commonalities were still important, despite differences, and the Church should build upon those "things human beings have in
common" that "tend to bring them together" (*NA* 1), rather than those things
that divide them. The interesting question is whether religious differences
need divide people. The Council clearly envisaged a dynamic relation between
being true to our beliefs and engaging with others honestly, respectfully, and
openly.

We started with the question: if Muslim piety was affirmed as worship-
ping the true God, then surely this must be either through or despite the
Qur'an and Muhammad. Which is it? At present, while some argue through
and hardly anyone argues despite, the mainstream response holds together
the through and despite, the latter always indicating the imperfect objective
truth of Islam, the former emphasizing the deep commonality, spirituality,
and riches found in both at the subjective and objective levels. The debate has
only just begun.

Conclusion

The reader should see that, in the reception of the Council, different creative
and positive pathways have been forged, and the Magisterium has continuously guided and encouraged, and sometimes admonished, theologians and
pastors in their desire to implement the Council. *LG* and *NA* remain founding charters for a path that the Catholic Church has begun to walk since
the mid-1960s. By examining some theological issues raised by *LG* and *NA*,
readers will realize that I have touched upon only the contours of a very
complex map. That map continues to be charted with a plethora of questions
arising at every turn. Perhaps the greatest blessings of the Council has been
friendships between individuals and groups, something we could not chart
here.[112]

NOTES

1. Gavin D'Costa, *Vatican II. Catholic Doctrines on Jews and Muslims* (Oxford: Oxford
University Press, 2014).

2. "Address at the Opening of Vatican II–11 October 1962," http://www.catholic-forum.com/saints/popeo26li.htm (all websites checked August 2014).

3. Interested readers should consult Martin Ganeri OP, "Catholicism and Hinduism" and Paul Williams OP, "Catholicism and Buddhism" in *The Catholic Church and the World Religions: A Theological and Phenomenological Account*, ed. Gavin D'Costa (London: T&T Clark, 2011), 106–41, 156–77, respectively; and consult on Hinduism: Mariasusai Dhavamony, *Hindu-Christian Dialogue: Theological Sounds and Perspectives* (Amsterdam: Rodopi, 2002); on Buddhism, see the proceedings of the four Buddhist-Christian Colloquia organized by the Pontifical Council for Interreligious Dialogue and published in their journal, *Pro Dialogo*: in Kaohsiung (1995), in Bangalore (1998), in Tokyo (2002) and in Rome (2013). This entire area raises a whole new set of doctrinal issues, given the Semitic non-theism of these religious traditions.

4. For its history and constitution, see http://www.vatican.va/roman_curia/pontifical_councils/interelg/documents/rc_pc_interelg_pro_20051996_en.html.

5. See *Pro Dialogo* 2 (1998); and Maria Diemling and Thomas Herbst, eds., *Interpreting the "Spirit of Assisi": Challenges to Interfaith Dialogue in a Pluralistic World* (Canterbury: Franciscan International Study Centre, 2013), showing the many areas opened up in this area of spiritual sharing. My essay in this collection covers some ground related to bishops' conferences on this matter. See also the Monastic Interreligious Dialogue movement: http://www.dimmid.org/.

6. Pope Benedict's concerns are expressed succinctly while he was a Cardinal. See his *Many Religions, One Covenant: Israel, the Church and the World*, trans. Graham Harrison (San Francisco: Ignatius Press, 1999), 106–12.

7. See "Final Report of the 1985 Synod," http://www.ewtn.com/library/CURIA/SYNFINAL.HTM.

8. Stated clearly in the important clarification of the Holy Office, *Letter to Feeney* (1949), http://www.ewtn.com/library/curia/cdffeeny.htm.

9. Instances can be found in Adrian Hastings, *A Concise Guide to the Documents of the Second Vatican Council* (London: Darton, Longman and Todd, 1968), 1:200–201; and for detailed analysis of a number of Catholic theologians who argue in this fashion, see my "Pluralist Arguments: Prominent Tendencies and Methods," in *Catholic Engagement with World Religions*, ed. Karl Josef Becker and Ilaria Morali (Maryknoll, NY: Orbis Books, 2010), 329–44.

10. Standard texts on the theology of religions perpetuate this view: see for example Paul Knitter, *No Other Name? A Critical Survey of Christian Attitudes Towards the World Religions* (London: SCM, 1985), 125: "If Vatican II is a watershed in Christian attitudes toward other religions, Karl Rahner is its chief engineer"; and see similarly, Alan Race, *Christians and Religious Pluralism* (London: SCM, 1983), 43–45; and Gerald R. McDermott and Harold A. Netland, *A Trinitarian Theology of Religions: An Evangelical Proposal* (New York: Oxford University Press, 2014), 30.

11. Karl Rahner, "On the Importance of the Non-Christian Religions for Salvation," in *Theological Investigations* (London: Darton, Longman & Todd, 1984), 18:288–95, 290–91.

12. See McDermott and Netland, *Trinitarian*, 30. Paul Knitter questionably claims that the "majority of Roman Catholic theologians interpret the Conciliar statements to affirm, implicitly but clearly, that the religions are ways of salvation," in "Roman Catholic Approaches to Other Religions: Developments and Tensions," *International Bulletin of Missionary Research* (1984): 30.

13. See Suso Brechter, "Decree on the Church's Missionary Activity," in *Commentary on the Documents of Vatican II*, ed. Herbert Vorgrimler (London: Burns

& Oates; New York: Herder & Herder [trans. Hilda Graer, W. J. O'Hara and Ronald Walls], 1969), 4:87–182, 122.

14. Jacques Dupuis, *Toward a Christian Theology of Religious Pluralism* (Maryknoll, NY: Orbis, 1997), citing *Redemptoris Missio* (1991), http://w2.vatican.va/content/john-paul-ii/en/encyclicals/documents/hf_jp-ii_enc_07121990_redemptoris-missio.html as most exemplary of these developments.

15. This position can be found in the work of Ilaria Morali, "Salvation, Religions, and Dialogue in the Roman Magisterium," in Becker and Morali, *Catholic Engagement*, 122–42; and in earlier influential theologians like de Lubac and Daniélou, without denigration to culture and religion as such (see Morali, "The Travail of Ideas in the Three Centuries Preceding Vatican II (1650–1964)," in Becker and Morali, *Catholic Engagement*, 91–121, esp. 110–18).

16. There is controversy about the type of causality operative here, with various proposals forwarded by Francis Sullivan, Jacques Dupuis, and Gavin D'Costa. See bibliographical details and discussion in my *Christianity and World Religions* (Oxford: Wiley-Blackwell, 2009), 180–86; and Gerard O'Collins's advancing that discussion in "Jacques Dupuis: The Ongoing Debate," *Theological Studies* 74 (2013): 632–54. O'Collins needs to clarify and justify his claims about the nature of "love" for his solution to be satisfactory.

17. Jacques Dupuis, *Christianity and the Religions* (New York: Orbis, 2002), 87–95, 255–58. His position is in constant danger of slipping toward pluralism, other than its constitutive Christology.

18. Hans Urs von Balthasar, *The Moment of Christian Witness*, trans. Richard Beckley (San Francisco: Ignatius Press, 1984).

19. See Morali, "Salvation"; and also Miikka Ruokanen, *The Catholic Doctrine on Non-Christian Religions According to the Second Vatican Council* (Leiden: Brill, 1992). This was also Yves Congar's reading in "The People of God," in *Vatican II: An Interfaith Appraisal*, ed. John Miller (Notre Dame and London: University of Notre Dame, 1966), 197–207; as well as De Lubac's and Daniélou's as noted above in note 15.

20. See Ralph Martin, *Will Many Be Saved? What Vatican II Actually Teaches and Its Implications for the New Evangelization* (Grand Rapids: William B. Eerdmans, 2012), 93–128; and for Rahner's comments on salvation optimism, see Rahner, "Observations on the Problem of the 'Anonymous Christian,'" in *Theological Investigations* (London: Darton, Longman & Todd, 1979), 14:280–94, 286.

21. Martin, *Will Many Be Saved?*, 14; but Martin is incorrect in claiming that this interpretation was held by the Magisterium. See my *Vatican II*, 107–12.

22. Morali, "Salvation," 133–37.

23. See Riccardo Lombardi, *The Salvation of the Unbeliever*, trans. Dorothy M. White (London: Burns & Oates, 1956). Lombardi outlines this solution and others that were current prior to the Council. None included seeing other religions as salvific.

24. ITC, *The Hope of Salvation for Infants who Die without Being Baptised* (2007). Vatican website. http://www.vatican.va/roman_curia/congregations/cfaith/cti_documents/rc_con_cfaith_doc_20070419_un-baptised-infants_en.html.

25. See Joseph A. DiNoia, *The Diversity of Religions: A Christian Perspective* (Washington, DC: The Catholic University Press of America, 1992); and D'Costa, *Christianity and World Religions*, 161–211; and Edward Oakes's criticisms of DiNoia's solution in "The Internal Logic of Holy Saturday in the Theology of Hans Urs von Balthasar," *International Journal of Systematic Theology* 9, no. 2 (2007): 184–99, at 188.

26. See for example Joseph Ratzinger, *Eschatology: Death and Eternal Life*, trans. Michael Waldstein (Washington, DC: The Catholic University Press of America, 1988),

esp. 48–50. However, individualism is not intrinsic to the proposed post-mortem solu-tions, but the individual acts as a test case to envisage the wider plan of an undoubted communal eschatological salvation.

27. See Paul Knitter, *No Other Name? A Critical Survey of Christian Attitudes Toward the World Religions* (London: SCM, 1985) for his move beyond Rahner.

28. See the debate between Knitter and Ruokanen in Ruokanen, *The Catholic Doctrine*, 144–48, 153–56; and Perry Schmidt-Leukel (who has since left the Catholic Church) in *Gott ohne Grenzen: eine christliche und pluralistische Theologie der Religionen* (Gütersloh: Gütersloher Verlaghaus, 2005); and the Jesuit Roger Haight in *Jesus the Symbol of God* (New York: Orbis Books, 1999).

29. See Paul F. Knitter, "Can We Put Our Theological Money Where Our Dialogical Mouth Is? Looking Back over the Past Fifty Years," *Journal of Ecumenical Studies* 49, no. 1 (2014): 166–73.

30. See Felix Wilfred, *Sunset in the East: Asian Challenges and Christian Involvement* (Madras: University of Madras Press, 1991) on Hinduism; and Aloysius Pieris, *An Asian Theology of Liberation* (New York: Orbis, 1988) on Buddhism. See my analysis of the problematic methodology of some Asian Catholic theologians in "Inculturation: India and Other Religions," *Studia Missionalia* 44 (1995): 121–48.

31. http://www.vatican.va/roman_curia/congregations/cfaith/documents/rc_con_cfaith_doc_20010124_dupuis_en.html. *Dominus Iesus*, published by the Congregation for the Doctrine of the Faith in 2000 was *personally* authorized by the Pope and thus carries the authority of the ordinary magisterium. Francis A. Sullivan, SJ, makes the point that it is not as authoritative as a papal encyclical and that it internally contains statements of differing weight—in Sullivan, "Introduction and Ecclesial Issues," in *Sic et Non. Encountering Dominus Iesus*, ed. Stephen J. Pope and Charles Hefling (Maryknoll, NY: Orbis, 2002), 47–56, at 47–48.

32. For "unnecessary" offense, see Philip A. Cunningham, "Implications for Catholic Magisterial Teaching on Jews and Judaism," in Pope and Hefling, *Sic et Non*, 134–49, 134–41. The use of neo-Scholastic terminology by the CDF when the wider theological community is not united in employing such language causes inevitable problems in reception.

33. *Redemptoris Missio*, 55—citing NA 2 and LG 16, although the actual quote comes from Pope Paul's VI, *Address at the Opening of the Second Session of the Second Vatican Ecumenical Council*, September 29, 1963: *Acta Apostolicae Sedis*, Vatican City, 55 (1963), 858, prior to the promulgation of either NA or LG.

34. See my detailed exegesis of Aquinas on this point in *Vatican II*, 89–99.

35. The CRRJ document "The Gifts and the Calling of God are Irrevocable" (2015) was published after this essay was completed (http://www.vatican.va/roman_curia/pontifical_councils/chrstuni/relations-jews-docs/rc_pc_chrstuni_doc_20151210_ebraismo-nostra-aetate_en.html).

36. It argued that Christian sins "seem graver in our case than it was in that of the Jews; for the Jews, as the same Apostle says, 'would never have crucified the Lord of glory if they had known him' (1 Cor 2.8). We ourselves maintain that we do know him, and yet we lay, as it were, violent hands on him by disowning him in our actions." See http://www.angelfire.com/art/cactussong/TridentineCatechism.htm, English transla-tion of *The Tridentine Catechism*, from John A. McHugh, OP, and Charles J. Callan, OP (1923).

37. See especially John M. Oesterreicher, "Declaration on the Relation of the Church to Non-Christian Religions," in *Commentary on the Documents of Vatican II*, ed. Herbert Vorgrimler (London: Burns & Oates, 1968), 3:1–154; and Augustin

Bea, *The Church and Jewish People: A Commentary on the Second Vatican Council's Declaration on the Relation of the Church to Non-Christian Religions*, trans. Philip Lovetz (London: Geoffrey Chapman, 1966).

38. Jules Isaac, *The Teaching of Contempt: Christian Roots of Anti-Semitism*, trans. Helen Weaver (New York: Holt, Rinehart and Winston, 1964).

39. Adam Gregerman, "Jewish Theology and Limits on Reciprocity in Catholic-Jewish Dialogue. A Response to Cardinal Kurt Koch's October 30, 2011 Keynote Address at Seton Hall University during the 10th Annual Meeting of the Council of Centers on Christian-Jewish Relations," *Studies in Christian-Jewish Relations* 7 (2012): 1–13, at 2.

40. See, for example, the seasoned Vatican observers soon after the Council: March H. Tannenbaum, "A Jewish Reaction to Catholic Positions in Vatican II," *Proceedings of the Catholic Theological Society of America* (1966): 303–13, http://ejournals.bc.edu/ojs/index.php/ctsa/article/view/2612/2248; and forty years after: David Rosen, "Jewish and Israeli Perspectives 40 Years after Vatican II," in *Nostra Aetate: Origins, Promulgation, Impact on Jewish–Catholic Relations*, ed. Neville Lamdan and Alberto Melloni (Berlin: LIT Verlag, 2007), 175–88.

41. See for example, Mary Boys, *Redeeming Our Sacred Story: The Death of Jesus and Relations between Jews and Christians* (New York: Paulist Books, 2013); and Rosemary Ruether, *Faith and Fratricide: The Theological Roots of Anti-Semitism* (New York: Seabury Press, 1980).

42. See *Supported by One Root*, 1995, http://www.sacredheart.edu/faithservice/centerforchristianandjewishunderstanding/documentsandstatements/statementbythecatholicbishopsinthenetherlandssupportedbyoneroot1995/.

43. *Declaration of Repentance*, September 30, 1997, http://www.sacredheart.edu/faithservice/centerforchristianandjewishunderstanding/documentsandstatements/declarationofrepentancebytheromancatholicbishopsoffranceseptember301997/.

See also the statements from the bishops of Switzerland (1997), Italy (1998) and the United States (2001), found at http://www.catholic.co.il/index.php?option=com_content&view=article&id=40%3Ajewish-christian-relations-catholic-church-documents&catid=11%3Abibliography&Itemid=17&lang=en.

44. See collected statements (until 1998) in *John Paul II and Interreligious Dialogue*, ed. Byron L. Sherwin and Harold Kasimow (Maryknoll, NY: Orbis Books, 1999), 70–84; and two Jewish responses from David M. Gordis, "John Paul II and the Jews," 125–38; and Byron L. Sherwin, "John Paul II's Catholic Theology of Judaism," 139–69. For later statements as well as a fuller listing, see *Interreligious Dialogue: The Official Teaching of the Catholic Church from the Second Vatican Council to John Paul II (1963–2005)*, ed. Francesco DeGoia (Boston: Pauline Books & Media, 2006).

45. At: http://www.vatican.va/roman_curia/pontifical_councils/chrstuni/documents/rc_pc_chrstuni_doc_16031998_shoah_en.html.

46. *We Remember*, section 3.

47. *We Remember*, section 4. See the interesting critique of the Catholic Church by Jewish scholars on this issue: Eugene Korn, "A Jewish Response to 'Theological Questions and Perspectives in Jewish-Catholic Dialogue' by Cardinal Kurt Koch," *Studies in Christian-Jewish Relations* 7 (2012): 1–7; and Adam Gregerman, "Jewish Theology and Limits on Reciprocity." Note 16 of *We Remember* also indicated that the Church did not accept any serious criticism of Pope Pius XII.

48. See some of the different positions outlined in Avery Dulles, "Should the Church Repent?," *First Things*, December 1998, http://www.firstthings.com/article/1998/12/should-the-church-repent; and for a very sympathetic Jewish reflection on *We*

Remember, which shows a subtle appreciation of the position outlined in this essay, see David Novak, "Jews and Catholics: Beyond Apologies," *First Things*, December 1998,   http://www.firstthings.com/article/1999/01/002-jews-and-catholics-beyond-apologies. Novak is rightly critical of some Jewish responses on Jewish theological grounds, such as the criticism of the Anti-Defamation League (March 16, 1998); see http://archive.adl.org/presrele/holna_52/4020-52.html.

49. See Jewish critics from 1966 to 2012 cited above: Tannenbaum, Rosen, Gordis, Sherwin, Gregerman, and Korn.

50. See Matthew Levering, *Christ's Fulfillment of Torah and Temple: Salvation according to Thomas Aquinas* (South Bend, IN: University of Notre Dame Press, 2002) for a Thomist view that fruitfully engages with our question.

51. *The 1974 Guidelines and Suggestions for Implementing the Conciliar Declaration Nostra Aetate*, 4, http://www.vatican.va/roman_curia/pontifical_councils/chrstuni/relations-jews-docs/rc_pc_chrstuni_doc_19741201_nostra-aetate_en.html; *The 1985 Notes on the Correct Way to Present Jews and Judaism in Preaching and Teaching in the Roman Catholic Church*, http://www.vatican.va/roman_curia/pontifical_councils/chrstuni/relations-jews-docs/rc_pc_chrstuni_doc_19820306_jews-judaism_en.html; and *We Remember: A Reflection on the Shoah* (1998). For the history of this commission, see Cardinal Jorge Maria Mejía, "The Creation and Work of the Commission for Religious Relations with the Jews," in *The Catholic Church and the Jewish People: Recent Reflections from Rome*, ed. Philip A. Cunningham, Norbert J. Hofmann, and Joseph Sievers (New York: Fordham University Press, 2007), 152–58; and, in the same collection, for the Commission's interaction with Jewish agencies, see Pier Francesco Fumagalli, "The Commission for Religious Relations with the Jews and the International Catholic-Jewish Liaison Committee," 159–66.

52. Particularly *The Jewish People and Their Sacred Scriptures in the Christian Bible* (2001), http://www.vatican.va/roman_curia/congregations/cfaith/pcb_documents/rc_con_cfaith_doc_20020212_popolo-ebraico_en.html.

53. See DeGoia, *Interreligious Dialogue*.

54. See Avery Cardinal Dulles, "Covenant and Mission," *America*, October 21, 2002,   http://americamagazine.org/issue/408/article/covenant-and-mission;   and Morali, "Salvation, Religions, and Dialogue in the Roman Magisterium."

55. PCRRJ, *Notes*, VI, 25.

56. Philip A. Cunningham, "Official Ecclesial Documents to Implement Vatican II on Relations with Jews: Study Them, Become Immersed in Them, and Put Them into Practice," *Studies in Christian-Jewish Relations* 4 (2009): 1–36, at 5; and more significantly, R. Kendall Soulen, "The Priority of the Present Tense for Jewish-Christian Relations," in *In Between Gospel and Election: Explorations in the Interpretation of Romans 9–11*, ed. Florian Wilk and J. Ross Wagner (Tübingen: Mohr Siebeck, 2010), 497–504.

57. The PCRRJ document, "The Gifts and the Calling of God are Irrevocable" (2015) December 2015, was published just after this was written. I believe it supports claims made in this essay about the post-conciliar magisterium, even though this document is not a magisterial teaching document.

58. Korn, "A Jewish Response," 2.

59. See David Hartman, *Israelis and the Jewish Tradition: An Ancient People Debating Its Future* (New Haven, CT: Yale University, 2000), 12–13.

60. Address at the Great Synagogue of Rome, April 13, 1986.

61. Elias Friedman, *Jewish Identity* (New York: The Miriam Press: 1987), 90–93; and see also the current Latin Patriarchal Vicar of Jerusalem's Hebrew Catholics,

David M. Neuhaus SJ, "Engaging the Jewish People: Forty Years since *Nostra Aetate*," in *Catholic Engagement*, 395–413. For a challenging Messianic Jewish critique of *Lumen Gentium* and a robust response, see Mark S. Kinzer and Matthew Levering, "Messianic Gentiles & Messianic Jews," *First Things*, January 2009, http://www.firstthings.com/article/2009/01/005-messianic-gentiles-messianic-jews.

62. See the references collected by Philip A. Cunningham, "Themes in Catholic Post-*Nostra Aetate* Theology," *Current Dialogue* 53 (2012): 10–20, esp. 15–18; and P. Cunningham, J. Sievers, M. Boys, H. Henrix, and J. Svartvik, eds., *Christ Jesus and the Jewish People Today: New Explorations of Theological Interrelationships* (Grand Rapids: Eerdmans, 2011). This trajectory "seems" close to pluralism as discussed in section A of this chapter, but it would be premature to give it this label unambiguously.

63. This position has its roots in Franz Rosenzweig, *The Star of Redemption*, trans. William W. Hallo (1930; 2nd ed., Boston: Beacon Paperbacks, 1972).

64. Kurt Cardinal Koch, "Theological Questions and Perspectives in Jewish-Catholic Dialogue. October 30, 2011 Keynote Address at Seton Hall University during the 10th Annual Meeting of the Council of Centers on Christian-Jewish Relations," *Studies in Christian-Jewish Relations* 7 (2012): 1–12, esp. 6–9. See also PCCRJ, "The Gifts and the Calling of God are Irrevocable," 32.

65. Kasper said, "The only thing I wish to say is that the document *Dominus Iesus* does not state that everybody needs to become a Catholic in order to be saved by God. On the contrary, it declares that God's grace, which is the grace of Jesus Christ according to our faith, is available to all. Therefore, the Church believes that Judaism, i.e. the faithful response of the Jewish people to God's irrevocable covenant, is salvific for them, because God is faithful to his promises." In Walter Cardinal Kasper, "*Dominus Iesus*" (2001), https://www.bc.edu/dam/files/research_sites/cjl/texts/cjrelations/resources/articles/kasper_dominus_iesus.htm. I am unable to find any text that says that Judaism is "salvific" for Jews, and in *DI* 21 it says, "It would be contrary to the faith to consider the Church as one way of salvation alongside those constituted by the other religions."

The PCRRJ *Notes* say, "Jesus affirms (ibid. 10:16) that 'there shall be one flock and one shepherd.' Church and Judaism cannot then be seen as two parallel ways of salvation and the Church must witness to Christ as the Redeemer for all, 'while maintaining the strictest respect for religious liberty in line with the teaching of the Second Vatican Council (Declaration Dignitatis Humanae)' (Guidelines and Suggestions, I)" (I.7). Ratzinger defending *DI* confirms this at the "objective level," in "Answers to Main Objections Against *Dominus Iesus*," *Frankfurter Allgemeine Zeitung*, September 22, 2000, http://www.ewtn.com/library/Theology/OBDOMIHS.HTM; and see also Cardinal Avery Dulles, "Covenant and Mission."

66. Koch, "Theological Questions and Perspectives in Jewish-Catholic Dialogue," 4–10.

67. See Franz Mussner, *Tractate on the Jews: The Significance of Judaism for Christian Faith*, trans. Leonard Swidler (Philadelphia: Fortress, 1984); and Otfried Hofius, "Das Evangelium und Israel: Erwägungen zu Römer 9–11," *Zeitschrift für Theologie und Kirche* 83 (1986): 319–20.

68. See Michael G. Vanlaningham, "Should the Church Evangelize Israel? A Response to Franz Mussner and Other Sonderweg Proponents," *Trinity Journal* 22, no. 2 (2001): 197–217; and the many alternatives mapped out by Joseph Sievers, "A History of the Interpretation of Romans 11:29," *Annali di storia dell'esegesi* 14 (1997): 381–442. Mark S. Kinzer (*Post-Missionary Messianic Judaism. Redefining Christian Engagement with the Jewish People* [Grand Rapids, MI: Brazos, 2005]) presents

a most important challenge to the Churches from Messianic Judaism, also echoed by the Catholic Friedman, *Jewish Identity*, 90–93. Only Jews who follow Jesus can carry out mission to the Jewish people.

69. Koch, "Theological Questions," 9. Repeated in PCCJR, "The Gifts and the Calling of God are Irrevocable," 40.

70. See Hans Hermann Henrix, "The Controversy Surrounding the 2008 Good Friday Prayer in Europe: The Discussion and Its Theological Implications," *Studies in Christian–Jewish Relations* 3 (2008): 1–19.

71. At: http://www.usccb.org/beliefs-and-teachings/ecumenical-and-interreligious/jewish/upload/Reflections-on-Covenant-and-Mission.pdf.

72. At:http://www.usccb.org/about/doctrine/publications/upload/note-on-ambiguities-contained-in-reflections-on-covenant-and-mission.pdf.

73. The deleted sentence was this: "Though Christian participation in inter-religious dialogue would not normally include an explicit invitation to baptism and entrance into the Church, the Christian dialogue partner is always giving witness to the following of Christ, to which all are implicitly invited." See Philip A. Cunningham, "Discerning the Stumbling Block," *Studies in Christian-Jewish Relations* 7 (2012): 1–9, at 4. See Cunningham's longer analysis in "Official Ecclesial Documents," 26–31; and my criticism of Cunningham in "What does the Catholic Church Teach about Mission to the Jewish People?," *Theological Studies* 73, no. 3 (2012): 590–613 (plus two responses in the same issue: Edward Kessler, "A Jewish Response to Gavin D'Costa," 614–28; and John T. Pawlikowski, "A Catholic Response to Gavin D'Costa," 629–40). Michael McGarry, "Can Catholics Make an Exception? Jews and 'The New Evangelization,'" (1994, Remembering for the Future II, Conference at Berlin, Germany) shows this ambivalence in *Redemptor Missio*, https://www.bc.edu/content/dam/files/research_sites/cjl/texts/cjrelations/resources/articles/mcgarry.htm.

74. PCCJR, "A Reflection," 36 notes that this tension "is and remains an unfath-omable divine mystery."

75. Koch, "Theological Questions," 8. I am not sure that the statement is "unques-tionable." Koch does not specify invincible ignorance as a condition of this possibility, nor does he differentiate between different and possibly incompatible Judaisms.

76. Christian W. Troll, "Changing Catholic Views of Islam," in Jacques Waardenburg, *Islam and Christianity: Mutual Perceptions since the Mid-20th Century* (Leuven: Peeters Press, 1998), 19–77, at 25–26. This is a masterly survey of Catholic views on Islam since the Council. Protestant views in the modern period can be found in the same volume; see J. C. Basset, "New Wineskins: Changing Protestant Views of Islam," 79–96.

77. See the following commentaries on the Council's teachings on Islam and the background: Georges C. Anawati, "Excursus on Islam," in *Commentary on the Documents of Vatican II*, 3:151–55; Joseph Farrugia, *The Church and the Muslims: The Church's Consideration of Islam and the Muslims in the Documents of the Second Vatican* (Malta: Gozo Press, 1988); and Andrew Unsworth, "A Historical and Textual-Critical Analysis of the Magisterial Documents of the Catholic Church on Islam: Towards a Hetero-Descriptive Account of Muslim Belief and Practice" (PhD diss., Heythrop College, 2007).

78. I outline the background to these two documents and their teachings on Islam in *Vatican II*, 160–211.

79. *Christian Lives Given to the Study of Islam*, ed. Christian W. Troll and C. T. R. Hewer (New York: Fordham University Press, 2012), contains many key Catholic

theologians (and an ecumenical spectrum) reflecting on the fact that the Council has opened new avenues to Islam through the life stories of some leading theologians.

80. See Mahmut Aydin, *Modern Western Christian Theological Understandings of Muslims Since the Second Vatican Council* (Washington DC: Council for Research in Values and Philosophy, 2002), chap. 2, "Post Vatican II Developments in the Catholic Church's Teaching on Non-Christians in General and Muslims in Particular," 49–87 for a good overview of the development of the Muslim desk; and also the PCID's then Secretary, Michael Fitzgerald's "Christian Muslim Dialogue—A Survey of Recent Developments," April 10, 2000, http://sedosmission.org/old/eng/fitzgerald.htm; and see Felix Körner's analysis of three pontificates in their relation to Islam: "Ecclesiastical Magisterium, Catholic Theology, Today's Islam: Proposals for Solutions to Key Issues," *Stimmen der Zeit* 3 (2010): 169–81 (English translation: http://www.con-spiration.de/texte/english/2010/koerner-e.html).

81. Published by Paulist Press, New York, 1981.

82. See Borrman's later reflections: "Islam as It Understands Itself," in Becker and Morali, *Catholic Engagement*, 487–508, especially, 500–508.

83. *Guidelines for Dialogue between Christians and Muslims*, 115–22.

84. *A Common Word* website gives many links to the many initiatives that grew out of the document: see http://www.acommonword.com/.

85. See, for example, Karim Lahham, *The Roman Catholic Church's Position on Islam after Vatican II*, Tabah Papers Series, Number 2, July 2008 (AbuDhabi, UAE: Tabah Foundation); Mahmoud Ayoub, "Pope John Paul on Islam," in *Pope John Paul II*, ed. Sherwin, 171–86; Adnan Silajdži, "Islam and Muslims in the Document Nostra Aetate: Challenges and Prospects," *International Symposium on Islam*, Samsun, November 26–28, 2010, 125–130.

86. *Vatican II*, 167–75.

87. Henrich Denzinger and Adolf Schönmetzer, eds., *Enchiridion Symbolorum. Definitionum et Declarationnum de Rebus Fidei et Morum*, 36th edition (Freiburg: Herder, 1976).

88. Ruokanen, *Catholic Doctrine*, 77. It should be noted that he is a Lutheran.

89. See David Marshall, *God, Muhammad and the Unbeliever: A Qur'anic Study* (Surrey: Curzon, 1999) for a rigorous textual treatment of this question.

90. See Ovey N. Mohammed, *Muslim-Christian Relations: Past, Present, Future* (Eugene, Oregon: Wipf & Stock, 2008), 55.

91. For example, Robert Caspar, "Islam According to Vatican II," in *Signs of Dialogue: Christian Encounter with Mulims*, eds. Michael L. Fitzgerald and Robert Caspar (Zamboanga, PH: Sillsilah Publications, 1992), 233–45.

92. Thomas Michel, "Christianity and Islam: Reflections on Recent Teachings of the Church," *Encounter* 112 (1985): 13; and see Michel's directions for the future in "Where to Now? Ways Forward for Interreligious Dialogue: Images of Abraham as Models of Interreligious Encounter," *The Muslim World* 100, no. 4 (2010): 530–38.

93. See the speech by Archbishop Descuffi: ASCOV = *Acta Synodalia Sacrosancti Concilii Oecumenici Vaticani II* (Vatican: Polyglot Press, 1975), 3/3, 53–55.

94. The latter argument is advanced by Miroslav Volf, *Allah: A Christian Response* (New York: Harper Collins, 2011), 127–85; and see also David Burrell's excellent essay "Trinity in Judaism and Islam," in *The Cambridge Companion to the Trinity*, ed. Peter Phan (Cambridge: Cambridge University Press, 2011), 344–64, and his classic *Knowing the Unknowable God: Ibn-Sina, Maimonides, Aquinas* (South Bend, IN: University of Notre Dame, 2004). See Troll, "Changing Catholic Views"; and Troll, *Muslims Ask,*

Christians Answer, trans. David Marshall (New York: New City Press, 2002), 9–19 on Christology and 45–54 on the Trinity.

95. See Risto Jukko, *Trinity in Unity in Christian-Muslim Relations: The Work of the Pontifical Council for Interreligious Dialogue* (Leiden: Brill, 2007), which is a helpful analysis of the PCID in this area but does not focus in depth on the Trinity as such, despite the title.

96. See Hussein Abdul-Raof, *Schools of Qur'anic Exegesis: Genesis and Development* (London: Routledge, 2010) for a historical overview and thus possibilities of change.

97. See Norman Daniels, *Islam and the West: The Making of an Image* (Edinburgh: Edinburgh University Press, 1960); and Thomas E. Burman, *Reading the Qur'ān in Latin Christendom, 1140–1560* (Philadelphia: University of Pennsylvania Press, 2007), a corrective to Daniels's classic regarding positive appreciations of the Qur'an. Sidney H. Griffith (*The Church in the Shadow of the Mosque: Christians and Muslims in the World of Islam* [Princeton, NJ: Princeton University Press, 2008]) explores the picture among Eastern Churches.

98. I am indebted to Troll, "Changing Catholic Views," and David Marshall's two articles: "Muhammad in Contemporary Christian Theological Reflection," *Islam and Christian–Muslim Relations* 24, no. 2 (2013): 2–13, 161–72, doi: 10.1080/09596410.2012.761405; and "Roman Catholic Approaches to the Qur'an since Vatican II," *Islam and Christian–Muslim Relations* 25, no. 1 (2014): 89–100.

99. See Georges C. Anawati, "An Assessment of the Christian–Islamic Dialogue," in *The Vatican, Islam, and the Middle East*, ed. Kalil C. Ellis (Syracuse: Syracuse University Press, 1987), 52–68. Anawati locates four problems in post-Conciliar reception (57–59), two of which are advanced by Caspar.

100. See Muslim-Christian Research Group, *The Challenge of the Scriptures: The Bible and the Qur'ān* (Maryknoll, NY: Orbis, 1989), especially 47–76.

101. Muslim-Christian Research Group, *The Challenge of the Scriptures*, 66.

102. Dupuis, *Towards*, 245.

103. Hans Küng holds a similar position in *Islam: Past, Present and Future* (Oxford: Oneworld, 2007), 124; and see also Hans Küng, Josef van Ess, Heinrich von Stietencron, and Heinz Bechert, *Christianity and the World Religions: Paths of Dialogue with Islam, Hinduism, and Buddhism*, trans. Peter Heinegg (London: Collins, 1987).

104. See Giulio Bassetti-Sani, *The Koran in the Light of Christ: A Christian Interpretation of the Sacred Book of Islam* (Chicago: Franciscan Herald Press, 1977).

105. See, for example, Jacques Jomier, *The Bible and the Qur'an* (San Francisco: Ignatius Press, 2002); Christian W. Troll, *Dialogue and Difference: Clarity in Christian-Muslim Relations*, trans. David Marshall (New York: Orbis, 2009); Samir Khalil Samir, SJ, *111 Questions on Islam: Samir Khalil Samir, S.J. on Islam and the West* (San Francisco: Ignatius Press, 2008); and a collection of authors named above and others in *Understanding and Discussion: Approaches to Muslim-Christian Dialogue*, ed. Peter Hans-Kolvenbach et al. (Rome: Pontificia Università Gregoriana, 1988).

106. See http://www.usccb.org/beliefs-and-teachings/ecumenical-and-interreligious/interreligious/islam/vatican-council-and-papal-statements-on-islam.cfm, listing the major statements made by Pope John Paul II on Islam; and DeGoia, *Interreligious Dialogue* for comprehensive coverage on Islam.

107. Thomas Michel, "Where to Now?" The commonality and complexity of this "Abrahamic link" is thoroughly outlined in the second edition of the classic work by F. E. Peters, *The Children of Abraham: Judaism, Christianity, Islam: A New Edition* (Princeton, NJ: Princeton University Press, 2004).

108. John Paul II, Address to the Catholic Community of Ankara, Turkey, November 29, 1979. http://www.usccb.org/beliefs-and-teachings/ecumenical-and-interreligious/interreligious/islam/vatican-council-and-papal-statements-on-islam.cfm.

109. See also his Visit to the Umayyad Great Mosque, May 6, 2001: "As we make our way through life toward our heavenly destiny, Christians feel the company of Mary, the mother of Jesus; and Islam too pays tribute to Mary and hails her as 'chosen above the women of the world' (Qur'an, 3:42). The virgin of Nazareth, the Lady of Saydnâya, has taught us that God protects the humble and 'scatters the proud in the imagination of their hearts' (Luke 1:51)." https://w2.vatican.va/content/john-paul-ii/en/speeches/2001/may/documents/hf_jp-ii_spe_20010506_omayyadi.html.

110. Pope John Paul II, *Crossing the Threshold of Hope* (London: Jonathan Cape, 1994), 92.

111. See George A. Lindbeck, *The Nature of Doctrine: Religion and Theology in a Postliberal Age* (London: SPCK, 1984), esp. 46–72.

112. Special thanks to Dr. Adam Gregerman and Rev. Dr. Damian Howard, SJ, for their critical comments on an earlier draft of this chapter.

Index